OFFICIAL GUIDE
TO THE
PLAYERS
OF THE
HOCKEY HALL OF FAME

HOCKEY HALL *of* FAME

Compiled by James Duplacey and Eric Zweig

FIREFLY BOOKS

A FIREFLY BOOK

Published by Firefly Books Ltd. 2010

First printing

Publisher Cataloging-in-Publication Data (U.S.)
Official guide to the players of the Hockey Hall of Fame
/ Hockey Hall of Fame ; compiled by James Duplacey
and Eric Zweig.
[ ] p. : col. photos. ; cm.
Includes index.
Summary: Profiles all 244 hockey players honored
by the Hockey Hall of Fame. Includes statistics and
archival photos for each player.
ISBN-13: 978-1-55407-662-8 (pbk.)
ISBN-10: 1-55407-662-5 (pbk.)
1. National Hockey League — Biography.
2. Hockey players — Biography.
I. Hockey Hall of Fame. II. Duplacey, James.
III. Zweig, Eric. IV. Title.
796.962/092 dc22 GV848.5.A1034 2010

Library and Archives Canada Cataloguing in
Publication
Official guide to the players of the Hockey Hall of Fame
/ Hockey Hall of Fame ; compiled by James Duplacey
and Eric Zweig.
Includes index.
ISBN-13: 978-1-55407-662-8 (pbk.)
ISBN-10: 1-55407-662-5 (pbk.)
1. Hockey Hall of Fame--Photograph collections.
2. Hockey players — Pictorial works.
3. Hockey players — Statistics.
4. Hockey — History — Pictorial works.
5. National Hockey League — History — Pictorial works.
6. Photograph collections — Ontario — Toronto.
I. Duplacey, James II. Zweig, Eric, 1963-
III. Hockey Hall of Fame
GV847.8.N3034 2010   796.962'640222   C2010-
903283-7

Cover and interior design by
Gareth Lind, LINDdesign

Published in the United States by
Firefly Books (U.S.) Inc.
P.O. Box 1338, Ellicott Station
Buffalo, New York 14205

Published in Canada by
Firefly Books Ltd.
66 Leek Crescent
Richmond Hill, Ontario L4B 1H1

The publisher gratefully
acknowledges the financial support
for our publishing program by the
Canada Book Fund as administered
by the Department of Canadian
Heritage.

Printed in China

FSC
Mixed Sources
Product group from well-managed
forests and other controlled sources

Cert no. SGS-COC-003853
www.fsc.org
© 1996 Forest Stewardship Council

Contents

The honor of being inducted into The Hockey Hall of Fame was one of the biggest highlights of my life. It was an incredible surprise when I found out I was being inducted into the Hall. When you hear the words "Hall of Fame" you immediately think of "the best of the best." For me that meant players like Jean Béliveau and Ted Lindsay, or one of my childhood favorites, Bill Cowley.

I've always thought that it was quite incredible that I was even considered for induction. I was demoted to the minors three times early in my career, and I don't have the NHL playoff pedigree that many other Hall of Famers have because I was on a team that rarely made the postseason. For 11 of the 17 years that I played in the NHL I was a right-winger for the New York Rangers. At that time the league consisted of only six teams, and the Rangers finished the season out of the hunt more often than not. Between 1952–53 and 1962–63 we only made the playoffs four times, never going

past the first round. My only Stanley Cup win came in 1963–64 after I was traded to the Toronto Maple Leafs.

I wasn't a household name in the same way as Rocket Richard or Gordie Howe was; I was just a hard working player on a less than stellar team. Despite our record in New York, I had the opportunity to play with some amazing teammates, like Dean Prentice and Larry Popein. These two men were definitely inspirational to me. It didn't matter where we were in the standings, these fine gentlemen always gave 100 percent and it forced me to step up my game to another level. Without line mates like this, I would never have won the Hart Trophy in 1959, nor would I have been named twice to the First All-Star Team and twice to the Second All-Star Team.

My nomination and induction into the Hockey Hall of Fame was truly a team effort, and for all those I skated alongside, I'm thankful.

The greatest honor that can be bestowed upon any athlete is induction into the Hall of Fame of his or her respective sport. It was a most humbling experience for me to be recognized as one of hockey's all-time elite performers by my peers and the experts who closely follow the game.

I was born in St. Louis, Missouri, and moved to Williams Lake, Michigan, when I was seven, and the best I ever hoped to achieve through hockey was a college scholarship. I had great teammates, coaches and trainers throughout my career and I did my best and tried to honor this great game every time I took the ice. It was a privilege to have ever skated in the NHL, and when my career was over, I thought that was the end.

But when I got the call that I had been inducted into the pinnacle of hockey, it gave me a chance to reflect on all the people that had helped me in my career, and of my personal support system: my wife, my three kids, my mom and dad, my in-laws, my brother and sister, and my good friend Don Meehan. Without them I would not have had a shot at the NHL, let alone the Hall. Each, in their own special way, has touched

me and contributed to the person that I have become. My induction took on even greater significance when I lost my mom six months after the ceremony. I'll never forget her smile that night as she enjoyed that special moment. It was the last time I was able to share a "hockey" moment with her. I humbly wear my Hall of Fame ring — and I usually only pull it out for very special occasions — and each and every time I slip that historic gold band on my finger I thank all of those who made a difference in my life.

I can honestly say that you only get a few surreal moments in your life. For me it was my wedding day, the birth of each of my three children and that moment that I stood at the podium in the Hockey Hall of Fame for my induction speech. Seven years have passed since the night I was introduced at the Hall by Bill Hay, but I still pinch myself whenever I'm introduced as a "Hall of Famer." There's not a day that goes by that I don't feel extremely blessed to have played this great game, for it has taught and provided me so much. I work hard every day to honor the game and give back to it as much as I can.

Explaining what it is like to be a member of the Hockey Hall of Fame is very difficult — I never set out to accomplish anything so grand. My dream was to play in the NHL and my goal was to be a better hockey player each day.

At the beginning of my career there weren't many people who thought I would make it to the NHL, let alone thrive. But all it took was one scout, Alex Smart. He saw potential in me, and his confidence in my game gave me a chance to show what I could do. I worked tirelessly to prove to him, and to myself, that I had what it took to be in the NHL.

After retirement you have four years to think about the possibility of your being inducted into the Hall alongside your heroes. And while it is nice to think about such things, induction was still a dream I never thought possible. To actually get in and be immortalized as a Hall of Famer is an absolutely amazing accomplishment, and while each and every "milestone" of my career — scoring 600 goals, hitting 1,000 points, winning a Stanley Cup — was amazing, it really is impossible for me to compare one to another. Induction was the best possible ending I could have ever wished for my career.

When writing my speech for the Hall of Fame induction ceremony, I had time to reflect on my entire career and the people who got me here. There were so many people who were instrumental in my success, but I am forever indebted to Pat Burns. Pat taught me so many things about hockey and about life — most importantly, he helped me become the man I am proud to say that I am today.

When I was a kid, I dreamed of playing in the best hockey league in the world, and to now be alongside greats like Rocket Richard, Guy Lafleur and Wayne Gretzky in the Hall of Fame is a humbling experience more grand than anything I dreamt as a child.

I hope that my induction symbolizes what can happen when you follow your dreams and persevere through your challenges. Dreams can come true, and I hope that my induction can inspire today's young players.

Growing up in Val Marie, Saskatchewan, thousands of miles from "Le Temple de la Renommée," the Hockey Hall of Fame was a home for the greatest to ever play the game — my childhood heroes, players like: Gordie Howe, Jean Beliveau, Bobby Hull, Bobby Orr and Johnny Bower. These men inspired me every Saturday on *Hockey Night in Canada*. But my vision of the Hall of Fame also included my dad (my first coach) and my uncles John and Don Gardner, as well as my hometown idol Paul Emile Lebel. These men had such a powerful influence on my desire to play hockey from a very young age. Youth allowed me the rationale to include my mentors alongside my NHL heroes in my vision of the Hall. As I got older, the tremendous skill, the championships, the individual awards and the hockey intangibles that my NHL favorites possessed, all while performing against the best competition in the world, magnified the reality that the Hockey Hall of Fame was for a very special set of hockey players.

The Hockey Hall of Fame is an impressive fraternity of talent, leadership, skill and class whose honored members portray the purest aspects of the game with dignity and style. The members of the Hall have always been my role models — even today! On and off the ice they carry the invisible torch for all generations who wish to play with great joy and proficiency. They are hockey's proudest athletes and champions.

My career has been beyond wonderful: from the nervousness and excitement of pulling on my first NHL jersey, to the thrill and zest of playing in the All-Star Game my rookie season, to the ultimate sensation of victory as Bobby Nystrom scored the Game 6, overtime, Cup-clinching goal in 1980 that made me a Stanley Cup champion for the first time — my greatest on-ice moment. None of it would have been possible without the support of my parents, Buzz and Mary; my siblings: Monty, Rocky, Kathy and Carol; the two villages of Val Marie and Climax, Saskatchewan, and the countless coaches and teammates I've had over the years.

Not once during my NHL career was I so presumptuous to think that I would one day be inducted into the Hockey Hall of Fame along side my hockey idols and role models. I could dream of playing in the NHL, of scoring my first goal and even of winning a Stanley Cup. But I didn't dare dream of "making the Hockey Hall of Fame." To this day, being inducted is still the highest compliment and honor I have ever received.

When that goal went in, they all could relax. The fans could let the air out. Before that, it was still nip and tuck. More people remember that than the guy [Jim Pappin] who scored the winning goal, for crying out loud."

George Armstrong

commenting on the empty-net goal that sealed 1967 Stanley Cup win

A
B
C
D
E
F
G
H
I
J
K
L
M
N
O
P
Q
R
S
T
U
V
W
X
Y
Z

12

Alternate: 20

Center/Left Wing

Shoots: Left

Height: 5'-11"

Weight: 170 lbs.

Born: February 22, 1918: Melville, Saskatchewan

Died: February 7, 2000: Farmington Hills, Michigan

Played 14 NHL seasons from 1938–43, 1945–54

Sid Abel

HOCKEY HALL OF FAME CLASS: 1969

QUICK FACTS

- Played amateur hockey with Melville Millionaires (1936–37); Saskatoon Wesleys (1936–37); Flin Flon Bombers (1937–38)
- Led NHL in goals (28) in 1948–49
- Finished among NHL top-5 in assists in 1941–42 (31), 1947–48 (30), 1948–49 (26), 1949–50 (35), 1950–51 (38) and 1951–52 (36)
- Finished among NHL top-5 in points in 1941–42 (49), 1948–49 (54), 1949–50 (69) and 1950–51 (61)
- One of only six Hall of Fame members (with Doug Bentley, Dit Clapper, Neil Colville, Mark Messier and Alex Delvecchio) to be selected as an NHL All-Star at two different positions (Left Wing and Center)
- Nicknamed "Boot Nose" after Rocket Richard punched him in the nose and broke it
- Played in NHL All-Star Game (1949, 1950, 1951)
- Member of Detroit's famed Production Line with Ted Lindsay and Gordie Howe
- Traded to Chicago by Detroit for cash, July 22, 1952
- Served as player/coach of Chicago Black Hawks (1952–54)
- Coached Detroit Red Wings (1958–68, 1969–70)
- Served as General Manager of Detroit Red Wings (1962–71)
- Coached St. Louis Blues (1971–72); served as General Manager of St. Louis Blues (1972–73)
- Served as General Manager of Kansas City Scouts (1974–76)

> I kept telling my wife Gloria to pinch me. I felt sure I was going to wake up and find that I'd been having a wonderful dream."
> — Sid Abel, on winning the Hart Trophy

REGULAR SEASON

Season	Age	Team	Lg	GP	G	A	PTS	PIM
1938–39	20	Detroit Red Wings	NHL	15	1	1	2	0
1939–40	21	Detroit Red Wings	NHL	24	1	5	6	4
1940–41	22	Detroit Red Wings	NHL	47	11	22	33	29
1941–42	23	Detroit Red Wings	NHL	48	18	31	49	45
1942–43	24	Detroit Red Wings	NHL	49	18	24	42	33
1945–46	27	Detroit Red Wings	NHL	7	0	2	2	0
1946–47	28	Detroit Red Wings	NHL	60	19	29	48	29
1947–48	29	Detroit Red Wings	NHL	60	14	30	44	69
1948–49	30	Detroit Red Wings	NHL	60	28	26	54	49
1949–50	31	Detroit Red Wings	NHL	69	34	35	69	46
1950–51	32	Detroit Red Wings	NHL	69	23	38	61	30
1951–52	33	Detroit Red Wings	NHL	62	17	36	53	32
1952–53	34	Chicago Blackhawks	NHL	39	5	4	9	6
1953–54	35	Chicago Blackhawks	NHL	3	0	0	0	4
NHL Career – 14 Seasons				612	189	283	472	376

PLAYOFFS

Season	Age	Team	Lg	GP	G	A	PTS	PIM
1938–39	20	Detroit Red Wings	NHL	6	1	1	2	2
1939–40	21	Detroit Red Wings	NHL	5	0	3	3	21
1940–41	22	Detroit Red Wings	NHL	9	2	2	4	2
1941–42	23	Detroit Red Wings	NHL	12	4	2	6	8
1942–43	24	Detroit Red Wings	NHL	10	5	8	13	4
1945–46	27	Detroit Red Wings	NHL	3	0	0	0	0
1946–47	28	Detroit Red Wings	NHL	3	1	1	2	2
1947–48	29	Detroit Red Wings	NHL	10	0	3	3	16
1948–49	30	Detroit Red Wings	NHL	11	3	3	6	6
1949–50	31	Detroit Red Wings	NHL	14	6	2	8	6
1950–51	32	Detroit Red Wings	NHL	6	4	3	7	0
1951–52	33	Detroit Red Wings	NHL	7	2	2	4	12
1952–53	34	Chicago Blackhawks	NHL	1	0	0	0	0
NHL Career – 13 Seasons				97	28	30	58	79

TROPHY CASE

AWARDS

Hart Memorial Trophy (1949)

Stanley Cup (1942–43, 1949–50, 1951–52)

ALL-STAR SELECTIONS

First All-Star Team Center (1949, 1950)

Second All-Star Team Center (1951)

Second All-Star Team Left Wing (1942)

5

Jack Adams
HOCKEY HALL OF FAME CLASS: 1959

Alternates:
9, 4, 11, 8

Position: Center

Shoots: Right

Height: 5'-9"

Weight: 175 lbs.

Born: June
14, 1895: Fort
William, Ontario

Died: May 1, 1968:
Detroit, Michigan

Played 10
professional
seasons from
1917–27

QUICK FACTS

- Only person to have his name engraved on the Stanley Cup as a player (1918, 1927), coach (1936, 1937, 1943) and General Manager (1936, 1937, 1943, 1950, 1952, 1954, 1955)
- Nicknamed "Jolly Jack"
- Played amateur hockey with Fort William Collegiate (1909–10); Fort William YMCA (1910–12); Fort William CYMA (1912–14); Fort William Maple Leafs (1914–17); Calumet Miners (1915–16); Peterborough 247th (1916–17); Sarnia Sailors (1917–18)
- Led TBSHL in goals (11) and points (11) in 1912–13, goals (33) and points (33) in 1913–14 and goals (16) and points (16) in 1914–15
- Led OIHA in goals (19) and points (22) in 1916–17
- Signed as a free agent by Toronto Arenas, February 9, 1918
- Traded to Vancouver Millionaires (PCHA) by Toronto Arenas for cash, December 7, 1919
- Led PCHA in penalty minutes (60) in 1920–21; led PCHA in goals (26) and points (30) in 1922–23
- Lost in the Stanley Cup finals in each of his last two seasons with Vancouver against teams he would play for later in his career – the Ottawa Senators and Toronto St. Pats
- Traded to Toronto St. Pats by Vancouver Millionaires (PCHA) for the rights to Corb Denneny, December 18, 1922
- Led NHL in penalty minutes (64) in 1922–23

> "No one ever shook the jolly out of Jack and got away with it. Life with Jack was like that. You either laughed with him or snarled with him or forfeited your right to his company."
> — *Montreal Gazette* tribute

REGULAR SEASON

Season	Age	Team	Lg	GP	G	A	PTS	PIM
1917–18	22	Toronto Arenas	NHL	8	0	0	0	31
1918–19	23	Toronto Arenas	NHL	17	3	3	6	35
1919–20	24	Vancouver Mllionaires	PCHA	22	9	6	15	18
1920–21	25	Vancouver Millionaires	PCHA	24	17	12	29	60
1921–22	26	Vancouver Millionaires	PCHA	24	26	4	30	24
1922–23	27	Toronto St. Patricks	NHL	23	19	9	28	64
1923–24	28	Toronto St. Patricks	NHL	22	14	4	18	51
1924–25	29	Toronto St. Patricks	NHL	27	21	10	31	67
1925–26	30	Toronto St. Patricks	NHL	36	21	5	26	52
1926–27	31	Ottawa Senators	NHL	40	5	1	6	66
Career – 10 Seasons				243	135	54	189	468

PLAYOFFS

Season	Age	Team	Lg	GP	G	A	PTS	PIM
1917–18	22	Toronto Arenas	NHL	2	1	0	1	6
1919–20	24	Vancouver Millionaires	PCHA	2	0	0	0	0
1920–21	25	Vancouver Millionaires	PCHA	2	3	0	3	0
1920–21	25	Vancouver Millionaires	St-Cup	5	2	1	3	6
1921–22	26	Vancouver Millionaires	PCHA	2	1	0	1	0
1921–22	26	Vancouver Millionaires	St-Cup	5	6	1	7	18
1921–22	26	Vancouver Millionaires	West-P	2	0	0	0	12
1924–25	29	Toronto St. Patricks	NHL	2	1	0	1	7
1926–27	31	Ottawa Senators	NHL	6	0	0	0	0
Career – 6 Seasons				28	14	2	16	37

TROPHY CASE

AWARDS

Lester Patrick Trophy (1966)

Stanley Cup (1917–18, 1926–27)

ALL-STAR SELECTIONS

PCHA First All-Star Team Center (1921, 1922)

First All-Star Team Coach (1937, 1943)

Second All-Star Team Coach (1945)

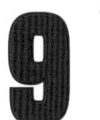

9

Retired by Edmonton

Glenn Anderson

HOCKEY HALL OF FAME CLASS: 2008

Alternates: 36, 10

Position:
Right Wing

Shoots: Left

Height: 6'-1"

Weight: 190 lbs.

Born: October 2, 1960: Vancouver, British Columbia

Drafted by the Edmonton Oilers 69th overall in 1979

Played 16 NHL seasons from 1980–96

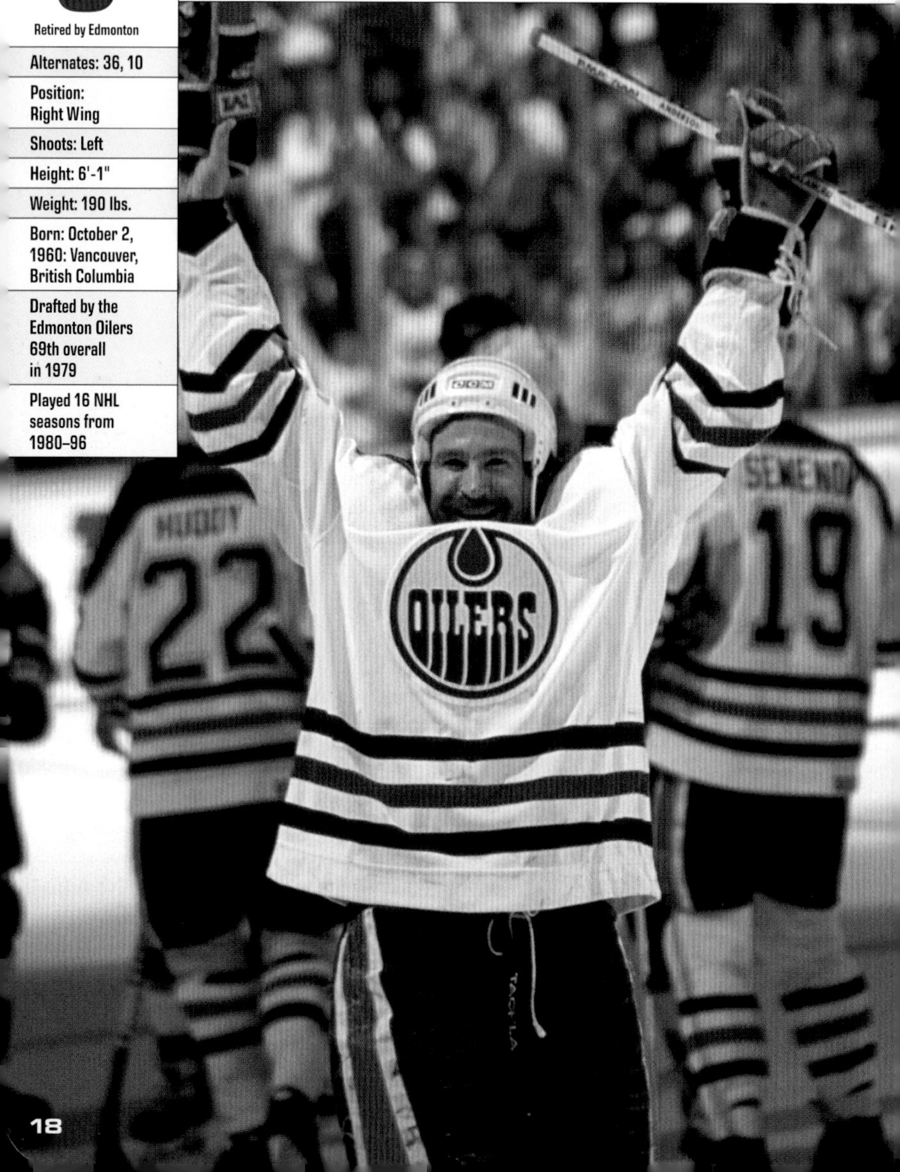

QUICK FACTS

- Shares NHL record for points in a single playoff period (4), established in Edmonton's 7–4 victory over Winnipeg Jets, April 6, 1988

- Played amateur hockey with Bellingham Blazers (1977–78); New Westminster Bruins (1977–78); Seattle Breakers (1978–80); University of Denver (1978–79); Canadian National Team (1979–80); Canadian Olympic Team (1979–80)

- Ranks fourth in NHL career playoff points (214)

- Ranks third in NHL career playoff overtime goals (5)

- Led NHL in game-winning goals (9) in 1985–86

- Played in NHL All-Star Game (1984, 1985, 1986, 1988)

- Scored 151 power-play goals, 85 game-winning goals and 13 shorthanded goals in 15-season career

- Finished among NHL top-5 in goals in 1983–84 (54) and 1985–86 (54)

- Registered 1,000th career NHL point in Toronto's 8–1 victory over Vancouver Canucks, February 22, 1993

- Played for Canada in 1980 Olympics, registering four points in six games

- Attempted to play for Canada in the 1994 Winter Olympics because he had negotiated that clause into his contract, but NHL Commissioner Gary Bettman vetoed it

- Played European pro hockey with Augsburger Panther (1995–96); HC Bolzano (1996–97) and HC La Chaux-de-Fonds (1996–97)

> The bond between the guys was very special. There was a closeness between us, the likes I have not seen on any other team I've played for."
>
> — Glenn Anderson, on the team unity of the Edmonton Oilers

REGULAR SEASON

Season	Age	Team	Lg	GP	G	A	PTS	+/-	PIM	ESG	PPG	SHG	GWG	SOG	S%
1980–81	20	Edmonton Oilers	NHL	58	30	23	53	4	24	17	10	3	5	160	18.8
1981–82	21	Edmonton Oilers	NHL	80	38	67	105	46	71	29	9	0	8	252	15.1
1982–83	22	Edmonton Oilers	NHL	72	48	56	104	41	70	37	11	0	10	243	19.8
1983–84	23	Edmonton Oilers	NHL	80	54	45	99	41	65	39	11	4	11	277	19.5
1984–85	24	Edmonton Oilers	NHL	80	42	39	81	24	69	29	12	1	6	258	16.3
1985–86	25	Edmonton Oilers	NHL	72	54	48	102	38	90	34	18	2	9	243	22.2
1986–87	26	Edmonton Oilers	NHL	80	35	38	73	27	65	27	7	1	5	188	18.6
1987–88	27	Edmonton Oilers	NHL	80	38	50	88	5	58	21	16	1	3	255	14.9
1988–89	28	Edmonton Oilers	NHL	79	16	48	64	-16	93	9	7	0	3	212	7.5
1989–90	29	Edmonton Oilers	NHL	73	34	38	72	-1	107	16	17	1	7	204	16.7
1990–91	30	Edmonton Oilers	NHL	74	24	31	55	-7	59	16	8	0	4	193	12.4
1991–92	31	Toronto Maple Leafs	NHL	72	24	33	57	-13	100	19	5	0	4	188	12.8
1992–93	32	Toronto Maple Leafs	NHL	76	22	43	65	19	117	11	11	0	3	161	13.7
1993–94	33	Toronto Maple Leafs	NHL	73	17	18	35	-6	50	12	5	0	3	127	13.4
1993–94	33	New York Rangers	NHL	12	4	2	6	1	12	2	2	0	0	22	18.2
1994–95	34	St. Louis Blues	NHL	36	12	14	26	9	37	12	0	0	3	54	22.2
1995–96	35	Edmonton Oilers	NHL	17	4	6	10	0	27	4	0	0	1	36	11.1
1995–96	35	St. Louis Blues	NHL	15	2	2	4	-11	6	0	2	0	0	35	5.7
NHL Career – 16 Seasons				1129	498	601	1099	201	1120	334	151	13	85	3108	16.0

PLAYOFFS

Season	Age	Team	L	GP	G	A	PTS	+/-	PIM	ESG	PPG	SHG	GWG	SOG	S%
1980–81	20	Edmonton Oilers	NHL	9	5	7	12		12	2	3	0	0		
1981–82	21	Edmonton Oilers	NHL	5	2	5	7		8	2	0	0	1		
1982–83	22	Edmonton Oilers	NHL	16	10	10	20		32	9	1	0	2		
1983–84	23	Edmonton Oilers	NHL	19	6	11	17	8	33	5	1	0	1	68	8.8
1984–85	24	Edmonton Oilers	NHL	18	10	16	26	11	38	8	2	0	1	47	21.3
1985–86	25	Edmonton Oilers	NHL	10	8	3	11	2	14	7	1	0	2	38	21.1
1986–87	26	Edmonton Oilers	NHL	21	14	13	27	13	59	10	4	0	2	62	22.6
1987–88	27	Edmonton Oilers	NHL	19	9	16	25	5	49	5	4	0	1	43	20.9
1988–89	28	Edmonton Oilers	NHL	7	1	2	3	-1	8	0	1	0	0	16	6.3
1989–90	29	Edmonton Oilers	NHL	22	10	12	22	12	20	8	2	0	2	46	21.7
1990–91	30	Edmonton Oilers	NHL	18	6	7	13	-2	41	3	3	0	0	31	19.4
1992–93	32	Toronto Maple Leafs	NHL	21	7	11	18	7	31	7	0	0	2	46	15.2
1993–94	33	New York Rangers	NHL	23	3	3	6	5	42	2	0	1	2	31	9.7
1994–95	34	St. Louis Blues	NHL	6	1	1	2	0	49	1	0	0	0	3	33.3
1995–96	35	St. Louis Blues	NHL	11	1	4	5	5	6	1	0	0	1	20	5.0
NHL Career – 15 Seasons				225	93	121	214	63	442	70	22	1	17	451	16.9

TROPHY CASE

AWARDS

Stanley Cup (1983–84, 1984–85, 1986–87, 1987–88, 1989–90, 1993–94)

INTERNATIONAL AWARDS

Canada Cup (1984, 1987)

10

Honored by Toronto

Syl Apps

HOCKEY HALL OF FAME CLASS: 1961

Center

Shoots: Left

Height: 6'

Weight: 185 lbs.

Born: January 18, 1915: Paris, Ontario

Died: December 24, 1998: Kingston, Ontario

Played 10 NHL seasons from 1936–43, 1945–48

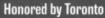

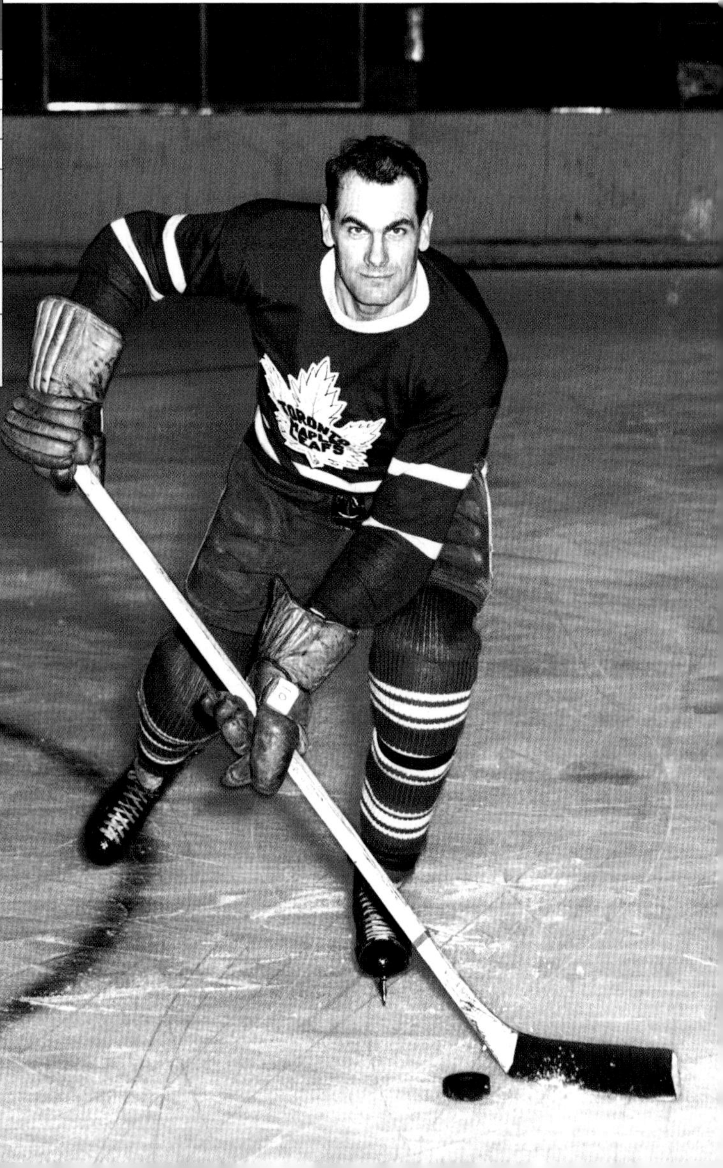

QUICK FACTS

- Played amateur hockey with Paris Greens (1930–31); McMaster University (1931–35); Hamilton Tigers (1935–36); Toronto Dominions (1935–36)

- Led OHA-Sr. in points (38) in 1935–36, led OHA-Sr. in playoff assists (7) and points (19) in 1935–36

- Won gold medal in pole vault representing Canada at 1934 British Empire Games in London, England

- Placed sixth in pole vault representing Canada at 1936 Summer Olympics in Berlin, Germany

- Led NHL in assists in 1936–37 (29) and 1937–38 (29)

- Finished second in NHL regular season points in 1936–37 (45), 1937–38 (50) and 1940–41 (44)

- Called "a Rembrandt on the ice, a Nijinsky at the goalmouth" by Montreal author Vincent D. Lunny

- Played in NHL All-Star Game (1947)

- Served as captain of Toronto Maple Leafs (1940–43, 1945–48)

- Played for Toronto Army Daggers (1943–44) and Ottawa All-Stars (1944–45) during World War II

- Father of Syl Apps Jr. who played in NHL with N.Y. Rangers, Pittsburgh and L.A. Kings from 1970–80

- Grandfather of Gillian Apps, member of the gold medal-winning Canadian Women's team at 2010 Winter Olympics

- Legacy honored by Canada Post, who issued a 47-cent stamp featuring his profile

> **(Apps) was getting $6,000 for the season and he came to me and said, 'Conn, I'm making more than I deserve. I want to give you this check.' Well, I almost died of heart failure. Of course, I refused his check. I felt that anyone who thought in such terms was bound to square off what he thought was a debt the following season."**
>
> — Conn Smythe, on Apps trying to return money after missing half a season with an injury

REGULAR SEASON

Season	Age	Team	Lg	GP	G	A	PTS	PIM
1936–37	22	Toronto Maple Leafs	NHL	48	16	29	45	10
1937–38	23	Toronto Maple Leafs	NHL	47	21	29	50	9
1938–39	24	Toronto Maple Leafs	NHL	44	15	25	40	4
1939–40	25	Toronto Maple Leafs	NHL	27	13	17	30	5
1940–41	26	Toronto Maple Leafs	NHL	41	20	24	44	6
1941–42	27	Toronto Maple Leafs	NHL	38	18	23	41	0
1942–43	28	Toronto Maple Leafs	NHL	29	23	17	40	2
1945–46	31	Toronto Maple Leafs	NHL	40	24	16	40	2
1946–47	32	Toronto Maple Leafs	NHL	54	25	24	49	6
1947–48	33	Toronto Maple Leafs	NHL	55	26	27	53	12
NHL Career — 10 Seasons				423	201	231	432	56

PLAYOFFS

Season	Age	Team	Lg	GP	G	A	PTS	PIM
1936–37	22	Toronto Maple Leafs	NHL	2	0	1	1	0
1937–38	23	Toronto Maple Leafs	NHL	7	1	4	5	0
1938–39	24	Toronto Maple Leafs	NHL	10	2	6	8	2
1939–40	25	Toronto Maple Leafs	NHL	10	5	2	7	2
1940–41	26	Toronto Maple Leafs	NHL	7	3	2	5	2
1941–42	27	Toronto Maple Leafs	NHL	13	5	9	14	2
1946–47	32	Toronto Maple Leafs	NHL	11	5	1	6	0
1947–48	33	Toronto Maple Leafs	NHL	9	4	4	8	0
NHL Career — 8 Seasons				69	25	29	54	8

TROPHY CASE

AWARDS

Calder Memorial Trophy (1937)

Lady Byng Memorial Trophy (1942)

Stanley Cup (1941–42, 1946–47, 1947–48)

ALL-STAR SELECTIONS

First All-Star Team Center (1939, 1942)

Second All-Star Team Center (1938, 1941, 1943)

10

Honored by Toronto

George Armstrong
HOCKEY HALL OF FAME CLASS: 1975

Alternates:
15, 20, 8

Right Wing

Shoots: Right

Height: 6'-1"

Weight: 204 lbs.

Born: July 6, 1930; Skead, Ontario

Played 21 NHL seasons from 1949–50, 1951–71

QUICK FACTS

- Holds Toronto Maple Leafs team record for career seasons (21) and games played (1,187)
- Holds Toronto Maple Leafs team record for career assists (417) and points (713) by a right wing
- Nicknamed "Chief" because of his Native heritage. Also known as "Chief-Shoot-The-Puck"
- Played amateur hockey with Copper Cliff Redmen (1946–47); Prince Albert Blackhawks (1946–47); Stratford Kroehlers (1947–48); Toronto Jr. Marlboros (1948–50); Toronto Sr. Marlboros (1948–50)
- Led OHA-Jr. in assists (43) and points (73) in 1947–48; led OHA-Jr. playoffs in goals (7), assists (10) and points (17) in 1948–49
- Led OHA-Jr. in goals (64) in 1949–50
- Member of Allan Cup-winning Toronto Sr. Marlboros (1950)
- Scored final goal of the "Original Six" era in Toronto's 3–1 victory over Montreal, May 2, 1967
- Played in NHL All-Star Game (1956, 1957, 1959, 1962, 1963, 1964, 1968)
- Served as captain of the Toronto Maple Leafs (1957–69)
- Coached Toronto Marlboros (1972–77); won Memorial Cup as coach of the Toronto Marlboros (1973, 1975)
- Served as scout with Quebec Nordiques (1978–87)
- Coached Toronto Maple Leafs (1988–89)

> "When that goal went in, they all could relax. The fans could let the air out. Before that, it was still nip and tuck. More people remember that than the guy (Jim Pappin) who scored the winning goal, for crying out loud."
> — George Armstrong, commenting on the empty-net goal that sealed 1967 Stanley Cup win

REGULAR SEASON

Season	Age	Team	Lg	GP	G	A	PTS	+/-	PIM	ESG	PPG	SHG	GWG	SOG	S%
1949–50	19	Toronto Maple Leafs	NHL	2	0	0	0		0						
1951–52	21	Toronto Maple Leafs	NHL	20	3	3	6		30						
1952–53	22	Toronto Maple Leafs	NHL	52	14	11	25		54						
1953–54	23	Toronto Maple Leafs	NHL	63	17	15	32		60						
1954–55	24	Toronto Maple Leafs	NHL	66	10	18	28		80						
1955–56	25	Toronto Maple Leafs	NHL	67	16	32	48		97						
1956–57	26	Toronto Maple Leafs	NHL	54	18	26	44		37						
1957–58	27	Toronto Maple Leafs	NHL	59	17	25	42		93						
1958–59	28	Toronto Maple Leafs	NHL	59	20	16	36		37						
1959–60	29	Toronto Maple Leafs	NHL	70	23	28	51		60						
1960–61	30	Toronto Maple Leafs	NHL	47	14	19	33		21						
1961–62	31	Toronto Maple Leafs	NHL	70	21	32	53		27						
1962–63	32	Toronto Maple Leafs	NHL	70	19	24	43		27						
1963–64	33	Toronto Maple Leafs	NHL	66	20	17	37		14	13	7	0	3		
1964–65	34	Toronto Maple Leafs	NHL	59	15	22	37		14	12	3	0	3		
1965–66	35	Toronto Maple Leafs	NHL	70	16	35	51		12	11	3	2	3		
1966–67	36	Toronto Maple Leafs	NHL	70	9	24	33		26	6	3	0	3		
1967–68	37	Toronto Maple Leafs	NHL	62	13	21	34	8	4	11	2	0	2	125	10.4
1968–69	38	Toronto Maple Leafs	NHL	53	11	16	27	-9	10	9	1	1	1	103	10.7
1969–70	39	Toronto Maple Leafs	NHL	49	13	15	28	9	12	11	2	0	3	93	14.0
1970–71	40	Toronto Maple Leafs	NHL	59	7	18	25	7	6	7	0	0	1	93	7.5
NHL Career — 21 Seasons				1187	296	417	713	15	721	80	21	3	19	414	10.6

PLAYOFFS

Season	Age	Team	Lg	GP	G	A	PTS	+/-	PIM	ESG	PPG	SHG	GWG	SOG	S%
1951–52	21	Toronto Maple Leafs	NHL	4	0	0	0		2						
1953–54	23	Toronto Maple Leafs	NHL	5	1	0	1		2						
1954–55	24	Toronto Maple Leafs	NHL	4	1	0	1		4						
1955–56	25	Toronto Maple Leafs	NHL	5	4	2	6		0						
1958–59	28	Toronto Maple Leafs	NHL	12	0	4	4		10						
1959–60	29	Toronto Maple Leafs	NHL	10	1	4	5		4						
1960–61	30	Toronto Maple Leafs	NHL	5	1	1	2		0						
1961–62	31	Toronto Maple Leafs	NHL	12	7	5	12		2						
1962–63	32	Toronto Maple Leafs	NHL	10	3	6	9		4						
1963–64	33	Toronto Maple Leafs	NHL	14	5	8	13		10						
1964–65	34	Toronto Maple Leafs	NHL	6	1	0	1		4						
1965–66	35	Toronto Maple Leafs	NHL	4	0	1	1		4						
1966–67	36	Toronto Maple Leafs	NHL	9	2	1	3		6						
1968–69	38	Toronto Maple Leafs	NHL	4	0	0	0		0	0	0	0	0		
1970–71	40	Toronto Maple Leafs	NHL	6	0	2	2		0	0	0	0	0		
NHL Career — 15 Seasons				110	26	34	60		52	0	0	0	0		

TROPHY CASE

AWARDS

Stanley Cup (1961–62, 1962–63, 1963–64, 1966–67)

I think a quick release is more important than aiming the puck. I always figured it was harder for a goalie to stop what he wasn't expecting than for me to look for a particular hole. Besides, in the NHL you almost never get the chance to pick a particular spot."

Mike Bossy

A
B
C
D
E
F
G
H
I
J
K
L
M
N
O
P
Q
R
S
T
U
V
W
X
Y
Z

Ace Bailey

HOCKEY HALL OF FAME CLASS: 1975

6

Retired by Toronto

Alternate: 12	
Right Wing	
Shoots: Right	
Height: 5'-10"	
Weight: 160 lbs.	
Born: July 3, 1903: Bracebridge, Ontario	
Died: April 7, 1992: Toronto, Ontario	
Played 8 NHL seasons from 1926–34	

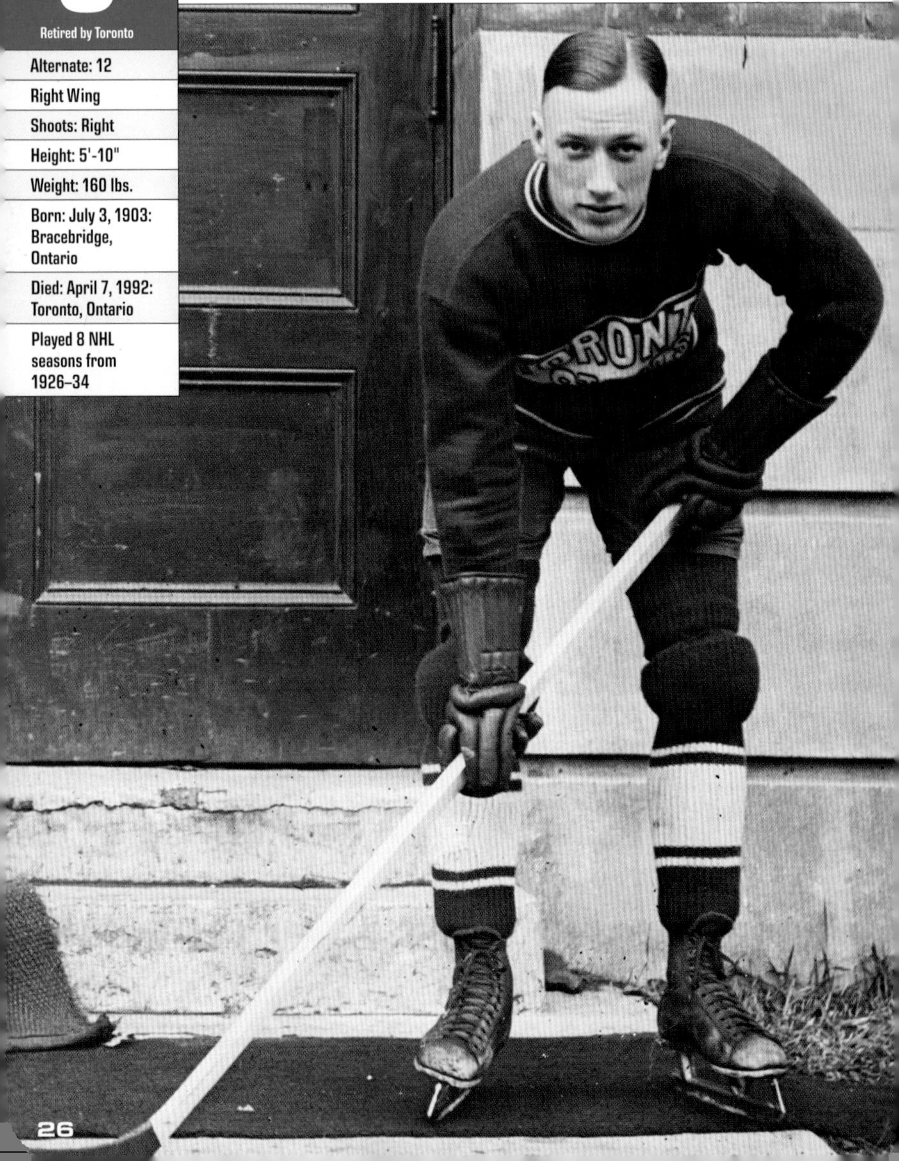

QUICK FACTS

- Played amateur hockey with Bracebridge Bird Mill (1918–22); Toronto St. Mary's (1922–24); Peterborough Petes (1924–25); Peterborough Seniors (1925–26)

- Signed as a free agent by Toronto St. Pats, November 3, 1926

- Led NHL in goals (22) and points (32) in 1928–29; led NHL playoffs in assists (2) and points (3) in 1928–29

- Scored Stanley Cup-winning goal in Toronto's 6–4 victory over N.Y. Rangers, April 9, 1932

- Suffered career-ending head injury in game vs. Boston, December 12, 1933, when tripped from behind by Bruins defenseman Eddie Shore

- First NHL All-Star Game held in his honor with the proceeds ($20,909) going to Bailey and his family, February 14, 1934

- In show of good sportsmanship, Bailey participated in a ceremonial handshake with Eddie Shore at center ice before the start of the Bailey Benefit Game

- Coached Toronto Dominions (1934–35)

- Coached University of Toronto Varsity Blues (1935–40, 1945–49)

- Worked as timekeeper at Maple Leaf Gardens (1938–84)

- Allowed his retired #6 to be worn by Maple Leafs' winger Ron Ellis from 1968–81 because he respected the way Ellis played the game

> I hold no grudge. I see Eddie often when he comes up to Toronto for the games. It was just one of those things that happens."
> — Ace Bailey, on the incident that ended his career

REGULAR SEASON

Season	Age	Team	Lg	GP	G	A	PTS	PIM
1926–27	23	Toronto St. Pats/Maple Leafs	NHL	42	15	13	28	82
1927–28	24	Toronto Maple Leafs	NHL	43	9	3	12	72
1928–29	25	Toronto Maple Leafs	NHL	44	22	10	32	78
1929–30	26	Toronto Maple Leafs	NHL	43	22	21	43	69
1930–31	27	Toronto Maple Leafs	NHL	40	23	19	42	46
1931–32	28	Toronto Maple Leafs	NHL	41	8	5	13	62
1932–33	29	Toronto Maple Leafs	NHL	47	10	8	18	52
1933–34	30	Toronto Maple Leafs	NHL	13	2	3	5	11
NHL Career – 8 Seasons				313	111	82	193	472

PLAYOFFS

Season	Age	Team	Lg	GP	G	A	PTS	PIM
1928–29	25	Toronto Maple Leafs	NHL	4	1	2	3	4
1930–31	27	Toronto Maple Leafs	NHL	2	1	1	2	0
1931–32	28	Toronto Maple Leafs	NHL	7	1	0	1	4
1932–33	29	Toronto Maple Leafs	NHL	8	0	1	1	4
NHL Career – 4 Seasons				21	3	4	7	12

TROPHY CASE

AWARDS

NHL Scoring Leader (1929)

Stanley Cup (1931–32)

Dan Bain

HOCKEY HALL OF FAME CLASS: 1945

Center

Shoots: Right

Height: 6'

Weight: 185 lbs.

Born: February 14, 1874: Belleville, Ontario

Died: August 15, 1962: Winnipeg, Manitoba

Played eight elite amateur seasons from 1894–1902

QUICK FACTS

- Helped Winnipeg Victorias win seven consecutive Manitoba Provincial Championships, from 1895 to 1902
- Led Manitoba Northwest League in goals (10) in 1895–96; led MNWHA in goals (7) and points (8) in 1896–97; led MNWHA in goals (11) and points (12) in 1898–99
- Scored Stanley Cup-winning goal in Winnipeg's 2–0 victory over Montreal Victorias, February 14, 1896
- First player to score a Stanley Cup-winning goal in overtime in Winnipeg's 2–1 victory over Montreal Shamrocks, January 31, 1901
- Won Campbell Trophy as Winnipeg Gymnastic champion (1891)
- Won Carruthers' Cup Cycling Championship (1984–96)
- Won Canadian trapshooting championship (1903)
- Named Canada's Top Athlete of the Half-Century (1900)
- Served as captain of Winnipeg Victorias (1998–1901)
- Inducted into Canada's Sports Hall of Fame (1971)
- Inducted into Manitoba Sports Hall of Fame (1981)

> "Those were the days of real athletes. When we passed, the puck never left the ice and if the wingman wasn't there to get it, it was because he had a broken leg."
> — Dan Bain, on the hockey of his era

REGULAR SEASON

Season	Age	Team	Lg	GP	G	A	PTS
1894-95	20	Winnipeg Victorias	MNWHA	3	10	0	10
1895-96	21	Winnipeg Victorias	MNWHA	5	10	3	13
1896-97	22	Winnipeg Victorias	MNWHA	5	7	1	8
1897-98	23	Winnipeg Victorias	MNWHA	5	13	1	14
1898-99	24	Winnipeg Victorias	MNWHA	3	11	1	12
1899-00	25	Winnipeg Victorias	MNWHA	2	9	1	10
1900-01	26	Winnipeg Victorias	MNWHA	3	3	0	3
1901-02	27	Winnipeg Victorias	MNWHA	1	3	0	3
Career – 8 Seasons				27	66	7	73

PLAYOFFS

Season	Age	Team	Lg	GP	G	A	PTS
1895-96	21	Winnipeg Victorias	St-Cup	2	3	0	3
1898-99	24	Winnipeg Victorias	St-Cup	1	0	0	0
1899-00	25	Winnipeg Victorias	St-Cup	3	4	0	4
1900-01	26	Winnipeg Victorias	St-Cup	2	3	0	3
1901-02	27	Winnipeg Victorias	St-Cup	3	0	0	0
Career – 5 Seasons				11	10	0	10

TROPHY CASE

AWARDS

Stanley Cup (1895-96, 1900-01, 1901-02)

Hobey Baker

HOCKEY HALL OF FAME CLASS: 1945

Rover

Shoots: Right

Height: 5'-9"

Weight: 160 lbs.

Born: January 15, 1892: Wissahickon, Pennsylvania

Died: December 21, 1918: Toul, France

Played 10 elite amateur seasons from 1906–16

QUICK FACTS

- Inaugural member of the Hockey Hall of Fame (1945)
- Inaugural member of the United States Hockey Hall of Fame (1973)
- Inducted into College Football Hall of Fame (1975)
- Legacy honored with The Hobey Baker Award, presented annually to the outstanding player in NCAA men's hockey since its introduction in 1981
- Players at St. Paul's Prep School compete for an award known simply as "Hobey's Stick"

- Member of the Ivy League champion Princeton University Tigers (1912, 1914)
- Served as captain of Princeton University Tigers in both football and hockey
- Hockey arena at Princeton University is named in his honor
- AAHL First All-Star Team Rover (1915, 1916)
- Led AAHL in goals (17) in 1914–15
- Served in U.S. Air Force during World War I and was awarded Croix de Guerre by the government of France for his service
- Died in an airplane crash while conducting a test flight after the completion of the war

> Baker is the greatest hockey player ever developed in the United States. Canadian experts maintain if he took up the game professionally he might rank as the greatest player in the world."
>
> — *Ottawa Citizen*, June 16, 1916

REGULAR SEASON

Season	Age	Team	Lg	GP	G	A	PTS	PIM
1906–07	15	St. Paul's School	High-NH					
1907–08	16	St. Paul's School	High-NH					
1908–09	17	St. Paul's School	High-NH					
1909–10	18	St. Paul's School	High-NH					
1910–11	19	Princeton University Tigers	Ivy					
1911–12	20	Princeton University Tigers	Ivy					
1912–13	21	Princeton University Tigers	Ivy					
1913–14	22	Princeton University Tigers	Ivy	11	12	0	12	2
1914–15	23	New York St. Nicholas	AAHL	8	17	0	17	
1915–16	24	New York St. Nicholas	AAHL	7	9	0	9	
Career – 10 Seasons				26	38	0	38	2

PLAYOFFS

Season	Age	Team	Lg	GP	G	A	PTS	PIM
1915–16	24	New York St. Nicholas	AAHL	3	1	0	1	
Career – 1 Season				3	1	0	1	

TROPHY CASE

AWARDS

Lester Patrick Trophy (1987)

7

Left Wing

Shoots: Left

Height: 6'

Weight: 195 lbs.

Born: July 11, 1952: Callander, Ontario

Drafted by the Philadelphia Flyers seventh overall in 1972

Played 12 NHL seasons from 1972–84

Bill Barber

HOCKEY HALL OF FAME CLASS: 1990

QUICK FACTS

- Shares NHL record (with Wayne Presley) for most short-handed goals in single playoff series (3), established in 1980
- Shares NHL record for most short-handed goals in single playoff season (3), established in 1980
- Holds Philadelphia Flyers team records for career goals (420) and regular season points by a left winger (112)
- Played amateur hockey with North Bay Trappers (1967–69); Kitchener Rangers (1969–72)
- Played minor pro hockey with Richmond Robins (1972–73)
- Led NHL in short-handed goals (6) in 1978–79; led NHL in shots-on-goal (380) in 1975–76

- Played in NHL All-Star Game (1975, 1976, 1978, 1980, 1981, 1982)
- Led World Hockey Championships in goals (8) in 1982
- World Championships First All-Star Team Left Wing (1982)
- Coached Hershey Bears (1984–85, 1995–96); coached Philadelphia Phantoms (1996–2000)
- Coached Calder Cup-winning Philadelphia Phantoms (1998)
- Served as assistant coach of Philadelphia Flyers (1985–88)
- Served as Philadelphia Flyers Director of Pro Scouting (1988–95)
- Coached Philadelphia Flyers (2000–02)

"You have to have a passion to play hockey and you have to express that passion for the people who come to watch you when you're playing."

REGULAR SEASON

Season	Age	Team	Lg	GP	G	A	PTS	+/-	PIM	ESG	PPG	SHG	GWG	SOG	S%
1972-73	20	Philadelphia Flyers	NHL	69	30	34	64	10	46	23	7	0	2	214	14.0
1973-74	21	Philadelphia Flyers	NHL	75	34	35	69	34	54	23	9	2	5	290	11.7
1974-75	22	Philadelphia Flyers	NHL	79	34	37	71	46	66	21	8	5	4	276	12.3
1975-76	23	Philadelphia Flyers	NHL	80	50	62	112	74	104	31	15	4	10	380	13.2
1976-77	24	Philadelphia Flyers	NHL	73	20	35	55	32	62	17	3	0	3	245	8.2
1977-78	25	Philadelphia Flyers	NHL	80	41	31	72	31	34	29	8	4	9	262	15.6
1978-79	26	Philadelphia Flyers	NHL	79	34	46	80	19	22	18	10	6	4	258	13.2
1979-80	27	Philadelphia Flyers	NHL	79	40	32	72	39	17	31	7	2	7	265	15.1
1980-81	28	Philadelphia Flyers	NHL	80	43	42	85	6	69	25	16	2	2	292	14.7
1981-82	29	Philadelphia Flyers	NHL	80	45	44	89	4	85	28	13	4	6	350	12.9
1982-83	30	Philadelphia Flyers	NHL	66	27	33	60	17	28	20	5	2	1	215	12.6
1983-84	31	Philadelphia Flyers	NHL	63	22	32	54	4	36	19	3	0	1	203	10.8
NHL Career – 12 Seasons				903	420	463	883	316	623	285	104	31	54	3250	12.9

PLAYOFFS

Season	Age	Team	Lg	GP	G	A	PTS	+/-	PIM	ESG	PPG	SHG	GWG	SOG	S%
1972-73	20	Philadelphia Flyers	NHL	11	3	2	5		22	3	0	0	0		
1973-74	21	Philadelphia Flyers	NHL	17	3	6	9		18	3	0	0	1		
1974-75	22	Philadelphia Flyers	NHL	17	6	9	15		8	6	0	0	0		
1975-76	23	Philadelphia Flyers	NHL	16	6	7	13		18	3	3	0	0		
1976-77	24	Philadelphia Flyers	NHL	10	1	4	5		2	1	0	0	0		
1977-78	25	Philadelphia Flyers	NHL	12	6	3	9		2	5	1	0	0		
1978-79	26	Philadelphia Flyers	NHL	8	3	4	7		10	3	0	0	0		
1979-80	27	Philadelphia Flyers	NHL	19	12	9	21		23	8	1	3	4		
1980-81	28	Philadelphia Flyers	NHL	12	11	5	16		0	7	3	1	1		
1981-82	29	Philadelphia Flyers	NHL	4	1	5	6		4	0	0	1	0		
1982-83	30	Philadelphia Flyers	NHL	3	1	1	2		2	0	1	0	0		
NHL Career – 11 Seasons				129	53	55	108		109	39	9	5	6		

TROPHY CASE

AWARDS
Jack Adams Award (2001)

Stanley Cup (1973–74, 1974–75)

ALL-STAR SELECTIONS
First All-Star Team Left Wing (1976)

Second All-Star Team Left Wing (1979, 1981)

INTERNATIONAL AWARDS
Canada Cup (1976)

Bronze Medal: World Championships (1982)

Marty Barry

HOCKEY HALL OF FAME CLASS: 1965

Alternates:
8, 10, 14, 11, 9

Center

Shoots: Left

Height: 5'-11"

Weight: 175 lbs.

Born: December 8, 1905: Quebec City, Quebec

Died: August 20, 1969: Halifax, Nova Scotia

Played 12 NHL seasons from 1927–28; 1929–40

QUICK FACTS

- Played amateur hockey with Montreal St-Ann's (1924–25); Montreal St-Anthony (1924–26); Montreal Bell Telephone (1926–27)

- Led Can-Am in goals (19) and points (29) in 1928–29

- Nicknamed "Goal-A-Game Barry"

- Finished among NHL top-5 in goals in 1932–33 (24), 1933–34 (27) and 1935–36 (21)

- Finished among NHL top-5 in assists in 1936–37 (27) and 1938–39 (28)

- Finished among NHL top-5 in points in 1933–34 (39), 1935–36 (40), 1936–37 (44) and 1938–39 (41)

- Led NHL playoffs in goals (4), assists (7) and points (11) in 1936–37

- Missed only two games in his first 10 NHL seasons

- Scored Stanley Cup-winning goal in Detroit's 3–0 victory over N.Y. Rangers, April 15, 1937

- Inducted into Detroit Red Wings' Hall of Fame (1944)

- Described in an article by Detroit Times' writer Bob Murphy as a player who "possesses that faculty of mechanical perfection"

- Played in NHL All-Star Game (1937)

- Served as player/coach of Minneapolis Millers (1940–41)

- Coached Minneapolis Millers (1941–42)

- Coached Halifax St. Mary's Saints (1947–52); coached St. Mary's Crescents (1947–49)

> "The rink seemed like it was miles long along about 10 minutes to 2 o'clock in the morning. Players of both teams were praying for somebody to score before we all fell from exhaustion."
>
> — Marty Barry, on the NHL's longest overtime game, March 24, 1936

REGULAR SEASON

Season	Age	Team	Lg	GP	G	A	PTS	PIM
1927–28	22	New York Americans	NHL	9	1	0	1	2
1929–30	24	Boston Bruins	NHL	44	18	15	33	34
1930–31	25	Boston Bruins	NHL	44	20	11	31	26
1931–32	26	Boston Bruins	NHL	48	21	17	38	22
1932–33	27	Boston Bruins	NHL	47	24	13	37	40
1933–34	28	Boston Bruins	NHL	48	27	12	39	12
1934–35	29	Boston Bruins	NHL	48	20	20	40	33
1935–36	30	Detroit Red Wings	NHL	48	21	19	40	16
1936–37	31	Detroit Red Wings	NHL	47	17	27	44	6
1937–38	32	Detroit Red Wings	NHL	48	9	20	29	34
1938–39	33	Detroit Red Wings	NHL	48	13	28	41	4
1939–40	34	Montreal Canadiens	NHL	30	4	10	14	2
NHL Career – 12 Seasons				509	195	192	387	231

PLAYOFFS

Season	Age	Team	Lg	GP	G	A	PTS	PIM
1928–29	23	New Haven Eagles	Can-Am	2	0	1	1	2
1929–30	24	Boston Bruins	NHL	6	3	3	6	14
1930–31	25	Boston Bruins	NHL	5	1	1	2	4
1932–33	27	Boston Bruins	NHL	5	2	2	4	6
1934–35	29	Boston Bruins	NHL	4	0	0	0	2
1935–36	30	Detroit Red Wings	NHL	7	2	4	6	6
1936–37	31	Detroit Red Wings	NHL	10	4	7	11	2
1938–39	33	Detroit Red Wings	NHL	6	3	1	4	0
NHL Career – 7 Seasons				43	15	18	33	34

TROPHY CASE

AWARDS

Lady Byng Memorial Trophy (1937)

Stanley Cup (1935–36, 1936–37)

ALL-STAR SELECTIONS

First All-Star Team Center (1937)

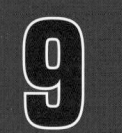

Andy Bathgate

HOCKEY HALL OF FAME CLASS: 1978

9

Retired by N.Y. Rangers

Alternates: 21, 14, 16

Right Wing

Shoots: Right

Height: 6'

Weight: 180 lbs.

Born: August 28, 1932: Winnipeg, Manitoba

Played 18 NHL and WHA seasons from 1952–68, 1970–71, 1974–75

"I couldn't run over people. I had to maneuver around them."

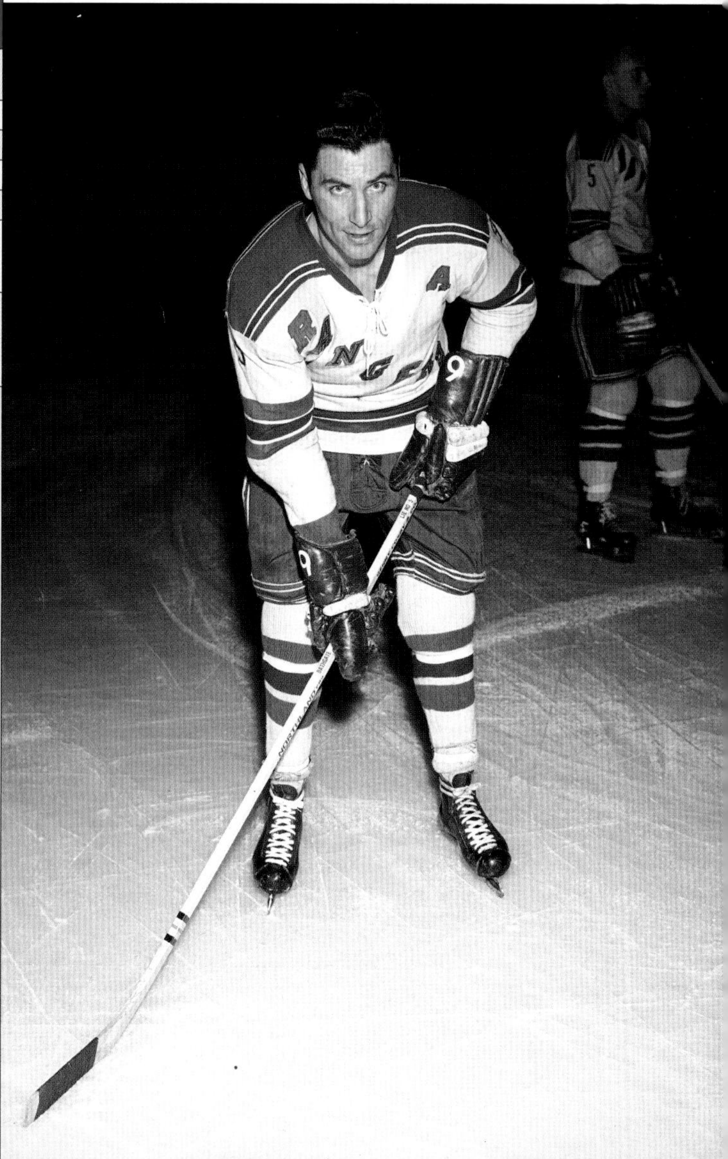

QUICK FACTS

- Played amateur hockey with Winnipeg Excelciors (1943–44); Winnipeg Rangers (1946–48); Winnipeg Black Hawks (1948–49); Guelph Biltmores (1949–53)

- Member of Memorial Cup-winning Guelph Biltmores (1952)

- Tied (with Bobby Hull) for NHL lead in points (84) in 1961–62; led NHL in assists in 1961–62 (56) and 1963–64 (58)

- Finished among NHL top-5 in goals in 1958–59 (40) and 1962–63 (35)

- Served as captain of N.Y. Rangers (1961–64)

- Traded to Toronto by N.Y. Rangers with Don McKenney for Dick Duff, Bob Nevin, Rod Seiling, Arnie Brown and Bill Collins, February 22, 1964

- Played in NHL All-Star Game (1957, 1958, 1959, 1960, 1961, 1962, 1963, 1964)

- Scored Stanley Cup-winning goal in Toronto's 4–0 victory over Detroit Red Wings, April 25, 1964

- Scored first goal in history of Pittsburgh Penguins franchise in 2–1 loss to Montreal Canadiens, October 11, 1967

- Traded to Detroit by Toronto with Billy Harris and Gary Jarrett for Marcel Pronovost, Eddie Joyal, Larry Jeffrey, Lowell McDonald and Aut Erickson, May 20, 1965; claimed by Pittsburgh from Detroit in Expansion Draft, June 6, 1967

- Member of Calder Cup-winning Cleveland Barons (1954); member of WHL champion Vancouver Canucks (1969, 1970)

MAPLE LEAFS

ANDY BATHGATE forward

Bathgate's 1964–65 "Tall Boy" hockey card.

REGULAR SEASON

Season	Age	Team	Lg	GP	G	A	PTS	+/-	PIM	ESG	PPG	SHG	GWG	SOG	S%
1952–53	20	New York Rangers	NHL	18	0	1	1		6						
1953–54	21	New York Rangers	NHL	20	2	2	4		18						
1954–55	22	New York Rangers	NHL	70	20	20	40		37						
1955–56	23	New York Rangers	NHL	70	19	47	66		59						
1956–57	24	New York Rangers	NHL	70	27	50	77		60						
1957–58	25	New York Rangers	NHL	65	30	48	78		42						
1958–59	26	New York Rangers	NHL	70	40	48	88		48						
1959–60	27	New York Rangers	NHL	70	26	48	74		28						
1960–61	28	New York Rangers	NHL	70	29	48	77		22						
1961–62	29	New York Rangers	NHL	70	28	56	84		44						
1962–63	30	New York Rangers	NHL	70	35	46	81		54						
1963–64	31	New York Rangers	NHL	56	16	43	59		26	12	4	0	1		
1963–64	31	Toronto Maple Leafs	NHL	15	3	15	18		8	3	0	0	0		
1964–65	32	Toronto Maple Leafs	NHL	55	16	29	45		34	10	6	0	1		
1965–66	33	Detroit Red Wings	NHL	70	15	32	47		25	11	4	0	3		
1966–67	34	Detroit Red Wings	NHL	60	8	23	31		24	8	0	0	1		
1967–68	35	Pittsburgh Penguins	NHL	74	20	39	59	-11	55	18	2	0	4	293	6.8
1970–71	38	Pittsburgh Penguins	NHL	76	15	29	44	-11	34	8	7	0	3	209	7.2
1974–75	42	Vancouver Blazers	WHA	11	1	6	7		2					12	8.3
Career – 18 Seasons				1080	350	630	980	-22	626	70	23	0	13	514	7.0

PLAYOFFS

Season	Age	Team	Lg	GP	G	A	PTS	+/-	PIM	ESG	PPG	SHG	GWG	SOG	S%
1955–56	23	New York Rangers	NHL	5	1	2	3		3						
1956–57	24	New York Rangers	NHL	5	2	0	2		27						
1957–58	25	New York Rangers	NHL	6	5	3	8		6						
1961–62	29	New York Rangers	NHL	6	1	2	3		4						
1963–64	31	Toronto Maple Leafs	NHL	14	5	4	9		25						
1964–65	32	Toronto Maple Leafs	NHL	6	1	0	1		6						
1965–66	33	Detroit Red Wings	NHL	12	6	3	9		6						
Career – 7 Seasons				54	21	14	35		76						

TROPHY CASE

AWARDS

Hart Memorial Trophy (1959)

Stanley Cup (1963–64)

ALL-STAR SELECTIONS

First All-Star Team Right Wing (1959, 1962)

Second All-Star Team Right Wing (1958, 1963)

Bobby Bauer

HOCKEY HALL OF FAME CLASS: 1996

Right Wing

Shoots: Right

Height: 5'-6"

Weight: 155 lbs.

Born: February 16, 1915: Waterloo, Ontario

Died: September 16, 1964: Kitchener, Ontario

Played nine NHL seasons from 1936–42, 1945–47, 1951–52

QUICK FACTS

- Played amateur hockey with St. Michael's Buzzers (1930–31); St. Michael's Majors (1931–34); Toronto British Consols (1934–35); Kitchener Greenshirts (1934–35); Kitchener-Waterloo Dutchmen (1947–50, 1951–52)

- Played minor pro with Boston Cubs (1935–36); Providence Reds (1936–37)

- Member of Boston's famed Kraut Line with Milt Schmidt and Woody Dumart

- Scored Stanley Cup-winning goal in Boston's 3–1 victory over Detroit Red Wings, April 12, 1941

- Played with Ottawa RCAF Flyers (1941–42); Dartmouth RCAF (1942–43) and Toronto People's Credit (1944–45) during World War II

- Member of Allan Cup-winning Ottawa RCAF Flyers (1941–42)

- Came out of retirement to play one game with Boston when the team honored the Kraut Line and scored a goal and assisted on Milt Schmidt's 200th career goal, March 18, 1952

- Coached Guelph Biltmores (1947–48)

- Served as coach, General Manager and/or President of Kitchener-Waterloo Dutchmen (1952–64)

- Coached Allan Cup-winning Kitchener-Waterloo Dutchmen (1952–53, 1955–56)

- Coached Kitchener-Waterloo Dutchmen team that represented Canada at 1956 and 1960 Winter Olympic Games

- Brother of Father David Bauer, founder and first coach of the Canadian National Team program

> There was no better person than Bobby. [He] gave everything he had. He was the brains of the line, always thinking, and a very clever playmaker."
> — Woody Dumart, Kraut Line teammate

REGULAR SEASON

Season	Age	Team	Lg	GP	G	A	PTS	PIM
1936–37	21	Boston Bruins	NHL	1	1	0	1	0
1937–38	22	Boston Bruins	NHL	48	20	14	34	9
1938–39	23	Boston Bruins	NHL	48	13	18	31	4
1939–40	24	Boston Bruins	NHL	48	17	26	43	2
1940–41	25	Boston Bruins	NHL	48	17	22	39	2
1941–42	26	Boston Bruins	NHL	36	14	22	35	11
1945–46	30	Boston Bruins	NHL	39	11	10	21	4
1946–47	31	Boston Bruins	NHL	58	30	24	54	4
1951–52	36	Boston Bruins	NHL	1	1	1	2	0
NHL Career – 9 Seasons				327	123	137	260	36

PLAYOFFS

Season	Age	Team	Lg	GP	G	A	PTS	PIM
1936–37	21	Boston Bruins	NHL	1	0	0	0	0
1937–38	22	Boston Bruins	NHL	3	0	0	0	2
1938–39	23	Boston Bruins	NHL	12	3	2	5	0
1939–40	24	Boston Bruins	NHL	6	1	0	1	2
1940–41	25	Boston Bruins	NHL	11	2	2	4	0
1945–46	30	Boston Bruins	NHL	10	4	3	7	2
1946–47	31	Boston Bruins	NHL	5	1	1	2	0
NHL Career – 7 Seasons				48	11	8	19	6

TROPHY CASE

AWARDS

Lady Byng Memorial Trophy (1940, 1941, 1947)

Stanley Cup (1938–39, 1940–41)

ALL-STAR SELECTIONS

Second All-Star Team Right Wing (1939, 1940, 1941, 1947)

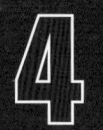

Jean Béliveau

HOCKEY HALL OF FAME CLASS: 1972

4

Retired by Montreal

Alternates: 12, 17, 20
Center
Shoots: Left
Height: 6'-3"
Weight: 205 lbs.
Born: August 31, 1931: Trois Rivieres, Quebec
Played 20 NHL seasons from 1950–51, 1952–71

"I always said a captain has three roles on the team: one, is during a game, when the fans and referees are watching him; two, his role between management and the players and three, a captain must represent his team and city well."

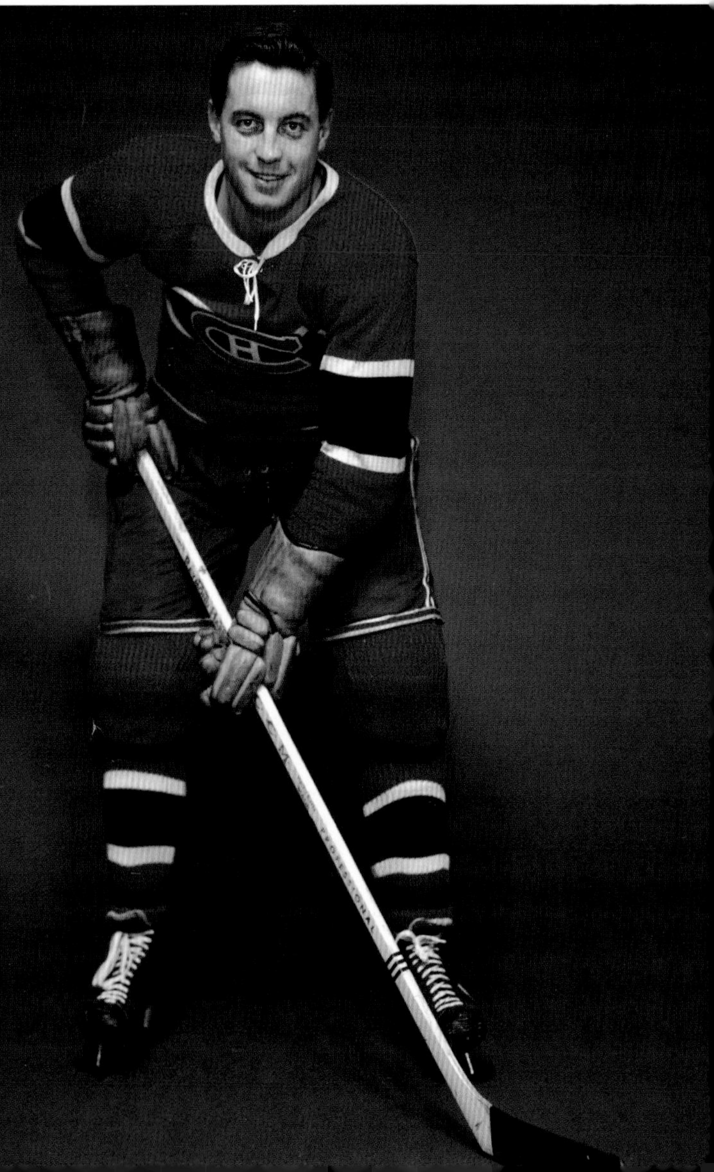

QUICK FACTS

- Holds NHL record for fastest Stanley Cup-winning goal (14 seconds) in Montreal's 4–0 victory over Chicago Black Hawks, April 14, 1965

- First winner of Conn Smythe Trophy as NHL playoff MVP (1965)

- Played amateur hockey with Victoriaville Tigers (1947–49); Quebec Citadelles (1949–51)

- Named QJHL Rookie of the Year (1949); QMHL First All-Star Team Center (1951, 1953)

- Led QJHL in goals (48) in 1948–49; led QJHL playoffs in goals (22) and points (31) in 1949–50; led QJHL in goals (63) and points (124) in 1950–51; led QJHL playoffs in goals (12), assists (14) and points (26) in 1950–51

- Led NHL in goals in 1955–56 (47) and 1958–59 (45)

- Led NHL in assists in 1960–61 (58) and 1965–66 (48)

- Led NHL in points (88) in 1955–56

- Played in NHL All-Star Game (1953, 1954, 1955, 1956, 1957, 1958, 1959, 1960, 1963, 1964, 1965, 1968, 1969)

- Registered 1,000th career NHL point in Montreal's 5–2 loss to Detroit Red Wings, March 3, 1968; recorded 500th career NHL goal in Montreal's 6–2 victory over Minnesota North Stars, February 11, 1971

- Nicknamed "Le Gros Bill" after a character in Quebec folklore

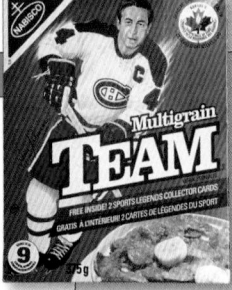

A breakfast with the captain: 1992 special edition Nabisco Multigrain Team cereal.

REGULAR SEASON

Season	Age	Team	Lg	GP	G	A	PTS	+/-	PIM	ESG	PPG	SHG	GWG	SOG	S%
1950–51	19	Montreal Canadiens	NHL	2	1	1	2		0						
1952–53	21	Montreal Canadiens	NHL	3	5	0	5		0						
1953–54	22	Montreal Canadiens	NHL	44	13	21	34		22						
1954–55	23	Montreal Canadiens	NHL	70	37	36	73		58						
1955–56	24	Montreal Canadiens	NHL	70	47	41	88		143						
1956–57	25	Montreal Canadiens	NHL	69	33	51	84		105						
1957–58	26	Montreal Canadiens	NHL	55	27	32	59		93						
1958–59	27	Montreal Canadiens	NHL	64	45	46	91		67						
1959–60	28	Montreal Canadiens	NHL	60	34	40	74		57						
1960–61	29	Montreal Canadiens	NHL	69	32	58	90		57						
1961–62	30	Montreal Canadiens	NHL	43	18	23	41		36						
1962–63	31	Montreal Canadiens	NHL	69	18	49	67		68						
1963–64	32	Montreal Canadiens	NHL	68	28	50	78		42	15	13	0	2		
1964–65	33	Montreal Canadiens	NHL	58	20	23	43		76	11	9	0	1		
1965–66	34	Montreal Canadiens	NHL	67	29	48	77		50	16	13	0	7		
1966–67	35	Montreal Canadiens	NHL	53	12	26	38		22	10	2	0	0		
1967–68	36	Montreal Canadiens	NHL	59	31	37	68	27	28	22	9	0	3	206	15.0
1968–69	37	Montreal Canadiens	NHL	69	33	49	82	15	55	26	7	0	5	235	14.0
1969–70	38	Montreal Canadiens	NHL	63	19	30	49	1	10	16	3	0	1	169	11.2
1970–71	39	Montreal Canadiens	NHL	70	25	51	76	24	40	18	7	0	4	172	14.5
NHL Career – 20 Seasons				1125	507	712	1219	67	1029	134	63	0	23	782	13.8

PLAYOFFS

Season	Age	Team	Lg	GP	G	A	PTS	+/-	PIM	ESG	PPG	SHG	GWG	SOG	S%
1953–54	22	Montreal Canadiens	NHL	10	2	8	10		4						
1954–55	23	Montreal Canadiens	NHL	12	6	7	13		18						
1955–56	24	Montreal Canadiens	NHL	10	12	7	19		22						
1956–57	25	Montreal Canadiens	NHL	10	6	6	12		15						
1957–58	26	Montreal Canadiens	NHL	10	4	8	12		10						
1958–59	27	Montreal Canadiens	NHL	3	1	4	5		4						
1959–60	28	Montreal Canadiens	NHL	8	5	2	7		6						
1960–61	29	Montreal Canadiens	NHL	6	0	5	5		0						
1961–62	30	Montreal Canadiens	NHL	6	2	1	3		4						
1962–63	31	Montreal Canadiens	NHL	5	2	1	3		2						
1963–64	32	Montreal Canadiens	NHL	5	2	0	2		18						
1964–65	33	Montreal Canadiens	NHL	13	8	8	16		34						
1965–66	34	Montreal Canadiens	NHL	10	5	5	10		6						
1966–67	35	Montreal Canadiens	NHL	10	6	5	11		26						
1967–68	36	Montreal Canadiens	NHL	10	7	4	11		6	4	3	0	1		
1968–69	37	Montreal Canadiens	NHL	14	5	10	15		8	4	1	0	1		
1970–71	39	Montreal Canadiens	NHL	20	6	16	22		28	4	2	0	0		
NHL Career – 17 Seasons				162	79	97	176		211	12	6	0	2		

1

Clint Benedict
HOCKEY HALL OF FAME CLASS: 1965

Alternate: 9

Goaltender

Catches: Left

Height: 6'-4"

Weight: 200 lbs.

Born: September 26, 1882: Ottawa, Ontario

Died: November 12, 1976: Ottawa, Ontario

Played 18 professional seasons from 1912–30

> (Benedict) devised an elaborate series of ruses to allow him to get to his knees — ruses that other goaltenders began copying. One routine allegedly saw him dropping to his knees to give thanks to God — a play that gave rise among outraged Toronto fans to the nickname 'Praying Bennie'."
> — Douglas Hunter, *A Breed Apart*

QUICK FACTS

- First NHL goaltender to win the Stanley Cup with two different teams: Ottawa Senators (1920–21, 1922–23), and Montreal Maroons (1925–26)

- First NHL goaltender to wear mask in a NHL game during Montreal Maroons' 3–3 tie with N.Y. Americans, February 20, 1930. He discarded the mask after five games because it affected his vision

- First NHL goaltender to record three consecutive shutouts in a single playoff season (1926)

- First NHL goaltender to record four shutouts in a single playoff season (1926)

- Nicknamed "Praying Bennie" because he was the first goaltender to fall to his knees to make a save

- Played amateur hockey with Ottawa Stewartons (1909–10), Ottawa New Edinburghs (1910–12) and Windsor Bulldogs (1930–31)

- Led NHL in wins in 1918–19 (12), 1919–20 (19), 1920–21 (14), 1921–22 (14), 1922–23 (14) and 1923–24 (15)

- Led NHL in shutouts in 1917–18 (1), 1918–19 (2), 1919–20 (5), 1920–21 (2), 1921–22 (2), 1922–23 (4), 1923–24 (3)

- Led NHL in goals-against-average in 1918–19 (2.76), 1919–20 (2.66), 1920–21 (3.08), 1921–22 (3.34), 1922–23 (2.18) and 1926–27 (1.42)

- Traded to Montreal Maroons by Ottawa with Punch Broadbent for cash, October 20, 1924

Benedict's famous mask from 1930, the first mask worn in NHL action.

TROPHY CASE

AWARDS

Stanley Cup: (1920–21, 1922–23, 1925–26)

REGULAR SEASON

Season	Age	Team	Lg	GP	W	L	T	SO	GA	GAA	G	A	PTS	PIM
1912–13	20	Ottawa Senators	NHA	10	7	2	1	1	16	3.49				
1913–14	21	Ottawa Senators	NHA	9	5	3	0	0	29	3.67				
1914–15	22	Ottawa Senators	NHA	20	14	6	0	0	65	3.14				
1915–16	23	Ottawa Senators	NHA	24	13	11	0	1	72	2.99				
1916–17	24	Ottawa Senators	NHA	18	14	4	0	1	50	2.72				
1917–18	25	Ottawa Senators	NHL	22	9	13	0	1	114	5.12	0	0	0	0
1918–19	26	Ottawa Senators	NHL	18	12	6	0	2	53	2.76	0	0	0	3
1919–20	27	Ottawa Senators	NHL	24	19	5	0	5	64	2.66	0	0	0	0
1920–21	28	Ottawa Senators	NHL	24	14	10	0	2	75	3.08	0	0	0	0
1921–22	29	Ottawa Senators	NHL	24	14	8	2	2	84	3.34	0	0	0	0
1922–23	30	Ottawa Senators	NHL	24	14	9	1	4	54	2.18	0	0	0	2
1923–24	31	Ottawa Senators	NHL	22	15	7	0	3	45	1.99	0	0	0	0
1924–25	32	Montreal Maroons	NHL	30	9	19	2	2	65	2.12	0	0	0	2
1925–26	33	Montreal Maroons	NHL	36	20	11	5	6	73	1.91	0	0	0	0
1926–27	34	Montreal Maroons	NHL	43	20	19	4	13	65	1.42	0	0	0	0
1927–28	35	Montreal Maroons	NHL	44	24	14	6	6	76	1.70	0	0	0	0
1928–29	36	Montreal Maroons	NHL	37	14	16	7	11	57	1.49	0	0	0	0
1929–30	37	Montreal Maroons	NHL	14	6	6	1	0	38	3.03	0	0	0	0
Career — 18 Seasons				443	243	169	29	60	1095	2.47	0	0	0	7

PLAYOFFS

Season	Age	Team	Lg	GP	W	L	T	SO	GA	GAA	G	A	PTS	PIM
1914–15	22	Ottawa Senators	NHA	2	1	1	0	1	2	1.00				
1914–15	22	Ottawa Senators	St-Cup	3	0	3	0	0	26	8.67				
1916–17	24	Ottawa Senators	NHA	2	1	1	0	0	7	3.50				
1918–19	26	Ottawa Senators	NHL	5	1	4	0	0	26	2.50	0	0	0	0
1919–20	27	Ottawa Senators	St-Cup	5	3	2	0	1	11	2.20				
1920–21	28	Ottawa Senators	NHL	2	2	0	0	2	0	0.00	0	0	0	0
1920–21	28	Ottawa Senators	St-Cup	5	3	2	0	0	12	2.40				
1921–22	29	Ottawa Senators	NHL	2	0	1	1	1	5	2.50	0	0	0	0
1922–23	30	Ottawa Senators	NHL	2	1	1	0	1	2	1.00	0	0	0	0
1922–23	30	Ottawa Senators	St-Cup	6	5	1	0	1	8	1.33				
1923–24	31	Ottawa Senators	NHL	2	0	2	0	0	5	2.50	0	0	0	0
1925–26	33	Montreal Maroons	NHL	4	2	0	2	1	5	1.25	0	0	0	0
1925–26	33	Montreal Maroons	St-Cup	4	3	1	0	3	3	0.75				
1926–27	34	Montreal Maroons	NHL	2	0	1	1	0	2	0.91	0	0	0	0
1927–28	35	Montreal Maroons	NHL	9	5	3	1	4	8	0.86	0	0	0	0
Career — 11 Seasons				55	27	23	5	15	122	2.22	0	0	0	0

7

Doug Bentley

HOCKEY HALL OF FAME CLASS: 1964

Alternates:
14, 19, 6

Left Wing/Center

Shoots: Left

Height: 5'-8"

Weight: 145 lbs.

Born: September
3, 1916: Delisle,
Saskatchewan

Died: November
24, 1972:
Saskatoon,
Saskatchewan

Played 13 NHL
seasons from
1939–44,
1945–52, 1953–54

**I thought
about
quitting, but
you know, I've
never liked the
word quit."**

QUICK FACTS

- Played amateur hockey with Delisle Tigers (1932–33); Saskatoon Wesleys (1933–34); Regina Victorias (1934–35); Moose Jaw Millers (1935–38); Drumheller Miners (1938–39)
- Led Southern Saskatchewan Senior League in assists (19) and points (37) in 1936–37; led S-SSHL in playoff assists (8) and points (14) in 1936–37
- Led ASHL in playoff goals (7) in 1938–39
- ASHL First All-Star Team Left Wing (1938–39)
- Member of the Chicago's famed Pony Line with brother Max Bentley and Bill Mosienko
- Member of the NHL's first all-brother line with Max and Reggie during the 1942–43 season

- Led NHL in goals in 1942–43 (33) and 1943–44 (38)
- Led NHL in assists in 1947–48 (37) and 1948–49 (43)
- Missed entire 1944–45 season after being given permission to stay home and tend to family farm by Canadian Armed Forces officials, September, 1944
- Played in NHL All-Star Game (1947, 1948, 1949, 1950, 1951)
- Served as captain of Chicago Black Hawks (1942–44)
- Traded to N.Y. Rangers by Chicago for cash, June 30, 1953
- Served as player/coach with Saskatoon Quakers (1951–56)

Bentley's 1947–48 Black Hawks jersey; he led Chicago in points that season with 57.

REGULAR SEASON

Season	Age	Team	Lg	GP	G	A	PTS	PIM
1939–40	23	Chicago Blackhawks	NHL	39	12	7	19	12
1940–41	24	Chicago Blackhawks	NHL	47	8	20	28	12
1941–42	25	Chicago Blackhawks	NHL	38	12	14	26	11
1942–43	26	Chicago Blackhawks	NHL	50	33	40	73	18
1943–44	27	Chicago Blackhawks	NHL	50	38	39	77	22
1945–46	29	Chicago Blackhawks	NHL	36	19	21	40	16
1946–47	30	Chicago Blackhawks	NHL	52	21	34	55	18
1947–48	31	Chicago Blackhawks	NHL	60	20	37	57	16
1948–49	32	Chicago Blackhawks	NHL	58	23	43	66	38
1949–50	33	Chicago Blackhawks	NHL	64	20	33	53	28
1950–51	34	Chicago Blackhawks	NHL	44	9	23	32	20
1951–52	35	Chicago Blackhawks	NHL	8	2	3	5	4
1953–54	37	New York Rangers	NHL	20	2	10	12	2
NHL Career – 13 Seasons				566	219	324	543	217

PLAYOFFS

Season	Age	Team	Lg	GP	G	A	PTS	PIM
1939–40	23	Chicago Blackhawks	NHL	2	0	0	0	0
1940–41	24	Chicago Blackhawks	NHL	5	1	1	2	4
1941–42	25	Chicago Blackhawks	NHL	3	0	1	1	4
1943–44	27	Chicago Blackhawks	NHL	9	8	4	12	4
1945–46	29	Chicago Blackhawks	NHL	4	0	2	2	0
NHL Career – 5 Seasons				23	9	8	17	12

TROPHY CASE

AWARDS

NHL Scoring Leader (1943)

ALL-STAR SELECTIONS

First All-Star Team Left Wing (1943, 1944, 1947)

Second All-Star Team Center (1949)

7

Max Bentley
HOCKEY HALL OF FAME CLASS: 1966

Alternates:
5, 18, 22

Center

Shoots: Left

Height: 5'-10"

Weight: 155 lbs.

Born: March 1,
1920: Delisle,
Saskatchewan

Died: January 19,
1984: Saskatoon,
Saskatchewan

Played 12 NHL
seasons from
1940–43, 1945–54

QUICK FACTS

- Shares NHL record for most goals in a single period (4), established in Chicago's 10–1 victory over N.Y. Rangers, January 28, 1943
- Nicknamed "The Dipsy-Doodle Dandy from Delisle"
- Played amateur hockey with Rosetown Red Wings (1935–37); Drumheller Miners (1937–39); Saskatoon Quakers (1939–40)
- Played with Victoria Navy, San Diego Skyhawks and Calgary Currie Army during World War II (1942–45)
- Led ASHL in points (43) in 1936–37; led ASHL in playoff goals (7) and points (8) in 1936–37
- Led SSHL in goals (37) in 1939–40
- Led ANDHL in goals (18), points (31) and penalty minutes (26) in 1942–43

- Played in NHL All-Star Game (1947, 1948, 1949, 1951)
- Led NHL in points in 1945–46 (61) and 1946–47 (72)
- Finished second in NHL assists in 1942–43 (44), 1945–46 (30) and 1946–47 (43)
- Finished among NHL top-5 in goals in 1945–46 (31), 1946–47 (29) and 1947–48 (26)
- Traded to Toronto by Chicago with Cy Thomas for Gus Bodnar, Bud Poile, Gaye Stewart, Ernie Dickens and Bob Goldham, November 2, 1947
- Brother of Doug Bentley, who played in NHL with Chicago and N.Y. Rangers from 1939–54; brother of Reggie Bentley, who played in NHL with Chicago in 1942–43

> He was the best, a dispy-doodler who could really skate and was tremendous with the puck."
> — Vic Lynn, teammate

REGULAR SEASON

Season	Age	Team	Lg	GP	G	A	PTS	PIM
1940–41	20	Chicago Blackhawks	NHL	36	7	10	17	6
1941–42	21	Chicago Blackhawks	NHL	39	13	17	30	2
1942–43	22	Chicago Blackhawks	NHL	47	26	44	70	2
1945–46	25	Chicago Blackhawks	NHL	47	31	30	61	6
1946–47	26	Chicago Blackhawks	NHL	60	29	43	72	12
1947–48	27	Chicago Blackhawks	NHL	6	3	3	6	4
1947–48	27	Toronto Maple Leafs	NHL	53	23	25	48	10
1948–49	28	Toronto Maple Leafs	NHL	60	19	22	41	18
1949–50	29	Toronto Maple Leafs	NHL	69	23	18	41	14
1950–51	30	Toronto Maple Leafs	NHL	67	21	41	62	34
1951–52	31	Toronto Maple Leafs	NHL	69	24	17	41	40
1952–53	32	Toronto Maple Leafs	NHL	36	12	11	23	16
1953–54	33	New York Rangers	NHL	57	14	18	32	15
NHL Career — 12 Seasons				646	245	299	544	179

PLAYOFFS

Season	Age	Team	Lg	GP	G	A	PTS	PIM
1940–41	20	Chicago Blackhawks	NHL	4	1	3	4	2
1941–42	21	Chicago Blackhawks	NHL	3	2	0	2	0
1945–46	25	Chicago Blackhawks	NHL	4	1	0	1	4
1947–48	27	Toronto Maple Leafs	NHL	9	4	7	11	0
1948–49	28	Toronto Maple Leafs	NHL	9	4	3	7	2
1949–50	29	Toronto Maple Leafs	NHL	7	3	3	6	0
1950–51	30	Toronto Maple Leafs	NHL	11	2	11	13	4
1951–52	31	Toronto Maple Leafs	NHL	4	1	0	1	2
NHL Career — 8 Seasons				51	18	27	45	14

TROPHY CASE

AWARDS

NHL Scoring Leader (1946, 1947)

Lady Byng Memorial Trophy (1943)

Hart Memorial Trophy (1946)

Stanley Cup (1947–48, 1948–49, 1950–51)

ALL-STAR SELECTIONS

First All-Star Team Center (1946)

Second All-Star Team Center (1947)

Toe Blake

HOCKEY HALL OF FAME CLASS: 1966

Alternates: 16, 21, 8

Left Wing

Shoots: Left

Height: 5'-10"

Weight: 165 lbs.

Born: August 21, 1912: Victoria Mines, Ontario

Died: May 17, 1995: Montreal, Quebec

Played 14 NHL seasons from 1934–48

QUICK FACTS

> If the day ever comes when I can swallow defeat, I'll quit."

- Ranks second in Stanley Cup championships won by a coach (8)
- Played amateur hockey with Cochrane Dunlops (1929–30); Sudbury Cub Wolves (1930–32); Sudbury CIL (1930–31); Sudbury Wolves (1930–31); Falconbridge Falcons (1931–32); Hamilton Tigers (1932–35)
- Played minor pro hockey with Providence Reds (1935–36); Buffalo Bisons (1948–49); Valleyfield Braves (1949–51)
- Led NOJHL in goals (5) in 1931–32; led NBHL in goals (8) in 1931–32; led OHA-Sr. in playoff assists (4) and points (7) in 1933–34
- Led NHL in points (47) in 1938–39; led NHL playoffs in assists (11) and points (18) in 1943–44; led NHL playoffs in goals (7) in 1945–46; led NHL playoffs in assists (7) in 1946–47
- Finished among NHL top-5 in goals in 1938–39 (24); 1944–45 (29) and 1945–46 (29)
- Member of Montreal Canadiens' famed Punch Line with Maurice Richard and Elmer Lach
- Served as captain of Montreal Canadiens (1940–47, 1947–48)
- Scored Stanley Cup-winning overtime goal in Montreal's 5–4 victory over Chicago Black Hawks, April 13, 1944; scored Stanley Cup-winning goal in Montreal's 6–3 victory over Boston Bruins, April 9, 1946
- Acquired the nickname "Old Lamplighter" early in his career because of his scoring talent

REGULAR SEASON

Season	Age	Team	Lg	GP	G	A	PTS	PIM
1934–35	22	Montreal Maroons	NHL	8	0	0	0	0
1935–36	23	Montreal Canadiens	NHL	11	1	2	3	28
1936–37	24	Montreal Canadiens	NHL	43	10	12	22	12
1937–38	25	Montreal Canadiens	NHL	43	17	16	33	33
1938–39	26	Montreal Canadiens	NHL	48	24	23	47	10
1939–40	27	Montreal Canadiens	NHL	48	17	19	36	48
1940–41	28	Montreal Canadiens	NHL	48	12	20	32	49
1941–42	29	Montreal Canadiens	NHL	48	17	28	45	19
1942–43	30	Montreal Canadiens	NHL	48	23	36	59	26
1943–44	31	Montreal Canadiens	NHL	41	26	33	59	10
1944–45	32	Montreal Canadiens	NHL	49	29	38	67	25
1945–46	33	Montreal Canadiens	NHL	50	29	21	50	2
1946–47	34	Montreal Canadiens	NHL	60	21	29	50	6
1947–48	35	Montreal Canadiens	NHL	32	9	15	24	4
NHL Career – 14 Seasons				577	235	292	527	272

PLAYOFFS

Season	Age	Team	Lg	GP	G	A	PTS	PIM
1934–35	22	Montreal Maroons	NHL	1	0	0	0	0
1936–37	24	Montreal Canadiens	NHL	5	1	0	1	0
1937–38	25	Montreal Canadiens	NHL	3	3	1	4	2
1938–39	26	Montreal Canadiens	NHL	3	1	1	2	2
1940–41	28	Montreal Canadiens	NHL	3	0	3	3	5
1941–42	29	Montreal Canadiens	NHL	3	0	3	3	2
1942–43	30	Montreal Canadiens	NHL	5	4	3	7	0
1943–44	31	Montreal Canadiens	NHL	9	7	11	18	2
1944–45	32	Montreal Canadiens	NHL	6	0	2	2	5
1945–46	33	Montreal Canadiens	NHL	9	7	6	13	5
1946–47	34	Montreal Canadiens	NHL	11	2	7	9	0
NHL Career – 11 Seasons				58	25	37	62	23

TROPHY CASE

AWARDS

NHL Scoring Leader (1939)

Hart Memorial Trophy (1939)

Lady Byng Memorial Trophy (1946)

Stanley Cup (1934–35, 1943–44, 1945–46)

ALL-STAR SELECTIONS

First All-Star Team Left Wing (1939, 1940, 1945)

Second All-Star Team Left Wing (1938, 1946)

20

Leo Boivin
HOCKEY HALL OF FAME CLASS: 1986

Alternates:
19, 2, 5, 4, 18

Defense

Shoots: Left

Height: 5'-8"

Weight: 183 lbs.

Born: August 2, 1932: Prescott, Ontario

Played 19 NHL seasons from 1951–70

QUICK FACTS

- Played amateur hockey with Inkerman Rockets (1948–49); Port Arthur West End Bruins (1949–51)
- Served as captain of Boston Bruins (1963–66)
- Played in NHL All-Star Game (1961, 1962, 1964)
- Traded to Toronto by Boston with Fernie Flaman, Ken Smith and Phil Maloney for Bill Ezinicki and Vic Lynn, November 16, 1950
- Traded to Boston by Toronto for Joe Klukay, November 9, 1954
- Traded to Detroit by Boston with Dean Prentice for Gary Doak, Ron Murphy, Bill Lesuk and future considerations (Steve Atkinson, June 6, 1966), February 16, 1966
- Claimed by Pittsburgh from Detroit in Expansion Draft, June 6, 1967
- Traded to Minnesota by Pittsburgh for Duane Rupp, January 24, 1969
- Served as scout for Minnesota North Stars (1970–72)
- Coached Ottawa 67's (1972–74)
- Served as scout and assistant coach of St. Louis Blues (1974–76, 1978–84)
- Coached St. Louis Blues (1975–76, 1977–78)
- Renowned for his stay-at-home, hard-rock hitting style
- One of several Hall of Fame players who never won a Stanley Cup

> My dream was to win the Stanley Cup, but I never did win it. It's just the way it goes."

TROPHY CASE

REGULAR SEASON

Season	Age	Team	Lg	GP	G	A	PTS	+/-	PIM	ESG	PPG	SHG	GWG	SOG	S%
1951-52	19	Toronto Maple Leafs	NHL	2	0	1	1		0						
1952-53	20	Toronto Maple Leafs	NHL	70	2	13	15		97						
1953-54	21	Toronto Maple Leafs	NHL	58	1	6	7		81						
1954-55	22	Toronto Maple Leafs	NHL	7	0	0	0		8						
1954-55	22	Boston Bruins	NHL	59	6	11	17		105						
1955-56	23	Boston Bruins	NHL	68	4	16	20		80						
1956-57	24	Boston Bruins	NHL	55	2	8	10		55						
1957-58	25	Boston Bruins	NHL	33	0	4	4		54						
1958-59	26	Boston Bruins	NHL	70	5	16	21		94						
1959-60	27	Boston Bruins	NHL	70	4	21	25		66						
1960-61	28	Boston Bruins	NHL	57	6	17	23		50						
1961-62	29	Boston Bruins	NHL	65	5	18	23		70						
1962-63	30	Boston Bruins	NHL	62	2	24	26		48						
1963-64	31	Boston Bruins	NHL	65	10	14	24		42	8	1	1	0		
1964-65	32	Boston Bruins	NHL	67	3	10	13		68	3	0	0	1		
1965-66	33	Boston Bruins	NHL	46	0	5	5		34	0	0	0	0		
1965-66	33	Detroit Red Wings	NHL	16	0	5	5		16	0	0	0	0		
1966-67	34	Detroit Red Wings	NHL	69	4	17	21		78	4	0	0	1		
1967-68	35	Pittsburgh Penguins	NHL	73	9	13	22	-15	74	5	4	0	1	163	5.5
1968-69	36	Pittsburgh Penguins	NHL	41	5	13	18	-6	26	3	2	0	1	74	6.8
1968-69	36	Minnesota North Stars	NHL	28	1	6	7	-19	16	0	1	0	0	64	1.6
1969-70	37	Minnesota North Stars	NHL	69	3	12	15	-2	30	3	0	0	0	95	3.2
NHL Career – 19 Seasons				1150	72	250	322	-42	1192	26	8	1	4	396	4.5

PLAYOFFS

Season	Age	Team	Lg	GP	G	A	PTS	+/-	PIM	ESG	PPG	SHG	GWG	SOG	S%
1953-54	21	Toronto Maple Leafs	NHL	5	0	0	0		2						
1954-55	22	Boston Bruins	NHL	5	0	1	1		4						
1956-57	24	Boston Bruins	NHL	10	2	3	5		12						
1957-58	25	Boston Bruins	NHL	12	0	3	3		21						
1958-59	26	Boston Bruins	NHL	7	1	2	3		4						
1965-66	33	Detroit Red Wings	NHL	12	0	1	1		16						
1969-70	37	Minnesota North Stars	NHL	3	0	0	0		0	0	0	0	0		
NHL Career – 7 Seasons				54	3	10	13		59	0	0	0	0		

Dickie Boon

HOCKEY HALL OF FAME CLASS: 1952

Defense

Shoots: Right

Height: 5'-5"

Weight: 130 lbs

Born: January 10, 1878: Belleville, Ontario

Died: May 3, 1961: Montreal, Quebec

Played six elite amateur seasons from 1899–1905

QUICK FACTS

- Renowned for his ability to use the poke check to steal pucks from rival players
- Won Junior Amateur Speedskating championship in 1892
- Began playing organized hockey as a 16-year-old in 1894
- Starred on defense for the 1902 Montreal Amateur Athletic Association team that defeated the Winnipeg Victorias in a thrilling three-game series for the Stanley Cup and earned the nickname "Little Men of Iron" for the tenacious way they hung on for a 2–1 victory in the final game
- One of several Montreal AAA stars recruited to join the Montreal Wanderers when the team was formed in 1903–04
- Served as player/manager of Montreal Wanderers (1903–04, 1904–05)
- Manager of Stanley Cup-winning Montreal Wanderers (1905–06, 1906–07, 1907–08, 1909–10)
- Coached New Glasgow Miners (1905–06)
- Coached Montreal Wanderers (1906–16)

> "Last year, Dickie was named to the Hockey Hall of Fame, a popular salute by those who remembered him, to a 'Little Man of Iron' who weighed only 115 pounds when he was the game's composite Rocket Richard and Gordie Howe."
>
> — Vern DeGeer, *Montreal Gazette*, January 10, 1953

REGULAR SEASON

Season	Age	Team	Lg	GP	G	A	PTS	PIM
1899–00	22	Montreal AAA	CAHL	8	2	0	2	
1900–01	23	Montreal AAA	CAHL	7	3	0	3	
1901–02	24	Montreal AAA	CAHL	8	2	0	2	6
1902–03	25	Montreal AAA	CAHL	7	3	0	3	6
1903–04	26	Montreal Wanderers	FAHL	4	0	0	0	0
1904–05	27	Montreal Wanderers	FAHL	8	0	0	0	6
Career – 6 Seasons				42	10	0	10	18

PLAYOFFS

Season	Age	Team	Lg	GP	G	A	PTS	PIM
1901–02	24	Montreal AAA	St-Cup	3	0	0	0	3
1902–03	25	Montreal AAA	St-Cup	4	0	0	0	10
Career – 2 Seasons				7	0	0	0	13

TROPHY CASE

AWARDS

Stanley Cup (1901–02, 1902–03)

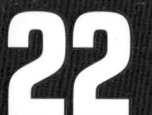

22

Retired by the N.Y. Islanders

Mike Bossy

HOCKEY HALL OF FAME CLASS: 1991

Right Wing

Shoots: Right

Height: 6'

Weight: 186 lbs.

Born: January 22, 1957: Montreal, Quebec

Drafted by the New York Islanders 15th overall in 1977

Played 10 NHL seasons from 1977–87

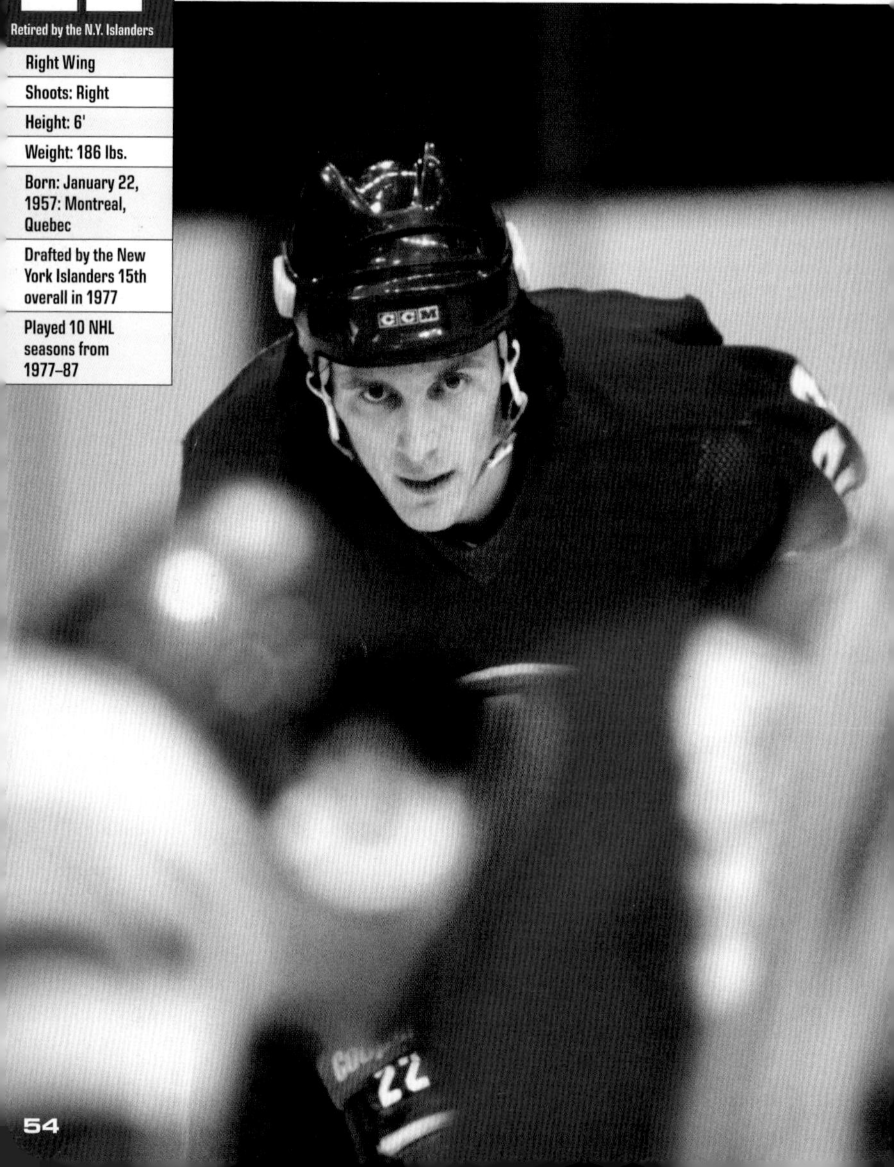

QUICK FACTS

- First NHL rookie to score 50 goals in the regular season (1977–78)
- Became second player in NHL history (with Maurice Richard) to score 50 goals in 50 games in N.Y. Islanders' 7–4 victory over Quebec Nordiques, January 24, 1981
- Holds NHL record for most consecutive 50-or-more goal seasons (9)
- Holds NHL record for most game-winning goals in a single playoff series (4), established in 1983
- Shares NHL record (with Cam Neely) for most power-play goals in a single playoff season (9), established in 1981
- Shares NHL record (with Wayne Gretzky) for most 50-or-more goal seasons (9); shares NHL record (with Wayne Gretzky) for most 60-or-more goal seasons (5)
- Played amateur hockey with Montreal-Bourassa Canadiens (1972–73); Laval Nationale (1972–77)
- Led QMJHL in goals (84) in 1974–75
- Scored Stanley Cup-winning goal in N.Y. Islanders' 3–1 victory over Vancouver Canucks, May 16, 1982
- Scored Stanley Cup-winning goal in N.Y. Islanders' 4–2 victory over Edmonton Oilers, May 17, 1983
- Played in NHL All-Star Game (1978, 1980–86)
- Led NHL in game-winning goals in 1980–81 (10) and 1985–86 (9); led NHL in power-play goals in 1977–78 (25), 1978–79 (27) and 1980–81 (28)

> I think a quick release is more important than aiming the puck. I always figured it was harder for a goalie to stop what he wasn't expecting than for me to look for a particular hole. Besides, in the NHL you almost never get the chance to pick a particular spot.

REGULAR SEASON

Season	Age	Team	Lg	GP	G	A	PTS	+/-	PIM	ESG	PPG	SHG	GWG	SOG	S%
1977–78	21	New York Islanders	NHL	73	53	38	91	31	6	28	25	0	5	235	22.6
1978–79	22	New York Islanders	NHL	80	69	57	126	63	25	42	27	0	9	279	24.7
1979–80	23	New York Islanders	NHL	75	51	41	92	28	12	35	16	0	8	244	20.9
1980–81	24	New York Islanders	NHL	79	68	51	119	37	32	38	28	2	10	315	21.6
1981–82	25	New York Islanders	NHL	80	64	83	147	69	22	47	17	0	10	301	21.3
1982–83	26	New York Islanders	NHL	79	60	58	118	27	20	41	19	0	8	272	22.1
1983–84	27	New York Islanders	NHL	67	51	67	118	66	8	45	6	0	11	246	20.7
1984–85	28	New York Islanders	NHL	76	58	59	117	37	38	40	14	4	7	285	20.4
1985–86	29	New York Islanders	NHL	80	61	62	123	30	14	39	21	1	9	302	20.2
1986–87	30	New York Islanders	NHL	63	38	37	75	-7	33	29	8	1	5	226	16.8
NHL Career – 10 Seasons				752	573	553	1126	381	210	384	181	8	82	2705	21.2

PLAYOFFS

Season	Age	Team	Lg	GP	G	A	PTS	+/-	PIM	ESG	PPG	SHG	GWG	SOG	S%
1977–78	21	New York Islanders	NHL	7	2	2	4		2	2	0	0	1		
1978–79	22	New York Islanders	NHL	10	6	2	8		2	4	2	0	1		
1979–80	23	New York Islanders	NHL	16	10	13	23		8	4	6	0	1		
1980–81	24	New York Islanders	NHL	18	17	18	35		4	8	9	0	3		
1981–82	25	New York Islanders	NHL	19	17	10	27		0	11	6	0	3		
1982–83	26	New York Islanders	NHL	19	17	9	26		10	11	6	0	5		
1983–84	27	New York Islanders	NHL	21	8	10	18	6	4	6	2	0	3	62	12.9
1984–85	28	New York Islanders	NHL	10	5	6	11	1	4	3	2	0	0	32	15.6
1985–86	29	New York Islanders	NHL	3	1	2	3	-2	4	1	0	0	0	14	7.1
1986–87	30	New York Islanders	NHL	6	2	3	5	-2	0	0	2	0	0	10	20.0
NHL Career – 10 Seasons				129	85	75	160	3	38	50	35	0	17	118	13.6

TROPHY CASE

AWARDS

Calder Memorial Trophy (1978)

Conn Smythe Trophy (1982)

Lady Byng Memorial Trophy (1983, 1984, 1986)

Stanley Cup (1979–80, 1980–81, 1981–82, 1982–83)

ALL-STAR SELECTIONS

First All-Star Team Right Wing (1981, 1982, 1983, 1984, 1986)

Second All-Star Team Right Wing (1978, 1979, 1985)

INTERNATIONAL AWARDS

Canada Cup (1984)

Retired by Montreal

Alternate: 17	
Defense	
Shoots: Right	
Height: 6'-2"	
Weight: 205 lbs.	
Born: September 4, 1919: Montreal, Quebec	
Played 15 NHL seasons from 1941–56	

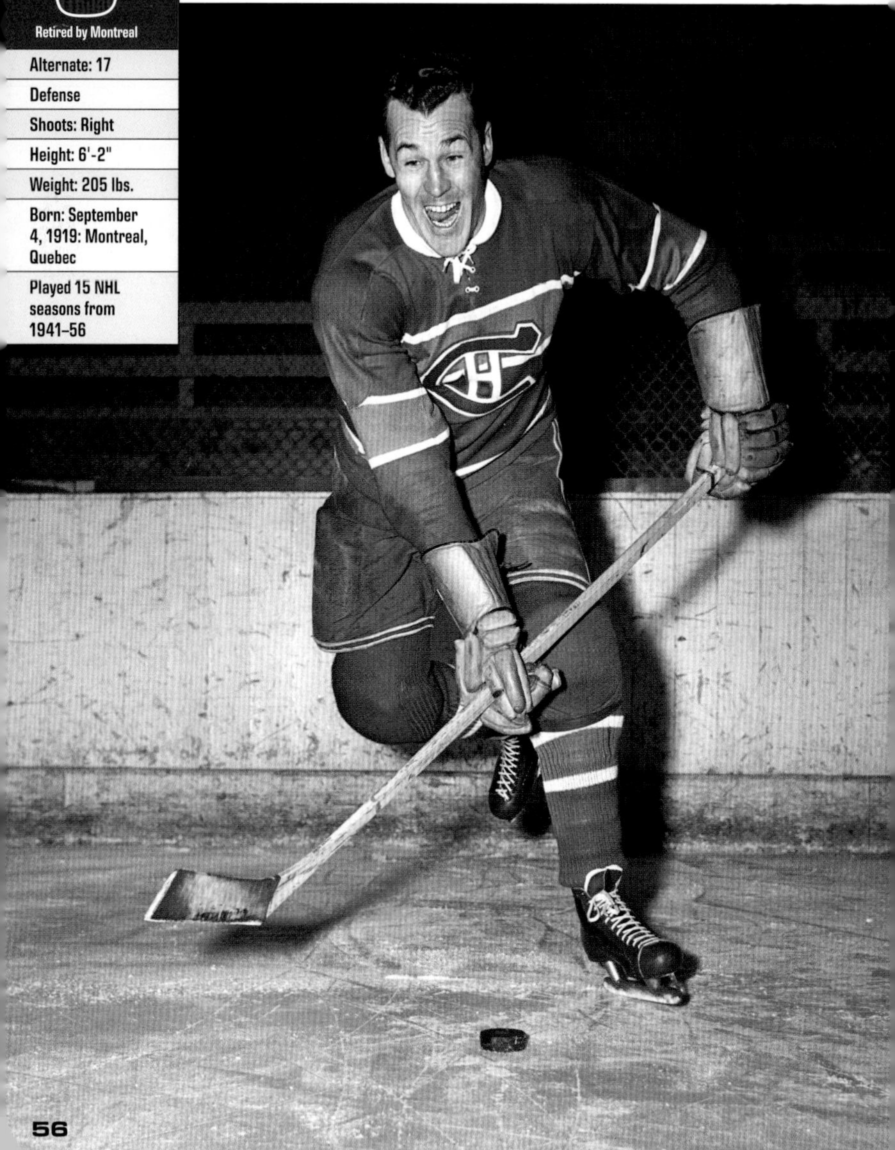

Butch Bouchard

HOCKEY HALL OF FAME CLASS: 1966

QUICK FACTS

- Played amateur hockey with Verdun Jr. Maple Leafs (1937–39); Verdun Sr. Maple Leafs (1939–40); Montreal Sr. Canadiens (1940–41)
- Played minor pro hockey with AHL's Providence Reds (1940–41)
- Signed as a free agent by Montreal Canadiens, February 21, 1941
- Nicknamed "Butch" by a junior teammate who said his last name was similar to the English word butcher
- Served as captain of Montreal Canadiens (1948–56)
- Played in NHL All-Star Game (1947, 1948, 1950, 1951, 1952, 1953)
- Renowned for his size, physical play and defensive domination

- Combined with Doug Harvey, the preeminent rushing defenseman of his time, to form one of the top backline pairs in the history of the game
- Served as President of the Montreal Royals AAA baseball club when the Royals won the Governors' Cup as champions of the International League (1958)
- Served as Municipal Council member for the city of Longueil (1960–62)
- Served as President of Montreal Metropolitan Junior "A" Hockey League (1968)
- Received the National Order of Quebec Chevalier (2008)
- Received the Order of Canada (2009)

> I was a determined, enthusiastic, young fellow. That's what you need to make a success in life. You work hard, you're enthusiastic, and very disciplined at your game."

REGULAR SEASON

Season	Age	Team	Lg	GP	G	A	PTS	PIM
1941–42	22	Montreal Canadiens	NHL	44	0	6	6	38
1942–43	23	Montreal Canadiens	NHL	45	2	16	18	47
1943–44	24	Montreal Canadiens	NHL	39	5	14	19	52
1944–45	25	Montreal Canadiens	NHL	50	11	23	34	34
1945–46	26	Montreal Canadiens	NHL	45	7	10	17	52
1946–47	27	Montreal Canadiens	NHL	60	5	7	12	60
1947–48	28	Montreal Canadiens	NHL	60	4	6	10	78
1948–49	29	Montreal Canadiens	NHL	27	3	3	6	42
1949–50	30	Montreal Canadiens	NHL	69	1	7	8	88
1950–51	31	Montreal Canadiens	NHL	52	3	10	13	80
1951–52	32	Montreal Canadiens	NHL	60	3	9	12	45
1952–53	33	Montreal Canadiens	NHL	58	2	8	10	55
1953–54	34	Montreal Canadiens	NHL	70	1	10	11	89
1954–55	35	Montreal Canadiens	NHL	70	2	15	17	81
1955–56	36	Montreal Canadiens	NHL	36	0	0	0	22
NHL Career — 15 Seasons				785	49	144	193	863

PLAYOFFS

Season	Age	Team	Lg	GP	G	A	PTS	PIM
1941–42	22	Montreal Canadiens	NHL	3	1	1	2	0
1942–43	23	Montreal Canadiens	NHL	5	0	1	1	4
1943–44	24	Montreal Canadiens	NHL	9	1	3	4	4
1944–45	25	Montreal Canadiens	NHL	6	3	4	7	4
1945–46	26	Montreal Canadiens	NHL	9	2	1	3	17
1946–47	27	Montreal Canadiens	NHL	11	0	3	3	21
1948–49	29	Montreal Canadiens	NHL	7	0	0	0	6
1949–50	30	Montreal Canadiens	NHL	5	0	2	2	2
1950–51	31	Montreal Canadiens	NHL	11	1	1	2	2
1951–52	32	Montreal Canadiens	NHL	11	0	2	2	14
1952–53	33	Montreal Canadiens	NHL	12	1	1	2	6
1953–54	34	Montreal Canadiens	NHL	11	2	1	3	4
1954–55	35	Montreal Canadiens	NHL	12	0	1	1	37
1955–56	36	Montreal Canadiens	NHL	1	0	0	0	0
NHL Career — 14 Seasons				113	11	21	32	121

TROPHY CASE

AWARDS

Stanley Cup
(1943–44, 1945–46, 1952–53, 1955–56)

ALL-STAR SELECTIONS

First All-Star Team
Defense (1945, 1946, 1947)
Second All-Star Team
Defense (1944)

Frank Boucher

HOCKEY HALL OF FAME CLASS: 1958

Alternates: 8, 17	
Center	
Shoots: Left	
Height: 5'-9"	
Weight: 185 lbs.	
Born: October 7, 1901: Ottawa, Ontario	
Died: December 12, 1977: Ottawa, Ontario	
Played 18 professional seasons from 1921–38, 1943–44	

QUICK FACTS

- Held NHL record for career assists (263), surpassed by Bill Cowley in 1943–44

- Played amateur hockey with Ottawa New Edinburghs (1916–19); Ottawa Munitions (1917–18); Lethbridge Vets (1919–20)

- Nicknamed "Raffles" after the gentlemanly thief in E.W. Hornung's books because of his ability to steal the puck from opposing players and overall clean play

- Signed as a free agent by Ottawa Senators, December 6, 1921; traded to Vancouver Maroons (PCHA) by Ottawa for cash, September 19, 1922

- Renowned for his ability to draw opposition players toward him and deftly pass to his linemates and is credited with perfecting the drop pass

- Member of the N.Y. Rangers' famed Bread Line with Bill and Bun Cook

- Assisted on the first goal scored in the history of the N.Y. Rangers franchise in Rangers' 1–0 victory over Montreal Maroons, November 16, 1926

- Scored Stanley Cup–winning goal in N.Y. Rangers' 2–1 victory over Montreal Maroons, April 14, 1928

- Played in NHL All-Star Game (1937)

- Led NHL playoffs in goals (7) and points (10) in 1927–28

- Led NHL in assists in 1928–29 (16), 1929–30 (36) and 1932–33 (28)

- Coached N.Y. Rovers (1938–39); coached N.Y. Rangers (1939–49, 1953–54)

> My thought was that hockey had become a see-saw affair. Defending teams were jammed in their own end for minutes because they couldn't pass their way out against the new five-man attack."
>
> — Frank Boucher, commenting on his idea to introduce the red line to hockey

REGULAR SEASON

Season	Age	Team	Lg	GP	G	A	PTS	PIM
1921–22	20	Ottawa Senators	NHL	24	8	2	10	4
1922–23	21	Vancouver Maroons	PCHA	29	11	9	20	2
1923–24	22	Vancouver Maroons	PCHA	28	15	5	20	10
1924–25	23	Vancouver Maroons	WCHL	27	16	12	28	6
1925–26	24	Vancouver Maroons	WHL	29	15	7	22	14
1926–27	25	New York Rangers	NHL	44	13	15	28	17
1927–28	26	New York Rangers	NHL	44	23	12	35	15
1928–29	27	New York Rangers	NHL	44	10	16	26	8
1929–30	28	New York Rangers	NHL	42	26	36	62	16
1930–31	29	New York Rangers	NHL	44	12	27	39	20
1931–32	30	New York Rangers	NHL	48	12	23	35	18
1932–33	31	New York Rangers	NHL	46	7	28	35	4
1933–34	32	New York Rangers	NHL	48	14	30	44	4
1934–35	33	New York Rangers	NHL	48	13	32	45	2
1935–36	34	New York Rangers	NHL	48	11	18	29	2
1936–37	35	New York Rangers	NHL	44	7	13	20	5
1937–38	36	New York Rangers	NHL	18	0	1	1	2
1943–44	42	New York Rangers	NHL	15	4	10	14	2
Career — 18 Seasons				670	217	296	513	151

PLAYOFFS

Season	Age	Team	Lg	GP	G	A	PTS	PIM
1921–22	20	Ottawa Senators	NHL	1	0	0	0	0
1922–23	21	Vancouver Maroons	PCHA	2	0	1	1	2
1922–23	21	Vancouver Maroons	St-Cup	4	2	0	2	0
1923–24	22	Vancouver Maroons	PCHA	2	1	0	1	0
1923–24	22	Vancouver Maroons	St-Cup	2	1	1	2	2
1923–24	22	Vancouver Millionaires	West-P	3	1	0	1	0
1926–27	25	New York Rangers	NHL	2	0	0	0	4
1927–28	26	New York Rangers	NHL	9	7	3	10	2
1928–29	27	New York Rangers	NHL	6	1	0	1	0
1929–30	28	New York Rangers	NHL	3	1	1	2	0
1930–31	29	New York Rangers	NHL	4	0	2	2	0
1931–32	30	New York Rangers	NHL	7	3	6	9	0
1932–33	31	New York Rangers	NHL	8	2	2	4	6
1933–34	32	New York Rangers	NHL	2	0	0	0	0
1934–35	33	New York Rangers	NHL	4	0	3	3	0
1936–37	35	New York Rangers	NHL	9	2	3	5	0
Career — 13 Seasons				68	21	22	43	16

TROPHY CASE

AWARDS

Lady Byng Memorial Trophy (1928, 1929, 1930, 1931, 1933, 1934, 1935)

Lester Patrick Trophy (1993)

Stanley Cup (1927–28, 1932–33)

ALL-STAR SELECTIONS

PCHA First All-Star Team Center (1923, 1924)

WCHL First All-Star Team Center (1925)

First All-Star Team Center (1933, 1934, 1935)

Second All-Star Team Center (1931)

First All-Star Team Coach (1942)

Second All-Star Team Coach (1940)

George Boucher

HOCKEY HALL OF FAME CLASS: 1960

Alternates:
9, 4, 12, 15

**Defense/
Left Wing**

Shoots: Left

Height: 5'-9"

Weight: 169 lbs.

**Born: August 19,
1896: Ottawa,
Ontario**

**Died: October 17,
1960: Ottawa,
Ontario**

**Played:
17 professional
seasons from
1915–32**

QUICK FACTS

- Played amateur hockey with Ottawa New Edinburghs (1913–15); Ottawa Royal Canadians (1914–15); Montreal La Casquette (1915–16)
- Played running back with Ottawa Rough Riders football club (1913–15)
- Began professional career as a forward with Senators but switched to defense in his third season
- Led NHL in assists (10) in 1923–24; led NHL in penalty minutes (95) in 1924–25
- Traded to Montreal Maroons by Ottawa for Joe Lamb, February 14, 1929; claimed on waivers by Chicago from Montreal Maroons, November 27, 1931
- Coached Montreal Maroons (1930–31); coached Ottawa Senators (1933–34); coached St. Louis Eagles (1934–35)
- Coached Boston Cubs (1932–33)
- Coached Springfield Indians (1936–1938); coached Noranda Eagles (1938–39); coached Quebec Beavers (1939–40); coached Ottawa Senators (1946–49)
- Coached Allan Cup-winning Ottawa Senators (1949)
- Coached Boston Bruins (1949–50)
- Helped assemble and coach Ottawa RCAF team that represented Canada at the 1948 Winter Olympic Games and captured the gold medal
- Brother of Hall of Fame member Frank Boucher
- Brother of Bobby Boucher, who played in NHL with Montreal Canadiens in 1923–24; brother of Billy Boucher, who played in NHL with Montreal Canadiens, N.Y. Americans and Boston from 1921–28

> "He is what I know to be an honest player and an honest sportsman. He lifted us off the floor and carried us through the playoffs."
> — Dave MacKell, Ottawa Senators President

REGULAR SEASON

Season	Age	Team	Lg	GP	G	A	PTS	PIM
1915–16	19	Ottawa Senators	NHA	19	9	1	10	62
1916–17	20	Ottawa Senators	NHA	18	10	5	15	27
1917–18	21	Ottawa Senators	NHL	21	9	8	17	46
1918–19	22	Ottawa Senators	NHL	17	3	2	5	29
1919–20	23	Ottawa Senators	NHL	22	9	8	17	55
1920–21	24	Ottawa Senators	NHL	23	11	8	19	53
1921–22	25	Ottawa Senators	NHL	23	13	12	25	12
1922–23	26	Ottawa Senators	NHL	24	14	9	23	58
1923–24	27	Ottawa Senators	NHL	21	13	10	23	38
1924–25	28	Ottawa Senators	NHL	28	15	5	20	95
1925–26	29	Ottawa Senators	NHL	36	8	4	12	64
1926–27	30	Ottawa Senators	NHL	40	8	3	11	115
1927–28	31	Ottawa Senators	NHL	43	7	5	12	78
1928–29	32	Ottawa Senators	NHL	29	3	1	4	60
1928–29	32	Montreal Maroons	NHL	12	1	1	2	10
1929–30	33	Montreal Maroons	NHL	37	2	6	8	50
1930–31	34	Montreal Maroons	NHL	30	0	0	0	25
1931–32	35	Chicago Black Hawks	NHL	43	1	5	6	50
Career — 17 Seasons				486	136	93	229	927

PLAYOFFS

Season	Age	Team	Lg	GP	G	A	PTS	PIM
1916–17	20	Ottawa Senators	NHA	2	1	0	1	8
1918–19	22	Ottawa Senators	NHL	5	2	0	2	9
1919–20	23	Ottawa Senators	St-Cup	5	2	0	2	2
1920–21	24	Ottawa Senators	NHL	2	3	0	3	10
1920–21	24	Ottawa Senators	St-Cup	5	2	0	2	9
1921–22	25	Ottawa Senators	NHL	2	0	0	0	4
1922–23	26	Ottawa Senators	NHL	2	0	1	1	2
1922–23	26	Ottawa Senators	St-Cup	6	2	1	3	6
1923–24	27	Ottawa Senators	NHL	2	0	1	1	4
1925–26	29	Ottawa Senators	NHL	2	0	0	0	10
1926–27	30	Ottawa Senators	NHL	6	0	0	0	43
1927–28	31	Ottawa Senators	NHL	2	0	0	0	4
1929–30	33	Montreal Maroons	NHL	3	0	0	0	2
1931–32	35	Chicago Black Hawks	NHL	2	0	1	1	0
Career — 12 Seasons				46	12	4	16	113

TROPHY CASE

AWARDS

Stanley Cup (1920–21, 1922–23, 1926–27)

77

Ray Bourque

HOCKEY HALL OF FAME CLASS: 2004

Retired by Boston & Colorado

Alternate: 7	
Defense	
Shoots: Left	
Height: 5'-11"	
Weight: 219 lbs.	

Born: December 28, 1960: Montreal, Quebec

Drafted by the Boston Bruins eighth overall in 1979

Played 22 NHL seasons from 1979–2001

"I loved what I did and I enjoyed the game. I had a passion for it. I think that is what kept me going."

QUICK FACTS

- Holds NHL records for career points by a defenseman (1,579), career goals by a defenseman (410), career assists by a defenseman (1,169), career years in playoffs (21), career playoff assists by a defenseman (139)

- Holds NHL record for most career shots-on-goal (6,206)

- Holds Boston Bruins team records for career games (1,518), assists (1,111) and points (1,506); holds Boston Bruins team record for career goals (395) by a defenseman

- Ranks fourth in NHL career assists (1,169); ranks eighth in NHL career games (1,612); ranks 11th in NHL career points (1,579)

- Played amateur hockey with Trois-Rivieres Draveurs (1976–77); Sorel Eperviers (1976–77); Verdun Eperviers (1977–79)

- QMJHL First All-Star Team Defense (1978, 1979); named QMJHL Defenseman of the Year (1979)

- Played in NHL All-Star Game (1981–86, 1988–94, 1996–2001)

Bourque notched his 1,000th career point with this puck on March 1, 1992, with an assist in a 4–1 victory over the Washington Capitals.

REGULAR SEASON

Season	Age	Team	Lg	GP	G	A	PTS	+/-	PIM	ESG	PPG	SHG	GWG	SOG	S%
1979–80	19	Boston Bruins	NHL	80	17	48	65	52	73	12	3	2	1	185	9.2
1980–81	20	Boston Bruins	NHL	67	27	29	56	29	96	17	9	1	6	207	13.0
1981–82	21	Boston Bruins	NHL	65	17	49	66	22	51	13	4	0	2	211	8.1
1982–83	22	Boston Bruins	NHL	65	22	51	73	49	20	15	7	0	5	205	10.7
1983–84	23	Boston Bruins	NHL	78	31	65	96	51	57	18	12	1	5	340	9.1
1984–85	24	Boston Bruins	NHL	73	20	66	86	30	53	9	10	1	1	333	6.0
1985–86	25	Boston Bruins	NHL	74	19	58	77	17	68	8	11	0	3	289	6.6
1986–87	26	Boston Bruins	NHL	78	23	72	95	44	36	16	6	1	3	334	6.9
1987–88	27	Boston Bruins	NHL	78	17	64	81	34	72	9	7	1	5	344	4.9
1988–89	28	Boston Bruins	NHL	60	18	43	61	20	52	12	6	0	0	243	7.4
1989–90	29	Boston Bruins	NHL	76	19	65	84	31	50	11	8	0	3	310	6.1
1990–91	30	Boston Bruins	NHL	76	21	73	94	33	75	14	7	0	3	323	6.5
1991–92	31	Boston Bruins	NHL	80	21	60	81	11	56	13	7	1	2	334	6.3
1992–93	32	Boston Bruins	NHL	78	19	63	82	38	40	11	8	0	7	330	5.8
1993–94	33	Boston Bruins	NHL	72	20	71	91	26	58	7	10	3	1	386	5.2
1994–95	34	Boston Bruins	NHL	46	12	31	43	3	20	3	9	0	2	210	5.7
1995–96	35	Boston Bruins	NHL	82	20	62	82	31	58	9	9	2	2	390	5.1
1996–97	36	Boston Bruins	NHL	62	19	31	50	-11	18	10	8	1	3	230	8.3
1997–98	37	Boston Bruins	NHL	82	13	35	48	2	80	4	9	0	3	264	4.9
1998–99	38	Boston Bruins	NHL	81	10	47	57	-7	34	2	8	0	3	262	3.8
1999–00	39	Boston Bruins	NHL	65	10	28	38	-11	20	4	6	0	0	217	4.6
1999–00	39	Colorado Avalanche	NHL	14	8	6	14	9	6	1	7	0	0	43	18.6
2000–01	40	Colorado Avalanche	NHL	80	7	52	59	25	48	3	2	2	0	216	3.2
NHL Career – 22 Seasons				1612	410	1169	1579	528	1141	221	173	16	60	6206	6.6

PLAYOFFS

Season	Age	Team	Lg	GP	G	A	PTS	+/-	PIM	ESG	PPG	SHG	GWG	SOG	S%
1979–80	19	Boston Bruins	NHL	10	2	9	11		27	2	0	0	0		
1980–81	20	Boston Bruins	NHL	3	0	1	1		2	0	0	0	0		
1981–82	21	Boston Bruins	NHL	9	1	5	6		16	1	0	0	1		
1982–83	22	Boston Bruins	NHL	17	8	15	23		10	6	2	0	1		
1983–84	23	Boston Bruins	NHL	3	0	2	2	-3	0	0	0	0	0	10	0.0
1984–85	24	Boston Bruins	NHL	5	0	3	3	1	4	0	0	0	0	15	0.0
1985–86	25	Boston Bruins	NHL	3	0	0	0	0	0	0	0	0	0	7	0.0
1986–87	26	Boston Bruins	NHL	4	1	2	3	-1	0	1	0	0	0	22	4.5
1987–88	27	Boston Bruins	NHL	23	3	18	21	16	26	3	0	0	1	65	4.6
1988–89	28	Boston Bruins	NHL	10	0	4	4	-1	6	0	0	0	0	40	0.0
1989–90	29	Boston Bruins	NHL	17	5	12	17	11	16	4	1	0	0	64	7.8
1990–91	30	Boston Bruins	NHL	19	7	18	25	-4	12	4	3	0	0	84	8.3
1991–92	31	Boston Bruins	NHL	12	3	6	9	-10	12	1	2	0	0	51	5.9
1992–93	32	Boston Bruins	NHL	4	1	1	2	-2	2	0	1	0	0	20	5.0
1993–94	33	Boston Bruins	NHL	13	2	8	10	-5	0	1	1	0	0	64	3.1
1994–95	34	Boston Bruins	NHL	5	0	3	3	-5	0	0	0	0	0	15	0.0
1995–96	35	Boston Bruins	NHL	5	1	6	7	-4	2	0	1	0	0	28	3.6
1997–98	37	Boston Bruins	NHL	6	1	4	5	-2	2	0	1	0	0	42	2.4
1998–99	38	Boston Bruins	NHL	12	1	9	10	1	14	1	0	0	0	44	2.3
1999–00	39	Boston Bruins	NHL	13	1	8	9	4	8	1	0	0	0	28	3.6
2000–01	40	Boston Bruins	NHL	21	4	6	10	9	12	1	3	0	1	49	8.2
NHL Career – 21 Seasons				214	41	139	180	5	171	26	15	0	4	648	4.6

TROPHY CASE

AWARDS

Calder Memorial Trophy (1980)

James Norris Memorial Trophy (1987, 1988, 1990, 1991, 1994)

King Clancy Trophy (1992)

Lester Patrick Trophy (2003)

Stanley Cup (2000–01)

ALL-STAR SELECTIONS

First All-Star Team Defense (1980, 1982, 1984, 1985, 1987, 1988, 1990, 1991, 1992, 1993, 1994, 1996, 2001)

Second All-Star Team Defense (1981, 1983, 1986, 1989, 1995, 1999)

INTERNATIONAL AWARDS

Canada Cup (1984, 1987)

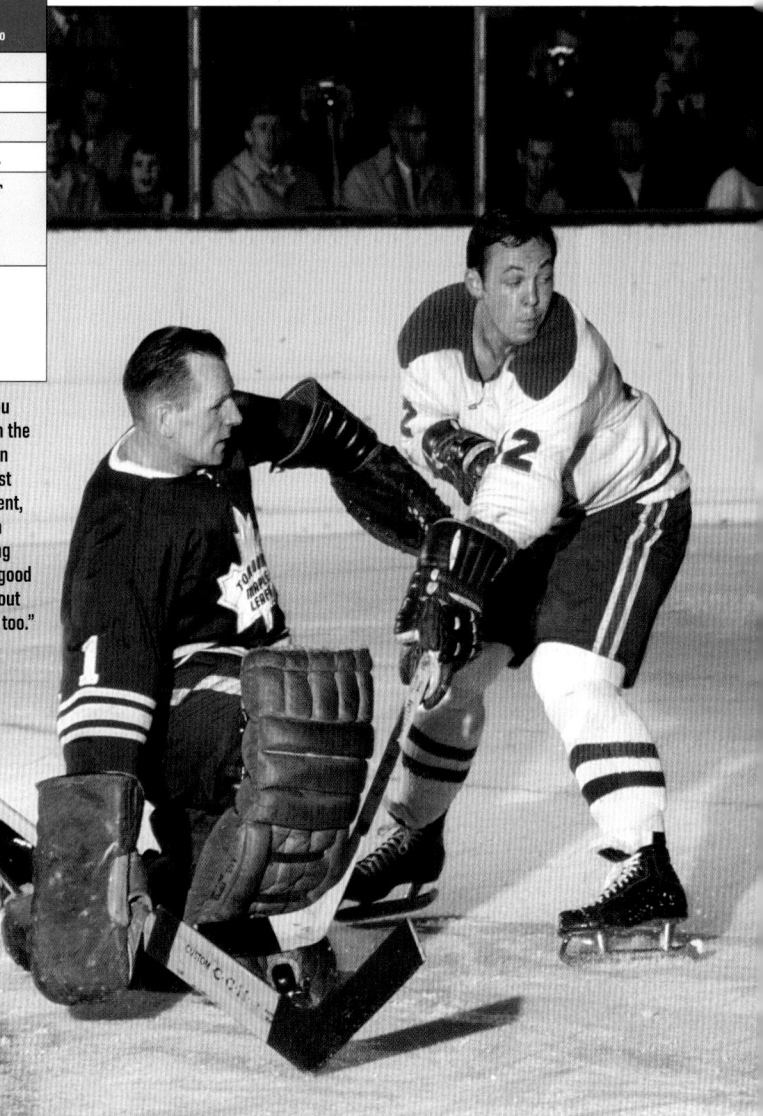

1

Goaltender
Catches: Left
Height: 5'- 11"
Weight: 189 lbs.
Born: November 8, 1924; Prince Albert, Saskatchewan
Played 15 NHL seasons from 1953–55, 1956–57, 1958–70

Johnny Bower

HOCKEY HALL OF FAME CLASS: 1976

"When you played in the American league, you just had to be patient, wait your turn for a rebuilding team. A lot of good goalies came out of our league, too."

QUICK FACTS

- Holds AHL record for career shutouts (45); holds AHL record for career wins (359)
- Played amateur hockey with Prince Albert Blackhawks (1944–45); Laura Beavers (1944–45)
- Played minor pro hockey with Providence Reds (1945–46); Cleveland Barons (1945–53); Vancouver Canucks (1954–55)
- Led AHL in wins in 1949–50 (38), 1950–51 (44), 1952–53 (40) and 1955–56 (45); led AHL in shutouts in 1949–50 (5) and 1952–53 (6); led AHL in goals-against-average in 1956–57 (2.37) and 1957–58 (2.17)
- Led WHL in shutouts (7) and goals-against-average (2.71) in 1954–55
- AHL First All-Star Team Goaltender (1952, 1953, 1956, 1957, 1958); AHL Second All-Star Team Goaltender (1952)

- Named AHL Most Valuable Player (1956, 1957, 1958); named WHL Top Goaltender (1954–55)
- Traded to N.Y. Rangers by Cleveland (AHL) with Eldred Kobussen for Emile Francis, Neil Strain and cash, July 20, 1953; claimed by Toronto from Cleveland (AHL) in Inter-League Draft, June 3, 1958
- Led NHL in wins (33) in 1960–61; led NHL in goals-against-average in 1963–64 (2.11), 1964–65 (2.38) and 1965–66 (2.25)
- Played in NHL All-Star Game (1961, 1962, 1963, 1964)
- Nicknamed "China Wall" because of his age and the fact he didn't play regularly in the NHL until the age of 34

Bower's musical debut "Honky the Christmas Goose" reached number 29 on the 1050 CHUM Radio (Toronto) chart in December 1965.

REGULAR SEASON

Season	Age	Team	Lg	GP	W	L	T	SO	GA	GAA	G	A	PTS	PIM
1953-54	29	New York Rangers	NHL	70	29	31	10	5	182	2.60	0	0	0	0
1954-55	30	New York Rangers	NHL	5	2	2	1	0	13	2.60	0	0	0	0
1956-57	32	New York Rangers	NHL	2	0	2	0	0	6	3.00	0	0	0	0
1958-59	34	Toronto Maple Leafs	NHL	39	15	17	7	3	106	2.72	0	0	0	2
1959-60	35	Toronto Maple Leafs	NHL	66	34	24	8	5	177	2.68	0	0	0	4
1960-61	36	Toronto Maple Leafs	NHL	58	33	15	10	2	145	2.50	0	0	0	0
1961-62	37	Toronto Maple Leafs	NHL	59	31	18	10	2	151	2.56	0	1	1	4
1962-63	38	Toronto Maple Leafs	NHL	42	20	15	7	1	109	2.60	0	0	0	2
1963-64	39	Toronto Maple Leafs	NHL	51	24	16	11	5	106	2.11	0	0	0	4
1964-65	40	Toronto Maple Leafs	NHL	34	13	13	8	3	81	2.38	0	0	0	6
1965-66	41	Toronto Maple Leafs	NHL	35	18	10	5	3	75	2.25	0	1	1	0
1966-67	42	Toronto Maple Leafs	NHL	27	12	9	3	2	63	2.64	0	0	0	0
1967-68	43	Toronto Maple Leafs	NHL	43	14	18	7	4	84	2.25	0	1	1	14
1968-69	44	Toronto Maple Leafs	NHL	20	5	4	3	2	37	2.85	0	0	0	0
1969-70	45	Toronto Maple Leafs	NHL	1	0	1	0	0	5	5.00	0	0	0	0
NHL Career – 15 Seasons				552	250	195	90	37	1340	2.51	0	3	3	36

PLAYOFFS

Season	Age	Team	Lg	GP	W	L	T	SO	GA	GAA	G	A	PTS	PIM
1958-59	34	Toronto Maple Leafs	NHL	12	5	7		0	38	3.06	0	0	0	0
1959-60	35	Toronto Maple Leafs	NHL	10	4	6		0	31	2.88	0	0	0	0
1960-61	36	Toronto Maple Leafs	NHL	3	0	3		0	8	2.67	0	0	0	2
1961-62	37	Toronto Maple Leafs	NHL	10	6	3		0	20	2.07	0	0	0	0
1962-63	38	Toronto Maple Leafs	NHL	10	8	2		2	16	1.60	0	1	1	0
1963-64	39	Toronto Maple Leafs	NHL	14	8	6		2	30	2.12	0	0	0	0
1964-65	40	Toronto Maple Leafs	NHL	5	2	3		0	13	2.43	0	0	0	0
1965-66	41	Toronto Maple Leafs	NHL	2	0	2		0	8	4.00	0	0	0	0
1966-67	42	Toronto Maple Leafs	NHL	4	2	0		1	5	1.64	0	0	0	2
1968-69	44	Toronto Maple Leafs	NHL	4	0	2		0	11	4.29	0	0	0	0
NHL Career – 10 Seasons				74	35	34		5	180	2.47	0	1	1	4

TROPHY CASE

AWARDS

Vezina Trophy (1961, 1965)

Stanley Cup (1961–62, 1962–63, 1963–64, 1966–67)

ALL-STAR SELECTIONS

First All-Star Team Goaltender (1961)

Dubbie Bowie

HOCKEY HALL OF FAME CLASS: 1945

Rover/Center

Shoots: Unknown

Height: 5'-5"

Weight: 122 lbs.

Born: August 24, 1880: Montreal, Quebec

Died: April 8, 1959: Montreal, Quebec

Played 12 elite amateur seasons from 1898–1910

QUICK FACTS

- Played amateur hockey with Montreal St. John's (1892–93); Montreal Tucker's Academy (1893–95); Montreal Comets (1894–97)

- Averaged nearly three goals per game during the course of his career, a statistic matched only by Frank McGee as the greatest scorer of his era

- ECAHA First All-Star Team Rover (1905, 1909)

- ECAHA Second All-Star Team Rover (1907)

- Led CAHL in goals in 1900–01 (24), 1902–03 (22), 1903–04 (27) and 1904–05 (27)

- Led ECAHA in goals (31) in 1907–08

- Scored eight goals in Montreal Victorias' 16–5 victory over Montreal Shamrocks, January 16, 1907

- Scored seven goals in a game twice in his career and had six goals in a game on five occasions

- Despite his individual prowess, he only won the Stanley Cup as a rookie when the Montreal Victorias successfully defended a midseason challenge from Winnipeg in February 1899

- Though he played in an era when professionalism first came to hockey, he refused to give up his amateur status, once turning down an offer of $1,000 (a huge amount of money at the time) to play just two games

- The music-loving Bowie refused the offer of a grand piano to turn professional with the Montreal Wanderers

> I am an amateur, was an amateur, and will die an amateur. I played for fun."
> — Russell Bowie, who refused all offers to play for money during his career

REGULAR SEASON

Season	Age	Team	Lg	GP	G	A	PTS	PIM
1898–99	18	Montreal Victorias	CAHL	7	11	0	11	
1899–00	19	Montreal Victorias	CAHL	7	15	0	15	
1900–01	20	Montreal Victorias	CAHL	7	24	0	24	
1901–02	21	Montreal Victorias	CAHL	7	13	0	13	
1902–03	22	Montreal Victorias	CAHL	7	22	0	22	
1903–04	23	Montreal Victorias	CAHL	8	27	0	27	
1904–05	24	Montreal Victorias	CAHL	8	27	0	27	9
1905–06	25	Montreal Victorias	ECAHA	9	30	0	30	8
1906–07	26	Montreal Victorias	ECAHA	10	39	0	39	13
1907–08	27	Montreal Victorias	ECAHA	10	31	0	31	19
1908–09	28	Montreal Victorias	IPAHU	5	21	0	21	19
1909–10	29	Montreal Victorias	IPAHU	3	6	0	6	0
Career – 12 Seasons				88	266	0	266	68

PLAYOFFS

Season	Age	Team	Lg	GP	G	A	PTS	PIM
1898–99	18	Montreal Victorias	St-Cup	2	1	0	1	
1902–03	22	Montreal Victorias	CAHL	2	0	0	0	3
1909–10	29	Montreal Victorias	IPAHU	2	5	0	5	8
Career – 3 Seasons				6	6	0	6	11

TROPHY CASE

AWARDS

Stanley Cup (1898–99)

1

Frank Brimsek

HOCKEY HALL OF FAME CLASS: 1966

Alternates: 10, 17

Goaltender

Catches: Left

Height: 5'-9"

Weight: 170 lbs.

Born: September 26, 1915: Eveleth, Minnesota

Died: November 11, 1998: Virginia, Minnesota

Played 10 NHL seasons from 1938–43, 1945–50

QUICK FACTS

> "The kid had the fastest hands I ever saw — like lightning."
> — Art Ross

- Played amateur hockey with Eveluth Rangers (1934–35); Pittsburgh Yellowjackets (1934–37)
- Renowned for using his stick to knock opposition players off their feet if they skated too close to his crease
- First goaltender to win the Calder Trophy and Vezina Trophy in the same season
- Earned the nickname "Mr. Zero" after recording six shutouts in his first seven NHL games
- Led EAHL in wins (20) and shutouts (8) in 1935–36; led IAHL in goals-against-average (1.75) and playoff wins (5) in 1937–38
- Signed as free agent by Boston Bruins and assigned to IAHL's Providence Reds, October 27, 1937

- EAHL First All-Star Team (1936); IAHL First All-Star Team Goaltender (1938)
- Led NHL in wins in 1938–39 (33) and 1939–40 (31)
- Led NHL in shutouts in 1938–39 (10) and 1940–41 (6); led NHL in goals-against-average in 1938–39 (1.56) and 1941–42 (2.35)
- Led NHL in playoff wins (8) and goals-against-average (1.25) in 1938–39; playoff wins (8), shutouts (1) and goals-against-average (2.04) in 1941–42
- Played for U.S. Coast Guard Cutters (1943–44) during World War II
- Played in NHL All-Star Game (1947, 1948)
- Traded to Chicago by Boston for cash, September 8, 1949

REGULAR SEASON

Season	Age	Team	Lg	GP	W	L	T	SO	GA	GAA	G	A	PTS	PIM
1938–39	23	Boston Bruins	NHL	43	33	9	1	10	68	1.56	0	0	0	0
1939–40	24	Boston Bruins	NHL	48	31	12	5	6	98	1.99	0	0	0	0
1940–41	25	Boston Bruins	NHL	48	27	8	13	6	102	2.01	0	0	0	0
1941–42	26	Boston Bruins	NHL	47	24	17	6	3	115	2.35	0	0	0	0
1942–43	27	Boston Bruins	NHL	50	24	17	9	1	176	3.52	0	0	0	0
1945–46	30	Boston Bruins	NHL	34	16	14	4	2	111	3.26	0	0	0	0
1946–47	31	Boston Bruins	NHL	60	26	23	11	3	175	2.92	0	0	0	2
1947–48	32	Boston Bruins	NHL	60	23	24	13	3	168	2.80	0	0	0	0
1948–49	33	Boston Bruins	NHL	54	26	20	8	1	147	2.72	0	0	0	2
1949–50	34	Chicago Blackhawks	NHL	70	22	38	10	5	244	3.49	0	0	0	2
NHL Career – 10 Seasons				514	252	182	80	40	1404	2.70	0	0	0	6

PLAYOFFS

Season	Age	Team	Lg	GP	W	L	T	SO	GA	GAA	G	A	PTS	PIM
1938–39	23	Boston Bruins	NHL	12	8	4		1	18	1.25	0	0	0	0
1939–40	24	Boston Bruins	NHL	6	2	4		0	15	2.50	0	0	0	0
1940–41	25	Boston Bruins	NHL	11	8	3		1	23	2.04	0	0	0	0
1941–42	26	Boston Bruins	NHL	5	2	3		0	16	3.13	0	0	0	0
1942–43	27	Boston Bruins	NHL	9	4	5		0	33	3.54	0	0	0	0
1945–46	30	Boston Bruins	NHL	10	5	5		0	29	2.67	0	0	0	0
1946–47	31	Boston Bruins	NHL	5	1	4		0	16	2.80	0	0	0	0
1947–48	32	Boston Bruins	NHL	5	1	4		0	20	3.79	0	0	0	0
1948–49	33	Boston Bruins	NHL	5	1	4		0	16	3.04	0	0	0	0
NHL Career – 9 Seasons				68	32	36		2	186	2.54	0	0	0	0

TROPHY CASE

AWARDS

Calder Memorial Trophy (1939)

Vezina Trophy (1939, 1942)

Stanley Cup (1938–39, 1940–41)

ALL-STAR SELECTIONS

First All-Star Team Goaltender (1939, 1942)

Second All-Star Team Goaltender (1940, 1941, 1943, 1946, 1947, 1948)

Punch Broadbent

HOCKEY HALL OF FAME CLASS: 1962

Alternates:
9, 6, 7, 8

Right Wing

Shoots: Right

Height: 5'-7"

Weight: 183 lbs.

Born: July 13, 1892: Ottawa, Ontario

Died: March 5, 1971: Ottawa, Ontario

Played 14 professional seasons from 1912–15, 1918–29

QUICK FACTS

- Holds NHL record for most consecutive regular season games with at least one goal (16), established from December 21, 1921 to February 15, 1922

- Played amateur hockey with Ottawa Emmetts (1908–09); Ottawa Seconds (1909–10); Ottawa Cliffsides (1909–11); Hull Volants (1909–10); Ottawa New Edinburghs (1911–12)

- Served in the Canadian RCAF during World War I and earned Military Medal for heroism in combat

- Renowned for his ability to dance around or skate over an opponent, he was considered to be one of the first true power-forwards in the game

- Nicknamed "Punch" because he had a knockout scoring punch and a knack for scoring at clutch times

- Nicknamed "Old Elbows" because he used his elbows to intimidate opposition players

- Led NHL in goals (32) and points (46) in 1921–??

- Scored Stanley Cup-winning goal in Ottawa's 1–0 victory over Edmonton Eskimos, March 23, 1923

- Traded to Montreal Maroons by Ottawa with Clint Benedict for cash, October 20, 1924; traded to Ottawa by Montreal Maroons with $22,500 for Hooley Smith, October 7, 1927; traded to N.Y. Americans by Ottawa for cash, October 15, 1928

- Coached Ottawa Rideaus (1931–35)

> "It's an unfortunate thing, but Punch might have left an even greater record if it hadn't been for the war. He lost four of his best seasons in his career because of service in World War One, and it was tribute to his ability that he came back and still did so well in hockey."
>
> — Sportswriter Baz O'Meara

TROPHY CASE

AWARDS

NHL Scoring Leader (1922)

Stanley Cup (1919–20, 1920–21, 1922–23, 1925–26)

REGULAR SEASON

Season	Age	Team	Lg	GP	G	A	PTS	PIM
1912–13	20	Ottawa Senators	NHA	20	20	0	20	15
1913–14	21	Ottawa Senators	NHA	17	6	7	13	61
1914–15	22	Ottawa Senators	NHA	20	24	3	27	115
1918–19	26	Ottawa Senators	NHL	8	4	-3	7	12
1919–20	27	Ottawa Senators	NHL	21	19	6	25	40
1920–21	28	Ottawa Senators	NHL	9	4	1	5	10
1921–22	29	Ottawa Senators	NHL	24	32	14	46	28
1922–23	30	Ottawa Senators	NHL	24	14	1	15	34
1923–24	31	Ottawa Senators	NHL	22	9	4	13	44
1924–25	32	Montreal Maroons	NHL	30	14	6	20	75
1925–26	33	Montreal Maroons	NHL	36	12	5	17	112
1926–27	34	Montreal Maroons	NHL	42	9	5	14	88
1927–28	35	Ottawa Senators	NHL	43	3	2	5	62
1928–29	36	New York Americans	NHL	44	1	4	5	59
Career – 14 Seasons				360	171	61	232	755

PLAYOFFS

Season	Age	Team	Lg	GP	G	A	PTS	PIM
1914–15	22	Ottawa Senators	NHA	5	3	0	3	26
1918–19	26	Ottawa Senators	NHL	5	2	2	4	28
1919–20	27	Ottawa Senators	St-Cup	4	0	0	0	3
1920–21	28	Ottawa Senators	NHL	2	0	2	2	4
1920–21	28	Ottawa Senators	St-Cup	4	2	0	2	0
1921–22	29	Ottawa Senators	NHL	2	0	1	1	8
1922–23	30	Ottawa Senators	NHL	2	0	0	0	2
1922–23	30	Ottawa Senators	St-Cup	6	6	1	7	10
1923–24	31	Ottawa Senators	NHL	2	0	0	0	2
1925–26	33	Montreal Maroons	NHL	4	2	1	3	14
1925–26	33	Montreal Maroons	St-Cup	4	1	0	1	22
1926–27	34	Montreal Maroons	NHL	2	0	0	0	0
1927–28	35	Ottawa Senators	NHL	2	0	0	0	0
1928–29	36	New York Americans	NHL	2	0	0	0	2
Career – 11 Seasons				46	16	7	23	121

Turk Broda

HOCKEY HALL OF FAME CLASS: 1967

1

Honored by Toronto

Alternate: 19

Goaltender

Catches: Left

Height: 5'-9"

Weight: 180 lbs.

Born: May 15, 1914: Brandon, Manitoba

Died: October 17, 1972: Toronto, Ontario

Played 14 NHL seasons from 1936–43, 1945–52

"The bonus money for winning wasn't much but I always needed it. Or maybe I was just too dumb to know the situation was serious."

— Turk Broda, commenting on his well-deserved image as a "money" goaltender

QUICK FACTS

- Holds Toronto Maple Leafs team goaltending records for career games (629), wins (302) and shutouts (62)

- Holds Toronto Maple Leafs team goaltending records for career playoff games (101), playoff wins (60) and playoff shutouts (13)

- First goaltender in NHL history to play 100 playoff games, March 27, 1952

- Played amateur hockey with Brandon Native Sons (1932–33); Winnipeg Monarchs (1933–34); Detroit Farm Crest (1934–35); Detroit Olympics (1935–36)

- Led IHL in wins (26) and goals-against-average (2.10) in 1935–36; led IHL playoffs in wins (6), shutouts (1) and goals-against-average (1.32)

- Traded to Toronto Maple Leafs by Detroit Olympics for $8,000 on May 6, 1936

- Played in NHL All-Star Game (1947, 1948, 1949, 1950)

- Led NHL in wins in 1940–41 (28) and 1947–48 (32)

- Led NHL in shutouts in 1941–42 (6) and 1949–50 (9)

- Led NHL in goals-against-average in 1940–41 (2.00) and 1947–48 (2.38)

- Nicknamed "Turk" because his freckles resembled the surface of a turkey egg

- Renowned for his comedic wit and ability to play his best in the playoffs when "the real money" was on the line

- Inducted into Manitoba Hockey Hall of Fame (1967); inducted into Manitoba Sports Hall of Fame (1985)

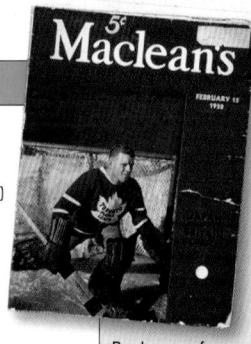

Broda poses for *Maclean's* in February 1938, his second NHL season.

REGULAR SEASON

Season	Age	Team	Lg	GP	W	L	T	SO	GA	GAA	G	A	PTS	PIM
1936–37	22	Toronto Maple Leafs	NHL	45	22	19	4	3	106	2.30	0	0	0	0
1937–38	23	Toronto Maple Leafs	NHL	48	24	15	9	6	127	2.56	0	0	0	0
1938–39	24	Toronto Maple Leafs	NHL	48	19	20	9	8	107	2.15	0	0	0	0
1939–40	25	Toronto Maple Leafs	NHL	47	25	17	5	4	108	2.23	0	0	0	0
1940–41	26	Toronto Maple Leafs	NHL	48	28	14	6	5	99	2.00	0	0	0	0
1941–42	27	Toronto Maple Leafs	NHL	48	27	18	3	6	136	2.76	0	0	0	0
1942–43	28	Toronto Maple Leafs	NHL	50	22	19	9	1	159	3.18	0	0	0	0
1945–46	31	Toronto Maple Leafs	NHL	15	6	6	3	0	53	3.53	0	0	0	0
1946–47	32	Toronto Maple Leafs	NHL	60	31	19	10	4	172	2.87	0	0	0	0
1947–48	33	Toronto Maple Leafs	NHL	60	32	15	13	5	143	2.38	0	0	0	2
1948–49	34	Toronto Maple Leafs	NHL	60	22	25	13	5	161	2.68	0	0	0	0
1949–50	35	Toronto Maple Leafs	NHL	68	30	25	12	9	167	2.48	0	0	0	2
1950–51	36	Toronto Maple Leafs	NHL	31	14	11	5	6	68	2.23	0	0	0	4
1951–52	37	Toronto Maple Leafs	NHL	1	0	1	0	0	3	6.00	0	0	0	0
NHL Career – 14 Seasons				629	302	224	101	62	1609	2.53	0	0	0	8

PLAYOFFS

Season	Age	Team	Lg	GP	W	L	T	SO	GA	GAA	G	A	PTS	PIM
1936–37	22	Toronto Maple Leafs	NHL	2	0	2		0	5	2.26	0	0	0	0
1937–38	23	Toronto Maple Leafs	NHL	7	4	3		1	13	1.73	0	0	0	0
1938–39	24	Toronto Maple Leafs	NHL	10	5	5		2	20	1.94	0	0	0	0
1939–40	25	Toronto Maple Leafs	NHL	10	6	4		1	19	1.74	0	0	0	0
1940–41	26	Toronto Maple Leafs	NHL	7	3	4		0	15	2.05	0	0	0	0
1941–42	27	Toronto Maple Leafs	NHL	13	8	5		1	31	2.38	0	0	0	0
1942–43	28	Toronto Maple Leafs	NHL	6	2	4		0	20	2.73	0	0	0	0
1946–47	32	Toronto Maple Leafs	NHL	11	8	3		1	27	2.38	0	0	0	10
1947–48	33	Toronto Maple Leafs	NHL	9	8	1		1	20	2.15	0	0	0	10
1948–49	34	Toronto Maple Leafs	NHL	9	8	1		1	15	1.57	0	0	0	2
1949–50	35	Toronto Maple Leafs	NHL	7	3	4		3	10	1.33	0	0	0	0
1950–51	36	Toronto Maple Leafs	NHL	8	5	1		2	9	1.10	0	0	0	0
1951–52	37	Toronto Maple Leafs	NHL	2	0	2		0	7	3.50	0	0	0	0
NHL Career – 13 Seasons				101	60	39		13	211	1.98	0	0	0	12

TROPHY CASE

AWARDS

Vezina Trophy (1941, 1948)

Stanley Cup (1941–42, 1946–47, 1947–48, 1948–49, 1950–51)

ALL-STAR SELECTIONS

First All-Star Team Goaltender (1941, 1948)

Second All-Star Team Goaltender (1942)

John Bucyk

HOCKEY HALL OF FAME CLASS: 1981

9

Retired by Boston

Alternate: 20	
Left Wing	
Shoots: Left	
Height: 6'	
Weight: 215 lbs.	
Born: May 12, 1935: Edmonton, Alberta	
Played 23 NHL seasons from 1955–78	

QUICK FACTS

- Holds record as oldest NHL player to score 50 goals in regular season, established in 1970–71
- Holds Boston Bruins team record for career goals (545)
- Holds Boston Bruins team record for consecutive games played (418), established 1969–1975
- Played amateur hockey with Edmonton Maple Leafs (1949–52); Edmonton Oil Kings (1951–54)
- Traded to Boston by Detroit with cash for Terry Sawchuk, June 10, 1957
- Played minor pro hockey with Edmonton Flyers (1953–56)
- Named WHL Rookie of the Year (1955)
- Registered 1,000th career NHL point in Boston's 8–3 victory over Detroit Red Wings, November 9, 1972; recorded 500th career NHL goal in Boston's 3–2 victory over St. Louis Blues, October 30, 1975
- Served as captain of Boston Bruins (1966–67, 1973–77)
- Member of Boston Bruins' famed Uke Line with Vic Stasiuk and Bronco Horvath
- Played in NHL All-Star Game (1955, 1963, 1964, 1965, 1968, 1970, 1971)
- Led NHL in shooting percentage in 1970–71 (22.7%), 1972–73 (23.8%) and 1973–74 (22.3%)

> I played physical but clean hockey. Most people think that the only reason a player wins the Lady Byng is because he is gentlemanly, but I had the ability to play physical and not draw penalties. I contributed offensively and stayed out of the penalty box."

TROPHY CASE

AWARDS

Lady Byng Memorial Trophy (1971, 1974)

Lester Patrick Trophy (1977)

Stanley Cup (1969–70, 1971–72)

ALL-STAR SELECTIONS

First All-Star Team Left Wing (1971)

Second All-Star Team Left Wing (1968)

REGULAR SEASON

Season	Age	Team	Lg	GP	G	A	PTS	+/-	PIM	ESG	PPG	SHG	GWG	SOG	S%
1955–56	20	Detroit Red Wings	NHL	38	1	8	9		20						
1956–57	21	Detroit Red Wings	NHL	66	10	11	21		41						
1957–58	22	Boston Bruins	NHL	68	21	31	52		57						
1958–59	23	Boston Bruins	NHL	69	24	36	60		36						
1959–60	24	Boston Bruins	NHL	56	16	36	52		26						
1960–61	25	Boston Bruins	NHL	70	19	20	39		48						
1961–62	26	Boston Bruins	NHL	67	20	40	60		32						
1962–63	27	Boston Bruins	NHL	69	27	39	66		36						
1963–64	28	Boston Bruins	NHL	62	18	36	54		36	17	1	0	2		
1964–65	29	Boston Bruins	NHL	68	26	29	55		24	19	7	0	2		
1965–66	30	Boston Bruins	NHL	63	27	30	57		12	24	3	0	5		
1966–67	31	Boston Bruins	NHL	59	18	30	48		12	14	4	0	1		
1967–68	32	Boston Bruins	NHL	72	30	39	69	18	8	23	6	1	4	172	17.4
1968–69	33	Boston Bruins	NHL	70	24	42	66	-3	18	13	11	0	3	192	12.5
1969–70	34	Boston Bruins	NHL	76	31	38	69	19	13	17	14	0	6	190	16.3
1970–71	35	Boston Bruins	NHL	78	51	65	116	36	8	29	22	0	5	225	22.7
1971–72	36	Boston Bruins	NHL	78	32	51	83	16	4	19	13	0	7	174	18.4
1972–73	37	Boston Bruins	NHL	78	40	53	93	18	12	30	10	0	10	168	23.8
1973–74	38	Boston Bruins	NHL	76	31	44	75	13	8	19	12	0	9	139	22.3
1974–75	39	Boston Bruins	NHL	78	29	52	81	11	10	20	9	0	4	167	17.4
1975–76	40	Boston Bruins	NHL	77	36	47	83	22	20	23	13	0	9	151	23.8
1976–77	41	Boston Bruins	NHL	49	20	23	43	-2	12	14	6	0	2	98	20.4
1977–78	42	Boston Bruins	NHL	53	5	13	18	-2	4	0	5	0	0	47	10.6
NHL Career — 23 Seasons				1540	556	813	1369	146	497	281	136	1	69	1723	19.1

PLAYOFFS

Season	Age	Team	Lg	GP	G	A	PTS	+/-	PIM	ESG	PPG	SHG	GWG	SOG	S%
1955–56	20	Detroit Red Wings	NHL	10	1	1	2		8						
1956–57	21	Detroit Red Wings	NHL	5	0	1	1		0						
1957–58	22	Boston Bruins	NHL	12	0	4	4		16						
1958–59	23	Boston Bruins	NHL	7	2	4	6		6						
1967–68	32	Boston Bruins	NHL	3	0	2	2		0	0	0	0	0		
1968–69	33	Boston Bruins	NHL	10	5	6	11		0	3	2	0	1		
1969–70	34	Boston Bruins	NHL	14	11	8	19		2	7	4	0	1		
1970–71	35	Boston Bruins	NHL	7	2	5	7		0	2	0	0	0		
1971–72	36	Boston Bruins	NHL	15	9	11	20		6	4	5	0	0		
1972–73	37	Boston Bruins	NHL	5	0	3	3		0	0	0	0	0		
1973–74	38	Boston Bruins	NHL	16	8	10	18		4	5	3	0	1		
1974–75	39	Boston Bruins	NHL	3	1	0	1		0	1	0	0	0		
1975–76	40	Boston Bruins	NHL	12	2	7	9		0	0	2	0	0		
1976–77	41	Boston Bruins	NHL	5	0	0	0		0	0	0	0	0		
NHL Career — 14 Seasons				124	41	62	103		42	22	16	0	3		

Billy Burch

HOCKEY HALL OF FAME CLASS: 1974

Alternates:
4, 9, 6, 12, 8

Center/Left Wing

Shoots: Left

Height: 6'

Weight: 200 lbs.

Born: November 20, 1900: Yonkers, New York

Died: November 30, 1950: Toronto, Ontario

Played 11 NHL seasons from 1922–33

QUICK FACTS

- First United States-born player to become a star in the NHL
- Born in Yonkers — but trained in Toronto — he was still promoted by N.Y. Americans management as "the Babe Ruth of hockey" to arouse hockey interest in New York
- Played amateur hockey with Toronto Canoe Club Paddlers (1919–20); Toronto Aura Lee (1920–22)
- Member of Memorial Cup-winning Toronto Canoe Club (1920)
- Led Memorial Cup playoffs in goals (42), assists (12) and points (54)
- Led OHA-Jr. in assists (10) and points (23) in 1921–22
- Played quarterback for Toronto Central YMCA, Canadian Junior Football Champions (1920)

- Played lacrosse with Toronto Maitlands
- Served as captain of N.Y. Americans (1925–32)
- Scored first goal in history of N.Y. Americans franchise in 2–1 victory over Pittsburgh Pirates, December 2, 1925
- Member of Hamilton Tigers team that refused to participate in 1925 playoffs without extra pay — often considered to be the first players strike in NHL history
- Transferred to N.Y. Americans after NHL club purchased Hamilton franchise, September 25, 1925
- Traded to Boston by N.Y. Americans for cash, April 13, 1932; traded to Chicago by Boston for Vic Ripley, January 17, 1933
- Coached Timmins Black Shirts (1935–36)

> He broke in and played in the days when the going was rough and a player had to be good to stick. If you didn't make it, there was no going back to the amateur ranks. Billy turned pro and never looked back. He was a major leaguer all the way."
>
> — Tommy Shields, *Montreal Gazette* columnist

REGULAR SEASON

Season	Age	Team	Lg	GP	G	A	PTS	PIM
1922–23	22	Hamilton Tigers	NHL	10	6	3	9	4
1923–24	23	Hamilton Tigers	NHL	24	16	6	22	6
1924–25	24	Hamilton Tigers	NHL	27	20	7	27	10
1925–26	25	New York Americans	NHL	36	22	3	25	33
1926–27	26	New York Americans	NHL	43	19	8	27	40
1927–28	27	New York Americans	NHL	32	10	2	12	34
1928–29	28	New York Americans	NHL	44	11	5	16	45
1929–30	29	New York Americans	NHL	35	7	3	10	22
1930–31	30	New York Americans	NHL	44	14	8	22	35
1931–32	31	New York Americans	NHL	48	7	15	22	20
1932–33	32	Boston Bruins	NHL	23	3	1	4	4
1932–33	32	Chicago Black Hawks	NHL	24	2	0	2	2
NHL Career — 11 Seasons				390	137	61	198	255

PLAYOFFS

Season	Age	Team	Lg	GP	G	A	PTS	PIM
1928–29	28	New York Americans	NHL	2	0	0	0	0
NHL Career — 1 Season				2	0	0	0	0

TROPHY CASE

AWARDS

Hart Memorial Trophy (1925)

Lady Byng Memorial Trophy (1927)

People think we exaggerate when we say it was like a war out there but that's exactly what it was. It was more than just a series of eight hockey games. It was a clash of different ideals and ways of life. It was an amazing experience and something I'll never forget."

Yvan Cournoyer

on the Summit Series of 1972

A
B
C
D
E
F
G
H
I
J
K
L
M
N
O
P
Q
R
S
T
U
V
W
X
Y
Z

2

Harry Cameron

HOCKEY HALL OF FAME CLASS: 1962

Alternate: 15

Defense

Shoots: Right

Height: 5'-10"

Weight: 155 lbs.

Born: February 6, 1890: Pembroke, Ontario

Died: October 20, 1953

Played 14 professional seasons from 1912–26

QUICK FACTS

> Ornery? You bet. Mean? At times. But he was the best when he was at his best."
> — Charlie Querrie

- First NHL defenseman to score four goals in a single game twice — in Toronto's 7–5 victory over Montreal Canadiens, December 26, 1917, and Montreal Canadiens' 16–3 victory over Quebec, March 3, 1920

- One of three natives of Pembroke, Ontario (with Frank Nighbor and Hugh Lehman), to be inducted into the Hall of Fame

- Played amateur hockey with Pembroke Debaters (1908–11); Port Arthur Lake City (1911–12)

- Led UOVHL in goals (9) and points (10) in 1910–11; led UOVHL playoffs in assists (4) and points (8) in 1910–11

- Signed as a free agent by Toronto Blueshirts (NHA), November 23, 1912

- Led NHL in assists in 1917–18 (10) and 1921–22 (17)

- Traded to Montreal Canadiens by Toronto St. Pats for Goldie Prodgers, January 14, 1920

- Renowned for developing hockey's first curved shot with a straight blade

- One of the original rushing defensemen in the history of the game, noted for end-to-end rushes

- Believed to be the first player in NHL history to record a goal, assist and fight in the same game, later called the Gordie Howe hat trick, in Toronto's 6–3 loss to Ottawa, December 22, 1920

- Played minor pro with Saskatoon Sheiks (1926–27), Minneapolis Millers (1927–28), St. Louis Flyers (1928–31) and Saskatoon Crescents (1932–33) after retiring as an NHL player

REGULAR SEASON

Season	Age	Team	Lg	GP	G	A	PTS	PIM
1912–13	22	Toronto Blueshirts	NHA	20	9	0	9	20
1913–14	23	Toronto Blueshirts	NHA	19	15	4	19	22
1914–15	24	Toronto Blueshirts	NHA	17	12	8	20	43
1915–16	25	Toronto Blueshirts	NHA	24	8	3	11	70
1916–17	26	Toronto Blueshirts	NHA	14	8	4	12	20
1916–17	26	Montreal Wanderers	NHA	6	1	1	2	9
1917–18	27	Toronto Arenas	NHL	21	17	10	27	28
1918–19	28	Toronto Arenas	NHL	7	6	2	8	9
1918–19	28	Ottawa Senators	NHL	7	5	1	6	26
1919–20	29	Toronto St. Patricks	NHL	7	3	0	3	6
1919–20	29	Montreal Canadiens	NHL	16	12	5	17	36
1920–21	30	Toronto St. Patricks	NHL	24	18	9	27	35
1921–22	31	Toronto St. Patricks	NHL	24	18	17	35	22
1922–23	32	Toronto St. Patricks	NHL	22	9	7	16	27
1923–24	33	Saskatoon Crescents	WCHL	29	10	10	20	16
1924–25	34	Saskatoon Crescents	WCHL	28	13	7	20	21
1925–26	35	Saskatoon Crescents	WHL	30	9	3	12	12
Career – 14 Seasons				315	173	91	264	422

PLAYOFFS

Season	Age	Team	Lg	GP	G	A	PTS	PIM
1913–14	23	Toronto Blueshirts	NHA	2	0	2	2	6
1913–14	23	Toronto Blueshirts	St-Cup	3	1	0	1	4
1917–18	27	Toronto Arenas	NHL	2	1	2	3	0
1917–18	27	Toronto Arenas	St-Cup	5	3	1	4	12
1918–19	28	Ottawa Senators	NHL	5	4	0	4	6
1920–21	30	Toronto St. Patricks	NHL	2	0	0	0	2
1921–22	31	Toronto St. Patricks	NHL	2	0	2	2	8
1921–22	31	Toronto St. Patricks	St-Cup	4	0	2	2	14
1924–25	34	Saskatoon Crescents	WCHL	2	1	0	1	0
1925–26	35	Saskatoon Crescents	WHL	2	0	0	0	0
Career – 7 Seasons				29	10	9	19	52

TROPHY CASE

AWARDS

Stanley Cup: (1913–14, 1917–18, 1921–22)

ALL-STAR SELECTIONS

NHA First All-Star Team Defense (1914)

30

Gerry Cheevers
HOCKEY HALL OF FAME CLASS: 1985

Alternates: 31, 1

Goaltender

Catches: Left

Height: 5'-11"

Weight: 180 lbs.

Born: December 7, 1940: St. Catharines, Ontario

Played 17 NHL and WHA seasons from 1961–80

"If you see a white mask today, it stands out. I hated white. It reminded me of purity, which was not the case the way I played goal."

QUICK FACTS

- Holds NHL record for longest winning streak (32 games) by a goaltender in regular season, established in 1971–72
- Played amateur hockey with St. Michael's Majors (1956–60)
- Renowned for his signature "stitch" mask that featured painted black replications of the stitches he would have had without wearing a mask
- Led OHA-Jr. in shutouts (5) and goals-against-average (3.08); led OHA-Jr. playoffs in shutouts (1) and goals-against-average (2.60) in 1960–61
- Played eight games as left winger for St. Michael's Majors during 1960–61 season
- AHL First All-Star Team Goaltender (1965)
- Led NHL playoffs in shutouts (3) in 1968–69
- Played in NHL All-Star Game (1969)

- Finished second in NHL wins in 1967–68 (23) and 1968–69 (28)
- Led WHA in shutouts in 1972–73 (5), 1973–74 (4) and 1974–75 (4); led WHA in goals-against-average (2.84) in 1972–73
- Won Ben Haskins Trophy (Top WHA Goaltender) in 1973
- Member of Team Canada '74 that played eight game summit series against the Soviet Union
- Member of Team NHL in 1979 Challenge Cup Series between NHL All-Stars and Soviet Union
- Owned Royal Ski, one of the top two-year-old thoroughbred horses in North America, in 1972
- Coached Boston Bruins (1980–85)

Goaltender
by GERRY CHEEVERS
with Trent Frayne

Published in 1971, *Goaltender* chronicles the Boston Bruins' 1970–71 season, including Boston's first-round playoff loss to the Montreal Canadiens.

REGULAR SEASON

Season	Age	Team	Lg	GP	W	L	T	SO	GA	GAA	G	A	PTS	PIM
1961–62	21	Toronto Maple Leafs	NHL	2	1	1	0	0	6	3.00	0	0	0	0
1965–66	25	Boston Bruins	NHL	7	0	4	1	0	34	6.00	0	0	0	0
1966–67	26	Boston Bruins	NHL	22	5	10	6	1	72	3.33	0	0	0	12
1967–68	27	Boston Bruins	NHL	47	23	17	5	3	125	2.83	0	2	2	8
1968–69	28	Boston Bruins	NHL	52	28	12	12	3	145	2.80	0	0	0	14
1969–70	29	Boston Bruins	NHL	41	24	8	8	4	108	2.72	0	0	0	4
1970–71	30	Boston Bruins	NHL	40	27	8	5	3	109	2.72	0	0	0	4
1971–72	31	Boston Bruins	NHL	41	27	5	8	2	101	2.50	0	2	2	25
1972–73	32	Cleveland Crusaders	WHA	52	32	20	0	5	149	2.84	0	1	1	30
1973–74	33	Cleveland Crusaders	WHA	59	30	20	6	4	180	3.03	0	0	0	30
1974–75	34	Cleveland Crusaders	WHA	52	26	24	2	4	167	3.26	0	1	1	59
1975–76	35	Cleveland Crusaders	WHA	28	11	14	1	1	95	3.63	0	0	0	15
1975–76	35	Boston Bruins	NHL	15	8	2	5	1	41	2.73	0	0	0	2
1976–77	36	Boston Bruins	NHL	45	30	10	5	3	137	3.04	0	4	4	46
1977–78	37	Boston Bruins	NHL	21	10	5	2	1	48	2.65	0	1	1	14
1978–79	38	Boston Bruins	NHL	43	23	9	10	1	132	3.16	0	2	2	23
1979–80	39	Boston Bruins	NHL	42	24	11	7	4	116	2.81	0	0	0	62
Career — 17 Seasons				609	329	180	83	40	1765	2.90	0	13	13	348

PLAYOFFS

Season	Age	Team	Lg	GP	W	L	T	SO	GA	GAA	G	A	PTS	PIM
1967–68	27	Boston Bruins	NHL	4	0	4		0	15	3.75	0	0	0	4
1968–69	28	Boston Bruins	NHL	9	6	3		3	16	1.68	0	0	0	17
1969–70	29	Boston Bruins	NHL	13	12	1		0	29	2.23	0	1	1	2
1970–71	30	Boston Bruins	NHL	6	3	3		0	21	3.50	0	0	0	4
1971–72	31	Boston Bruins	NHL	8	6	2		2	21	2.61	0	0	0	0
1972–73	32	Cleveland Crusaders	WHA	9	5	4		0	22	2.41	0	0	0	4
1973–74	33	Cleveland Crusaders	WHA	5	1	4		0	18	3.56	0	0	0	6
1974–75	34	Cleveland Crusaders	WHA	5	1	4		0	23	4.60	0	0	0	0
1975–76	35	Boston Bruins	NHL	6	2	4		1	14	2.14	0	0	0	4
1976–77	36	Boston Bruins	NHL	14	8	5		1	44	3.08	0	0	0	4
1977–78	37	Boston Bruins	NHL	12	8	4		1	35	2.87	0	0	0	6
1978–79	38	Boston Bruins	NHL	6	4	2		0	15	2.50	0	0	0	0
1979–80	39	Boston Bruins	NHL	10	4	6		0	32	3.10	0	0	0	0
Career — 13 Seasons				107	60	46		8	305	2.85	0	1	1	47

TROPHY CASE

AWARDS

Stanley Cup (1969–70, 1971–72)

ALL-STAR SELECTIONS

WHA First All-Star Team Goaltender (1973)

WHA Second All-Star Team Goaltender (1974, 1975)

20

Dino Ciccarelli
HOCKEY HALL OF FAME CLASS: 2010

Alternate: 22
Right Wing
Shoots: Right
Height: 5'-10"
Weight: 185 lbs.
Born: February 8, 1960: Sarnia, Ontario
Played 19 NHL seasons from 1980–99

QUICK FACTS

- Holds NHL record for goals by a rookie in a single playoff year (14), established in 1980–81
- Shares NHL record (with Ville Leino) for points by a rookie in a single playoff year (21)
- Played amateur hockey with Sarnia Army Vets (1974–75); Sarnia Bees (1975–76); London Knights (1976–80)
- Played minor pro hockey with Oklahoma City Stars (1979–81)
- OMJHL Second All-Star Team Right Wing (1978)
- Suffered serious leg injury in 1978–79 season and was not selected in the annual NHL Amateur Draft

- Signed as a free agent by Minnesota North Stars, September 29, 1979
- Played in NHL All-Star Game (1982, 1983, 1989, 1997)
- Finished among NHL top-10 in goals (55), power-play goals (20) and points (106) in 1981–82; goals (52), power-play goals (22) and points (103) in 1986–87
- Finished among NHL top-10 in game-winning goals in 1988–89 (8), 1991–92 (7) and 1992–93 (10)
- Traded to Washington by Minnesota North Stars with Bob Rouse for Mike Gartner and Larry Murphy, March 7, 1989; traded to Detroit by Washington for Kevin Miller, June 20, 1992

> "In our sport, you only get to celebrate the ultimate when you win the Cup. You don't celebrate winning a division or a conference, so that leaves a lot of people out of celebrating an accomplishment. That's why this is so special."
> — Dino Ciccarelli, commenting on his Hall of Fame induction

REGULAR SEASON

Season	Age	Team	Lg	GP	G	A	PTS	+/-	PIM	ESG	PPG	SHG	GWG	SOG	S%
1980–81	20	Minnesota North Stars	NHL	32	18	12	30	2	29	10	8	0	0	126	14.3
1981–82	21	Minnesota North Stars	NHL	76	55	51	106	14	138	35	20	0	4	289	19.0
1982–83	22	Minnesota North Stars	NHL	77	37	38	75	16	94	23	14	0	4	210	17.6
1983–84	23	Minnesota North Stars	NHL	79	38	33	71	1	58	22	16	0	2	211	18.0
1984–85	24	Minnesota North Stars	NHL	51	15	17	32	-10	41	10	5	0	0	133	11.3
1985–86	25	Minnesota North Stars	NHL	75	44	45	89	12	51	25	19	0	5	262	16.8
1986–87	26	Minnesota North Stars	NHL	80	52	51	103	10	88	30	22	0	5	255	20.4
1987–88	27	Minnesota North Stars	NHL	67	41	45	86	-29	79	27	13	1	2	262	15.6
1988–89	28	Minnesota North Stars	NHL	65	32	27	59	-16	64	19	13	0	5	208	15.4
1988–89	28	Washington Capitals	NHL	11	12	3	15	0	12	9	3	0	3	39	30.8
1989–90	29	Washington Capitals	NHL	80	41	38	79	-5	122	31	10	0	6	267	15.4
1990–91	30	Washington Capitals	NHL	54	21	18	39	-17	66	19	2	0	2	186	11.3
1991–92	31	Washington Capitals	NHL	78	38	38	76	-10	78	25	13	0	7	279	13.6
1992–93	32	Detroit Red Wings	NHL	82	41	56	97	2	81	20	21	0	8	200	20.5
1993–94	33	Detroit Red Wings	NHL	66	28	29	57	10	73	16	12	0	1	153	18.3
1994–95	34	Detroit Red Wings	NHL	42	16	27	43	12	39	10	6	0	3	106	15.1
1995–96	35	Detroit Red Wings	NHL	64	22	21	43	14	99	9	13	0	5	107	20.6
1996–97	36	Tampa Bay Lightning	NHL	77	35	25	60	-11	116	23	12	0	6	229	15.3
1997–98	37	Tampa Bay Lightning	NHL	34	11	6	17	-14	42	8	3	0	3	104	10.6
1997–98	37	Florida Panthers	NHL	28	5	11	16	-2	28	3	2	0	1	57	8.8
1998–99	38	Florida Panthers	NHL	14	6	1	7	-1	27	1	5	0	1	23	26.1
NHL Career – 19 Seasons				1232	608	592	1200	-2	1425	375	232	1	73	3706	16.4

PLAYOFFS

Season	Age	Team	Lg	GP	G	A	PTS	+/-	PIM	ESG	PPG	SHG	GWG	SOG	S%
1980–81	20	Minnesota North Stars	NHL	19	14	7	21		25	9	5	0	3		
1981–82	21	Minnesota North Stars	NHL	4	3	1	4		2	1	2	0	1		
1982–83	22	Minnesota North Stars	NHL	9	4	6	10		11	3	1	0	2		
1983–84	23	Minnesota North Stars	NHL	16	4	5	9	-6	27	3	1	0	1	38	10.5
1984–85	24	Minnesota North Stars	NHL	9	3	3	6	-4	8	2	1	0	0	36	8.3
1985–86	25	Minnesota North Stars	NHL	5	0	1	1	-6	6	0	0	0	0	8	0.0
1988–89	28	Washington Capitals	NHL	6	3	3	6	-2	12	0	3	0	0	16	18.8
1989–90	29	Washington Capitals	NHL	8	8	3	11	0	6	7	1	0	1	28	28.6
1990–91	30	Washington Capitals	NHL	11	5	4	9	-3	22	2	3	0	2	44	11.4
1991–92	31	Washington Capitals	NHL	7	5	4	9	-1	14	4	1	0	0	12	41.7
1992–93	32	Detroit Red Wings	NHL	7	4	2	6	-6	16	1	3	0	0	17	23.5
1993–94	33	Detroit Red Wings	NHL	7	5	2	7	1	14	4	1	0	0	22	22.7
1994–95	34	Detroit Red Wings	NHL	16	9	2	11	-4	22	3	6	0	2	49	18.4
1995–96	35	Detroit Red Wings	NHL	17	6	2	8	-6	26	0	6	0	1	36	16.7
NHL Career – 14 Seasons				141	73	45	118	-37	211	39	34	0	13	306	17.0

TROPHY CASE

INTERNATIONAL AWARDS

Bronze Medal: World Championships (1982)

King Clancy
HOCKEY HALL OF FAME CLASS: 1958

Alternate: 9

Defense

Shoots: Left

Height: 5'-7"

Weight: 155 lbs.

Born: February 25, 1903: Ottawa, Ontario

Died: November 8, 1986: Toronto, Ontario

Played 16 NHL seasons from 1921–37

QUICK FACTS

- Played amateur hockey with Ottawa Sandy Hill (1916–17); Ottawa St. Joseph's (1916–17); Ottawa Munitions (1917–18); Ottawa College (1917–18); Ottawa St. Brigands (1918–21)

- Nicknamed "King" because that was his father's nickname

- First defenseman in NHL to score on a penalty shot, established in Toronto's 6–2 victory over Chicago Black Hawks, November 14, 1936

- Only player in NHL history to play all four positions (defense, forward, rover and goaltender) in a single Stanley Cup playoff game in Ottawa's 1–0 victory over Edmonton Eskimos, March 31, 1923

- Replaced goaltender Alex Connell in Ottawa's 4–3 victory over Toronto St. Pats, December 27, 1924

- Replaced goaltender Lorne Chabot in Toronto Maple Leafs' 6–2 loss to Boston Bruins, March 15, 1932

- Played in NHL All-Star Game (1934, 1937)

- Toronto Maple Leafs owner Conn Smythe used the winnings from the money he bet on one of his horses, Rare Jewel, a 200–1 shot, to buy Clancy from Ottawa for $35,000 plus players Eric Pettinger and Art Smith

- Coached Montreal Maroons (1937–38)

- Served as NHL and AHL official (1938–49)

- Coached Cincinnati Mohawks (1949–51)

- Coached Pittsburgh Hornets (1951–53)

- Coached Toronto Maple Leafs (1953–56)

- Substituted for Punch Imlach as Toronto coach (February 18 to March 11, 1967); substituted for John McLellan as Toronto coach (February 23 to March 22, 1972)

> Everybody says I have a gift for the gab and I suppose it's true that I never take a backseat to anyone when it comes to conversation. In fact, a sportswriter once described me as '135 pounds of muscle and conversation.'"

REGULAR SEASON

Season	Age	Team	Lg	GP	G	A	PTS	PIM
1921–22	18	Ottawa Senators	NHL	24	4	6	10	21
1922–23	19	Ottawa Senators	NHL	24	3	2	5	20
1923–24	20	Ottawa Senators	NHL	24	8	8	16	26
1924–25	21	Ottawa Senators	NHL	29	14	7	21	61
1925–26	22	Ottawa Senators	NHL	35	8	4	12	80
1926–27	23	Ottawa Senators	NHL	43	9	10	19	78
1927–28	24	Ottawa Senators	NHL	39	8	7	15	73
1928–29	25	Ottawa Senators	NHL	44	13	2	15	89
1929–30	26	Ottawa Senators	NHL	44	17	23	40	83
1930–31	27	Toronto Maple Leafs	NHL	44	7	14	21	63
1931–32	28	Toronto Maple Leafs	NHL	48	10	9	19	61
1932–33	29	Toronto Maple Leafs	NHL	48	13	12	25	79
1933–34	30	Toronto Maple Leafs	NHL	46	11	17	28	62
1934–35	31	Toronto Maple Leafs	NHL	47	5	16	21	53
1935–36	32	Toronto Maple Leafs	NHL	47	5	10	15	61
1936–37	33	Toronto Maple Leafs	NHL	6	1	0	1	4
NHL Career — 16 Seasons				592	136	147	283	914

PLAYOFFS

Season	Age	Team	Lg	GP	G	A	PTS	PIM
1921–22	18	Ottawa Senators	NHL	2	0	0	0	2
1922–23	19	Ottawa Senators	NHL	2	0	0	0	0
1922–23	19	Ottawa Senators	St-Cup	6	1	0	1	4
1923–24	20	Ottawa Senators	NHL	2	0	0	0	6
1925–26	22	Ottawa Senators	NHL	2	1	0	1	4
1926–27	23	Ottawa Senators	NHL	6	1	1	2	4
1927–28	24	Ottawa Senators	NHL	2	0	0	0	6
1929–30	26	Ottawa Senators	NHL	2	0	1	1	2
1930–31	27	Toronto Maple Leafs	NHL	2	1	0	1	0
1931–32	28	Toronto Maple Leafs	NHL	7	2	1	3	14
1932–33	29	Toronto Maple Leafs	NHL	9	0	3	3	14
1933–34	30	Toronto Maple Leafs	NHL	3	0	0	0	8
1934–35	31	Toronto Maple Leafs	NHL	7	1	0	1	8
1935–36	32	Toronto Maple Leafs	NHL	9	2	2	4	10
NHL Career — 13 Seasons				61	9	8	17	92

TROPHY CASE

AWARDS

Stanley Cup (1922–23, 1926–27, 1931–32)

ALL-STAR SELECTIONS

First All-Star Team Defense (1931, 1934)

Second All-Star Team Defense (1932, 1933)

Dit Clapper

HOCKEY HALL OF FAME CLASS: 1947

Alternates: 12, 3

Defense/
Right Wing

Shoots: Right

Height: 6'-2"

Weight: 195 lbs.

Born: February 9,
1907: Newmarket,
Ontario

Died: January
21, 1978:
Peterborough,
Ontario

Played 20 NHL
seasons from
1927–47

> Clapper
> diagnosed
> the plays like
> a great infielder
> in baseball. He put
> himself where the
> puck had to come."
>
> — Tiny Thompson,
> Boston goaltender

QUICK FACTS

- First player in NHL history to be named to the NHL All-Star Team at two different positions — right wing and defense
- First player in NHL history to play 20 seasons
- One of his given names is Victor, but because of a childhood lisp, his name became Dit
- Played amateur hockey with Parkdale Canoe Club (1925–26) and Boston Tigers (1926–27)
- Traded to Boston Bruins by Boston Tigers (Can-Am) for cash, October 25, 1927
- Played nine seasons on right wing and 11 seasons on defense
- Member of Boston's famed Dynamite Line with Dutch Gainor and Cooney Weiland

- Played in NHL All-Star Game (1937, 1939)
- Well-liked by players and fans throughout the NHL because of the tough way he played the game and his class and character off the ice
- Served as captain of Boston Bruins (1932–38, 1939–47)
- Coached Boston Bruins (1945–49)
- Coached Buffalo Bisons (1959–60)
- Elected to Hockey Hall of Fame immediately after his retirement
- Grandfather of Greg Theberge, who played in NHL with Washington from 1979–84

Clapper's commemorative sweater for the Boston Bruins' 1928–29 Stanley Cup victory, Boston's first.

REGULAR SEASON

Season	Age	Team	Lg	GP	G	A	PTS	PIM
1927–28	20	Boston Bruins	NHL	40	4	1	5	20
1928–29	21	Boston Bruins	NHL	40	9	2	11	48
1929–30	22	Boston Bruins	NHL	44	41	20	61	48
1930–31	23	Boston Bruins	NHL	43	22	8	30	50
1931–32	24	Boston Bruins	NHL	48	17	22	39	21
1932–33	25	Boston Bruins	NHL	48	14	14	28	42
1933–34	26	Boston Bruins	NHL	48	10	12	22	8
1934–35	27	Boston Bruins	NHL	48	21	16	37	21
1935–36	28	Boston Bruins	NHL	44	12	13	25	14
1936–37	29	Boston Bruins	NHL	48	17	8	25	25
1937–38	30	Boston Bruins	NHL	46	6	9	15	24
1938–39	31	Boston Bruins	NHL	42	13	13	26	22
1939–40	32	Boston Bruins	NHL	44	10	18	28	25
1940–41	33	Boston Bruins	NHL	48	8	18	26	24
1941–42	34	Boston Bruins	NHL	32	3	12	15	31
1942–43	35	Boston Bruins	NHL	38	5	18	23	12
1943–44	36	Boston Bruins	NHL	50	6	25	31	13
1944–45	37	Boston Bruins	NHL	46	8	14	22	16
1945–46	38	Boston Bruins	NHL	30	2	3	5	0
1946–47	39	Boston Bruins	NHL	6	0	0	0	0
NHL Career — 20 Seasons				833	228	246	474	462

PLAYOFFS

Season	Age	Team	Lg	GP	G	A	PTS	PIM
1927–28	20	Boston Bruins	NHL	2	0	0	0	2
1928–29	21	Boston Bruins	NHL	5	1	0	1	0
1929–30	22	Boston Bruins	NHL	6	4	0	4	4
1930–31	23	Boston Bruins	NHL	5	2	4	6	4
1932–33	25	Boston Bruins	NHL	5	1	1	2	2
1934–35	27	Boston Bruins	NHL	3	1	0	1	0
1935–36	28	Boston Bruins	NHL	2	0	1	1	0
1936–37	29	Boston Bruins	NHL	3	2	0	2	5
1937–38	30	Boston Bruins	NHL	3	0	0	0	12
1938–39	31	Boston Bruins	NHL	12	0	1	1	6
1939–40	32	Boston Bruins	NHL	5	0	2	2	2
1940–41	33	Boston Bruins	NHL	11	0	5	5	4
1942–43	35	Boston Bruins	NHL	9	2	3	5	9
1944–45	37	Boston Bruins	NHL	7	0	0	0	0
1945–46	38	Boston Bruins	NHL	4	0	0	0	0
NHL Career — 15 Seasons				82	13	17	30	50

TROPHY CASE

AWARDS

Stanley Cup (1928–29, 1938–39, 1940–41)

ALL-STAR SELECTIONS

First All-Star Team Defense (1939, 1940, 1941)

Second All-Star Team Right Wing (1931, 1935)

Second All-Star Team Defense (1944)

16

Retired by Philadelphia

Bobby Clarke
HOCKEY HALL OF FAME CLASS: 1987

Alternate: 36

Center

Shoots: Left

Height: 5'-10"

Weight: 176 lbs.

Born: August 13, 1949: Flin Flon, Manitoba

Drafted by the Philadelphia Flyers 17th overall in 1969

Played 15 NHL seasons from 1969–84

QUICK FACTS

- First player from an expansion-era team (post-1967) to win Hart Trophy as NHL MVP (1974, 1975)
- Played amateur hockey with Flin Flon Midget Bombers (1965–66); Flin Flon Bombers (1965–69)
- Led MJHL in goals (71), assists (112) and points (183) in 1966–67
- Led WCJHL in assists (117) and points (168) in 1967–68, assists (86) and points (137) in 1968–69
- Led WCJHL playoffs in assists (16) and points (25) in 1968–69; named WCJHL MVP in 1968–69
- Overlooked by many NHL teams in Amateur Draft because he suffered from juvenile diabetes

- Led NHL in assists in 1974–75 (89) and 1975–76 (89)
- Led NHL in plus/minus (+83) in 1975–76
- Led NHL in short-handed goals in 1973–74 (5) and 1976–77 (6)
- Finished among NHL top-5 in points in 1972–73 (104), 1973–74 (87) and 1975–76 (119)
- Registered 1,000th career NHL point in Philadelphia's 5–3 victory over Boston Bruins, March 19, 1981
- Served as captain of Philadelphia Flyers (1972–79, 1982–84)
- Served as General Manager of Philadelphia Flyers (1985–90, 1994–2006), Florida Panthers (1993–94) and Minnesota North Stars (1990–92)

> "We take the shortest route to the puck and arrive in ill humor."
> — Bobby Clarke, talking about the Broad Street Bullies

REGULAR SEASON

Season	Age	Team	Lg	GP	G	A	PTS	+/-	PIM	ESG	PPG	SHG	GWG	SOG	S%
1969–70	20	Philadelphia Flyers	NHL	76	15	31	46	1	68	9	5	1	0	214	7.0
1970–71	21	Philadelphia Flyers	NHL	77	27	36	63	9	78	16	10	1	5	185	14.6
1971–72	22	Philadelphia Flyers	NHL	78	35	46	81	22	87	23	11	1	3	225	15.6
1972–73	23	Philadelphia Flyers	NHL	78	37	67	104	32	80	25	10	2	4	231	16.0
1973–74	24	Philadelphia Flyers	NHL	77	35	52	87	35	113	20	10	5	5	221	15.8
1974–75	25	Philadelphia Flyers	NHL	80	27	89	116	79	125	14	10	3	4	193	14.0
1975–76	26	Philadelphia Flyers	NHL	76	30	89	119	83	136	16	10	4	2	194	15.5
1976–77	27	Philadelphia Flyers	NHL	80	27	63	90	39	71	15	6	6	3	158	17.1
1977–78	28	Philadelphia Flyers	NHL	71	21	68	89	47	83	14	5	2	1	131	16.0
1978–79	29	Philadelphia Flyers	NHL	80	16	57	73	12	68	10	5	1	1	143	11.2
1979–80	30	Philadelphia Flyers	NHL	76	12	57	69	42	65	9	1	2	2	139	8.6
1980–81	31	Philadelphia Flyers	NHL	80	19	46	65	17	140	13	5	1	2	150	12.7
1981–82	32	Philadelphia Flyers	NHL	62	17	46	63	28	154	14	2	1	3	110	15.5
1982–83	33	Philadelphia Flyers	NHL	80	23	62	85	37	115	16	6	1	2	164	14.0
1983–84	34	Philadelphia Flyers	NHL	73	17	43	60	23	70	13	3	1	1	129	13.2
NHL Career – 15 Seasons				1144	358	852	1210	506	1453	227	99	32	38	2587	13.8

PLAYOFFS

Season	Age	Team	Lg	GP	G	A	PTS	+/-	PIM	ESG	PPG	SHG	GWG	SOG	S%
1970–71	21	Philadelphia Flyers	NHL	4	0	0	0		2	0	0	0	0		
1972–73	23	Philadelphia Flyers	NHL	11	2	6	8		6	0	2	0	1		
1973–74	24	Philadelphia Flyers	NHL	17	5	11	16		42	3	2	0	2		
1974–75	25	Philadelphia Flyers	NHL	17	4	12	16		16	1	2	1	2		
1975–76	26	Philadelphia Flyers	NHL	16	2	14	16		28	1	1	0	0		
1976–77	27	Philadelphia Flyers	NHL	10	5	5	10		8	3	2	0	0		
1977–78	28	Philadelphia Flyers	NHL	12	4	7	11		8	3	1	0	0		
1978–79	29	Philadelphia Flyers	NHL	8	2	4	6		8	1	1	0	0		
1979–80	30	Philadelphia Flyers	NHL	19	8	12	20		16	5	3	0	2		
1980–81	31	Philadelphia Flyers	NHL	12	3	3	6		6	2	0	1	0		
1981–82	32	Philadelphia Flyers	NHL	4	4	2	6		4	2	1	1	0		
1982–83	33	Philadelphia Flyers	NHL	3	1	0	1		2	1	0	0	0		
1983–84	34	Philadelphia Flyers	NHL	3	2	1	3	-1	6	2	0	0	0	8	25.0
NHL Career – 13 Seasons				136	42	77	119	-1	152	24	15	3	7	8	25.0

TROPHY CASE

AWARDS

Bill Masterton Memorial Trophy (1972)

Hart Memorial Trophy (1973, 1975, 1976)

Lester B. Pearson Award (1973)

Frank J. Selke Trophy (1983)

Lester Patrick Trophy (1980)

Stanley Cup (1974–75, 1975–76)

ALL-STAR SELECTIONS

First All-Star Team Center (1975, 1976)

Second All-Star Team Center (1973, 1974)

INTERNATIONAL AWARDS

Summit Series (1972)

Canada Cup (1976)

Bronze Medal: World Championships (1982)

Sprague Cleghorn

HOCKEY HALL OF FAME CLASS: 1958

Alternates: 2, 1

Defense

Shoots: Left

Height: 5'-10"

Weight: 190 lbs.

Born: March 11, 1890: Montreal, Quebec

Died: July 12, 1956: Montreal, Quebec

Played 17 professional seasons from 1910–17, 1918–28

QUICK FACTS

- Played amateur hockey with Montreal Canadian Rubber (1908–09); New York Wanderers (1909–10)

- Nicknamed "Peg"

- Renowned for his questionable on ice antics, it was noted that he played the game with "vigilante vigor"

- Missed entire 1917–18 season recovering from broken leg suffered in off-ice accident, January 13, 1918

- Served as "unofficial" captain of Boston Bruins (1925–27); served as player/ assistant coach of Boston Bruins (1927–28)

- Led NHL in penalty minutes (80) in 1921–22

- Signed as a free agent by Ottawa Senators after securing his release from Toronto St. Pats and allowed to play in Stanley Cup playoffs, March 15, 1921

- Rights transferred to Hamilton by NHL, April 6, 1921; traded to Montreal Canadiens by Hamilton for Harry Mummery and Amos Arbour, November 26, 1921; traded to Boston by Montreal Canadiens for $5,000, November 8, 1925

- Served as player/coach of Newark Bulldogs (1928–29)

- Coached Providence Reds (1930–31)

- Coached Montreal Maroons (1931–32)

- Coached Verdun Maple Leafs (1932–34); coached Edmonton Eskimos (1934–35); coached Pittsburgh Shamrocks (1935–36); coached Cornwall Cougars (1946–47)

- Brother of Odie Cleghorn, who played in NHL with Montreal Canadiens and Pittsburgh Pirates from 1917–28

> He typified the old-time, driving hockey player, of which there are too few in the game today."
> — Frank Selke

REGULAR SEASON

Season	Age	Team	Lg	GP	G	A	PTS	PIM
1910–11	20	Renfrew Hockey Club	NHA	12	5	0	5	27
1911–12	21	Montreal Wanderers	NHA	18	9	0	9	40
1912–13	22	Montreal Wanderers	NHA	19	12	0	12	46
1913–14	23	Montreal Wanderers	NHA	20	12	8	20	17
1914–15	24	Montreal Wanderers	NHA	19	21	12	33	51
1915–16	25	Montreal Wanderers	NHA	8	9	4	13	22
1916–17	26	Montreal Wanderers	NHA	19	16	9	25	62
1918–19	28	Ottawa Senators	NHL	18	7	6	13	27
1919–20	29	Ottawa Senators	NHL	21	16	5	21	85
1920–21	30	Toronto St. Patricks	NHL	13	3	5	8	31
1921–22	31	Montreal Canadiens	NHL	24	17	9	26	80
1922–23	32	Montreal Canadiens	NHL	24	9	8	17	34
1923–24	33	Montreal Canadiens	NHL	23	8	4	12	45
1924–25	34	Montreal Canadiens	NHL	27	8	10	18	89
1925–26	35	Boston Bruins	NHL	28	6	5	11	49
1926–27	36	Boston Bruins	NHL	44	7	1	8	84
1927–28	37	Boston Bruins	NHL	37	2	2	4	14
Career — 17 Seasons				374	167	88	255	803

Season	Age	Team	Lg	GP	G	A	PTS	PIM
1914–15	24	Montreal Wanderers	NHA	2	0	0	0	17
1918–19	28	Ottawa Senators	NHL	5	2	1	3	9
1919–20	29	Ottawa Senators	St-Cup	5	0	1	1	4
1920–21	30	Toronto St. Patricks	NHL	1	0	0	0	0
1920–21	30	Ottawa Senators	St-Cup	5	1	2	3	38
1922–23	32	Montreal Canadiens	NHL	1	0	0	0	7
1923–24	33	Montreal Canadiens	NHL	2	0	0	0	0
1923–24	33	Montreal Canadiens	St-Cup	4	2	1	3	2
1924–25	34	Montreal Canadiens	NHL	2	1	2	3	2
1924–25	34	Montreal Canadiens	St-Cup	4	0	0	0	2
1926–27	36	Boston Bruins	NHL	8	1	0	1	8
1927–28	37	Boston Bruins	NHL	2	0	0	0	0
Career — 9 Seasons				41	7	7	14	89

TROPHY CASE

AWARDS

Stanley Cup (1919–20, 1920–21, 1923–24)

7

Retired by Edmonton

Alternates: 77, 74	
Defense	
Shoots: Left	
Height: 6'	
Weight: 205 lbs.	
Born: June 1, 1961; Weston, Ontario	
Drafted by the Edmonton Oilers sixth overall in 1980	
Played 21 NHL seasons from 1980–2001	

Paul Coffey
HOCKEY HALL OF FAME CLASS: 2004

Retired by Edmonton

QUICK FACTS

- Holds NHL record for goals in a single season by a defenseman (48), established in 1985–86; holds NHL record for career playoff goals (59) and career playoff points (196) by a defenseman

- Holds Edmonton Oilers team records for career goals (209), assists (460), points (669) and career playoff points (103) by a defenseman; holds Edmonton Oilers' team records for points in a single season by a defenseman (138)

- Holds Detroit Red Wings team record for assists (63) and points (77) in a single season by a defenseman

- Holds Pittsburgh Penguins team records for career goals (108), assists (332) and points (440) by a defenseman (440); holds Pittsburgh Penguins team records for goals (30), assists (83) and points (113) in a single season by a defenseman

- Ranks fifth in NHL career assists (1,135); ranks 12th in NHL career points (1,531)

- Played amateur hockey with North York Rangers (1977–78); Kingston Canadians (1977–78); Sault Ste. Marie Greyhounds (1978–80); Kitchener Rangers (1979–80)

- OMJHL Second All-Star Team Defense (1980)

> "We were very lucky to have a general manager at that time, and he ended up being our coach, who allowed us to be ourselves; who allowed us to express ourselves whether it was on or off the ice. We had a simple set of rules: be on time, don't embarrass the coach and work hard, and we tried to do that."
> — Paul Coffey, on his Edmonton Oiler days

REGULAR SEASON

Season	Age	Team	Lg	GP	G	A	PTS	+/-	PIM	ESG	PPG	SHG	GWG	SOG	S%
1980–81	19	Edmonton Oilers	NHL	74	9	23	32	4	130	7	2	0	0	113	8.0
1981–82	20	Edmonton Oilers	NHL	80	29	60	89	35	106	16	13	0	1	234	12.4
1982–83	21	Edmonton Oilers	NHL	80	29	67	96	52	87	19	9	1	2	259	11.2
1983–84	22	Edmonton Oilers	NHL	80	40	86	126	52	104	25	14	1	4	258	15.5
1984–85	23	Edmonton Oilers	NHL	80	37	84	121	55	97	23	12	2	6	264	13.0
1985–86	24	Edmonton Oilers	NHL	79	48	90	138	61	120	30	9	9	3	307	15.6
1986–87	25	Edmonton Oilers	NHL	59	17	50	67	12	49	5	10	2	3	165	10.3
1987–88	26	Pittsburgh Penguins	NHL	46	15	52	67	-1	93	7	6	2	2	193	7.8
1988–89	27	Pittsburgh Penguins	NHL	75	30	83	113	-10	195	19	11	0	2	342	8.8
1989–90	28	Pittsburgh Penguins	NHL	80	29	74	103	-25	95	19	10	0	3	324	9.0
1990–91	29	Pittsburgh Penguins	NHL	76	24	69	93	-18	128	16	8	0	3	240	10.0
1991–92	30	Pittsburgh Penguins	NHL	54	10	54	64	4	62	5	5	0	1	207	4.8
1991–92	30	Los Angeles Kings	NHL	10	1	4	5	-3	25	1	0	0	0	25	4.0
1992–93	31	Los Angeles Kings	NHL	50	8	49	57	9	50	6	2	0	0	182	4.4
1992–93	31	Detroit Red Wings	NHL	30	4	26	30	7	27	1	3	0	0	72	5.6
1993–94	32	Detroit Red Wings	NHL	80	14	63	77	28	106	9	5	0	3	278	5.0
1994–95	33	Detroit Red Wings	NHL	45	14	44	58	18	72	9	4	1	2	181	7.7
1995–96	34	Detroit Red Wings	NHL	76	14	60	74	19	90	10	3	1	3	234	6.0
1996–97	35	Hartford Whalers	NHL	20	3	5	8	0	18	2	1	0	1	39	7.7
1996–97	35	Philadelphia Flyers	NHL	37	6	20	26	11	20	5	0	1	1	71	8.5
1997–98	36	Philadelphia Flyers	NHL	57	2	27	29	3	30	1	1	0	1	107	1.9
1998–99	37	Chicago Blackhawks	NHL	10	0	4	4	-6	0	0	0	0	0	8	0.0
1998–99	37	Carolina Hurricanes	NHL	44	2	8	10	-1	28	1	1	0	0	79	2.5
1999–00	38	Carolina Hurricanes	NHL	69	11	29	40	-6	40	5	6	0	3	155	7.1
2000–01	39	Boston Bruins	NHL	18	0	4	4	-6	30	0	0	0	0	28	0.0
NHL Career — 21 Seasons				1409	396	1135	1531	294	1802	241	135	20	44	4385	9.0

PLAYOFFS

Season	Age	Team	Lg	GP	G	A	PTS	+/-	PIM	ESG	PPG	SHG	GWG	SOG	S%
1980–81	19	Edmonton Oilers	NHL	9	4	3	7		22	3	1	0	0		
1981–82	20	Edmonton Oilers	NHL	5	1	1	2		6	0	1	0	0		
1982–83	21	Edmonton Oilers	NHL	16	7	7	14		14	3	2	2	0		
1983–84	22	Edmonton Oilers	NHL	19	8	14	22	21	21	6	2	0	1	66	12.1
1984–85	23	Edmonton Oilers	NHL	18	12	25	37	26	44	8	3	1	4	66	18.2
1985–86	24	Edmonton Oilers	NHL	10	1	9	10	0	30	0	1	0	0	33	3.0
1986–87	25	Edmonton Oilers	NHL	17	3	8	11	7	30	2	1	0	1	43	7.0
1988–89	27	Pittsburgh Penguins	NHL	11	2	13	15	-7	31	0	2	0	1	48	4.2
1990–91	29	Pittsburgh Penguins	NHL	12	2	9	11	-1	6	2	0	0	0	37	5.4
1991–92	30	Los Angeles Kings	NHL	6	4	3	7		5	2	1	3	0	28	14.3
1992–93	31	Detroit Red Wings	NHL	7	2	9	11	-3	2	2	0	0	0	24	8.3
1993–94	32	Detroit Red Wings	NHL	7	1	6	7	6	8	1	0	0	0	23	4.3
1994–95	33	Detroit Red Wings	NHL	18	6	12	18	4	10	3	2	1	0	74	8.1
1995–96	34	Detroit Red Wings	NHL	17	5	9	14	-3	30	0	3	2	1	49	10.2
1996–97	35	Philadelphia Flyers	NHL	17	1	8	9	-3	6	1	0	0	0	37	2.7
1998–99	37	Carolina Hurricanes	NHL	5	0	1	1	0	2	0	0	0	0	8	0.0
NHL Career — 16 Seasons				194	59	137	196	42	264	32	21	6	8	536	8.8

TROPHY CASE

AWARDS

James Norris Memorial Trophy (1985, 1986, 1995)

Stanley Cup (1983–84, 1984–85, 1986–87, 1990–91)

ALL-STAR SELECTIONS

First All-Star Team Defense (1985, 1986, 1989, 1995)

Second All-Star Team Defense (1982, 1983, 1984, 1990)

INTERNATIONAL AWARDS

Canada Cup (1984, 1987, 1991)

Neil Colville

HOCKEY HALL OF FAME CLASS: 1967

Center/Defense

Shoots: Right

Height: 5'-11"

Weight: 175 lbs.

Born: August 4, 1914: Edmonton, Alberta

Died: December 26, 1987: Richmond, British Columbia

Played 12 NHL seasons from 1935–42, 1944–49

QUICK FACTS

" A neat puck manipulator, a smart ice general, the gray-thatched center has given local customers more thrills per game than any other member of the hockey cast."
— *Ottawa Citizen*

- Played amateur hockey with Edmonton Eharcos (1929–30); Edmonton Canadians (1930–31); Edmonton Poolers (1931–33); Edmonton Athletic Club (1933–34); N.Y.-Hamilton Crescents (1934–35)

- Led Edmonton City Junior League in goals (14) and points (18) in 1933–34; led ECJHL playoffs in goals (4), assists (2) and points (6) in 1933–34

- Led EAHL in goals (24) and points (35) in 1934–35; led EAHL playoffs in goals (8) in 1934–35

- EAHL First All-Star Team Center (1935)

- One of six Hall of Fame members (with Sid Abel, Doug Bentley, Dit Clapper, Alex Delvecchio and Mark Messier) to be selected as NHL All-Star at two different positions

- Played in NHL All-Star Game (1939, 1948)

- Member of N.Y. Rangers' famed Bread Line with Mac Colville and Alex Shibicky

- Played with Ottawa Commandos (1942–44); Ottawa RCAF Corps (1942–43); Winnipeg RCAF Bombers (1944–45); Quebec Aces (1944–45) during World War II

- Member of Allan Cup-winning Ottawa Commandos (1942–43)

- Led QSHL in assists (32) in 1942–43; led QSHL playoffs in goals (11), assists (7) and points (18) in 1942–43

- Led Allan Cup playoffs in goals (14), assists (14) and points (28) in 1942–43

- Served as captain of N.Y. Rangers (1945–49)

- Switched from center to defense after returning to NHL from World War II

- Coached N.Y. Rangers (1950–52)

REGULAR SEASON

Season	Age	Team	Lg	GP	G	A	PTS	PIM
1935–36	21	New York Rangers	NHL	1	0	0	0	0
1936–37	22	New York Rangers	NHL	45	10	18	28	33
1937–38	23	New York Rangers	NHL	45	17	19	36	11
1938–39	24	New York Rangers	NHL	47	18	19	37	12
1939–40	25	New York Rangers	NHL	48	19	19	38	22
1940–41	26	New York Rangers	NHL	48	14	28	42	28
1941–42	27	New York Rangers	NHL	48	8	25	33	37
1944–45	30	New York Rangers	NHL	4	0	1	1	2
1945–46	31	New York Rangers	NHL	49	5	4	9	25
1946–47	32	New York Rangers	NHL	60	4	16	20	16
1947–48	33	New York Rangers	NHL	55	4	12	16	25
1948–49	34	New York Rangers	NHL	14	0	5	5	2
NHL Career – 12 Seasons				464	99	166	265	213

PLAYOFFS

Season	Age	Team	Lg	GP	G	A	PTS	PIM
1936–37	22	New York Rangers	NHL	9	3	3	6	0
1937–38	23	New York Rangers	NHL	3	0	1	1	0
1938–39	24	New York Rangers	NHL	7	0	2	2	2
1939–40	25	New York Rangers	NHL	12	2	7	9	18
1940–41	26	New York Rangers	NHL	3	1	1	2	0
1941–42	27	New York Rangers	NHL	6	0	5	5	6
1947–48	33	New York Rangers	NHL	6	1	0	1	6
NHL Career – 7 Seasons				46	7	19	26	32

TROPHY CASE

AWARDS

Stanley Cup (1939–40)

ALL-STAR SELECTIONS

Second All-Star Team Center (1939, 1940)

Second All-Star Team Defense (1948)

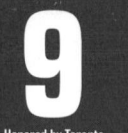

Charlie Conacher

HOCKEY HALL OF FAME CLASS: 1961

9

Honored by Toronto

Alternates: 17, 6, 4
Right Wing
Shoots: Right
Height: 6'-1"
Weight: 195 lbs.
Born: December 20, 1909: Toronto, Ontario
Died: December 30, 1967: Toronto, Ontario
Played 12 NHL seasons from 1929–41

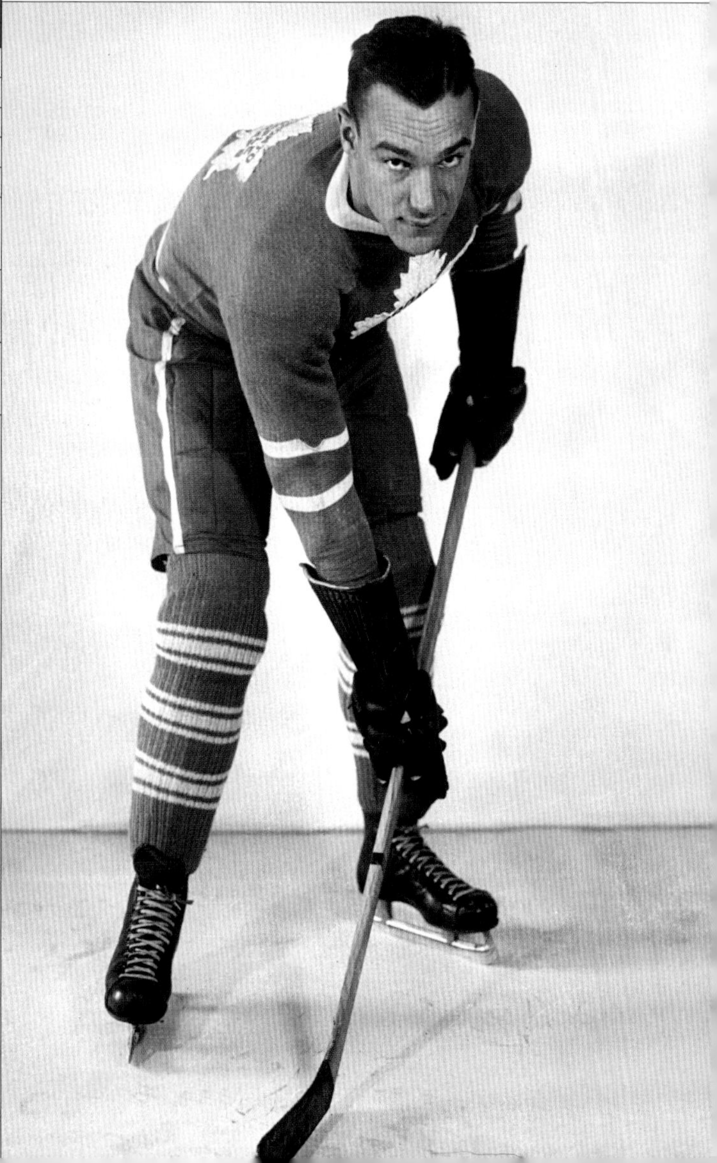

Syl Apps, Hap Day, George Hainsworth, Joe Hall, Percy LeSueur, Frank Rankin, Maurice Richard, Milt Schmidt, Oliver Seibert, Bruce Stuart

QUICK FACTS

- Holds NHL record for fastest game-winning goal (6 seconds), established in Toronto's 6–0 victory over Boston, February 6, 1932
- One of three Conacher brothers (along with Roy and Lionel) to be inducted into the Hockey Hall of Fame
- Nicknamed "The Big Bomber" because of his explosive shot
- Played amateur hockey with North Toronto Juniors (1926–27); North Toronto Seniors (1926–27); Toronto Marlboros (1927–29)
- Led OHA-Jr. in goals (18) and points (21) in 1928–29; led Memorial Cup playoffs in goals (28) and points (36) in 1929
- Signed as a free agent by Toronto, October 7, 1929

- Led NHL in goals in 1930–31 (31), 1931–32 (34), 1933–34 (32), 1934–35 (36) and 1935–36 (23)
- First player in Toronto Maple Leaf history to score five goals in one game in 11–3 victory over N.Y. Americans, January 19, 1932
- Played in NHL All-Star Game (1934, 1937)
- Coached Chicago Black Hawks (1947–48)
- His legacy is remembered through the Charlie Conacher Research Fund for cancer
- Inducted into Canada's Sports Hall of Fame (1975)
- NHL presented an award in his name from 1968 to 1984 to the player best exhibiting outstanding humanitarian and public service contributions

> I never had a finer friend in Toronto than Charlie. He was my protection as a Maple Leaf ... He didn't go looking for trouble, but if it came along, he would clear it up."
>
> — King Clancy, commenting on his teammate

REGULAR SEASON

Season	Age	Team	Lg	GP	G	A	PTS	PIM
1929–30	20	Toronto Maple Leafs	NHL	38	20	9	29	48
1930–31	21	Toronto Maple Leafs	NHL	37	31	12	43	78
1931–32	22	Toronto Maple Leafs	NHL	44	34	14	48	66
1932–33	23	Toronto Maple Leafs	NHL	40	14	19	33	64
1933–34	24	Toronto Maple Leafs	NHL	42	32	20	52	38
1934–35	25	Toronto Maple Leafs	NHL	47	36	21	57	24
1935–36	26	Toronto Maple Leafs	NHL	44	23	15	38	74
1936–37	27	Toronto Maple Leafs	NHL	15	3	5	8	13
1937–38	28	Toronto Maple Leafs	NHL	19	7	9	16	6
1938–39	29	Detroit Red Wings	NHL	40	8	15	23	39
1939–40	30	New York Americans	NHL	47	10	18	28	41
1940–41	31	New York Americans	NHL	46	7	16	23	32
NHL Career – 12 Seasons				459	225	173	398	523

PLAYOFFS

Season	Age	Team	Lg	GP	G	A	PTS	PIM
1930–31	21	Toronto Maple Leafs	NHL	2	0	1	1	0
1931–32	22	Toronto Maple Leafs	NHL	7	6	2	8	6
1932–33	23	Toronto Maple Leafs	NHL	9	1	1	2	10
1933–34	24	Toronto Maple Leafs	NHL	5	3	2	5	0
1934–35	25	Toronto Maple Leafs	NHL	7	1	4	5	6
1935–36	26	Toronto Maple Leafs	NHL	9	3	2	5	12
1936–37	27	Toronto Maple Leafs	NHL	2	0	0	0	5
1938–39	29	Detroit Red Wings	NHL	5	2	5	7	2
1939–40	30	New York Americans	NHL	3	1	1	2	8
NHL Career – 9 Seasons				49	17	18	35	49

TROPHY CASE

AWARDS

NHL Scoring Leader (1934, 1935)

Stanley Cup (1931–32)

ALL-STAR SELECTIONS

First All-Star Team Right Wing (1934, 1935, 1936)

Second All-Star Team Right Wing (1931, 1932)

3

Lionel Conacher
HOCKEY HALL OF FAME CLASS: 1994

Alternates: 2, 15

Defense

Shoots: Left

Height: 6'-2"

Weight: 195 lbs.

Born: May 24, 1901: Toronto, Ontario

Died: May 26, 1954: Ottawa, Ontario

Played 12 NHL seasons from 1925–37

" The cost to the professional athlete of his success is most invariably overlooked when he is exposed to the glamour created by roaring crowds, breezy headlines and over-enthusiastic ballyhoo. But is the climb worthwhile? Sometimes I wonder, especially after contemplating this inventory of injuries which I've picked up during my athletic career."

QUICK FACTS

- Played amateur hockey with Toronto Century Rovers (1916–17); Toronto Aura Lee (1917–19, 1920–22); Toronto Canoe Club (1919–20); North Toronto Seniors (1922–23); Pittsburgh Yellowjackets (1923–25)
- Member of Memorial Cup-winning Toronto Canoe Club (1919–20)
- Member of USAHA champion Pittsburgh Yellowjackets (1923–24, 1924–25)
- Named Canada's Athlete of the Half-Century (1950)
- Played professional baseball as an outfielder for the Toronto Maple Leafs of the International League (1926)
- Played professional lacrosse with Montreal Maroons of the International Indoor Professional Lacrosse League (1931)

- Played professional football with Toronto Crosse and Blackwell Chefs (1933) and Wrigley Aromints (1934)
- Won Grey Cup (Canadian Football championship) as a member of the Toronto Argonauts (1921)
- Inducted into Canadian Lacrosse Hall of Fame (1965); inducted into Canadian Football Hall of Fame (1963); inducted into Canada's Sports Hall of Fame (1955)
- Won Canadian amateur light heavyweight boxing championship (1921)
- Nicknamed "Big Train" because of his endless energy and stamina

Montreal Maroons jersey worn by Conacher in his last NHL season, 1936–37.

REGULAR SEASON

Season	Age	Team	Lg	GP	G	A	PTS	PIM
1925–26	24	Pittsburgh Pirates	NHL	33	9	4	13	64
1926–27	25	Pittsburgh Pirates	NHL	9	0	0	0	12
1926–27	25	New York Americans	NHL	30	8	9	17	81
1927–28	26	New York Americans	NHL	35	11	6	17	82
1928–29	27	New York Americans	NHL	44	5	2	7	132
1929–30	28	New York Americans	NHL	40	4	6	10	73
1930–31	29	Montreal Maroons	NHL	36	4	3	7	57
1931–32	30	Montreal Maroons	NHL	45	7	9	16	60
1932–33	31	Montreal Maroons	NHL	47	7	21	28	61
1933–34	32	Chicago Black Hawks	NHL	48	10	13	23	87
1934–35	33	Montreal Maroons	NHL	38	2	6	8	44
1935–36	34	Montreal Maroons	NHL	46	7	7	14	65
1936–37	35	Montreal Maroons	NHL	47	6	19	25	64
NHL Career – 12 Seasons				498	80	105	185	882

PLAYOFFS

Season	Age	Team	Lg	GP	G	A	PTS	PIM
1925–26	24	Pittsburgh Pirates	NHL	2	0	0	0	0
1928–29	27	New York Americans	NHL	2	0	0	0	10
1930–31	29	Montreal Maroons	NHL	2	0	0	0	2
1931–32	30	Montreal Maroons	NHL	4	0	0	0	2
1932–33	31	Montreal Maroons	NHL	2	0	1	1	0
1933–34	32	Chicago Black Hawks	NHL	8	2	0	2	4
1934–35	33	Montreal Maroons	NHL	7	0	0	0	14
1935–36	34	Montreal Maroons	NHL	3	0	0	0	0
1936–37	35	Montreal Maroons	NHL	5	0	1	1	2
NHL Career – 9 Seasons				35	2	2	4	34

TROPHY CASE

AWARDS

Stanley Cup (1933–34, 1934–35)

ALL-STAR SELECTIONS

First All-Star Team Defense (1934)

Second All-Star Team Defense (1933, 1937)

9

Roy Conacher
HOCKEY HALL OF FAME CLASS: 1998

Alternates: 11, 8

Left Wing

Shoots: Left

Height: 6'-2"

Weight: 175 lbs.

Born: October 5, 1916: Toronto, Ontario

Died: December 29, 1984: Victoria, British Columbia

Played 11 NHL seasons from 1938–42, 1945–52

"He was a man self-effacing, who believed that merit should speak for itself. My father became, at least for one season, certainly the best in the world at what he did. He was driven to that pinnacle by a deeply-rooted motivation — a desire for perfection."

— Roy Conacher's son, speaking at his father's posthumous induction into the Hockey Hall of Fame

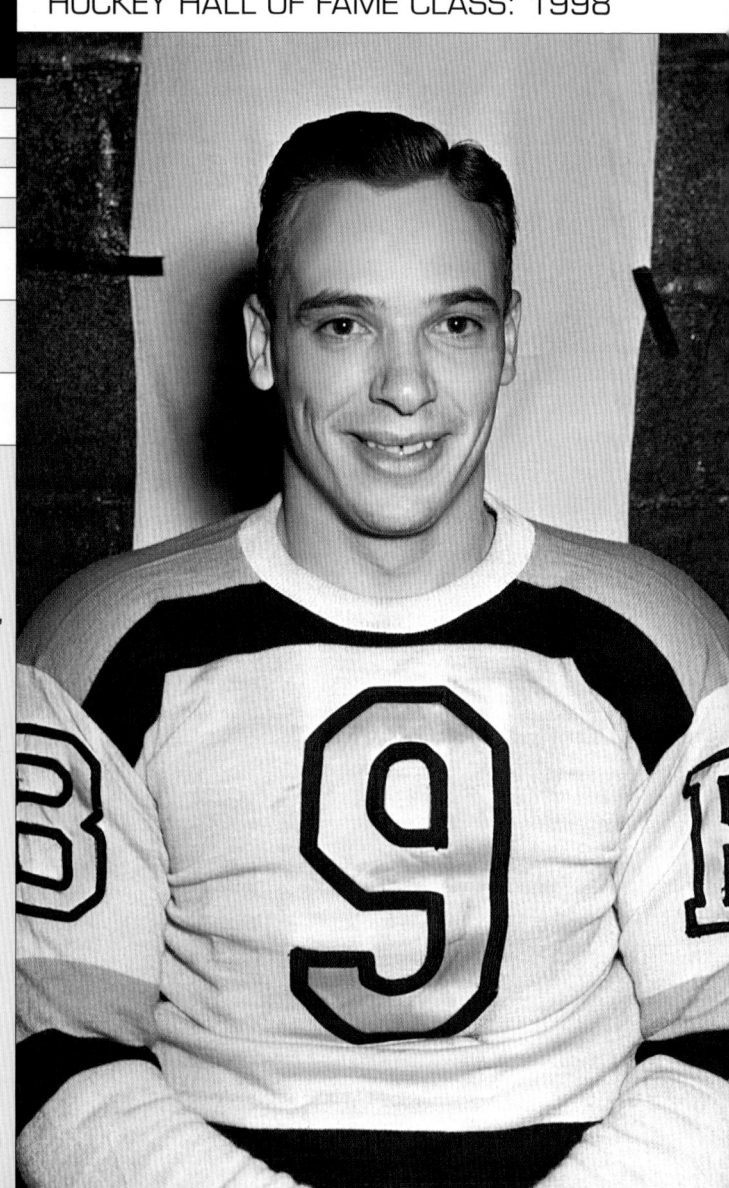

QUICK FACTS

- First rookie in NHL history in lead league in goals (1938–39)
- Played amateur hockey with West Toronto Nationals (1933–36); Toronto Dominions (1936–37); Kirkland Lake Wright-Hargreaves (1937–38)
- Led OHA-Jr. in goals (12) in 1935–36
- Signed as a free agent by Boston, October 23, 1938
- Member of Memorial Cup-winning West Toronto Nationals (1935–36); recorded 8 goals and 13 points in Memorial Cup playoffs
- Played with Saskatoon RCAF (1942–43); Dartmouth RCAF (1943–45); Millward RCAF (1944–45) during World War II
- Led Halifax City League in goals (9) in 1943–44
- Traded to Detroit by Boston for Joe Carveth, June 25, 1946
- Led NHL in goals (26) in 1938–39; led NHL in points (68) in 1948–49
- Finished second in NHL goals in 1940–41 (24), 1941–42 (24), 1946–47 (30) and 1948–49 (26)
- Scored Stanley Cup-winning goal in Boston's 3–1 victory over Toronto Maple Leafs, April 16, 1939
- Brother of Hall of Fame member Charlie Conacher, who played in NHL with Toronto, N.Y. Americans and Detroit from 1929–41; brother of Hall of Fame member Lionel Conacher, who played in NHL with Pittsburgh Pirates, N.Y. Americans, Montreal Maroons and Chicago from 1925–37

Conacher's Black Hawks cardigan from his time in the Windy City, 1947–52.

REGULAR SEASON

Season	Age	Team	Lg	GP	G	A	PTS	PIM
1938–39	22	Boston Bruins	NHL	47	26	11	37	12
1939–40	23	Boston Bruins	NHL	31	18	12	30	9
1940–41	24	Boston Bruins	NHL	41	24	14	38	7
1941–42	25	Boston Bruins	NHL	43	24	13	37	12
1945–46	29	Boston Bruins	NHL	4	2	1	3	0
1946–47	30	Detroit Red Wings	NHL	60	30	24	54	6
1947–48	31	Chicago Black Hawks	NHL	52	22	27	49	4
1948–49	32	Chicago Black Hawks	NHL	60	26	42	68	8
1949–50	33	Chicago Black Hawks	NHL	70	25	31	56	16
1950–51	34	Chicago Black Hawks	NHL	70	26	24	50	16
1951–52	35	Chicago Black Hawks	NHL	12	3	1	4	0
NHL Career – 11 Seasons				490	226	200	426	90

PLAYOFFS

Season	Age	Team	Lg	GP	G	A	PTS	PIM
1938–39	22	Boston Bruins	NHL	12	6	4	10	12
1939–40	23	Boston Bruins	NHL	6	2	1	3	0
1940–41	24	Boston Bruins	NHL	11	1	5	6	0
1941–42	25	Boston Bruins	NHL	5	2	1	3	0
1945–46	29	Boston Bruins	NHL	3	0	0	0	0
1946–47	30	Detroit Red Wings	NHL	5	4	4	8	2
NHL Career – 6 Seasons				42	15	15	30	14

TROPHY CASE

AWARDS

Art Ross Trophy (1949)

Stanley Cup (1938–39, 1940–41)

ALL-STAR SELECTIONS

First All-Star Team Left Wing (1949)

1

Alex Connell
HOCKEY HALL OF FAME CLASS: 1958

Goaltender

Catches: Left

Height: 5'-9"

Weight: 150 lbs.

Born: February 8, 1902: Ottawa, Ontario

Died: May 10, 1958: Ottawa, Ontario

Played 12 NHL seasons from 1924–35, 1936–37

> He's a little man, as fast as a flash and as cool-headed as Georges Vezina of the Canadiens."
>
> — Tommy Gorman, general manager of the Ottawa Senators, on signing Connell to a professional contract

QUICK FACTS

- Holds NHL record for longest shutout sequence by a goaltender in the regular season (461:29), established from January 31, 1928, to February 18, 1928

- Only goaltender in NHL history to record 15 or more shutouts in regular season twice, 1926–27 (15) and 1927–28 (15)

- Ranks sixth in NHL career shutouts (81)

- Played amateur hockey with Kingston Ponies (1916–17); Kingston Frontenacs (1917–19); Ottawa Cliffsides (1919–20); Ottawa St. Brigands (1920–21, 1922–24); Ottawa Gunners (1921–22)

- Signed as a free agent by the Ottawa Senators in 1924

- Led NHL in shutouts in 1924–25 (7), 1925–26 (15), 1927–28 (15) and 1934–35 (9)

- Led NHL in wins in 1925–26 (24) and 1926–27 (30)

- Led NHL in goals-against-average (1.12) in 1925–26

- Nicknamed "The Ottawa Fireman" because he was the Secretary of the Ottawa Fire Department in the off-season

- Loaned to N.Y. Americans by Ottawa to replace injured Roy Worters in N.Y. Americans' 3–2 victory over Ottawa, March 15, 1934

- Traded to Montreal Maroons by Ottawa for future considerations (Glenn Brydson), October 2, 1934

- Elected to Ottawa Sports Hall of Fame (1968)

An early O-Pee-Chee card featuring Alex Connell, then of the Ottawa Senators.

REGULAR SEASON

Season	Age	Team	Lg	GP	W	L	T	SO	GA	GAA	G	A	PTS	PIM
1924–25	22	Ottawa Senators	NHL	30	17	12	1	7	66	2.14	0	0	0	2
1925–26	23	Ottawa Senators	NHL	36	24	8	4	15	42	1.12	0	0	0	0
1926–27	24	Ottawa Senators	NHL	44	30	10	4	13	69	1.49	0	0	0	2
1927–28	25	Ottawa Senators	NHL	44	20	14	10	15	57	1.24	0	0	0	0
1928–29	26	Ottawa Senators	NHL	44	14	17	13	7	67	1.43	0	0	0	0
1929–30	27	Ottawa Senators	NHL	44	21	15	8	3	118	2.55	0	0	0	0
1930–31	28	Ottawa Senators	NHL	36	10	22	4	3	110	3.01	0	0	0	0
1931–32	29	Detroit Falcons	NHL	48	18	20	10	6	108	2.12	0	0	0	0
1932–33	30	Ottawa Senators	NHL	15	4	8	2	1	36	2.56	0	0	0	0
1933–34	31	New York Americans	NHL	1	1	0	0	0	2	3.00	0	0	0	0
1934–35	32	Montreal Maroons	NHL	48	24	19	5	9	92	1.86	0	0	0	0
1936–37	34	Montreal Maroons	NHL	27	10	11	6	2	63	2.21	0	0	0	0
NHL Career – 12 Seasons				417	193	156	67	81	830	1.91	0	0	0	4

PLAYOFFS

Season	Age	Team	Lg	GP	W	L	T	SO	GA	GAA	G	A	PTS	PIM
1925–26	23	Ottawa Senators	NHL	2	0	1	1	0	2	1.00	0	0	0	0
1926–27	24	Ottawa Senators	NHL	6	3	0	3	2	4	0.60	0	0	0	0
1927–28	25	Ottawa Senators	NHL	2	0	2	0	0	3	1.50	0	0	0	0
1929–30	27	Ottawa Senators	NHL	2	0	1	1	0	6	3.00	0	0	0	0
1931–32	29	Detroit Falcons	NHL	2	0	1	1	0	3	1.50	0	0	0	0
1934–35	32	Montreal Maroons	NHL	7	5	0	2	2	8	1.12	0	0	0	0
NHL Career – 6 Seasons				21	8	5	8	4	26	1.19	0	0	0	0

TROPHY CASE

AWARDS

Stanley Cup (1926–27, 1934–35)

Bill Cook

HOCKEY HALL OF FAME CLASS: 1952

Right Wing

Shoots: Right

Height: 5'-10"

Weight: 170 lbs.

Born: October 8, 1896: Brantford, Ontario

Died: May 5, 1986: Kingston, Ontario

Played 15 professional seasons from 1922–37

QUICK FACTS

- Oldest player in NHL history (37 years, 5 months) to win scoring title (1932–33)

- Played amateur hockey with Kingston Frontenacs (1913–15, 1919–20); Sault Ste. Marie Greyhounds (1920–22)

- Led OHA-Sr. in goals (12) and points (19) in 1919–20; led AAHA in goals (20) and points (28) in 1921–22

- Led WCHL in goals (26), assists (14) and points (40) in 1923–24; led WHL in goals (31) and points (44) in 1925–26; led WHL playoffs in goals (2) in 1925–26

- Member of N.Y. Rangers' famed Bread Line with Bun Cook and Frank Boucher

- Served as captain of N.Y. Rangers (1926–37)

- Scored first goal in history of N.Y. Rangers franchise in 1–0 victory over Montreal Maroons, November 16, 1926

- Scored Stanley Cup-winning goal in N.Y. Rangers' 1–0 victory over Toronto Maple Leafs, April 13, 1933

- Led NHL in goals in 1926–27 (33), 1931–32 (34) and 1932–33 (28); led NHL in points in 1926–27 (37) and 1932–33 (50)

- Coached Cleveland Barons (1937–43); coached Minneapolis Millers (1947–50); coached Denver Falcons (1950–51); coached Saskatoon Quakers (1951–52); coached N.Y. Rangers (1951–53)

- Coached Cleveland Barons to AHL championship (1938–39, 1940–41); coached Minneapolis Millers to USHL championship (1949–50)

> Bill's cry was the most amazing half-grunt, half-moan, half-yell that I ever heard. He'd let this weird sound out of him, meaning that he was in the clear. And he'd say in these skull-sessions of ours, 'When I yell, I want the puck then, don't look up to see where I am. Just put it there and I'll be there.'"
>
> — Frank Boucher, commenting on his teammate

REGULAR SEASON

Season	Age	Team	Lg	GP	G	A	PTS	PIM
1922–23	26	Saskatoon Sheiks	WCHL	30	9	16	25	19
1923–24	27	Saskatoon Crescents	WCHL	30	26	14	40	20
1924–25	28	Saskatoon Crescents	WCHL	27	22	10	32	79
1925–26	29	Saskatoon Crescents	WHL	30	31	13	44	26
1926–27	30	New York Rangers	NHL	44	33	4	37	58
1927–28	31	New York Rangers	NHL	43	18	6	24	42
1928–29	32	New York Rangers	NHL	43	15	8	23	41
1929–30	33	New York Rangers	NHL	44	29	30	59	56
1930–31	34	New York Rangers	NHL	43	30	12	42	39
1931–32	35	New York Rangers	NHL	48	34	14	48	33
1932–33	36	New York Rangers	NHL	48	28	22	50	51
1933–34	37	New York Rangers	NHL	48	13	13	26	21
1934–35	38	New York Rangers	NHL	48	21	15	36	23
1935–36	39	New York Rangers	NHL	44	7	10	17	16
1936–37	40	New York Rangers	NHL	21	1	4	5	6
Career – 15 Seasons				591	317	191	508	530

PLAYOFFS

Season	Age	Team	Lg	GP	G	A	PTS	PIM
1924–25	28	Saskatoon Crescents	WCHL	2	0	0	0	4
1925–26	29	Saskatoon Crescents	WHL	2	2	0	2	26
1926–27	30	New York Rangers	NHL	2	1	0	1	6
1927–28	31	New York Rangers	NHL	9	2	3	5	26
1928–29	32	New York Rangers	NHL	6	0	0	0	6
1929–30	33	New York Rangers	NHL	4	0	1	1	11
1930–31	34	New York Rangers	NHL	4	3	0	3	4
1931–32	35	New York Rangers	NHL	7	3	3	6	2
1932–33	36	New York Rangers	NHL	8	3	2	5	4
1933–34	37	New York Rangers	NHL	2	0	0	0	2
1934–35	38	New York Rangers	NHL	4	1	2	3	7
Career – 11 Seasons				50	15	11	26	98

TROPHY CASE

AWARDS

NHL Scoring Leader (1927, 1933)

Stanley Cup (1927–28, 1932–33)

ALL-STAR SELECTIONS

First All-Star Team Right Wing (1931, 1932, 1933)

Second All-Star Team Right Wing (1934)

WCHL First All-Star Team Right Wing (1924, 1925)

WHL First All-Star Team Right Wing (1926)

Bun Cook

HOCKEY HALL OF FAME CLASS: 1995

Alternates: 5, 8, 10

Left Wing

Shoots: Left

Height: 5'-11"

Weight: 180 lbs.

Born: September 18, 1903: Kingston, Ontario

Died: March 19, 1988: Kingston, Ontario

Played 13 professional seasons from 1924–37

QUICK FACTS

- Played amateur hockey with Sault Ste. Marie Greyhounds (1921–24)
- Earned nickname "Bun" when a journalist noted that he was "quick as a bunny"
- Signed as a free agent by Saskatoon Crescents (WCHL), September 20, 1924
- Traded to N.Y. Rangers by Saskatoon (WHL) for cash, October 18, 1926
- Assisted on first goal in N.Y. Rangers' franchise history in N.Y. Rangers' 1–0 victory over Montreal Maroons, November 16, 1926
- Member of N.Y. Rangers' famed Bread Line with Bill Cook and Frank Boucher
- Line scored every goal for the N.Y. Rangers in the Stanley Cup finals against Montreal Maroons in 1928

- Traded to Boston by N.Y. Rangers for cash, September 10, 1936
- IAHL First All-Star Team Coach (1939, 1940)
- AHL First All-Star Team Coach (1941, 1942, 1944, 1945)
- Coached Providence Reds (1937–43); coached Cleveland Barons (1943–56); coached Sault Ste. Marie Greyhounds (1956–57)
- Won Calder Cup (AHL Championship) as coach (1938, 1940, 1945, 1948, 1953, 1954)
- Credited with helping pioneer the drop pass and the slapshot

> Although we didn't get paid much, it was a lot of fun. We played with intensity. All in all, hockey has been real good to me."

REGULAR SEASON

Season	Age	Team	Lg	GP	G	A	PTS	PIM
1924–25	21	Saskatoon Crescents	WCHL	28	17	4	21	44
1925–26	22	Saskatoon Crescents	WHL	30	8	4	12	22
1926–27	23	New York Rangers	NHL	44	14	9	23	42
1927–28	24	New York Rangers	NHL	44	14	14	28	45
1928–29	25	New York Rangers	NHL	43	13	5	18	70
1929–30	26	New York Rangers	NHL	43	24	18	42	55
1930–31	27	New York Rangers	NHL	44	18	17	35	72
1931–32	28	New York Rangers	NHL	45	14	20	34	43
1932–33	29	New York Rangers	NHL	48	22	15	37	35
1933–34	30	New York Rangers	NHL	48	18	15	33	36
1934–35	31	New York Rangers	NHL	48	13	21	34	26
1935–36	32	New York Rangers	NHL	26	4	5	9	12
1936–37	33	Boston Bruins	NHL	40	4	5	9	8
Career – 13 Seasons				531	183	152	335	510

PLAYOFFS

Season	Age	Team	Lg	GP	G	A	PTS	PIM
1924–25	21	Saskatoon Crescents	WCHL	2	0	1	1	0
1925–26	22	Saskatoon Crescents	WHL	2	0	0	0	0
1926–27	23	New York Rangers	NHL	2	0	0	0	6
1927–28	24	New York Rangers	NHL	9	2	1	3	10
1928–29	25	New York Rangers	NHL	6	1	0	1	12
1929–30	26	New York Rangers	NHL	4	2	0	2	2
1930–31	27	New York Rangers	NHL	4	0	0	0	2
1931–32	28	New York Rangers	NHL	7	6	2	8	12
1932–33	29	New York Rangers	NHL	8	2	0	2	4
1933–34	30	New York Rangers	NHL	2	0	0	0	2
1934–35	31	New York Rangers	NHL	4	2	0	2	0
Career – 11 Seasons				50	15	4	19	50

TROPHY CASE

AWARDS

Stanley Cup (1927–28, 1932–33)

ALL-STAR SELECTIONS

Second All-Star Team Left Wing (1931)

Art Coulter

HOCKEY HALL OF FAME CLASS: 1974

Alternates: 17, 21, 18

Defense

Shoots: Right

Height: 5'-11"

Weight: 185 lbs.

Born: May 31, 1909: Winnipeg, Manitoba

Died: October 14, 2000: Mobile, Alabama

Played 11 NHL seasons from 1931–42

QUICK FACTS

- Nicknamed "The Trapper" because of his love of fishing and hunting
- Played amateur hockey with Winnipeg Pilgrims (1925–27)
- Played minor pro with Philadelphia Arrows (1929–32)
- Led Can-Am in penalty minutes (109) in 1930–31
- Traded to Chicago by Philadelphia Arrows (Can-Am) for cash and the loan of Frank Ingram, February, 1932
- Traded to N.Y. Rangers by Chicago for Earl Seibert, January 15, 1936
- Led NHL in penalty minutes (90) in 1937–38; finished second in NHL penalty minutes (68) in 1939–40
- Served as captain of the N.Y. Rangers (1937–42)
- Ranked number 30 on list of the 100 Greatest New York Rangers
- Joined U.S. Navy and played with Coast Guard Clippers during World War II
- Member of the American Amateur champion Coast Guard Cutters (1943, 1944)
- Inducted into Manitoba Hockey Hall of Fame (1985)
- Inducted into Manitoba Sports Hall of Fame (2009)
- Operated a hardware store in Miami, Florida, after retiring from the NHL
- Brother of Tom Coulter, who played in the NHL with Chicago Black Hawks in 1933–34

> "Art Coulter was our best player. He was a leader ... he could really carry the puck. But he had to head-man the puck. That's the way we played."
> — Clint Smith, Art Coulter's teammate on the 1940 Rangers

REGULAR SEASON

Season	Age	Team	Lg	GP	G	A	PTS	PIM
1931–32	22	Chicago Black Hawks	NHL	13	0	1	1	23
1932–33	23	Chicago Black Hawks	NHL	46	3	2	5	53
1933–34	24	Chicago Black Hawks	NHL	46	5	2	7	39
1934–35	25	Chicago Black Hawks	NHL	48	4	8	12	68
1935–36	26	Chicago Black Hawks	NHL	25	0	2	2	18
1935–36	26	New York Rangers	NHL	23	1	5	6	26
1936–37	27	New York Rangers	NHL	47	1	5	6	27
1937–38	28	New York Rangers	NHL	43	5	10	15	90
1938–39	29	New York Rangers	NHL	44	4	8	12	58
1939–40	30	New York Rangers	NHL	48	1	9	10	68
1940–41	31	New York Rangers	NHL	35	5	14	19	42
1941–42	32	New York Rangers	NHL	47	1	16	17	31
NHL Career — 11 Seasons				465	30	82	112	543

PLAYOFFS

Season	Age	Team	Lg	GP	G	A	PTS	PIM
1931–32	22	Chicago Black Hawks	NHL	2	1	0	1	0
1933–34	24	Chicago Black Hawks	NHL	8	1	0	1	10
1934–35	25	Chicago Black Hawks	NHL	2	0	0	0	5
1936–37	27	New York Rangers	NHL	9	0	3	3	15
1938–39	29	New York Rangers	NHL	7	1	1	2	6
1939–40	30	New York Rangers	NHL	12	1	0	1	21
1940–41	31	New York Rangers	NHL	3	0	0	0	0
1941–42	32	New York Rangers	NHL	6	0	1	1	4
NHL Career — 8 Seasons				49	4	5	9	61

TROPHY CASE

AWARDS

Stanley Cup (1933–1934, 1939–1940)

ALL-STAR SELECTIONS

Second All-Star Team Defense (1935, 1938, 1939, 1940)

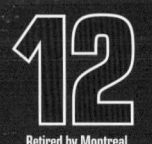

12

Retired by Montreal

Alternate: 25

Right Wing

Shoots: Left

Height: 5'-7"

Weight: 178 lbs.

Born: November 22, 1943; Drummondville, Quebec

Played 16 NHL seasons from 1963–79

Yvan Cournoyer
HOCKEY HALL OF FAME CLASS: 1982

QUICK FACTS

- Played amateur hockey with Lachine Maroons (1960–61); Montreal Jr. Canadiens (1961–64)
- Led OHA-Jr. in goals (63) in 1963–64; led OHA-Jr. playoffs in goals (19) in 1963–64
- Played minor pro hockey with Quebec Aces (1964–65)
- Nicknamed "The Roadrunner" because of his outstanding speed
- Ranks fourth in Montreal Canadiens career regular season goals (428); ranks sixth in Montreal Canadiens career regular season assists (435) and ranks third in Montreal Canadiens career playoff goals (64)
- Played in NHL All-Star Game (1967, 1971, 1972, 1973, 1974, 1978)
- Led NHL in power-play goals (20) in 1966–67
- Led NHL in game-winning goals in 1966–67 (7) and 1975–76 (12)
- Finished second in NHL shooting percentage in 1971–72 (22.6%) and finished third in 1973–74 (21.4%)
- Scored Stanley Cup-winning goal in Montreal's 6–4 victory over Chicago Black Hawks, May 10, 1973
- Served as captain of Montreal Canadiens (1975–79)
- Coached Montreal Roadrunners (named after him) of the Roller Hockey International League (1994–95)
- Served as assistant coach of Montreal Canadiens (1996–97)

> People think we exaggerate when we say it was like a war out there but that's exactly what it was. It was more than just a series of eight hockey games. It was a clash of different ideals and ways of life. It was an amazing experience and something I'll never forget."
>
> — Yvan Cournoyer, on the Summit Series of 1972

REGULAR SEASON

Season	Age	Team	Lg	GP	G	A	PTS	+/-	PIM	ESG	PPG	SHG	GWG	SOG	S%
1963-64	20	Montreal Canadiens	NHL	5	4	0	4		0	3	1	0	0		
1964-65	21	Montreal Canadiens	NHL	55	7	10	17		10	3	4	0	0		
1965-66	22	Montreal Canadiens	NHL	65	18	11	29		8	2	16	0	0		
1966-67	23	Montreal Canadiens	NHL	69	25	15	40		14	5	20	0	7		
1967-68	24	Montreal Canadiens	NHL	64	28	32	60	19	23	20	7	1	4	222	12.6
1968-69	25	Montreal Canadiens	NHL	76	43	44	87	19	31	29	14	0	8	245	17.6
1969-70	26	Montreal Canadiens	NHL	72	27	36	63	1	23	17	10	0	4	233	11.6
1970-71	27	Montreal Canadiens	NHL	65	37	36	73	20	21	19	18	0	5	197	18.8
1971-72	28	Montreal Canadiens	NHL	73	47	36	83	23	15	29	18	0	5	208	22.6
1972-73	29	Montreal Canadiens	NHL	67	40	39	79	50	18	34	6	0	4	194	20.6
1973-74	30	Montreal Canadiens	NHL	67	40	33	73	16	18	30	10	0	9	187	21.4
1974-75	31	Montreal Canadiens	NHL	76	29	45	74	15	32	18	11	0	2	176	16.5
1975-76	32	Montreal Canadiens	NHL	71	32	36	68	37	20	24	8	0	12	163	19.6
1976-77	33	Montreal Canadiens	NHL	60	25	28	53	27	8	19	6	0	2	122	20.5
1977-78	34	Montreal Canadiens	NHL	68	24	29	53	39	12	20	4	0	6	125	19.2
1978-79	35	Montreal Canadiens	NHL	15	2	5	7	5	2	2	0	0	0	23	8.7
NHL Career – 16 Seasons				968	428	435	863	271	255	274	153	1	68	2095	17.9

PLAYOFFS

Season	Age	Team	Lg	GP	G	A	PTS	+/-	PIM	ESG	PPG	SHG	GWG	SOG	S%
1964-65	21	Montreal Canadiens	NHL	12	3	1	4		0						
1965-66	22	Montreal Canadiens	NHL	10	2	3	5		2						
1966-67	23	Montreal Canadiens	NHL	10	2	3	5		6						
1967-68	24	Montreal Canadiens	NHL	13	6	8	14		4	3	3	0	1		
1968-69	25	Montreal Canadiens	NHL	14	4	7	11		5	2	2	0	2		
1970-71	27	Montreal Canadiens	NHL	20	10	12	22		6	8	2	0	1		
1971-72	28	Montreal Canadiens	NHL	6	2	1	3		2	2	0	0			
1972-73	29	Montreal Canadiens	NHL	17	15	10	25		2	12	3	0	3		
1973-74	30	Montreal Canadiens	NHL	6	5	2	7		2	5	0	0	2		
1974-75	31	Montreal Canadiens	NHL	11	5	6	11		4	3	2	0	0		
1975-76	32	Montreal Canadiens	NHL	13	3	6	9		4	1	2	0	1		
1977-78	34	Montreal Canadiens	NHL	15	7	4	11		10	7	0	0	2		
NHL Career – 12 Seasons				147	64	63	127		47	43	14	0	12		

TROPHY CASE

AWARDS

Conn Smythe Trophy (1973)

Stanley Cup (1964–65, 1965–66, 1967–68, 1968–69, 1970–71, 1972–73, 1975–76, 1976–77 1977–78, 1978–79)

ALL-STAR SELECTIONS

Second All-Star Team Right Wing (1969, 1971, 1972, 1973)

INTERNATIONAL AWARDS

Summit Series (1972)

10

Bill Cowley
HOCKEY HALL OF FAME CLASS: 1968

Alternates: 17, 15

Center

Shoots: Left

Height: 5'-10"

Weight: 165 lbs.

Born: June 12, 1912: Bristol, Quebec

Died: December 31, 1993: Ottawa, Ontario

Played 13 NHL seasons from 1934–47

QUICK FACTS

- Held NHL record for highest points-per-game average (1.97) in regular season (71 points in 36 games in 1943–44); surpassed by Wayne Gretzky in 1980–81 (2.05)

- Held NHL record for career points in the regular season (548); surpassed by Elmer Lach, February 23, 1953

- Held NHL record for career assists in the regular season (353); surpassed by Elmer Lach in 1951–52

- Held NHL record for assists in the regular season (45); surpassed by Clint Smith in 1943–44

- Played amateur hockey with Ottawa Glebe Collegiate (1929–30); Ottawa Primrose (1930–31); Ottawa Shamrocks (1931–33); Halifax Wolverines (1933–34)

- One of only two players (with Wayne Gretzky) to record more assists than next leading scorer had points (1940–41)

- Led Ottawa City Junior League in playoff goals (4) in 1930–31; led OCJHL in playoff goals (4), assists (4) and points (8) in 1931–32

- Led Maritime Senior League in goals (25), assists (25) and points (50) in 1933–34

- Led NHL in assists in 1938–39 (34), 1940–41 (45) and 1942–43 (45); led NHL in points (62) in 1940–41

- Led NHL playoffs in points (14) in 1938–39

- Coached Ottawa Army (1947–48); coached Vancouver Canucks (1948–49)

- Only Hall of Fame member to have started his NHL career with the St. Louis Eagles

> "Two points a game over an 80-game schedule, that would be amazing. I never thought I'd see the day when a player would do that. I always thought that would be impossible."
>
> — Bill Cowley, commenting on Wayne Gretzky breaking his point-per-game record

REGULAR SEASON

Season	Age	Team	Lg	GP	G	A	PTS	PIM
1934–35	22	St. Louis Eagles	NHL	41	5	7	12	10
1935–36	23	Boston Bruins	NHL	48	11	10	21	17
1936–37	24	Boston Bruins	NHL	46	13	22	35	4
1937–38	25	Boston Bruins	NHL	48	17	22	39	8
1938–39	26	Boston Bruins	NHL	34	8	34	42	2
1939–40	27	Boston Bruins	NHL	48	13	27	40	24
1940–41	28	Boston Bruins	NHL	46	17	45	62	16
1941–42	29	Boston Bruins	NHL	28	4	23	27	6
1942–43	30	Boston Bruins	NHL	48	27	45	72	10
1943–44	31	Boston Bruins	NHL	36	30	41	71	12
1944–45	32	Boston Bruins	NHL	49	25	40	65	12
1945–46	33	Boston Bruins	NHL	26	12	12	24	6
1946–47	34	Boston Bruins	NHL	51	13	25	38	16
NHL Career – 13 Seasons				549	195	353	548	143

PLAYOFFS

Season	Age	Team	Lg	GP	G	A	PTS	PIM
1935–36	23	Boston Bruins	NHL	2	2	1	3	2
1936–37	24	Boston Bruins	NHL	3	0	3	3	0
1937–38	25	Boston Bruins	NHL	3	2	0	2	0
1938–39	26	Boston Bruins	NHL	12	3	11	14	2
1939–40	27	Boston Bruins	NHL	6	0	1	1	7
1940–41	28	Boston Bruins	NHL	2	0	0	0	0
1941–42	29	Boston Bruins	NHL	5	0	3	3	5
1942–43	30	Boston Bruins	NHL	9	1	7	8	4
1944–45	32	Boston Bruins	NHL	7	3	3	6	0
1945–46	33	Boston Bruins	NHL	10	1	3	4	2
1946–47	34	Boston Bruins	NHL	5	0	2	2	0
NHL Career – 11 Seasons				64	12	34	46	22

TROPHY CASE

AWARDS

NHL Scoring Leader (1941)

Hart Memorial Trophy (1941, 1943)

Stanley Cup (1938–39, 1940–41)

ALL-STAR SELECTIONS

First All-Star Team Center (1938, 1941, 1943, 1944)

Second All-Star Team Center (1945)

8

Rusty Crawford

HOCKEY HALL OF FAME CLASS: 1962

Alternate: 5

Left Wing

Shoots: Left

Height: 5'-11"

Weight: 165 lbs.

Born: November 7, 1885: Cardinal, Ontario

Died: December 19, 1971: Prince Albert, Saskatchewan

Played 16 professional and elite amateur seasons from 1910–26

QUICK FACTS

- Played amateur hockey with Montreal Montagnards (1907–08); Newington Ontarios (1908–09); Prince Albert Mintos (1909–11); Saskatoon Hoo Hoos (1911–12); Saskatoon Wholesalers (1911–12); Prince Albert Mintos (1930–31)

- Sask-Pro First All-Star Team Left Wing (1912)

- Played minor pro hockey with Minneapolis Millers (1926–30)

- Both his Prince Albert (1911) and Saskatoon (1912) teams challenged for the Stanley Cup, but were eliminated from competition before facing the defending champions

- Signed as a free agent by Quebec Bulldogs, December 12, 1912

- Renowned for his speed and longevity, he played competitive hockey until the age of 45

- Quebec Bulldogs were already Stanley Cup champions when he signed with them and helped them defend their title in 1912–13

- Signed as a free agent by Toronto, February 9, 1918; signed as a free agent by Ottawa, December 2, 1918

- Signed as a free agent by Saskatoon (WCHL), November 12, 1921; traded to Calgary (WCHL) by Saskatoon (WCHL) for cash, February 10, 1923; traded to Vancouver (WHL) by Calgary (WHL) for Fern Headley, November 3, 1925

> "Rusty Crawford played a hard effective game while he was on, showing lots of speed and aggressiveness."
> — *Quebec Daily Telegraph*, January 19, 1913

REGULAR SEASON

Season	Age	Team	Lg	GP	G	A	PTS	PIM
1910–11	25	Prince Albert Mintos	Sask-Pro	7	26	0	26	
1911–12	26	Saskatoon Hoo-Hoos	Sask-Pro	7	7	0	7	
1911–12	26	Saskatoon Wholesalers	Sask-Pro	1	2	0	2	
1912–13	27	Quebec Bulldogs	NHA	19	4	0	4	29
1913–14	28	Quebec Bulldogs	NHA	19	15	10	25	14
1914–15	29	Quebec Bulldogs	NHA	20	18	8	26	30
1915–16	30	Quebec Bulldogs	NHA	22	18	5	23	54
1916–17	31	Quebec Bulldogs	NHA	19	11	9	20	77
1917–18	32	Ottawa Senators	NHL	12	2	2	4	15
1917–18	32	Toronto Arenas	NHL	8	1	2	3	51
1918–19	33	Toronto Arenas	NHL	18	7	4	11	51
1919–20	34	Saskatoon Crescents	SSHL	12	3	3	6	14
1920–21	35	Saskatoon Crescents	SSHL	14	11	7	18	12
1921–22	36	Saskatoon/Moose Jaw	WCHL	24	8	8	16	29
1922–23	37	Saskatoon Sheiks	WCHL	19	7	6	13	10
1922–23	37	Calgary Tigers	WCHL	11	3	1	4	7
1923–24	38	Calgary Tigers	WCHL	26	4	4	8	21
1924–25	39	Calgary Tigers	WCHL	27	12	2	14	27
1925–26	40	Vancouver Maroons	WHL	14	0	0	0	8
Career — 16 Seasons				299	159	71	230	449

PLAYOFFS

Season	Age	Team	Lg	GP	G	A	PTS	PIM
1910–11	25	Prince Albert Mintso	Sask-Pro	4	4	0	4	26
1911–12	26	Saskatoon Wholesalers	Sask-Pro	2	2	0	2	12
1912–13	27	Quebec Bulldogs	St-Cup	1	0	0	0	0
1917–18	32	Toronto Arenas	NHL	2	2	1	3	9
1920–21	35	Saskatoon Crescents	SSHL	4	2	2	4	4
1923–24	38	Calgary Tigers	St-Cup	2	0	0	0	0
1923–24	38	Calgary Tigers	WCHL	2	1	0	1	2
1923–24	38	Calgary Tigers	West-P	3	1	0	1	4
1924–25	39	Calgary Tigers	WCHL	2	0	0	0	4
Career — 7 Seasons				22	11	4	152	61

TROPHY CASE

AWARDS

Stanley Cup (1912–13, 1917–18)

117

I think it took me so long to want to be part of the team because I was afraid of a team. Afraid of always having to do what a team does; afraid of losing my own right to be different. When I realized I could be part of a team, and still be different, I could then be less different. Then I realized I wasn't very different at all."

Ken Dryden

A
B
C
D
E
F
G
H
I
J
K
L
M
N
O
P
Q
R
S
T
U
V
W
X
Y
Z

7

Jack Darragh
HOCKEY HALL OF FAME CLASS: 1962

Alternate: 5

Right Wing

Shoots: Right

Height: 5'-10"

Weight: 168 lbs.

Born: December 4, 1890: Ottawa, Ontario

Died: June 25, 1924: Ottawa, Ontario

Played 13 professional seasons from 1910–21, 1922–24

QUICK FACTS

- Played amateur hockey with Ottawa Stewartons (1908–11); Ottawa Cliffsides (1909–10); Fort Coulonge Bankers (1909–10)

- Scored a goal in professional debut against Georges Vezina in Ottawa's 5–3 victory over Montreal Canadiens in opening game of the NHA, December 31, 1910

- Scored game-winning goal in all three of the Ottawa Senators' wins in the 1919–20 Stanley Cup series against Seattle

- Scored Stanley Cup–winning goal in Ottawa's 6–1 victory over Seattle, April 1, 1920; scored Stanley Cup–winning goal in Ottawa's 2–1 victory over Vancouver, April 4, 1921

- One of only two players (with Mike Bossy) to score Stanley Cup–winning goal in back-to-back seasons

- Led NHL in assists (15) in 1920–21

- Renowned for his backhand shot, blistering speed and clever stickhandling skills

- Surprisingly retired following 1920–21 season and coached Ottawa Gunners (1921–22) during his year away from the game

- Worked for Ottawa Dairy Company while he was playing for the Senators

- Died of a ruptured appendix following the 1923–24 season, June 25, 1924

- Brother of Harold Darragh, who played in the NHL with Pittsburgh, Philadelphia, Boston and Toronto from 1925–32

> I have always wanted to make good on the Ottawa team and now, feeling in my prime, I thought it all out and decided to jump the amateur ranks. I believe what I have done, under the circumstances, was just and fair."
>
> — Jack Darragh, on his decision to turn pro

REGULAR SEASON

Season	Age	Team	Lg	GP	G	A	PTS	PIM
1910-11	20	Ottawa Senators	NHA	16	18	0	18	36
1911-12	21	Ottawa Senators	NHA	17	15	0	15	10
1912-13	22	Ottawa Senators	NHA	20	15	0	15	16
1913-14	23	Ottawa Senators	NHA	20	23	5	28	69
1914-15	24	Ottawa Senators	NHA	18	11	2	13	32
1915-16	25	Ottawa Senators	NHA	21	16	5	21	41
1916-17	26	Ottawa Senators	NHA	20	24	4	28	17
1917-18	27	Ottawa Senators	NHL	18	14	5	19	26
1918-19	28	Ottawa Senators	NHL	14	11	3	14	33
1919-20	29	Ottawa Senators	NHL	23	22	14	36	22
1920-21	30	Ottawa Senators	NHL	24	11	15	26	20
1922-23	32	Ottawa Senators	NHL	24	6	9	15	10
1923-24	33	Ottawa Senators	NHL	18	2	0	2	2
Career — 13 Seasons				253	188	62	250	334

PLAYOFFS

Season	Age	Team	Lg	GP	G	A	PTS	PIM
1910-11	20	Ottawa Senators	St-Cup	2	0	0	0	6
1914-15	24	Ottawa Senators	NHA	5	4	0	4	9
1916-17	26	Ottawa Senators	NHA	2	2	0	2	3
1918-19	28	Ottawa Senators	NHL	5	2	0	2	3
1919-20	29	Ottawa Senators	St-Cup	5	5	2	7	3
1920-21	30	Ottawa Senators	NHL	2	0	0	0	2
1920-21	30	Ottawa Senators	St-Cup	5	5	0	5	12
1922-23	32	Ottawa Senators	NHL	2	1	0	1	2
1923-24	33	Ottawa Senators	NHL	2	0	0	0	2
Career — 8 Seasons				30	19	2	21	42

TROPHY CASE

AWARDS

Stanley Cup (1910–11, 1919–20, 1920–21, 1922–23)

ALL-STAR SELECTIONS

NHA First All-Star Team Right Wing (1914)

3

Scotty Davidson
HOCKEY HALL OF FAME CLASS: 1950

Right Wing

Shoots: Right

Height: 6'-1"

Weight: 195 lbs.

Born: March 6, 1891: Kingston, Ontario

Died: June 16, 1915: Killed in action, Belgium

Played six professional and elite amateur seasons from 1908–14

QUICK FACTS

- Led OHA-Sr. in goals (8) in 1908–09
- Led NHA playoffs in penalty minutes (11) in 1913–14
- Had a brief but brilliant hockey career before losing his life in World War I
- Learned the game in his hometown of Kingston under the coaching of James T. Sutherland, who often is called "The Father of Hockey"
- Member of Ontario Junior champion Kingston Frontenacs (1910, 1911)
- Ranked among NHA top-10 in goals in 1912–13 (19) and 1913–14 (23)

- Ranked second in NHA assists (13) in 1913–14
- Served as captain of Stanley Cup-winning Toronto Blueshirts (1913–14)
- First professional hockey player to enlist in the Canadian Army following the outbreak of World War I
- Legacy commemorated on the Vimy Memorial
- Selected as Right Wing on *Maclean's Magazine* All-Time All-Star Team (1925)

> Young players of the caliber of Davidson are the making of the game, and play much better hockey than the old-timers, who have nothing but their reputations of years gone by to travel on."
>
> — The *Toronto Daily Star*, November 13, 1912

REGULAR SEASON

Season	Age	Team	Lg	GP	G	A	PTS	PIM
1908–09	17	Kingston 14th Regiment	OHA-Sr.	4	8	0	8	11
1909–10	18	Kingston Frontenacs	OHA-Jr.					
1910–11	19	Kingston Frontenacs	OHA-Jr.					
1911–12	20	Calgary Athletics	S-ASHL	4	3	0	3	
1912–13	21	Toronto Blueshirts	NHA	20	19	0	19	69
1912–13	21	Toronto Tecumsehs	Exhib.	2	0	0	0	0
1913–14	22	Toronto Blueshirts	NHA	20	23	13	36	64
Career – 6 Seasons				50	53	13	66	210

PLAYOFFS

Season	Age	Team	Lg	GP	G	A	PTS	PIM
1908–09	17	Kingston 14th Regiment	OHA-Sr.	4	4	0	4	6
1911–12	20	Calgary Athletics	S-ASHL	3	3	0	3	6
1913–14	22	Toronto Blueshirts	NHA	2	2	0	2	11
1913–14	22	Toronto Blueshirts	St-Cup	2	1	0	1	7
Career – 3 Seasons				11	10	0	10	30

TROPHY CASE

AWARDS

Stanley Cup (1913–14)

Hap Day

HOCKEY HALL OF FAME CLASS: 1961

4

Honored by Toronto

Defense/
Left Wing

Shoots: Left

Height: 5'-11"

Weight: 175 lbs.

Born: June 14,
1901: Owen
Sound, Ontario

Died: February 17,
1990: Toronto,
Ontario

Played 14 NHL
seasons from
1924–38

"Fame is
fleeting, no
matter how
many Cups you've
won. I remember
once I saw Reg
Bentley, brother
of Max and Doug,
at a hockey game.
I said, 'Hi ya, Reg.'
He looked at me
kind of puzzled.
I said, 'Happy Day.'
'Oh,' he said, 'Same
to you'."

Syl Apps, Charlie Conacher, George Hainsworth, Joe Hall, Percy LeSueur, Frank Rankin, Maurice Richard, Milt Schmidt, Oliver Seibert, Bruce Stuart

QUICK FACTS

- Only member of the Toronto Maple Leafs to serve as captain, coach and general manager

- Played amateur hockey with Collingwood Seniors (1921–22); Hamilton Tigers (1922–24)

- OHA-Sr. First All-Star Team Defense (1923)

- Played in NHL All-Star Game (1934, 1937)

- Nicknamed "Happy" — later shortened to "Hap" — because of his cheery disposition

- Graduated with a degree in pharmacy from the University of Toronto

- Signed by Toronto St. Pats owner Charlie Querrie for salary of $5,000 and the promise he wouldn't miss too many classes

- Traded to New York Americans for cash in September, 1937

- Played left wing on a line with future Hall of Famers Jack Adams and Babe Dye before switching to defense in his fourth season

- Owned a drugstore during his playing days that was located inside Maple Leaf Gardens

- Served as captain of Toronto Maple Leafs (1927–37)

- Coached Toronto Maple Leafs (1940–50); coached Toronto Maple Leafs to Stanley Cup championship (1942, 1945, 1947, 1948, 1949)

- Served as General Manager of Toronto Maple Leafs (1957–58)

- Scored first Stanley Cup Final goal in Toronto Maple Leafs franchise history, April 15, 1932

Commemorative puck given to Day after the 1931–32 Stanley Cup championship, the first at Maple Leaf Gardens.

REGULAR SEASON

Season	Age	Team	Lg	GP	G	A	PTS	PIM
1924–25	23	Toronto St. Patricks	NHL	26	10	12	22	33
1925–26	24	Toronto St. Patricks	NHL	36	14	2	16	26
1926–27	25	Toronto St. Pats/Maple Leafs	NHL	44	11	5	16	50
1927–28	26	Toronto Maple Leafs	NHL	22	9	8	17	48
1928–29	27	Toronto Maple Leafs	NHL	44	6	6	12	84
1929–30	28	Toronto Maple Leafs	NHL	43	7	14	21	77
1930–31	29	Toronto Maple Leafs	NHL	44	1	13	14	56
1931–32	30	Toronto Maple Leafs	NHL	47	7	8	15	33
1932–33	31	Toronto Maple Leafs	NHL	47	6	14	20	46
1933–34	32	Toronto Maple Leafs	NHL	48	9	10	19	35
1934–35	33	Toronto Maple Leafs	NHL	45	2	4	6	38
1935–36	34	Toronto Maple Leafs	NHL	44	1	13	14	41
1926–37	35	Toronto Maple Leafs	NHL	48	3	4	7	20
1937–38	36	New York Americans	NHL	43	0	3	3	14
NHL Career — 14 Seasons				581	86	116	202	601

PLAYOFFS

Season	Age	Team	Lg	GP	G	A	PTS	PIM
1924–25	23	Toronto St. Patricks	NHL	2	0	0	0	0
1928–29	27	Toronto Maple Leafs	NHL	4	1	0	1	4
1930–31	29	Toronto Maple Leafs	NHL	2	0	3	3	7
1931–32	30	Toronto Maple Leafs	NHL	7	3	3	6	6
1932–33	31	Toronto Maple Leafs	NHL	9	0	1	1	21
1933–34	32	Toronto Maple Leafs	NHL	5	0	0	0	6
1934–35	33	Toronto Maple Leafs	NHL	7	0	0	0	4
1935–36	34	Toronto Maple Leafs	NHL	9	0	0	0	8
1936–37	35	Toronto Maple Leafs	NHL	2	0	0	0	0
1937–38	36	New York Americans	NHL	6	0	0	0	0
NHL Career — 10 Seasons				53	4	7	11	56

TROPHY CASE

AWARDS
Stanley Cup (1931–32)

10
Retired by Detroit

Alex Delvecchio
HOCKEY HALL OF FAME CLASS: 1977

Alternates: 17, 15

Center/Left Wing

Shoots: Left

Height: 6'

Weight: 195 lbs.

Born: December 4, 1932: Fort William, Ontario

Played 24 NHL seasons from 1950–74

QUICK FACTS

- One of only four players (with Stan Mikita, Steve Yzerman and Mike Modano) to play at least 20 seasons with only one organization
- Played amateur hockey with Fort William Hurricane-Rangers (1946–50); Port Arthur West End Bruins (1948–49); Oshawa Generals (1950–51)
- Led TBJHL in penalty minutes (53) in 1948–49; led TBJHL in assists (20) in 1949–50; led OHA-Jr. in assists (62) in 1950–51
- Served as captain of Detroit Red Wings (1962–74)
- Holds Detroit team record for consecutive games played (548), established from 1956–64

- Ranks 10th in NHL career games played (1,549)
- Led NHL in short-handed goals (4) in 1965–66
- Finished among NHL top-5 in assists in 1952–53 (43), 1961–62 (43), 1964–65 (42), 1967–68 (48) and 1968–69 (58)
- Finished among NHL top-5 in points in 1952–53 (59) and 1964–65 (67)
- Number retired by Detroit on November 10, 1991
- Played in NHL All-Star Game (1953, 1954, 1955, 1956, 1957, 1958, 1959, 1961, 1962, 1963, 1964, 1965, 1967)

> The goals are nice, of course, but I've always taken a lot of priade in assists. It's a centerman's job to get assists."

REGULAR SEASON

Season	Age	Team	Lg	GP	G	A	PTS	+/-	PIM	ESG	PPG	SHG	GWG	SOG	S%
1950–51	18	Detroit Red Wings	NHL	1	0	0	0		0						
1951–52	19	Detroit Red Wings	NHL	65	15	22	37		22						
1952–53	20	Detroit Red Wings	NHL	70	16	43	59		28						
1953–54	21	Detroit Red Wings	NHL	69	11	18	29		34						
1954–55	22	Detroit Red Wings	NHL	69	17	31	48		37						
1955–56	23	Detroit Red Wings	NHL	70	25	26	51		24						
1956–57	24	Detroit Red Wings	NHL	48	16	25	41		8						
1957–58	25	Detroit Red Wings	NHL	70	21	38	59		22						
1958–59	26	Detroit Red Wings	NHL	70	19	35	54		6						
1959–60	27	Detroit Red Wings	NHL	70	19	28	47		8						
1960–61	28	Detroit Red Wings	NHL	70	27	35	62		26						
1961–62	29	Detroit Red Wings	NHL	70	26	43	69		18						
1962–63	30	Detroit Red Wings	NHL	70	20	44	64		8						
1963–64	31	Detroit Red Wings	NHL	70	23	30	53		11	17	6	0	2		
1964–65	32	Detroit Red Wings	NHL	68	25	42	67		16	19	6	0	7		
1965–66	33	Detroit Red Wings	NHL	70	31	38	69		16	18	9	4	6		
1966–67	34	Detroit Red Wings	NHL	70	17	38	55		10	12	4	1	2		
1967–68	35	Detroit Red Wings	NHL	74	22	48	70	8	14	19	3	0	2	212	10.4
1968–69	36	Detroit Red Wings	NHL	72	25	58	83	43	8	18	7	0	2	221	11.3
1969–70	37	Detroit Red Wings	NHL	73	21	47	68	26	24	17	4	0	3	218	9.6
1970–71	38	Detroit Red Wings	NHL	77	21	34	55	-18	6	15	6	0	2	171	12.3
1971–72	39	Detroit Red Wings	NHL	75	20	45	65	-19	22	11	9	0	5	123	16.3
1972–73	40	Detroit Red Wings	NHL	77	18	53	71	6	13	10	8	0	3	130	13.8
1973–74	41	Detroit Red Wings	NHL	11	1	4	5	-13	2	0	1	0	0	9	11.1
NHL Career — 24 Seasons				1549	456	825	1281	33	383	156	63	5	34	1084	11.8

PLAYOFFS

Season	Age	Team	Lg	GP	G	A	PTS	+/-	PIM	ESG	PPG	SHG	GWG	SOG	S%
1951–52	19	Detroit Red Wings	NHL	8	0	3	3		4						
1952–53	20	Detroit Red Wings	NHL	6	2	4	6		2						
1953–54	21	Detroit Red Wings	NHL	12	2	7	9		7						
1954–55	22	Detroit Red Wings	NHL	11	7	8	15		2						
1955–56	23	Detroit Red Wings	NHL	10	7	3	10		2						
1956–57	24	Detroit Red Wings	NHL	5	3	2	5		2						
1957–58	25	Detroit Red Wings	NHL	4	0	1	1		0						
1959–60	27	Detroit Red Wings	NHL	6	2	6	8		0						
1960–61	28	Detroit Red Wings	NHL	11	4	5	9		0						
1962–63	30	Detroit Red Wings	NHL	11	3	6	9		2						
1963–64	31	Detroit Red Wings	NHL	14	3	8	11		0						
1964–65	32	Detroit Red Wings	NHL	7	2	3	5		4						
1965–66	33	Detroit Red Wings	NHL	12	0	11	11		4						
1969–70	37	Detroit Red Wings	NHL	4	0	2	2		0	0	0	0	0		
NHL Career — 14 Seasons				121	35	69	104		29	0	0	0	0		

TROPHY CASE

AWARDS

Lady Byng Memorial Trophy (1959, 1966, 1969)

Lester Patrick Trophy (1974)

Stanley Cup (1951–52, 1953–54, 1954–55)

ALL-STAR SELECTIONS

Second All-Star Team Center (1953)

Second All-Star Team Left Wing (1959)

5

Cy Denneny

HOCKEY HALL OF FAME CLASS: 1959

Alternates:
6, 10, 16

Left Wing

Shoots: Left

Height: 5'-7"

Weight: 168 lbs.

Born: December
23, 1891: Farrow's
Point, Ontario

Died: September
9, 1970: Ottawa,
Ontario

Played 15
professional
seasons from
1914–29

QUICK FACTS

- Held NHL record for career goals (248) and career points (333); goals record surpassed by Howie Morenz in 1933–34; points record surpassed by Morenz in 1931–32

- One of four players (with Joe Malone, Newsy Lalonde and Evgeni Malkin) to score in their first six NHL games

- Played amateur hockey with Cornwall Internationals (1910–12); Russell Athletics (1912–13); Cobalt O'Brien Mines (1913–14); Russell H.C. (1914–15)

- One of the first players to experiment with a curved stick, using hot water to shape and bend the blade

- Nicknamed "The Cornwall Colt" because of his tremendous speed and feisty manner

- Coached Boston Bruins to the first Stanley Cup title in franchise history (1929)

- Led NHL in goals (22) and points (24) in 1923–24; led NHL in assists in 1917–18 (10) and 1924–25 (15)

- Fifth player in NHL history to score six goals in a single game in Ottawa Senators' 12–5 victory over Hamilton Tigers, March 7, 1921

- Scored Stanley Cup-winning goal in Ottawa's 3–1 victory over Boston Bruins, April 13, 1927

- Served as NHL on-ice official (1929–31)

- Coached Boston Bruins (1928–29); coached Ottawa Senators (1932–33)

- Brother of Corb Denneny, who played in NHL with Toronto Arenas, Toronto St. Pats, Hamilton Tigers and Chicago from 1917–28

- Denneny brothers combined to score 475 goals, the top total by a brother duo in the pre-World War II era

> "When I was a rookie, a lad had to earn his berth on a pro club the hard way. They slammed me down at every opportunity and really gave me the business. But, after that, I was on my way."

REGULAR SEASON

Season	Age	Team	Lg	GP	G	A	PTS	PIM
1914–15	23	Toronto Shamrocks	NHA	8	6	0	6	43
1915–16	24	Toronto Blueshirts	NHA	24	24	4	28	57
1916–17	25	Ottawa Senators	NHA	10	3	0	3	17
1917–18	26	Ottawa Senators	NHL	20	36	10	46	80
1918–19	27	Ottawa Senators	NHL	18	18	4	22	58
1919–20	28	Ottawa Senators	NHL	24	16	6	22	31
1920–21	29	Ottawa Senators	NHL	24	34	5	39	10
1921–22	30	Ottawa Senators	NHL	22	27	12	39	20
1922–23	31	Ottawa Senators	NHL	24	23	11	34	28
1923–24	32	Ottawa Senators	NHL	22	22	2	24	10
1924–25	33	Ottawa Senators	NHL	29	27	15	42	16
1925–26	34	Ottawa Senators	NHL	36	24	12	36	18
1926–27	35	Ottawa Senators	NHL	42	17	6	23	16
1927–28	36	Ottawa Senators	NHL	44	3	0	3	12
1928–29	37	Boston Bruins	NHL	23	1	2	3	2
Career – 15 Seasons				370	281	89	370	418

PLAYOFFS

Season	Age	Team	Lg	GP	G	A	PTS	PIM
1916–17	25	Ottawa Senators	NHA	2	1	0	1	8
1918–19	27	Ottawa Senators	NHL	5	3	2	5	6
1919–20	28	Ottawa Senators	St-Cup	5	0	2	2	3
1920–21	29	Ottawa Senators	NHL	2	2	0	2	5
1920–21	29	Ottawa Senators	St-Cup	5	2	2	4	13
1921–22	30	Ottawa Senators	NHL	2	2	0	2	4
1922–23	31	Ottawa Senators	NHL	2	2	0	2	2
1922–23	31	Ottawa Senators	St-Cup	6	1	2	3	10
1923–24	32	Ottawa Senators	NHL	2	2	0	2	2
1925–26	34	Ottawa Senators	NHL	2	0	0	0	4
1926–27	35	Ottawa Senators	NHL	6	5	0	5	0
1927–28	36	Ottawa Senators	NHL	2	0	0	0	0
1928–29	37	Boston Bruins	NHL	2	0	0	0	0
Career – 11 Seasons				43	20	8	28	57

TROPHY CASE

AWARDS

NHL Scoring Leader (1924)

Stanley Cup (1919–1920, 1920–21, 1922–23, 1926–27, 1928–29)

16

Marcel Dionne
HOCKEY HALL OF FAME CLASS: 1992

Alternates: 5, 12	
Center	
Shoots: Right	
Height: 5'-9"	
Weight: 190 lbs.	

Born: August 3, 1951: Drummondville, Quoboo

Drafted by the Detroit Red Wings second overall in 1971

Played 18 NHL seasons from 1971–89

> People ask if I regret not winning a Stanley Cup, but winning the series against the Soviet Union was the best. It was the greatest experience of my hockey career."

QUICK FACTS

- Ranks fourth in NHL career goals (731); ranks fifth in NHL career points (1,771)
- Ranks seventh in NHL career power-play goals (234); ranks second in NHL career shots-on-goal (5,366)
- Played amateur hockey with Montreal Laurentides (1966–67); Drummondville Rangers (1967–68); St. Catharines Black Hawks (1968–71)
- Led QJHL in playoff goals (14) in 1967–68; led OHA-Jr. in goals (55), assists (77) and points (132) in 1969–70; led OHA-Jr. in points (143) in 1970–71; led OHA-Jr. in playoff goals (25), assists (26) and points (55) in 1970–71
- OHA-Jr. Second All-Star Team Center (1970); OHA-Jr. First All-Star Team Center (1971)
- Played in NHL All-Star Game (1975, 1975, 1977, 1978, 1980, 1981, 1983, 1985)
- Led NHL in points (137) in 1979–80; led NHL in short-handed goals (10) in 1974–75
- Led NHL in shots-on-goal in 1976–77 (378), 1978–79 (362), 1979–80 (348) and 1980–81 (342)
- Finished among NHL top-5 in goals in 1974–75 (47), 1976–77 (53), 1978–79 (59), 1979–80 (53), 1980–81 (58), 1982–83 (56)
- Finished among NHL top-5 in power-play goals in 1976–77 (14), 1978–79 (19), 1979–80 (17), 1980–81 (23), 1984–85 (16) and 1987–88 (22)

Dionne scored his 700th goal with this puck on October 31, 1987. Unfortunately, his Rangers lost 8–2.

REGULAR SEASON

Season	Age	Team	Lg	GP	G	A	PTS	+/-	PIM	ESG	PPG	SHG	GWG	SOG	S%
1971-72	20	Detroit Red Wings	NHL	78	28	49	77	0	14	21	7	0	2	268	10.4
1972-73	21	Detroit Red Wings	NHL	77	40	50	90	-4	21	30	10	0	6	282	14.2
1973-74	22	Detroit Red Wings	NHL	74	24	54	78	-31	10	21	3	0	1	280	8.6
1974-75	23	Detroit Red Wings	NHL	80	47	74	121	-15	14	22	15	10	2	378	12.4
1975-76	24	Los Angeles Kings	NHL	80	40	54	94	2	38	32	7	1	6	329	12.2
1976-77	25	Los Angeles Kings	NHL	80	53	69	122	10	12	38	14	1	5	378	14.0
1977-78	26	Los Angeles Kings	NHL	70	36	43	79	-8	37	27	9	0	4	294	12.2
1978-79	27	Los Angeles Kings	NHL	80	59	71	130	23	30	40	19	0	7	362	16.3
1979-80	28	Los Angeles Kings	NHL	80	53	84	137	35	32	36	17	0	6	348	15.2
1980-81	29	Los Angeles Kings	NHL	80	58	77	135	55	70	31	23	4	9	342	17.0
1981-82	30	Los Angeles Kings	NHL	78	50	67	117	-10	50	32	17	1	5	351	14.2
1982-83	31	Los Angeles Kings	NHL	80	56	51	107	10	22	38	17	1	7	345	16.2
1983-84	32	Los Angeles Kings	NHL	66	39	53	92	8	28	26	13	0	2	278	14.0
1984-85	33	Los Angeles Kings	NHL	80	46	80	126	11	46	29	16	1	2	316	14.6
1985-86	34	Los Angeles Kings	NHL	80	36	58	94	-22	42	25	11	0	4	284	12.7
1986-87	35	Los Angeles Kings	NHL	67	24	50	74	-8	54	15	9	0	2	224	10.7
1986-87	35	New York Rangers	NHL	14	4	6	10	-8	6	3	1	0	0	49	8.2
1987-88	36	New York Rangers	NHL	67	31	34	65	-14	54	9	22	0	4	184	16.8
1988-89	37	New York Rangers	NHL	37	7	16	23	-6	20	3	4	0	0	74	9.5
NHL Career - 18 Seasons				1348	731	1040	1771	28	600	478	234	19	74	5366	13.6

PLAYOFFS

Season	Age	Team	Lg	GP	G	A	PTS	+/-	PIM	ESG	PPG	SHG	GWG	SOG	S%
1975-76	24	Los Angeles Kings	NHL	9	6	1	7		0	3	3	0	0		
1976-77	25	Los Angeles Kings	NHL	9	5	9	14		2	4	1	0	1		
1977-78	26	Los Angeles Kings	NHL	2	0	0	0		0	0	0	0	0		
1978-79	27	Los Angeles Kings	NHL	2	0	1	1		0	0	0	0	0		
1979-80	28	Los Angeles Kings	NHL	4	0	3	3		4	0	0	0	0		
1980-81	29	Los Angeles Kings	NHL	4	1	3	4		7	0	1	0	0		
1981-82	30	Los Angeles Kings	NHL	10	7	4	11		0	3	4	0	0		
1984-85	33	Los Angeles Kings	NHL	3	1	2	3	-1	2	0	1	0	0	13	7.7
1986-87	35	New York Rangers	NHL	6	1	1	2	-4	2	0	1	0	0	15	6.7
NHL Career - 9 Seasons				49	21	24	45	-5	17	10	11	0	1	28	7.1

TROPHY CASE

AWARDS

Lady Byng Memorial Trophy (1975, 1977)

Lester B. Pearson Award (1979, 1980)

Art Ross Trophy (1980)

Lester Patrick Trophy (2006)

ALL-STAR SELECTIONS

First All-Star Team Center (1977, 1980)

Second All-Star Team Center (1979, 1981)

INTERNATIONAL AWARDS

Bronze Medal: World Championships (1978, 1983, 1986)

Canada Cup (1976)

131

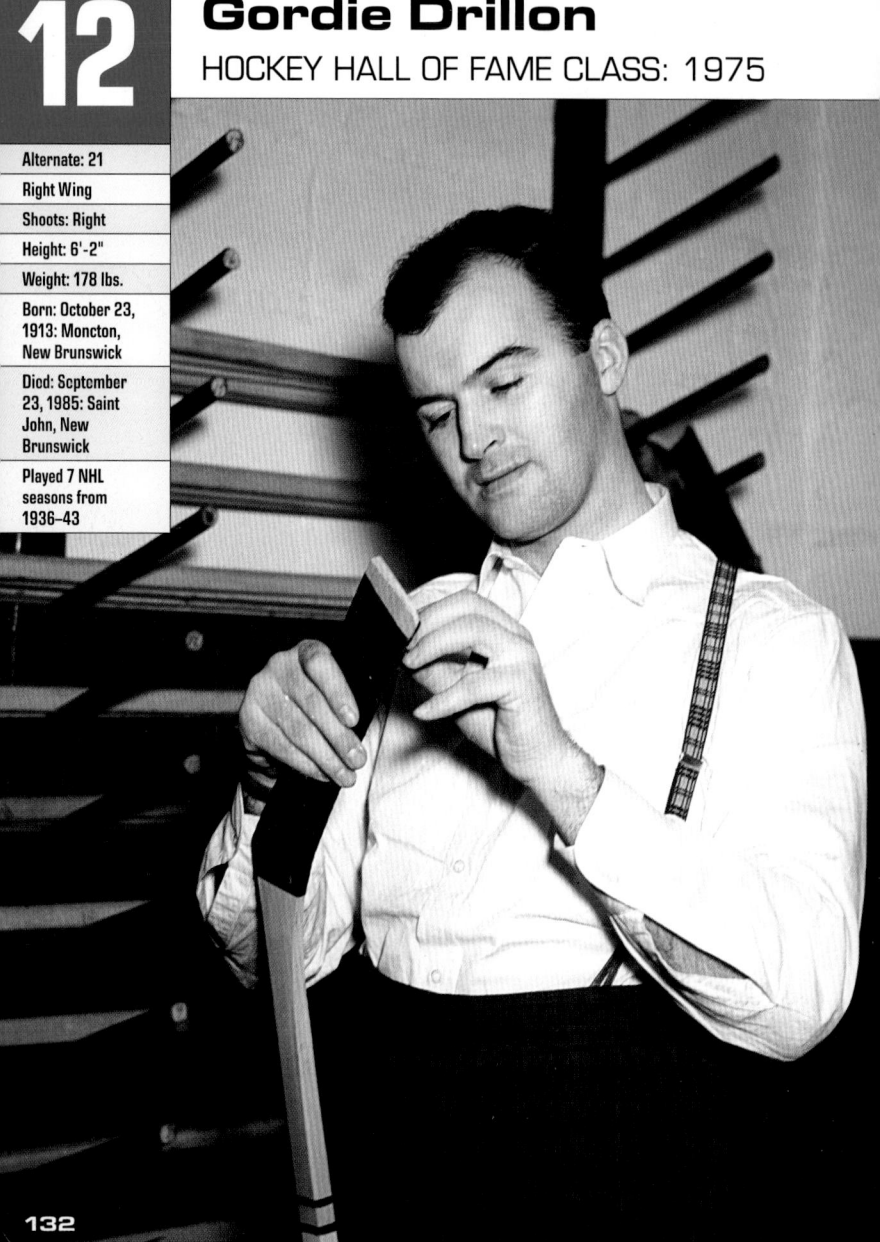

12

Gordie Drillon
HOCKEY HALL OF FAME CLASS: 1975

Alternate: 21

Right Wing

Shoots: Right

Height: 6'-2"

Weight: 178 lbs.

Born: October 23, 1913: Moncton, New Brunswick

Died: September 23, 1985: Saint John, New Brunswick

Played 7 NHL seasons from 1936–43

QUICK FACTS

> I spent ten years playing in the slot before anyone invented a name for it."

- First New Brunswick native to be inducted into Hockey Hall of Fame

- Played amateur hockey with Moncton Athletics (1930–31); Moncton Wheelers (1931–32); Moncton Hawks (1932–33); Toronto Young Rangers (1933–34); Toronto Lions (1934–36); Toronto Dominions (1933–35); Saint John Beavers (1949–50)

- Led Moncton City Junior League in goals (15) and points (19) in 1930–31; led Moncton Commercial League playoffs in goals (13) and points (17) in 1932–33

- Played minor pro hockey with Pittsburgh Yellowjackets (1935–36); Syracuse Stars (1936–37)

- Last member of the Toronto Maple Leafs to win NHL scoring title (1937–38)

- Played in NHL All-Star Game (1939)

- Played with Toronto Army Daggers (1943–44); Valleyfield Braves (1944–45); Dartmouth RCAF (1944–45); Halifax Army (1945–46) during World War II

- Led NHL in goals (26) and points (52) in 1937–38

- Led NHL playoffs in goals in 1937–38 (7) and 1938–39 (7)

- Renowned for being one of the "star" players benched by coach Hap Day during Toronto's historic comeback in 1942 Stanley Cup Finals against Detroit

- Traded to Montreal Canadiens by Toronto for cash, October 4, 1942

- Inducted into New Brunswick Sports Hall of Fame (1970); inducted into Canada's Sport Hall of Fame (1989)

REGULAR SEASON

Season	Age	Team	Lg	GP	G	A	PTS	PIM
1936–37	23	Toronto Maple Leafs	NHL	41	16	17	33	2
1937–38	24	Toronto Maple Leafs	NHL	48	26	26	52	4
1938–39	25	Toronto Maple Leafs	NHL	40	18	16	34	15
1939–40	26	Toronto Maple Leafs	NHL	43	21	19	40	13
1940–41	27	Toronto Maple Leafs	NHL	42	23	21	44	2
1941–42	28	Toronto Maple Leafs	NHL	48	23	18	41	6
1942–43	29	Montreal Canadiens	NHL	49	28	22	50	14
NHL Career – 7 Seasons				311	155	139	294	56

PLAYOFFS

Season	Age	Team	Lg	GP	G	A	PTS	PIM
1936–37	23	Toronto Maple Leafs	NHL	2	0	0	0	0
1937–38	24	Toronto Maple Leafs	NHL	7	7	1	8	2
1938–39	25	Toronto Maple Leafs	NHL	10	7	6	13	4
1939–40	26	Toronto Maple Leafs	NHL	10	3	1	4	0
1940–41	27	Toronto Maple Leafs	NHL	7	3	2	5	2
1941–42	28	Toronto Maple Leafs	NHL	9	2	3	5	2
1942–43	29	Montreal Canadiens	NHL	5	4	2	6	0
NHL Career – 7 Seasons				50	26	15	41	10

TROPHY CASE

AWARDS

NHL Scoring Leader (1937–38)

Lady Byng Memorial Trophy (1938)

Stanley Cup (1941–42)

ALL-STAR SELECTIONS

First All-Star Team Right Wing (1938, 1939)

Second All-Star Team Right Wing (1942)

Graham Drinkwater

HOCKEY HALL OF FAME CLASS: 1950

Rover

Shoots: Right

Height: 5'-11"

Weight: 165 lbs

Born: February 22, 1875: Montreal, Quebec

Died: September 26, 1946: Montreal, Quebec

Played six elite amateur seasons from 1892–93, 1894–99

QUICK FACTS

- Renowned as a smooth skater and slick stickhandler who could play forward or defense will equal skill
- Played football at McGill University
- Won a junior hockey championship with the Montreal Amateur Athletic Association in 1892–93, the same year he made his senior debut with the Montreal Victorias
- Member of Stanley Cup-winning Montreal Victorias team that was awarded championship after winning Amateur Hockey Association league title, March, 1895
- After losing a Stanley Cup challenge to the Winnipeg Victorias in February of 1896, he scored a goal in the rematch won 6–5 by the Montreal Victorias in December of 1896

- Scored career-high 10 goals during Montreal Victorias' perfect 8–0 season in 1897–98 which resulted in another Stanley Cup championship
- Served as captain of Montreal Victorias (1898–99)
- Helped Montreal Victorias successfully defend Stanley Cup title against Winnipeg Victorias before losing their league title (and the Cup) to the Montreal Shamrocks
- Served as an original trustee for the Allan Cup, donated in 1908 to recognize Canada's amateur hockey champion

> "Bob MacDougall, Graham Drinkwater and Norman Rankin formed the astonishing forward line which delighted the Vic's admirers … Drinkwater and MacDougall are dead sure shots."
>
> — Montreal's *Metropolitan* newspaper, April 13, 1895

REGULAR SEASON

Season	Age	Team	Lg	GP	G	A	PTS
1892–93	17	Montreal Victorias	AHAC	3	1	0	1
1894–95	19	Montreal Victorias	AHAC	8	9	0	9
1895–96	20	Montreal Victorias	AHAC	8	7	0	7
1896–97	21	Montreal Victorias	AHAC	4	3	0	3
1897–98	22	Montreal Victorias	AHAC	8	10	0	10
1898–99	23	Montreal Victorias	CAHL	6	0	0	0
Career — 6 Seasons				37	30	0	30

PLAYOFFS

Season	Age	Team	Lg	GP	G	A	PTS
1895–96	20	Montreal Victorias	St-Cup	1	1	0	1
1896–97	21	Montreal Victorias	St-Cup	1	0	0	0
1898–99	23	Montreal Victorias	St-Cup	2	1	0	1
Career — 3 Seasons				4	2	0	2

TROPHY CASE

AWARDS

Stanley Cup (1894–95, 1895–96, 1896–97, 1897–98, 1898–99)

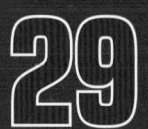

29

Retired by Montreal

Ken Dryden

HOCKEY HALL OF FAME CLASS: 1983

Goaltender

Catches: Left

Height: 6'-4"

Weight: 205 lbs.

Born: August 8, 1947: Hamilton, Ontario

Drafted by the Boston Bruins 14th overall in 1964

Played 8 NHL seasons from 1970–72, 1973–79

"I think it took me so long to want to be part of the team because I was afraid of a team. Afraid of always having to do what a team does; afraid of losing my own right to be different. When I realized I could be part of a team, and still be different, I could then be less different. Then I realized I wasn't very different at all."

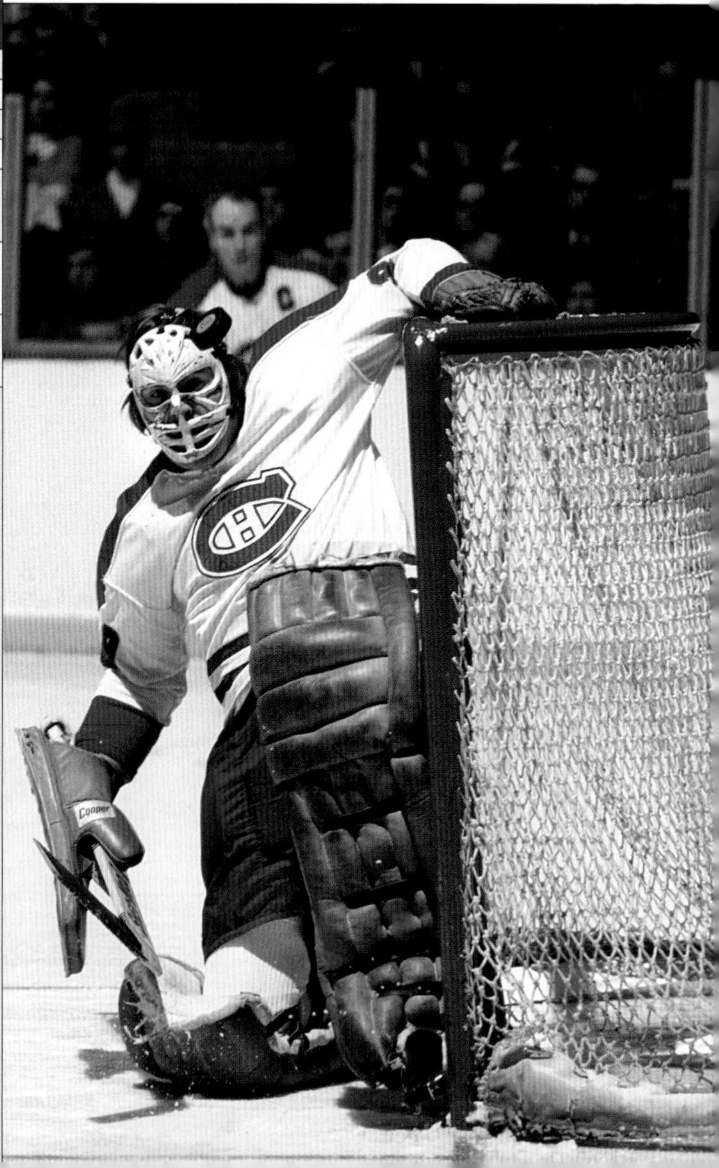

QUICK FACTS

- Only player in NHL history to win a major award (Conn Smythe Trophy) before winning the Calder Trophy as top rookie (1971)
- Played amateur hockey with Humber Valley Packers (1963–64); Etobicoke Indians (1964–65); Cornell University Big Red (1966–69); Canadian National Team (1969–70)
- NCAA All-Tournament Team (1967); NCAA All-America First Team (1966–67, 1967–68, 1968–69)
- Rights traded to Montreal by Boston Bruins with Alex Campbell for Guy Allen and Paul Reid, June 28, 1964
- Sat out the entire 1973–74 season because of a contract dispute and spent the year articling at a Toronto law firm

- Played in NHL All-Star Game (1972, 1975, 1976, 1977, 1978)
- Led NHL in wins in 1971–72 (39), 1972–73 (33), 1975–76 (42) and 1976–77 (41)
- Led NHL in shutouts in 1972–73 (6), 1975–76 (8), 1976–77 (10) and 1978–79 (5); led NHL in goals-against-average in 1972–73 (2.26), 1975–76 (2.03), 1977–78 (2.05) and 1978–79 (2.30)
- Wrote *The Game*, considered to be the most definitive book ever written about hockey
- Served as President of the Toronto Maple Leafs (1997–2004)
- Served as Ontario Youth Commissioner (1984–86); elected as Liberal Member of Parliament for York Centre (2004, 2006)

This pretzel mask came with Dryden to the NHL as a rookie in 1970–71.

REGULAR SEASON

Season	Age	Team	Lg	GP	W	L	T	SO	GA	GAA	G	A	PTS	PIM
1970–71	23	Montreal Canadiens	NHL	6	6	0	0	0	9	1.65	0	0	0	0
1971–72	24	Montreal Canadiens	NHL	64	39	8	15	8	142	2.24	0	3	3	4
1972–73	25	Montreal Canadiens	NHL	54	33	7	13	6	119	2.26	0	4	4	2
1974–75	27	Montreal Canadiens	NHL	56	30	9	16	4	149	2.69	0	3	3	2
1975–76	28	Montreal Canadiens	NHL	62	42	10	8	8	121	2.03	0	2	2	0
1976–77	29	Montreal Canadiens	NHL	56	41	6	8	10	117	2.14	0	2	2	0
1977–78	30	Montreal Canadiens	NHL	52	37	7	7	5	105	2.05	0	2	2	0
1978–79	31	Montreal Canadiens	NHL	47	30	10	7	5	108	2.30	0	3	3	4
NHL Career – 8 Seasons				397	258	57	74	46	870	2.24	0	19	19	12

PLAYOFFS

Season	Age	Team	Lg	GP	W	L	T	SO	GA	GAA	G	A	PTS	PIM
1970–71	23	Montreal Canadiens	NHL	20	12	8		0	61	3.00	0	1	1	0
1971–72	24	Montreal Canadiens	NHL	6	2	4		0	17	2.83	0	0	0	0
1972–73	25	Montreal Canadiens	NHL	17	12	5		1	50	2.89	0	0	0	2
1974–75	27	Montreal Canadiens	NHL	11	6	5		2	29	2.53	0	0	0	0
1975–76	28	Montreal Canadiens	NHL	13	12	1		1	25	1.92	0	0	0	0
1976–77	29	Montreal Canadiens	NHL	14	12	2		4	22	1.55	0	0	0	0
1977–78	30	Montreal Canadiens	NHL	15	12	3		2	29	1.89	0	0	0	0
1978–79	31	Montreal Canadiens	NHL	16	12	4		0	41	2.48	0	3	3	2
NHL Career – 8 Seasons				112	80	32		10	274	2.40	0	4	4	4

TROPHY CASE

AWARDS

Conn Smythe Trophy (1971)

Calder Memorial Trophy (1972)

Vezina Trophy (1973, 1976, 1977, 1978, 1979)

Stanley Cup (1970–71, 1972–73, 1975–76, 1976–77, 1977–78, 1978–79)

ALL-STAR SELECTIONS

First All-Star Team Goaltender (1973, 1976, 1977, 1978, 1979)

Second All-Star Team Goaltender (1972)

INTERNATIONAL AWARDS

Summit Series (1972)

9

Dick Duff
HOCKEY HALL OF FAME CLASS: 2006

Alternates:
17, 20, 8, 7, 24

Left Wing

Shoots: Left

Height: 5'-9"

Weight: 166 lbs.

Born: February
18, 1936: Kirkland
Lake, Ontario

Played 18 NHL
seasons from
1954–72

QUICK FACTS

- Holds NHL record for scoring fastest two goals (1:08) from the start of a playoff game, established in Toronto's 4–2 victory over Detroit, April 9, 1963

- Played amateur hockey with St. Michael's Buzzers (1952–53); St. Michael's Majors (1952–55)

- One of only six players in NHL history (with Red Kelly, Frank Mahovlich, Bryan Trottier, Patrick Roy and Larry Murphy) to win two-or-more Stanley Cup championships with two-or-more teams

- Played in NHL All-Star Game (1956, 1957, 1958, 1962, 1963, 1965, 1967)

- Scored Stanley Cup-winning goal in Toronto's 2–1 victory over Chicago Black Hawks, April 22, 1962

- Traded to N.Y. Rangers by Toronto with Bob Nevin, Rod Seiling, Arnie Brown, and Bill Collins for Andy Bathgate and Don McKenney, February 22, 1964

- Traded to Montreal by N.Y. Rangers with Dave McComb for Bill Hicke and the loan of Jean-Guy Morissette for remainder of 1964–65 season, December 22, 1964

- Led NHL in game-winning goals (8) in 1967–68; led NHL in shooting percentage (22.5%) in 1967–68

- Coached Toronto Maple Leafs (1979–80)

- Served as assistant coach of Toronto Maple Leafs (1979–81)

> "The thing that I always kept to myself was that when the best players were playing for the best prize (the Stanley Cup), I could compete with them all. When the end of the year was coming around, they wanted me there for the playoffs ... I just wanted to be good at the end when it counted."

TROPHY CASE

AWARDS

Stanley Cup (1961–62, 1962–63, 1964–65, 1965–66, 1967–68, 1968–69)

REGULAR SEASON

Season	Age	Team	Lg	GP	G	A	PTS	+/-	PIM	ESG	PPG	SHG	GWG	SOG	S%
1954–55	18	Toronto Maple Leafs	NHL	3	0	0	0		2						
1955–56	19	Toronto Maple Leafs	NHL	69	18	19	37		74						
1956–57	20	Toronto Maple Leafs	NHL	70	26	14	40		50						
1957–58	21	Toronto Maple Leafs	NHL	65	26	23	49		79						
1958–59	22	Toronto Maple Leafs	NHL	69	29	24	53		73						
1959–60	23	Toronto Maple Leafs	NHL	67	19	22	41		51						
1960–61	24	Toronto Maple Leafs	NHL	67	16	17	33		54						
1961–62	25	Toronto Maple Leafs	NHL	51	17	20	37		37						
1962–63	26	Toronto Maple Leafs	NHL	69	16	19	35		56						
1963–64	27	Toronto Maple Leafs	NHL	52	7	10	17		59	5	2	0	0		
1963–64	27	New York Rangers	NHL	14	4	4	8		2	2	2	0	0		
1964–65	28	New York Rangers	NHL	29	3	9	12		20	2	1	0	0		
1964–65	28	Montreal Canadiens	NHL	40	9	7	16		16	9	0	0	3		
1965–66	28	Montreal Canadiens	NHL	63	21	24	45		78	16	5	0	2		
1966–67	30	Montreal Canadiens	NHL	51	12	11	23		23	9	3	0	2		
1967–68	31	Montreal Canadiens	NHL	66	25	21	46	6	21	19	6	0	8	111	22.5
1968–69	32	Montreal Canadiens	NHL	68	19	21	40	-13	24	14	5	0	2	138	13.8
1969–70	33	Montreal Canadiens	NHL	17	1	1	2	-5	4	1	0	0	0		
1969–70	33	Los Angeles Kings	NHL	32	5	8	13	-15	8	5	0	0	0	37	13.5
1970–71	34	Los Angeles Kings	NHL	7	1	0	1	-2	0	1	0	0	0	4	25.0
1970–71	34	Buffalo Sabres	NHL	53	7	13	20	-16	12	7	0	0	1	67	10.4
1971–72	34	Buffalo Sabres	NHL	8	2	2	4	-2	0	2	0	0	0	5	40.0
NHL Career — 18 Seasons				1030	283	289	572	-47	743	92	24	0	18	383	15.7

PLAYOFFS

Season	Age	Team	Lg	GP	G	A	PTS	+/-	PIM	ESG	PPG	SHG	GWG	SOG	S%
1955–56	19	Toronto Maple Leafs	NHL	5	1	4	5		2						
1958–59	22	Toronto Maple Leafs	NHL	12	4	3	7		8						
1959–60	23	Toronto Maple Leafs	NHL	10	2	4	6		6						
1960–61	24	Toronto Maple Leafs	NHL	5	0	1	1		2						
1961–62	25	Toronto Maple Leafs	NHL	12	3	10	13		20						
1962–63	26	Toronto Maple Leafs	NHL	10	4	1	5		2						
1964–65	28	Montreal Canadiens	NHL	13	3	6	9		17						
1965–66	28	Montreal Canadiens	NHL	10	2	5	7		2						
1966–67	30	Montreal Canadiens	NHL	10	2	3	5		4						
1967–68	31	Montreal Canadiens	NHL	13	3	4	7		4	3	0	0	1		
1968–69	32	Montreal Canadiens	NHL	14	6	8	14		11	3	3	0	1		
NHL Career — 11 Seasons				114	30	49	79		78	6	3	0	2		

Woody Dumart

HOCKEY HALL OF FAME CLASS: 1992

Alternate: 10

Left Wing

Shoots: Left

Height: 6'

Weight: 190 lbs.

Born: December 23, 1916: Berlin, Ontario

Died October 20, 2001: Needham, Massachusetts

Played 16 NHL seasons from 1935–42, 1945–54

> He used to kid me a lot that I couldn't see out of my left eye because, of course, Woody was on the left side."
>
> — Milt Schmidt, on his Kraut Line teammate

QUICK FACTS

- Played amateur hockey with Kitchener Empires (1933–34); Kitchener Greenshirts (1934–35)
- Led OHA-Jr. playoffs in assists (3) in 1933–34
- Led OHA-Jr. in points (28) in 1934–35
- Played with Ottawa RCAF (1941–43) and Millward RCAF (1942–43) during World War II
- Member of the Allan Cup-winning Ottawa RCAF Flyers (1942), scoring 14 goals in 13 Allan Cup playoff games
- Signed as a free agent by Boston Bruins, October 9, 1935
- Played in NHL All-Star Game (1947, 1948)
- Member of Boston's famed Kraut Line with Milt Schmidt and Bobby Bauer

- Providence Reds coach Albert "Battleship" Leduc originally labeled the Bruins' trio "The Sauerkraut Line" in reference to their German ancestry
- Renowned for his checking and defensive ability, he "shadowed" Gordie Howe during the Boston-Detroit semi-finals in 1953 and held the scoring champion to two goals as Boston won the series
- Nicknamed "Porky"
- Finished second in NHL goals (22) in 1939–40; finished second in NHL points (43) in 1939–40
- Played with AHL's Providence Reds (1954–55) after retiring from NHL

Dumart's tube skates.

REGULAR SEASON

Season	Age	Team	Lg	GP	G	A	PTS	PIM
1935–36	19	Boston Bruins	NHL	1	0	0	0	0
1936–37	20	Boston Bruins	NHL	17	4	4	8	2
1937–38	21	Boston Bruins	NHL	48	13	14	27	6
1938–39	22	Boston Bruins	NHL	46	14	15	29	2
1939–40	23	Boston Bruins	NHL	48	22	21	43	16
1940–41	24	Boston Bruins	NHL	40	18	15	33	2
1941–42	25	Boston Bruins	NHL	35	14	15	29	8
1945–46	29	Boston Bruins	NHL	50	22	12	34	2
1946–47	30	Boston Bruins	NHL	60	24	28	52	12
1947–48	31	Boston Bruins	NHL	59	21	16	37	14
1948–49	32	Boston Bruins	NHL	59	11	12	23	6
1949–50	33	Boston Bruins	NHL	69	14	25	39	14
1950–51	34	Boston Bruins	NHL	70	20	21	41	7
1951–52	35	Boston Bruins	NHL	39	5	8	13	0
1952–53	36	Boston Bruins	NHL	62	5	9	14	2
1953–54	37	Boston Bruins	NHL	69	4	3	7	6
NHL Career — 16 Seasons				772	211	218	429	99

PLAYOFFS

Season	Age	Team	Lg	GP	G	A	PTS	PIM
1936–37	20	Boston Bruins	NHL	3	0	0	0	0
1937–38	21	Boston Bruins	NHL	3	0	0	0	0
1938–39	22	Boston Bruins	NHL	12	1	3	4	6
1939–40	23	Boston Bruins	NHL	6	1	0	1	0
1940–41	24	Boston Bruins	NHL	11	1	3	4	9
1945–46	29	Boston Bruins	NHL	10	4	3	7	0
1946–47	30	Boston Bruins	NHL	5	1	1	2	8
1947–48	31	Boston Bruins	NHL	5	0	0	0	0
1948–49	32	Boston Bruins	NHL	5	3	0	3	0
1950–51	34	Boston Bruins	NHL	6	1	2	3	0
1951–52	35	Boston Bruins	NHL	7	0	1	1	0
1952–53	36	Boston Bruins	NHL	11	0	2	2	0
1953–54	37	Boston Bruins	NHL	4	0	0	0	0
NHL Career — 13 Seasons				88	12	15	27	23

TROPHY CASE

AWARDS

Stanley Cup (1938–39, 1940–41)

ALL-STAR SELECTIONS

Second All-Star Team Left Wing (1940, 1941, 1947)

Tommy Dunderdale

HOCKEY HALL OF FAME CLASS: 1974

Alternates: 4, 5

Center

Shoots: Right

Height: 5'-8"

Weight: 160 lbs.

Born: May 6, 1887: Benella, Australia

Died: December 15, 1960: Winnipeg, Manitoba

Played 18 professional seasons from 1906–24

QUICK FACTS

- Holds PCHA record for career goals (198)
- Holds PCHA record for penalty minutes in a single season (141) in 1916–17
- Holds PCHA record for game-winning goals in a single season (6) in 1913–14
- Holds PCHA record for most consecutive games with at least one goal (15), established in 1913–14
- Played amateur hockey with Winnipeg Ramblers (1905–06)
- Led Manitoba Pro League in penalty minutes (44) in 1906–07
- Led MHL-Pro in assists (7) and points (24) in 1908–09
- Led PCHA in goals in 1912–13 (24), 1913–14 (24) and 1919–20 (26)
- Led PCHA in points in 1912–13 (29) and 1919–20 (33); led PCHA in penalty minutes in 1916–17 (141), 1917–18 (57) and 1921–22 (37)
- Born in Australia, he came to Canada in 1894 and was raised in Ottawa
- Scored goals in 15 straight games in 1913–14 and tied Cyclone Taylor for the league lead with 24 goals
- Member of PCHA champion Victoria Aristocrats (1913, 1914)
- Member of PCHA champion Portland Rosebuds (1916)

> "More excitement was caused over the arrival of Tommy Dunderdale, who will play this season at Victoria, than any other player from the east to go west this winter."
> — Toronto World, December 25, 1911

REGULAR SEASON

Season	Age	Team	Lg	GP	G	A	PTS	PIM
1906–07	19	Winnipeg Strathconas	MHL-Pro	10	8	0	8	
1907–08	20	Winnipeg Maple Leafs	MHL-Pro	3	1	0	1	3
1907–08	20	Strathcona-Alberta	MHL-Pro	5	11	1	12	17
1908–09	21	Winnipeg Shamrocks	MHL-Pro	9	17	7	24	9
1909–10	22	Montreal Shamrocks	CHA	3	7	0	7	5
1909–10	22	Montreal Shamrocks	NHA	12	14	0	14	19
1910–11	23	Quebec Bulldogs	NHA	9	13	0	13	25
1911–12	24	Victoria Aristocrats	PCHA	16	24	0	24	25
1912–13	25	Victoria Aristocrats	PCHA	15	24	5	29	36
1913–14	26	Victoria Aristocrats	PCHA	16	24	4	28	34
1914–15	27	Victoria Aristocrats	PCHA	17	17	10	27	22
1915–16	28	Portland Rosebuds	PCHA	18	14	3	17	45
1916–17	29	Portland Rosebuds	PCHA	24	22	4	26	141
1917–18	30	Portland Rosebuds	PCHA	18	14	6	20	57
1918–19	31	Victoria Aristocrats	PCHA	20	5	4	9	28
1919–20	32	Victoria Aristocrats	PCHA	22	26	7	33	35
1920–21	33	Victoria Aristocrats	PCHA	24	9	11	20	18
1921–22	34	Victoria Cougars	PCHA	24	13	6	19	37
1922–23	35	Victoria Cougars	PCHA	27	2	0	2	16
1923–24	36	Saskatoon Crescents	WCHL	6	1	0	1	4
1923–24	36	Edmonton Eskimos	WCHL	11	1	1	2	5
Career – 18 Seasons				314	249	69	318	581

PLAYOFFS

Season		Team	Lg	GP	G	A	PTS	PIM
1907–08		Strathcona-Alberta	MHL-Pro	3	6	1	7	3
1908–09		Winnipeg Shamrocks	MHL-Pro	3	3	0	3	6
1913–14		Victoria Aristocrats	St-Cup	3	2	0	2	11
1915–16		Portland Rosebuds	St-Cup	5	1	1	2	9
1922–23		Victoria Cougars	PCHA	2	0	1	1	0
Career – 3 Seasons				16	12	3	15	29

TROPHY CASE

ALL-STAR SELECTIONS

PCHA First All-Star Team Center (1912, 1913, 1914, 1915, 1920, 1921)

Bill Durnan

HOCKEY HALL OF FAME CLASS: 1964

Goaltender

Catches:
Right/Left

Height: 6'

Weight: 190 lbs.

Born: January 22,
1916: Toronto,
Ontario

Died: October 31,
1972: Toronto,
Ontario

Played 7 NHL
seasons from
1943–50

"He's the best
goaler in 20
years in the
National Hockey
League because
he has the most
competitive spirit
and is the least
temperamental
and he's the
greatest of all
goalers under fire."
— Dick Irvin Sr.,
Montreal coach

QUICK FACTS

- First rookie in NHL history to win Vezina Trophy (1944)
- Last goaltender to serve as on-ice captain of NHL team (1947–48)
- Only ambidextrous goaltender in NHL history
- Played amateur hockey with North Toronto Juniors (1931–32); Sudbury Cub Wolves (1932–33); Toronto British Consols (1933–34); Toronto McColl-Frontenacs (1934–35); Toronto Dominions (1935–36); Kirkland Lake Blue Devils (1936–40); Montreal Royals (1940–43)
- Led North Bay Junior League in shutouts (2) and goals-against-average (1.00) in 1932–33
- TMHL First All-Star Team Goaltender (1934); NOHA First All-Star Team Goaltender (1937)

- Led NOHA in wins (8) and goals-against-average (2.66) in 1937–38; led NOHA in wins (7), shutouts (3) and goals-against-average (1.00) in 1938–39
- Member of Allan Cup-winning Kirkland Lake Blue Devils (1939–40)
- Led QSHL in wins (21), playoff wins (6) and playoff shutouts (1) in 1940–41
- Signed as a free agent by Montreal Canadiens, October 30, 1943
- Played in NHL All-Star Game (1947, 1948, 1949)
- Led NHL in wins in 1943–44 (38), 1944–45 (38), 1945–46 (24) and 1946–47 (34)
- Led NHL in shutouts in 1945–46 (4) and 1948–49 (10)

Bill Durnan's felt arm pads.

REGULAR SEASON

Season	Age	Team	Lg	GP	W	L	T	SO	GA	GAA	G	A	PTS	PIM
1943–44	28	Montreal Canadiens	NHL	50	38	5	7	2	109	2.18	0	0	0	0
1944–45	29	Montreal Canadiens	NHL	50	38	8	4	1	121	2.42	0	0	0	0
1945–46	30	Montreal Canadiens	NHL	40	24	11	5	4	104	2.60	0	0	0	0
1946–47	31	Montreal Canadiens	NHL	60	34	16	10	4	138	2.30	0	0	0	0
1947–48	32	Montreal Canadiens	NHL	59	20	28	10	5	162	2.77	0	0	0	5
1948–49	33	Montreal Canadiens	NHL	60	28	23	9	10	126	2.10	0	0	0	0
1949–50	34	Montreal Canadiens	NHL	64	26	21	17	8	141	2.20	0	1	1	2
NHL Career – 7 Seasons				383	208	112	62	34	901	2.36	0	1	1	7

PLAYOFFS

Season	Age	Team	Lg	GP	W	L	T	SO	GA	GAA	G	A	PTS	PIM
1943–44	28	Montreal Canadiens	NHL	9	8	1		1	14	1.53	0	0	0	0
1944–45	29	Montreal Canadiens	NHL	6	2	4		0	15	2.41	0	0	0	0
1945–46	30	Montreal Canadiens	NHL	9	8	1		0	20	2.07	0	0	0	0
1946–47	31	Montreal Canadiens	NHL	11	6	5		1	23	1.92	0	0	0	0
1948–49	33	Montreal Canadiens	NHL	7	3	4		0	17	2.18	0	0	0	0
1949–50	34	Montreal Canadiens	NHL	3	0	3		0	10	3.33	0	0	0	0
NHL Career – 6 Seasons				45	27	18		2	99	2.07	0	0	0	0

TROPHY CASE

AWARDS

Vezina Trophy (1944, 1945, 1946, 1947, 1949, 1950)

Stanley Cup (1943–44, 1945–46)

ALL-STAR SELECTIONS

First All-Star Team Goaltender (1944, 1945, 1946, 1947, 1949, 1950)

Red Dutton

HOCKEY HALL OF FAME CLASS: 1958

Alternates: 3, 8

Defense

Shoots: Right

Height: 6'

Weight: 185 lbs.

Born: July 23, 1897: Russell, Manitoba

Died: March 15, 1987: Calgary, Alberta

Played 15 professional seasons from 1921–36

QUICK FACTS

> I wasn't a good hockey player, but I was a good competitor."

- Played amateur hockey with Winnipeg St. John's (1914–15); Winnipeg Winnipegs (1919–20); Calgary Canadians (1920–21)

- Served in World War I with the Princess Light Infantry (1915–19)

- Severely wounded during the Battle of Vimy Ridge, April 11, 1917

- Led Big-4 in penalty minutes (38) in 1920–21

- Signed as a free agent by Calgary (WCHL) in November, 1921

- Led WCHL in penalty minutes in 1921–22 (73) and 1923–24 (54); led Stanley Cup playoffs in penalty minutes (8) in 1923–24

- Played in NHL All-Star Game (1934)

- Traded to Montreal Maroons by Calgary Tigers (WHL) for cash, September 11, 1926

- Traded to N.Y. Americans by Montreal Maroons with Mike Neville, Hap Emms and Frank Carson for $35,000, May 14, 1930

- Led NHL in penalty minutes in 1928–29 (139) and 1931–32 (107)

- Real name was Norman Alexander Dutton, but he was commonly known as "Mervyn"

- Served as a Trustee of the Stanley Cup (1950–87)

- Served as second President of the National Hockey League (1943–46)

- Coached N.Y. Americans (1934–40)

- Served as General Manager of N.Y. Americans (1940–42)

- Performed the official face-off prior to Calgary Flames' first home game on October 9, 1980

REGULAR SEASON

Season	Age	Team	Lg	GP	G	A	PTS	PIM
1921–22	23	Calgary Tigers	WCHL	22	16	5	21	73
1922–23	24	Calgary Tigers	WCHL	18	2	4	6	24
1923–24	25	Calgary Tigers	WCHL	30	6	7	13	54
1924–25	26	Calgary Tigers	WCHL	23	8	4	12	72
1925–26	27	Calgary Tigers	WHL	30	10	5	15	87
1926–27	28	Montreal Maroons	NHL	44	4	4	8	108
1927–28	29	Montreal Maroons	NHL	42	7	6	13	94
1928–29	30	Montreal Maroons	NHL	44	1	3	4	139
1929–30	31	Montreal Maroons	NHL	43	3	13	16	98
1930–31	32	New York Americans	NHL	44	1	11	12	71
1931–32	33	New York Americans	NHL	47	3	5	8	107
1932–33	34	New York Americans	NHL	43	0	2	2	74
1933–34	35	New York Americans	NHL	48	2	8	19	65
1934–35	36	New York Americans	NHL	48	3	7	10	46
1935–36	37	New York Americans	NHL	46	5	8	13	69
Career — 15 Seasons				572	71	92	163	1181

PLAYOFFS

Season	Age	Team	Lg	GP	G	A	PTS	PIM
1921–22	23	Calgary Tigers	WCHL	2	0	0	0	2
1923–24	25	Calgary Tigers	St-Cup	2	0	0	0	6
1923–24	25	Calgary Tigers	WCHL	2	0	1	1	2
1923–24	25	Calgary Tigers	West-P	3	1	0	1	2
1924–25	26	Calgary Tigers	WCHL	2	0	0	0	8
1926–27	28	Montreal Maroons	NHL	2	0	0	0	4
1927–28	29	Montreal Maroons	NHL	9	1	0	1	27
1929–30	31	Montreal Maroons	NHL	4	0	0	0	2
1935–36	37	New York Americans	NHL	3	0	0	0	0
Career — 7 Seasons				29	2	1	3	53

TROPHY CASE

AWARDS

Lester Patrick Trophy (1993)

ALL-STAR SELECTIONS

WCHL First All-Star Team Defense (1922, 1923)
Second All-Star Team Coach (1939)

6

Babe Dye

HOCKEY HALL OF FAME CLASS: 1970

Alternates:
4, 7, 9, 14

Right Wing

Shoots: Right

Height: 5'-8"

Weight: 150 lbs.

Born: May 13,
1898: Hamilton,
Ontario

Died: January 3,
1962: Chicago,
Illinois

Played 11 NHL
seasons from
1919–29, 1930–31

WORLDS
CHAMPIONS
1922-23

QUICK FACTS

- Holds NHL record for most goals in a Stanley Cup Final series (9), established in Toronto St. Pats' five game series victory over Vancouver Millionaires in 1922

- Played amateur hockey with Toronto Aura Lee (1916–17); Toronto De LaSalle (1917–18); Toronto Sr. St. Pats' (1918–19)

- Led OHA-Jr. in goals (31) in 1916–17

- Led OHA-Sr. in points (14) in 1918–19; OHA-Sr. Second All-Star Team Right Wing (1919)

- Played professional baseball with Buffalo Bisons and Baltimore Orioles in the International League and turned down the opportunity to play baseball with the Philadelphia Athletics in 1921

- Nicknamed "Babe" by his teammates because of his love of baseball

- Played halfback with the Toronto Argonauts football club (1917–20)

- Signed as a free agent by Toronto St. Pats, December 15, 1919

- Led NHL in goals in 1920–21 (35), 1922–23 (26) and 1924–25 (38)

- Lcd NHL in points in 1922–23 (37) and 1924–25 (46)

- Traded to Chicago Black Hawks by Toronto for $15,000, October 18, 1926; traded to N.Y. Americans by Chicago for $15,000, October 17, 1928; traded to New Haven (Can-Am) by N.Y. Americans for George Massecar, November 13, 1929

- Coached St. Louis Flyers (1930–31)

- Coached Chicago Shamrocks (1931–32)

> I think I could do even better today with these long schedules. I could always fire a puck and I knew where it was going. I could skate when I had to. The big difference, as I see it, is the crowds are bigger and the boys are getting a lot more money then we ever did."
>
> — Babe Dye, 1961

TROPHY CASE

AWARDS

NHL Scoring Leader (1923, 1925)

Stanley Cup (1921–22)

REGULAR SEASON

Season	Age	Team	Lg	GP	G	A	PTS	PIM
1919–20	21	Toronto St. Patricks	NHL	23	11	3	14	10
1920–21	22	Hamilton Tigers	NHL	1	2	0	2	0
1920–21	22	Toronto St. Patricks	NHL	23	33	5	38	32
1921–22	23	Toronto St. Patricks	NHL	24	31	7	38	39
1922–23	24	Toronto St. Patricks	NHL	22	26	11	37	19
1923–24	25	Toronto St. Patricks	NHL	19	16	3	19	23
1924–25	26	Toronto St. Patricks	NHL	29	38	8	46	41
1925–26	27	Toronto St. Patricks	NHL	31	18	5	23	26
1926–27	28	Chicago Black Hawks	NHL	41	25	5	30	14
1927–28	29	Chicago Black Hawks	NHL	10	0	0	0	0
1928–29	30	New York Americans	NHL	42	1	0	1	17
1930–31	32	Toronto Maple Leafs	NHL	6	0	0	0	0
NHL Career — 11 Seasons				271	201	47	248	221

PLAYOFFS

Season	Age	Team	Lg	GP	G	A	PTS	PIM
1920–21	22	Toronto St. Patricks	NHL	2	0	0	0	7
1921–22	23	Toronto St. Patricks	NHL	2	2	0	2	2
1921–22	23	Toronto St. Patricks	St-Cup	5	9	1	10	3
1924–25	26	Toronto St. Patrcisk	NHL	2	0	0	0	0
1926–27	28	Chicago Black Hawks	NHL	2	0	0	0	2
1928–29	30	New York Americans	NHL	2	0	0	0	0
NHL Career — 5 Seasons				15	11	1	12	14

I was a lucky guy. There is nothing better than good teammates. I don't care what anybody says, you can't do it alone. It takes a good team for you to be a good player."

Phil Esposito

A
B
C
D
E
F
G
H
I
J
K
L
M
N
O
P
Q
R
S
T
U
V
W
X
Y
Z

7

Alternates: 77, 12

Center

Shoots: Left

Height: 6'-1"

Weight: 205 lbs.

Born: February 20, 1942: Sault Ste. Marie, Ontario

Played 18 NHL seasons from 1963–81

Phil Esposito
HOCKEY HALL OF FAME CLASS: 1984

QUICK FACTS

> I was a lucky guy. There is nothing better than good teammates. I don't care what anybody says, you can't do it alone. It takes a good team for you to be a good player."

- Holds NHL record for shots-on-goal in a single season (550), established in 1970–71
- Held NHL record for goals in regular season (76); surpassed by Wayne Gretzky (92), February 24, 1982; held NHL record for points in regular season (152); surpassed by Wayne Gretzky (164) in 1980–81
- Ranks first in NHL career game-winning goals (118); ranks third in NHL career power-play goals (249); ranks fifth in NHL career goals (717); ranks tenth in NHL career points (1,590)
- Played amateur hockey with Sault Ste. Marie Tagonas (1959–60); Sarnia Legionnaires (1960–61); Sault Ste. Marie Thunderbirds (1961–62); St. Catharines Teepees (1961–62)
- Played minor pro hockey with St. Louis Braves (1962–64)

- Led NHL in short-handed goals (5) in 1972–73; led NHL in game-winning goals in 1970–71 (16), 1971–72 (16) and 1972–73 (11); led NHL in shots-on-goal in 1970–71 (540), 1971–72 (426), 1972–73 (411) and 1973–74 (393)
- Registered 1,000th career NHL point in Boston's 4–2 victory over Vancouver Canucks, February 15, 1974; recorded 500th career NHL goal in Boston's 5–4 victory over Detroit Red Wings, December 22, 1974; recorded 700th career NHL goal in N.Y. Rangers' 6–3 victory over Washington Capitals, February 2, 1980
- Played in NHL All-Star Game (1969, 1970, 1971, 1972, 1973, 1974, 1975, 1977, 1978, 1980)

REGULAR SEASON

Season	Age	Team	Lg	GP	G	A	PTS	+/-	PIM	ESG	PPG	SHG	GWG	SOG	S%
1963-64	21	Chicago Blackhawks	NHL	27	3	2	5		2	3	0	0	0		
1964-65	22	Chicago Blackhawks	NHL	70	23	32	55		44	17	5	1	9		
1965-66	23	Chicago Blackhawks	NHL	69	27	26	53		49	20	7	0	6		
1966-67	24	Chicago Blackhawks	NHL	69	21	40	61		40	18	2	1	3		
1967-68	25	Boston Bruins	NHL	74	35	49	84	19	21	25	9	1	3	284	12.3
1968-69	26	Boston Bruins	NHL	74	49	77	126	56	79	37	10	2	9	351	14.0
1969-70	27	Boston Bruins	NHL	76	43	56	99	28	50	24	18	1	5	405	10.6
1970-71	28	Boston Bruins	NHL	78	76	76	152	71	71	50	25	1	16	550	13.8
1971-72	29	Boston Bruins	NHL	76	66	67	133	55	76	36	28	2	16	426	15.5
1972-73	30	Boston Bruins	NHL	78	55	75	130	6	87	31	19	5	11	411	13.4
1973-74	31	Boston Bruins	NHL	78	68	77	145	51	58	50	14	4	9	393	17.3
1974-75	32	Boston Bruins	NHL	79	61	66	127	18	62	30	27	4	8	347	17.6
1975-76	33	Boston Bruins	NHL	12	6	10	16	-1	8	3	3	0	0	57	10.5
1975-76	33	New York Rangers	NHL	62	29	38	67	-39	28	12	16	1	2	217	13.4
1976-77	34	New York Rangers	NHL	80	34	46	80	-28	52	19	15	0	4	344	9.9
1977-78	35	New York Rangers	NHL	79	38	43	81	-22	53	17	21	0	5	259	14.7
1978-79	36	New York Rangers	NHL	80	42	36	78	-1	37	28	14	0	7	215	19.5
1979-80	37	New York Rangers	NHL	80	34	44	78	-13	73	21	13	0	5	245	13.9
1980-81	38	New York Rangers	NHL	41	7	13	20	-13	20	4	3	0	0	91	7.7
NHL Career — 18 Seasons				1282	717	873	1590	197	910	445	249	23	118	4595	14.0

PLAYOFFS

Season	Age	Team	Lg	GP	G	A	PTS	+/-	PIM	ESG	PPG	SHG	GWG	SOG	S%
1963-64	21	Chicago Blackhawks	NHL	4	0	0	0		0						
1964-65	22	Chicago Blackhawks	NHL	13	3	3	6		15						
1965-66	23	Chicago Blackhawks	NHL	6	1	1	2		2						
1966-67	24	Chicago Blackhawks	NHL	6	0	0	0		7						
1967-68	25	Boston Bruins	NHL	4	0	3	3		0	0	0	0	0		
1968-69	26	Boston Bruins	NHL	10	8	10	18		8	3	5	0	2		
1969-70	27	Boston Bruins	NHL	14	13	14	27		16	9	4	0	2		
1970-71	28	Boston Bruins	NHL	7	3	7	10		6	1	2	0	0		
1971-72	29	Boston Bruins	NHL	15	9	15	24		24	7	2	0	3		
1972-73	30	Boston Bruins	NHL	2	0	1	1		2	0	0	0	0		
1973-74	31	Boston Bruins	NHL	16	9	5	14		25	5	4	0	2		
1974-75	32	Boston Bruins	NHL	3	4	1	5		0	3	1	0	0		
1977-78	35	New York Rangers	NHL	3	0	1	1		5	0	0	0	0		
1978-79	36	New York Rangers	NHL	18	8	12	20		20	6	2	0	2		
1979-80	37	New York Rangers	NHL	9	3	3	6		8	2	1	0	1		
NHL Career — 15 Seasons				130	61	76	137		138	36	21	0	12		

TROPHY CASE

AWARDS

Art Ross Trophy (1969, 1971, 1972, 1973, 1974)

Hart Memorial Trophy (1969, 1974)

Lester B. Pearson Award (1971, 1974)

Lester Patrick Trophy (1978)

Stanley Cup (1969–70, 1971–72)

ALL-STAR SELECTIONS

First All-Star Team Center (1969, 1970, 1971, 1972, 1973, 1974)

Second All-Star Team Center (1968, 1975)

INTERNATIONAL AWARDS

Summit Series (1972)

Canada Cup (1976)

35

Retired by Chicago

Alternates: 29, 1
Goaltender
Catches: Right
Height: 5'-11"
Weight: 185 lbs.
Born: April 23, 1943; Sault Ste. Marie, Ontario
Played 16 NHL seasons from 1968–84

Tony Esposito
HOCKEY HALL OF FAME CLASS: 1988

QUICK FACTS

- Ranks seventh in career NHL games played by a goaltender (886); ranks seventh in career NHL wins (423); ranks ninth in career NHL shutouts (76)
- First NHL rookie to win Vezina Trophy since Frank Brimsek (1970)
- Played amateur hockey with Sault Ste. Marie Greyhounds (1962–63); Michigan Tech University Huskies (1963–67)
- WCHA First All-Star Team Goaltender (1965, 1966, 1967)
- NCAA West First All-American Team Goaltender (1965, 1966, 1967); NCAA Championship All-Tournament Team Goaltender (1965)
- Played minor pro hockey with Vancouver Canucks (1967–68)
- Claimed by Chicago from Montreal in Intra-League Draft, June 11, 1969
- Signed as a free agent by Montreal (Cleveland-AHL), September 29, 1967; loaned to Vancouver Canucks (WHL) by Montreal for cash, October 1967
- Played in NHL All-Star Game (1970, 1971, 1972, 1973, 1974, 1980)
- Led NHL in wins in 1969–70 (38) and 1970–71 (35); led NHL in shutouts in 1969–70 (15), 1971–72 (9) and 1979–80 (6); led NHL in goals-against-average (1.77) in 1971–72
- Acquired American citizenship and played for Team U.S.A. in 1981 Canada Cup tournament

REGULAR SEASON

Season	Age	Team	Lg	GP	W	L	T	SO	GA	GAA	G	A	PTS	PIM
1968–69	25	Montreal Canadiens	NHL	13	5	4	4	2	34	2.73	0	0	0	0
1969–70	26	Chicago Black Hawks	NHL	63	38	17	8	15	136	2.17	0	2	2	2
1970–71	27	Chicago Black Hawks	NHL	57	35	14	6	6	126	2.27	0	1	1	4
1971–72	28	Chicago Black Hawks	NHL	48	31	10	6	9	82	1.77	0	1	1	2
1972–73	29	Chicago Black Hawks	NHL	56	32	17	7	4	140	2.51	0	2	2	0
1973–74	30	Chicago Black Hawks	NHL	70	34	14	21	10	141	2.04	0	1	1	0
1974–75	31	Chicago Black Hawks	NHL	71	34	30	7	6	193	2.74	0	1	1	11
1975–76	32	Chicago Black Hawks	NHL	68	30	23	13	4	198	2.97	0	1	1	2
1976–77	33	Chicago Black Hawks	NHL	69	25	36	8	2	234	3.45	0	2	2	6
1977–78	34	Chicago Black Hawks	NHL	64	28	22	14	5	168	2.63	0	4	4	0
1978–79	35	Chicago Black Hawks	NHL	63	24	28	11	4	206	3.27	0	1	1	2
1979–80	36	Chicago Black Hawks	NHL	69	31	22	16	6	205	2.97	0	1	1	2
1980–81	37	Chicago Black Hawks	NHL	66	29	23	14	0	246	3.75	0	3	3	0
1981–82	38	Chicago Black Hawks	NHL	52	19	25	8	1	231	4.52	0	2	2	0
1982–83	39	Chicago Black Hawks	NHL	39	23	11	5	1	135	3.46	0	0	0	0
1983–84	40	Chicago Black Hawks	NHL	18	5	10	3	1	88	4.82	0	3	3	0
NHL Career — 16 Seasons				886	423	306	151	76	2563	2.92	0	25	25	31

PLAYOFFS

Season	Age	Team	Lg	GP	W	L	T	SO	GA	GAA	G	A	PTS	PIM
1969–70	26	Chicago Black Hawks	NHL	8	4	4		0	27	3.38	0	0	0	0
1970–71	27	Chicago Black Hawks	NHL	18	11	7		2	42	2.19	0	0	0	0
1971–72	28	Chicago Black Hawks	NHL	5	2	3		0	16	3.20	0	0	0	0
1972–73	29	Chicago Black Hawks	NHL	15	10	5		1	46	3.08	0	0	0	0
1973–74	30	Chicago Black Hawks	NHL	10	6	4		2	28	2.88	0	0	0	0
1974–75	31	Chicago Black Hawks	NHL	8	3	5		0	34	4.32	0	0	0	0
1975–76	32	Chicago Black Hawks	NHL	4	0	4		0	13	3.25	0	0	0	0
1976–77	33	Chicago Black Hawks	NHL	2	0	2		0	6	3.00	0	0	0	0
1977–78	34	Chicago Black Hawks	NHL	4	0	4		0	19	4.52	0	0	0	0
1978–79	35	Chicago Black Hawks	NHL	4	0	4		0	14	3.46	0	0	0	0
1979–80	36	Chicago Black Hawks	NHL	6	3	3		0	14	2.25	0	0	0	0
1980–81	37	Chicago Black Hawks	NHL	3	0	3		0	15	4.19	0	0	0	0
1981–82	38	Chicago Black Hawks	NHL	7	3	3		1	16	2.52	0	0	0	0
1982–83	39	Chicago Black Hawks	NHL	5	3	2		0	18	3.47	0	0	0	0
NHL Career — 14 Seasons				99	45	53		6	308	3.07	0	0	0	0

TROPHY CASE

AWARDS

Calder Memorial Trophy (1970)

Vezina Trophy (1970, 1972, 1974)

Stanley Cup (1968–69)

ALL-STAR SELECTIONS

First All-Star Team Goaltender (1970, 1972, 1980)

Second All-Star Team Goaltender (1973, 1974)

INTERNATIONAL AWARDS

Summit Series (1972)

Arthur Farrell

HOCKEY HALL OF FAME CLASS: 1965

Forward

Shoots: Unknown

Height: Unknown

Weight: Unkown

Born: February 8, 1877: Montreal, Quebec

Died: February 7, 1909: Montreal, Quebec

Played five elite amateur seasons from 1896–1901

QUICK FACTS

- Played school hockey with Montreal St. Mary's College (1893–96)

- Wrote what is believed to be the first book about hockey — *Hockey: Canada's Royal Winter Game* (1899)

- Wrote books about hockey for the Spalding Sports Series in the early 1900s

- Member of Montreal Shamrocks team that also featured future Hall of Fame members Harry Trihey and Fred Scanlan

- One of the men responsible for moving the focus of hockey from individual play to a team-oriented game

- Credited with scoring five goals in a game versus the Quebec Bulldogs on January 19, 1901

- Scored 33 goals in 25 league games for the Shamrocks over four seasons

- Scored two goals in a 6–2 victory over Queen's University in a one-game Stanley Cup challenge on March 14, 1899, and had 10 goals in five games during two sets of challenges in 1900, including a pair of four-goal games

- Went into business with his father after retiring from hockey and died of tuberculosis at age 32

> "A team should feel that it can defeat any seven that opposes it ... A team that goes on the ice thinking that defeat is probable is already beaten."
>
> — Art Farrell, in *Hockey: Canada's Royal Winter Game*

REGULAR SEASON

Season	Age	Team	Lg	GP	G	A	PTS	PIM
1896–97	19	Montreal Shamrocks	AHAC	2	2	0	2	
1897–98	20	Berlin Hockey Club	OHA	2	6	0	6	
1898–99	21	Montreal Shamrocks	CAHL	8	8	0	8	
1899–00	22	Montreal Shamrocks	CAHL	7	13	0	13	
1900–01	23	Montreal Shamrocks	CAHL	8	10	0	10	
Career – 5 Seasons				27	39	0	39	

PLAYOFFS

Season	Age	Team	Lg	GP	G	A	PTS	PIM
1898–99	21	Montreal Shamrocks	St-Cup	1	2	0	2	0
1899–00	22	Montreal Shamrocks	St-Cup	5	10	0	10	0
1900–01	23	Montreal Shamrocks	St-Cup	2	1	0	1	0
Career – 3 Seasons				8	13	0	13	

TROPHY CASE

AWARDS

Stanley Cup (1898–99, 1899–1900)

24

Alternate: 42	
Center	
Shoots: Left	
Height: 6'	
Weight: 178 lbs.	
Born: May 12, 1956: Foam Lake, Saskatchewan	
Drafted by the St. Louis Blues seventh overall in 1976	
Played 14 NHL seasons from 1976–90	

Bernie Federko

HOCKEY HALL OF FAME CLASS: 2002

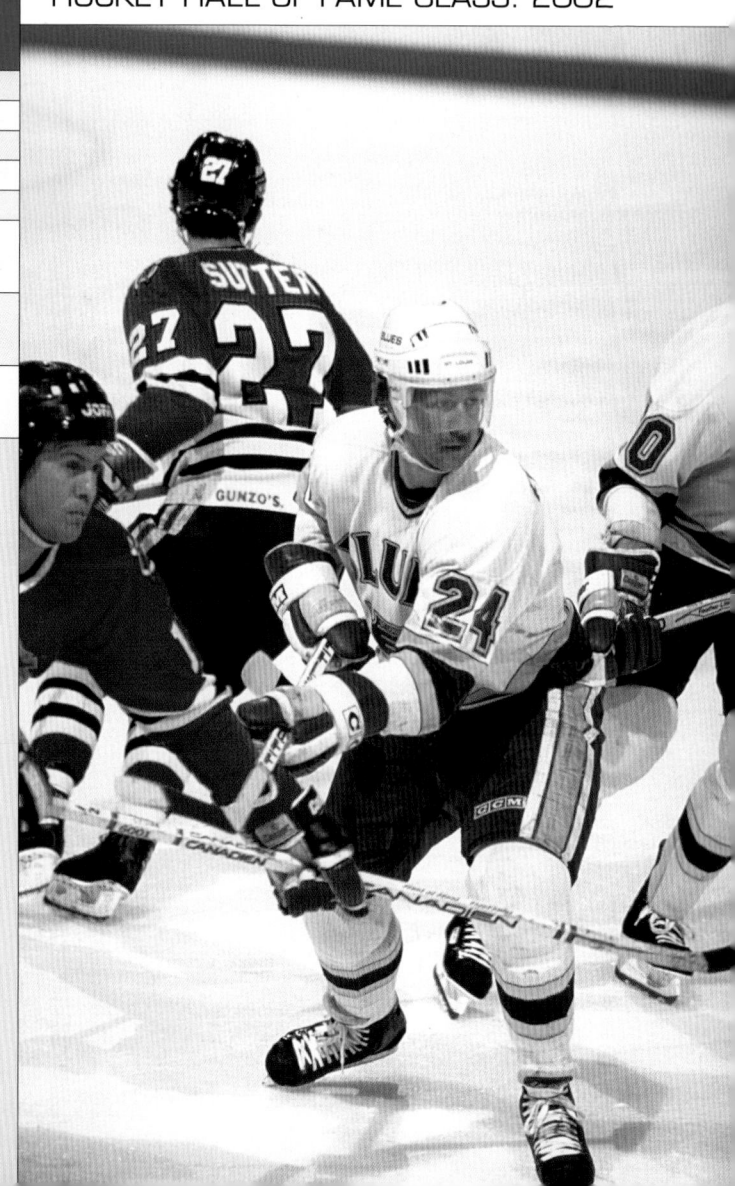

QUICK FACTS

- Holds St. Louis Blues team records for career seasons (13), games played (927), assists (721) and points (1,073)

- Ranks eleventh in NHL career assists-per-game (0.76)

- Played amateur hockey with Foam Lake Flyers (1972–73); Saskatoon Blades (1973–76)

- Led WHL in assists (115) and points (187) in 1975–76; led WHL playoffs in goals (15) in 1974–75; led WHL playoffs in assists (27) and points (45) in 1975–76

- Named WHL Player of the Year (1976); WHL First All-Star team Center (1976)

- Played minor pro hockey with Kansas City Blues (1976–77)

- Named CHL Rookie of the Year (1977); CHL Second All-Star Team Center (1977)

- First player in NHL history to record at least 50 assists in 10 consecutive seasons

- Played in NHL All-Star Game (1980, 1981)

- Led NHL playoffs in points (21) in 1985–86

- Served as captain of St. Louis Blues (1988–89)

- Registered 1,000th career NHL point in St. Louis' 5–3 loss to Hartford Whalers, March 18, 1988

- Traded to Detroit by St. Louis Blues with Tony McKegney for Adam Oates and Paul MacLean, June 15, 1989

- Nicknamed "The Magician" because of his wizardry behind the net

> I was given the opportunity by Emile Francis to be the nucleus of the Blues. I just always felt it was my job to be consistent and that they were relying on me to make sure we were going to compete all of the time."

TROPHY CASE

REGULAR SEASON

Season	Age	Team	Lg	GP	G	A	PTS	+/-	PIM	ESG	PPG	SHG	GWG	SOG	S%
1976-77	20	St. Louis Blues	NHL	31	14	9	23	-6	15	8	6	0	3	67	20.9
1977-78	21	St. Louis Blues	NHL	72	17	24	41	-35	27	13	4	0	1	128	13.3
1978-79	22	St. Louis Blues	NHL	74	31	64	95	-15	14	24	7	0	1	156	19.9
1979-80	23	St. Louis Blues	NHL	79	38	56	94	3	24	31	7	0	4	184	20.7
1980-81	24	St. Louis Blues	NHL	78	31	73	104	9	47	20	9	2	4	170	18.2
1981-82	25	St. Louis Blues	NHL	74	30	62	92	-10	70	19	11	0	6	177	16.9
1982-83	26	St. Louis Blues	NHL	75	24	60	84	-10	24	15	9	0	1	184	13.0
1983-84	27	St. Louis Blues	NHL	79	41	66	107	-3	43	27	14	0	4	197	20.8
1984-85	28	St. Louis Blues	NHL	76	30	73	103	-10	27	24	6	0	3	174	17.2
1985-86	29	St. Louis Blues	NHL	80	34	68	102	10	34	18	16	0	2	167	20.4
1986-87	30	St. Louis Blues	NHL	64	20	52	72	-25	32	11	9	0	3	130	15.4
1987-88	31	St. Louis Blues	NHL	79	20	69	89	-12	52	11	9	0	2	119	16.8
1988-89	32	St. Louis Blues	NHL	66	22	45	67	-20	54	13	9	0	6	115	19.1
1989-90	33	Detroit Red Wings	NHL	73	17	40	57	-8	24	14	3	0	0	108	15.7
NHL Career – 14 Seasons				1000	369	761	1130	-132	487	248	119	2	40	2076	17.8

PLAYOFFS

Season	Age	Team	Lg	GP	G	A	PTS	+/-	PIM	ESG	PPG	SHG	GWG	SOG	S%
1976-77	20	St. Louis Blues	NHL	4	1	1	2		2	1	0	0	0		
1979-80	23	St. Louis Blues	NHL	3	1	0	1		2	1	0	0	0		
1980-81	24	St. Louis Blues	NHL	11	8	10	18		2	4	4	0	1		
1981-82	25	St. Louis Blues	NHL	10	3	15	18		10	2	1	0	1		
1982-83	26	St. Louis Blues	NHL	4	2	3	5		0	1	1	0	0		
1983-84	27	St. Louis Blues	NHL	11	4	4	8	-5	10	3	1	0	1	26	15.4
1984-85	28	St. Louis Blues	NHL	3	0	2	2	1	4	0	0	0	0	3	0.0
1985-86	29	St. Louis Blues	NHL	19	7	14	21	2	17	6	1	0	1	34	20.6
1986-87	30	St. Louis Blues	NHL	6	3	3	6	0	18	2	1	0	0	9	33.3
1987-88	31	St. Louis Blues	NHL	10	2	6	8	-6	18	0	2	0	0	8	25.0
1988-89	32	St. Louis Blues	NHL	10	4	8	12	-2	0	2	2	0	0	19	21.1
NHL Career – 11 Seasons				91	35	66	101	-10	83	22	13	0	4	99	20.2

2

Viacheslav Fetisov
HOCKEY HALL OF FAME CLASS: 2001

Defense

Shoots: Left

Height: 6'-1"

Weight: 220 lbs.

Born: April 20, 1958: Moscow, Union of Soviet Socialist Republics

Drafted by the Montreal Canadiens 201st overall in 1978

Drafted by the New Jersey Devils 150th overall in 1983 (re-entry)

Played nine NHL seasons from 1989–98

QUICK FACTS

- Shares New Jersey Devils team record (with Tom Kurvers and Bruce Driver) for points in a regular season game by a defenseman (5), March 29, 1990
- Played amateur hockey with CSKA Moscow (1974–89)
- Named USSR Player of Year (1986); USSR First All-Star Team Defense (1984, 1985, 1986, 1987, 1988)
- Won Golden Stick Award (European Player of Year) in 1984, 1986 and 1990
- Canada Cup First All-Star Team Defense (1987)
- Named World Championships Most Valuable Player (1989); named World Championships Best Defenseman (1985, 1986, 1989)
- Won USSR Pravda Trophy (most points by a defenseman) in 1984, 1986, 1987, 1988

- World Championships First All-Star Team Defense (1985, 1986, 1987, 1989, 1990, 1991)
- Among a group of eight Soviet players who were allowed to play in the NHL in 1989 on the provision they continue to play internationally for the Soviet Union
- Played in NHL All-Star Game (1997, 1998)
- Served as assistant coach with New Jersey (1998–2002)
- Received IOC Olympic Order (2000); inducted into IIHF Hall of Fame (2005)
- Coached bronze medal-winning Team Russia at 2002 Winter Olympic Games in Salt Lake City, Utah
- Came out of retirement after 11 years at age 51 to play for CSKA Moscow for one game, December 11, 2009

> I was the first Soviet to sign a direct contract with the NHL, and I'm proud to say that not only hockey players followed me. The door opened for people in every profession."

REGULAR SEASON

Season	Age	Team	Lg	GP	G	A	PTS	+/-	PIM	ESG	PPG	SHG	GWG	SOG	S%
1989-90	31	New Jersey Devils	NHL	72	8	34	42	9	52	6	2	0	0	108	7.4
1990-91	32	New Jersey Devils	NHL	67	3	16	19	5	62	2	1	0	0	71	4.2
1991-92	33	New Jersey Devils	NHL	70	3	23	26	11	108	3	0	0	1	70	4.3
1992-93	34	New Jersey Devils	NHL	76	4	23	27	7	158	2	1	1	0	63	6.3
1993-94	35	New Jersey Devils	NHL	52	1	14	15	14	30	1	0	0	0	36	2.8
1994-95	36	New Jersey Devils	NHL	4	0	1	1	-2	0	0	0	0	0	1	0.0
1994-95	36	Detroit Red Wings	NHL	14	3	11	14	3	2	0	3	0	0	36	8.3
1995-96	37	Detroit Red Wings	NHL	69	7	35	42	37	96	5	1	1	1	127	5.5
1996-97	38	Detroit Red Wings	NHL	64	5	23	28	26	76	5	0	0	1	95	5.3
1997-98	39	Detroit Red Wings	NHL	58	2	12	14	4	72	2	0	0	1	55	3.6
NHL Career – 9 Seasons				546	36	192	228	114	656	26	8	2	4	662	5.4

PLAYOFFS

Season	Age	Team	Lg	GP	G	A	PTS	+/-	PIM	ESG	PPG	SHG	GWG	SOG	S%
1989-90	31	New Jersey Devils	NHL	6	0	2	2	-5	10	0	0	0	0	11	0.0
1990-91	32	New Jersey Devils	NHL	7	0	0	0	-3	17	0	0	0	0	7	0.0
1991-92	33	New Jersey Devils	NHL	6	0	3	3	5	8	0	0	0	0	3	0.0
1992-93	34	New Jersey Devils	NHL	5	0	2	2	-3	4	0	0	0	0	2	0.0
1993-94	35	New Jersey Devils	NHL	14	1	0	1	-1	8	1	0	0	0	14	7.1
1994-95	36	Detroit Red Wings	NHL	18	0	8	8	1	14	0	0	0	0	31	0.0
1995-96	37	Detroit Red Wings	NHL	19	1	4	5	3	34	1	0	0	1	24	4.2
1996-97	38	Detroit Red Wings	NHL	20	0	4	4	2	42	0	0	0	0	27	0.0
1997-98	39	Detroit Red Wings	NHL	21	0	3	3	4	10	0	0	0	0	14	0.0
NHL Career – 9 Seasons				116	2	26	28	3	147	2	0	0	1	133	1.5

TROPHY CASE

AWARDS

Stanley Cup (1996–97, 1997–98)

INTERNATIONAL AWARDS

Canada Cup (1981)

Gold Medal: Winter Olympics (1984, 1988)

Silver Medal: Winter Olympics (1980)

Gold Medal: World Championships (1978, 1981, 1982, 1983, 1986, 1989, 1990)

Silver Medal: World Championships (1987)

Bronze Medal: World Championships (1977, 1985, 1991)

14

Fernie Flaman

HOCKEY HALL OF FAME CLASS: 1990

Alternates:
10, 12, 15, 4, 3, 6

Defense

Shoots: Right

Height: 5'-10"

Weight: 190 lbs.

Born: January
25, 1927: Dysart,
Saskatchewan

Played 17 NHL
seasons from
1944–61

QUICK FACTS

- Played amateur hockey with Regina Abbots (1942–43)

- Played first regular-season game for Boston at age 18 and became a full-time player late in his third year

- Considered the toughest defenseman of his era, he was noted for his body-checking and shot-blocking

- Traded to Toronto by Boston with Ken Smith, Phil Maloney and Leo Boivin for Bill Ezinicki and Vic Lynn, November 16, 1950

- Traded to Boston by Toronto for Dave Creighton, July 20, 1954

- Served as captain of Boston Bruins (1956–61)

- Led NHL in penalty minutes (150) in 1954–55

- One of the founders of the first NHL Players Association in 1958

- Served as player/coach/General Manager of Rhode Island/Providence Reds (1961–65)

- Coached Los Angeles Blades (1966–67)

- Served as coach/GM of the Fort Worth Red Wings (1967–69)

- Served as scout for Boston Bruins (1969–70)

- Coached Northeastern University Huskies (1970–89); coached Northeastern University to Hockey East championship (1989)

- Named ECAC and NCAA Division I Coach of the Year (1982)

> "Fernie was the toughest guy out there. Strong on his skates. I tell you, he didn't lose too many."
> — NHL official Art Skov

REGULAR SEASON

Season	Age	Team	Lg	GP	G	A	PTS	PIM
1944–45	18	Boston Bruins	NHL	1	0	0	0	0
1945–46	19	Boston Bruins	NHL	1	0	0	0	0
1946–47	20	Boston Bruins	NHL	23	1	4	5	41
1947–48	21	Boston Bruins	NHL	56	4	6	10	69
1948–49	22	Boston Bruins	NHL	60	4	12	16	62
1949–50	23	Boston Bruins	NHL	69	2	5	7	122
1950–51	24	Boston Bruins	NHL	14	1	1	2	37
1950–51	24	Toronto Maple Leafs	NHL	39	2	6	8	64
1951–52	25	Toronto Maple Leafs	NHL	61	0	7	7	110
1952–53	26	Toronto Maple Leafs	NHL	66	2	6	8	110
1953–54	27	Toronto Maple Leafs	NHL	62	0	8	8	84
1954–55	28	Boston Bruins	NHL	70	4	14	18	150
1955–56	29	Boston Bruins	NHL	62	4	17	21	70
1956–57	30	Boston Bruins	NHL	68	6	25	31	108
1957–58	31	Boston Bruins	NHL	66	0	15	15	71
1958–59	32	Boston Bruins	NHL	70	0	21	21	101
1959–60	33	Boston Bruins	NHL	60	2	18	20	112
1960–61	34	Boston Bruins	NHL	62	2	9	11	59
NHL Career – 17 Seasons				910	34	174	208	1370

PLAYOFFS

Season	Age	Team	Lg	GP	G	A	PTS	PIM
1946–47	20	Boston Bruins	NHL	5	0	0	0	8
1947–48	21	Boston Bruins	NHL	5	0	0	0	12
1948–49	22	Boston Bruins	NHL	5	0	1	1	8
1950–51	24	Toronto Maple Leafs	NHL	9	1	0	1	8
1951–52	25	Toronto Maple Leafs	NHL	4	0	2	2	18
1953–54	27	Toronto Maple Leafs	NHL	2	0	0	0	0
1954–55	28	Boston Bruins	NHL	4	1	0	1	2
1956–57	30	Boston Bruins	NHL	10	0	3	3	19
1957–58	31	Boston Bruins	NHL	12	2	2	4	10
1958–59	32	Boston Bruins	NHL	7	0	0	0	8
NHL Career – 10 Seasons				63	4	8	12	93

TROPHY CASE

AWARDS

Stanley Cup (1950–51)

ALL-STAR SELECTIONS

Second All-Star Team Defense (1955, 1957, 1958)

4

Frank Foyston
HOCKEY HALL OF FAME CLASS: 1958

Alternates:
10, 5, 9

Center/
Right Wing

Shoots: Left

Height: 5'-9"

Weight: 158 lbs.

Born: February 2,
1891: Minesing,
Ontario

Died: January 19,
1966: Seattle,
Washington

Played 16
professional
seasons from
1912–28

"You missed one of the all-time greats if you never saw Frank Foyston perform with a hockey stick. He wielded it like [conductor] Fritz Kreisler his bow, Willie Mays his bat and Arnold Palmer his two-iron."

— Eulogy in the *Seattle Post-Intelligencer*

QUICK FACTS

- Played amateur hockey with Barrie Athletic Club (1908–11); Toronto Eatons (1911–12)
- OHA-Jr. First All-Star Team Center (1909)
- Led OHA-Sr. playoffs in goals (5) in 1911–12
- Led PCHA playoffs in goals (3) in 1918–19
- Led Stanley Cup playoffs in goals (9) and points (10) in 1918–19; goals (6) and points (7) in 1919–20
- Led PCHA in goals in 1919–20 (26) and 1920–21 (26)
- One of several Toronto players lured to the Pacific Coast Hockey Association when the Seattle Metropolitans were added to the league in 1915–16
- Named PCHA Most Valuable Player (1917)
- Ranked third in the PCHA with a career-high 36 goals in 1916–17

- Member of Stanley Cup-winning Seattle Metropolitans — first American-based team to win the Stanley Cup (1916–17)
- Member of PCHA champion Seattle Metropolitans (1917, 1919, 1920)
- Member of WHL champion Victoria Cougars (1925, 1926)
- Member of Stanley Cup-winning Victoria Cougars — last non-NHL club to win the Stanley Cup (1924–25)
- Served as player/coach of Detroit Olympics (1927–28, 1928–30)
- Coached Bronx Tigers (1931–32); coached Seattle Seahawks (1934–36)

Foyston's 1923–24 Seattle Metropolitans jersey, the last season for the Mets.

REGULAR SEASON

Season	Age	Team	Lg	GP	G	A	PTS	PIM
1912–13	21	Toronto Blueshirts	NHA	16	8	0	8	8
1913–14	22	Toronto Blueshirts	NHA	19	16	2	18	8
1914–15	23	Toronto Blueshirts	NHA	20	13	9	22	11
1915–16	24	Toronto Blueshirts	NHA	1	0	0	0	0
1915–16	24	Seattle Metropolitans	PCHA	18	9	4	13	6
1916–17	25	Seattle Metropolitans	PCHA	24	36	12	48	51
1917–18	26	Seattle Metropolitans	PCHA	13	9	5	14	9
1918–19	27	Seattle Metropolitans	PCHA	18	15	4	19	0
1919–20	28	Seattle Metropolitans	PCHA	22	26	3	29	3
1920–21	29	Seattle Metropolitans	PCHA	23	26	4	30	10
1921–22	30	Seattle Metropolitans	PCHA	24	16	7	23	25
1922–23	31	Seattle Metropolitans	PCHA	30	20	8	28	21
1923–24	32	Seattle Metropolitans	PCHA	30	17	6	23	8
1924–25	33	Victoria Cougars	WCHL	27	6	5	11	6
1925–26	34	Victoria Cougars	WHL	12	6	3	9	8
1926–27	35	Detroit Cougars	NHL	41	10	5	15	16
1927–28	36	Detroit Cougars	NHL	23	7	2	9	16
Career — 16 Seasons				361	240	79	319	206

PLAYOFFS

Season	Age	Team	Lg	GP	G	A	PTS	PIM
1913–14	22	Toronto Blueshirts	NHA	2	1	0	1	0
1913–14	22	Toronto Blueshirts	St-Cup	3	2	0	2	3
1916–17	25	Seattle Metropolitans	St-Cup	4	7	3	10	3
1917–18	26	Seattle Metropolitans	PCHA	2	0	0	0	3
1918–19	27	Seattle Metropolitans	PCHA	2	3	0	3	0
1918–19	27	Seattle Metropolitans	St-Cup	5	9	1	10	0
1919–20	28	Seattle Metropolitans	PCHA	2	3	1	4	0
1919–20	28	Seattle Metropolitans	St-Cup	5	6	1	7	7
1920–21	29	Seattle Metropolitans	PCHA	2	1	0	1	0
1921–22	30	Seattle Metropolitans	PCHA	2	0	0	0	3
1923–24	32	Seattle Metropolitans	PCHA	2	1	0	1	0
1924–25	33	Victoria Cougars	St-Cup	4	1	0	1	0
1924–25	33	Victoria Cougars	WCHL	4	1	1	2	2
1925–26	34	Victoria Cougars	St-Cup	4	0	0	0	2
1925–26	34	Victoria Cougars	WHL	3	2	0	2	4
Career — 10 Seasons				46	42	7	49	27

TROPHY CASE

AWARDS

Stanley Cup (1913–14, 1916–17, 1924–25)

ALL-STAR SELECTIONS

PCHA First All-Star Team Center (1917, 1918, 1920, 1921, 1923, 1924)

PCHA Second All-Star Team Center (1919, 1922)

Ron Francis
HOCKEY HALL OF FAME CLASS: 2007

10

Retired by Carolina/Hartford

Alternates:
9, 4, 21

Center

Shoots: Left

Height: 6'-3"

Weight: 200 lbs.

Born: March 1,
1963: Sault Ste.
Marie, Ontario

Drafted by
the Hartford
Whalers fourth
overall in 1981

Played 23 NHL
seasons from
1981–2004

QUICK FACTS

- Shares NHL record (with Gordie Howe) for most consecutive seasons with at least 50 points (22)
- Holds Hartford/Carolina team records for career games (1,186), seasons (16), goals (382), assists (793) and points (1,175)
- Holds Hartford/Carolina team records for career playoff assists (25) and points (39)
- Ranks fourth in NHL career points (1,798); ranks second in NHL career assists (1,249)
- Played amateur hockey with Sault Ste. Marie Legionnaires (1979–80); Sault Ste. Marie Greyhounds (1980–82)

- Led NHL in assists in 1994–95 (48) and 1995–96 (92)
- Led NHL in plus/minus (+30) in 1994–95
- Nicknamed "Ronnie Franchise"
- Served as captain of Hartford Whalers (1984–85, 1985–91); served as captain of Pittsburgh Penguins (1994–95, 1997–98)
- Served as captain of Carolina Hurricanes (1999–2000, 2000–04)
- Only player in NHL history to captain two separate franchises (Hartford/Carolina and Pittsburgh) on two separate occasions

> As a kid growing up in the little city of Sault Ste. Marie, Ontario, I dreamed of one day playing in the NHL, but never did I expect it to be as much fun as it turned out to be."

REGULAR SEASON

Season	Age	Team	Lg	GP	G	A	PTS	+/-	PIM	ESG	PPG	SHG	GWG	SOG	S%
1981–82	18	Hartford Whalers	NHL	59	25	43	68	-13	51	13	12	0	1	163	15.3
1982–83	19	Hartford Whalers	NHL	79	31	59	90	-25	60	25	4	2	4	212	14.6
1983–84	20	Hartford Whalers	NHL	72	23	60	83	-10	45	18	5	0	5	202	11.4
1984–85	21	Hartford Whalers	NHL	80	24	57	81	-23	66	20	4	0	1	195	12.3
1985–86	22	Hartford Whalers	NHL	53	24	53	77	8	24	16	7	1	4	120	20.0
1986–87	23	Hartford Whalers	NHL	75	30	63	93	10	45	23	7	0	7	189	15.9
1987–88	24	Hartford Whalers	NHL	80	25	50	75	-8	87	13	11	1	3	172	14.5
1988–89	25	Hartford Whalers	NHL	69	29	48	77	4	36	21	8	0	4	156	18.6
1989–90	26	Hartford Whalers	NHL	80	32	69	101	13	73	16	15	1	5	170	18.8
1990–91	27	Hartford Whalers	NHL	67	21	55	76	-2	51	10	10	1	6	149	14.1
1990–91	27	Pittsburgh Penguins	NHL	14	2	9	11	0	21	2	0	0	1	25	8.0
1991–92	28	Pittsburgh Penguins	NHL	70	21	33	54	-7	30	15	5	1	2	121	17.4
1992–93	29	Pittsburgh Penguins	NHL	84	24	76	100	6	68	13	9	2	4	215	11.2
1993–94	30	Pittsburgh Penguins	NHL	82	27	66	93	-3	62	19	8	0	2	216	12.5
1994–95	31	Pittsburgh Penguins	NHL	44	11	48	59	30	18	8	3	0	1	94	11.7
1995–96	32	Pittsburgh Penguins	NHL	77	27	92	119	25	56	14	12	1	4	158	17.1
1996–97	33	Pittsburgh Penguins	NHL	81	27	63	90	7	20	16	10	1	2	183	14.8
1997–98	34	Pittsburgh Penguins	NHL	81	25	62	87	12	20	18	7	0	5	189	13.2
1998–99	35	Carolina Hurricanes	NHL	82	21	31	52	-2	34	13	8	0	2	133	15.8
1999–00	36	Carolina Hurricanes	NHL	78	23	50	73	10	18	16	7	0	4	150	15.3
2000–01	37	Carolina Hurricanes	NHL	82	15	50	65	-15	32	8	7	0	4	130	11.5
2001–02	38	Carolina Hurricanes	NHL	80	27	50	77	4	18	13	14	0	5	165	16.4
2002–03	39	Carolina Hurricanes	NHL	82	22	35	57	-22	30	13	8	1	1	156	14.1
2003–04	40	Carolina Hurricanes	NHL	68	10	20	30	-12	14	5	5	0	1	79	12.7
2003–04	40	Toronto Maple Leafs	NHL	12	3	7	10	3	0	1	2	0	1	12	25.0
NHL Career — 23 Seasons				1731	549	1249	1798	-10	979	349	188	12	79	3754	14.6

PLAYOFFS

Season	Age	Team	Lg	GP	G	A	PTS	+/-	PIM	ESG	PPG	SHG	GWG	SOG	S%
1985–86	22	Hartford Whalers	NHL	10	1	2	3	-1	4	1	0	0	0	27	3.7
1986–87	23	Hartford Whalers	NHL	6	2	2	4	-1	6	1	1	0	0	15	13.3
1987–88	24	Hartford Whalers	NHL	6	2	5	7	5	2	1	1	0	0	8	25.0
1988–89	25	Hartford Whalers	NHL	4	0	2	2	-2	0	0	0	0	0	10	0.0
1989–90	26	Hartford Whalers	NHL	7	3	3	6	2	8	2	1	0	0	14	14.3
1990–91	27	Pittsburgh Penguins	NHL	24	7	10	17	13	24	7	0	0	4	48	14.6
1991–92	28	Pittsburgh Penguins	NHL	21	8	19	27	6	6	6	2	0	2	58	13.8
1992–93	29	Pittsburgh Penguins	NHL	12	6	11	17	5	19	5	1	0	1	26	23.1
1993–94	30	Pittsburgh Penguins	NHL	6	0	2	2	-2	6	0	0	0	0	9	0.0
1994–95	31	Pittsburgh Penguins	NHL	12	6	13	19	3	4	4	2	0	0	30	20.0
1995–96	32	Pittsburgh Penguins	NHL	11	3	6	9	3	4	1	2	0	1	23	13.0
1996–97	33	Pittsburgh Penguins	NHL	5	1	2	3	-7	2	1	0	0	0	6	16.7
1997–98	34	Pittsburgh Penguins	NHL	6	1	5	6	5	2	1	0	0	0	19	5.3
1998–99	35	Carolina Hurricanes	NHL	3	0	1	1	1	0	0	0	0	0	4	0.0
2000–01	37	Carolina Hurricanes	NHL	3	0	0	0	-2	0	0	0	0	0	5	0.0
2001–02	38	Carolina Hurricanes	NHL	23	6	10	16	-2	6	2	4	0	3	51	11.8
2003–04	40	Toronto Maple Leafs	NHL	12	0	4	4	0	2	0	0	0	0	14	0.0
NHL Career — 17 Seasons				171	46	97	143	28	95	31	15	0	11	374	12.3

TROPHY CASE

AWARDS

Frank J. Selke Trophy (1995)

Lady Byng Memorial Trophy (1995, 1998, 2002)

King Clancy Memorial Trophy (2002)

Stanley Cup (1990–91, 1991–92)

INTERNATIONAL AWARDS

Silver Medal: World Championship (1985)

5

Frank Fredrickson

HOCKEY HALL OF FAME CLASS: 1958

Alternates:
4, 10, 7, 17

Center

Shoots: Left

Height: 5'-11"

Weight: 180 lbs.

Born: June 11, 1895: Winnipeg, Manitoba

Died: May 28, 1979: Vancouver, British Columbia

Played 11 professional seasons from 1920–31

QUICK FACTS

- Played amateur hockey with Winnipeg Falcons (1913–16, 1919–20); Winnipeg 223rd Battalion (1916–17)
- Studied Law and Liberal Arts at the University of Manitoba before enlisting in the armed forces
- Led Manitoba Senior league in goals (13) and points (16) in 1915–16, goals (17) and points (20) in 1916–17, goals (23) and points (28) in 1919–20
- Captained the Winnipeg Falcon team that represented Canada and captured the gold medal at the 1920 Olympics, in which hockey was a demonstration sport
- Signed as a free agent by Victoria Aristocrats (PCHA), December 23, 1920
- Led PCHA in goals (39), assists (16) and points (55) in 1922–23

- Rights transferred to Detroit after NHL club purchased Victoria (WHL) franchise, May 15, 1926
- Traded to Boston by Detroit with Harry Meeking for Duke Keats and Archie Briden, January 7, 1927
- Traded to Pittsburgh by Boston for Mickey MacKay and $12,000, December 21, 1928
- Coached Pittsburgh Pirates (1929–30)
- Coached Princeton University (1933–35); coached Sea Island Flyers (1940–45); coached University of British Columbia (1945–50)
- Inducted into UBC Sports Hall of Fame (1983); inducted into Manitoba Sports Hall of Fame (1980); inducted into Canadian Olympic Hall of Fame (2006)

"My best outlet was hockey. I got my first pair of skates when I was five and had a great time learning to play. In 1914 I enrolled at the University of Manitoba, took liberal arts courses, and a year later was named captain of the hockey team."

REGULAR SEASON

Season	Age	Team	Lg	GP	G	A	PTS	PIM
1920–21	25	Victoria Aristocrats	PCHA	21	20	12	32	3
1921–22	26	Victoria Aristocrats	PCHA	24	15	10	25	26
1922–23	27	Victoria Cougars	PCHA	30	39	16	55	26
1923–24	28	Victoria Cougars	PCHA	30	19	8	27	28
1924–25	29	Victoria Cougars	WCHL	28	22	8	30	43
1925–26	30	Victoria Cougars	WHL	30	16	8	24	89
1926–27	31	Detroit Cougars	NHL	16	4	6	10	12
1926–27	31	Boston Bruins	NHL	28	14	7	21	33
1927–28	32	Boston Bruins	NHL	41	10	4	14	83
1928–29	33	Boston Bruins	NHL	12	3	1	4	24
1928–29	33	Pittsburgh Pirates	NHL	31	3	7	10	28
1929–30	34	Pittsburgh Pirates	NHL	9	4	7	11	20
1930–31	35	Detroit Falcons	NHL	24	1	2	3	6
Career — 11 Seasons				324	170	96	266	421

PLAYOFFS

Season	Age	Team	Lg	GP	G	A	PTS	PIM
1922–23	27	Victoria Cougars	PCHA	2	2	0	2	4
1924–25	29	Victoria Cougars	St-Cup	4	3	2	5	6
1924–25	29	Victoria Cougars	WCHL	4	3	1	4	2
1925–26	30	Victoria Cougars	St-Cup	4	1	1	2	10
1925–26	30	Victoria Cougars	WHL	4	2	1	3	6
1926–27	31	Boston Bruins	NHL	8	2	2	4	20
1927–28	32	Boston Bruins	NHL	2	0	1	1	4
Career — 5 Seasons				28	13	8	21	52

TROPHY CASE

AWARDS

Stanley Cup
(1924–1925)

ALL-STAR SELECTIONS

PCHA First All-Star Team Center (1921, 1922, 1923, 1924)

WHL First All-Star Team Center (1926)

INTERNATIONAL AWARDS

Gold Medal: Winter Olympics (1920)

31

Retired by Edmonton

Alternate: 1
Goaltender
Catches: Right
Height: 5'-10"
Weight: 201 lbs.
Born: September 28, 1962: Spruce Grove, Alberta
Drafted by the Edmonton Oilers eighth overall in 1981
Played 19 NHL seasons from 1981–2000

Grant Fuhr
HOCKEY HALL OF FAME CLASS: 2003

> It was a great honor as a kid to get drafted to the National Hockey League, but for me it was kind of a bonus. I got drafted to my hometown."

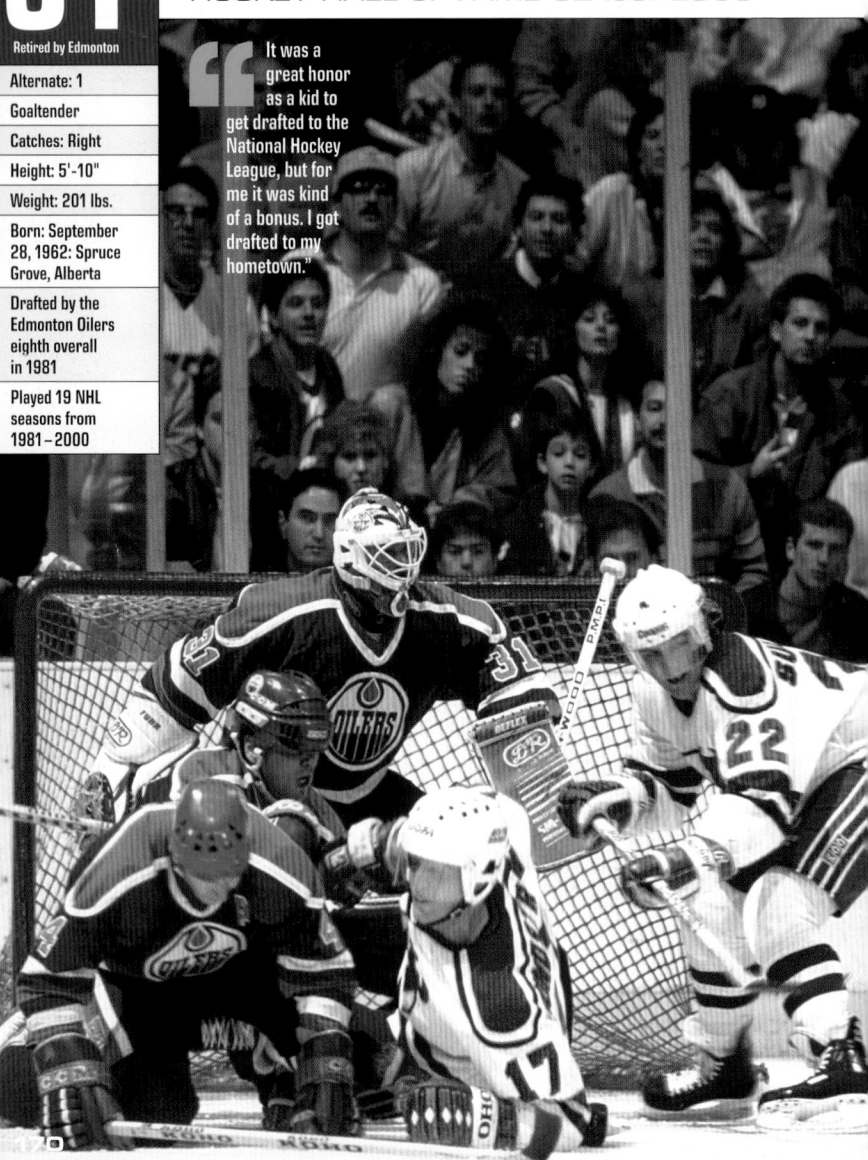

QUICK FACTS

- Holds NHL record for most games played by a goaltender in regular season (79) and most consecutive starts by a goaltender in regular season (76), established in 1995–96
- Holds NHL record for assists (14) and points (14) by a goaltender in regular season, established in 1983–84
- Shares NHL record for most wins in a single playoff season (16), established in 1987–88
- Ranks third in all-time NHL playoff wins (92)
- Ranks ninth in NHL career wins (403)
- Ranks eighth in NHL career shots against (21,873)
- Played amateur hockey with Sherwood Park Crusaders (1978–79); Victoria Cougars (1979–81)
- Named WHL Rookie of the Year (1980); Named WHL Top Goaltender (1981)
- WHL First All-Star Team Goaltender (1980, 1981)
- Led WHL in wins (48), shutouts (4) and goals-against-average (2.78) in 1980–81; led WHL playoffs in wins (12), shutouts (1) and goals-against-average (3.00)
- Played in NHL All-Star Game (1982, 1984, 1985, 1986, 1988, 1989)
- Led NHL in wins in 1983–84 (30) and 1987–88 (40); led NHL in shutouts (4) in 1987–88
- Traded to Toronto by Edmonton with Glenn Anderson and Craig Berube for Vincent Damphousse, Peter Ing, Scott Thornton and Luke Richardson, September 19, 1991

Fuhr's last traditional-style mask, which he wore in 1984–85.

REGULAR SEASON

Season	Age	Team	Lg	GP	W	L	T	SO	GA	GAA	G	A	PTS	PIM
1981–82	19	Edmonton Oilers	NHL	48	28	5	14	0	157	3.31	0	0	0	0
1982–83	20	Edmonton Oilers	NHL	32	13	12	5	0	129	4.29	0	0	0	6
1983–84	21	Edmonton Oilers	NHL	45	30	10	4	1	171	3.91	0	14	14	6
1984–85	22	Edmonton Oilers	NHL	46	26	8	7	1	165	3.87	0	3	3	6
1985–86	23	Edmonton Oilers	NHL	40	29	8	0	0	143	3.93	0	2	2	0
1986–87	24	Edmonton Oilers	NHL	44	22	13	3	0	137	3.44	0	2	2	6
1987–88	25	Edmonton Oilers	NHL	75	40	24	9	4	246	3.43	0	8	8	16
1988–89	26	Edmonton Oilers	NHL	59	23	26	6	1	213	3.83	0	1	1	6
1989–90	27	Edmonton Oilers	NHL	21	9	7	3	1	70	3.89	0	0	0	2
1990–91	28	Edmonton Oilers	NHL	13	6	4	3	1	39	3.01	0	0	0	0
1991–92	29	Toronto Maple Leafs	NHL	66	25	33	5	2	230	3.66	0	1	1	4
1992–93	30	Toronto Maple Leafs	NHL	29	13	9	4	1	87	3.14	0	0	0	0
1992–93	30	Buffalo Sabres	NHL	29	11	15	2	0	98	3.47	0	0	0	10
1993–94	31	Buffalo Sabres	NHL	32	13	12	3	2	106	3.68	0	4	4	16
1994–95	32	Buffalo Sabres	NHL	3	1	2	0	0	12	4.00	0	0	0	0
1994–95	32	Los Angeles Kings	NHL	14	1	7	3	0	47	4.04	0	0	0	2
1995–96	33	St. Louis Blues	NHL	79	30	28	16	3	209	2.87	0	1	1	8
1996–97	34	St. Louis Blues	NHL	73	33	27	11	3	193	2.72	0	2	2	6
1997–98	35	St. Louis Blues	NHL	58	29	21	6	3	138	2.53	0	2	2	6
1998–99	36	St. Louis Blues	NHL	39	16	11	8	2	89	2.44	0	0	0	12
1999–00	37	Calgary Flames	NHL	23	5	13	2	0	77	3.83	0	0	0	2
NHL Career — 19 Seasons				868	403	295	114	25	2756	3.38	0	40	40	114

PLAYOFFS

Season	Age	Team	Lg	GP	W	L	T	SO	GA	GAA	G	A	PTS	PIM
1981–82	19	Edmonton Oilers	NHL	5	2	3		0	26	5.05	0	1	1	0
1982–83	20	Edmonton Oilers	NHL	1	0	0		0	0	0.00	0	0	0	0
1983–84	21	Edmonton Oilers	NHL	16	11	4		1	44	2.99	0	3	3	4
1984–85	22	Edmonton Oilers	NHL	18	15	3		0	55	3.10	0	3	3	2
1985–86	23	Edmonton Oilers	NHL	9	5	4		0	28	3.11	0	1	1	0
1986–87	24	Edmonton Oilers	NHL	19	14	5		0	47	2.46	0	1	1	0
1987–88	25	Edmonton Oilers	NHL	19	16	2		0	55	2.90	0	1	1	6
1988–89	26	Edmonton Oilers	NHL	7	3	4		1	24	3.45	0	0	0	0
1990–91	28	Edmonton Oilers	NHL	17	8	7		0	51	3.00	0	2	2	2
1992–93	30	Buffalo Sabres	NHL	8	3	4		1	27	3.42	0	0	0	2
1995–96	33	St. Louis Blues	NHL	2	1	0		0	1	0.87	0	0	0	0
1996–97	34	St. Louis Blues	NHL	6	2	4		2	13	2.18	0	0	0	4
1997–98	35	St. Louis Blues	NHL	10	6	4		0	28	2.73	0	1	1	2
1998–99	36	St. Louis Blues	NHL	13	6	6		1	31	2.35	0	1	1	2
NHL Career — 14 Seasons				150	92	50		6	430	2.92	0	14	14	24

TROPHY CASE

AWARDS

Vezina Trophy (1988)

William M. Jennings Trophy (1994)

Stanley Cup (1983–84, 1984–85, 1986–87, 1987–88, 1989–90)

ALL-STAR SELECTIONS

First All-Star Team Goaltender (1988)

Second All-Star Team Goaltender (1982)

INTERNATIONAL AWARDS

Canada Cup (1984, 1987)

Bronze Medal: World Championships (1988)

A good hockey player plays where the puck is. A great hockey player plays where the puck is going to be."

Wayne Gretzky

A
B
C
D
E
F
G
H
I
J
K
L
M
N
O
P
Q
R
S
T
U
V
W
X
Y
Z

Bill Gadsby

HOCKEY HALL OF FAME CLASS: 1970

Alternate: 16	
Defense	
Shoots: Left	
Height: 6'	
Weight: 180 lbs.	
Born: August 8, 1927; Calgary, Alberta	
Played 20 NHL seasons from 1946–66	

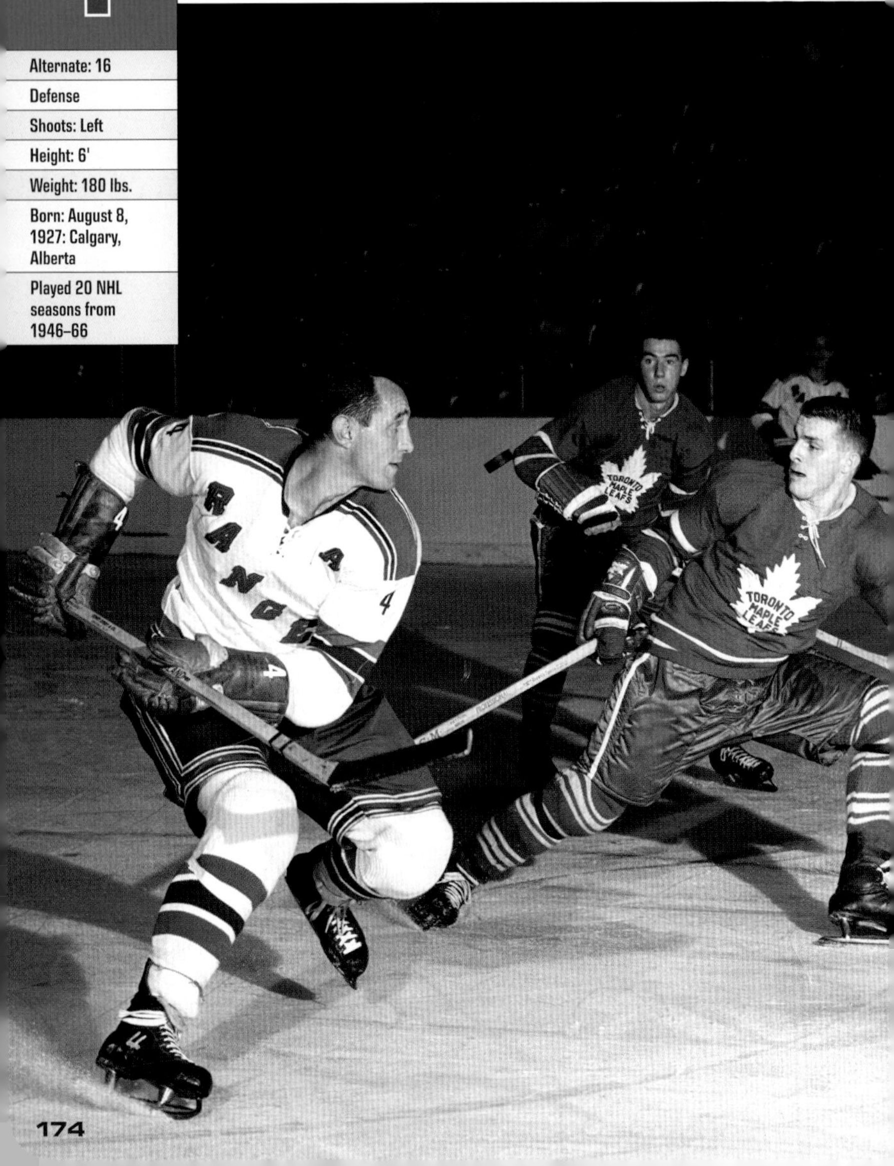

QUICK FACTS

- Held NHL record for regular season assists by a defenseman (46); surpassed by Bobby Orr (87) in 1969–70

- Held NHL record for career games played by a defenseman (1,248); surpassed by Harry Howell in 1969–70

- First NHL defenseman to record 500 regular season career points (1961–62)

- First NHL player to play at least 300 games with three different teams (Chicago, New York, Detroit)

- Played amateur hockey with Calgary Grills (1943–44); Edmonton Canadiens (1944–46)

- Led Memorial Cup playoffs in goals (12) in 1945–46

- Led NHL playoffs in penalty minutes (36) in 1962–63

- Played in NHL All-Star Game (1953, 1954, 1956, 1957, 1958, 1959, 1960, 1965)

- Signed as a free agent by Chicago Black Hawks, July 14, 1946

- Traded to N.Y. Rangers by Chicago with Pete Conacher for Allan Stanley, Nick Mickoski and Rich Lamoureux, November 23, 1954; traded to Detroit Red Wings by N.Y. Rangers for Les Hunt, June 12, 1961

- Finished among NHL top-10 in assists in 1955–56 (42), 1956–57 (37) and 1958–59 (46)

- Coached Detroit Red Wings (1968–69, 1969–70)

> When the Red Wings acquired me at age 34 in 1961, (Boston Bruins' great) Eddie Shore said, 'He will play three to five more years. He is virtually indestructible.' That kind of praise means plenty to me because it meant that I never cheated on my effort.

REGULAR SEASON

Season	Age	Team	Lg	GP	G	A	PTS	PIM	ESG	PPG	SHG	GWG
1946–47	19	Chicago Black Hawks	NHL	48	8	10	18	31				
1947–48	20	Chicago Black Hawks	NHL	60	6	10	16	66				
1948–49	21	Chicago Black Hawks	NHL	50	3	10	13	85				
1949–50	22	Chicago Black Hawks	NHL	70	10	25	35	138				
1950–51	23	Chicago Black Hawks	NHL	25	3	7	10	32				
1951–52	24	Chicago Black Hawks	NHL	59	7	15	22	87				
1952–53	25	Chicago Black Hawks	NHL	68	2	20	22	84				
1953–54	26	Chicago Black Hawks	NHL	70	12	29	41	108				
1954–55	27	Chicago Black Hawks	NHL	18	3	5	8	17				
1954–55	27	New York Rangers	NHL	52	8	8	16	44				
1955–56	28	New York Rangers	NHL	70	9	42	51	84				
1956–57	29	New York Rangers	NHL	70	4	37	41	72				
1957–58	30	New York Rangers	NHL	65	14	32	46	48				
1958–59	31	New York Rangers	NHL	70	5	46	51	56				
1959–60	32	New York Rangers	NHL	65	9	22	31	60				
1960–61	33	New York Rangers	NHL	65	9	26	35	49				
1961–62	34	Detroit Red Wings	NHL	70	7	30	37	88				
1962–63	35	Detroit Red Wings	NHL	70	4	24	28	116				
1963–64	36	Detroit Red Wings	NHL	64	2	16	18	80	2	0	0	0
1964–65	37	Detroit Red Wings	NHL	61	0	12	12	122	0	0	0	0
1965–66	38	Detroit Red Wings	NHL	58	5	12	17	72	5	0	0	0
NHL Career — 20 Seasons				1248	130	438	568	1539	7	0	0	0

PLAYOFFS

Season	Age	Team	Lg	GP	G	A	PTS	PIM	ESG	PPG	SHG	GWG
1952–53	25	Chicago Black Hawks	NHL	7	0	1	1	4				
1955–56	28	New York Rangers	NHL	5	1	3	4	4				
1956–57	29	New York Rangers	NHL	5	1	2	3	2				
1957–58	30	New York Rangers	NHL	6	0	3	3	4				
1962–63	35	Detroit Red Wings	NHL	11	1	4	5	36				
1963–64	36	Detroit Red Wings	NHL	14	0	4	4	22				
1964–65	37	Detroit Red Wings	NHL	7	0	3	3	8				
1965–66	38	Detroit Red Wings	NHL	12	1	3	4	12				
NHL Career — 8 Seasons				67	4	23	27	92				

TROPHY CASE

ALL-STAR SELECTIONS

First All-Star Team
Defense (1956, 1958, 1959)

Second All-Star Team
Defense (1953, 1954, 1957, 1965)

23

Retired by Montreal

Left Wing

Shoots: Left

Height: 6'-2"

Weight: 200 lbs.

Born: December 13, 1953: Peterborough, Ontario

Drafted by the Montreal Canadiens eighth overall in 1973

Played 16 NHL seasons from 1973–89

Bob Gainey

HOCKEY HALL OF FAME CLASS: 1992

QUICK FACTS

- Played amateur hockey with Peterborough TPT's (1970–73)
- Played minor pro hockey with Nova Scotia Voyageurs (1973–74)
- Served as player/coach of Epinal Squirrels (France II) in 1989–90
- Inaugural winner of Frank J. Selke Trophy for NHL's top defensive forward
- Played in NHL All-Star Game (1977, 1978, 1980, 1981)
- Finished even or better in plus/minus rating in 16 of 18 NHL seasons
- Served as captain of Montreal Canadiens (1981–89)
- Coached Minnesota North Stars/Dallas Stars (1990–95, 1995–96)
- Coached Minnesota North Stars to Clarence Campbell Conference championship (1990–91)
- Served as General Manager of Dallas Stars (1992–2001, 2001–02)
- Coached Montreal Canadiens (2005–06, 2008–09)
- Served as General Manager of Montreal Canadiens (2003–09, 2009–10)
- Won Stanley Cup as General Manager of Dallas Stars (1998–99)
- Number 23 jersey retired by Montreal Canadiens, October 19, 2007

> "One of the aspects of the [Frank Selke Trophy] I've always appreciated the most was that it was named after Mr. Selke. He really was strong in his belief that style of player needs to be recognized."
> — Bob Gainey, on recognition for defensive forwards

REGULAR SEASON

Season	Age	Team	Lg	GP	G	A	PTS	+/-	PIM	ESG	PPG	SHG	GWG	SOG	S%
1973–74	20	Montreal Canadiens	NHL	66	3	7	10	-9	34	3	0	0	0	55	5.5
1974–75	21	Montreal Canadiens	NHL	80	17	20	37	23	49	16	1	0	2	132	12.9
1975–76	22	Montreal Canadiens	NHL	78	15	13	28	20	57	12	1	2	1	155	9.7
1976–77	23	Montreal Canadiens	NHL	80	14	19	33	31	41	13	0	1	3	143	9.8
1977–78	24	Montreal Canadiens	NHL	66	15	16	31	11	57	13	0	2	1	140	10.7
1978–79	25	Montreal Canadiens	NHL	79	20	18	38	11	44	18	1	1	1	153	13.1
1979–80	26	Montreal Canadiens	NHL	64	14	19	33	-2	32	9	4	1	3	153	9.2
1980–81	27	Montreal Canadiens	NHL	78	23	24	47	13	36	15	5	3	3	181	12.7
1981–82	28	Montreal Canadiens	NHL	79	21	24	45	37	24	17	1	3	1	172	12.2
1982–83	29	Montreal Canadiens	NHL	80	12	18	30	7	43	11	0	1	3	150	8.0
1983–84	30	Montreal Canadiens	NHL	77	17	22	39	10	41	17	0	0	3	125	13.6
1984–85	31	Montreal Canadiens	NHL	79	19	13	32	13	40	16	0	3	3	166	11.4
1985–86	32	Montreal Canadiens	NHL	80	20	23	43	10	20	18	0	2	4	135	14.8
1986–87	33	Montreal Canadiens	NHL	47	8	8	16	0	19	7	0	1	3	73	11.0
1987–88	34	Montreal Canadiens	NHL	78	11	11	22	8	14	11	0	0	1	101	10.9
1988–89	35	Montreal Canadiens	NHL	49	10	7	17	13	34	9	1	0	2	65	15.4
NHL Career — 16 Seasons				1160	239	262	501	196	585	205	14	20	34	2099	11.4

PLAYOFFS

Season	Age	Team	Lg	GP	G	A	PTS	+/-	PIM	ESG	PPG	SHG	GWG	SOG	S%
1973–74	20	Montreal Canadiens	NHL	6	0	0	0		6	0	0	0	0		
1974–75	21	Montreal Canadiens	NHL	11	2	4	6		4	2	0	0	1		
1975–76	22	Montreal Canadiens	NHL	13	1	3	4		20	1	0	0	0		
1976–77	23	Montreal Canadiens	NHL	14	4	1	5		25	3	0	1	1		
1977–78	24	Montreal Canadiens	NHL	15	2	7	9		14	1	0	1	0		
1978–79	25	Montreal Canadiens	NHL	16	6	10	16		10	6	0	0	1		
1979–80	26	Montreal Canadiens	NHL	10	1	1	2		4	1	0	0	0		
1980–81	27	Montreal Canadiens	NHL	3	0	0	0		2	0	0	0	0		
1981–82	28	Montreal Canadiens	NHL	5	0	1	1		8	0	0	0	0		
1982–83	29	Montreal Canadiens	NHL	3	0	0	0		4	0	0	0	0		
1983–84	30	Montreal Canadiens	NHL	15	1	5	6	5	9	1	0	0	0	10	10.0
1984–85	31	Montreal Canadiens	NHL	12	1	3	4	-7	13	1	0	0	0	15	16.7
1985–86	32	Montreal Canadiens	NHL	20	5	5	10	3	12	4	0	1	3	36	13.9
1986–87	33	Montreal Canadiens	NHL	17	1	3	4	-7	6	1	0	0	0	26	3.8
1987–88	34	Montreal Canadiens	NHL	6	0	1	1	-4	6	0	0	0	0	5	0.0
1988–89	35	Montreal Canadiens	NHL	16	1	4	5	0	8	1	0	0	0	14	7.1
NHL Career — 16 Seasons				182	25	48	73	-10	151	22	0	3	7	106	8.5

TROPHY CASE

AWARDS

Frank J. Selke Trophy (1978, 1979, 1980, 1981)

Conn Smythe Trophy (1979)

Stanley Cup (1975–76, 1976–77, 1977–78, 1978–79, 1985–86)

INTERNATIONAL AWARDS

Canada Cup (1976)

Bronze Medal: World Championships (1982, 1983)

Chuck Gardiner

HOCKEY HALL OF FAME CLASS: 1945

Goaltender

Catches: Right

Height: 5'-9"

Weight: 176 lbs.

Born: December 31, 1904: Edinburgh, Scotland, United Kingdom

Died: June 13, 1934: Winnipeg, Manitoba

Played seven NHL seasons from 1927–34

QUICK FACTS

- Played amateur hockey with Winnipeg Assiniboia (1919–21); Winnipeg Tigers (1921–24); Selkirk Fisherman (1924–25)

- Signed as a free agent by Winnipeg Maroons, November 3, 1926

- Made professional debut with American Hockey Association's Winnipeg Maroons (1926–27)

- Traded to Chicago by Winnipeg Maroons (AHA) with Cecil Browne and Nick Wasnie for $17,500, April 8, 1927

- First right-handed catching goaltender to win the Vezina Trophy

- Named captain of the Black Hawks in November of 1933, he is the only NHL goaltender to captain his team to a Stanley Cup victory

- Played in All-Star Game (1934)

- Led NHL in shutouts in 1930–31 (12); 1933–34 (10); led NHL in goals-against-average in 1931–32 (1.85)

- A renowned vocalist who gave numerous radio recitals, he was also noted for his skills as a trapshooter

- After backstopping Black Hawks to the 1934 Stanley Cup championship, he was carried through Chicago's downtown Loop in a wheelbarrow

- Died of a brain hemorrhage only two months after leading the Chicago Black Hawks to the franchise's first Stanley Cup championship, June 13, 1934

- Inducted into Manitoba Sports Hall of Fame (1989)

> "Chuck was always a cheery soul and a real inspiration to the team in front of him. He was a sportsman from his head to his heels as well as one of the greatest goalkeepers the game has ever produced."
> — Frank Calder, NHL president

REGULAR SEASON

Season	Age	Team	Lg	GP	W	L	T	SO	GA	GAA	G	A	PTS	PIM
1927–28	23	Chicago Black Hawks	NHL	40	6	32	2	3	114	2.83	0	0	0	0
1928–29	24	Chicago Black Hawks	NHL	44	7	29	8	5	85	1.85	0	0	0	0
1929–30	25	Chicago Black Hawks	NHL	44	21	18	5	3	111	2.42	0	0	0	0
1930–31	26	Chicago Black Hawks	NHL	44	24	17	3	12	78	1.73	0	0	0	0
1931–32	27	Chicago Black Hawks	NHL	48	18	19	11	4	92	1.85	0	0	0	0
1932–33	28	Chicago Black Hawks	NHL	48	16	20	12	5	101	2.01	0	0	0	0
1933–34	29	Chicago Black Hawks	NHL	48	20	17	11	10	83	1.63	0	0	0	0
NHL Career – 7 Seasons				316	112	152	52	42	664	2.02	0	0	0	0

PLAYOFFS

Season	Age	Team	Lg	GP	W	L	T	SO	GA	GAA	G	A	PTS	PIM
1929–30	25	Chicago Black Hawks	NHL	2	0	1	1	0	3	1.05	0	0	0	0
1930–31	26	Chicago Black Hawks	NHL	9	5	3	1	2	14	1.32	0	0	0	0
1931–32	27	Chicago Black Hawks	NHL	2	1	1	0	1	6	3.00	0	0	0	0
1933–34	29	Chicago Black Hawks	NHL	8	6	1	1	2	12	1.33	0	0	0	0
NHL Career – 4 Seasons				21	12	6	3	5	35	1.43	0	0	0	0

TROPHY CASE

AWARDS

Vezina Trophy (1932, 1934)

Stanley Cup (1933–34)

ALL-STAR SELECTIONS

First All-Star Team Goaltender (1931, 1932, 1934)

Second All-Star Team Goaltender (1933)

Herb Gardiner

HOCKEY HALL OF FAME CLASS: 1958

Alternates: 1, 3

Defense

Shoots: Left

Height: 5'-10"

Weight: 190 lbs.

Born: May 8, 1891: Winnipeg, Manitoba

Died: January 11, 1972: Philadelphia, Pennsylvania

Played eight professional seasons from 1921–29

QUICK FACTS

- First non-goaltender in NHL history to wear #1 (1926–28); first Montreal Canadiens player to wear #1 after Georges Vezina

- First defenseman to win Hart Trophy as NHL MVP

- One of only two players (with Wayne Gretzky) to win Hart Trophy in their first NHL season

- Played amateur hockey with Winnipeg Merchants Bank (1906–08); Winnipeg Victorias (1908–10); Winnipeg Northern Crowns (1910); Calgary Monarchs (1914–15); Calgary Rotarians (1918–19); Calgary Wanderers (1919–21)

- Signed as a free agent by Calgary (WCHL), November 4, 1921

- Rights traded to Montreal Canadiens by Calgary Tigers (WHL) for cash, October 20, 1926

- Member of WCHL champion Calgary Tigers team that lost Stanley Cup challenge series to the Ottawa Senators two games to none in 1924. Calgary had defeated the Regina Capitals four goals to two in the two-game, total-goal series to win the WCHL title to earn the right to challenge the Senators

- Named to the "Unofficial" NHL Second All-Star Team Defense (1927)

- Loaned to Chicago by Montreal Canadiens and named playing coach of Black Hawks, August 27, 1928; recalled by Montreal Canadiens from Chicago, February 12, 1929

- Traded to Boston by Montreal Canadiens for cash, May 13, 1929

> "Herb Gardiner is a wonderful story, beginning with the fabled reports that, as a 35-year-old rookie, he played every second of all 48 Canadiens games that 1926–27 season to win the Hart Trophy as the NHL's most valuable player."
> — Sportswriter Dave Stubbs, *Montreal Gazette*

REGULAR SEASON

Season	Age	Team	Lg	GP	G	A	PTS	PIM
1921–22	30	Calgary Tigers	WCHL	24	4	1	5	6
1922–23	31	Calgary Tigers	WCHL	29	9	3	12	9
1923–24	32	Calgary Tigers	WCHL	22	5	5	10	4
1924–25	33	Calgary Tigers	WCHL	28	12	8	20	18
1925–26	34	Calgary Tigers	WHL	27	3	1	4	10
1926–27	35	Montreal Canadiens	NHL	44	6	6	12	26
1927–28	36	Montreal Canadiens	NHL	44	4	3	7	26
1928–29	37	Chicago Black Hawks	NHL	13	0	0	0	0
1928–29	37	Montreal Canadiens	NHL	7	0	0	0	0
Career – 8 Seasons				238	43	27	70	99

PLAYOFFS

Season	Age	Team	Lg	GP	G	A	PTS	PIM
1921–22	30	Calgary Tigers	WCHL	2	0	0	0	0
1923–24	32	Calgary Tigers	St-Cup	2	1	0	1	0
1923–24	32	Calgary Tigers	WCHL	2	1	0	1	0
1923–24	32	Calgary Tigers	West-P	3	1	1	2	0
1924–25	33	Calgary Tigers	WCHL	2	0	0	0	0
1926–27	35	Montreal Canadiens	NHL	4	0	0	0	10
1927–28	36	Montreal Canadiens	NHL	2	0	1	1	4
1928–29	37	Montreal Canadiens	NHL	3	0	0	0	2
Career – 6 Seasons				20	3	2	5	16

TROPHY CASE

AWARDS

Hart Memorial Trophy (1927)

ALL-STAR SELECTIONS

WCHL First All-Star Team Defense (1923, 1925)

Jimmy Gardner

HOCKEY HALL OF FAME CLASS: 1962

Alternate: 9

Left Wing

Shoots: Left

Height: 5'-9"

Weight: 180 lbs.

Born: May 21, 1881: Montreal, Quebec

Died: November 6, 1940: Montreal, Quebec

Played 15 elite amateur and professional seasons from 1900–15

QUICK FACTS

- Played amateur hockey with Montreal AAA (1899–1903); Montreal AAA-2 (1900–02)
- Member of CAHL intermediate champions Montreal AAA-2 (1900, 1901)
- Led Stanley Cup playoffs in penalty minutes in 1901–02 (12) and 1908–09 (13)
- Led ECAHA in penalty minutes (42) in 1907–08; led NHA in penalty minutes (67) in 1909–10
- Learned to play hockey growing up in Montreal with future Hall of Fame member Dickie Boon
- Member of IHL champion Calumet Miners (1905)

- Member of the Stanley Cup-winning Montreal Amateur Athletic Association team that became known as the "Little Men of Iron" (1902)
- Served as player/coach with Montreal Canadiens (1913–14, 1914–15)
- Served as on-ice official in WCHL (1923–24)
- Coached Hamilton Tigers (1924–25); coached Providence Reds (1928–31); coached Chicoutimi Carabins (1931–32); coached Sherbrooke Red Raiders (1937–38); coached Verdun Maple Leafs (1939–40)

> It is not often that in hockey's history can be found a player who figured on more than one 'great' championship team. Jimmy Gardner, is however, a notable example."
> — D.A.L. MacDonald, *Montreal Gazette.* January 16, 1934

REGULAR SEASON

Season	Age	Team	Lg	GP	G	A	PTS	PIM
1900–01	19	Montreal AAA	CAHL	1	0	0	0	0
1901–02	20	Montreal AAA	CAHL	8	1	0	1	16
1902–03	21	Montreal AAA	CAHL	3	3	0	3	9
1903–04	22	Montreal Wanderers	FAHL	6	5	0	5	12
1904–05	23	Calumet Miners	IHL	23	16	0	16	33
1905–06	24	Calumet Miners	IHL	19	3	0	3	30
1906–07	25	Pittsburgh Professionals	IHL	20	10	8	18	61
1907–08	26	Montreal Shamrocks	ECAHA	10	7	0	7	42
1908–09	27	Montreal Wanderers	ECHA	12	11	0	11	61
1909–10	28	Montreal Wanderers	NHA	13	13	0	13	67
1910–11	29	Montreal Wanderers	NHA	14	5	0	5	35
1911–12	30	New Westminster Royals	PCHA	15	8	0	8	50
1912–13	31	New Westminster Royals	PCHA	13	3	4	7	21
1913–14	32	Montreal Canadiens	NHA	15	10	9	19	12
1914–15	33	Montreal Canadiens	NHA	2	0	0	0	0
Career – 15 Seasons				174	95	21	116	452

PLAYOFFS

Season	Age	Team	Lg	GP	G	A	PTS	PIM
1901–02	20	Montreal AAA	St-Cup	3	0	0	0	12
1902–03	21	Montreal AAA	St-Cup	2	1	0	1	6
1903–04	22	Montreal Wanderers	St-Cup	1	1	0	1	0
1908–09	27	Montreal Wanderers	St-Cup	2	0	0	0	13
1909–10	28	Montreal Wanderers	NHA	1	3	0	3	9
1909–10	28	Montreal Wanderers	St-Cup	1	0	0	0	6
Career – 5 Seasons				10	5	0	5	46

TROPHY CASE

AWARDS

Stanley Cup (1901–02, 1902–03, 1909–10)

ALL-STAR SELECTIONS

IHL Second All-Star Team Left Wing (1905)

11

Mike Gartner

HOCKEY HALL OF FAME CLASS: 2001

Alternate: 22

Right Wing

Shoots: Right

Height: 6'

Weight: 187 lbs.

Born: October 29, 1959: Ottawa, Ontario

Drafted by the Washington Capitals fourth overall in 1979

Played 20 WHA and NHL seasons from 1978–98

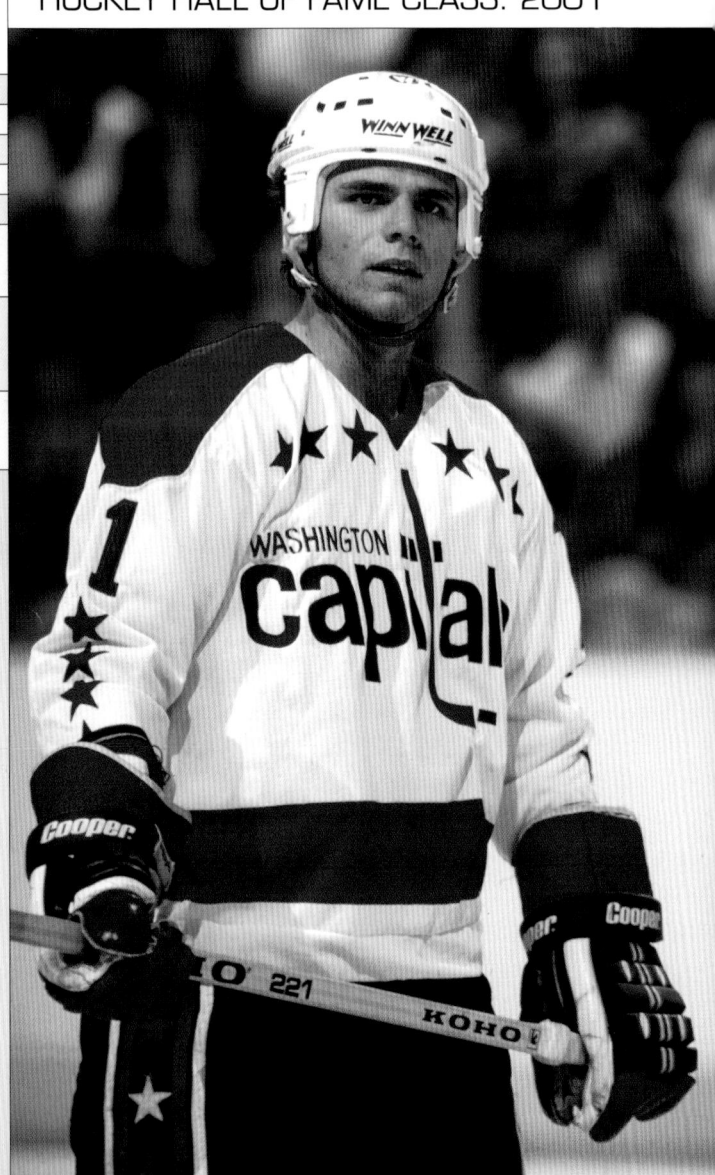

QUICK FACTS

- Holds NHL record for most seasons with at least 30 goals (17)

- Shares NHL record (with Jaromir Jagr) for most consecutive seasons with at least 30 goals (15)

- Holds Washington Capitals team record for consecutive games with at least one point (17), established in 1980–81

- Ranks sixth in NHL career regular season goals (708)

- Ranks fourth in NHL career shots-on-goal (5,090); ranks tenth in NHL career power-play goals (217); ranks 14th in NHL career game-winning goals (90)

- Played amateur hockey with Barrie Co-Op (1974–75); Mississauga Reps (1974–75); Toronto Young Nationals (1975–76); St. Catharines Black Hawks (1975–76); Niagara Falls Flyers (1976–78)

- OMJHL First All-Star Team Right Wing (1978)

- Only player in NHL history to record 500th goal, 500th assist, 1,000th point and play in his 1,000th game in the same season (1991–92)

- Registered 1,000th career NHL point in N.Y. Rangers' 6–4 loss to New Jersey Devils, January 4, 1992; recorded 500th career NHL goal in N.Y. Rangers' 5–3 loss to Washington Capitals, October 14, 1991

> "When I went there, hockey was in no way the number one sport. In fact, it wasn't number two, three or four either! Yet, it was a great experience for me."
> — Mike Gartner, on playing for the Washington Capitals

REGULAR SEASON

Season	Age	Team	Lg	GP	G	A	PTS	+/-	PIM	ESG	PPG	SHG	GWG	SOG	S%
1978–79	19	Cincinnati Stingers	WHA	78	27	25	52	-18	123	18	9	0		227	11.9
1979–80	20	Washington Capitals	NHL	77	36	32	68	15	66	32	4	0	3	228	15.8
1980–81	21	Washington Capitals	NHL	80	48	46	94	-5	100	35	13	0	3	326	14.7
1981–82	22	Washington Capitals	NHL	80	35	45	80	-11	121	28	5	2	5	300	11.7
1982–83	23	Washington Capitals	NHL	73	38	38	76	-2	54	27	10	1	3	269	14.1
1983–84	24	Washington Capitals	NHL	80	40	45	85	22	90	32	8	0	7	286	14.0
1984–85	25	Washington Capitals	NHL	80	50	52	102	17	71	33	17	0	11	330	15.2
1985–86	26	Washington Capitals	NHL	74	35	40	75	-5	63	22	11	2	4	279	12.5
1986–87	27	Washington Capitals	NHL	78	41	32	73	1	61	30	5	6	10	317	12.9
1987–88	28	Washington Capitals	NHL	80	48	33	81	20	73	29	19	0	7	316	15.2
1988–89	29	Washington Capitals	NHL	56	26	29	55	8	71	20	6	0	1	190	13.7
1988–89	29	Minnesota North Stars	NHL	13	7	7	14	3	2	4	3	0	0	33	21.2
1989–90	30	Minnesota North Stars	NHL	67	34	36	70	-8	32	15	15	4	2	240	14.2
1989–90	30	New York Rangers	NHL	12	11	5	16	4	6	5	6	0	3	48	22.9
1990–91	31	New York Rangers	NHL	79	49	20	69	-9	53	26	22	1	4	262	18.7
1991–92	32	New York Rangers	NHL	76	40	41	81	11	55	25	15	0	6	286	14.0
1992–93	33	New York Rangers	NHL	84	45	23	68	-4	59	32	13	0	3	323	13.9
1993–94	34	New York Rangers	NHL	71	28	24	52	11	58	13	10	5	4	245	11.4
1993–94	34	Toronto Maple Leafs	NHL	10	6	6	12	9	4	5	1	0	0	30	20.0
1994–95	35	Toronto Maple Leafs	NHL	38	12	8	20	0	6	9	2	1	1	91	13.2
1995–96	36	Toronto Maple Leafs	NHL	82	35	19	54	5	52	20	15	0	4	275	12.7
1996–97	37	Phoenix Coyotes	NHL	82	32	31	63	-11	38	18	13	1	7	271	11.8
1997–98	38	Phoenix Coyotes	NHL	60	12	15	27	-4	24	8	4	0	2	145	8.3
Career — 20 Seasons				1510	735	652	1387	49	1282	486	226	23	90	5317	13.8

PLAYOFFS

Season	Age	Team	Lg	GP	G	A	PTS	+/-	PIM	ESG	PPG	SHG	GWG	SOG	S%
1978–79	19	Cincinnati Stingers	WHA	3	0	0	0	-2	2					0	
1982–83	23	Washington Capitals	NHL	4	0	0	0		4	0	0	0	0		
1983–84	24	Washington Capitals	NHL	8	3	7	10	1	16	1	2	0	0	30	10.0
1984–85	25	Washington Capitals	NHL	5	4	3	7	3	9	3	1	0	1	23	17.4
1985–86	26	Washington Capitals	NHL	9	2	10	12	6	4	2	0	0	0	26	7.7
1986–87	27	Washington Capitals	NHL	7	4	3	7	0	14	4	0	0	0	33	12.1
1987–88	28	Washington Capitals	NHL	14	3	4	7	-7	14	2	1	0	0	45	6.7
1988–89	29	MinnesotaNorthStars	NHL	5	0	0	0	-4	6	0	0	0	0	14	0.0
1989–90	30	New York Rangers	NHL	10	5	3	8	0	12	1	4	0	1	26	19.2
1990–91	31	New York Rangers	NHL	6	1	1	2	-4	0	0	1	0	0	22	4.5
1991–92	32	New York Rangers	NHL	13	8	8	16	3	4	5	3	0	1	66	12.1
1993–94	34	Toronto Maple Leafs	NHL	18	5	6	11	3	14	4	1	0	3	53	9.4
1994–95	35	Toronto Maple Leafs	NHL	5	2	2	4	4	2	2	0	0	0	10	20.0
1995–96	36	Toronto Maple Leafs	NHL	6	4	1	5	-5	4	2	2	0	1	18	22.2
1996–97	37	Phoenix Coyotes	NHL	7	1	2	3	-1	4	1	0	0	0	17	4.9
1997–98	38	Phoenix Coyotes	NHL	5	1	0	1	-2	18	0	1	0	0	11	9.1
Career — 16 Seasons				125	43	50	93	-5	127	27	16	0	7	394	10.9

TROPHY CASE

INTERNATIONAL AWARDS

Canada Cup (1984, 1987)

Bronze Medal: World Championships (1982, 1983)

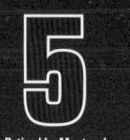

Bernie Geoffrion

HOCKEY HALL OF FAME CLASS: 1972

5

Retired by Montreal

Right Wing

Shoots: Right

Height: 5'-9"

Weight: 166 lbs.

Born: February 16, 1931: Montreal, Quebec

Died: March 11, 2006: Atlanta, Georgia

Played 16 NHL seasons from 1950–64, 1966–68

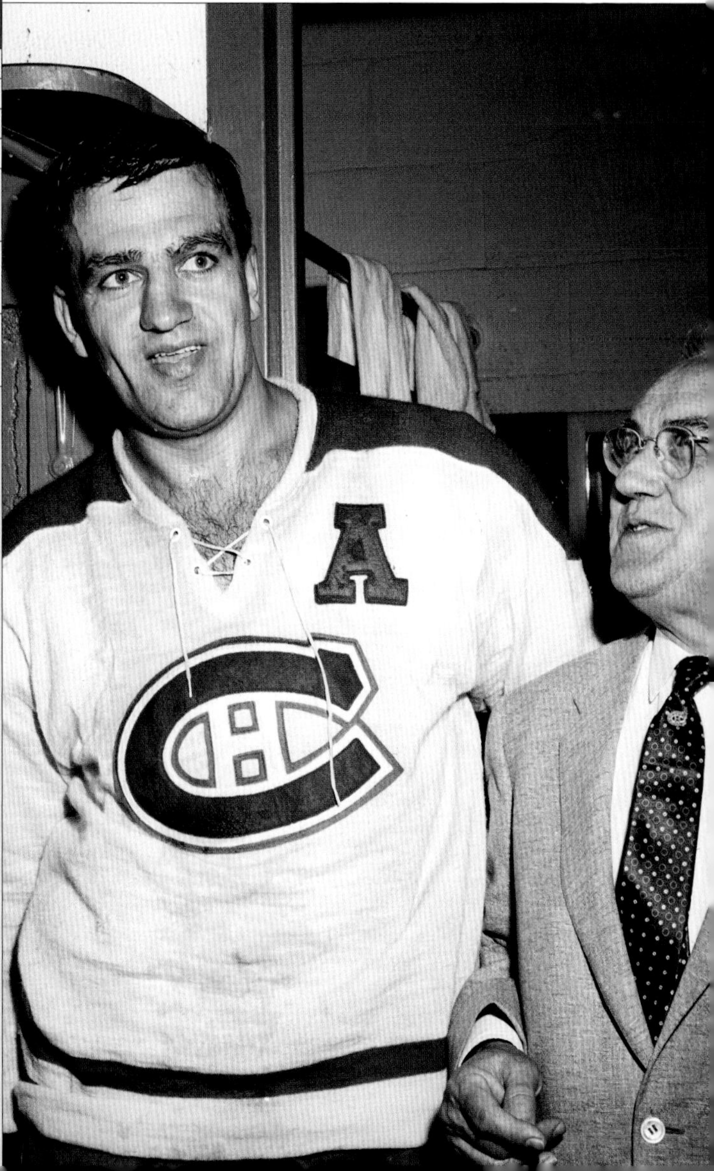

QUICK FACTS

- Nicknamed "Boom Boom" because of the sound his stick blade made when it struck the puck and the sound his shot made when it missed the net and struck the boards

- Played amateur hockey with Montreal–St. Louis College (1945–46); Montreal Concordia Civics (1946–47); Montreal Nationale (1947–51); Montreal Royals (1948–50); Laval Nationale (1949–50)

- Led QJHL in goals (52) and points (86) in 1949–50

- QJHL First All-Star Team Right Wing (1949, 1950, 1951)

- Signed as a free agent by Montreal, February 14, 1951

- Second player in NHL history to score 50 goals in the regular season (1960–61)

- Led NHL playoffs in goals (6) in 1952–53; led NHL playoffs in goals (11) and points (18) in 1956–57; led NHL playoffs in assists (10) and points (12) in 1959–60

- Led NHL in goals (38) and points (75) in 1954–55, goals (50) and points (95) in 1960–61

- Claimed on waivers by N.Y. Rangers from Montreal, June 9, 1966

- Coached Quebec Aces (1964–66)

- Coached N.Y. Rangers (1968–69); coached Atlanta Flames (1972–75); coached Montreal Canadiens (1979–80)

- Son-in-law of Hall of Fame member Howie Morenz

- Father of Danny Geoffrion, who played in NHL with Montreal Canadiens and Winnipeg Jets from 1979–82

> "Look, the Montreal Canadiens were very good to me, but I was very good to them too. There are things I wish could have been different but I have no regrets ... I got to play hockey for my favorite team."

REGULAR SEASON

Season	Age	Team	Lg	GP	G	A	PTS	+/-	PIM	ESG	PPG	SHG	GWG	SOG	S%
1950–51	19	Montreal Canadiens	NHL	18	8	6	14		9						
1951–52	20	Montreal Canadiens	NHL	67	30	24	54		66						
1952–53	21	Montreal Canadiens	NHL	65	22	17	39		37						
1953–54	22	Montreal Canadiens	NHL	54	29	25	54		87						
1954–55	23	Montreal Canadiens	NHL	70	38	37	75		57						
1955–56	24	Montreal Canadiens	NHL	59	29	33	62		66						
1956–57	25	Montreal Canadiens	NHL	41	19	21	40		18						
1957–58	26	Montreal Canadiens	NHL	42	27	23	50		51						
1958–59	27	Montreal Canadiens	NHL	59	22	44	66		30						
1959–60	28	Montreal Canadiens	NHL	59	30	41	71		36						
1960–61	29	Montreal Canadiens	NHL	64	50	45	95		29						
1961–62	30	Montreal Canadiens	NHL	62	23	36	59		36						
1962–63	31	Montreal Canadiens	NHL	51	23	18	41		73						
1963–64	32	Montreal Canadiens	NHL	55	21	18	39		41	16	5	0	9		
1966–67	35	New York Rangers	NHL	58	17	25	42		42	12	5	0	2		
1967–68	36	New York Rangers	NHL	59	5	16	21	1	11	1	4	0	0	84	6.0
NHL Career — 16 Seasons				883	393	429	822	1	689	29	14	0	11	84	6.0

PLAYOFFS

Season	Age	Team	Lg	GP	G	A	PTS	+/-	PIM	ESG	PPG	SHG	GWG	SOG	S%
1950–51	19	Montreal Canadiens	NHL	11	1	1	2		6						
1951–52	20	Montreal Canadiens	NHL	11	3	1	4		6						
1952–53	21	Montreal Canadiens	NHL	12	6	4	10		12						
1953–54	22	Montreal Canadiens	NHL	11	6	5	11		18						
1954–55	23	Montreal Canadiens	NHL	12	8	5	13		8						
1955–56	24	Montreal Canadiens	NHL	10	5	9	14		6						
1956–57	25	Montreal Canadiens	NHL	10	11	7	18		2						
1957–58	26	Montreal Canadiens	NHL	10	6	5	11		2						
1958–59	27	Montreal Canadiens	NHL	11	5	8	13		10						
1959–60	28	Montreal Canadiens	NHL	8	2	10	12		4						
1960–61	29	Montreal Canadiens	NHL	4	2	1	3		0						
1961–62	30	Montreal Canadiens	NHL	5	0	1	1		6						
1962–63	31	Montreal Canadiens	NHL	5	0	1	1		4						
1963–64	32	Montreal Canadiens	NHL	7	1	1	2		4						
1966–67	35	New York Rangers	NHL	4	2	0	2		0						
1967–68	36	New York Rangers	NHL	1	0	1	1		0	0	0	0	0		
NHL Career — 16 Seasons				132	58	60	118		88	0	0	0	0		

TROPHY CASE

AWARDS

Calder Memorial Trophy (1952)

Art Ross Trophy (1955, 1961)

Hart Memorial Trophy (1961)

Stanley Cup (1952–53, 1955–56, 1956–57, 1957–58, 1958–59, 1959–60)

ALL-STAR SELECTIONS

First All-Star Team Right Wing (1961)

Second All-Star Team Right Wing (1955, 1960)

8

Eddie Gerard
HOCKEY HALL OF FAME CLASS: 1945

Alternates: 2, 12

Left Wing/Defense

Shoots: Left

Height: 5'-9"

Weight: 168 lbs.

Born: February 22, 1890: Ottawa, Ontario

Died: August 7, 1937: Ottawa, Ontario

Played 10 professional seasons from 1913–23

QUICK FACTS

- Played amateur hockey with Ottawa Seconds (1907–10); Ottawa New Edinburghs (1910–14)
- Led IPAHU in goals (16) in 1912–13
- Signed as a free agent by Ottawa Senators, November 20, 1913
- Began career in Ottawa playing on a forward line with Jack Darragh and Skene Ronan, then switched to defense three years later
- Served as captain of Ottawa Senators (1919–23)
- Served as player/coach of Ottawa Senators (1917–18)
- Loaned to Toronto St. Pats by Ottawa for fourth game of Stanley Cup finals between Toronto and Vancouver on emergency injury basis, March 25, 1922
- Led NHL in assists (13) in 1922–23
- Coached Montreal Maroons (1924–29, 1932–34); coached N.Y. Americans (1930–32); coached St. Louis Eagles (1934–35)
- Coach of Stanley Cup-winning Montreal Maroons (1926)
- Retired following the 1922–23 season because of a growth in throat that limited his breathing, an ailment that ultimately caused his early death
- Played half-back for the Ottawa Rough Riders Football Club (1909–13)
- Inducted into Ottawa Sports Hall of Fame (1968)

> He has an unblemished career in sports. He was never a publicity seeker but will live long in the memory of every person who had the pleasure of his acquaintance. He was a man."
> — Gerard Obituary, *Ottawa Citizen*

REGULAR SEASON

Season	Age	Team	Lg	GP	G	A	PTS	PIM
1913-14	23	Ottawa Senators	NHA	11	6	7	13	34
1914-15	24	Ottawa Senators	NHA	20	9	10	19	39
1915-16	25	Ottawa Senators	NHA	24	13	5	18	57
1916-17	26	Ottawa Senators	NHA	19	18	16	34	48
1917-18	27	Ottawa Senators	NHL	20	13	7	20	26
1918-19	28	Ottawa Senators	NHL	18	4	6	10	17
1919-20	29	Ottawa Senators	NHL	22	9	7	16	19
1920-21	30	Ottawa Senators	NHL	24	11	4	15	18
1921-22	31	Ottawa Senators	NHL	21	7	11	18	16
1922-23	32	Ottawa Senators	NHL	23	6	13	19	12
Career – 10 Seasons				202	96	86	182	286

PLAYOFFS

Season	Age	Team	Lg	GP	G	A	PTS	PIM
1914-15	24	Ottawa Senators	NHA	5	1	0	1	6
1916-17	26	Ottawa Senators	NHA	2	1	2	3	6
1918-19	28	Ottawa Senators	NHL	5	3	0	3	3
1919-20	29	Ottawa Senators	St-Cup	5	2	1	3	3
1920-21	30	Ottawa Senators	NHL	2	1	0	1	6
1920-21	30	Ottawa Senators	St-Cup	5	0	0	0	44
1921-22	31	Ottawa Senators	NHL	2	0	0	0	8
1921-22	31	Toronto St. Patricks	St-Cup	1	0	0	0	0
1922-23	32	Ottawa Senators	NHL	2	0	0	0	0
1922-23	32	Ottawa Senators	St-Cup	6	1	0	1	4
Career – 7 Seasons				35	9	3	12	80

TROPHY CASE

AWARDS

Stanley Cup (1919–20, 1920–21, 1922–23)

Eddie Giacomin

HOCKEY HALL OF FAME CLASS: 1987

1

Retired by N.Y. Rangers

Alternate: 31	
Goaltender	
Catches: Left	
Height: 5'-11"	
Weight: 180 lbs.	
Born: June 6, 1939; Sudbury, Ontario	
Played 13 NHL seasons from 1965–78	

"I really loved being a Ranger and being in New York. I guess it showed. It's hard for me even today to sign Detroit Red Wings' hockey cards. It isn't natural because I never felt like I was a Red Wing."

QUICK FACTS

- Nicknamed "Fast Eddie" because of his penchant for leaving the net to reach loose pucks before incoming forwards
- Played amateur hockey with Commack Comets (1957–58); Sudbury Bell Telephone (1958–59); Clinton Comets (1958-60); N.Y. Rovers (1959–61); Washington Presidents (1958–59)
- Suffered serious burns as a teenager but he recovered and played in an industrial men's league in Sudbury and a senior team in the Nickel Belt League
- Traded to N.Y. Rangers by Providence Reds (AHL) for Marcel Paille, Aldo Guidolin, Sandy McGregor and Jim Mikol, May 18, 1965
- Led NHL in wins in 1966–67 (30), 1967–68 (36) and 1968–69 (37)

- Led NHL in shutouts in 1966–67 (9), 1967–68 (8) and 1970–71 (8)
- Played in NHL All-Star Game (1967, 1968, 1969, 1970, 1971, 1973)
- Started wearing a mask in the 1970–71 season, even though he had been critical of it the year before saying it would hurt his style because he liked to shoot the puck
- Claimed on waivers by Detroit from N.Y. Rangers, October 31, 1975
- Served as N.Y. Rangers' goaltending coach (1986–89)

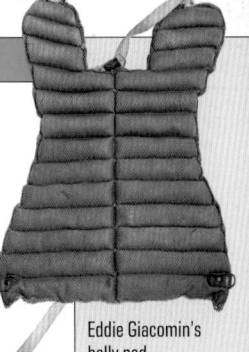

Eddie Giacomin's belly pad.

REGULAR SEASON

Season	Age	Team	Lg	GP	W	L	T	SO	GA	GAA	G	A	PTS	PIM
1965-66	26	New York Rangers	NHL	35	8	20	6	0	125	3.68	0	0	0	8
1966-67	27	New York Rangers	NHL	68	30	27	11	9	173	2.61	0	0	0	8
1967-68	28	New York Rangers	NHL	66	36	20	10	8	160	2.44	0	0	0	4
1968-69	29	New York Rangers	NHL	70	37	23	7	7	175	2.55	0	0	0	2
1969-70	30	New York Rangers	NHL	70	35	21	14	6	163	2.36	0	2	2	2
1970-71	31	New York Rangers	NHL	45	27	10	7	8	95	2.16	0	0	0	4
1971-72	32	New York Rangers	NHL	44	24	10	9	1	115	2.70	0	3	3	4
1972-73	33	New York Rangers	NHL	43	26	11	6	4	125	2.91	0	2	2	6
1973-74	34	New York Rangers	NHL	56	30	15	10	5	168	3.07	0	1	1	4
1974-75	35	New York Rangers	NHL	37	13	12	8	1	120	3.48	0	0	0	20
1975-76	36	New York Rangers	NHL	4	0	3	1	0	19	4.75	0	0	0	0
1975-76	36	Detroit Red Wings	NHL	29	12	14	3	2	100	3.45	0	0	0	0
1976-77	37	Detroit Red Wings	NHL	33	8	18	3	3	107	3.58	0	1	1	4
1977-78	38	Detroit Red Wings	NHL	9	3	5	1	0	27	3.14	0	0	0	0
NHL Career – 13 Seasons				609	289	209	96	54	1672	2.82	0	9	9	66

PLAYOFFS

Season	Age	Team	Lg	GP	W	L	T	SO	GA	GAA	G	A	PTS	PIM
1966-67	27	New York Rangers	NHL	4	0	4		0	14	3.41	0	0	0	0
1967-68	28	New York Rangers	NHL	6	2	4		0	18	3.00	0	0	0	0
1968-69	29	New York Rangers	NHL	3	0	3		0	10	3.33	0	0	0	5
1969-70	30	New York Rangers	NHL	5	2	3		0	19	4.07	0	0	0	0
1970-71	31	New York Rangers	NHL	12	7	5		0	28	2.21	0	0	0	2
1971-72	32	New York Rangers	NHL	10	6	4		0	27	2.70	0	0	0	2
1972-73	33	New York Rangers	NHL	10	5	4		1	23	2.56	0	0	0	4
1973-74	34	New York Rangers	NHL	13	7	6		0	37	2.82	0	0	0	6
1974-75	35	New York Rangers	NHL	2	0	2		0	4	2.79	0	0	0	4
NHL Career – 9 Seasons				65	29	35		1	180	2.81	0	0	0	23

TROPHY CASE

AWARDS

Vezina Trophy (1971)

ALL-STAR SELECTIONS

First All-Star Team Goaltender (1967, 1971)

Second All-Star Team Goaltender (1968, 1969, 1970)

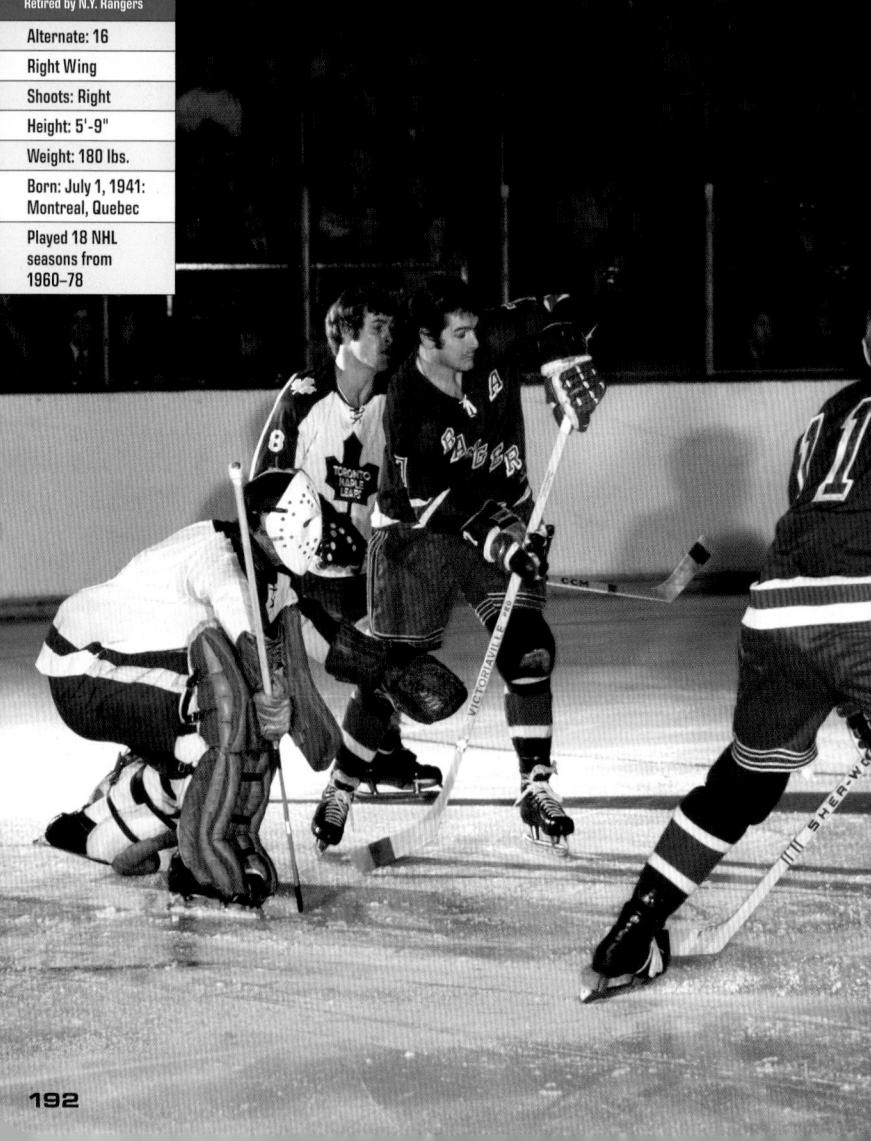

7

Retired by N.Y. Rangers

Alternate: 16

Right Wing

Shoots: Right

Height: 5'-9"

Weight: 180 lbs.

Born: July 1, 1941: Montreal, Quebec

Played 18 NHL seasons from 1960–78

Rod Gilbert
HOCKEY HALL OF FAME CLASS: 1982

QUICK FACTS

- Held NHL record for most shots-on-goal in a single game (16); surpassed by Ray Bourque (19), March 21, 1991

- Holds N.Y. Rangers team records for career seasons (18), goals (406) and points (1,021)

- Played amateur hockey with Guelph Biltmores (1957–60); Guelph Royals (1960–61)

- Led OHA-Jr. in goals (54) and points (103) in 1960–61

- OHA-Jr. First All-Star Team Right Wing (1961)

- Played minor pro hockey with Trois-Rivieres Lions (1959–60); Kitchener-Waterloo Beavers (1961–62)

- Member of N.Y. Rangers' famed GAG (Goal-a-Game) Line with Jean Ratelle and Vic Hadfield

- Registered 1,000th career NHL point in N.Y. Rangers' 5–2 loss to N.Y. Islanders, February 19, 1977

- First player in N.Y. Rangers history to have his number retired, October 14, 1979

- Recorded one goal and four points in 1972 Summit Series, including key assist on Bill White's tying goal in second period of Game 8

- Hampered by back troubles most of his career, he underwent delicate spinal fusion surgery in 1961 and again in 1965

- Officially announced retirement, December 6, 1977

> I would have loved to have played on a Stanley Cup winner; that's for sure. But I had my share of thrills and, in a lot of ways, I was very lucky guy considering my dream of making the NHL and being able to do what I did with all those back problems."

REGULAR SEASON

Season	Age	Team	Lg	GP	G	A	PTS	+/-	PIM	ESG	PPG	SHG	GWG	SOG	S%
1960-61	19	New York Rangers	NHL	1	0	1	1		2						
1961-62	20	New York Rangers	NHL	1	0	0	0		0						
1962-63	21	New York Rangers	NHL	70	11	20	31		20						
1963-64	22	New York Rangers	NHL	70	24	40	64		62	17	7	0	0		
1964-65	23	New York Rangers	NHL	70	25	36	61		52	15	10	0	3		
1965-66	24	New York Rangers	NHL	34	10	15	25		20	7	3	0	2		
1966-67	25	New York Rangers	NHL	64	28	18	46		12	23	5	0	5		
1967-68	26	New York Rangers	NHL	73	29	48	77	13	12	21	8	0	6	281	10.3
1968-69	27	New York Rangers	NHL	66	28	49	77	12	22	20	8	0	5	301	9.3
1969-70	28	New York Rangers	NHL	72	16	37	53	2	22	13	3	0	1	230	7.0
1970-71	29	New York Rangers	NHL	78	30	31	61	22	65	22	8	0	5	226	13.3
1971-72	30	New York Rangers	NHL	73	43	54	97	51	64	37	6	0	4	238	18.1
1972-73	31	New York Rangers	NHL	76	25	59	84	12	25	19	6	0	4	183	13.7
1973-74	32	New York Rangers	NHL	75	36	41	77	11	20	20	16	0	8	168	21.4
1974-75	33	New York Rangers	NHL	76	36	61	97	1	22	25	11	0	1	239	15.1
1975-76	34	New York Rangers	NHL	70	36	50	86	-8	32	27	9	0	4	211	17.1
1976-77	35	New York Rangers	NHL	77	27	48	75	-17	50	20	7	0	2	187	14.4
1977-78	36	New York Rangers	NHL	19	2	7	9	-10	6	1	1	0	0	27	7.4
NHL Career – 18 Seasons				1065	406	615	1021	89	508	287	108	0	50	2291	13.4

PLAYOFFS

Season	Age	Team	Lg	GP	G	A	PTS	+/-	PIM	ESG	PPG	SHG	GWG	SOG	S%
1961-62	20	New York Rangers	NHL	4	2	3	5		4						
1966-67	25	New York Rangers	NHL	4	2	2	4		6						
1967-68	26	New York Rangers	NHL	6	5	0	5		4	5	0	0	0		
1968-69	27	New York Rangers	NHL	4	1	0	1		2	1	0	0	0		
1969-70	28	New York Rangers	NHL	6	4	5	9		0	1	3	0	0		
1970-71	29	New York Rangers	NHL	13	4	6	10		8	3	1	0	1		
1971-72	30	New York Rangers	NHL	16	7	8	15		11	3	4	0	2		
1972-73	31	New York Rangers	NHL	10	5	1	6		2	5	0	0	1		
1973-74	32	New York Rangers	NHL	13	3	5	8		4	2	1	0	1		
1974-75	33	New York Rangers	NHL	3	1	3	4		2	1	0	0	0		
NHL Career – 10 Seasons				79	34	33	67		43	21	9	0	5		

TROPHY CASE

AWARDS

Bill Masterton Memorial Trophy (1976)

ALL-STAR SELECTIONS

First All-Star Team Right Wing (1972)

Second All-Star Team Right Wing (1968)

INTERNATIONAL AWARDS

Summit Series (1972)

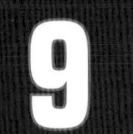

9

Retired by the N.Y. Islanders

Alternates: 39, 90

Left Wing

Shoots: Left

Height: 6'-3"

Weight: 215 lbs.

Born: April 7, 1954: Moose Jaw, Saskatchewan

Drafted by the New York Islanders fourth overall in 1974

Played 14 NHL seasons from 1974–88

Clark Gillies

HOCKEY HALL OF FAME CLASS: 2002

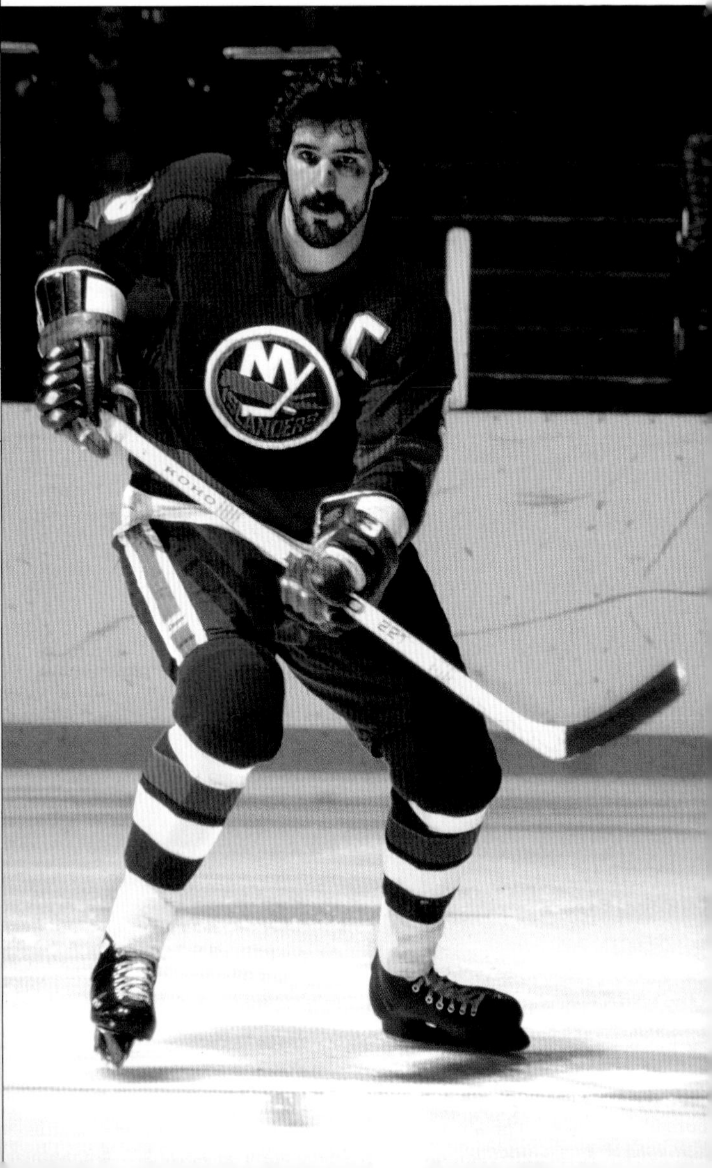

QUICK FACTS

- Played amateur hockey with Moose Jaw Canucks (1969–71); Regina Pats (1971–74)

- Member of the Memorial Cup-winning Regina Pats (1974), registering four points in three games during tournament

- WCJHL First All-Star Team Left Wing (1974)

- Played in NHL All-Star Game (1978)

- Served as captain of N.Y. Islanders (1976–79)

- Member of the N.Y. Islanders' Long Island Lightning Company line with Billy Harris and Bryan Trottier

- Recorded three consecutive game-winning goals against Buffalo Sabres in 1977 quarterfinals to tie NHL record

- Scored 93 powerplay and 44 game-winning goals in 14-year career

- Member of Team NHL that played Soviet Union in 1979 Challenge Cup; member of Team Canada in 1981 Canada Cup tournament

- Nicknamed "Jethro" by New York Islanders teammates because of his resemblance to the character on the *Beverly Hillbillies* TV show

- Claimed by Buffalo from N.Y. Islanders in waiver draft, October 6, 1986

- Uncle of Colton Gilllies, a first round draft selection of the Minnesota Wild in 2007

- Played three seasons of minor-league baseball as a first baseman and outfielder in the Houston Astros organization (1970–72)

- Inducted into Saskatchewan Sports Hall of Fame (2000)

> "When we got beat by Edmonton for that fifth Cup, it really took a lot of the heart and soul out of me. It took me a while to even want to play the game again."

REGULAR SEASON

Season	Age	Team	Lg	GP	G	A	PTS	+/-	PIM	ESG	PPG	SHG	GWG	SOG	S%
1974-75	20	New York Islanders	NHL	80	25	22	47	-4	66	17	8	0	4	165	15.2
1975-76	21	New York Islanders	NHL	80	34	27	61	20	96	19	15	0	6	210	16.2
1976-77	22	New York Islanders	NHL	70	33	22	55	18	93	21	12	0	5	215	15.3
1977-78	23	New York Islanders	NHL	80	35	50	85	49	76	26	9	0	2	277	12.6
1978-79	24	New York Islanders	NHL	75	35	56	91	57	68	24	11	0	5	210	16.7
1979-80	25	New York Islanders	NHL	73	19	35	54	29	49	12	7	0	5	175	10.9
1980-81	26	New York Islanders	NHL	80	33	45	78	26	99	24	9	0	3	188	17.6
1981-82	27	New York Islanders	NHL	79	38	39	77	39	75	30	8	0	5	200	19.0
1982-83	28	New York Islanders	NHL	70	21	20	41	9	76	17	4	0	2	145	14.5
1983-84	29	New York Islanders	NHL	76	12	16	28	5	65	9	3	0	2	138	8.7
1984-85	30	New York Islanders	NHL	54	15	1/	32	0	73	10	5	0	2	125	12.0
1985-86	31	New York Islanders	NHL	55	4	10	14	-8	55	3	1	0	0	74	5.4
1986-87	32	Buffalo Sabres	NHL	61	10	17	27	0	81	9	1	0	2	106	9.4
1987-88	33	Buffalo Sabres	NHL	25	5	2	7	1	51	5	0	0	0	23	21.7
NHL Career – 14 Seasons				958	319	378	697	241	1023	226	93	0	44	2251	14.2

PLAYOFFS

Season	Age	Team	Lg	GP	G	A	PTS	+/-	PIM	ESG	PPG	SHG	GWG	SOG	S%
1974-75	20	New York Islanders	NHL	17	4	2	6		36	4	0	0	2		
1975-76	21	New York Islanders	NHL	13	2	4	6		16	2	0	0	1		
1976-77	22	New York Islanders	NHL	12	4	4	8		15	4	0	0	4		
1977-78	23	New York Islanders	NHL	7	2	0	2		15	1	1	0	0		
1978-79	24	New York Islanders	NHL	10	1	2	3		11	1	0	0	0		
1979-80	25	New York Islanders	NHL	21	6	10	16		63	5	1	0	2		
1980-81	26	New York Islanders	NHL	18	6	9	15		28	3	3	0	0		
1981-82	27	New York Islanders	NHL	19	8	6	14		34	4	4	0	3		
1982-83	28	New York Islanders	NHL	8	0	2	2		10	0	0	0	0		
1983-84	29	New York Islanders	NHL	21	12	7	19	2	19	9	3	0	0	41	29.3
1984-85	30	New York Islanders	NHL	10	1	0	1	0	9	1	0	0	0	13	7.7
1985-86	31	New York Islanders	NHL	3	1	0	1	-2	6	1	0	0	0	7	14.3
1987-88	33	Buffalo Sabres	NHL	5	0	1	1	-3	25	0	0	0	0	5	0.0
NHL Career – 13 Seasons				164	47	47	94	-3	287	35	12	0	12	66	21.2

TROPHY CASE

AWARDS

Stanley Cup (1979–80, 1980–81, 1981–82, 1982–83)

ALL-STAR SELECTIONS

First All-Star Team Left Wing (1978, 1979)

Billy Gilmour

HOCKEY HALL OF FAME CLASS: 1962

Right Wing

Shoots: Unknown

Height: Unknown

Weight: Unknown

Born: March 21, 1885: Ottawa, Ontario

Died: March 13, 1959: Montreal, Quebec

Played eight elite amateur and professional seasons from 1902–09, 1915–16

QUICK FACTS

> Billy Gilmour is easily the finest stickhandler on the Ottawa professional squad."
> — Ottawa Citizen, December 24, 1908

- Played amateur hockey with Ottawa Aberdeens (1900–02)

- Member of prominent Ottawa family that featured brothers Dave and Suddy Gilmour, who also played for Ottawa's famed "Silver Seven"

- Played as an amateur throughout the majority of his career

- Member of Stanley Cup-winning Ottawa "Silver Seven" while playing hockey and studying engineering at McGill University (1902–03, 1903–04, 1904–05)

- MCHL First All-Star Team Right Wing (1907); ECAHA First All-Star Team Right Wing (1908); ECHA First All-Star Team Right Wing (1909)

- Led ECHA in penalty minutes (74) in 1908–09

- Did not play hockey after 1908–09 until making brief comeback during the 1915–16 season

- Signed as a free agent by Ottawa Senators, January 15, 1916

- Scored final goal of his career against future Hockey Hall of Fame member Georges Vezina in Ottawa's 5–2 victory over Montreal Canadiens, January 15, 1916

- Enlisted in Canadian Army for service in World War I (1916)

REGULAR SEASON

Season	Age	Team	Lg	GP	G	A	PTS	PIM
1902–03	21	Ottawa Silver Seven	CAHL	7	10	0	10	3
1903–04	22	McGill Redmen	MCHL	4	5	0	5	12
1904–05	23	McGill Redmen	MCHL	4	5	0	5	12
1904–05	23	Ottawa Silver Seven	FAHL	1	0	0	0	0
1905–06	24	Ottawa Silver Seven	ECAHA	1	0	0	0	0
1905–06	24	McGill Redmen	MCHL	4	5	0	5	21
1906–07	25	McGill Redmen	MCHL	3	2	0	2	8
1907–08	26	Montreal Victorias	ECAHA	10	5	0	5	33
1908–09	27	Ottawa Senators	ECHA	11	9	0	9	74
1915–16	34	Ottawa Senators	NHA	2	1	0	1	0
Career — 8 Seasons				47	42	0	42	163

PLAYOFFS

Season	Age	Team	Lg	GP	G	A	PTS	PIM
1902–03	21	Ottawa Silver Seven	CAHL	2	1	0	1	
1902–03	21	Ottawa Silver Seven	St-Cup	2	4	0	4	3
1903–04	22	Ottawa Silver Seven	St-Cup	3	1	0	1	0
1904–05	23	Ottawa Silver Seven	St-Cup	2	1	0	1	8
Career — 3 Seasons				9	7	0	7	11

TROPHY CASE

AWARDS

Stanley Cup (1902–03, 1903–04, 1904–05, 1908–09)

Moose Goheen

HOCKEY HALL OF FAME CLASS: 1952

Left Wing

Shoots: Left

Height: 6'

Weight: 220 lbs.

Born: February 8, 1894: White Bear Lake, Minnesota

Died: November 13, 1979: Maplewood, Minnesota

Played 16 elite amateur and professional seasons from 1914–32

QUICK FACTS

- Played amateur hockey with St. Paul Athletic Club (1914–22); St. Paul Saints (1922–26); White Bear Lakers (1916–17)

- Served with the U.S. Army signal corps during World War I (1917–19)

- Graduate of Valparaiso (Indiana) University

- Scored seven goals in four games for the United States at the 1920 Olympics

- Played professional hockey with St. Paul Saints (1926–32); Buffalo Majors (1930–31)

- Turned down offer to join Boston Bruins in 1926 to remain at home and continue off-ice career with Northern States Power Company

- Second American-born and trained player to be elected to Hockey Hall of Fame (after Hobey Baker)

- Inducted into Minnesota Sports Hall of Fame (1958)

- Inducted into the United States Hockey Hall of Fame (1973)

- Member of MacNaughton Cup (U.S. amateur) champion St. Paul AC (1916, 1920). St. Paul defeated American Soo three games to none to win the 1916 championship and shared the 1920 title with Canadian Soo after both teams completed the season with identical 9–3 records

- In 1916, Goheen and his St. Paul AC team defeated Lachine 7–6 to win the Art Ross Cup — symbolic of amateur hockey supremacy in Eastern Canada — but the victory was overturned when it was determined that two "borrowed" players — Ray Bonney and Duke Wellington — were ineligible

> He had terrific speed and fight. I coined the term, 'Moose.' He had a chest like a house and huge strong legs, with thighs as big as [teammate] Emmy Garrett's waist. No man ever trained more.
>
> — Tony Conroy, teammate on the St. Paul AC

REGULAR SEASON

Season	Age	Team	Lg	GP	G	A	PTS	PIM
1922–23	28	St. Paul Saints	USAHA	20	11	0	11	
1923–24	29	St. Paul Saints	USAHA	20	10	4	14	
1924–25	30	St. Paul Saints	USAHA	32	6	0	6	
1925–26	31	St. Paul Saints	CHL	36	13	10	23	87
1926–27	32	St. Paul Saints	AHA	27	2	7	9	40
1927–28	33	St. Paul Saints	AHA	39	19	5	24	96
1928–29	34	St. Paul Saints	AHA	28	7	4	11	39
1929–30	35	St. Paul Saints	AHA	35	9	6	15	47
1930–31	36	Buffalo Majors	AHA	2	0	0	0	0
1931–32	37	St. Paul Saints	CHL	20	2	7	9	17
Career — 10 Seasons				259	79	53	122	326

PLAYOFFS

Season	Age	Team	Lg	GP	G	A	PTS	PIM
1922–23	28	St. Paul Saints	USAHA	4	3	0	3	
1923–24	29	St. Paul Saints	USAHA	8	1	3	4	
1928–29	34	St. Paul Saints	AHA	8	2	0	2	20
Career — 3 Seasons				20	6	3	9	20

TROPHY CASE

INTERNATIONAL AWARDS

Silver Medal: Winter Olympics (1920)

5

Ebbie Goodfellow

HOCKEY HALL OF FAME CLASS: 1963

Alternate: 10

Defense/Center

Shoots: Left

Height: 6'

Weight: 175 lbs.

Born: April 9, 1906;
Ottawa, Ontario

Died: September
10, 1985;
Sarasota, Florida

Played 14 NHL
seasons from
1929–43

QUICK FACTS

- Played amateur hockey with Ottawa Montagnards (1926–28)

- Member of the Ottawa City champion Ottawa Montagnards, leading all playoff scorers in goals (4) and points (5) in 1928

- Signed as a free agent by Saskatoon Sheiks (WCHL), December 25, 1924; traded to Detroit by Saskatoon Sheiks (PrHL) for $4,000, February 2, 1927

- Made professional debut with Detroit Olympics (1928–29)

- Led Can-Pro League in goals (26) and points (34) in 1928–29

- Held Detroit franchise record for points as a rookie (34) in 1929–30; surpassed by Steve Wojciechowski (39) in 1944–45

- Finished second (48 points) to Howie Morenz in NHL scoring race (1930–31); finished among NHL top-5 in goals (25) in 1930–31

- Played center before becoming an All-Star defenseman after the 1934–35 season

- Scored series-winning goal in Detroit's 1–0 victory over the Toronto Maple Leafs in the fifth and deciding game of semi-final series, March 30, 1934

- Served as captain of Detroit Red Wings (1934–35, 1938–41)

- Served as player/assistant coach of Detroit Red Wings (1941–42)

- Kept his day job as a tool and die salesman while he was player/assistant coach for Detroit in 1941 and 1942

> "Playing forward and defense, I saw both sides of the action. Forward seemed a better position because a man can make more mistakes there and not be criticized as much for it. When you're back on defense and someone skates past you, then you're the goat."

REGULAR SEASON

Season	Age	Team	Lg	GP	G	A	PTS	PIM
1929–30	22	Detroit Cougars	NHL	44	17	17	34	54
1930–31	23	Detroit Falcons	NHL	44	25	23	48	32
1931–32	24	Detroit Falcons	NHL	48	14	16	30	56
1932–33	25	Detroit Red Wings	NHL	41	12	8	20	47
1933–34	26	Detroit Red Wings	NHL	48	13	13	26	45
1934–35	27	Detroit Red Wings	NHL	48	12	24	36	44
1935–36	28	Detroit Red Wings	NHL	48	5	18	23	69
1936–37	29	Detroit Red Wings	NHL	48	9	16	25	43
1937–38	30	Detroit Red Wings	NHL	30	0	7	7	13
1938–39	31	Detroit Red Wings	NHL	48	8	8	16	36
1939–40	32	Detroit Red Wings	NHL	43	11	17	28	31
1940–41	33	Detroit Red Wings	NHL	47	5	17	22	35
1941–42	34	Detroit Red Wings	NHL	9	2	2	4	2
1942–43	35	Detroit Red Wings	NHL	11	1	4	5	4
NHL Career – 14 Seasons				557	134	190	324	511

PLAYOFFS

Season	Age	Team	Lg	GP	G	A	PTS	PIM
1931–32	24	Detroit Falcons	NHL	2	0	0	0	0
1932–33	25	Detroit Red Wings	NHL	4	1	0	1	11
1933–34	26	Detroit Red Wings	NHL	9	4	3	7	12
1935–36	28	Detroit Red Wings	NHL	7	1	0	1	4
1936–37	29	Detroit Red Wings	NHL	9	2	2	4	12
1938–39	31	Detroit Red Wings	NHL	6	0	0	0	8
1939–40	32	Detroit Red Wings	NHL	5	0	2	2	9
1940–41	33	Detroit Red Wings	NHL	3	0	1	1	9
NHL Career – 9 Seasons				45	8	8	16	65

TROPHY CASE

AWARDS

Hart Memorial Trophy (1940)

Stanley Cup (1935–36, 1936–37, 1942–43)

ALL-STAR SELECTIONS

First All-Star Team Defense (1937, 1940)

Second All-Star Team Defense (1936)

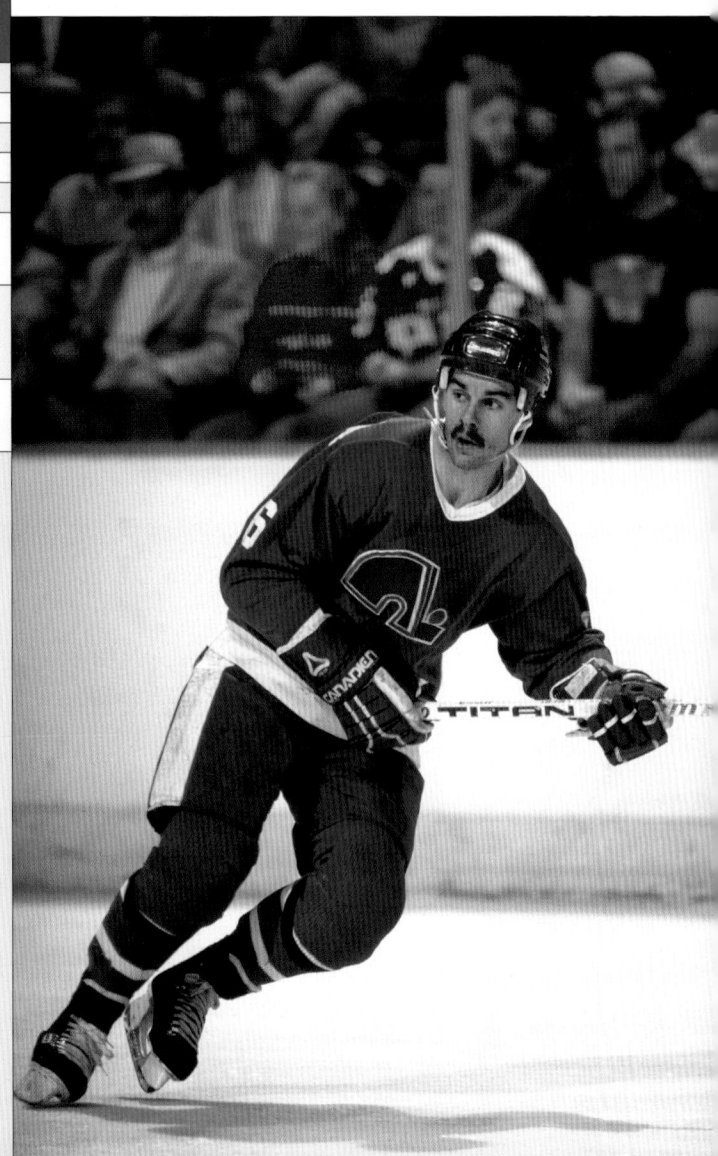

16

Alternate: 9
Left Wing
Shoots: Left
Height: 6'-1"
Weight: 195 lbs.
Born: April 21, 1960: Peribonka, Quebec
Drafted by the Quebec Nordiques 20th overall in 1979
Played 16 WHA and NHL seasons from 1978–94

Michel Goulet

HOCKEY HALL OF FAME CLASS: 1998

QUICK FACTS

- Played amateur hockey with Mistassinni Majors (1976–77); Quebec Remparts (1976–78)

- QMJHL Second All-Star Team Left Wing (1978)

- Holds Quebec Nordiques/Colorado Avalanche team record for regular season plus/minus (+62), established in 1983–84

- Holds Quebec Nordiques/Colorado Avalanche record for goals in regular season (57), established in 1982–83

- Played in NHL All-Star Game (1983, 1984, 1985, 1986, 1988)

- Made professional debut as an underage free agent in the World Hockey Association with the Birmingham Bulls in 1978

- One of six teenage players on Birmingham Bulls team, who were collectively known as the "Baby Bulls"

- Led NHL in short-handed goals (6) in 1981–82; led NHL in game-winning goals (16) in 1983–84

- Finished second in NHL power-play goals in 1984–85 (17), 1985–86 (28) and 1987–88 (29)

- Registered nine points in 10 games at 1983 World Hockey Championships in West Germany

- Traded to Chicago by Quebec with Greg Millen and Quebec's 6th round choice (Kevin St. Jacques) in 1991 Entry Draft for Mario Doyon, Everett Sanipass and Dan Vincelette, March 5, 1990

> It was a dream come true. I really enjoyed the city and the fans in Quebec City. For me, to start my NHL career there in Quebec City was the best. I knew there was something good there, and during my 10 years we did pretty well."

REGULAR SEASON

Season	Age	Team	Lg	GP	G	A	PTS	+/-	PIM	ESG	PPG	SHG	GWG	SOG	S%
1978–79	18	Birmingham Bulls	WHA	78	28	30	58	13	65	25	3	0		146	19.2
1979–80	19	Quebec Nordiques	NHL	77	22	32	54	-10	48	17	5	0	2	267	13.2
1980–81	20	Quebec Nordiques	NHL	76	32	39	71	0	45	27	3	2	3	265	12.1
1981–82	21	Quebec Nordiques	NHL	80	42	42	84	35	48	29	7	6	3	251	16.7
1982–83	22	Quebec Nordiques	NHL	80	57	48	105	31	51	43	10	4	4	256	22.3
1983–84	23	Quebec Nordiques	NHL	75	56	65	121	62	76	43	11	2	16	239	23.4
1984–85	24	Quebec Nordiques	NHL	69	55	40	95	10	55	38	17	0	6	257	21.4
1985–86	25	Quebec Nordiques	NHL	75	53	51	104	6	64	25	28	0	3	244	21.7
1986–87	26	Quebec Nordiques	NHL	75	49	47	96	-12	61	32	17	0	6	276	17.8
1987–88	27	Quebec Nordiques	NHL	80	48	58	106	-31	56	18	29	1	4	284	16.9
1988–89	28	Quebec Nordiques	NHL	69	26	38	64	-20	67	15	11	0	2	162	16.0
1989–90	29	Quebec Nordiques	NHL	57	16	29	45	-33	42	8	8	0	0	144	11.1
1989–90	29	Chicago Blackhawks	NHL	8	4	1	5	1	9	2	1	1	0	10	40.0
1990–91	30	Chicago Blackhawks	NHL	74	27	38	65	27	65	18	9	0	1	167	16.2
1991–92	31	Chicago Blackhawks	NHL	75	22	41	63	20	69	13	9	0	4	176	12.5
1992–93	32	Chicago Blackhawks	NHL	63	23	21	44	10	43	13	10	0	5	125	18.4
1993–94	33	Chicago Blackhawks	NHL	56	16	14	30	1	26	13	3	0	6	120	13.3
Career – 16 Seasons				1167	576	634	1210	110	890	379	181	16	64	3289	17.5

PLAYOFFS

Season	Age	Team	Lg	GP	G	A	PTS	+/-	PIM	ESG	PPG	SHG	GWG	SOG	S%
1980–81	20	Quebec Nordiques	NHL	4	3	4	7		7	3	0	0	1		
1981–82	21	Quebec Nordiques	NHL	16	8	5	13		6	4	2	2	0		
1982–83	22	Quebec Nordiques	NHL	4	0	0	0		6	0	0	0	0		
1983–84	23	Quebec Nordiques	NHL	9	2	4	6	1	17	2	0	0	0	17	11.8
1984–85	24	Quebec Nordiques	NHL	17	11	10	21	3	17	4	7	0	0	51	21.6
1985–86	25	Quebec Nordiques	NHL	3	1	2	3	-2	10	0	1	0	0	12	8.3
1986–87	26	Quebec Nordiques	NHL	13	9	5	14	-2	35	5	4	0	2	40	22.5
1989–90	29	Chicago Blackhawks	NHL	14	2	4	6	2	6	2	0	0	0	18	11.1
1991–92	31	Chicago Blackhawks	NHL	9	3	4	7	4	6	3	0	0	1	19	15.8
1992–93	32	Chicago Blackhawks	NHL	3	0	1	1	-1	0	0	0	0	0	1	0.0
Career – 10 Seasons				92	39	39	78	5	110	23	14	2	4	158	17.7

TROPHY CASE

ALL-STAR SELECTIONS

First All-Star Team Left Wing (1984, 1986, 1987)

Second All-Star Team Left Wing (1983, 1988)

INTERNATIONAL AWARDS

Canada Cup (1984, 1987)

Bronze Medal: World Championships (1983)

21

Cammi Granato
HOCKEY HALL OF FAME CLASS: 2010

Right Wing/Center

Shoots: Right

Height: 5'-7"

Weight: 140 lbs.

Born: March 25, 1971: Downers Grove, Illinois

Played 16 elite amateur seasons from 1989–2005

QUICK FACTS

- Played amateur hockey with Providence College Friars (1989–93); U.S. National Women's Team (1990–2005); Concordia University Stingers (1995–97); Vancouver Griffins (2002–03); B.C. Breakers (2004–05)

- Holds Providence College records for single-season goals (48), assists (43) and points (84)

- Holds Providence College records for career goals (139) and career points (256)

- Named ECAC Women's Player of the Year (1991, 1992, 1993)

- Named U.S.A. Women's Player of the Year (1996)

- IIHF All-Tournament Team (1992, 1997, 2002); named IIHF Best Forward (1992); named IIHF All-Tournament Player (1997)

- Inducted into International Ice Hockey Hall of Fame (2008); inducted into U.S. Hockey Hall of Fame (2008)

- Sister of Tony Granato, who played 13 NHL seasons with N.Y. Rangers, L.A. Kings and San Jose from 1988–2001; spouse of Ray Ferraro, who played 18 NHL seasons with Hartford Whalers, N.Y. Islanders, N.Y. Rangers, L.A. Kings, Atlanta Thrashers and St. Louis from 1984–2002

- Served as captain of U.S. Women's Olympic Team (1998)

- Honored as U.S. flag bearer during the 1998 Winter Olympics' closing ceremony in Nagano, Japan

- Invited to the New York Islanders' training camp in 1997 but turned down the offer because she was worried about getting hurt

> "As a kid I was an equal. I never thought of myself any different. I wanted to be a Chicago Blackhawk exactly like my brothers."
> — Cammi Granato, commenting on her childhood ambitions

CAREER STATS

Season	Age	Team	Lg	GP	G	A	PTS	PIM
1989–90	18	Providence College	ECAC	24	24	22	46	
1989–90	18	U.S. National Team	WWC	5	9	5	14	4
1990–91	19	Providence College	ECAC	22	26	20	46	
1991–92	20	Providence College	ECAC	25	48	32	80	
1991–92	20	U.S. National Team	WWC	5	8	2	10	2
1992–93	21	Providence College	ECAC	28	41	43	84	
1993–94	22	U.S. National Team	WWC	5	5	7	12	6
1994–95	23	U.S. National Team	Pacific Rim	5	4	7	11	4
1995–96	24	Concordia Stingers	QSSF					
1995–96	24	U.S. National Team	Pacific Rim	5	5	3	8	0
1996–97	25	Concordia Stingers	QSSF					
1996–97	25	U.S. National Team	WWC	5	5	3	8	4
1997–98	26	U.S. National Team	Nat-Team	33	14	19	33	
1997–98	26	U.S. National Team	Olympics	6	4	4	8	0
1998–99	27	U.S. National Team	WWC	5	3	5	8	0
1999–00	28	U.S. National Team	Nat-Team	20	17	25	42	
1999–00	28	U.S. National Team	WWC	5	7	6	13	0
2000–01	29	U.S. National Team	Nat-Team	38	36	32	68	
2001–02	30	U.S. National Team	Nat-Team	25	27	21	48	
2001–02	30	U.S. National Team	Olympics	5	6	4	10	0
2002–03	31	Vancouver Griffins	NWHL	16	18	14	32	6
2003–04	32	U.S. National Team	WWC	3	0	2	2	0
2004–05	33	B.C. Breakers	NWHL	21	8	11	19	30
2004–05	33	U.S. National Team	WWC	5	1	3	4	2
Career – 16 Seasons				306	323	287	610	58

PLAYOFFS

Season	Age	Team	Lg	GP	G	A	PTS	PIM
2002–03		Vancouver Griffins	NWHL	1	0	1	1	0
Career – 1 Season				1	0	1	1	0

TROPHY CASE

AWARDS

Lester Patrick Trophy (2007)

INTERNATIONAL AWARDS

Gold Medal: Winter Olympics (1998)

Silver Medal: Winter Olympics (2002)

Gold Medal: World Championships (2005)

Silver Medal: World Championships (1990, 1992, 1994, 1997, 1999, 2000, 2001, 2004)

Mike Grant

HOCKEY HALL OF FAME CLASS: 1950

Defense

Shoots: Unknown

Height: Unknown

Weight: Unknown

Born: November 27, 1873: Montreal, Quebec

Died: August 20, 1955: St. Lambert, Quebec

Played nine elite amateur seasons from 1893–1902

QUICK FACTS

- Renowned as the first rushing defenseman in hockey history
- Champion speedskater in his youth, he also played lacrosse growing up in Montreal
- Member of Montreal City Junior champion Montreal Jr. Crystals (1890–91); member of Montreal City Intermediate champion Montreal Crystals (1891–92, 1892–93)
- Served as captain of Stanley Cup-winning Montreal Victorias (1894–95, December 1896, 1897, 1898, February 1899)
- After losing a challenge to the Winnipeg Victorias in February of 1896, the Montreal "Vics" quickly won back their title and defended it successfully into the 1898–99 season

- Famously served as a referee during the 1905 Stanley Cup series between Ottawa and the Rat Portage Thistles, wearing a hard hat on his head during a rough series played on soft ice
- After retiring, he gave demonstrations and organized hockey exhibitions in the United States
- Joined Montreal Shamrocks as emergency replacement for Frank Tansey and played in Stanley Cup challenge series against Winnipeg Victorias, January 1901

> "Mike Grant … has the rare qualities that make him at once a good player and a good captain."
> — *The Metropolitan*, Montreal, April 13, 1895

REGULAR SEASON

Season	Age	Team	Lg	GP	G	A	PTS
1893–94	20	Montreal Maples	MCJHL				
1893–94	20	Montreal Victorias	AHAC	5	0	0	0
1894–95	21	Montreal Victorias	AHAC	8	1	0	1
1895–96	22	Montreal Victorias	AHAC	8	3	0	3
1896–97	23	Montreal Victorias	AHAC	8	3	0	3
1897–98	24	Montreal Victorias	AHAC	8	1	0	1
1898–99	25	Montreal Victorias	CAHL	7	2	0	2
1899–00	26	Montreal Victorias	CAHL	2	0	0	0
1900–01	27	Montreal Shamrocks	CAHL	2	0	0	0
1901–02	28	Montreal Victorias	CAHL	7	0	0	0
Career – 9 Seasons				55	10	0	10

PLAYOFFS

Season	Age	Team	Lg	GP	G	A	PTS
1893–94	20	Montreal Victorias	AHAC	1	0	0	0
1895–96	22	Montreal Victorias	St-Cup	2	0	0	0
1896–97	23	Montreal Victorias	St-Cup	1	0	0	0
1898–99	25	Montreal Victorias	St-Cup	2	0	0	0
1900–01	27	Montreal Shamrocks	St-Cup	2	0	0	0
Career – 5 Seasons				8	0	0	0

TROPHY CASE

AWARDS

Stanley Cup (1894–95, 1895–96, 1896–97, 1897–98, 1898–99)

8

Shorty Green

HOCKEY HALL OF FAME CLASS: 1962

Alternates: 16, 6

Right Wing

Shoots: Right

Height: 5'-10"

Weight: 152 lbs.

Born: July 17, 1896: Sudbury, Ontario

Died: April 19, 1960: Sudbury, Ontario

Played nine elite amateur and NHL seasons from 1918–27

QUICK FACTS

- Played amateur hockey with Sudbury All-Stars (1914–16); Hamilton 227th (1916–17); Hamilton Tigers (1918–19); Sudbury Wolves (1919–23)

- Led OHA-Sr. in playoff goals (5) and points (8) in 1918–19; led Northern Ontario Hockey Association in goals (23) and points (27) in 1919–20

- Served overseas in World War I and was injured in a gas attack, prompting his return to Canada in December of 1918

- Member of Allan Cup-winning Hamilton Tigers (1919), scoring three goals in Hamilton's 7–6 two-game, total-goal series win over the Winnipeg Selkirks

- Signed as a free agent by Hamilton Tigers (NHL), November 22, 1923

- Captain of the Hamilton Tigers when the team went on strike before the playoffs to protest not receiving extra pay for post-season play. The entire team was suspended by NHL president Frank Calder and the franchise was relocated to New York and renamed the Americans before the start of the 1925–26 season

- Transferred to New York Americans after NHL club purchased Hamilton franchise, September 25, 1925

- Scored first goal in history of Madison Square Garden in N.Y. Americans 3–1 loss to the Montreal Canadiens, December 15, 1925

- Suffered a career-ending kidney injury in game against N.Y. Rangers, February 28, 1928. Green had his kidney removed and was administered the last rites before recovering

> Professional hockey is a money-making affair. The promoters are in the game for what they can make out of it and the players wouldn't be in the game if they didn't look at matters in the same light."

REGULAR SEASON

Season	Age	Team	Lg	GP	G	A	PTS	PIM
1918–19	22	Hamilton Tigers	OHA-Sr	8	12	13	15	
1919–20	23	Sudbury Wolves	NOHA	6	23	4	27	16
1920–21	24	Sudbury Wolves	NOHA	4	4	2	6	7
1921–22	25	Sudbury Wolves	NOHA	9	5	4	9	9
1922–23	26	Sudbury Wolves	NOHA	7	3	1	4	16
1923–24	27	Hamilton Tigers	NHL	22	7	6	13	31
1924–25	28	Hamilton Tigers	NHL	28	18	9	27	63
1925–26	29	New York Americans	NHL	32	6	4	10	40
1926–27	30	New York Americans	NHL	21	2	1	3	17
Career – 9 Seasons				137	80	34	114	199

PLAYOFFS

Season	Age	Team	Lg	GP	G	A	PTS	PIM
1918–19	22	Hamilton Tigers	OHA-Sr	4	5	3	8	
1919–20	23	Sudbury Wolves	NOHA	7	13	4	17	8
1922–23	26	Sudbury Wolves	NOHA	1	0	1	1	2
Career – 3 Seasons				12	18	8	26	10

TROPHY CASE

Wayne Gretzky

HOCKEY HALL OF FAME CLASS: 1999

99

Retired by Edmonton, Los Angeles and the NHL

Center

Shoots: Left

Height: 6'

Weight: 185 lbs.

Born: January 26, 1961: Brantford, Ontario

Played 21 WHA and NHL seasons from 1978–99

" A good hockey player plays where the puck is. A great hockey player plays where the puck is going to be."

Only player inducted into the Hall of Fame Class of 1999

QUICK FACTS

- At time of retirement in 1999, held 40 regular season NHL records, 15 playoff records and six All-Star Game records
- Only player in NHL history to have his number (99) retired by the league
- Holds NHL records for career goals (894), short-handed goals (73), assists (1,963) and points (2,857); holds NHL records for single season goals (92), assists (163) and points (212); holds NHL records for career playoff goals (122), assists (260) and points (382)
- Shares NHL record (with Brett Hull) for career playoff game-winning goals (24)

- Registered 1,000th career NHL point in Edmonton's 7–4 victory over L.A. Kings, December 19, 1984; registered 2,000th career NHL point in L.A. Kings' 6–2 loss to Winnipeg Jets, October 26, 1990; recorded 802nd career NHL goal in L.A. Kings' 6–3 loss to Vancouver Canucks, March 23, 1994
- Traded to Los Angeles by Edmonton with Mike Krushelnyski and Marty McSorley for Jimmy Carson, Martin Gelinas, Los Angeles' first round choices in 1989 (later traded to New Jersey; New Jersey selected Jason Miller), 1991 (Martin Rucinsky) and 1993 (Nick Stajduhar) and cash, August 9, 1988

The skates Gretzky wore as 10-year-old in Brantford, Ontario.

REGULAR SEASON

Season	Age	Team	Lg	GP	G	A	PTS	+/-	PIM	ESG	PPG	SHG	GWG	SOG	S%
1978–79	18	Indianapolis Racers	WHA	8	3	3	6	-3	0	3	0	0		17	17.6
1978–79	18	Edmonton Oilers	WHA	72	43	61	104	23	19	34	9	0		253	17.0
1979–80	19	Edmonton Oilers	NHL	79	51	86	137	15	21	37	13	1	6	284	18.0
1980–81	20	Edmonton Oilers	NHL	80	55	109	164	41	28	36	15	4	3	261	21.1
1981–82	21	Edmonton Oilers	NHL	80	92	120	212	81	26	68	18	6	12	369	24.9
1982–83	22	Edmonton Oilers	NHL	80	71	125	196	60	59	47	18	6	9	348	20.4
1983–84	23	Edmonton Oilers	NHL	74	87	118	205	76	39	55	20	12	11	324	26.9
1984–85	24	Edmonton Oilers	NHL	80	73	135	208	98	52	54	8	11	7	358	20.4
1985–86	25	Edmonton Oilers	NHL	80	52	163	215	71	46	38	11	3	6	350	14.9
1986–87	26	Edmonton Oilers	NHL	79	62	121	183	70	28	42	13	7	4	288	21.5
1987–88	27	Edmonton Oilers	NHL	64	40	109	149	39	24	26	9	5	3	211	19.0
1988–89	28	Los Angeles Kings	NHL	78	54	114	168	15	26	38	11	5	5	303	17.8
1989–90	29	Los Angeles Kings	NHL	73	40	102	142	8	42	26	10	4	4	236	16.9
1990–91	30	Los Angeles Kings	NHL	78	41	122	163	30	16	33	8	0	5	212	19.3
1991–92	31	Los Angeles Kings	NHL	74	31	90	121	-12	34	17	12	2	2	215	14.4
1992–93	32	Los Angeles Kings	NHL	45	16	49	65	6	6	14	0	2	1	141	11.3
1993–94	33	Los Angeles Kings	NHL	81	38	92	130	-25	20	20	14	4	0	233	16.3
1994–95	34	Los Angeles Kings	NHL	48	11	37	48	-20	6	8	3	0	1	142	7.7
1995–96	35	Los Angeles Kings	NHL	62	15	66	81	-7	32	10	5	0	2	144	10.4
1995–96	35	St. Louis Blues	NHL	18	8	13	21	-6	2	6	1	1	1	51	15.7
1996–97	36	New York Rangers	NHL	82	25	72	97	12	28	19	6	0	2	286	8.7
1997–98	37	New York Rangers	NHL	82	23	67	90	-11	28	17	6	0	4	201	11.4
1998–99	38	New York Rangers	NHL	70	9	53	62	-23	14	6	3	0	3	132	6.8
Career – 21 Seasons				1587	940	2027	2967	538	596	654	213	73	91	5359	17.5

PLAYOFFS

Season	Age	Team	Lg	GP	G	A	PTS	+/-	PIM	ESG	PPG	SHG	GWG	SOG	S%
1978–79	18	Edmonton Oilers	WHA	13	10	10	20	8	2				1		
1979–80	19	Edmonton Oilers	NHL	3	2	1	3		0	0	2	0	0		
1980–81	20	Edmonton Oilers	NHL	9	7	14	21		4	4	2	1	1		
1981–82	21	Edmonton Oilers	NHL	5	5	7	12		8	3	1	1			
1982–83	22	Edmonton Oilers	NHL	16	12	26	38		4	7	2	3	3		
1983–84	23	Edmonton Oilers	NHL	19	13	22	35	18	12	11	2	0	3	86	15.1
1984–85	24	Edmonton Oilers	NHL	18	17	30	47	28	4	11	4	2	3	67	25.4
1985–86	25	Edmonton Oilers	NHL	10	8	11	19	0	2	3	4	1	2	42	19.0
1986–87	26	Edmonton Oilers	NHL	21	5	29	34	10	6	3	2	0	0	55	9.1
1987–88	27	Edmonton Oilers	NHL	19	12	31	43	9	16	6	5	1	3	62	19.4
1988–89	28	Los Angeles Kings	NHL	11	5	17	22	-4	0	3	1	1	0	42	11.9
1989–90	29	Los Angeles Kings	NHL	7	3	7	10	-4	0	2	1	1	0	13	23.1
1990–91	30	Los Angeles Kings	NHL	12	4	11	15	0	2	3	1	0	2	26	15.4
1991–92	31	Los Angeles Kings	NHL	6	2	5	7	-3	2	1	1	0	0	11	18.2
1992–93	32	Los Angeles Kings	NHL	24	15	25	40	6	4	10	4	1	3	76	19.7
1995–96	35	St. Louis Blues	NHL	13	2	14	16	2	0	1	1	0	1	25	8.0
1996–97	36	New York Rangers	NHL	15	10	10	20	5	2	7	3	0	2	44	22.7
Career – 17 Seasons				221	132	270	402	73	68	77	34	11	25	549	17.5

TROPHY CASE

AWARDS

Hart Memorial Trophy (1980–87, 1989)

Art Ross Trophy (1981–87, 1990, 1991, 1994)

Lady Byng Memorial Trophy (1980, 1991, 1992, 1994, 1999)

Conn Smythe Trophy (1985, 1988)

Lester B. Pearson Award (1982, 1983, 1984, 1985, 1987)

Lester Patrick Trophy (1994)

Stanley Cup (1983–84, 1984–85, 1986–87, 1987–88)

ALL-STAR SELECTIONS

First All-Star Team Center (1981–87, 1991)

Second All-Star Team Center (1980, 1988–90, 1994, 1997, 1998)

INTERNATIONAL AWARDS

Canada Cup (1984, 1987, 1991)

6

Si Griffis

HOCKEY HALL OF FAME CLASS: 1950

Alternate: 5

Defense/Rover

Shoots: Left

Height: 6'-1"

Weight: 195 lbs.

Born: September 22, 1883: Onega, Kansas

Died: July 9, 1950: Vancouver, British Columbia

Played 13 elite amateur and professional seasons from 1902–07, 1911–19

QUICK FACTS

- Born in Kansas, he was raised in St. Catharines and Rat Portage (Kenora), Ontario
- Renowned as one of the fastest skaters of his era and one of the game's largest players
- Starred on local school and junior teams in Rat Portage (Kenora) with future Hall of Fame members Tommy Phillips, Tom Hooper and Billy McGimisie
- Member of MNWHA champion Rat Portage Thistles (1902–03, 1904–05)
- Challenged for Stanley Cup with Rat Portage in 1903 and 1905 but lost to the Ottawa "Silver Seven" on both occasions
- Member of MHL champion Kenora Thistles (1905–06)
- Member of Stanley Cup-winning Kenora Thistles team that defeated Montreal Wanderers in January of 1907
- Signed as a free agent by Vancouver Millionaires, November 6, 1911
- Served as captain of PCHA champion Vancouver Millionaires but was unable to play in the Stanley Cup series against Ottawa Senators due to a broken leg (1914–15)
- Returned to play two more full seasons and parts of two others before retiring in 1919

> "Of the visitors, Griffis is probably the star at rover. He is a big fellow and a rattling good stickhandler and his rushes are a continual feature of the game."
> — *Manitoba Free Press*, March 10, 1904

REGULAR SEASON

Season	Age	Team	Lg	GP	G	A	PTS	PIM
1902–03	19	Rat Portage Thistles	MNWHA	5	5	0	5	
1903–04	20	Rat Portage Thistles	MNWHA	12	12	2	14	
1904–05	21	Rat Portage Thistles	MHL	8	15	0	15	3
1905–06	22	Kenora Thistles	MHL	9	9	0	9	
1906–07	23	Kenora Thistles	MHL-Pro	6	5	0	5	
1911–12	28	Vancouver Millionaires	PCHA	15	8	0	8	18
1912–13	29	Vancouver Millionaires	PCHA	14	10	3	13	30
1913–14	30	Vancouver Millionaires	PCHA	13	2	3	5	21
1914–15	31	Vancouver Millionaires	PCHA	17	2	3	5	32
1915–16	32	Vancouver Millionaires	PCHA	18	7	5	12	12
1916–17	33	Vancouver Millionaires	PCHA	23	7	4	11	34
1917–18	34	Vancouver Millionaires	PCHA	8	2	6	8	0
1918–19	35	Vancouver Millionaires	PCHA	2	0	2	2	0
Career – 13 Seasons				150	84	28	112	150

PLAYOFFS

Season	Age	Team	Lg	GP	G	A	PTS	PIM
1902–03	19	Rat Portage Thistles	St-Cup	2	0	0	0	
1904–05	21	Rat Portage Thistles	St-Cup	3	3	0	3	3
1906–07	23	Kenora Thistles	St-Cup	4	1	0	1	6
1917–18	34	Vancouver Millionaires	PCHA	2	0	0	0	0
1917–18	34	Vancouver Millionaires	St-Cup	5	1	0	1	9
1918–19	35	Vancouver Millionaires	PCHA	2	1	1	2	0
Career – 5 Seasons				18	6	1	7	18

TROPHY CASE

AWARDS

Stanley Cup (1906–07, 1914–15)

> You've got to love what you're doing. If you love it, you can overcome any handicap or the soreness or all the aches and pains, and continue to play for a long, long time."
>
> Gordie Howe

A
B
C
D
E
F
G
H
I
J
K
L
M
N
O
P
Q
R
S
T
U
V
W
X
Y
Z

1

George Hainsworth
HOCKEY HALL OF FAME CLASS: 1961

Alternates: 12, 17

Goaltender

Catches: Left

Height: 5'-6"

Weight: 150 lbs.

Born: June 26, 1895: Toronto, Ontario

Died: October 9, 1950: Gravenhurst, Ontario

Played 14 professional seasons from 1923–37

QUICK FACTS

- Holds NHL record for shutouts in regular season (22), established in 1928–29
- Holds NHL record for consecutive shutout minutes in a single playoff season (270:08) established in 1930; shares NHL record for consecutive shutouts in a single playoff season (3), established in 1926
- Shares NHL record for shutouts in a single calendar month (6), established in February of 1929; record tied by Dominic Hasek in December of 1997
- Ranks third in career NHL shutouts (94)
- Ranks second in professional career shutouts (104) with 94 NHL shutouts and 10 WCHL/WHL shutouts
- Led OHA-Sr. in wins in 1912–13 (3), 1913–14 (7), 1914–15 (5), 1915–16 (8), 1917–18 (9) and 1919–20 (6)
- Played amateur hockey with Berlin Mavericks (1910–11); Berlin Union Jacks (1911–12); Berlin City Seniors (1913–16); Toronto Kew Beach (1916–17); Kitchener Greenshirts (1918–23)
- Led OHA-Sr. in shutouts in 1915–16 (1), 1919–20 (1), 1920–21 (3) and 1921–22 (1)
- Led OHA-Sr. in goals-against-average in 1913–14 (1.57), 1914–15 (1.80), 1917–18 (3.44) and 1919–20 (2.00)
- Signed as a free agent by Saskatoon Crescents (WCHL), October 11, 1923
- Led WCHL in shutouts (4) in 1923–24
- Traded to Montreal Canadiens by Saskatoon Crescents, August 23, 1926
- Traded to Toronto by Montreal Canadiens for Lorne Chabot, October 1, 1933

> I'm sorry I can't put on a show like some of the other goaltenders. I can't look excited because I'm not. I can't shout at other players because that's not my style. I can't dive on easy shots and make them look hard. I guess all I can do is stop pucks."
> — George Hainsworth, 1931

REGULAR SEASON

Season	Age	Team	Lg	GP	W	L	T	SO	GA	GAA	G	A	PTS	PIM
1923–24	28	Saskatoon Crescents	WCHL	30	15	12	3	4	73	2.34				
1924–25	29	Saskatoon Crescents	WCHL	28	16	11	1	2	75	2.65				
1925–26	30	Saskatoon Crescents	WHL	30	18	11	1	4	64	2.11				
1926–27	31	Montreal Canadiens	NHL	44	28	14	2	14	67	1.47	0	0	0	0
1927–28	32	Montreal Canadiens	NHL	44	26	11	7	13	48	1.05	0	0	0	0
1928–29	33	Montreal Canadiens	NHL	44	22	7	15	22	43	0.92	0	0	0	0
1929–30	34	Montreal Canadiens	NHL	42	20	13	9	4	108	2.42	0	0	0	0
1930–31	35	Montreal Canadiens	NHL	44	26	10	8	8	89	1.95	0	0	0	0
1931–32	36	Montreal Canadiens	NHL	48	25	16	7	6	110	2.20	0	0	0	2
1932–33	37	Montreal Canadiens	NHL	48	18	25	5	8	115	2.32	0	0	0	0
1933–34	38	Toronto Maple Leafs	NHL	48	26	13	9	3	119	2.37	0	0	0	0
1934–35	39	Toronto Maple Leafs	NHL	48	30	14	4	8	111	2.25	0	0	0	0
1935–36	40	Toronto Maple Leafs	NHL	48	23	19	6	8	106	2.12	0	0	0	0
1936–37	41	Toronto Maple Leafs	NHL	3	0	2	1	0	9	2.84	0	0	0	0
1936–37	41	Montreal Canadiens	NHL	4	2	1	1	0	12	2.67	0	0	0	0
Career – 14 Seasons				553	295	179	79	104	1149	2.08	0	0	0	2

PLAYOFFS

Season	Age	Team	Lg	GP	W	L	T	SO	GA	GAA	G	A	PTS	PIM
1924–25	29	Saskatoon Crescents	WCHL	2	0	1	1	0	6	3.00				
1925–26	30	Saskatoon Crescents	WHL	2	0	1	1	0	4	1.86				
1926–27	31	Montreal Canadiens	NHL	4	1	1	2	1	6	1.43	0	0	0	0
1927–28	32	Montreal Canadiens	NHL	2	0	1	1	0	3	1.41	0	0	0	0
1928–29	33	Montreal Canadiens	NHL	3	0	3	0	0	5	1.67	0	0	0	0
1929–30	34	Montreal Canadiens	NHL	6	5	0	1	3	6	0.75	0	0	0	0
1930–31	35	Montreal Canadiens	NHL	10	6	4	0	2	21	1.75	0	0	0	0
1931–32	36	Montreal Canadiens	NHL	4	1	3	0	0	13	2.60	0	0	0	0
1932–33	37	Montreal Canadiens	NHL	2	0	1	1	0	8	4.00	0	0	0	0
1933–34	38	Toronto Maple Leafs	NHL	5	2	3	0	0	11	2.19	0	0	0	0
1934–35	39	Toronto Maple Leafs	NHL	7	3	4	0	2	12	1.57	0	0	0	0
1935–36	40	Toronto Maple Leafs	NHL	9	4	5	0	0	27	2.99	0	0	0	0
Career – 12 Seasons				56	22	27	7	8	122	2.18	0	0	0	0

TROPHY CASE

AWARDS

Vezina Trophy (1927, 1928, 1929)

Stanley Cup (1929–30, 1930–31)

ALL-STAR SELECTIONS

WHL First All-Star Team Goaltender (1926)

Glenn Hall

HOCKEY HALL OF FAME CLASS: 1975

Alternate: 22

Goaltender

Catches: Left

Height: 5'-11"

Weight: 180 lbs.

Born: October 3, 1931: Humboldt, Saskatchewan

Played 18 NHL seasons from 1952–53, 1954–71

> **Our first priority was staying alive. Our second was stopping the puck."**
> — Glenn Hall, on the reality of playing goal without a mask

QUICK FACTS

- Holds NHL record for consecutive games played by a goaltender (502), established from 1952–62
- Ranks fourth in NHL career shutouts (84)
- Played amateur hockey with Homboldt Indians (1947–49); Windsor Spitfires (1949–51)
- Led OHA-Jr. in shutouts (6) in 1950–51
- Played minor pro with Indianapolis Capitols (1951–52); Edmonton Flyers (1952–55)
- Led WHL in wins (38) in 1954–55; led WHL in playoff wins (10) in 1952–53
- WHL First All-Star Team Goaltender (1954–55); WHL Second All-Star Team Goaltender (1952–53)
- Led NHL in wins in 1956–57 (38), 1962–63 (30), 1963–64 (34) and 1965–66 (34)
- Led NHL in goals-against-average (2.38) in 1966–67
- Led NHL in shutouts in 1955–56 (12), 1959–60 (6), 1960–61 (6), 1961–62 (9), 1962–63 (5) and 1968–69 (8)
- Played in NHL All-Star Game (1955, 1956, 1957, 1958, 1960, 1961, 1962, 1963, 1964, 1965, 1967, 1968, 1969)
- Traded to Chicago by Detroit with Ted Lindsay for Johnny Wilson, Forbes Kennedy, Bill Preston and Hank Bassen, July 23, 1957
- Claimed by St. Louis from Chicago in Expansion Draft, June 6, 1967
- Second player from losing team (with Roger Crozier) to be awarded Conn Smythe Trophy
- Renowned for reporting late to training camp because he was home "painting the barn"

Painting celebrating Hall's record 502 consecutive games; one of many works featuring hockey greats in the Hockey Hall of Fame archives by an artist known only as "Thompson."

REGULAR SEASON

Season	Age	Team	Lg	GP	W	L	T	SO	GA	GAA	G	A	PTS	PIM
1952–53	21	Detroit Red Wings	NHL	6	4	1	1	1	10	1.67	0	0	0	0
1954–55	23	Detroit Red Wings	NHL	2	2	0	0	1	2	1.00	0	0	0	0
1955–56	24	Detroit Red Wings	NHL	70	30	24	16	12	147	2.10	0	0	0	14
1956–57	25	Detroit Red Wings	NHL	70	38	20	12	4	155	2.21	0	0	0	2
1957–58	26	Chicago Blackhawks	NHL	70	24	39	7	7	200	2.86	0	0	0	10
1958–59	27	Chicago Blackhawks	NHL	70	28	29	13	1	208	2.97	0	0	0	0
1959–60	28	Chicago Blackhawks	NHL	70	28	29	13	6	179	2.56	0	1	1	2
1960–61	29	Chicago Blackhawks	NHL	70	29	24	17	6	176	2.51	0	1	1	0
1961–62	30	Chicago Blackhawks	NHL	70	31	26	13	9	184	2.63	0	0	0	12
1962–63	31	Chicago Blackhawks	NHL	66	30	20	15	5	161	2.47	0	0	0	0
1963–64	32	Chicago Blackhawks	NHL	65	34	19	11	7	148	2.30	0	2	2	2
1964–65	33	Chicago Blackhawks	NHL	41	18	17	5	4	99	2.43	0	0	0	2
1965–66	34	Chicago Blackhawks	NHL	64	34	21	7	4	164	2.63	0	2	2	14
1966–67	35	Chicago Blackhawks	NHL	32	19	5	2	5	66	2.38	0	0	0	10
1967–68	36	St. Louis Blues	NHL	49	19	21	9	5	118	2.48	0	0	0	0
1968–69	37	St. Louis Blues	NHL	41	19	12	8	8	85	2.17	0	2	2	20
1969–70	38	St. Louis Blues	NHL	18	7	8	3	1	49	2.91	0	0	0	0
1970–71	39	St. Louis Blues	NHL	32	13	11	8	2	71	2.42	0	1	1	0
NHL Career – 18 Seasons				906	407	326	163	84	2222	2.49	0	9	9	88

PLAYOFFS

Season	Age	Team	Lg	GP	W	L	T	SO	GA	GAA	G	A	PTS	PIM
1955–56	24	Detroit Red Wings	NHL	10	5	5		0	28	2.78	0	0	0	0
1956–57	25	Detroit Red Wings	NHL	5	1	4		0	15	3.00	0	0	0	10
1958–59	27	Chicago Blackhawks	NHL	6	2	4		0	21	3.50	0	0	0	0
1959–60	28	Chicago Blackhawks	NHL	4	0	4		0	14	3.37	0	0	0	0
1960–61	29	Chicago Blackhawks	NHL	12	8	4		2	26	2.02	0	0	0	0
1961–62	30	Chicago Blackhawks	NHL	12	6	6		2	31	2.58	0	0	0	0
1962–63	31	Chicago Blackhawks	NHL	6	2	4		0	25	4.17	0	0	0	0
1963–64	32	Chicago Blackhawks	NHL	7	3	4		0	22	3.24	0	0	0	0
1964–65	33	Chicago Blackhawks	NHL	13	7	6		1	28	2.21	0	0	0	0
1965–66	34	Chicago Blackhawks	NHL	6	2	4		0	22	3.80	0	0	0	0
1966–67	35	Chicago Blackhawks	NHL	3	1	2		0	8	2.73	0	0	0	0
1967–68	36	St. Louis Blues	NHL	18	8	10		1	45	2.43	0	0	0	0
1968–69	37	St. Louis Blues	NHL	3	0	2		0	5	2.29	0	0	0	0
1969–70	38	St. Louis Blues	NHL	7	4	3		0	21	2.99	0	0	0	0
1970–71	39	St. Louis Blues	NHL	3	0	3		0	9	3.00	0	1	1	0
NHL Career – 15 Seasons				115	49	65		6	320	2.78	0	0	0	10

TROPHY CASE

AWARDS

Calder Memorial Trophy (1956)

Conn Smythe Trophy (1968)

Vezina Trophy (1963, 1967, 1969)

Stanley Cup (1960–61)

ALL-STAR SELECTIONS

First All-Star Team Goaltender (1957, 1958, 1960, 1963, 1964, 1966, 1969)

Second All-Star Team Goaltender (1956, 1961, 1962, 1967)

219

3

Joe Hall
HOCKEY HALL OF FAME CLASS: 1961

Defense

Shoots: Right

Height: 5'-10"

Weight: 175 lbs.

Born: May 3, 1882: Staffordshire, England

Died: April 5, 1919: Seattle, Washington

Played 17 elite amateur and professional seasons from 1902–19

> Well, I'm one of those fellows able to take care of himself if anybody starts anything. But I don't think I am as bad as I am painted."
> — Joe Hall, on his reputation

QUICK FACTS

- Played amateur hockey with Brandon HC (1900–03); Winnipeg Rowing Club (1903–04); Brandon Wheat Cities (1904–05)
- Member of Manitoba Intermediate champion Brandon Hockey Club (1901–02)
- Signed as a free agent by Portage Lakes (IHL), November 2, 1906
- Led IHL in penalty minutes (98) in 1905–06
- Member of IHL champion Portage Lakes (1905–06)
- Led MHL-Pro in playoff goals (5) in 1906–07
- Moved to Canada at age of two and was raised in Winnipeg
- Nicknamed "Bad Joe" or simply "The Bad Man" because of his temper, though teammates would later say his tough guy reputation was overrated

- Played forward early in his career but later became a star defenseman
- Member of Stanley Cup-winning Kenora Thistles team that defeated Montreal Wanderers in January of 1907 although he did not see action in the series
- Scored 7 goals in a single game for the Montreal Shamrocks in the short-lived Canadian Hockey Association on January 11, 1910
- Member of Stanley Cup-winning Quebec Bulldogs (1911–12, 1912–13); named Quebec Bulldogs' Most Popular Player by fans (1913–14)
- Joined the Montreal Canadiens for the inaugural NHL season of 1917–18 when Quebec chose not to operate its team and helped them win the NHL championship in 1918–19

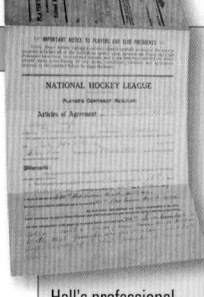

Hall's professional contract with the 1918–19 Montreal Canadiens; Hall would succumb to complications from the Spanish influenza on April 5, 1919.

REGULAR SEASON

Season	Age	Team	Lg	GP	G	A	PTS	PIM
1902–03	20	Brandon Elks	MNWHA	6	8	0	8	
1903–04	21	Winnipeg Rowing Club	WCAHA	6	6	3	9	10
1904–05	22	Brandon Elks	MHL	8	11	0	11	
1905–06	23	Portage Lakes	IHL	20	33	0	33	98
1906–07	24	Brandon Elks	MHL-Pro	9	14	0	14	32
1907–08	25	Montreal AAA	ECAHA	4	5	0	5	11
1907–08	25	Montreal Shamrocks	ECAHA	4	4	0	4	6
1908–09	26	Edmonton Professionals	APHL	1	8	0	8	6
1908–09	26	Montreal Wanderers	ECHA	5	10	0	10	18
1908–09	26	Winnipeg Maple Leafs	MHL-Pro	2	2	1	3	0
1909–10	27	Montreal Shamrocks	CHA	1	7	0	7	6
1909–10	27	Montreal Shamrocks	NHA	10	8	0	8	47
1910–11	28	Quebec Bulldogs	NHA	10	0	1	1	24
1911–12	29	Quebec Bulldogs	NHA	18	15	1	16	43
1912–13	30	Quebec Bulldogs	NHA	18	6	2	8	78
1913–14	31	Quebec Bulldogs	NHA	19	13	4	17	61
1914–15	32	Quebec Bulldogs	NHA	20	3	2	5	52
1915–16	33	Quebec Bulldogs	NHA	23	1	2	3	89
1916–17	34	Quebec Bulldogs	NHA	19	6	5	11	95
1917–18	35	Montreal Canadiens	NHL	21	8	7	15	100
1918–19	36	Montreal Canadiens	NHL	16	7	2	9	135
Career — 17 Seasons				240	175	30	205	911

PLAYOFFS

Season	Age	Team	Lg	GP	G	A	PTS	PIM
1903–04	21	Winnipeg Rowing Club	St-Cup	3	1	0	1	
1906–07	24	Brandon Elks	MHL-Pro	2	5	0	5	5
1908–09	26	Winnipeg Maple Leafs	MHL-Pro	2	2	1	3	9
1911–12	29	Quebec Bulldogs	NHA	2	2	0	2	0
1911–12	29	Quebec Bulldogs	St-Cup	2	2	0	2	2
1912–13	30	Quebec Bulldogs	NHA	2	3	0	3	0
1912–13	30	Quebec Bulldogs	St-Cup	2	3	0	3	0
1917–18	35	Montreal Canadiens	NHL	2	0	1	1	12
1918–19	36	Montreal Canadiens	St-Cup	5	0	0	0	6
1918–19	36	Montreal Canadiens	NHL	5	0	0	0	26
Career — 7 Seasons				27	18	2	20	80

TROPHY CASE

AWARDS

Stanley Cup (1906–07, 1911–12, 1912–13)

ALL-STAR SELECTIONS

IHL First All-Star Team Defense (1906)

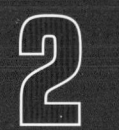

2

Retired by Montreal

Alternates: 5, 6, 17

Defense

Shoots: Left

Height: 5'-11"

Weight: 187 lbs.

Born: December 19, 1924: Montreal, Quebec

Died: December 26, 1989: Montreal, Quebec

Played 19 NHL seasons from 1947–64, 1966–67, 1968–69

Doug Harvey

HOCKEY HALL OF FAME CLASS: 1973

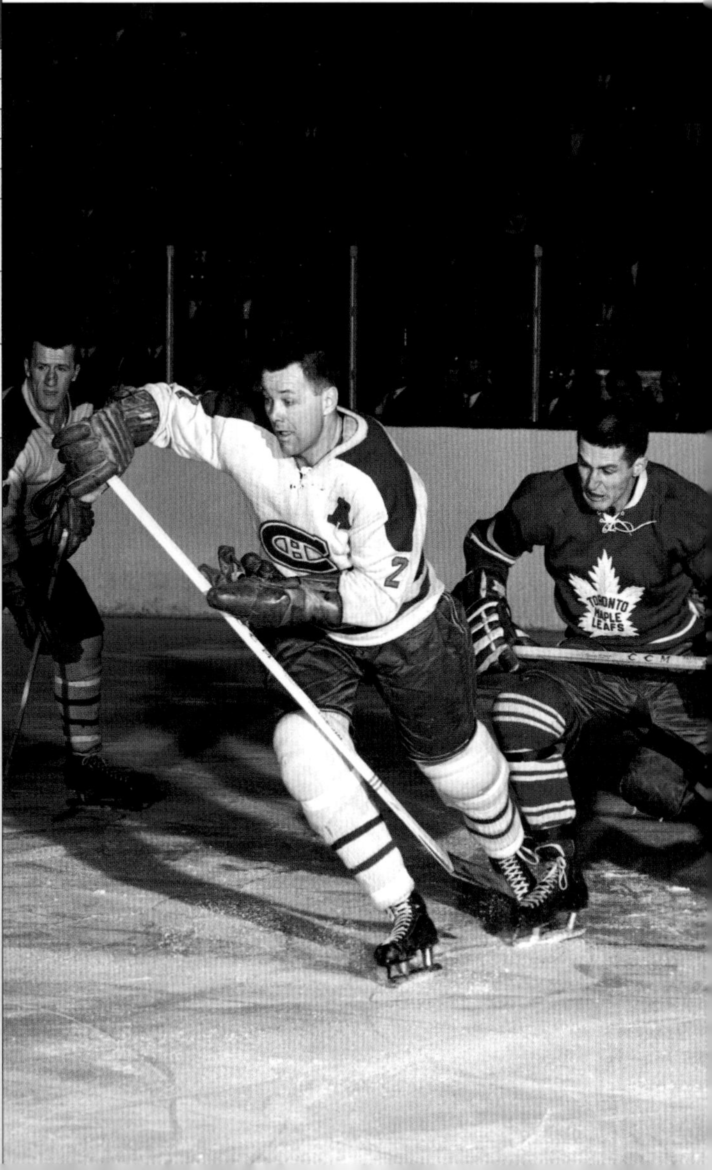

QUICK FACTS

- Played amateur hockey with Montreal Navy (1942–45); Montreal Jr. Royals (1942–45); Montreal Royals (1942–45)
- Played in NHL All-Star Game (1951, 1952, 1953, 1954, 1955, 1956, 1957, 1958, 1959, 1960, 1961, 1962, 1969)
- Originated the spin-a-rama move to avoid checking defenders later popularized by Canadiens' defenseman Serge Savard
- Traded to N.Y. Rangers by Montreal for Lou Fontinato, June 13, 1961
- Served as captain of Montreal Canadiens (1960–61)
- Coached N.Y. Rangers (1961–62)
- Signed as a free agent by Quebec Aces, November 26, 1963

- AHL Second All-Star Team Defense (1964)
- Played minor pro hockey with St. Paul Rangers (1963–64); Quebec Aces (1963–65); Baltimore Clippers (1966–67); Pittsburgh Hornets (1966–67); Kansas City Blues (1967–68)
- Signed as a free agent by Detroit and assigned to AHL's Pittsburgh Hornets, January 6, 1967
- Played two games for the Detroit Red Wings in the 1966–67 season when called up from the team's AHL affiliate in Pittsburgh
- Signed as a free agent by St. Louis and named playing coach of Kansas City Blues, June 1, 1967
- Coached Laval Saints (1969–70); coached Houston Aeros (1973–75)

> "I'm not throwing any pucks away. I'm trying to do what's best for the team. That's why I take my time and make the play."
> — Doug Harvey, describing his puck-moving style that changed the way the game is played

REGULAR SEASON

Season	Age	Team	Lg	GP	G	A	PTS	+/-	PIM	ESG	PPG	SHG	GWG	SOG	S%
1947–48	23	Montreal Canadiens	NHL	35	4	4	8		32						
1948–49	24	Montreal Canadiens	NHL	55	3	13	16		87						
1949–50	25	Montreal Canadiens	NHL	70	4	20	24		76						
1950–51	26	Montreal Canadiens	NHL	70	5	24	29		93						
1951–52	27	Montreal Canadiens	NHL	68	6	23	29		82						
1952–53	28	Montreal Canadiens	NHL	69	4	30	34		67						
1953–54	29	Montreal Canadiens	NHL	68	8	29	37		110						
1954–55	30	Montreal Canadiens	NHL	70	6	43	49		58						
1955–56	31	Montreal Canadiens	NHL	62	5	39	44		60						
1956–57	32	Montreal Canadiens	NHL	70	6	44	50		92						
1957–58	33	Montreal Canadiens	NHL	68	9	32	41		131						
1958–59	34	Montreal Canadiens	NHL	61	4	16	20		61						
1959–60	35	Montreal Canadiens	NHL	66	6	21	27		45						
1960–61	36	Montreal Canadiens	NHL	58	6	33	39		48						
1961–62	37	New York Rangers	NHL	69	6	24	30		42						
1962–63	38	New York Rangers	NHL	68	4	35	39		92						
1963–64	39	New York Rangers	NHL	14	0	2	2		10	0	0	0	0		
1966–67	42	Detroit Red Wings	NHL	2	0	0	0		0	0	0	0	0		
1968–69	44	St. Louis Blues	NHL	70	2	20	22	11	30	1	1	0	0	46	4.3
NHL Career — 19 Seasons				1113	88	452	540	11	1216	1	1	0	0	46	4.3

PLAYOFFS

Season	Age	Team	Lg	GP	G	A	PTS	+/-	PIM	ESG	PPG	SHG	GWG	SOG	S%
1948–49	24	Montreal Canadiens	NHL	7	0	1	1		10						
1949–50	25	Montreal Canadiens	NHL	5	0	2	2		10						
1950–51	26	Montreal Canadiens	NHL	11	0	5	5		12						
1951–52	27	Montreal Canadiens	NHL	11	0	3	3		8						
1952–53	28	Montreal Canadiens	NHL	12	0	5	5		8						
1953–54	29	Montreal Canadiens	NHL	10	0	2	2		12						
1954–55	30	Montreal Canadiens	NHL	12	0	8	8		6						
1955–56	31	Montreal Canadiens	NHL	10	2	5	7		10						
1956–57	32	Montreal Canadiens	NHL	10	0	7	7		10						
1957–58	33	Montreal Canadiens	NHL	10	2	9	11		16						
1958–59	34	Montreal Canadiens	NHL	11	1	11	12		22						
1959–60	35	Montreal Canadiens	NHL	8	3	0	3		6						
1960–61	36	Montreal Canadiens	NHL	6	0	1	1		8						
1961–62	37	New York Rangers	NHL	6	0	1	1		2						
1967–68	43	St. Louis Blues	NHL	8	0	4	4		12						
NHL Career — 15 Seasons				137	8	64	72		152						

TROPHY CASE

AWARDS

James Norris Memorial Trophy (1955, 1956, 1957, 1958, 1960, 1961, 1962)

Stanley Cup (1952–53, 1955–56, 1956–57, 1957–58, 1958–59, 1959–60)

ALL-STAR SELECTIONS

First All-Star Team Defense (1952, 1953, 1954, 1955, 1956, 1957, 1958, 1960, 1961, 1962)

Second All-Star Team Defense (1959)

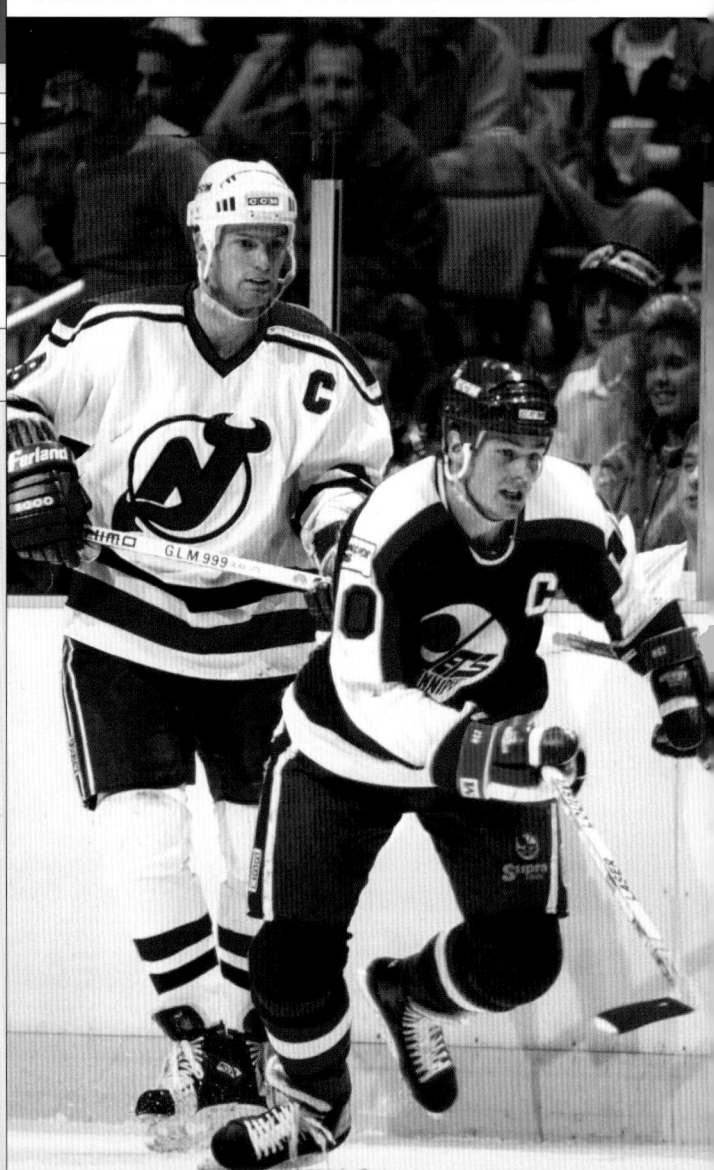

10

Center

Shoots: Left

Height: 5'-11"

Weight: 190 lbs.

Born: April 4, 1963: Toronto, Ontario

Drafted by the Winnipeg Jets first overall in 1981

Played 16 NHL seasons from 1981–97

Dale Hawerchuk

HOCKEY HALL OF FAME CLASS: 2001

QUICK FACTS

- Held NHL record as youngest player to register 100-point season (1981–82); surpassed by Sidney Crosby in 2005–06

- Played amateur hockey with Oshawa Legionnaires (1978–79); Cornwall Royals (1979–81)

- Led QMJHL in goals (81), assists (102) and points (183) in 1980–81; led QMJHL playoffs in goals (20), assists (25) and points (45) in 1979–80

- Member of Memorial Cup-winning Cornwall Royals (1980, 1981)

- Led Memorial Cup tournament in goals (8) and points (12) in 1981

- Memorial Cup All-Star Team (1980, 1981)

- Named Memorial Cup Most Valuable Player (1981); named Memorial Cup Most Sportsmanlike Player (1980)

- QMJHL First All-Star Team Center (1981); CMJHL Player of the Year (1981)

- Scored a goal and recorded two assists in third game of the 1987 Canada Cup final series against the Soviet Union

- Inducted into the Phoenix Coyotes' Ring of Honor (2007)

- Played in NHL All-Star Game (1982, 1985, 1986, 1988, 1997)

- Served as captain of Winnipeg Jets (1984–89)

- Registered 1,000th career NHL point in Buffalo's 5–3 victory over Chicago Blackhawks, March 8, 1991; recorded 500th career NHL goal in St. Louis' 4–0 victory over Toronto Maple Leafs, January 31, 1996

> "We won [the 1987 Canada Cup] because we jelled into a very good team. Each man did whatever the coaches asked him to do and every player on the roster was very important in the whole picture of the team."

REGULAR SEASON

Season	Age	Team	Lg	GP	G	A	PTS	+/-	PIM	ESG	PPG	SHG	GWG	SOG	S%
1981–82	18	Winnipeg Jets	NHL	80	45	58	103	-4	47	33	12	0	2	339	13.3
1982–83	19	Winnipeg Jets	NHL	79	40	51	91	-17	31	26	13	1	3	297	13.5
1983–84	20	Winnipeg Jets	NHL	80	37	65	102	-14	73	27	10	0	4	256	14.5
1984–85	21	Winnipeg Jets	NHL	80	53	77	130	22	74	33	17	3	4	280	18.9
1985–86	22	Winnipeg Jets	NHL	80	46	59	105	-27	44	26	18	2	2	313	14.7
1986–87	23	Winnipeg Jets	NHL	80	47	53	100	3	52	37	10	0	4	267	17.6
1987–88	24	Winnipeg Jets	NHL	80	44	77	121	-9	59	21	20	3	4	292	15.1
1988–89	25	Winnipeg Jets	NHL	75	41	55	96	-30	28	24	14	3	4	239	17.2
1989–90	26	Winnipeg Jets	NHL	79	26	55	81	-11	60	18	8	0	2	211	12.3
1990–91	27	Buffalo Sabres	NHL	80	31	58	89	2	32	19	12	0	1	194	16.0
1991–92	28	Buffalo Sabres	NHL	77	23	75	98	-22	27	10	13	0	4	242	9.5
1992–93	29	Buffalo Sabres	NHL	81	16	80	96	-17	52	8	8	0	2	259	6.2
1993–94	30	Buffalo Sabres	NHL	81	35	51	86	10	91	21	13	1	7	227	15.4
1994–95	31	Buffalo Sabres	NHL	23	5	11	16	-2	2	3	2	0	2	56	8.9
1995–96	32	St. Louis Blues	NHL	66	13	28	41	5	22	8	5	0	1	136	9.6
1995–96	32	Philadelphia Flyers	NHL	16	4	16	20	10	4	3	1	0	1	44	9.1
1996–97	33	Philadelphia Flyers	NHL	51	12	22	34	9	32	6	6	0	2	102	11.8
NHL Career — 16 Seasons				1188	518	891	1409	-92	730	323	182	13	49	3754	13.8

PLAYOFFS

Season	Age	Team	Lg	GP	G	A	PTS	+/-	PIM	ESG	PPG	SHG	GWG	SOG	S%
1981–82	18	Winnipeg Jets	NHL	4	1	7	8		5	1	0	0	0		
1982–83	19	Winnipeg Jets	NHL	3	1	4	5		8	0	1	0	0		
1983–84	20	Winnipeg Jets	NHL	3	1	1	2	-6	0	0	1	0	0	15	6.7
1984–85	21	Winnipeg Jets	NHL	3	2	1	3	1	4	1	1	0	0	8	25.0
1985–86	22	Winnipeg Jets	NHL	3	0	3	3	-2	0	0	0	0	0	10	0.0
1986–87	23	Winnipeg Jets	NHL	10	5	8	13	-4	4	2	3	0	0	39	12.8
1987–88	24	Winnipeg Jets	NHL	5	3	4	7	-4	16	1	2	0	0	16	18.8
1989–90	26	Winnipeg Jets	NHL	7	3	5	8	5	2	3	0	0	1	21	14.3
1990–91	27	Buffalo Sabres	NHL	6	2	4	6	-3	10	1	1	0	0	19	10.5
1991–92	28	Buffalo Sabres	NHL	7	2	5	7	3	0	2	0	0	0	24	8.3
1992–93	29	Buffalo Sabres	NHL	8	5	9	14	0	2	2	3	0	0	31	16.1
1993–94	30	Buffalo Sabres	NHL	7	0	7	7	-1	4	0	0	0	0	16	0.0
1994–95	31	Buffalo Sabres	NHL	2	0	0	0	-1	0	0	0	0	0	3	0.0
1995–96	32	Philadelphia Flyers	NHL	12	3	6	9	0	12	2	1	0	0	48	6.3
1996–97	33	Philadelphia Flyers	NHL	17	2	5	7	-2	0	1	1	0	1	24	8.3
NHL Career — 15 Seasons				97	30	69	99	-14	67	16	14	0	2	274	10.2

TROPHY CASE

AWARDS

Calder Memorial Trophy (1982)

ALL-STAR SELECTIONS

Second All-Star Team Center (1985)

INTERNATIONAL AWARDS

Canada Cup (1987, 1991)

Bronze Medal: World Championships (1982, 1986)

Silver Medal: World Championships (1989)

5

George Hay
HOCKEY HALL OF FAME CLASS: 1958

Alternates: 4, 7, 8

Left Wing

Shoots: Left

Height: 5'-10"

Weight: 155 lbs.

Born: January 10, 1898: Listowel, Ontario

Died: July 13, 1975: Stratford, Ontario

Played 12 professional seasons from 1921–31, 1932–34

Frank Boucher, King Clancy, Sprague Cleghorn, Alex Connell, Red Dutton, Frank Foyston, Frank Frederickson, Herb Gardiner, Dick Irvin, Ching Johnson, Duke Keats, Hugh Lehman, George McNamara, Paddy Moran

QUICK FACTS

- Although he was born in Ontario, earned the nickname "The Western Wizard" because of his stickhandling expertise and scoring exploits in Western Canada

- Played amateur hockey with the Winnipeg Strathconas (1914–15); Winnipeg Monarchs (1915–17); Regina Victorias (1919–21)

- Signed as a free agent by Regina Capitals (WCHL), December 1, 1921

- Rights transferred to Portland (WHL) after Regina (WCHL) franchise relocated, September 1, 1925; rights transferred to Chicago after NHL club purchased Portland (WHL) franchise, May 15, 1926

- Scored first goal in history of Chicago Black Hawks franchise in 4–1 victory over Toronto St. Pats, November 17, 1926

- Traded to Detroit Cougars by Chicago with Percy Traub for $15,000, April 11, 1927

- Named to "Unofficial" NHL First All-Star Team Left Wing (1928)

- Finished second to New York Rangers center Frank Boucher in voting for the Lady Byng Trophy (1928)

- Scored first playoff goal in Detroit franchise history in 3–1 loss to Toronto St. Pats, March 20, 1929

- Served as captain of Detroit Falcons (1930–31)

- Served as player/coach of Detroit Olympics (1931–32) and didn't play in the NHL for the entire season

- Coached London Tecumsehs (1935–36); coached Listowel Intermediates (1938–39)

> "I've seen a lot of good ones, but none who had more stuff than George. He was one of the easiest players to handle I ever had, always in condition, always on the job, always willing to play any position. He never got into any trouble on the ice and was rarely sent to the penalty box."
> — Jack Adams

REGULAR SEASON

Season	Age	Team	Lg	GP	G	A	PTS	PIM
1921–22	24	Regina Capitals	WCHL	25	21	11	32	9
1922–23	25	Regina Capitals	WCHL	30	28	8	36	12
1923–24	26	Regina Capitals	WCHL	25	20	11	31	8
1924–25	27	Regina Capitals	WCHL	20	16	6	22	6
1925–26	28	Portland Rosebuds	WHL	30	19	12	31	4
1926–27	29	Chicago Black Hawks	NHL	35	14	8	22	12
1927–28	30	Detroit Cougars	NHL	42	22	13	35	20
1928–29	31	Detroit Cougars	NHL	39	11	8	19	14
1929–30	32	Detroit Cougars	NHL	44	18	15	33	8
1930–31	33	Detroit Falcons	NHL	44	8	10	18	24
1932–33	35	Detroit Red Wings	NHL	34	6	7	6	6
1933–34	36	Detroit Red Wings	NHL	1	0	0	0	0
Career – 12 Seasons				369	178	108	286	130

PLAYOFFS

Season	Age	Team	Lg	GP	G	A	PTS	PIM
1921–22	24	Regina Capitals	WCHL	4	0	0	0	4
1921–22	24	Regina Capitals	West-P	2	0	1	1	0
1922–23	25	Regina Capitals	WCHL	2	1	0	1	0
1923–24	26	Regina Capitals	WCHL	2	1	1	2	0
1926–27	29	Chicago Black Hawks	NHL	2	1	2	3	2
1928–29	31	Detroit Cougars	NHL	2	1	0	1	0
1932–33	35	Detroit Red Wings	NHL	4	0	1	1	0
Career – 7 Seasons				18	4	5	9	6

TROPHY CASE

ALL-STAR SELECTIONS

WCHL First All-Star Team Left Wing (1922, 1923, 1924)

WHL First All-Star Team Left Wing (1926)

Riley Hern

HOCKEY HALL OF FAME CLASS: 1962

Goaltender

Catches: Left

Height: 5'-9"

Weight: 170 lbs.

Born: December 5, 1880: St. Marys, Ontario

Died: June 24, 1929: Montreal, Quebec

Played 10 elite amateur and professional seasons from 1901–11

QUICK FACTS

- Played amateur hockey with Stratford HC (1898–01)
- Played as both a goaltender and forward with Stratford (1900–01)
- Member of Western Pennsylvania Hockey League champion Pittsburgh Keystones (1901–03)
- Member of IHL champion with Portage Lakes (1903–04, 1905–06)
- WPHL First All-Star Team Goaltender (1902)
- Led WPHL in wins (14) in 1901–02
- Led IHL in shutouts (2) and goals-against-average (3.54) in 1904–05
- ECAHA First All-Star Team Goaltender (1907)
- ECHA First All-Star Team Goaltender (1909)

- Led ECAHA in wins in 1906–07 (10) and 1907–08 (8); led Stanley Cup playoff in wins (5) in 1907–08
- Led NHA in wins (10) in 1906–07
- Retired after the 1910–11 season but remained in the game as a goal judge and referee
- Made his permanent home in Montreal after joining the Wanderers and was prominent in many sporting clubs and business organizations there for the rest of his life

> "Hern was without a doubt one of the greatest drawing cards hockey has ever known, and the success of the Wanderers in winning the world's championship [three] times during his [five] years on the team is adequate evidence of his ability."
> — Montreal Gazette, June 25, 1929

REGULAR SEASON

Season	Age	Team	Lg	GP	W	L	T	SO	GA	GAA
1901–02	23	Pittsburgh Keystones	WPHL	19	14	5	0	2	40	3.08
1902–03	24	Pittsburgh Keystones	WPHL	12	1	10	0	0	61	·7.96
1903–04	25	Portage Lakes	Exhib.	14	13	1	0	4	21	1.50
1904–05	26	Portage Lakes	IHL	24	15	7	2	2	81	3.54
1905–06	27	Portage Lakes	IHL	20	15	5	0	1	70	3.46
1906–07	28	Montreal Wanderers	ECAHA	10	10	0	0	0	39	3.84
1907–08	29	Montreal Wanderers	ECAHA	10	8	2	0	0	52	5.11
1908–09	30	Montreal Wanderers	ECHA	12	9	3	0	0	61	5.03
1909–10	31	Montreal Wanderers	NHA	13	12	1	0	1	47	3.62
1910–11	32	Montreal Wanderers	NHA	16	7	9	0	0	88	5.43
Career – 10 Seasons				150	104	43	2	10	560	3.73

PLAYOFFS

Season	Age	Team	Lg	GP	W	L	T	SO	GA	GAA
1901–02	23	Pittsburgh Keystones	WPHL	1	1	0	0	1	1.50	
1906–07	28	Montreal Wanderers	St-Cup	6	3	3	0	0	25	4.17
1907–08	29	Montreal Wanderers	St-Cup	5	5	0	0	0	16	3.20
1908–09	30	Montreal Wanderers	St-Cup	2	1	1	0	0	10	5.00
1909–10	31	Montreal Wanderers	St-Cup	1	1	0	0	0	3	3.00
Career – 5 Seasons				15	11	4	0	1	55	3.92

TROPHY CASE

AWARDS

Stanley Cup (1906–07, 1907–08, 1909–10)

ALL-STAR SELECTIONS

IHL First All-Star Team Goaltender (1905)

12

Bryan Hextall
HOCKEY HALL OF FAME CLASS: 1969

Alternates: 19, 15

Right Wing

Shoots: Left

Height: 5'-10"

Weight: 180 lbs.

Born: July 31, 1913: Grenfell, Saskatchewan

Died: July 25, 1984: Portage La Prairie, Manitoba

Played 11 NHL seasons from 1936–44, 1945–48

QUICK FACTS

- Played amateur hockey with Winnipeg Monarchs (1931–32); Portage Terriers (1932–34); Vancouver Lions (1933–36); St. Catharines Saints (1944–45); Poplar Point Memorials (1949–52, 1953–54)

- Led MJHL in assists (8) and points (18) in 1932–33

- Played minor pro hockey with Philadelphia Ramblers (1936–37); Cleveland Barons (1948–49); Washington Lions (1948–49)

- Led NWHL in goals (29) in 1935–36; led IAHL in goals (27) in 1936–37

- Rights sold to the N.Y. Rangers by the Victoria Lions (NWHL) in 1936

- Led NHL in goals in 1939–40 (24) and 1940–41 (26); led NHL in points (56) in 1941–42

- Scored Stanley Cup-winning overtime goal in N.Y. Rangers' 3–2 victory over Toronto Maple Leafs, April 13, 1940

- Renowned for great speed, stickhandling ability and toughness

- Coached Saint Boniface Canadiens (1952–53)

- Served as player/coach of Minnedosa Jets (1954–55)

- Father of Bryan Hextall Jr., who played in NHL with N.Y. Rangers, Pittsburgh, Atlanta Flames, Detroit and Minnesota North Stars from 1962–63, 1970–76

- Father of Dennis Hextall, who played in NHL with N.Y. Rangers, L.A. Kings, California, Minnesota North Stars, Detroit and Washington from 1967–80

> He was the hardest bodychecking forward I had seen in more than forty years of watching hockey."
> — Herb Goren, *N.Y. Sun* reporter

REGULAR SEASON

Season	Age	Team	Lg	GP	G	A	PTS	PIM
1936–37	23	New York Rangers	NHL	3	0	1	1	0
1937–38	24	New York Rangers	NHL	48	17	4	21	6
1938–39	25	New York Rangers	NHL	48	20	15	35	18
1939–40	26	New York Rangers	NHL	48	24	15	39	52
1940–41	27	New York Rangers	NHL	48	26	18	44	16
1941–42	28	New York Rangers	NHL	48	24	32	56	30
1942–43	29	New York Rangers	NHL	50	27	32	59	28
1943–44	30	New York Rangers	NHL	50	21	33	54	41
1945–46	32	New York Rangers	NHL	3	0	1	1	0
1946–47	33	New York Rangers	NHL	60	20	10	30	18
1947–48	34	New York Rangers	NHL	43	8	14	22	18
NHL Career — 11 Seasons				449	187	175	362	227

PLAYOFFS

Season	Age	Team	Lg	GP	G	A	PTS	PIM
1937–38	24	New York Rangers	NHL	3	2	0	2	0
1938–39	25	New York Rangers	NHL	7	0	1	1	4
1939–40	26	New York Rangers	NHL	12	4	3	7	11
1940–41	27	New York Rangers	NHL	3	0	1	1	0
1941–42	28	New York Rangers	NHL	6	1	1	2	4
1947–48	34	New York Rangers	NHL	6	1	3	4	0
NHL Career — 6 Seasons				37	8	9	17	19

TROPHY CASE

AWARDS

NHL Scoring Leader (1942)

Stanley Cup (1939–40)

ALL-STAR SELECTIONS

First All-Star Team Right Wing (1940, 1941, 1942)

Second All-Star Team Right Wing (1943)

Hap Holmes

HOCKEY HALL OF FAME CLASS: 1972

Goaltender

Catches: Left

Height: 5'-10"

Weight: 170 lbs.

Born: February 21, 1888: Aurora, Ontario

Died: June 27, 1941: Fort Lauderdale, Florida

Played 16 professional seasons from 1912–28

QUICK FACTS

- Played amateur hockey with Toronto Young Torontos (1907–08); Parkdale Canoe Club (1908–11); Toronto Tecumsehs (1911–12)

- Starred in all five (NHA, NHL, WCHL, WHL, PCHA) of professional hockey's top leagues during his career

- Led NHA in wins (13) in 1913–14

- Led PCHA in wins in 1916–17 (16), 1921–22 (12), 1922–23 (15) and 1923–24 (14)

- Led PCHA in shutouts in 1916–17 (2), 1919–20 (4), 1923–24 (2) and 1924–25 (3)

- Appeared in the Stanley Cup Finals seven times, winning with four teams (Toronto Blueshirts, Toronto Arenas, Seattle, Victoria) in four different leagues (NHA, NHL, PCHA, WHL)

- Member of Stanley Cup-winning Victoria Cougars — last non-NHL club to win the Stanley Cup (1924–25)

- Signed as a free agent by Victoria (WCHL), November 7, 1924; rights transferred to Detroit after NHL club purchased Victoria (WHL) franchise, May 26, 1926

- Coached Cleveland Indians (1929–35); coached Cleveland Falcons (1935–36)

- Legacy honored by the American Hockey League with the Harry "Hap" Holmes Memorial Trophy, presented annually to the league's top goaltender

> Jack Marshall of the Torontos thinks a lot of Harry Holmes as a goaltender and says that with coaching he will be as good as any net guardian in the NHA."
> — *Toronto World*, January 7, 1913

REGULAR SEASON

Season	Age	Team	Lg	GP	W	L	T	SO	GA	GAA	G	A	PTS	PIM
1912–13	24	Toronto Blueshirts	NHA	15	6	7	0	1	58	4.47				
1913–14	25	Toronto Blueshirts	NHA	20	13	7	0	1	65	3.24				
1914–15	26	Toronto Blueshirts	NHA	20	8	12	0	0	84	4.14				
1915–16	27	Seattle Metropolitans	PCHA	18	9	9	0	0	66	3.67				
1916–17	28	Seattle Metropolitans	PCHA	24	16	8	0	2	80	3.28				
1917–18	29	Toronto Arenas	NHL	16	9	7	0	0	76	4.73	0	0	0	0
1918–19	30	Toronto Arenas	NHL	2	0	2	0	0	9	4.50	0	0	0	0
1918–19	30	Seattle Metropolitans	PCHA	20	11	9	0	0	46	2.25				
1919–20	31	Seattle Metropolitans	PCHA	22	12	10	0	4	55	2.46				
1920–21	32	Seattle Metropolitans	PCHA	24	12	11	1	0	68	2.63				
1921–22	33	Seattle Metropolitans	PCHA	24	12	11	1	4	64	2.60				
1922–23	34	Seattle Metropolitans	PCHA	30	15	15	0	2	106	3.45				
1923–24	35	Seattle Metropolitans	PCHA	30	14	16	0	2	99	3.28				
1924–25	36	Victoria Cougars	WCHL	28	16	12	0	3	63	2.25				
1925–26	37	Victoria Cougars	WHL	30	15	11	4	4	53	1.68				
1926–27	38	Detroit Cougars	NHL	41	11	26	4	6	100	2.23	0	0	0	0
1927–28	39	Detroit Cougars	NHL	44	19	19	6	11	79	1.73	0	0	0	0
NHL Career—18 Seasons				408	198	192	16	40	1170	2.87	0	0	0	0

PLAYOFFS

Season	Age	Team	Lg	GP	W	L	T	SO	GA	GAA	G	A	PTS	PIM
1913–14	25	Toronto Blueshirts	NHA	2	1	1	0	1	2	1.00				
1913–14	25	Toronto Blueshirts	St-Cup	3	3	0	0	0	8	2.46				
1916–17	28	Seattle Metropolitans	St-Cup	4	3	1	0	0	11	2.75				
1917–18	29	Toronto Arenas	St-Cup	5	3	2		0	21	4.20				
1917–18	29	Toronto Arenas	NHA	2	1	1	0	0	7	3.50	0	0	0	0
1918–19	30	Seattle Metropolitans	PCHA	2	1	1	0	0	5	2.50				
1918–19	30	Seattle Metropolitans	St-Cup	5	2	2	1	2	10	1.79				
1919–20	31	Seattle Metropolitans	PCHA	2	1	1	0	1	3	1.50				
1919–20	31	Seattle Metropolitans	St-Cup	5	2	3	0	0	15	3.00				
1920–21	32	Seattle Metropolitans	PCHA	2	0	2	0	0	13	6.50				
1921–22	33	Seattle Metropolitans	PCHA	2	0	2	0	0	2	1.00				
1923–24	35	Seattle Metropolitans	PCHA	2	0	1	1	0	4	1.79				
1924–25	36	Victoria Cougars	St-Cup	4	3	1	0	0	8	2.00				
1924–25	36	Victoria Cougars	WCHL	4	2	0	2	1	5	1.25				
1925–26	37	Victoria Cougars	St-Cup	4	1	3	0	0	10	2.50				
1925–26	37	Victoria Cougars	WHL	4	2	0	2	1	6	1.45				
Career—10 Seasons				52	25	21	7	6	139	2.67	0	0	0	0

TROPHY CASE

AWARDS

Stanley Cup (1913–14, 1916–17, 1917–18, 1924–25)

ALL-STAR SELECTIONS

PCHA Second All-Star Team Goaltender (1916, 1917, 1919, 1920, 1922, 1923)

WHL First All-Star Team Goaltender (1925)

Tom Hooper

HOCKEY HALL OF FAME CLASS: 1962

Rover

Shoots: Right

Height: 5'-10"

Weight: 175 lbs.

Born: November 24, 1883: Rat Portage, Ontario

Died: March 23, 1960: Unknown

Played seven elite amateur and professional seasons from 1901–08

QUICK FACTS

- Starred on local school and junior teams in Rat Portage (Kenora) with future Hall of Fame members Tommy Phillips, Si Griffis and Billy McGimisie

- Member of Manitoba Northwest champion Rat Portage Thistles (1902–03)

- Lost Stanley Cup challenge to the Ottawa "Silver Seven" (1902–03, 1904–05)

- Member of Manitoba Senior league champion Kenora Thistles (1905–06)

- Member of Stanley Cup-winning Kenora Thistles team that defeated Montreal Wanderers in January of 1907

- Scored three goals in Kenora Thistles' Stanley Cup-clinching 8–6 victory over Montreal Wanderers, January 21, 1907

- Injured and unable to play when the Thistles lost a Stanley Cup rematch to the Wanderers in March of 1907

- Member of Stanley Cup-winning Montreal Wanderers team that defeated Ottawa, Toronto, Winnipeg and Edmonton (1907–08)

> He was born in Rat Portage, learned the game there and has been a mainstay of the team for several years. He is considered the cleverest all-round performer on the team. Though on the forward line, he can play any position with equal efficiency and played [defense] for two seasons."
> — Montreal Gazette, March 7, 1905

REGULAR SEASON

Season	Age	Team	Lg	GP	G	A	PTS	PIM
1901–02	18	Rat Portage Thistles	MNWHA-Int	8	9	0	9	17
1902–03	19	Rat Portage Thistles	MNWHA	5	5	1	6	
1903–04	20	Rat Portage Thistles	MNWHA	10	2	1	3	
1904–05	21	Rat Portage Thistles	MHL	8	9	0	9	
1905–06	22	Kenora Thistles	MHL	9	4	0	4	
1906–07	23	Kenora Thistles	MHL-Pro	3	4	0	4	
1907–08	24	Montreal AAA	ECAHA	7	9	0	9	5
1907–08	24	Pembroke Lumber Kings	UOVHL	1	0	0	0	0
1907–08	24	Montreal Wanderers	ECAHA	2	1	0	1	0
Career — 7 Seasons				53	43	2	45	22

PLAYOFFS

Season	Age	Team	Lg	GP	G	A	PTS	PIM
1902–03	19	Rat Portage Thistles	St-Cup	2	0	0	0	0
1904–05	21	Rat Portage Thistles	St-Cup	3	2	0	2	12
1906–07	23	Kenora Thistles	MHL-Pro	2	0	0	0	11
1906–07	23	Kenora Thistles	St-Cup	3	3	0	3	0
1907–08	24	Montreal Wanderers	St-Cup	2	0	0	0	3
Career — 4 Seasons				12	5	0	5	26

TROPHY CASE

AWARDS

Stanley Cup (1906–07, 1907–08)

2

Red Horner

HOCKEY HALL OF FAME CLASS: 1965

Alternates: 11, 15

Defense

Shoots: Right

Height: 6'

Weight: 190 lbs.

Born: May 28, 1909: Lynden, Ontario

Died: April 27, 2005: Toronto, Ontario

Played 12 NHL seasons from 1928–40

QUICK FACTS

- Held NHL record for penalty minutes in regular season (167); surpassed by N.Y. Rangers' Lou Fontinato, who registered 202 penalty minutes in 1955-56

- Played amateur hockey with Toronto Marlboros (1926–28) and Solway Mills Bankers (1926–28)

- Registered seven goals and 12 points in 1928 Memorial Cup playoffs with Toronto Jr. Marlboros

- Signed as a free agent by Toronto, December 22, 1929 and made his NHL debut that evening in a 3–2 loss to Pittsburgh Pirates. Horner had played a junior game for the Toronto Marlboros the night before and a commercial game with Solway Mills that afternoon

- Replaced penalized goaltender Lorne Chabot in net for the Maple Leafs in a 6–2 loss to Boston on March 15, 1932. Horner allowed one goal in the one minute he "pinch hit" for Chabot

- Led the league in penalty minutes for eight consecutive seasons (1933–40)

- Played in NHL All-Star Game (1934, 1937)

- Served as captain of Toronto Maple Leafs (1938–40)

- Worked for two seasons as a NHL linesman and later owned and operated the Canada Coal Company

- At the time of his death in 2005, he was the oldest living NHL player and oldest living member of the Hockey Hall of Fame

> I asked Mrs. Selke if she thought her husband would mind if I came down and tried out for the Marlboro Juniors ... Twenty or thirty young fellas were trying to make the team ... At the first of the season back in those days, they had the SPA — the Sportsmen's Patriotic Association. If you lost a game, you were out."

REGULAR SEASON

Season	Age	Team	Lg	GP	G	A	PTS	PIM
1928–29	19	Toronto Maple Leafs	NHL	22	0	0	0	30
1929–30	20	Toronto Maple Leafs	NHL	33	2	7	9	96
1930–31	21	Toronto Maple Leafs	NHL	42	1	11	12	71
1931–32	22	Toronto Maple Leafs	NHL	42	7	9	16	97
1932–33	23	Toronto Maple Leafs	NHL	48	3	8	11	144
1933–34	24	Toronto Maple Leafs	NHL	40	11	10	21	146
1934–35	25	Toronto Maple Leafs	NHL	46	4	8	12	125
1935–36	26	Toronto Maple Leafs	NHL	43	2	9	11	167
1936–37	27	Toronto Maple Leafs	NHL	48	3	9	12	124
1937–38	28	Toronto Maple Leafs	NHL	47	4	20	24	82
1938–39	29	Toronto Maple Leafs	NHL	48	4	10	14	85
1939–40	30	Toronto Maple Leafs	NHL	31	1	9	10	87
NHL Career – 12 Seasons				490	42	110	152	1254

PLAYOFFS

Season	Age	Team	Lg	GP	G	A	PTS	PIM
1928–29	19	Toronto Maple Leafs	NHL	4	1	0	1	2
1930–31	21	Toronto Maple Leafs	NHL	2	0	0	0	4
1931–32	22	Toronto Maple Leafs	NHL	7	2	2	4	20
1932–33	23	Toronto Maple Leafs	NHL	9	1	0	1	10
1933–34	24	Toronto Maple Leafs	NHL	5	1	0	1	6
1934–35	25	Toronto Maple Leafs	NHL	7	0	1	1	4
1935–36	26	Toronto Maple Leafs	NHL	9	1	2	3	22
1936–37	27	Toronto Maple Leafs	NHL	2	0	0	0	7
1937–38	28	Toronto Maple Leafs	NHL	7	0	1	1	14
1938–39	29	Toronto Maple Leafs	NHL	10	1	2	3	26
1939–40	30	Toronto Maple Leafs	NHL	9	0	2	2	55
NHL Career – 11 Seasons				71	7	10	17	170

TROPHY CASE

AWARDS

Stanley Cup (1931–32)

7

2 (Retired by Buffalo)
Alternates:
16, 20, 26

Defense

Shoots: Right

Height: 5'-10"

Weight: 180 lbs.

Born: January 12, 1930: Cochrane, Ontario

Died: February 21, 1974: St. Catharines, Ontario

Played 24 NHL seasons from 1949–50, 1951–74

Tim Horton

HOCKEY HALL OF FAME CLASS: 1977

QUICK FACTS

- Held NHL record for games played by a defenseman (1,446); surpassed by Larry Murphy, February 5, 1999

- Renowned throughout Canada and the United States for chain of restaurants that bear his name

- Played amateur hockey with Cooper Cliff Redmen (1946–47); St. Michael's Majors (1947–49); Toronto Swansea Sentinals (1947–48)

- Led OHA-Jr. in penalty minutes (137) in 1947–48

- AHL First All-Star Team Defense (1951–52)

- Nicknamed "Mister Magoo" because of his poor eyesight and "Superman" because of his strength

- Renowned for his "Tim Horton Bear Hug," a ploy he would use instead of engaging in fisticuffs

- Led all NHL defensemen in game-winning goals (7) in 1963–64

- Played in NHL All-Star Game (1954, 1961, 1962, 1963, 1964, 1968, 1969)

- Regarded as one of the toughest, strongest and most durable defensive defensemen in NHL history

> "Horton's the hardest body-checker I've ever come up against. He's as strong as an ox and hits with terrific force."
> — John Ferguson

REGULAR SEASON

Season	Age	Team	Lg	GP	G	A	PTS	+/-	PIM	ESG	PPG	SHG	GWG	SOG	S%
1949–50	20	Toronto Maple Leafs	NHL	1	0	0	0		2						
1951–52	22	Toronto Maple Leafs	NHL	4	0	0	0		8						
1952–53	23	Toronto Maple Leafs	NHL	70	2	14	16		85						
1953–54	24	Toronto Maple Leafs	NHL	70	7	24	31		94						
1954–55	25	Toronto Maple Leafs	NHL	67	5	9	14		84						
1955–56	26	Toronto Maple Leafs	NHL	35	0	5	5		36						
1956–57	27	Toronto Maple Leafs	NHL	66	6	19	25		72						
1957–58	28	Toronto Maple Leafs	NHL	53	6	20	26		39						
1958–59	29	Toronto Maple Leafs	NHL	70	5	21	26		76						
1959–60	30	Toronto Maple Leafs	NHL	70	3	29	32		69						
1960–61	31	Toronto Maple Leafs	NHL	57	6	15	21		75						
1961–62	32	Toronto Maple Leafs	NHL	70	10	28	38		88						
1962–63	33	Toronto Maple Leafs	NHL	70	6	19	25		69						
1963–64	34	Toronto Maple Leafs	NHL	70	9	20	29		71	7	2	0	7		
1964–65	35	Toronto Maple Leafs	NHL	70	12	16	28		95	9	2	1	2		
1965–66	36	Toronto Maple Leafs	NHL	70	6	22	28		76	3	3	0	2		
1966–67	37	Toronto Maple Leafs	NHL	70	8	17	25		70	5	3	0	1		
1967–68	38	Toronto Maple Leafs	NHL	69	4	23	27	20	82	2	1	1	0	179	2.2
1968–69	39	Toronto Maple Leafs	NHL	74	11	29	40	14	107	8	3	0	1	169	6.5
1969–70	40	Toronto Maple Leafs	NHL	59	3	19	22	4	91	2	1	0	1	116	2.6
1969–70	40	New York Rangers	NHL	15	1	5	6	-7	16	0	1	0	0	41	2.4
1970–71	41	New York Rangers	NHL	78	2	18	20	28	57	1	1	0	1	124	1.6
1971–72	42	Pittsburgh Penguins	NHL	44	2	9	11	5	40	2	0	0	1	84	2.4
1972–73	43	Buffalo Sabres	NHL	69	1	16	17	12	56	1	0	0	0	73	1.4
1973–74	44	Buffalo Sabres	NHL	55	0	6	6	5	53	0	0	0	0	59	0.0
NHL Career — 24 Seasons				1446	115	403	518	81	1611	40	17	2	16	845	2.8

PLAYOFFS

Season	Age	Team	Lg	GP	G	A	PTS	+/-	PIM	ESG	PPG	SHG	GWG	SOG	S%
1949–50	20	Toronto Maple Leafs	NHL	1	0	0	0		2						
1953–54	24	Toronto Maple Leafs	NHL	5	1	1	2		4						
1955–56	26	Toronto Maple Leafs	NHL	2	0	0	0		4						
1958–59	29	Toronto Maple Leafs	NHL	12	0	3	3		16						
1959–60	30	Toronto Maple Leafs	NHL	10	0	1	1		6						
1960–61	31	Toronto Maple Leafs	NHL	5	0	0	0		0						
1961–62	32	Toronto Maple Leafs	NHL	12	3	13	16		16						
1962–63	33	Toronto Maple Leafs	NHL	10	1	3	4		10						
1963–64	34	Toronto Maple Leafs	NHL	14	0	4	4		20						
1964–65	35	Toronto Maple Leafs	NHL	6	0	2	2		13						
1965–66	36	Toronto Maple Leafs	NHL	4	1	0	1		12						
1966–67	37	Toronto Maple Leafs	NHL	12	3	5	8		25						
1968–69	39	Toronto Maple Leafs	NHL	4	0	0	0		7	0	0	0	0		
1969–70	40	New York Rangers	NHL	6	1	1	2		28	1	0	0	0		
1970–71	41	New York Rangers	NHL	13	1	4	5		14	1	0	0	0		
1971–72	42	Pittsburgh Penguins	NHL	4	0	1	1		2	0	0	0	0		
1972–73	43	Buffalo Sabres	NHL	6	0	1	1		4	0	0	0	0		
NHL Career — 17 Seasons				126	11	39	50		183	2	0	0	0		

TROPHY CASE

AWARDS

Stanley Cup (1961–62, 1962–63, 1963–64, 1966–67)

ALL-STAR SELECTIONS

First All-Star Team Defense (1964, 1968, 1969)

Second All-Star Team Defense (1954, 1963, 1967)

Gordie Howe

HOCKEY HALL OF FAME CLASS: 1972

9

Retired by Detroit

Alternate: 17

Right Wing

Shoots: Right

Height: 6'

Weight: 205 lbs.

Born: March 31, 1928: Floral, Saskatchewan

Played 32 NHL and WHA seasons from 1946–1971, 1973–1980

"You've got to love what you're doing. If you love it, you can overcome any handicap or the soreness or all the aches and pains, and continue to play for a long, long time."

QUICK FACTS

- Holds NHL record for seasons played (26) from 1946–1971, 1979–80; holds NHL record for career games played (1,767)
- Holds NHL record for goals (801), assists (1,049) and points (1,850) by a right wing
- Registered 2,000th professional point in Houston Aeros' 8–0 victory over Winnipeg Jets, March 27, 1975
- Signed a one-game contract with IHL's Detroit Vipers and played a single shift to become hockey's first six decade player, October 3, 1997
- Played on a line with sons Mark and Marty in Hartford's 4–4 tie with Detroit Red Wings, March 12, 1980
- Brother of Vic Howe, who played in NHL with N.Y. Rangers from 1950–54

Howe's gloves from the 1952–53 season; Howe recorded 49 goals, the highest total of his career.

TROPHY CASE

AWARDS

Art Ross Trophy (1951, 1952, 1953, 1954, 1957, 1963)

Hart Memorial Trophy (1952, 1953, 1957, 1958, 1960, 1963)

Lester Patrick Trophy (1967)

Stanley Cup (1949–50, 1951–52, 1953–54, 1954–55)

ALL-STAR SELECTIONS

First All-Star Team Right Wing (1951, 1952, 1953, 1954, 1957, 1958, 1960, 1963, 1966, 1968, 1969, 1970)

Second All-Star Team Right Wing (1949, 1950, 1956, 1959, 1961, 1962, 1964, 1965, 1967)

REGULAR SEASON

Season	Age	Team	Lg	GP	G	A	PTS	PIM
1946–47	18	Detroit Red Wings	NHL	58	7	15	22	52
1947–48	19	Detroit Red Wings	NHL	60	16	28	44	63
1948–49	20	Detroit Red Wings	NHL	40	12	25	37	57
1949–50	21	Detroit Red Wings	NHL	70	35	33	68	69
1950–51	22	Detroit Red Wings	NHL	70	43	43	86	74
1951–52	23	Detroit Red Wings	NHL	70	47	39	86	78
1952–53	24	Detroit Red Wings	NHL	70	49	46	95	57
1953–54	25	Detroit Red Wings	NHL	70	33	48	81	109
1954–55	26	Detroit Red Wings	NHL	64	29	33	62	68
1955–56	27	Detroit Red Wings	NHL	70	38	41	79	100
1956–57	28	Detroit Red Wings	NHL	70	44	45	89	72
1957–58	29	Detroit Red Wings	NHL	64	33	44	77	40
1958–59	30	Detroit Red Wings	NHL	70	32	46	78	57
1959–60	31	Detroit Red Wings	NHL	70	28	45	73	46
1960–61	32	Detroit Red Wings	NHL	64	23	49	72	30
1961–62	33	Detroit Red Wings	NHL	70	33	44	77	54
1962–63	34	Detroit Red Wings	NHL	70	38	48	86	100
1963–64	35	Detroit Red Wings	NHL	69	26	47	73	70
1964–65	36	Detroit Red Wings	NHL	70	29	47	76	104
1965–66	37	Detroit Red Wings	NHL	70	29	46	75	83
1966–67	38	Detroit Red Wings	NHL	69	25	40	65	53
1967–68	39	Detroit Red Wings	NHL	74	39	43	82	53
1968–69	40	Detroit Red Wings	NHL	76	44	59	103	58
1969–70	41	Detroit Red Wings	NHL	76	31	40	71	58
1970–71	42	Detroit Red Wings	NHL	63	23	29	52	38
1973–74	45	Houston Aeros	WHA	70	31	69	100	46
1974–75	46	Houston Aeros	WHA	75	34	65	99	84
1975–76	47	Houston Aeros	WHA	78	32	70	102	76
1976–77	48	Houston Aeros	WHA	62	24	44	68	57
1977–78	49	New England Whalers	WHA	76	34	62	96	85
1978–79	50	New England Whalers	WHA	58	19	24	43	51
1979–80	51	Hartford Whalers	NHL	80	15	26	41	42
Career — 32 Seasons				2186	975	1383	2358	2084

PLAYOFFS

Season	Age	Team	Lg	GP	G	A	PTS	PIM
1946–47	18	Detroit Red Wings	NHL	5	0	0	0	18
1947–48	19	Detroit Red Wings	NHL	10	1	1	2	11
1948–49	20	Detroit Red Wings	NHL	11	8	3	11	19
1949–50	21	Detroit Red Wings	NHL	1	0	0	0	7
1950–51	22	Detroit Red Wings	NHL	6	4	3	7	4
1951–52	23	Detroit Red Wings	NHL	8	2	5	7	2
1952–53	24	Detroit Red Wings	NHL	6	2	5	7	2
1953–54	25	Detroit Red Wings	NHL	12	4	5	9	31
1954–55	26	Detroit Red Wings	NHL	11	9	11	20	24
1955–56	27	Detroit Red Wings	NHL	10	3	9	12	8
1956–57	28	Detroit Red Wings	NHL	5	2	5	7	6
1957–58	29	Detroit Red Wings	NHL	4	1	1	2	0
1959–60	31	Detroit Red Wings	NHL	6	1	5	6	4
1960–61	32	Detroit Red Wings	NHL	11	4	11	15	10
1962–63	34	Detroit Red Wings	NHL	11	7	9	16	22
1963–64	35	Detroit Red Wings	NHL	14	9	10	19	16
1964–65	36	Detroit Red Wings	NHL	7	4	2	6	20
1965–66	37	Detroit Red Wings	NHL	12	4	6	10	12
1969–70	41	Detroit Red Wings	NHL	4	2	0	2	2
1973–74	45	Houston Aeros	WHA	13	3	14	17	34
1974–75	46	Houston Aeros	WHA	13	8	12	20	20
1975–76	47	Houston Aeros	WHA	17	4	8	12	31
1976–77	48	Houston Aeros	WHA	11	5	3	8	11
1977–78	49	New England Whalers	WHA	14	5	5	10	15
1978–79	50	New England Whalers	WHA	10	3	1	4	4
1979–80	51	Hartford Whalers	NHL	3	1	1	2	2
Career — 26 Seasons				235	96	135	231	335

8

Syd Howe
HOCKEY HALL OF FAME CLASS: 1965

Alternates: 15, 11

Center/Left Wing

Shoots: Left

Height: 5'-9"

Weight: 165 lbs.

Born: September 28, 1911: Ottawa, Ontario

Died: May 20, 1976: Ottawa, Ontario

Played 17 NHL seasons from 1929–46

QUICK FACTS

- Played amateur hockey with Glebe Collegiate (1925–26); Landsdowne Park Juveniles (1925–26); Ottawa Gunners (1927–28); Ottawa Rideaus (1928–30)

- Became sixth player — and first in hockey's modern era — to score six goals in a single game in Detroit's 12–2 victory over N.Y. Rangers, February 3, 1944

- Held NHL record for scoring fastest playoff overtime goal (25 seconds), established in Detroit's 2–1 victory over N.Y. Americans, March 19, 1940; surpassed by Ted Irvine (19 seconds), April 2, 1969

- Played with Ottawa Senators (1946–47) and Ottawa Army (1948–49) after retiring from NHL

- Finished second in NHL points in 1934–35 (47) and 1940–41 (44)

- Held NHL record for career regular season points (528); surpassed by Bill Cowley, February 12, 1947

- Played in NHL All-Star Game (1939)

- Signed as a free agent by Ottawa, January 16, 1930

- Claimed by Toronto from Ottawa for 1931–32 season in Dispersal Draft, September 26, 1931

- Transferred to St. Louis after Ottawa franchise relocated, September 22, 1934; traded to Detroit by St. Louis with Ralph Bowman for Teddy Graham and $50,000, February 11, 1935

- On the ice when Mud Bruneteau scored in the sixth overtime period to give Detroit a 1–0 win over Montreal Maroons in longest game in NHL history

"I'll never forget the night Detroit fans gave me toward the end of my career. I got a lot of gifts, including a piano. You know how it is when they give you a night. It usually turns out that team gets beat and you can't come close to scoring. I was a lot luckier. We beat the Black Hawks, 2–0 and I scored both goals."

REGULAR SEASON

Season	Age	Team	Lg	GP	G	A	PTS	PIM
1929–30	18	Ottawa Senators	NHL	12	1	1	2	0
1930–31	19	Philadelphia Quakers	NHL	44	9	11	20	20
1931–32	20	Toronto Maple Leafs	NHL	3	0	0	0	0
1932–33	21	Ottawa Senators	NHL	48	12	12	24	17
1933–34	22	Ottawa Senators	NHL	42	13	7	20	18
1934–35	23	St. Louis Eagles	NHL	36	14	13	27	23
1934–35	23	Detroit Red Wings	NHL	14	8	12	20	11
1935–36	24	Detroit Red Wings	NHL	48	16	14	30	26
1936–37	25	Detroit Red Wings	NHL	45	17	10	27	10
1937–38	26	Detroit Red Wings	NHL	48	8	19	27	14
1938–39	27	Detroit Red Wings	NHL	48	16	20	36	11
1939–40	28	Detroit Red Wings	NHL	46	14	23	37	17
1940–41	29	Detroit Red Wings	NHL	48	20	24	44	8
1941–42	30	Detroit Red Wings	NHL	48	16	19	35	6
1942–43	31	Detroit Red Wings	NHL	50	20	35	55	10
1943–44	32	Detroit Red Wings	NHL	46	32	28	60	6
1944–45	33	Detroit Red Wings	NHL	46	17	36	53	6
1945–46	34	Detroit Red Wings	NHL	26	4	7	11	9
NHL Career — 17 Seasons				698	237	291	528	212

PLAYOFFS

Season	Age	Team	Lg	GP	G	A	PTS	PIM
1929–30	18	Ottawa Senators	NHL	2	0	0	0	0
1935–36	24	Detroit Red Wings	NHL	7	3	3	6	2
1936–37	25	Detroit Red Wings	NHL	10	2	5	7	0
1938–39	27	Detroit Red Wings	NHL	6	3	1	4	4
1939–40	28	Detroit Red Wings	NHL	5	2	2	4	2
1940–41	29	Detroit Red Wings	NHL	9	1	7	8	0
1941–42	30	Detroit Red Wings	NHL	12	3	5	8	0
1942–43	31	Detroit Red Wings	NHL	7	1	2	3	0
1943–44	32	Detroit Red Wings	NHL	5	2	2	4	0
1944–45	33	Detroit Red Wings	NHL	7	0	0	0	2
NHL Career — 10 Seasons				70	17	27	44	10

TROPHY CASE

AWARDS

Stanley Cup (1935–36, 1936–37, 1942–43)

ALL-STAR SELECTIONS

Second All-Star Team Center (1945)

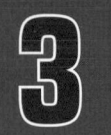

3

Retired by N.Y. Rangers

Alternate: 5

Defense

Shoots: Left

Height: 6'-1"

Weight: 195 lbs.

Born: December 28, 1932: Hamilton, Ontario

Played 25 NHL and WHA seasons from 1952–76

Harry Howell

HOCKEY HALL OF FAME CLASS: 1979

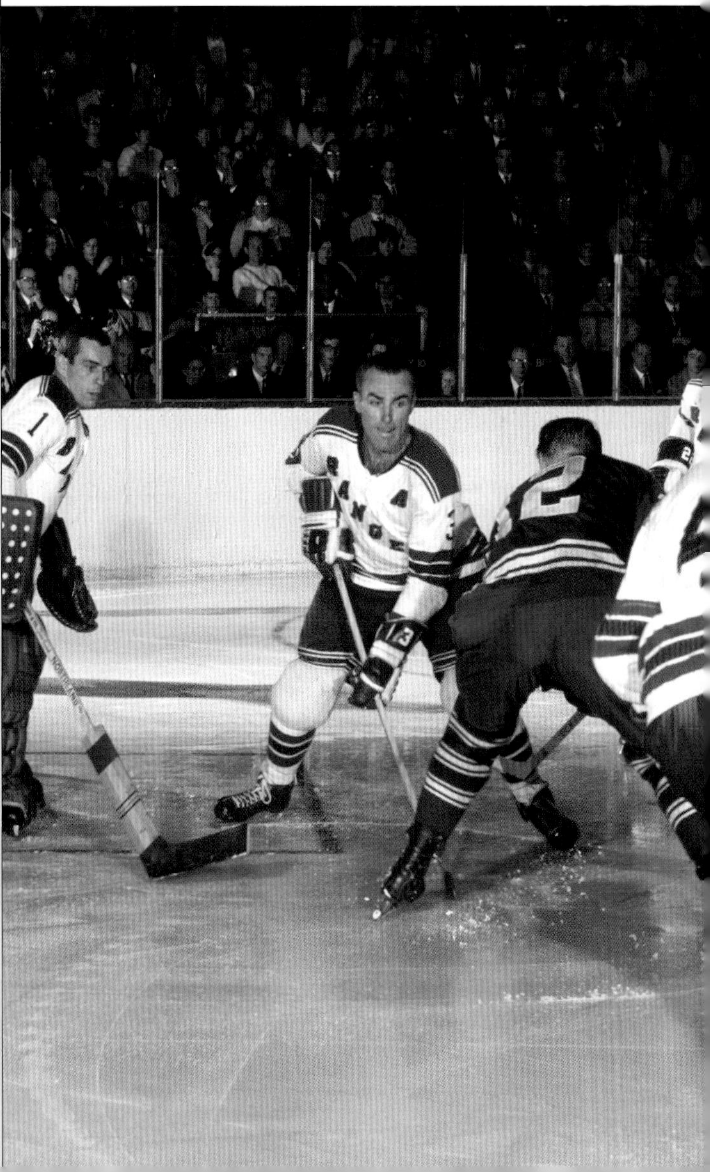

QUICK FACTS

- Holds N.Y. Rangers team record for career games played (1,160)
- Played amateur hockey with Guelph Biltmores (1949–52)
- Member of Memorial Cup-winning Guelph Biltmores (1952); recorded five goals and ten points in 1952 Memorial Cup playoffs
- Nicknamed "Harry the Horse" because of his work ethic and the fact he missed only 20 games in his first 16 NHL seasons
- Scored first NHL goal in first NHL game on first NHL shot in N.Y. Rangers' 4–3 loss to Toronto, October 18, 1952
- Last player to win the Norris Trophy before Bobby Orr — who won the award for the next eight seasons

- Played in NHL All-Star Game (1954, 1963, 1964, 1965, 1967, 1968, 1970)
- Served as captain of N.Y. Rangers (1955–57)
- Never won the Stanley Cup as a player, but did win as a scout with the Edmonton Oilers in 1990
- Underwent spinal fusion surgery in 1969 and recovered to play another seven professional seasons in the NHL and WHA
- Traded to Oakland Seals by N.Y. Rangers for cash, June 10, 1969; traded to Los Angeles by California Seals for cash, February 5, 1971
- Coached N.Y. Golden Blades/Jersey Knights (1973–74); coached San Diego Mariners (1974–75)

> We played mostly road hockey, and if someone was fortunate enough to have a rink in their backyard, that's where we headed. That was it until I was seven or eight years old."

REGULAR SEASON

Season	Age	Team	Lg	GP	G	A	PTS	+/-	PIM	ESG	PPG	SHG	GWG	SOG	S%
1952–53	20	New York Rangers	NHL	67	3	8	11		46						
1953–54	21	New York Rangers	NHL	67	7	9	16		58						
1954–55	22	New York Rangers	NHL	70	2	14	16		87						
1955–56	23	New York Rangers	NHL	70	3	15	18		77						
1956–57	24	New York Rangers	NHL	65	2	10	12		70						
1957–58	25	New York Rangers	NHL	70	4	7	11		62						
1958–59	26	New York Rangers	NHL	70	4	10	14		101						
1959–60	27	New York Rangers	NHL	67	7	6	13		58						
1960–61	28	New York Rangers	NHL	70	7	10	17		62						
1961–62	29	New York Rangers	NHL	66	6	15	21		89						
1962–63	30	New York Rangers	NHL	70	5	20	25		55						
1963–64	31	New York Rangers	NHL	70	5	31	36		75	3	2	0	2		
1964–65	32	New York Rangers	NHL	68	2	20	22		63	2	0	0	0		
1965–66	33	New York Rangers	NHL	70	4	29	33		92	3	1	0	0		
1966–67	34	New York Rangers	NHL	70	12	28	40		54	10	2	0	0		
1967–68	35	New York Rangers	NHL	74	5	24	29	12	62	4	1	0	2	220	2.3
1968–69	36	New York Rangers	NHL	56	4	7	11	2	36	3	1	0	1	140	2.9
1969–70	37	Oakland Seals	NHL	55	4	16	20	-14	52	1	3	0	3	147	2.7
1970–71	38	California Golden Seals	NHL	28	0	9	9	-20	14	0	0	0	0	51	0.0
1970–71	38	Los Angeles Kings	NHL	18	3	8	11	1	4	2	1	0	0	33	9.1
1971–72	39	Los Angeles Kings	NHL	77	1	17	18	-34	53	1	0	0	0	138	0.7
1972–73	40	Los Angeles Kings	NHL	73	4	11	15	-4	28	4	0	0	0	97	4.1
1973–74	41	N.Y. Golden Blades/ New Jersey Knights	WHA	65	3	23	26		24	3	0	0	2		
1974–75	42	San Diego Mariners	WHA	74	4	10	14	28	28	3	0	1		78	5.1
1975–76	43	Calgary Cowboys	WHA	31	0	3	3	4	6	0	0	0	0	26	0.0
Career — 24 Seasons				1581	101	360	461	-25	1356	39	11	1	10	930	3.00

PLAYOFFS

Season	Age	Team	Lg	GP	G	A	PTS	+/-	PIM	ESG	PPG	SHG	GWG	SOG	S%
1955–56	23	New York Rangers	NHL	5	0	1	1		4						
1956–57	24	New York Rangers	NHL	5	1	0	1		6						
1957–58	25	New York Rangers	NHL	6	1	0	1		8						
1961–62	29	New York Rangers	NHL	6	0	1	1		8						
1966–67	34	New York Rangers	NHL	4	0	0	0		4						
1967–68	35	New York Rangers	NHL	6	1	0	1		0	0	1	0	1		
1968–69	36	New York Rangers	NHL	2	0	0	0		0	0	0	0	0		
1969–70	37	Oakland Seals	NHL	4	0	1	1		2	0	0	0	0		
1974–75	42	San Diego Mariners	WHA	5	1	0	1		10				0		
1975–76	43	Calgary Cowboys	WHA	2	0	0	0	1	2						
Career –10 Seasons				45	4	3	7	1	44	0	1	0	1		

TROPHY CASE

AWARDS

James Norris Memorial Trophy (1967)

ALL-STAR SELECTIONS

First All-Star Team Defense (1967)

Bobby Hull
HOCKEY HALL OF FAME CLASS: 1983

Alternate: 16

Left Wing

Shoots: Left

Height: 5'-10"

Weight: 195 lbs.

Born: January 3, 1939: Point Anne, Ontario

Played 23 NHL and WHA seasons from 1957–80

" All I've done all my life is just tried to better the game for our players and for those people watching."

QUICK FACTS

- First player in NHL history to record more than 50 goals in a season, March 12, 1966
- Held NHL record for goals in regular season (58); surpassed by Phil Esposito, March 11, 1971
- Only Hall of Fame member to play in all seven seasons of WHA's existence
- Played amateur hockey with Galt Black Hawks (1953–54); Hespeler Shamrocks (1953–54); Woodstock Warriors (1954–55); St. Catharines Teepees (1955–57)
- Led NHL in power-play goals in 1965–66 (22) and 1968–69 (20); led NHL in game-winning goals in 1968–69 (11) and 1969–70 (8)

- Named WHA Most Valuable Player (1973, 1974); WHA First All-Star Team Left Wing (1973, 1974, 1975); WHA Second All-Star Team Left Wing (1976, 1977); member of WHA champion Winnipeg Jets (1976, 1977, 1978)
- Led NHL in goals seven times (1959–60, 1961–62, 1963–64, 1965–66, 1966–67, 1967–68, 1968–69); led NHL in short-handed goals (4) in 1963–64
- Led NHL playoffs in goals in 1961–62 (8), 1962–63 (8), 1964–65 (10); led WHA in goals (77) in 1974–75

Hull used this stick to score his 500th NHL goal during the 4–2 victory over the N.Y. Rangers on February 21, 1970.

REGULAR SEASON

Season	Age	Team	Lg	GP	G	A	PTS	+/-	PIM	ESG	PPG	SHG	GWG	SOG	S%
1957–58	19	Chicago Black Hawks	NHL	70	13	34	47		62						
1958–59	20	Chicago Black Hawks	NHL	70	18	32	50		50						
1959–60	21	Chicago Black Hawks	NHL	70	39	42	81		68						
1960–61	22	Chicago Black Hawks	NHL	67	31	25	56		43						
1961–62	23	Chicago Black Hawks	NHL	70	50	34	84		35						
1962–63	24	Chicago Black Hawks	NHL	65	31	31	62		27						
1963–64	25	Chicago Black Hawks	NHL	70	43	44	87		50	27	12	4	5		
1964–65	26	Chicago Black Hawks	NHL	61	39	32	71		32	27	10	2	5		
1965–66	27	Chicago Black Hawks	NHL	65	54	43	97		70	31	22	1	7		
1966–67	28	Chicago Black Hawks	NHL	66	52	28	80		52	32	18	2	3		
1967–68	29	Chicago Black Hawks	NHL	71	44	31	75	14	39	34	8	2	6	364	12.1
1968–69	30	Chicago Black Hawks	NHL	74	58	49	107	-7	48	36	20	2	11	414	14.0
1969–70	31	Chicago Black Hawks	NHL	61	38	29	67	20	8	26	10	2	8	289	13.1
1970–71	32	Chicago Black Hawks	NHL	78	44	52	96	34	32	33	11	0	11	378	11.6
1971–72	33	Chicago Black Hawks	NHL	78	50	43	93	54	24	39	8	3	9	336	14.9
1972–73	34	Winnipeg Jets	WHA	63	51	52	103		37	35	14	2	7		
1973–74	35	Winnipeg Jets	WHA	75	53	42	95		38	43	9	1	9		
1974–75	36	Winnipeg Jets	WHA	78	77	65	142	55	41	50	27	0		556	13.6
1975–76	37	Winnipeg Jets	WHA	80	53	70	123	62	30	39	14	0	10	416	12.7
1976–77	38	Winnipeg Jets	WHA	34	21	32	53	16	14	14	7	0		102	20.6
1977–78	39	Winnipeg Jets	WHA	77	46	71	117	55	23	36	10	0		257	17.9
1978–79	40	Winnipeg Jets	WHA	4	2	3	5	1	0	1	1	0		12	16.7
1979–80	41	Winnipeg Jets	NHL	18	4	6	10	-7	0	3	1	0	0	25	16.0
1979–80	41	Hartford Whalers	NHL	9	2	5	7	-3	0	1	1	0	0	13	15.4
Career — 23 Seasons				1474	913	895	1808	294	823	507	203	21	91	3162	17.1

PLAYOFFS

Season	Age	Team	Lg	GP	G	A	PTS	+/-	PIM	ESG	PPG	SHG	GWG	SOG	S%
1958–59	20	Chicago Black Hawks	NHL	6	1	1	2		2						
1959–60	21	Chicago Black Hawks	NHL	3	1	0	1		2						
1960–61	22	Chicago Black Hawks	NHL	12	4	10	14		4						
1961–62	23	Chicago Black Hawks	NHL	12	8	6	14		12						
1962–63	24	Chicago Black Hawks	NHL	5	8	2	10		4						
1963–64	25	Chicago Black Hawks	NHL	7	2	5	7		2						
1964–65	26	Chicago Black Hawks	NHL	14	10	7	17		27						
1965–66	27	Chicago Black Hawks	NHL	6	2	2	4		10						
1966–67	28	Chicago Black Hawks	NHL	6	4	2	6		0	2	1	1	1		
1967–68	29	Chicago Black Hawks	NHL	11	4	6	10		15	3	0	0	0		
1969–70	31	Chicago Black Hawks	NHL	8	3	8	11		2	5	6	0	4		
1970–71	32	Chicago Black Hawks	NHL	18	11	14	25		16	3	0	1	0		
1971–72	33	Chicago Black Hawks	NHL	8	4	4	8		6	7	2	0	3		
1972–73	34	Winnipeg Jets	WHA	14	9	16	25		16				0		
1973–74	35	Winnipeg Jets	WHA	4	1	1	2	15	4						
1975–76	37	Winnipeg Jets	WHA	13	12	8	20	6	4				2		
1976–77	38	Winnipeg Jets	WHA	8	8	3	11	5	12				2		
1979–80	41	Hartford Whalers	NHL	3	0	0	0		0	0	0	0	0		
Career — 19 Seasons				179	105	104	209	26	140	20	9	2	12		

TROPHY CASE

AWARDS

Art Ross Trophy (1960, 1962, 1966)

Hart Memorial Trophy (1965, 1966)

Lady Byng Memorial Trophy (1965)

Stanley Cup (1960–61)

ALL-STAR SELECTIONS

First All-Star Team Left Wing (1960, 1962, 1964, 1965, 1966, 1967, 1968, 1969, 1970, 1972)

Second All-Star Team Left Wing (1963, 1971)

INTERNATIONAL AWARDS

Canada Cup (1976)

Brett Hull

HOCKEY HALL OF FAME CLASS: 2009

Alternates:
17, 22, 9, 15

Right Wing

Shoots: Right

Height: 5'-11"

Weight: 203 lbs.

Born: August 9, 1964: Belleville, Ontario

Drafted by the Calgary Flames 117th overall in 1984

Played 20 NHL seasons from 1985–2004, 2005–06

QUICK FACTS

"The game almost picked me. I didn't pick the game."

- Holds NHL record for career playoff power-play goals (38); holds NHL record for goals in a single season by right wing (86), established in 1990-91

- Shares NHL record (with Wayne Gretzky) for career playoff game-winning goals (24)

- Holds St. Louis Blues team record for career goals (527); holds St. Louis Blues team record for goals (86) and points (131) in a single season

- Ranks third in NHL career goals (741); ranks second in NHL career power-play goals (265); ranks third in NHL career game-winning goals (110), ranks seventh in NHL career shots-on-goal (4,876)

- Played amateur hockey with North Shore Winter Club (1981–82); Penticton Knights (1982–84); University of Minnesota-Duluth (1984–86)

- Scored Stanley Cup-winning overtime goal in Dallas' 2–1 victory over Buffalo Sabres, June 19, 1999

- Became fifth player in NHL history (with Maurice Richard, Mike Bossy, Wayne Gretzky and Mario Lemieux) to score 50 goals in 50-or-fewer games, January 25, 1991

- Led BCJHL in goals (105) and points (188) in 1983–84; WCHA First All-Star Team Right Wing (1986)

REGULAR SEASON

Season	Age	Team	Lg	GP	G	A	PTS	+/-	PIM	ESG	PPG	SHG	GWG	SOG	S%
1986–87	22	Calgary Flames	NHL	5	1	0	1	-1	0	1	0	0	1	5	20.0
1987–88	23	Calgary Flames	NHL	52	26	24	50	10	12	22	4	0	3	153	17.0
1987–88	23	St. Louis Blues	NHL	13	6	8	14	4	4	4	2	0	0	58	10.3
1988–89	24	St. Louis Blues	NHL	78	41	43	84	-17	33	25	16	0	6	305	13.4
1989–90	25	St. Louis Blues	NHL	80	72	41	113	-1	24	45	27	0	12	385	18.7
1990–91	26	St. Louis Blues	NHL	78	86	45	131	23	22	57	29	0	11	389	22.1
1991–92	27	St. Louis Blues	NHL	73	70	39	109	-2	48	45	20	5	9	408	17.2
1992–93	28	St. Louis Blues	NHL	80	54	47	101	-27	41	25	29	0	2	390	13.8
1993–94	29	St. Louis Blues	NHL	81	57	40	97	-3	38	29	25	3	8	392	14.5
1994–95	30	St. Louis Blues	NHL	48	29	21	50	13	10	17	9	3	6	200	14.5
1995–96	31	St. Louis Blues	NHL	70	43	40	83	4	30	22	16	5	6	327	13.1
1996–97	32	St. Louis Blues	NHL	77	42	40	82	-9	10	28	12	2	6	302	13.9
1997–98	33	St. Louis Blues	NHL	66	27	45	72	-1	26	17	10	0	6	211	12.8
1998–99	34	Dallas Stars	NHL	60	32	26	58	19	30	17	15	0	11	192	16.7
1999–00	35	Dallas Stars	NHL	79	24	35	59	-21	43	13	11	0	3	223	10.8
2000–01	36	Dallas Stars	NHL	79	39	40	79	10	18	28	11	0	8	219	17.8
2001–02	37	Detroit Red Wings	NHL	82	30	33	63	18	35	22	7	1	4	247	12.1
2002–03	38	Detroit Red Wings	NHL	82	37	39	76	11	22	24	12	1	4	262	14.1
2003–04	39	Detroit Red Wings	NHL	81	25	43	68	-4	12	15	10	0	6	200	12.5
2005–06	41	Phoenix Coyotes	NHL	5	0	1	1	-3	0	0	0	0	0	8	0.0
NHL Career — 19 Seasons				1269	741	650	1391	23	458	456	265	20	110	4876	15.2

PLAYOFFS

Season	Age	Team	Lg	GP	G	A	PTS	+/-	PIM	ESG	PPG	SHG	GWG	SOG	S%
1985–86	21	Calgary Flames	NHL	2	0	0	0	0	0	0	0	0	0	1	0.0
1986–87	22	Calgary Flames	NHL	4	2	1	3	4	0	2	0	0	0	18	11.1
1987–88	23	St. Louis Blues	NHL	10	7	2	9	1	4	3	4	0	3	39	17.9
1988–89	24	St. Louis Blues	NHL	10	5	5	10	-4	6	4	1	0	2	43	11.6
1989–90	25	St. Louis Blues	NHL	12	13	8	21	1	17	6	7	0	3	68	19.1
1990–91	26	St. Louis Blues	NHL	13	11	8	19	5	4	8	3	0	2	58	19.0
1991–92	27	St. Louis Blues	NHL	6	4	4	8	2	4	2	1	1	1	38	10.5
1992–93	28	St. Louis Blues	NHL	11	8	5	13	-2	2	3	5	0	2	52	15.4
1993–94	29	St. Louis Blues	NHL	4	2	1	3	1	0	1	1	0	0	22	9.1
1994–95	30	St. Louis Blues	NHL	7	6	2	8	0	0	4	2	0	0	34	17.6
1995–96	31	St. Louis Blues	NHL	13	6	5	11	2	10	3	2	1	1	52	11.5
1996–97	32	St. Louis Blues	NHL	6	2	7	9	4	2	2	0	0	0	25	8.0
1997–98	33	St. Louis Blues	NHL	10	3	3	6	-3	2	2	1	0	1	32	9.4
1998–99	34	Dallas Stars	NHL	22	8	7	15	3	4	5	3	0	2	86	9.3
1999–00	35	Dallas Stars	NHL	23	11	13	24	3	4	8	3	0	4	79	13.9
2000–01	36	Dallas Stars	NHL	10	2	5	7	-1	6	1	1	0	0	41	4.9
2001–02	37	Detroit Red Wings	NHL	23	10	8	18	1	4	5	3	2	2	61	16.4
2002–03	38	Detroit Red Wings	NHL	4	0	1	1	-4	0	0	0	0	0	15	0.0
2003–04	39	Detroit Red Wings	NHL	12	3	2	5	0	4	2	1	0	1	39	7.7
NHL Career — 19 Seasons				202	103	87	190	13	73	61	38	4	24	803	12.8

TROPHY CASE

AWARDS

Lady Byng Memorial Trophy (1990)

Hart Memorial Trophy (1991)

Lester B. Pearson Award (1991)

Stanley Cup (1998–99, 2001–02)

ALL-STAR SELECTIONS

First All-Star Team Right Wing (1990, 1991, 1992)

INTERNATIONAL AWARDS

World Cup (1996)

Silver Medal: Winter Olympics (2002)

Bouse Hutton

HOCKEY HALL OF FAME CLASS: 1962

Goaltender

Catches: Left

Height: Unknown

Weight: Unknown

Born: October 24, 1877: Ottawa, Ontario

Died: October 27, 1962: Ottawa, Ontario

Played seven elite amateur seasons from 1898–1904, 1908–09

QUICK FACTS

- Posted much lower goals-against-averages than many contemporaries, despite playing in an era when goalies wore little protection and had to remain standing when making saves
- Won national championships in lacrosse, football and hockey in the same season
- Played fullback with Ottawa Rough Riders football club
- Played goal with the Ottawa Capitals lacrosse club (1901–10)
- Made debut in senior hockey in 1898–99 but also led his Ottawa intermediate team to the Canadian Amateur Hockey League championship that season
- Member of CAHL champion Ottawa Hockey Club (1900–01)

- Earned shutout in Ottawa "Silver Seven" 8–0 victory over Montreal Victorias that clinched Ottawa's first Stanley Cup title, March 10, 1903
- Led CAHL in wins (6) in 1902–03
- Led Stanley Cup playoffs in wins (6) in 1903–04
- Signed professional contract to play lacrosse after winning his Stanley Cup title in 1903–04, which made him ineligible to play amateur hockey in Canada
- Continued to play lacrosse and coach hockey before returning to play hockey with Ottawa Senators in 1908–09
- Led FAHL in shutouts (1) in 1908–09

> "No one wants to hear about the Silver Seven days. There was nothing exciting about the old days. People want to read about today's stars."

REGULAR SEASON

Season	Age	Team	Lg	GP	W	L	T	SO	GA	GAA
1898–99	21	Ottawa Hockey Club	CAHL	2	1	1	0	0	11	5.50
1899–00	22	Ottawa Hockey Club	CAHL	7	4	3	0	0	19	2.71
1900–01	23	Ottawa Hockey Club	CAHL	7	7	0	0	0	20	2.50
1901–02	24	Ottawa Hockey Club	CAHL	8	5	3	0	2	15	1.88
1902–03	25	Ottawa Silver Seven	CAHL	8	6	2	0	0	26	3.25
1903–04	26	Ottawa Silver Seven	CAHL	4	4	0	0	0	15	3.75
1908–09	31	Ottawa Senators	FAHL	5	3	2	0	1	26	5.20
Career — 7 Seasons				41	30	11	0	3	132	3.14

PLAYOFFS

Season	Age	Team	Lg	GP	W	L	T	SO	GA	GAA
1902–03	25	Ottawa Silver Seven	CAHL	2	1	0	1	1	1	0.50
1902–03	25	Ottawa Silver Seven	St-Cup	2	2	0	0	0	4	2.00
1903–04	26	Ottawa Silver Seven	St-Cup	8	6	1	1	1	23	2.87
Career — 2 Seasons				12	9	1	2	2	28	2.33

TROPHY CASE

AWARDS

Stanley Cup (1902–03, 1903–04)

4

Harry Hyland

HOCKEY HALL OF FAME CLASS: 1962

Alternates: 7, 9

Right Wing

Shoots: Right

Height: 5'-6"

Weight: 156 lbs.

Born: January 2, 1889: Montreal, Quebec

Died: August 8, 1969: Montreal, Quebec

Played 10 professional seasons from 1908–18

QUICK FACTS

- Played amateur hockey with Montreal Shamrocks (1906–09)
- Led Montreal Shamrocks in goals (19) as an ECHA rookie (1908–09)
- Scored two goals in professional debut in Montreal Wanderers' 9–8 victory over Quebec Bulldogs, January 2, 1909
- Led Montreal Wanderers in goals (24) in 1909–10
- Signed as a free agent by New Westminster, November 12, 1911
- Finished second in PCHA in goals (26) in 1911–12
- Won national championship in lacrosse with New Westminster Salmonbellies (1912)
- Scored eight goals in Montreal Wanderers' 10–6 victory over Quebec Bulldogs, January 25, 1913
- Coached Montreal Shamrocks (1913–14) while engaged in contract dispute with Montreal Wanderers
- Scored five goals in Montreal Wanderers' 10–9 victory over Toronto Arenas on the first night in NHL history, December 19, 1917
- Claimed by Ottawa Senators in NHL Dispersal Draft after Montreal Wanderers club folded, January 4, 1918

> A fast skater and a powerful accurate shot, Hyland was a high scorer and dominant figure with [the Montreal Wanderers]."
>
> — *Montreal Gazette*, August 9, 1969

REGULAR SEASON

Season	Age	Team	Lg	GP	G	A	PTS	PIM
1908–09	20	Montreal Shamrocks	ECHA	11	19	0	19	36
1909–10	21	Montreal Wanderers	NHA	12	24	0	24	23
1910–11	22	Montreal Wanderers	NHA	15	14	0	14	43
1911–12	23	New Westminster Royals	PCHA	15	26	0	26	44
1912–13	24	Montreal Wanderers	NHA	20	27	0	27	38
1913–14	25	Montreal Wanderers	NHA	18	30	12	42	18
1914–15	26	Montreal Wanderers	NHA	19	23	6	29	49
1915–16	27	Montreal Wanderers	NHA	20	14	0	14	69
1916–17	28	Montreal Wanderers	NHA	13	12	2	14	21
1917–18	29	Montreal Wanderers	NHL	4	6	1	7	6
1917–18	29	Ottawa Senators	NHL	13	8	1	9	59
Career — 10 Seasons				160	203	22	225	414

PLAYOFFS

Season	Age	Team	Lg	GP	G	A	PTS	PIM
1909–10	21	Montreal Wanderers	St-Cup	1	3	0	3	3
1914–15	26	Montreal Wanderers	NHA	2	0	0	0	26
Career — 2 Seasons				3	3	0	3	29

TROPHY CASE

AWARDS

Stanley Cup (1909–10)

ALL-STAR SELECTIONS

PCHA First All-Star Team Right Wing (1912)

Most kids today slap the puck. The backhand takes time to learn. It's not something you do naturally. But it is an effective shot."

Dave Keon

3

Dick Irvin

HOCKEY HALL OF FAME CLASS: 1958

Alternate: 6

Center

Shoots: Left

Height: 5'-9"

Weight: 162 lbs.

Born: July 19, 1892: Hamilton, Ontario

Died: May 16, 1957: Montreal, Quebec

Played 12 elite amateur and professional seasons from 1916–18, 1919–29

QUICK FACTS

- Ranks third in all-time NHL games coached (1,449); ranks third in all-time wins by an NHL coach (627)

- Played amateur hockey with Winnipeg Strathconas-Jr. (1909–11); Winnipeg Strathconas-Sr. (1912–14); Winnipeg Monarchs (1911–16); Winnipeg Ypres (1917–18); Regina Victorias (1919–21)

- Led Western Senior League in goals (16) in 1911–12; led Manitoba Intermediate League in goals (32) in 1912–13

- Member of Allan Cup-winning Winnipeg Monarchs (1915); led all Allan Cup competitors in goals (17) and points (20) as Winnipeg defeated Fort William, Edmonton and Melville to win the Canadian Senior Hockey Championship

- Served as first captain of the Chicago Black Hawks (1926–29)

- Led Manitoba Senior League in goals (23) and points (24) in 1913–14; goals (23) and points (26) in 1914–15; goals (17) and points (20) in 1915–16; goals (29) and points (37) in 1917–18

- Led Southern Saskatchewan Senior League in goals (32) and points (36) in 1919–20; led WCHL in goals (31) in 1925–26

- Led NHL in assists (18) in 1926–27

- Coached Toronto Maple Leafs (1931–40); Montreal Canadiens (1940–55); Chicago Black Hawks (1928–29, 1930–31, 1955–56)

- Coached Toronto Maple Leafs to Stanley Cup championship (1931–32); coached Montreal Canadiens to Stanley Cup championship (1943–44, 1945–46, 1952–53)

- Inducted into Manitoba Sports Hall of Fame (1963)

> "Sometimes I think hockey players would be better off if there were no coaches. Kids today are over-coached. They don't develop a style of their own and most of them look alike out there on the ice."
> — Dick Irvin, 1957

REGULAR SEASON

Season	Age	Team	Lg	GP	G	A	PTS	PIM
1916–17	24	Portland Rosebuds	PCHA	23	35	10	45	24
1917–18	25	Winnipeg Ypres	MHL-Sr.	9	29	8	37	26
1919–20	27	Regina Victorias	SSHL	12	32	4	36	22
1920–21	28	Regina Victorias	SSHL	11	19	5	24	12
1921–22	29	Regina Capitals	WCHL	20	21	7	28	17
1922–23	30	Regina Capitals	WCHL	25	9	4	13	12
1923–24	31	Regina Capitals	WCHL	29	15	8	23	33
1924–25	32	Regina Capitals	WCHL	28	13	5	18	38
1925–26	33	Portland Rosebuds	WHL	30	31	5	36	29
1926–27	34	Chicago Black Hawks	NHL	43	18	18	36	34
1927–28	35	Chicago Black Hawks	NHL	12	5	4	9	14
1928–29	36	Chicago Black Hawks	NHL	39	6	1	7	30
Career – 12 Seasons				281	233	79	312	291

PLAYOFFS

Season	Age	Team	Lg	GP	G	A	PTS	PIM
1919–20	27	Regina Victorias	SSHL	2	1	0	1	4
1920–21	28	Regina Victorias	SSHL	4	8	0	8	4
1921–22	29	Regina Capitals	WCHL	4	3	0	3	2
1921–22	29	Regina Capitals	West-P	2	1	0	1	0
1922–23	30	Regina Capitals	WCHL	2	1	0	1	0
1923–24	31	Regina Capitals	WCHL	2	0	0	0	4
1926–27	34	Chicago Black Hawks	NHL	2	2	0	2	4
Career – 6 Seasons				18	16	0	16	18

TROPHY CASE

ALL-STAR SELECTIONS

PCHA Second All-Star Team Center (1917)

WCHL First All-Star Team All-Star Center (1924)

WCHL Second All-Star Team Center (1922)

WHL Second All-Star Team Center (1926)

NHL First All-Star Team Coach (1944, 1945, 1946)

NHL Second All-Star Team Coach (1931, 1932, 1933, 1934, 1935, 1941)

11

Busher Jackson

HOCKEY HALL OF FAME CLASS: 1971

Alternates: 18, 17

Left Wing/Defense

Shoots: Left

Height: 5'-11"

Weight: 195 lbs.

Born: January 19, 1911: Toronto, Ontario

Died: June 25, 1966: Toronto, Ontario

Played 15 NHL seasons from 1929–44

"[Maple Leafs trainer Tim] Daly asked me to carry the sticks for him. I told him I wasn't a stick boy, I was a hockey player. So he said I was nothing but a fresh busher [a term for someone who had just been called up from the minors] and the name stuck."

QUICK FACTS

- First NHL player to score four goals in a single period in Toronto's 5–2 victory over St. Louis Eagles, November 20, 1934
- Played amateur hockey with Humberside Collegiate (1925–27) and Toronto Marlboros (1927–29)
- Led OHA-Jr. league in playoff goals (7) and points (9) in 1928–29
- Member of Memorial Cup-winning Toronto Marlboros who defeated the Ottawa Shamrocks and Elmwood (Manitoba) Millionaires in 1929. Jackson scored 15 goals and registered 10 assists in 13 games during the Memorial Cup playoffs
- Signed as a free agent by Toronto Maple Leafs, December 6, 1929
- Member of Toronto's famed Kid Line with Joe Primeau and Charlie Conacher
- Played in NHL All-Star Game (1934, 1937, 1939)
- Led NHL in points (53) in 1931–32
- Youngest player to lead NHL in scoring (21 years, 3 months) until Wayne Gretzky (aged 20 years, 3 months) won scoring title in 1980–81
- Traded to N.Y. Americans by Toronto with Buzz Boll, Doc Romnes, Jimmy Fowler and Murray Armstrong for Sweeney Schriner, May 18, 1939; traded to Boston by N.Y. Americans for $7,500, January 4, 1942
- Played the occasional shift as a defenseman in his final season with the Boston Bruins
- Best known for his energetic skating, driving style of attack and lethal backhand, which he often employed while crisscrossing through the slot

A booster patch for fans of the 24-year-old Jackson in 1934–35.

REGULAR SEASON

Season	Age	Team	Lg	GP	G	A	PTS	PIM
1929–30	19	Toronto Maple Leafs	NHL	31	12	6	18	29
1930–31	20	Toronto Maple Leafs	NHL	43	18	13	31	81
1931–32	21	Toronto Maple Leafs	NHL	48	28	25	53	63
1932–33	22	Toronto Maple Leafs	NHL	48	27	17	44	43
1933–34	23	Toronto Maple Leafs	NHL	38	20	18	38	38
1934–35	24	Toronto Maple Leafs	NHL	42	22	22	44	27
1935–36	25	Toronto Maple Leafs	NHL	47	11	11	22	19
1936–37	26	Toronto Maple Leafs	NHL	46	21	19	40	12
1937–38	27	Toronto Maple Leafs	NHL	48	17	17	34	18
1938–39	28	Toronto Maple Leafs	NHL	41	10	17	27	12
1939–40	29	New York Americans	NHL	43	12	8	20	10
1940–41	30	New York Americans	NHL	46	8	18	26	4
1941–42	31	Boston Bruins	NHL	26	5	7	12	18
1942–43	32	Boston Bruins	NHL	44	19	15	34	38
1943–44	33	Boston Bruins	NHL	42	11	21	32	25
NHL Career – 15 Seasons				633	241	234	475	437

PLAYOFFS

Season	Age	Team	Lg	GP	G	A	PTS	PIM
1930–31	20	Toronto Maple Leafs	NHL	2	0	0	0	0
1931–32	21	Toronto Maple Leafs	NHL	7	5	2	7	13
1932–33	22	Toronto Maple Leafs	NHL	9	3	1	4	2
1933–34	23	Toronto Maple Leafs	NHL	5	1	0	1	8
1934–35	24	Toronto Maple Leafs	NHL	7	3	2	5	2
1935–36	25	Toronto Maple Leafs	NHL	9	3	2	5	4
1936–37	26	Toronto Maple Leafs	NHL	2	1	0	1	2
1937–38	27	Toronto Maple Leafs	NHL	6	1	0	1	8
1938–39	28	Toronto Maple Leafs	NHL	7	0	1	1	2
1939–40	29	New York Americans	NHL	3	0	1	1	2
1941–42	31	Boston Bruins	NHL	5	0	1	1	0
1942–43	32	Boston Bruins	NHL	9	1	2	3	10
NHL Career – 12 Seasons				71	18	12	30	53

TROPHY CASE

AWARDS

NHL Scoring Leader (1932)

Stanley Cup (1931–32)

ALL-STAR SELECTIONS

First All-Star Team Left Wing (1932, 1934, 1935, 1937)

Second All-Star Team Left Wing (1933)

Angela James

HOCKEY HALL OF FAME CLASS: 2010

8

Retired by Seneca College

Defense/Center

Shoots: Right

Height: 5'-5"

Weight: 147 lbs.

Born: December 22, 1964; Toronto, Ontario

Played 18 elite amateur seasons from 1982–2000

QUICK FACTS

- Holds Team Canada record for most goals in a single World Hockey Championship tournament (11), established in 1990
- Played amateur hockey with Brantford Nationals (1982–83); Seneca College (1983–85); Hamilton Golden Hawks (1985–90); Toronto Aeros (1990–96); Toronto Red Wings (1995–96); Newtonbrook Panthers (1996–97); North York/Beatrice Aeros (1997–2000)
- OCAA First All-Star Team Defense (1984, 1985); named OCAA Women's Hockey MVP (1983, 1984, 1985)
- Inducted into International Ice Hockey Hall of Fame (2008)
- Inducted into Black Hockey and Sports Hall of Fame (2006)
- Inducted into Ontario Colleges Athletic Association (OCAA) Hall of Fame (2005)
- Inducted into Canada's Sports Hall of Fame (2009)
- IIHF All-Tournament All-Star Team (1990, 1992)
- Named Best Forward at 1994 IIHF World Championships
- Registered 33 goals and 21 assists in 50 games during nine-year career with Canadian National Women's Team
- Member of National Women's Champion Toronto Aeros (1991, 1993)
- COWHL First All-Star Team Center (1991, 1992, 1993); named COWHL MVP (1991); named NWHL MVP (1999)

"She could do it all. She had end-to-end speed, she had finesse as a stick handler and her slap shot was harder and more accurate than any female player I have ever seen. She was a pure goal scorer like Mike Bossy and aggressive like Mark Messier. In her prime, she was referred to as the 'Wayne Gretzky of Women's Hockey'."
— Robin Brown, CBC commentator

CAREER STATS

Season	Age	Team	Lg	GP	G	A	PTS	PIM
1982–83	18	Seneca College	OCAA	8	15	10	25	
1983–84	19	Seneca College	OCAA	10	15	15	30	
1984–85	20	Seneca College	OCAA	14	50	23	73	
1989–90	25	Canada	WWC	5	11	2	13	10
1991–92	27	Canada	WWC	5	5	2	7	2
1992–93	28	Toronto Aeros	COWHL	23	16	18	34	67
1993–94	29	Canada	WWC	5	4	5	9	2
1993–94	29	Toronto Aeros	COWHL	28	30	40	70	41
1995–96	31	Canada	Pacific Rim	5	3	4	7	2
1995–96	31	Canada	3 Nations Cup	5	1	2	3	2
1995–96	31	Toronto Red Wings	COWHL	29	35	35	70	37
1996–97	32	Newtonbrook Panthers	COWHL	28	29	29	58	57
1996–97	32	Canada	WWC	5	2	3	5	2
1997–98	33	Toronto Aeros	COWHL	9	6	3	9	19
1997–98	33	Canada	Nat-Team	15	7	1	8	4
1998–99	34	North York/Beatrice Aeros	NWHL	31	36	19	55	30
1998–99	34	Canada	3 Nations Cup	3	0	2	2	0
1999–00	35	Canada	3 Nations Cup	2	0	0	0	0
1999–00	35	North York/Beatrice Aeros	NWHL	27	22	22	44	10
Career – 12 Seasons				257	281	235	516	285

TROPHY CASE

INTERNATIONAL AWARDS

Gold Medal: World Championships (1990, 1992, 1994, 1997)

3

Ching Johnson
HOCKEY HALL OF FAME CLASS: 1958

Alternate: 18

Defense

Shoots: Left

Height: 5'-11"

Weight: 210 lbs.

Born: December 7, 1898: Winnipeg, Manitoba

Died: June 16, 1979: Silver Spring, Maryland

Played 12 NHL seasons from 1926–38

" Ching Johnson's grin is as wide as ever ... He played with such buoyant zest that he was the idol of the galleries and he played with such consummate skill that he has won a niche in hockey's Hall of Fame."

— Arthur Daly, *New York Times*, on Johnson's induction into the Hockey Hall of Fame

QUICK FACTS

- Given name was Ivan; earned nickname because of his talents as a cook
- Played amateur hockey with Winnipeg Monarchs (1918–20); Eveleth Rangers (1920–23); Minneapolis Millers (1923–24, 1925–26); Minneapolis Rockets (1924–25)
- USAHA First All-Star Team Defense (1924); CHL First All-Star Team Defense (1926); AHA First All-Star Team Defense (1939)
- Signed as a free agent by N.Y. Rangers, September 2, 1926
- Finished second to Howie Morenz in voting for the Hart Trophy (1931–32)
- Played in NHL All-Star Game (1934)
- Signed as a free agent by N.Y. Americans, November 19, 1937
- Coached Washington Lions (1941–43); coached Hollywood Wolves (1943–44)

- Served as player/coach of Minneapolis Millers (1938); served as player/coach of Marquette Ironmen (1940–41)
- Worked as a AHL and EHL linesman (1944–45)
- Also known as "Ivan the Terrible" around the league because of his rugged style and bruising body checks.
- Led N.Y. Rangers team in penalty minutes in eight of his 11 seasons he played with New York
- Led NHL in playoff penalty minutes in 1928 (46) and 1932 (24)

Ching Johnson's gloves.

REGULAR SEASON

Season	Age	Team	Lg	GP	G	A	PTS	PIM
1926–27	28	New York Rangers	NHL	27	3	2	5	66
1927–28	29	New York Rangers	NHL	42	10	6	16	146
1928–29	30	New York Rangers	NHL	8	0	0	0	14
1929–30	31	New York Rangers	NHL	30	3	3	6	82
1930–31	32	New York Rangers	NHL	44	2	6	8	77
1931–32	33	New York Rangers	NHL	47	3	10	13	106
1932–33	34	New York Rangers	NHL	48	8	9	17	127
1933–34	35	New York Rangers	NHL	48	2	6	8	86
1934–35	36	New York Rangers	NHL	29	2	3	5	34
1935–36	37	New York Rangers	NHL	47	5	3	8	58
1936–37	38	New York Rangers	NHL	35	0	0	0	2
1937–38	39	New York Americans	NHL	31	0	0	0	10
NHL Career – 12 Seasons				436	38	48	86	808

PLAYOFFS

Season	Age	Team	Lg	GP	G	A	PTS	PIM
1926–27	28	New York Rangers	NHL	2	0	0	0	8
1927–28	29	New York Rangers	NHL	9	1	1	2	46
1928–29	30	New York Rangers	NHL	6	0	0	0	26
1929–30	31	New York Rangers	NHL	4	0	0	0	14
1930–31	32	New York Rangers	NHL	4	1	0	1	17
1931–32	33	New York Rangers	NHL	7	2	0	2	24
1932–33	34	New York Rangers	NHL	8	1	0	1	14
1933–34	35	New York Rangers	NHL	2	0	0	0	4
1934–35	36	New York Rangers	NHL	4	0	0	0	2
1936–37	38	New York Rangers	NHL	9	0	1	1	4
1937–38	39	New York Americans	NHL	6	0	0	0	2
NHL Career – 11 Seasons				58	3	2	5	155

TROPHY CASE

AWARDS

Stanley Cup (1927–28, 1932–33)

ALL-STAR SELECTIONS

First All-Star Team Defense (1932, 1933)

Second All-Star Team Defense (1931, 1934)

Ernie Johnson

HOCKEY HALL OF FAME CLASS: 1952

Defense/Left Wing

Shoots: Left

Height: 5'-11"

Weight: 185 lbs.

Born: February 26, 1886: Montreal, Quebec

Died: March 24, 1963: White Rock, British Columbia

Played 19 elite amateur and professional seasons from 1903–22

QUICK FACTS

- Played amateur hockey with Montreal St. Lawrence (1902–03); Montreal AAA (1903–05); Montreal Wanderers (1905–09)

- ECAHA Second All-Star Team Left Wing (1907); ECHA Second All-Star Team Left Wing (1908)

- Started his career as a winger with the Montreal Wanderers

- Teamed with Frank "Pud" Glass with the Montreal Wanderers and the pair were inseparable on and off the ice. Known as "The Hockey Twins," they were fined early and often for their "behavior" off the ice

- Scored four goals in Stanley Cup playoff game against Ottawa Vics, January 13, 1908; scored four goals in Stanley Cup playoff game against Winnipeg Maple Leafs, March 12, 1908

- Member of the Montreal Wanderers team that successfully defended the Stanley Cup seven times against Ottawa Silver Seven, New Glasgow, Edmonton, Ottawa Victorias, Winnipeg, Toronto and Berlin

- Notorious for signing and then rejecting contracts, he jumped, re-jumped and jumped back between the Montreal Wanderers and New Westminster Royals three times in less than a year

- Transferred to Portland (PCHA) when New Westminster franchise relocated, September, 1915; transferred to Victoria when Portland franchise relocated, August, 1918

- Worked as a brakeman for the Union Pacific Railway in Portland in the 1920s

- Switched from left wing to defense when he joined the PCHA

> I don't pay much attention to rules. There is only one rule that I really know — there is the puck and there's the net. Just put the puck in the net."

REGULAR SEASON

Season	Age	Team	Lg	GP	G	A	PTS	PIM
1903-04	17	Montreal AAA	CAHL	2	1	0	1	
1904-05	18	Montreal AAA	CAHL	9	8	0	8	9
1905-06	19	Montreal Wanderers	ECAHA	10	12	0	12	44
1906-07	20	Montreal Wanderers	ECAHA	10	15	0	15	42
1907-08	21	Montreal Wanderers	ECAHA	10	9	0	9	33
1908-09	22	Montreal Wanderers	ECHA	10	10	0	10	34
1909-10	23	Montreal Wanderers	NHA	1	0	0	0	6
1909-10	23	Montreal Wanderers	NHA	12	7	0	7	41
1910-11	24	Montreal Wanderers	NHA	16	6	0	6	60
1911-12	25	New Westminster Royals	PCHA	14	9	0	9	13
1912-13	26	New Westminster Royals	PCHA	13	7	3	10	15
1913-14	27	New Westminster Royals	PCHA	16	3	5	8	27
1914-15	28	Portland Rosebuds	PCHA	18	6	4	10	21
1915-16	29	Portland Rosebuds	PCHA	18	6	3	9	62
1916-17	30	Portland Rosebuds	PCHA	24	12	9	21	54
1917-18	31	Portland Rosebuds	PCHA	15	3	2	5	3
1918-19	32	Victoria Aristocrats	PCHA	15	3	3	6	0
1919-20	33	Victoria Aristocrats	PCHA	21	0	5	5	22
1920-21	34	Victoria Aristocrats	PCHA	24	5	2	7	26
1921-22	35	Victoria Cougars	PCHA	13	1	1	2	12
Career — 19 Seasons				271	123	37	160	524

PLAYOFFS

Season	Age	Team	Lg	GP	G	A	PTS	PIM
1905-06	19	Montreal Wanderers	ECAHA	2	1	0	1	3
1906-07	20	Montreal Wanderers	St-Cup	6	5	0	5	8
1907-08	21	Montreal Wanderers	St-Cup	5	11	0	11	28
1908-09	22	Montreal Wanderers	St-Cup	2	1	0	1	6
1909-10	23	Montreal Wanderers	St-Cup	1	0	0	0	9
1915-16	29	Portland Rosebuds	St-Cup	5	1	0	1	9
Career — 6 Seasons				21	19	0	19	63

TROPHY CASE

AWARDS

Stanley Cup (1905-06, 1906-07, 1907-08, 1909-10)

ALL-STAR SELECTIONS

PCHA First All-Star Team Defense (1912, 1913, 1915, 1916, 1917, 1918, 1919, 1921)

10

Tom Johnson
HOCKEY HALL OF FAME CLASS: 1970

Alternate: 22

Defense

Shoots: Left

Height: 6'

Weight: 180 lbs.

Born: February 18, 1928: Baldur, Manitoba

Died: November 21, 2007: Falmouth, Massachusetts

Played 16 NHL seasons from 1947–48, 1950–65

QUICK FACTS

- Played amateur hockey with Winnipeg Monarchs (1946–47); Montreal Royals (1947–48)
- Signed as a free agent by Montreal, April 30, 1947
- Played in NHL All-Star Game (1952, 1953, 1956, 1957, 1958, 1959, 1960)
- Inducted into Manitoba Hockey Hall of Fame (1985)
- Inducted into Manitoba Sports Hall of Fame (1993)
- Coached Boston Bruins (1971–73)
- Coached Boston Bruins to Stanley Cup championship (1971–72)

- Renowned for his abilities as a penalty killer and skill at stripping the puck from opposing players and feeding a perfect pass to teammates
- Nicknamed "Tomcat" because he was always on the prowl when he was on the ice
- Claimed by Boston Bruins from Montreal in Waiver Draft, June 4, 1963
- Suffered career-ending leg injury in game vs. Chicago, February 28, 1965
- Served as assistant General Manager (1970–71, 1973–79) and Vice-President of the Boston Bruins (1979–99)

> "I was classified as a defensive defenseman. I stayed back and minded the store. With the high powered scoring teams I was with, I just had to get them the puck and let them do the rest."

REGULAR SEASON

Season	Age	Team	Lg	GP	G	A	PTS	PIM	ESG	PPG	SHG	GWG
1947–48	19	Montreal Canadiens	NHL	1	0	0	0	0				
1950–51	22	Montreal Canadiens	NHL	70	2	8	10	128				
1951–52	23	Montreal Canadiens	NHL	67	0	7	7	76				
1952–53	24	Montreal Canadiens	NHL	70	3	8	11	63				
1953–54	25	Montreal Canadiens	NHL	70	7	11	18	85				
1954–55	26	Montreal Canadiens	NHL	70	6	19	25	74				
1955–56	27	Montreal Canadiens	NHL	64	3	10	13	75				
1956–57	28	Montreal Canadiens	NHL	70	4	11	15	59				
1957–58	29	Montreal Canadiens	NHL	66	3	18	21	75				
1958–59	30	Montreal Canadiens	NHL	70	10	29	39	76				
1959–60	31	Montreal Canadiens	NHL	64	4	25	29	59				
1960–61	32	Montreal Canadiens	NHL	70	1	15	16	54				
1961–62	33	Montreal Canadiens	NHL	62	1	17	18	45				
1962–63	34	Montreal Canadiens	NHL	43	3	5	8	28				
1963–64	35	Boston Bruins	NHL	70	4	21	25	33	4	0	0	1
1964–65	36	Boston Bruins	NHL	51	0	9	9	30	0	0	0	0
NHL Career — 16 Seasons				978	51	213	264	960	4	0	0	1

PLAYOFFS

Season	Age	Team	Lg	GP	G	A	PTS	PIM	ESG	PPG	SHG	GWG
1949–50	21	Montreal Canadiens	NHL	1	0	0	0	0				
1950–51	22	Montreal Canadiens	NHL	11	0	0	0	6				
1951–52	23	Montreal Canadiens	NHL	11	1	0	1	2				
1952–53	24	Montreal Canadiens	NHL	12	2	3	5	8				
1953–54	25	Montreal Canadiens	NHL	11	1	2	3	30				
1954–55	26	Montreal Canadiens	NHL	12	2	0	2	22				
1955–56	27	Montreal Canadiens	NHL	10	0	2	2	8				
1956–57	28	Montreal Canadiens	NHL	10	0	2	2	13				
1957–58	29	Montreal Canadiens	NHL	2	0	0	0	0				
1958–59	30	Montreal Canadiens	NHL	11	2	3	5	8				
1959–60	31	Montreal Canadiens	NHL	8	0	1	1	4				
1960–61	32	Montreal Canadiens	NHL	6	0	1	1	8				
1961–62	33	Montreal Canadiens	NHL	6	0	1	1	0				
NHL Career — 13 Seasons				111	8	15	23	109				

TROPHY CASE

AWARDS

James Norris Memorial Trophy (1959)

Stanley Cup (1952–53, 1955–56, 1956–57, 1957–58, 1958–59, 1959–60)

ALL-STAR SELECTIONS

First All-Star Team Defense (1959)

Second All-Star Team Defense (1956)

Aurele Joliat
HOCKEY HALL OF FAME CLASS: 1947

Left Wing

Shoots: Left

Height: 5'-7"

Weight: 136 lbs.

Born: August 29, 1901: Ottawa, Ontario

Died: June 2, 1986: Ottawa, Ontario

Played 16 NHL seasons from 1922–38

"One night [Eddie Shore] dislocated my shoulder and they carried me off in a lot of pain. Then I look around and Shore is leading a fancy rush. Forget the sore shoulder. I leaped over the boards and intercepted the big bugger. Hit him with a flyin' tackle. Hit him so hard he was out cold on the ice. He had it comin' I'd say."

QUICK FACTS

- Ranks second among Montreal Canadiens left wingers in career goals (270)
- Finished among NHL top-5 in goals in 1923–24 (15), 1924–25 (30), 1927–28 (28) and 1933–34 (22)
- Finished among NHL top-5 in assists in 1925–26 (9), 1927–28 (11), 1930–31 (22) and 1931–32 (24)
- Finished among NHL top-5 in points in 1923–24 (20), 1924–25 (41), 1925–26 (26) and 1927–28 (39)
- Known as both "The Little Giant" and "The Mighty Atom"
- Played amateur hockey with Ottawa New Edinburghs (1916–17, 1918–20); Ottawa Aberdeens (1917–18); Iroquois Falls Flyers (1920–21)
- Played football with Regina Boat Club in 1922 where he was first noticed by officials of the Saskatoon Sheiks hockey club
- Signed as a free agent by Saskatoon Sheiks (WCHL), September 1, 1922
- Rights traded to Montreal Canadiens by Saskatoon Sheiks (WCHL) with $3,500 for Newsy Lalonde, September 18, 1922
- Played in NHL All-Star Game (1934, 1937)
- Older brother, Homer, was killed in action in France during World War I
- Played in a benefit All-Star game in 1982 at the age of 80 and scored a hat-trick as the NHL Oldstars defeated his Ottawa Old-Pros 18–12

Joliat's profile from a Montreal Canadiens caricature book celebrating the club's 1930 Stanley Cup championship.

REGULAR SEASON

Season	Age	Team	Lg	GP	G	A	PTS	PIM
1922–23	21	Montreal Canadiens	NHL	24	12	9	21	37
1923–24	22	Montreal Canadiens	NHL	24	15	5	20	27
1924–25	23	Montreal Canadiens	NHL	25	30	11	41	85
1925–26	24	Montreal Canadiens	NHL	35	17	9	26	52
1926–27	25	Montreal Canadiens	NHL	43	14	4	18	79
1927–28	26	Montreal Canadiens	NHL	44	28	11	39	105
1928–29	27	Montreal Canadiens	NHL	44	12	5	17	59
1929–30	28	Montreal Canadiens	NHL	42	19	12	31	40
1930–31	29	Montreal Canadiens	NHL	43	13	22	35	73
1931–32	30	Montreal Canadiens	NHL	48	15	24	39	46
1932–33	31	Montreal Canadiens	NHL	48	18	21	39	53
1933–34	32	Montreal Canadiens	NHL	48	22	15	37	27
1934–35	33	Montreal Canadiens	NHL	48	17	12	29	18
1935–36	34	Montreal Canadiens	NHL	48	15	8	23	16
1936–37	35	Montreal Canadiens	NHL	47	17	15	32	30
1937–38	36	Montreal Canadiens	NHL	44	6	7	13	24
Career – 16 Seasons				655	270	190	460	771

PLAYOFFS

Season	Age	Team	Lg	GP	G	A	PTS	PIM
1922–23	21	Montreal Canadiens	NHL	2	1	0	1	11
1923–24	22	Montreal Canadiens	NHL	2	1	1	2	0
1923–24	22	Montreal Canadiens	St-Cup	4	3	1	4	6
1924–25	23	Montreal Canadiens	NHL	1	0	0	0	5
1924–25	23	Montreal Canadiens	St-Cup	4	2	0	2	16
1926–27	25	Montreal Canadiens	NHL	4	1	0	1	10
1927–28	26	Montreal Canadiens	NHL	2	0	0	0	4
1928–29	27	Montreal Canadiens	NHL	3	1	1	2	10
1929–30	28	Montreal Canadiens	NHL	6	0	2	2	6
1930–31	29	Montreal Canadiens	NHL	10	0	4	4	12
1931–32	30	Montreal Canadiens	NHL	4	2	0	2	4
1932–33	31	Montreal Canadiens	NHL	2	2	1	3	2
1933–34	32	Montreal Canadiens	NHL	2	0	1	1	0
1934–35	33	Montreal Canadiens	NHL	2	1	0	1	0
1936–37	35	Montreal Canadiens	NHL	5	0	3	3	2
Career – 13 Seasons				53	14	14	28	88

TROPHY CASE

AWARDS

Hart Memorial Trophy (1934)

Stanley Cup (1923–24, 1929–30, 1930–31)

ALL-STAR SELECTIONS

First All-Star Team Left Wing (1931)

Second All-Star Team Left Wing (1932, 1934, 1935)

5

Duke Keats

HOCKEY HALL OF FAME CLASS: 1958

Alternates: 3, 8, 4

Center

Shoots: Right

Height: 5'-11"

Weight: 195 lbs.

Born: March 21, 1895: Montreal, Quebec

Died: January 16, 1972: Victoria, British Columbia

Played 12 elite amateur and professional seasons from 1915–17, 1919–29

QUICK FACTS

- Nicknamed "The Iron Duke"
- Played amateur hockey with Cobalt McKinley Mines (1912–13); Cobalt O'Brien Mines (1913–14); North Bay Trappers (1913–14); Haileybury Hawks (1914–15); Edmonton Eskimos (1919–21)
- Became so angered by the poor performance of goaltender Billy Nicholson while playing for the Toronto Blueshirts of the NHA during the 1916–17 season, he strapped on the pads and took over in net himself for the next period
- Reinstated as an amateur and signed as a free agent by Edmonton Eskimos (Big-4), December, 1919
- Led Big-4 in goals (18), assists (14) and points (32) in 1919–20; led Big-4 in goals (23) and points (29) in 1920–21

- Signed as free agent by Edmonton Eskimos (WCHL), November 4, 1921
- Led WCHL in goals (31), assists (24) and points (55) in 1921–22
- Traded to Boston by Edmonton Eskimos (WHL) for cash, September 4, 1926; traded to Detroit by Boston with Archie Briden for Frank Fredrickson and Harry Meeking, January 7, 1927
- Scored the first hat trick in Detroit franchise history in 7–1 victory over Pittsburgh Pirates, March 10, 1927
- Traded to Chicago by Detroit for Gord Fraser and $5,000, December 16, 1927
- Traded to Tulsa Oilers (AHA) by Chicago for cash, November 28, 1928
- Led AHA in goals (22) and points (33) in 1928–29

> "You would have thought he had a nail in the end of his stick, the way he could carry that puck around. He was that good."
>
> — Lloyd McIntyre, Duke Keats' teammate with the Edmonton Eskimos

REGULAR SEASON

Season	Age	Team	Lg	GP	G	A	PTS	PIM
1915–16	20	Toronto Blueshirts	NHA	24	22	7	29	112
1916–17	21	Toronto Blueshirts	NHA	13	15	3	18	54
1919–20	24	Edmonton Eskimos	Big-4	12	18	14	32	41
1920–21	25	Edmonton Eskimos	Big-4	15	23	6	29	36
1921–22	26	Edmonton Eskimos	WCHL	25	31	24	55	47
1922–23	27	Edmonton Eskimos	WCHL	25	24	13	37	72
1923–24	28	Edmonton Eskimos	WCHL	29	19	12	31	41
1924–25	29	Edmonton Eskimos	WCHL	28	23	9	32	63
1925–26	30	Edmonton Eskimos	WHL	30	20	9	29	134
1926–27	31	Boston Bruins	NHL	17	4	7	11	20
1926–27	31	Detroit Cougars	NHL	25	12	1	13	32
1927–28	32	Detroit Cougars	NHL	5	0	2	2	6
1927–28	32	Chicago Black Hawks	NHL	32	14	8	22	55
1928–29	33	Chicago Black Hawks	NHL	3	0	1	1	0
Career – 12 Seasons				303	233	123	356	859

PLAYOFFS

Season	Age	Team	Lg	GP	G	A	PTS	PIM
1919–20	24	Edmonton Eskimos	Big-4	2	2	2	4	2
1921–22	26	Edmonton Eskimos	WCHL	2	0	1	1	6
1922–23	27	Edmonton Eskimos	WCHL	2	2	0	4	0
1925–26	30	Edmoton Eskimos	WHL	2	0	0	0	28
Careers – 4 Seasons				8	4	5	9	36

TROPHY CASE

ALL-STAR SELECTIONS

WCHL First All-Star Team Center (1922, 1923, 1924, 1925)

WHL First All-Star Team Center (1926)

Red Kelly

HOCKEY HALL OF FAME CLASS: 1969

4

Alternate: 20

Defense/Center

Shoots: Left

Height: 5'-11"

Weight: 180 lbs.

Born: July 9, 1927: Simcoe, Ontario

Played 20 NHL seasons from 1947–67

> [Coach] Joe Primeau taught me you don't win games in the penalty box. You've got to stay on the ice. Players would try to get you off the ice sometimes but you're more valuable to a team when you're on the ice."

QUICK FACTS

- First defenseman in NHL history to win Lady Byng Memorial Trophy
- Only player in NHL history to win Lady Byng Memorial Trophy as both a defenseman and a forward
- One of only six players in NHL history (with Dick Duff, Frank Mahovlich, Bryan Trottier, Patrick Roy and Larry Murphy) to win two-or-more Stanley Cup championships with two-or-more teams
- Played amateur hockey with St. Michael's Midgets (1943–44); St. Michael's Buzzers (1944–45); St. Michael's Majors (1944–47)
- Member of Memorial Cup-winning St. Michael's Majors (1946–47)
- Won four Stanley Cup championships as a defenseman and four as a forward
- Played in NHL All-Star Game (1950, 1951, 1952, 1953, 1954, 1955, 1956, 1957, 1958, 1960, 1962, 1963)
- Converted to center from defense when acquired by Toronto from Detroit, February 10, 1960
- Rights traded to L.A. Kings by Toronto on condition he would coach and not play, June 8, 1967

Kelly's jersey that he wore during the 1966–67 Stanley Cup final versus the Montreal Canadiens.

REGULAR SEASON

Season	Age	Team	Lg	GP	G	A	PTS	PIM	ESG	PPG	SHG	GWG
1947–48	20	Detroit Red Wings	NHL	60	6	14	20	13				
1948–49	21	Detroit Red Wings	NHL	59	5	11	16	10				
1949–50	22	Detroit Red Wings	NHL	70	15	25	40	9				
1950–51	23	Detroit Red Wings	NHL	70	17	37	54	24				
1951–52	24	Detroit Red Wings	NHL	67	16	31	47	16				
1952–53	25	Detroit Red Wings	NHL	70	19	27	46	8				
1953–54	26	Detroit Red Wings	NHL	62	16	33	49	18				
1954–55	27	Detroit Red Wings	NHL	70	15	30	45	28				
1955–56	28	Detroit Red Wings	NHL	70	16	34	50	39				
1956–57	29	Detroit Red Wings	NHL	70	10	25	35	18				
1957–58	30	Detroit Red Wings	NHL	61	13	18	31	26				
1958–59	31	Detroit Red Wings	NHL	67	8	13	21	34				
1959–60	32	Detroit Red Wings	NHL	50	6	12	18	10				
1959–60	32	Toronto Maple Leafs	NHL	18	6	5	11	8				
1960–61	33	Toronto Maple Leafs	NHL	64	20	50	70	12				
1961–62	34	Toronto Maple Leafs	NHL	58	22	27	49	6				
1962–63	35	Toronto Maple Leafs	NHL	66	20	40	60	8				
1963–64	36	Toronto Maple Leafs	NHL	70	11	34	45	16	10	1	0	2
1964–65	37	Toronto Maple Leafs	NHL	70	18	28	46	8	11	6	1	1
1965–66	38	Toronto Maple Leafs	NHL	63	8	24	32	12	8	0	0	2
1966–67	39	Toronto Maple Leafs	NHL	61	14	24	38	4	12	2	0	0
NHL Career — 20 Seasons				1316	281	542	823	327	41	9	1	5

PLAYOFFS

Season	Age	Team	Lg	GP	G	A	PTS	PIM	ESG	PPG	SHG	GWG
1947–48	20	Detroit Red Wings	NHL	10	3	2	5	2				
1948–49	21	Detroit Red Wings	NHL	11	1	1	2	10				
1949–50	22	Detroit Red Wings	NHL	14	1	3	4	2				
1950–51	23	Detroit Red Wings	NHL	6	0	1	1	0				
1951–52	24	Detroit Red Wings	NHL	5	1	0	1	0				
1952–53	25	Detroit Red Wings	NHL	6	0	4	4	0				
1953–54	26	Detroit Red Wings	NHL	12	5	1	6	0				
1954–55	27	Detroit Red Wings	NHL	11	2	4	6	17				
1955–56	28	Detroit Red Wings	NHL	10	2	4	6	2				
1956–57	29	Detroit Red Wings	NHL	5	1	0	1	0				
1957–58	30	Detroit Red Wings	NHL	4	0	1	1	2				
1959–60	32	Toronto Maple Leafs	NHL	10	3	8	11	2				
1960–61	33	Toronto Maple Leafs	NHL	2	1	0	1	0				
1961–62	34	Toronto Maple Leafs	NHL	12	4	6	10	0				
1962–63	35	Toronto Maple Leafs	NHL	10	2	6	8	6				
1963–64	36	Toronto Maple Leafs	NHL	14	4	9	13	4				
1964–65	37	Toronto Maple Leafs	NHL	6	3	2	5	2				
1965–66	38	Toronto Maple Leafs	NHL	4	0	2	2	0				
1966–67	39	Toronto Maple Leafs	NHL	12	0	5	5	2				
NHL Career — 19 Seasons				164	33	59	92	51				

TROPHY CASE

NHL AWARDS

Lady Byng Memorial Trophy (1951, 1953, 1954, 1961)

James Norris Memorial Trophy (1954)

Stanley Cup (1949–50, 1951–52, 1953–54, 1954–55, 1961–62, 1962–63, 1963–64, 1966–67)

ALL-STAR SELECTIONS

First All-Star Team Defense (1951, 1952, 1953, 1954, 1955, 1957)

Second All-Star Team Defense (1950, 1956)

273

9

Honored by Toronto

Alternate: 10	
Center	
Shoots: Right	
Height: 5'-10"	
Weight: 170 lbs.	
Born: December 12, 1925: Humberstone, Ontario	
Died: August 14, 2009: Port Colbourne, Ontario	
Played 14 NHL seasons from 1942–55, 1956–57	

Ted Kennedy

HOCKEY HALL OF FAME CLASS: 1966

QUICK FACTS

- Played amateur hockey with Port Colbourne Sailors (1942–43)
- Led OHA-Sr. in assists (29) in 1942–43
- Attended Montreal's training camp as a 16-year-old, but left early suffering from homesickness
- Rights traded to Toronto by Montreal for the rights to Frank Eddolls, September 10, 1943
- Scored Stanley Cup-winning goal in Toronto's 2–1 victory over Montreal Canadiens, April 19, 1947
- Leafs fan John Arnott, sitting high up in the stands, often shouted "C'mon Teeder" during a quiet moment at home games to rally the team. The rally cry continued to be heard at Maple Leaf Gardens until the building closed in 1998
- In 1953, Conn Smythe created the J.P. Bickell Trophy, given to the most valuable Maple Leaf, because Kennedy hadn't won a league award up to that point
- Played in NHL All-Star Game (1947, 1948, 1949, 1950, 1951, 1954)
- Finished among NHL top-5 in goals in 1944–45 (29) and 1946–47 (28)
- Finished among NHL top-5 in assists in 1946–47 (32), 1950–51 (43) and 1954–55 (42)
- Finished among NHL top-5 in points in 1944–45 (54), 1946–47 (60) and 1950–51 (61)
- Led NHL in assists (43) in 1950–51
- Served as captain of Toronto Maple Leafs (1948–55)

> I never had much speed, certainly not in the way Syl Apps or Max Bentley or Milt Schmidt, the great centers, did. So I compensated by using my wingers. To be able to pass reasonably well made up for my lack of speed."

REGULAR SEASON

Season	Age	Team	Lg	GP	G	A	PTS	PIM
1942-43	17	Toronto Maple Leafs	NHL	2	0	1	1	0
1943-44	18	Toronto Maple Leafs	NHL	49	26	23	49	2
1944-45	19	Toronto Maple Leafs	NHL	49	29	25	54	14
1945-46	20	Toronto Maple Leafs	NHL	21	3	2	5	4
1946-47	21	Toronto Maple Leafs	NHL	60	28	32	60	27
1947-48	22	Toronto Maple Leafs	NHL	60	25	21	46	32
1948-49	23	Toronto Maple Leafs	NHL	59	18	21	39	25
1949-50	24	Toronto Maple Leafs	NHL	53	20	24	44	34
1950-51	25	Toronto Maple Leafs	NHL	63	18	43	61	32
1951-52	26	Toronto Maple Leafs	NHL	70	19	33	52	33
1952-53	27	Toronto Maple Leafs	NHL	43	14	23	37	42
1953-54	28	Toronto Maple Leafs	NHL	67	15	23	38	78
1954-55	29	Toronto Maple Leafs	NHL	70	10	42	52	74
1956-57	31	Toronto Maple Leafs	NHL	30	6	16	22	35
NHL Career – 14 Seasons				696	231	329	560	432

PLAYOFFS

Season	Age	Team	Lg	GP	G	A	PTS	PIM
1943-44	18	Toronto Maple Leafs	NHL	5	1	1	2	4
1944-45	19	Toronto Maple Leafs	NHL	13	7	2	9	2
1946-47	21	Toronto Maple Leafs	NHL	11	4	5	9	4
1947-48	22	Toronto Maple Leafs	NHL	9	8	6	14	0
1948-49	23	Toronto Maple Leafs	NHL	9	2	6	8	2
1949-50	24	Toronto Maple Leafs	NHL	7	1	2	3	8
1950-51	25	Toronto Maple Leafs	NHL	11	4	5	9	6
1951-52	26	Toronto Maple Leafs	NHL	4	0	0	0	4
1953-54	28	Toronto Maple Leafs	NHL	5	1	1	2	2
1954-55	29	Toronto Maple Leafs	NHL	4	1	3	4	0
NHL Career – 10 Seasons				78	29	31	60	32

TROPHY CASE

NHL AWARDS

Hart Memorial Trophy (1955)

Stanley Cup (1944–45, 1945–46, 1946–47, 1947–48, 1948–49, 1950–51)

ALL-STAR SELECTIONS

Second All-Star Team Center (1950, 1951, 1954)

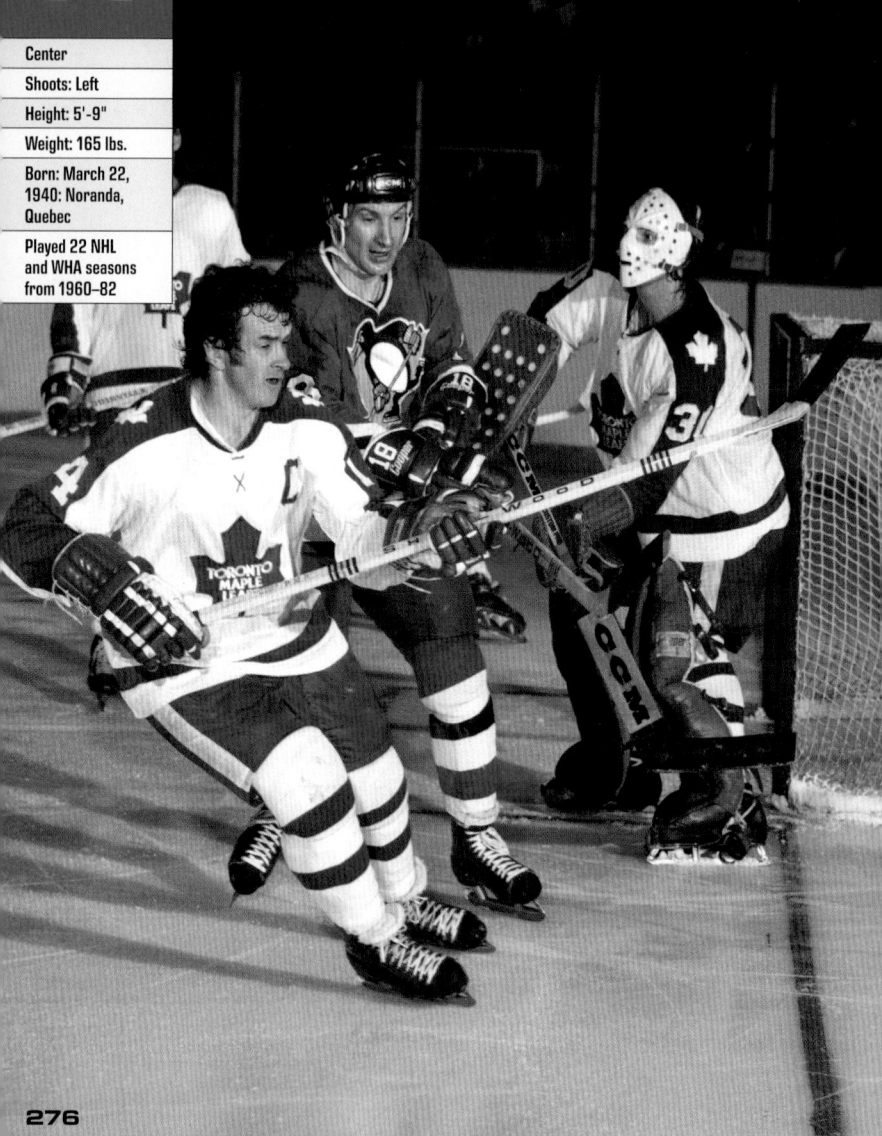

14

Dave Keon

HOCKEY HALL OF FAME CLASS: 1986

Center

Shoots: Left

Height: 5'-9"

Weight: 165 lbs.

Born: March 22, 1940; Noranda, Quebec

Played 22 NHL and WHA seasons from 1960–82

QUICK FACTS

- Shares NHL record for most short-handed goals (2) in a single playoff game, established in Toronto's 3–1 victory over Detroit Red Wings, April 18, 1963

- Played amateur hockey with St. Michael's Buzzers (1956–57); St. Michael's Majors (1956–59); Kitchener-Waterloo Dutchmen (1959–60); Sudbury Wolves (1959–60)

- Won OHA-Jr. B Rookie of the Year Award (1957)

- Played in NHL All-Star Game (1962, 1963, 1964, 1967, 1968, 1970, 1971, 1973)

- Won Paul Deneau Trophy (WHA Most Gentlemanly Player) in 1977 and 1978

- Led NHL in shorthanded goals in 1968–69 (6) and 1970–71 (8)

- Nicknamed "Mister Perpetual Motion" by legendary hockey announcer Foster Hewitt

- An excellent penalty killer and checker, he scored the majority of his goals with the backhand

- Only member of the Maple Leafs to win the Conn Smythe Trophy as playoff MVP

- Served as captain of Toronto Maple Leafs (1969–75)

- Number nine jersey retired by Mississauga (St. Michael's) Majors, December 14, 2008

> "Most kids today slap the puck. The backhand takes time to learn. It's not something you do naturally. But it is an effective shot."

REGULAR SEASON

Season	Age	Team	Lg	GP	G	A	PTS	+/-	PIM	ESG	PPG	SHG	GWG	SOG	S%
1960–61	20	Toronto Maple Leafs	NHL	70	20	25	45		6						
1961–62	21	Toronto Maple Leafs	NHL	64	26	35	61		2						
1962–63	22	Toronto Maple Leafs	NHL	68	28	28	56		2						
1963–64	23	Toronto Maple Leafs	NHL	70	23	37	60		6	16	7	0	2		
1964–65	24	Toronto Maple Leafs	NHL	65	21	29	50		10	14	6	1	2		
1965–66	25	Toronto Maple Leafs	NHL	69	24	30	54		4	18	6	0	5		
1966–67	26	Toronto Maple Leafs	NHL	66	19	33	52		2	13	5	1	2		
1967–68	27	Toronto Maple Leafs	NHL	67	11	37	48	16	4	10	1	0	3	196	5.6
1968–69	28	Toronto Maple Leafs	NHL	75	27	34	61	17	12	18	3	6	6	281	9.6
1969–70	29	Toronto Maple Leafs	NHL	72	32	30	62	-15	6	21	9	2	4	284	11.3
1970–71	30	Toronto Maple Leafs	NHL	76	38	38	76	24	4	25	5	8	9	277	13.7
1971–72	31	Toronto Maple Leafs	NHL	72	18	30	48	1	4	14	2	2	5	265	6.8
1972–73	32	Toronto Maple Leafs	NHL	76	37	36	73	4	2	27	8	2	6	277	13.4
1973–74	33	Toronto Maple Leafs	NHL	74	25	28	53	13	7	22	1	2	3	244	10.2
1974–75	34	Toronto Maple Leafs	NHL	78	16	43	59	3	4	14	1	1	2	183	8.7
1975–76	35	Minnesota Fighting Saints	WHA	57	26	38	64	14	4	19	5	2	3	144	18.1
1975–76	35	Indianapolis Racers	WHA	12	3	7	10	2	2	2	1	0	0	40	7.5
1976–77	36	Minnesota Fighting Saints	WHA	42	13	38	51	25	2	11	1	1	na	151	8.6
1976–77	36	New England Whalers	WHA	34	14	25	39	13	8	8	5	1	na	107	13.1
1977–78	37	New England Whalers	WHA	77	24	38	62	-4	2	18	1	5	na	169	14.2
1978–79	38	New England Whalers	WHA	79	22	43	65	4	2	15	7	0	na	189	11.6
1979–80	39	Hartford Whalers	NHL	76	10	52	62	-13	10	10	0	0	0	146	6.8
1980–81	40	Hartford Whalers	NHL	80	13	34	47	-31	26	11	2	0	0	131	9.9
1981–82	41	Hartford Whalers	NHL	78	8	11	19	-31	6	7	0	1	1	84	9.5
Career — 22 Seasons				1597	498	779	1277	42	137	313	76	35	1	3168	15.7

PLAYOFFS

Season	Age	Team	Lg	GP	G	A	PTS	+/-	PIM	ESG	PPG	SHG	GWG	SOG	S%
1960–61	20	Toronto Maple Leafs	NHL	5	1	1	2		0						
1961–62	21	Toronto Maple Leafs	NHL	12	5	3	8		0						
1962–63	22	Toronto Maple Leafs	NHL	10	7	5	12		0						
1963–64	23	Toronto Maple Leafs	NHL	14	7	2	9		2						
1964–65	24	Toronto Maple Leafs	NHL	6	2	2	4		2						
1965–66	25	Toronto Maple Leafs	NHL	4	0	2	2		0						
1966–67	26	Toronto Maple Leafs	NHL	12	3	5	8		0						
1968–69	28	Toronto Maple Leafs	NHL	4	1	3	4		2	0	0	1	0		
1970–71	30	Toronto Maple Leafs	NHL	6	3	2	5		0	3	0	0	0		
1971–72	31	Toronto Maple Leafs	NHL	5	2	3	5		0	2	0	0	0		
1973–74	33	Toronto Maple Leafs	NHL	4	1	2	3		0	1	0	0	0		
1974–75	34	Toronto Maple Leafs	NHL	7	0	5	5		0	0	0	0	0		
1975–76	35	Indianapolis Racers	WHA	7	2	2	4	0	2						
1976–77	36	New England Whalers	WHA	5	3	1	4	4	0				0		
1977–78	37	New England Whalers	WHA	15	5	11	16	2	4				1		
1978–79	38	New England Whalers	WHA	10	3	9	12	2	2				1		
1979–80	39	Hartford Whalers	NHL	3	0	1	1		0	0	0	0	0		
Career — 17 Seasons				128	45	59	104	8	14	6	0	1	2		

TROPHY CASE

NHL AWARDS

Calder Memorial Trophy (1961)

Lady Byng Memorial Trophy (1962, 1963)

Conn Smythe Trophy (1967)

Stanley Cup (1961–62, 1962–63, 1963–64, 1966–67)

ALL-STAR SELECTIONS

Second All-Star Team Center (1962, 1971)

Valeri Kharlamov

HOCKEY HALL OF FAME CLASS: 2005

Left Wing

Shoots: Left

Height: 5'-8"

Weight: 165 lbs.

Born: January 14, 1948: Moscow, Union of Soviet Socialist Republics

Died: August 27, 1981: Moscow, Union of Soviet Socialist Republics

Played 14 seasons of Russian elite amateur hockey from 1967–81

QUICK FACTS

- One of only two European-born and trained players (with Vladislav Tretiak) without NHL experience to be inducted into Hockey Hall of Fame

- Renowned for his performance during the 1972 Summit Series where he recorded three goals and seven points in seven games

- Played amateur hockey with Zvezda Chebarkul (1967–68); CSKA Moscow (1967–81)

- Led USSR Elite League in goals (40) in 1970–71

- Led USSR Elite League in points (42) in 1971–72

- Named USSR League Most Valuable Player (1972, 1973)

- USSR First All-Star Team Left Wing (1971, 1972, 1973, 1974, 1975, 1976, 1978)

- Named World Championships Best Forward (1976)

- World Championships First All-Star Team Left Wing (1972, 1973, 1975, 1976)

- Inducted into the International Ice Hockey Federation (IIHF) Hall of Fame (1998)

- Legacy honored by the Kharlamov Trophy, awarded to the best Russian NHL player as voted by Russian NHL players

- Died in an automobile accident on highway that connects St. Petersburg and Moscow, August 27, 1981

- At point of accident (kilometer marker #73) there is a memorial stone bearing the inscription: "The star of Russian hockey fell here."

> "His talents were God-given and he could do practically everything — a smart play, a tricky pass, a precise shot. Everything he did looked so easy, so elegant. His execution of hockey was aesthetic and he amazed millions."
> — Vladislav Tretiak

REGULAR SEASON

Season	Age	Team	Lg	GP	G	A	PTS	PIM
1967–68	20	CSKA Moscow	USSR	15	2	3	5	6
1968–69	21	CSKA Moscow	USSR	42	37	12	49	24
1969–70	22	CSKA Moscow	USSR	33	33	10	43	16
1970–71	23	CSKA Moscow	USSR	34	40	12	52	18
1971–72	24	CSKA Moscow	USSR	31	26	16	42	22
1972–73	25	CSKA Moscow	USSR	27	19	13	32	22
1973–74	26	CSKA Moscow	USSR	26	20	10	30	28
1974–75	27	CSKA Moscow	USSR	31	15	24	39	35
1975–76	28	CSKA Moscow	USSR	34	18	18	36	6
1976–77	29	CSKA Moscow	USSR	21	18	8	26	16
1977–78	30	CSKA Moscow	USSR	29	18	24	42	35
1978–79	31	CSKA Moscow	USSR	41	22	26	48	36
1979–80	32	CSKA Moscow	USSR	42	16	22	38	40
1980–81	33	CSKA Moscow	USSR	30	9	16	25	14
Career – 14 Seasons				436	293	214	507	318

TROPHY CASE

INTERNATIONAL AWARDS

Summit Series (1974)

Challenge Cup (1979)

Gold Medal: Winter Olympics (1972, 1976)

Silver Medal: Winter Olympics (1980)

Gold Medal: World Championships (1969, 1970, 1971, 1973, 1974, 1975, 1978, 1979)

Silver Medal: World Championships (1972, 1976)

Bronze Medal: World Championships (1977)

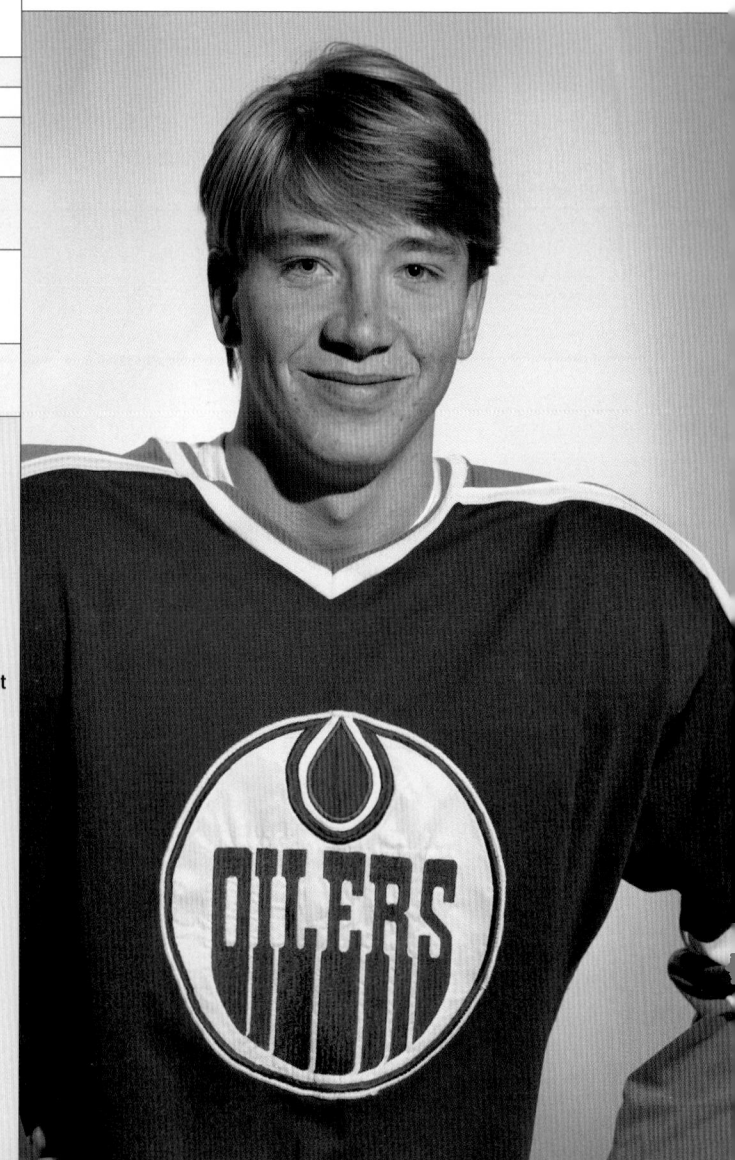

17

Retired by Edmonton

Right Wing	
Shoots: Right	
Height: 6'	
Weight: 194 lbs.	
Born: May 18, 1960: Helsinki, Finland	
Drafted by the Edmonton Oilers 69th overall in 1980	
Played 17 NHL seasons from 1980–90, 1991–98	

Jari Kurri

HOCKEY HALL OF FAME CLASS: 2001

> It took me a year to get to know the league, the systems and just being away from the old country, my parents and friends. It's not just the hockey that's different but a whole different lifestyle."

— Jari Kurri, on adjusting to the NHL

QUICK FACTS

- First European-born and trained player in NHL history to record 500 career goals, October 17, 1992
- Shares NHL record (with Reggie Leach) for goals in a single playoff year (19), established in 1984–85
- Ranks first in NHL assists (797) and points (1,398) by a European-trained player
- Ranks second in NHL goals by a European-trained player (601)
- Ranks sixth in NHL short-handed goals (39)
- Played amateur hockey with Jokerit Helsinki-Jr. (1974–80)
- Scored Stanley Cup-winning goal in Edmonton's 3–1 victory over Philadelphia Flyers, May 31, 1987
- World Championships All-Star Team (1991, 1994)

- Registered 1,000th career NHL point in Edmonton's 6–4 victory over St. Louis Blues, January 2, 1990; recorded 500th career NHL goal in L.A. Kings' 8–6 victory over Boston Bruins, October 17, 1992
- Played for Team Finland in 1980 Olympics, 1981 Canada Cup Tournament, 1982 World Championships, 1989 World Championships, 1991 Canada Cup Tournament, 1991 World Championships, 1994 World Championships, 1997 World Cup and 1998 Olympics
- Played in NHL All-Star Game (1983, 1985, 1986, 1988, 1989, 1990, 1993, 1998)
- Played with Milano Devils (Italy) in 1990–91

Kurri wore these gloves to score his 600th goal during a 5–1 route of the L.A. Kings on December 23, 1997.

REGULAR SEASON

Season	Age	Team	Lg	GP	G	A	PTS	+/-	PIM	ESG	PPG	SHG	GWG	SOG	S%
1980–81	20	Edmonton Oilers	NHL	75	32	43	75	26	40	23	9	0	1	202	15.8
1981–82	21	Edmonton Oilers	NHL	71	32	54	86	38	32	25	6	1	5	211	15.2
1982–83	22	Edmonton Oilers	NHL	80	45	59	104	47	22	34	10	1	3	218	20.6
1983–84	23	Edmonton Oilers	NHL	64	52	61	113	38	14	37	10	5	4	194	26.8
1984–85	24	Edmonton Oilers	NHL	73	71	64	135	76	30	54	14	3	13	261	27.2
1985–86	25	Edmonton Oilers	NHL	78	68	63	131	45	22	46	16	6	9	236	28.8
1986–87	26	Edmonton Oilers	NHL	79	54	54	108	35	41	37	12	5	10	211	25.6
1987–88	27	Edmonton Oilers	NHL	80	43	53	96	25	30	30	10	3	5	207	20.8
1988–89	28	Edmonton Oilers	NHL	76	44	58	102	19	69	29	10	5	8	214	20.6
1989–90	29	Edmonton Oilers	NHL	78	33	60	93	18	48	21	10	2	2	201	16.4
1991–92	31	Los Angeles Kings	NHL	73	23	37	60	-24	24	12	10	1	3	167	13.8
1992–93	32	Los Angeles Kings	NHL	82	27	60	87	19	38	13	12	2	3	210	12.9
1993–94	33	Los Angeles Kings	NHL	81	31	46	77	-24	48	13	14	4	3	198	15.7
1994–95	34	Los Angeles Kings	NHL	38	10	19	29	-17	24	8	2	0	0	84	11.9
1995–96	35	Los Angeles Kings	NHL	57	17	23	40	-12	37	11	5	1	0	131	13.0
1995–96	35	New York Rangers	NHL	14	1	4	5	-4	2	1	0	0	0	27	3.7
1996–97	36	Mighty Ducks of Anaheim	NHL	82	13	22	35	-13	12	10	3	0	3	109	11.9
1997–98	37	Colorado Avalanche	NHL	70	5	17	22	6	12	3	2	0	0	61	8.2
NHL Career — 17 Seasons				1251	601	797	1398	298	545	407	155	39	72	3142	19.1

PLAYOFFS

Season	Age	Team	Lg	GP	G	A	PTS	+/-	PIM	ESG	PPG	SHG	GWG	SOG	S%
1980–81	20	Edmonton Oilers	NHL	9	5	7	12		4	5	0	0	0		
1981–82	21	Edmonton Oilers	NHL	5	2	5	7		10	2	0	0	0		
1982–83	22	Edmonton Oilers	NHL	16	8	15	23		8	4	2	2	0		
1983–84	23	Edmonton Oilers	NHL	19	14	14	28	9	13	10	4	0	0	60	23.3
1984–85	24	Edmonton Oilers	NHL	18	19	12	31	24	6	16	1	2	2	89	21.3
1985–86	25	Edmonton Oilers	NHL	10	2	10	12	1	4	1	0	1	0	25	8.0
1986–87	26	Edmonton Oilers	NHL	21	15	10	25	11	20	10	4	1	5	52	28.8
1987–88	27	Edmonton Oilers	NHL	19	14	17	31	15	12	9	5	0	3	57	24.6
1988–89	28	Edmonton Oilers	NHL	7	3	5	8	-2	6	2	0	1	0	17	17.6
1989–90	29	Edmonton Oilers	NHL	22	10	15	25	13	18	4	6	0	3	58	17.2
1991–92	31	Los Angeles Kings	NHL	4	1	2	3	1	4	0	1	0	0	10	10.0
1992–93	32	Los Angeles Kings	NHL	24	9	8	17	2	12	5	2	2	0	50	18.0
1995–96	35	New York Rangers	NHL	11	3	5	8	-2	2	2	0	1	1	31	9.7
1996–97	36	Mighty Ducks of Anaheim	NHL	11	1	2	3	2	4	1	0	0	0	18	5.6
1997–98	37	Colorado Avalanche	NHL	4	0	0	0	-1	0	0	0	0	0	2	0.0
NHL Career — 15 Seasons				200	106	127	233	73	123	71	25	10	14	469	19.4

TROPHY CASE

AWARDS

Lady Byng Memorial Trophy (1985)

Stanley Cup (1983–84, 1984–85, 1986–87, 1987–88, 1989–90)

ALL-STAR SELECTIONS

First All-Star Team Right Wing (1985, 1987)

Second All-Star Team Right Wing (1984, 1986, 1989)

INTERNATIONAL AWARDS

Silver Medal: World Championships (1994)

Bronze Medal: Winter Olympics (1998)

All I can say to young players is enjoy every moment of it. Just enjoy every moment. Your career goes by very quickly."

Mario Lemieux

A
B
C
D
E
F
G
H
I
J
K
L
M
N
O
P
Q
R
S
T
U
V
W
X
Y
Z

Retired by Montreal

Alternates: 14, 10

Center

Shoots: Left

Height: 5'-10"

Weight: 165 lbs.

Born: January 22, 1918: Nokomis, Saskatchewan

Played 14 NHL seasons from 1940–54

Elmer Lach

HOCKEY HALL OF FAME CLASS: 1966

QUICK FACTS

- Held NHL record for career points (610); surpassed by Maurice Richard, December 12, 1953

- Played amateur hockey with Regina Abbots (1935–36); Weyburn Beavers (1936–38); Moose Jaw Millers (1938–40)

- SSHL First All-Star Team Center (1940)

- Centered Montreal's famed Punch Line with Toe Blake and Maurice "Rocket" Richard

- Nicknamed "Elegant Elmer" and the "Nokomis Flash"

- Solid two-way player with offensive flair, excellent speed and superb puck-handling skills

- Led NHL in points in 1944–45 (80) and 1947–48 (61); led NHL in assists in 1944–45 (54); 1945–46 (34) and 1951–52 (50)

- Led NHL playoffs in assists (11) in 1943–44; led NHL playoffs in assists (12) and points (17) in 1945–46

- Inaugural recipient of Art Ross Trophy for leading NHL in points (1948)

- Played in NHL All-Star Game (1948, 1952, 1953)

- Scored Stanley Cup-winning overtime goal in Montreal's 1–0 victory over Boston Bruins, April 16, 1953

- Had his number retired along with Butch Bouchard's on December 4, 2009, to coincide with the Canadiens' 100th anniversary

- Coached Montreal Jr. Canadiens (1954–55); coached Montreal Royals (1955–57)

> I would say scoring the winning goal when we beat Boston in overtime to end the series in 1953. It doesn't get any better than that!"
>
> — Elmer Lach, on the greatest moment of his career

REGULAR SEASON

Season	Age	Team	Lg	GP	G	A	PTS	PIM
1940–41	23	Montreal Canadiens	NHL	43	7	14	21	16
1941–42	24	Montreal Canadiens	NHL	1	0	1	1	0
1942–43	25	Montreal Canadiens	NHL	45	18	40	58	14
1943–44	26	Montreal Canadiens	NHL	48	24	48	72	23
1944–45	27	Montreal Canadiens	NHL	50	26	54	80	37
1945–46	28	Montreal Canadiens	NHL	50	13	34	47	34
1946–47	29	Montreal Canadiens	NHL	31	14	16	30	22
1947–48	30	Montreal Canadiens	NHL	60	30	31	61	72
1948–49	31	Montreal Canadiens	NHL	36	11	18	29	59
1949–50	32	Montreal Canadiens	NHL	64	15	33	48	33
1950–51	33	Montreal Canadiens	NHL	65	21	24	45	48
1951–52	34	Montreal Canadiens	NHL	70	15	50	65	36
1952–53	35	Montreal Canadiens	NHL	53	16	25	41	56
1953–54	36	Montreal Canadiens	NHL	48	5	20	25	28
NHL Career – 14 Seasons				664	215	408	623	478

PLAYOFFS

Season	Age	Team	Lg	GP	G	A	PTS	PIM
1940–41	23	Montreal Canadiens	NHL	3	1	0	1	0
1942–43	25	Montreal Canadiens	NHL	5	2	4	6	6
1943–44	26	Montreal Canadiens	NHL	9	2	11	13	4
1944–45	27	Montreal Canadiens	NHL	6	4	4	8	2
1945–46	28	Montreal Canadiens	NHL	9	5	12	17	4
1948–49	31	Montreal Canadiens	NHL	1	0	0	0	4
1949–50	32	Montreal Canadiens	NHL	5	1	2	3	4
1950–51	33	Montreal Canadiens	NHL	11	2	2	4	2
1951–52	34	Montreal Canadiens	NHL	11	1	2	3	4
1952–53	35	Montreal Canadiens	NHL	12	1	6	7	6
1953–54	36	Montreal Canadiens	NHL	4	0	2	2	0
NHL Career – 11 Seasons				76	19	45	64	36

TROPHY CASE

AWARDS

Art Ross Trophy (1948)

Hart Memorial Trophy (1945)

Stanley Cup (1943–44, 1945–46, 1952–53)

ALL-STAR SELECTIONS

First All-Star Team Center (1945, 1948, 1952)

Second All-Star Team Center (1944, 1946)

Retired by Montreal

Right Wing

Shoots: Right

Height: 6'

Weight: 185 lbs.

Born: September 20, 1951: Thurso, Quebec

Drafted by the Montreal Canadiens first overall in 1971

Played 17 NHL seasons from 1971–85, 1988–91

Guy Lafleur

HOCKEY HALL OF FAME CLASS: 1988

QUICK FACTS

- First player in NHL history to score at least 50 goals and register at least 100 points in six consecutive seasons (1974–80)

- Holds Montreal Canadiens' team record for career assists (728) and points (1,246); holds Montreal Canadiens' team record for points in regular season (136), established in 1976–77; shares Montreal Canadiens' team record (with Steve Shutt) for goals in regular season (60), established in 1977–78

- Played amateur hockey with Quebec Aces (1966–69); Quebec Remparts (1969–71)

- Member of Memorial Cup-winning Quebec Remparts (1971); led Memorial Cup playoffs in goals (9) and points (14) in 1971

- Led QMJHL in assists (103) in 1969–70; led QMJHL playoffs in goals (25) and points (43) in 1969–70

- Led QMJHL in assists (130) and points (209) in 1970–71; led QMJHL playoffs in goals (22), assists (21) and points (43) in 1970–71

- QMJHL First All-Star Team Right Wing (1970, 1971)

- Led NHL in goals (60) in 1977–78; led NHL in assists (80) in 1976–77; led NHL in points in 1975–76 (125), 1976–77 (136) and 1977–78 (132); led NHL in plus/minus (+73) in 1977–78

- Led NHL in game-winning goals in 1974–75 (11), 1975–76 (12), 1977–78 (12) and 1978–79 (12)

- One of only three players (with Gordie Howe and Mario Lemieux) to play in the NHL after being inducted into the Hall of Fame

- Played in NHL All-Star Game (1975, 1976, 1977, 1978, 1980, 1991)

> Go ahead, work hard and never be afraid to try something. Even if you don't make it, at least you can say you tried."

REGULAR SEASON

Season	Age	Team	Lg	GP	G	A	PTS	+/	PIM	ESG	PPG	SHG	GWG	SOG	S%
1971–72	20	Montreal Canadiens	NHL	73	29	35	64	27	48	24	5	0	5	187	15.5
1972–73	21	Montreal Canadiens	NHL	69	28	27	55	16	51	19	9	0	7	176	15.9
1973–74	22	Montreal Canadiens	NHL	73	21	35	56	10	29	17	3	1	2	167	12.6
1974–75	23	Montreal Canadiens	NHL	70	53	66	119	52	37	36	15	2	11	260	20.4
1975–76	24	Montreal Canadiens	NHL	80	56	69	125	68	36	38	18	0	12	303	18.5
1976–77	25	Montreal Canadiens	NHL	80	56	80	136	89	20	42	14	0	8	291	19.2
1977–78	26	Montreal Canadiens	NHL	78	60	72	132	73	26	45	15	0	12	307	19.5
1978–79	27	Montreal Canadiens	NHL	80	52	77	129	56	28	39	13	0	12	342	15.2
1979–80	28	Montreal Canadiens	NHL	74	50	75	125	40	12	35	15	0	7	323	15.5
1980–81	29	Montreal Canadiens	NHL	51	27	43	70	24	29	20	7	0	7	191	14.1
1981–82	30	Montreal Canadiens	NHL	66	27	57	84	33	24	18	9	0	3	233	11.6
1982–83	31	Montreal Canadiens	NHL	68	27	49	76	6	12	18	9	0	1	177	15.3
1983–84	32	Montreal Canadiens	NHL	80	30	40	70	-14	19	24	6	0	6	217	13.8
1984–85	33	Montreal Canadiens	NHL	19	2	3	5	-3	10	2	0	0	0	35	5.7
1988–89	37	New York Rangers	NHL	67	18	27	45	1	12	12	6	0	2	122	14.8
1989–90	38	Quebec Nordiques	NHL	39	12	22	34	-15	4	6	6	0	2	100	12.0
1990–91	39	Quebec Nordiques	NHL	59	12	16	28	-10	2	9	3	0	0	90	13.3
NHL Career – 17 Seasons				1126	560	793	1353	453	399	404	153	3	97	3521	15.9

PLAYOFFS

Season	Age	Team	Lg	GP	G	A	PTS	+/-	PIM	ESG	PPG	SHG	GWG	SOG	S%
1971–72	20	Montreal Canadiens	NHL	6	1	4	5		2	1	0	0	0		
1972–73	21	Montreal Canadiens	NHL	17	3	5	8		9	1	2	0	1		
1973–74	22	Montreal Canadiens	NHL	6	0	1	1		4	0	0	0	0		
1974–75	23	Montreal Canadiens	NHL	11	12	7	19		15	8	4	0	4		
1975–76	24	Montreal Canadiens	NHL	13	7	10	17		2	7	0	0	3		
1976–77	25	Montreal Canadiens	NHL	14	9	17	26		6	8	1	0	2		
1977–78	26	Montreal Canadiens	NHL	15	10	11	21		16	7	3	0	2		
1978–79	27	Montreal Canadiens	NHL	16	10	13	23		0	8	2	0	2		
1979–80	28	Montreal Canadiens	NHL	3	3	1	4		0	3	0	0	0		
1980–81	29	Montreal Canadiens	NHL	3	0	1	1		2	0	0	0	0		
1981–82	30	Montreal Canadiens	NHL	5	2	1	3		4	0	2	0	0		
1982–83	31	Montreal Canadiens	NHL	3	0	2	2		2	0	0	0	0		
1983–84	32	Montreal Canadiens	NHL	12	0	3	3	1	5	0	0	0	0	16	0.0
1988–89	37	New York Rangers	NHL	4	1	0	1	-3	0	0	1	0	0	10	10.0
NHL Career – 14 Seasons				128	58	76	134	-2	67	43	15	0	14	26	3.8

TROPHY CASE

AWARDS

Art Ross Trophy (1976, 1977, 1978)

Conn Smythe Trophy (1977)

Hart Memorial Trophy (1977, 1978)

Lester B. Pearson Award (1976, 1977, 1978)

Stanley Cup (1972–73, 1975–76, 1976–77, 1977–78, 1978–79)

ALL-STAR SELECTIONS

First All-Star Team Right Wing (1975, 1976, 1977, 1978, 1979, 1980)

INTERNATIONAL AWARDS

Canada Cup (1976)

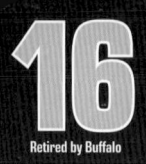

Pat LaFontaine

HOCKEY HALL OF FAME CLASS: 2003

16

Retired by Buffalo

Center

Shoots: Right

Height: 5'-10"

Weight: 182 lbs.

Born: February 22, 1965: St. Louis, Missouri

Drafted by the New York Islanders third overall in 1983

Played 15 NHL seasons from 1983–98

"That was a special feeling to win that Game 7 and be a part of some history as far as the National Hockey League. I look at that goal and it was really a stepping stone in my career."
— Pat LaFontaine, on his famous overtime goal

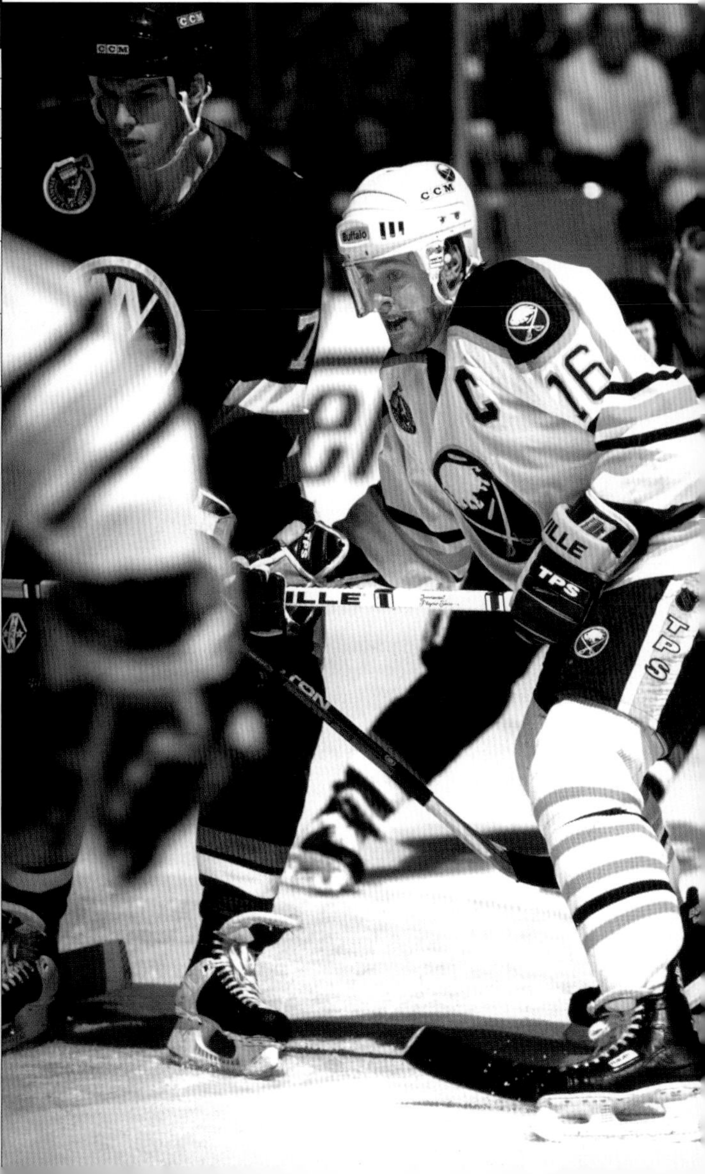

QUICK FACTS

- Holds NHL record for most points in regular season by a U.S.-born player (148), established 1992–93
- Holds NHL record for fastest two goals from start of a playoff period (35 seconds), established in N.Y. Islanders' 5–2 loss to Edmonton Oilers, May 19, 1984
- Holds Buffalo Sabres' record for points in regular season (148), established 1992–93
- Played amateur hockey with Detroit Compuware (1981–82); Verdun Juniors (1982–83); USA National Team (1983–84)
- Led QMJHL in goals (104), assists (130) and points (234) in 1982–83; led QMJHL playoffs in assists (24) and points (35) in 1982–83
- QMJHL First Team All-Star Center (1983)

- Named QMJHL MVP (1983); named QMJHL Playoff MVP (1983); named Canadian Junior Player of the Year (1983)
- Played in NHL All-Star Game (1988, 1989, 1990, 1991, 1993)
- Scored "Easter Epic" goal in fourth overtime period of N.Y. Islanders' 3–2 victory over Washington Capitals in Game Seven of 1987 Patrick Division Semifinals
- Registered 1,000th career NHL point in N.Y. Rangers' 4–3 loss to Philadelphia Flyers, January 22, 1998
- Suffered career-ending head injury in game vs. Ottawa, March 16, 1998
- Officially announced retirement, October 12, 1999

LaFontaine recorded his 1,000th point wearing these gloves in his last NHL season, 1997–98.

REGULAR SEASON

Season	Age	Team	Lg	GP	G	A	PTS	+/-	PIM	ESG	PPG	SHG	GWG	SOG	S%
1983–84	18	New York Islanders	NHL	15	13	6	19	9	6	12	1	0	0	35	37.1
1984–85	19	New York Islanders	NHL	67	19	35	54	9	32	18	1	0	1	173	11.0
1985–86	20	New York Islanders	NHL	65	30	23	53	16	43	28	2	0	4	172	17.4
1986–87	21	New York Islanders	NHL	80	38	32	70	-10	70	18	19	1	6	219	17.4
1987–88	22	New York Islanders	NHL	75	47	45	92	12	52	32	15	0	7	242	19.4
1988–89	23	New York Islanders	NHL	79	45	43	88	-8	26	29	16	0	4	288	15.6
1989–90	24	New York Islanders	NHL	74	54	51	105	-13	38	39	13	2	8	286	18.9
1990–91	25	New York Islanders	NHL	75	41	44	85	-6	42	27	12	2	5	225	18.2
1991–92	26	Buffalo Sabres	NHL	57	46	47	93	10	98	23	23	0	5	203	22.7
1992–93	27	Buffalo Sabres	NHL	84	53	95	148	11	63	31	20	2	7	306	17.3
1993–94	28	Buffalo Sabres	NHL	16	5	13	18	-4	2	4	1	0	0	40	12.5
1994–95	29	Buffalo Sabres	NHL	22	12	15	27	2	4	5	6	1	3	54	22.2
1995–96	30	Buffalo Sabres	NHL	76	40	51	91	-8	36	22	15	3	7	224	17.9
1996–97	31	Buffalo Sabres	NHL	13	2	6	8	-8	4	1	1	0	0	38	5.3
1997–98	32	New York Rangers	NHL	67	23	39	62	-16	36	12	11	0	2	160	14.4
NHL Career – 15 Seasons				865	468	545	1013	-4	552	301	156	11	59	2665	17.6

PLAYOFFS

Season	Age	Team	Lg	GP	G	A	PTS	+/-	PIM	ESG	PPG	SHG	GWG	SOG	S%
1983–84	18	New York Islanders	NHL	16	3	6	9	-2	8	3	0	0	0	21	14.3
1984–85	19	New York Islanders	NHL	9	1	2	3	-3	4	1	0	0	0	7	14.3
1985–86	20	New York Islanders	NHL	3	1	0	1	-2	0	0	1	0	0	7	14.3
1986–87	21	New York Islanders	NHL	14	5	7	12	-6	10	4	1	0	2	39	12.8
1987–88	22	New York Islanders	NHL	6	4	5	9	2	8	3	1	0	1	16	25.0
1989–90	24	New York Islanders	NHL	2	0	1	1	-1	0	0	0	0	0	5	0.0
1991–92	26	Buffalo Sabres	NHL	7	8	3	11	0	4	2	5	1	1	27	29.6
1992–93	27	Buffalo Sabres	NHL	7	2	10	12	0	0	1	1	0	0	13	15.4
1994–95	29	Buffalo Sabres	NHL	5	2	2	4	-2	2	1	1	0	0	11	18.2
NHL Career – 9 Seasons				69	26	36	62	-14	36	15	10	1	4	146	17.8

TROPHY CASE

AWARDS

Bill Masterton Memorial Trophy (1995)

ALL-STAR SELECTIONS

Second All-Star Team Center (1993)

INTERNATIONAL AWARDS

World Cup (1996)

4

Newsy Lalonde

HOCKEY HALL OF FAME CLASS: 1950

Alternate: 11

Center

Shoots: Right

Height: 5'-9"

Weight: 168 lbs.
Born: October 31,
1888: Cornwall,
Ontario

Died: November
21, 1971: Montreal,
Quebec

Played 21
professional
seasons from
1906–27

QUICK FACTS

- Shares NHL record for most goals in a single playoff game (5), established in Montreal's 6–3 victory over Ottawa Senators, March 1, 1919

- Scored first goal in Montreal Canadiens franchise history in 7–6 victory over Cobalt Creamery Kings, January 5, 1910

- Scored 11 goals in five games against Ottawa in the 1919 NHL final series, the second-highest total of goals in a single series in NHL history

- Earned nickname "Newsy" working in a local newsprint plant as a youth

- Played amateur hockey with Cornwall Victorias (1903–05); Cornwall HC (1904–05); Woodstock HC (1905–06)

- Led Ontario Professional League in goals (32) in 1907–08; led NHA in goals (38) in 1909–10

- Signed as a free agent by Vancouver Millionaires (PCHA), November 28, 1911; led PCHA in goals (27) in 1911–12

- Led NHA in goals (28) in 1915–16; led NHL in goals (23), assists (10) and points (33) in 1918–19; led NHL in points (43) in 1920–21

- Traded to Saskatoon (WCHL) by Montreal Canadiens for rights to Aurele Joliat and $3,500, September 18, 1922

- Led WCHL in goals (30) in 1922–23

- Coached Montreal Canadiens (1917–21, 1932–35); coached N.Y. Americans (1926–27); coached Ottawa Senators (1929–31)

> As I got more experience, I got less and less nervous and really began to enjoy professional hockey. The money was good and I was able to make extra cash playing professional lacrosse. I played in Vancouver and got $6,000 for 12 games.

REGULAR SEASON

Season	Age	Team	Lg	GP	G	A	PTS	PIM
1906–07	18	Canadian Soo	IHL	18	29	4	33	27
1907–08	19	Portage-la-Prarie	MHL-Pro	1	0	0	0	0
1907–08	19	Toronto Professionals	OPHL	9	32	0	32	37
1908–09	20	Toronto Professionals	OPHL	11	29	0	29	79
1909–10	21	Les Canadiens (Montreal)	NHA	1	2	0	2	3
1909–10	21	Les Canadiens (Montreal)	NHA	6	16	0	16	40
1909–10	21	Renfrew Hockey Club	NHA	5	22	0	22	16
1910–11	22	Montreal Canadiens	NHA	16	19	0	19	54
1911–12	23	Vancouver Millionaires	PCHA	15	27	0	27	60
1912–13	24	Montreal Canadiens	NHA	13	9	5	14	52
1913–14	25	Montreal Canadiens	NHA	14	22	5	27	34
1914–15	26	Montreal Canadiens	NHA	7	4	3	7	17
1915–16	27	Montreal Canadiens	NHA	24	28	6	34	78
1916–17	28	Montreal Canadiens	NHA	18	28	7	35	61
1917–18	29	Montreal Canadiens	NHL	14	23	7	30	51
1918–19	30	Montreal Canadiens	NHL	17	23	10	33	40
1919–20	31	Montreal Canadiens	NHL	23	37	9	46	34
1920–21	32	Montreal Canadiens	NHL	24	33	10	43	36
1921–22	33	Montreal Canadiens	NHL	20	9	5	14	20
1922–23	34	Saskatoon Sheiks	WCHL	29	30	4	34	44
1923–24	35	Saskatoon Crescents	WCHL	21	10	10	20	24
1924–25	36	Saskatoon Crescents	WCHL	22	8	6	14	42
1925–26	37	Saskatoon Crescents	WHL	3	0	0	0	2
1926–27	38	New York Americans	NHL	1	0	0	0	2
Career – 21 Seasons				332	440	91	531	853

PLAYOFFS

Season	Age	Team	Lg	GP	G	A	PTS	PIM
1907–08	19	Toronto Professionals	St-Cup	1	2	0	2	0
1907–08	19	Haileybury Hockey Club	TPHL	1	3	0	3	0
1913–14	25	Montreal Canadiens	NHA	1	0	0	0	2
1915–16	27	Montreal Canadiens	St-Cup	4	3	0	3	41
1916–17	28	Montreal Canadiens	NHA	1	1	0	1	23
1916–17	28	Montreal Canadiens	St-Cup	4	1	0	1	24
1917–18	29	Montreal Canadiens	NHL	2	4	2	6	17
1918–19	30	Montreal Canadiens	NHL	5	11	2	13	15
1918–19	31	Montreal Canadiens	St-Cup	5	6	0	6	3
1924–25	36	Saskatoon Crescents	WCHL	2	0	0	0	4
1925–26	37	Saskatoon Crescents	WHL	2	0	0	0	2
Career – 8 Seasons				28	31	4	35	131

TROPHY CASE

AWARDS

NHL Scoring Leader (1919, 1921)

Stanley Cup (1915–16)

ALL-STAR SELECTIONS

OPHL First All-Star Team Center (1908)

PCHA First All-Star Team Center (1912)

NHA First All-Star Team Center (1914)

WCHL First All-Star Team Center (1924)

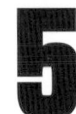

5

Retired by Washington

Alternate: 17

Defense

Shoots: Left

Height: 6'-3"

Weight: 218 lbs.

Born: May 3, 1957: Maag, Taiwan

Drafted by the Montreal Canadiens 36th overall in 1977

Played 16 WHA and NHL seasons from 1977–93

Rod Langway

HOCKEY HALL OF FAME CLASS: 2002

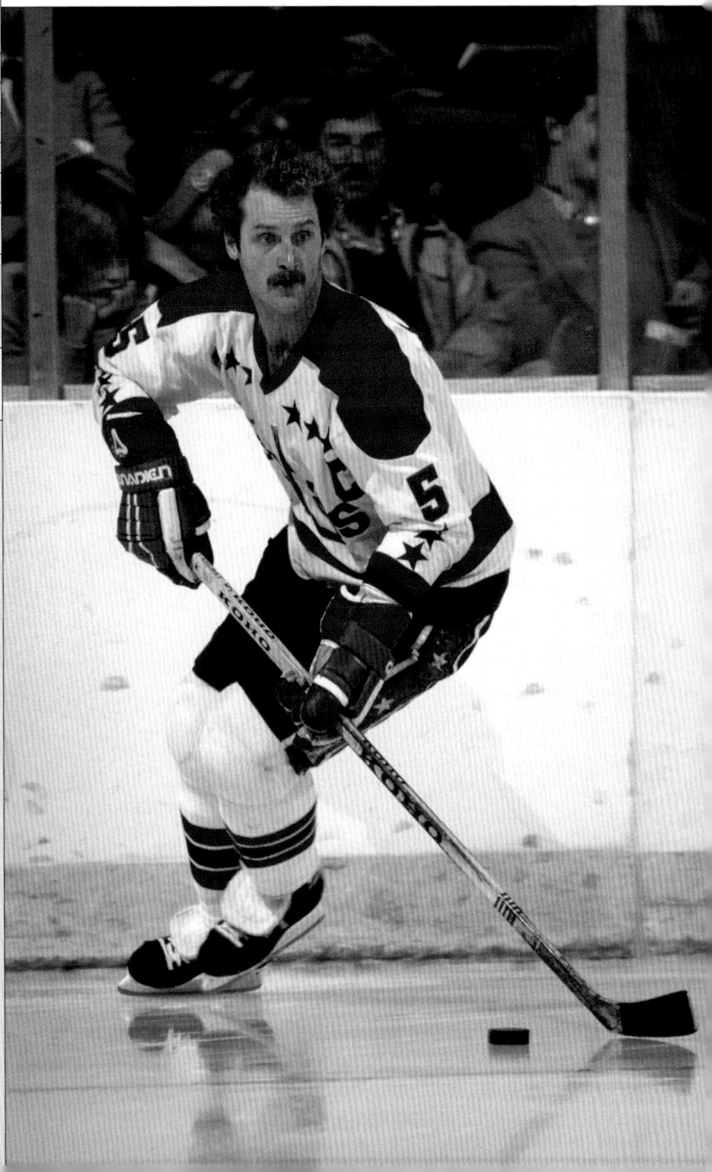

QUICK FACTS

- Played amateur hockey with Randolph Rockets (1972–75); University of New Hampshire (1975–77)
- Played football, baseball and hockey at Randolph High School (1972–75)
- Played minor pro hockey with Hampton Gulls (1977–78)
- Played linebacker in football and defense in hockey at University of New Hampshire (1975–77)
- Nicknamed "The Secretary of Defense" during his career in Washington
- Traded to Washington by Montreal with Doug Jarvis, Craig Laughlin and Brian Engblom for Ryan Walter and Rick Green, September 9, 1982
- Played in NHL All-Star Game (1981, 1982, 1983, 1984, 1985, 1986)
- Played with Team U.S.A. in 1981, 1984 and 1987 Canada Cup Tournament
- Named to the Canada Cup First All-Star Team Defense (1984)
- Only player in NHL history to be born in Taiwan
- Served as assistant coach with Richmond Renegades (1993–94, 1996–97, 2000–01)
- Served as assistant coach with Providence Bruins (1997–98)
- Served as player/coach with Richmond Renegades (1994–95); San Francisco Spiders (1995–96)
- Coached Richmond Renegades (2003–04)
- Number retired by Washington, November 26, 1997

> It was a case that it was simply my time. If I had stayed in Montreal, I would have been the same kind of player, but I wouldn't have received the accolades of winning the Norris Trophy because I would have been put into different situations.
> — Rod Langway, on being traded to Washington

REGULAR SEASON

Season	Age	Team	Lg	GP	G	A	PTS	+/-	PIM	ESG	PPG	SHG	GWG	SOG	S%
1977–78	20	Birmingham Bulls	WHA	52	3	18	21	10	52	0	0	0		75	4.0
1978–79	21	Montreal Canadiens	NHL	45	3	4	7	5	30	3	0	0	0	48	6.3
1979–80	22	Montreal Canadiens	NHL	77	7	29	36	36	81	7	0	0	1	112	6.3
1980–81	23	Montreal Canadiens	NHL	80	11	34	45	53	120	5	5	1	2	165	6.7
1981–82	24	Montreal Canadiens	NHL	66	5	34	39	66	116	4	1	0	1	139	3.6
1982–83	25	Washington Capitals	NHL	80	3	29	32	0	75	2	1	0	0	126	2.4
1983–84	26	Washington Capitals	NHL	80	9	24	33	14	61	6	1	2	2	168	5.4
1984–95	27	Washington Capitals	NHL	79	4	22	26	35	54	4	0	0	1	102	3.9
1985–86	28	Washington Capitals	NHL	71	1	17	18	27	61	0	1	0	0	54	1.9
1986–87	29	Washington Capitals	NHL	78	2	25	27	11	53	2	0	0	1	76	2.6
1987–88	30	Washington Capitals	NHL	63	3	13	16	1	28	3	0	0	1	49	6.1
1988–89	31	Washington Capitals	NHL	76	2	19	21	12	65	2	0	0	0	80	2.5
1989–90	32	Washington Capitals	NHL	58	0	8	8	7	39	0	0	0	0	46	0.0
1990–91	33	Washington Capitals	NHL	56	1	7	8	12	24	1	0	0	0	32	3.1
1991–92	34	Washington Capitals	NHL	64	0	13	13	11	22	0	0	0	0	32	0.0
1992–93	35	Washington Capitals	NHL	21	0	0	0	-13	20	0	0	0	0	6	0.0
Career — 16 Seasons				1046	54	296	350	287	901	42	9	3	9	1310	4.1

PLAYOFFS

Season	Age	Team	Lg	GP	G	A	PTS	+/-	PIM	ESG	PPG	SHG	GWG	SOG	S%
1977–78	20	Birmingham Bulls	WHA	4	0	0	0	-2	9				0		
1978–79	21	Montreal Canadiens	NHL	8	0	0	0		16	0	0	0	0		
1979–80	22	Montreal Canadiens	NHL	10	3	3	6		2	2	1	0	0		
1980–81	23	Montreal Canadiens	NHL	3	0	0	0		6	0	0	0	0		
1981–82	24	Montreal Canadiens	NHL	5	0	3	3		18	0	0	0	0		
1982–83	25	Washington Capitals	NHL	4	0	0	0		0	0	0	0	0		
1983–84	26	Washington Capitals	NHL	8	0	5	5	0	7	0	0	0	0	16	0.0
1984–85	27	Washington Capitals	NHL	5	0	1	1	-1	6	0	0	0	0	12	0.0
1985–86	28	Washington Capitals	NHL	9	1	2	3	4	6	0	1	0	0	17	5.9
1986–87	29	Washington Capitals	NHL	7	0	1	1	0	2	0	0	0	0	15	0.0
1987–88	30	Washington Capitals	NHL	6	0	0	0	2	8	0	0	0	0	7	0.0
1988–89	31	Washington Capitals	NHL	6	0	0	0	-4	6	0	0	0	0	10	0.0
1989–90	32	Washington Capitals	NHL	15	1	4	5	0	12	1	0	0	1	17	5.9
1990–91	33	Washington Capitals	NHL	11	0	2	2	1	6	0	0	0	0	12	0.0
1991–92	34	Washington Capitals	NHL	7	0	1	1	0	2	0	0	0	0	2	0.0
Career — 15 Seasons				108	5	22	27	0	106	3	2	0	1	108	1.9

TROPHY CASE

AWARDS

James Norris Memorial Trophy (1983, 1984)

Stanley Cup (1978–79)

ALL-STAR SELECTIONS

First All-Star Team Defense (1983, 1984)

Second All-Star Team Defense (1985)

2

Jacques Laperriere
HOCKEY HALL OF FAME CLASS: 1987

Alternates: 26

Defense

Shoots: Left

Height: 6'-2"

Weight: 190 lbs.

Born: November 22, 1941: Rouyn, Quebec

Played 12 NHL seasons from 1962–74

"You cover the area you're responsible for. You don't get caught out of position. You gain control of the puck. You pass it to somebody or else you carry it over the blueline and then pass it to somebody else."
— Jacques Laperierre, on defense

QUICK FACTS

- Played amateur hockey with St. Laurent Jets (1957–58); Hull-Ottawa Jr. Canadiens (1958–62); Brockville Canadiens (1959–60)

- Played minor pro hockey with Hull-Ottawa Canadiens (1959–63)

- EPHL Second All-Star Team Defense (1963)

- Played on six Stanley Cup-winning teams in 12 seasons as a player and won two more Stanley Cup championships (1986, 1993) in 16 seasons as an assistant coach with Montreal Canadiens

- Played in NHL All-Star Game (1964, 1965, 1967, 1968, 1970)

- Named to the NHL Second All-Star Team as a rookie

- A tall and mobile defenseman that broke up plays with his long reach, he possessed an excellent low, hard drive from the point

- Only player other than Bobby Orr to lead the NHL in plus/minus between 1969–75

- Led NHL in plus/minus (+78) in 1972–73

- Suffered career-ending knee injury in game vs. Boston, January 19, 1974

- Father of Dan Laperriere, who played in the NHL with St. Louis and Ottawa from 1993–96

- Coached Montreal Red, White and Blue (1975–76); coached Montreal Juniors (1976–77)

- Served as assistant coach with Montreal Canadiens (1981–97); Boston Bruins (1997–2000); N.Y. Islanders (2001–03); New Jersey Devils (2003–08)

The familiar No. 2 of Laperriere roamed the blueline in Montreal in 1963–64; before No. 2 he wore No. 26.

REGULAR SEASON

Season	Age	Team	Lg	GP	G	A	PTS	+/-	PIM	ESG	PPG	SHG	GWG	SOG	S%
1962-63	21	Montreal Canadiens	NHL	6	0	2	2		2						
1963-64	22	Montreal Canadiens	NHL	65	2	28	30		102	0	1	1	1		
1964-65	23	Montreal Canadiens	NHL	67	5	22	27		92	5	0	0	0		
1965-66	24	Montreal Canadiens	NHL	57	6	25	31		85	3	2	1	2		
1966-67	25	Montreal Canadiens	NHL	61	0	20	20		48	0	0	0	0		
1967-68	26	Montreal Canadiens	NHL	72	4	21	25	23	84	3	1	0	0	122	3.3
1968-69	27	Montreal Canadiens	NHL	69	5	26	31	49	45	5	0	0	0	166	3.0
1969-70	28	Montreal Canadiens	NHL	73	6	31	37	28	98	3	2	1	1	169	3.6
1970-71	29	Montreal Canadiens	NHL	49	0	16	16	24	20	0	0	0	0	65	0.0
1971-72	30	Montreal Canadiens	NHL	73	3	25	28	36	50	1	2	0	0	97	3.1
1972-73	31	Montreal Canadiens	NHL	57	7	16	23	78	34	5	2	0	0	88	8.0
1973-74	32	Montreal Canadiens	NHL	42	2	10	12	15	14	1	0	1	0	60	3.3
NHL Career – 12 Seasons				691	40	242	282	241	674	26	10	4	5	767	3.5

PLAYOFFS

Season	Age	Team	Lg	GP	G	A	PTS	+/-	PIM	ESG	PPG	SHG	GWG	SOG	S%
1962-63	21	Montreal Canadiens	NHL	5	0	1	1		4						
1963-64	22	Montreal Canadiens	NHL	7	1	1	2		8						
1964-65	23	Montreal Canadiens	NHL	6	1	1	2		16						
1966-67	25	Montreal Canadiens	NHL	9	0	1	1		9						
1967-68	26	Montreal Canadiens	NHL	13	1	3	4		20	1	0	0	0		
1968-69	27	Montreal Canadiens	NHL	14	1	3	4		28	0	1	0	0		
1970-71	29	Montreal Canadiens	NHL	20	4	9	13		12	3	1	0	1		
1971-72	30	Montreal Canadiens	NHL	4	0	0	0		2	0	0	0	0		
1972-73	31	Montreal Canadiens	NHL	10	1	3	4		2	1	0	0	0		
NHL Career – 9 Seasons				88	9	22	31		101	5	2	0	1		

TROPHY CASE

AWARDS

Calder Memorial Trophy (1964)

James Norris Memorial Trophy (1966)

Stanley Cup (1964–65, 1965–66, 1967–68, 1968–69, 1970–71, 1972–73)

ALL-STAR SELECTIONS

First All-Star Team Defense (1965, 1966)

Second All-Star Team Defense (1964, 1970)

Guy Lapointe

HOCKEY HALL OF FAME CLASS: 1993

Alternates:
17, 4, 27

Defense

Shoots: Left

Height: 6'

Weight: 205 lbs.

Born: March 18,
1948: Montreal,
Quebec

Played 16 NHL
seasons from
1968–84

QUICK FACTS

- Shares Montreal Canadiens team record (with Larry Robinson) for all-time playoff goals by a defenseman (25)

- Holds Montreal Canadiens team record for goals by a defenseman in regular season (28), established in 1974–75

- Holds Montreal Canadiens team record for goals by a rookie defenseman (15), established in 1970–71

- Played amateur hockey with Verdun Maple Leafs (1965–67); Montreal Jr. Canadiens (1967–68)

- Played in All-Star Game (1973, 1975, 1976, 1977)

- Became only fifth NHL defenseman to score 20 or more goals in regular season (1974–75)

- Member of Team NHL that played Soviet Union in 1979 Challenge Cup

- Member of Montreal's Big Three on defense with Serge Savard and Larry Robinson

- Scored 59 power-play goals and 22 game-winning goals in 16-season career

- Runner-up up to Bobby Orr in voting for the 1972–73 Norris Trophy

- Traded to St. Louis by Montreal for St. Louis' second round choice (Sergio Momesso) in 1983 Entry Draft, March 9, 1982

- Signed as a free agent by Boston, August 15, 1983

- Was awarded Dit Clapper's retired jersey #5 when he joined Boston, but switched after Clapper family protested

- Coached Longueuil Chevaliers (1985–86)

> I was a kid who grew up in Montreal about a half hour away from the Forum. You don't even think that one day you're going to play for the Montreal Canadiens."

REGULAR SEASON

Season	Age	Team	Lg	GP	G	A	PTS	+/-	PIM	ESG	PPG	SHG	GWG	SOG	S%
1968–69	20	Montreal Canadiens	NHL	1	0	0	0	0	2	0	0	0	0	0	
1969–70	21	Montreal Canadiens	NHL	5	0	0	0	0	4	0	0	0	0	0	
1970–71	22	Montreal Canadiens	NHL	78	15	29	44	28	107	10	5	0	1	228	6.6
1971–72	23	Montreal Canadiens	NHL	69	11	38	49	15	58	7	4	0	4	227	4.8
1972–73	24	Montreal Canadiens	NHL	76	19	35	54	51	117	16	3	0	2	196	9.7
1973–74	25	Montreal Canadiens	NHL	71	13	40	53	12	63	7	5	1	2	205	6.3
1974–75	26	Montreal Canadiens	NHL	80	28	47	75	46	88	16	11	1	1	219	12.8
1975–76	27	Montreal Canadiens	NHL	77	21	47	68	64	78	12	8	1	1	317	6.6
1976–77	28	Montreal Canadiens	NHL	77	25	51	76	69	53	15	10	0	6	289	8.7
1977–78	29	Montreal Canadiens	NHL	49	13	29	42	46	19	9	4	0	2	148	8.8
1978–79	30	Montreal Canadiens	NHL	69	13	42	55	27	43	7	6	0	1	209	6.2
1979–80	31	Montreal Canadiens	NHL	45	6	20	26	-2	29	6	0	0	0	124	4.8
1980–81	32	Montreal Canadiens	NHL	33	1	9	10	-6	79	0	1	0	1	47	2.1
1981–82	33	Montreal Canadiens	NHL	47	1	19	20	-3	72	1	0	0	0	97	1.0
1981–82	33	St. Louis Blues	NHL	8	0	6	6	-3	4	0	0	0	0	15	0.0
1982–83	34	St. Louis Blues	NHL	54	3	23	26	-12	43	1	1	0	1	106	2.8
1983–84	35	Boston Bruins	NHL	45	2	16	18	-3	34	1	1	0	1	57	3.5
NHL Career — 16 Seasons				884	171	451	622	329	893	108	59	4	22	2484	6.9

PLAYOFFS

Season	Age	Team	Lg	GP	G	A	PTS	+/-	PIM	ESG	PPG	SHG	GWG	SOG	S%
1970–71	22	Montreal Canadiens	NHL	20	4	5	9		34	3	1	0	2		
1971–72	23	Montreal Canadiens	NHL	6	0	1	1		0	0	0	0	0		
1972–73	24	Montreal Canadiens	NHL	17	6	7	13		20	4	2	0	1		
1973–74	25	Montreal Canadiens	NHL	6	0	2	2		4	0	0	0	0		
1974–75	26	Montreal Canadiens	NHL	11	6	4	10		4	2	3	1	0		
1975–76	27	Montreal Canadiens	NHL	13	3	3	6		12	2	1	0	1		
1976–77	28	Montreal Canadiens	NHL	12	3	9	12		4	2	1	0	0		
1977–78	29	Montreal Canadiens	NHL	14	1	6	7		16	0	1	0	0		
1978–79	30	Montreal Canadiens	NHL	10	2	6	8		10	1	1	0	0		
1979–80	31	Montreal Canadiens	NHL	2	0	0	0		0	0	0	0	0		
1980–81	32	Montreal Canadiens	NHL	1	0	0	0		17	0	0	0	0		
1981–82	33	St. Louis Blues	NHL	7	1	0	1		8	0	1	0	1		
1982–83	34	St. Louis Blues	NHL	4	0	1	1		9	0	0	0	0		
NHL Career — 13 Seasons				123	26	44	70		138	14	11	1	5		

TROPHY CASE

AWARDS

Stanley Cup (1970–71, 1972–73, 1975–76, 1976–77, 1977–78, 1978–79)

ALL-STAR SELECTIONS

First All-Star Team Defense (1973)

Second All-Star Team Defense (1975, 1976, 1977)

INTERNATIONAL AWARDS

Summit Series (1972)

Canada Cup (1976)

Edgar Laprade

HOCKEY HALL OF FAME CLASS: 1993

Center

Shoots: Right

Height: 5'-8"

Weight: 160 lbs.

Born: October 10, 1919: Port Arthur, Ontario

Played 10 NHL seasons from 1945–55

" I was taught early on that you can't score from the penalty box."

QUICK FACTS

- Nicknamed "Beaver" because of his work ethic and defensive abilities
- Played amateur hockey with Port Arthur Juniors (1935–37); Port Arthur Bearcats (1938–43)
- Member of the Allan Cup-winning Port Arthur Bearcats (1939); led Allan Cup playoffs in goals (22) and points (26)
- Led TBJHL in goals (19) and points (33) in 1936–37; goals (23) and points (34) in 1937–38
- Led TBSHL in goals (31) and points (40) in 1938–39; led TBSHL in goals (20); led TBSHL in goals (26), assists (21) and points (47) in 1940–41; led TBSHL in assists (23) and points (41) in 1941–42
- Played with Barriefield Bears during World War II (1944–45)

- Delayed starting his NHL career to serve in the Canadian Armed Forces during World War II
- Signed with N.Y. Rangers instead of Montreal Canadiens because they gave him a $5,000 bonus to pay for the mortgage on his house
- Third player (with Gus Bodnar and Gaye Stewart) in four years from the Port Arthur/Fort William area to win the Calder Trophy
- Distinguished himself as a solid two-way player who was adept at poke checking
- Played in NHL All-Star Game (1947, 1948, 1949, 1950)
- Recorded two or fewer penalty minutes in six of his 10 NHL seasons

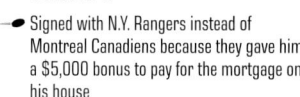

Socks Laprade wore as an All Star.

REGULAR SEASON

Season	Age	Team	Lg	GP	G	A	PTS	PIM
1945–46	26	New York Rangers	NHL	49	15	19	34	0
1946–47	27	New York Rangers	NHL	58	15	25	40	9
1947–48	28	New York Rangers	NHL	59	13	34	47	7
1948–49	29	New York Rangers	NHL	56	18	12	30	12
1949–50	30	New York Rangers	NHL	60	22	22	44	2
1950–51	31	New York Rangers	NHL	42	10	13	23	0
1951–52	32	New York Rangers	NHL	70	9	29	38	8
1952–53	33	New York Rangers	NHL	11	2	1	3	2
1953–54	34	New York Rangers	NHL	35	1	6	7	2
1954–55	35	New York Rangers	NHL	60	3	11	14	0
NHL Career — 10 Seasons				500	108	172	280	42

PLAYOFFS

Season	Age	Team	Lg	GP	G	A	PTS	PIM
1947–48	28	New York Rangers	NHL	6	1	4	5	0
1949–50	30	New York Rangers	NHL	12	3	5	8	4
NHL Career — 2 Seasons				18	4	9	13	4

TROPHY CASE

AWARDS

Calder Memorial Trophy (1946)

Lady Byng Memorial Trophy (1950)

8

Igor Larionov
HOCKEY HALL OF FAME CLASS: 2008

Alternates: 18, 7

Center

Shoots: Left

Height: 5'-9"

Weight: 170 lbs.

Born: December 3, 1960: Voskresensk, Union of Soviet Socialist Republics

Drafted by the Vancouver Canucks 214th overall in 1985

Played 14 NHL seasons from 1989–92, 1993–2004

QUICK FACTS

- Played amateur hockey with Khimik Voskresensk (1977–81); CSKA Moscow (1981–89)
- USSR First All-Star Team Center (1983, 1986, 1987, 1988)
- Named USSR Player of the Year (1988)
- Member of the Soviet Union's famed K-L-M Line with Vladimir Krutov and Sergei Makarov
- Played European pro hockey with HC Luogno (1992–93); Sierre Tigers (2004–05); Brunflo IK (2005–06)
- Nicknamed "The Professor" became of his scholarly approach to the game
- Played in NHL All-Star Game (1988)
- Became oldest player (41 years, seven months) in NHL history to score a game-winning goal in the Stanley Cup Finals in Detroit's 3–2 overtime victory over Carolina Hurricanes, June 8, 2002
- Claimed by San Jose from Vancouver in Waiver Draft, October 4, 1992
- Traded to Detroit by San Jose for Ray Sheppard, October 24, 1995; signed as a free agent by Florida, July 1, 2000
- Traded to Detroit by Florida for Yan Golubovsky, December 28, 2000; signed as a free agent by New Jersey, September 10, 2003
- Officially announced retirement, April 20, 2004
- Known as the "Russian Wayne Gretzky" in the Soviet Union

> I was quoted in the media and expressing myself quite openly that the day would come where I would play in the NHL, but I wasn't sure when. It took us a while to get the doors open for many of us to come to the National Hockey League."
>
> — Igor Larionov, on the struggle to gain his release to play in the NHL

REGULAR SEASON

Season	Age	Team	Lg	GP	G	A	PTS	+/-	PIM	ESG	PPG	SHG	GWG	SOG	S%
1989-90	29	Vancouver Canucks	NHL	74	17	27	44	-5	20	9	8	0	2	118	14.4
1990-91	30	Vancouver Canucks	NHL	64	13	21	34	-3	14	11	1	1	0	66	19.7
1991-92	31	Vancouver Canucks	NHL	72	21	44	65	7	54	8	10	3	4	97	21.6
1993-94	33	San Jose Sharks	NHL	60	18	38	56	20	40	13	3	2	2	72	25.0
1994-95	34	San Jose Sharks	NHL	33	4	20	24	-3	14	4	0	0	1	69	5.8
1995-96	35	San Jose Sharks	NHL	4	1	1	2	-6	0	0	1	0	0	5	20.0
1995-96	35	Detroit Red Wings	NHL	69	21	50	71	37	34	11	9	1	5	108	19.4
1996-97	36	Detroit Red Wings	NHL	64	12	42	54	31	26	9	2	1	4	95	12.6
1997-98	37	Detroit Red Wings	NHL	69	8	39	47	14	40	5	3	0	2	93	8.6
1998-99	38	Detroit Red Wings	NHL	75	14	49	63	13	48	8	4	2	2	83	16.9
1999-00	39	Detroit Red Wings	NHL	79	9	38	47	13	28	6	3	0	4	69	13.0
2000-01	40	Florida Panthers	NHL	26	5	6	11	-11	10	3	2	0	0	15	33.3
2000-01	40	Detroit Red Wings	NHL	39	4	25	29	6	28	2	2	0	1	31	12.9
2001-02	41	Detroit Red Wings	NHL	70	11	32	43	-5	50	7	4	0	1	50	22.0
2002-03	42	Detroit Red Wings	NHL	74	10	33	43	-7	48	5	5	0	3	50	20.0
2003-04	43	New Jersey Devils	NHL	49	1	10	11	3	20	1	0	0	0	25	4.0
NHL Career – 14 Seasons				921	169	475	644	104	474	102	57	10	31	1046	16.2

PLAYOFFS

Season	Age	Team	Lg	GP	G	A	PTS	+/-	PIM	ESG	PPG	SHG	GWG	SOG	S%
1990-91	30	Vancouver Canucks	NHL	6	1	0	1	-5	6	1	0	0	0	8	12.5
1991-92	31	Vancouver Canucks	NHL	13	3	7	10	1	4	2	1	0	0	12	25.0
1993-94	33	San Jose Sharks	NHL	14	5	13	18	-1	10	5	0	0	0	27	18.5
1994-95	34	San Jose Sharks	NHL	11	1	8	9	-4	2	1	0	0	0	19	5.3
1995-96	35	Detroit Red Wings	NHL	19	6	7	13	5	6	3	3	0	2	46	13.0
1996-97	36	Detroit Red Wings	NHL	20	4	8	12	8	8	1	3	0	1	29	13.8
1997-98	37	Detroit Red Wings	NHL	22	3	10	13	5	12	3	0	0	0	27	11.1
1998-99	38	Detroit Red Wings	NHL	7	0	2	2	-1	0	0	0	0	0	3	0.0
1999-00	39	Detroit Red Wings	NHL	9	1	2	3	-2	6	0	1	0	0	5	20.0
2000-01	40	Detroit Red Wings	NHL	6	1	3	4	-2	2	0	1	0	0	7	14.3
2001-02	41	Detroit Red Wings	NHL	18	5	6	11	5	4	5	0	0	1	24	20.8
2002-03	42	Detroit Red Wings	NHL	4	0	1	1	1	0	0	0	0	0	6	0.0
2003-04	43	New Jersey Devils	NHL	1	0	0	0	-1	0	0	0	0	0	0	0.0
NHL Career – 13 Seasons				150	30	67	97	9	60	21	9	0	4	213	14.1

TROPHY CASE

AWARDS

Stanley Cup (1996–97, 1997–98, 2001–02)

INTERNATIONAL AWARDS

Canada Cup (1981)

Gold Medal: Winter Olympics (1994, 1998)

Bronze Medal: Winter Olympics (2002)

Gold Medal: World Championships (1982, 1983, 1986, 1990)

Silver Medal: World Championships (1987)

Bronze Medal: World Championships (1985)

Jack Laviolette

HOCKEY HALL OF FAME CLASS: 1962

Alternates: 6, 7, 2

Defense/Forward

Shoots: Right

Height: 5'-11"

Weight: 170 lbs.

Born: July 27, 1879: Belleville, Ontario

Died: January 9, 1960: Montreal, Quebec

Played 14 professional seasons from 1904–18

QUICK FACTS

- Starred in both hockey and lacrosse and also was renowned as an automobile racer

- Played amateur hockey with Montreal Bell Telephone (1902–03); Montreal Nationals (1903–04)

- Signed as a free agent by Michigan Soo, November, 1904

- Signed as a free agent by Montreal Shamrocks, December 15, 1907

- Helped form, organize and manage the Montreal Canadiens in their inaugural season (1909–10)

- Replaced goaltender Pat Larochelle in net for the final five minutes of overtime in Montreal Canadiens' 5–4 victory over Montreal Shamrocks, March 11, 1910

- Served as first captain of Montreal Canadiens (1909–10)

- Nicknamed "The Speed Merchant" because of his legendary speed — a skill that prompted sportswriters to dub his Montreal Canadiens teammates "The Flying Frenchmen"

- Member of Stanley Cup-winning Montreal Canadiens (1915–16)

- Career came to an end when his right leg had to be amputated below the knee following an automobile accident, May 1, 1918

> I do not wish to discuss my personal merit as a player. The public is the judge of that. But I know that every time I put on a uniform to play hockey ... I put my whole heart, courage and desire to win into the game."

REGULAR SEASON

Season	Age	Team	Lg	GP	G	A	PTS	PIM
1903–04	24	Montreal Nationals	FAHL	6	8	0	8	
1904–05	25	Michigan Soo Indians	IHL	24	15	0	15	24
1905–06	26	Michigan Soo Indians	IHL	17	15	0	15	28
1906–07	27	Michigan Soo Indians	IHL	19	10	7	17	34
1907–08	28	Montreal Shamrocks	ECAHA	6	1	0	1	36
1908–09	29	Montreal Shamrocks	ECHA	9	1	0	1	36
1909–10	30	Les Canadiens (Montreal)	NHA	12	4	0	4	41
1910–11	31	Montreal Canadiens	NHA	16	0	0	0	24
1911–12	32	Montreal Canadiens	NHA	17	7	0	7	10
1912–13	33	Montreal Canadiens	NHA	20	8	0	8	77
1913–14	34	Montreal Canadiens	NHA	20	7	9	16	30
1914–15	35	Montreal Canadiens	NHA	18	6	3	9	35
1915–16	36	Montreal Canadiens	NHA	18	8	3	11	62
1916–17	37	Montreal Canadiens	NHA	17	7	3	10	24
1917–18	38	Montreal Canadiens	NHL	18	2	1	3	6
Career — 15 Seasons				237	99	26	125	467

PLAYOFFS

Season	Age	Team	Lg	GP	G	A	PTS	PIM
1913–14	34	Montreal Canadiens	NHA	2	0	1	1	0
1915–16	36	Montreal Canadiens	St-Cup	4	0	0	0	6
1916–17	37	Montreal Canadiens	NHA	2	0	0	0	0
1916–17	37	Montreal Canadiens	St-Cup	4	1	2	3	9
1917–18	38	Montreal Canadiens	NHL	2	0	0	0	0
Career — 4 Seasons				14	1	3	4	15

TROPHY CASE

AWARDS

Stanley Cup (1915–16)

ALL-STAR SELECTIONS

IHL First All-Star Team Right Wing (1905, 1907)

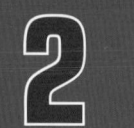

Brian Leetch

HOCKEY HALL OF FAME CLASS: 2009

2

Retired by N.Y. Rangers

Alternate: 22

Defense

Shoots: Left

Height: 6'

Weight: 185 lbs.

Born: March 3, 1968: Corpus Christi, Texas

Drafted by the New York Rangers ninth overall in 1986

Played 18 NHL seasons from 1987–2004, 2005–06

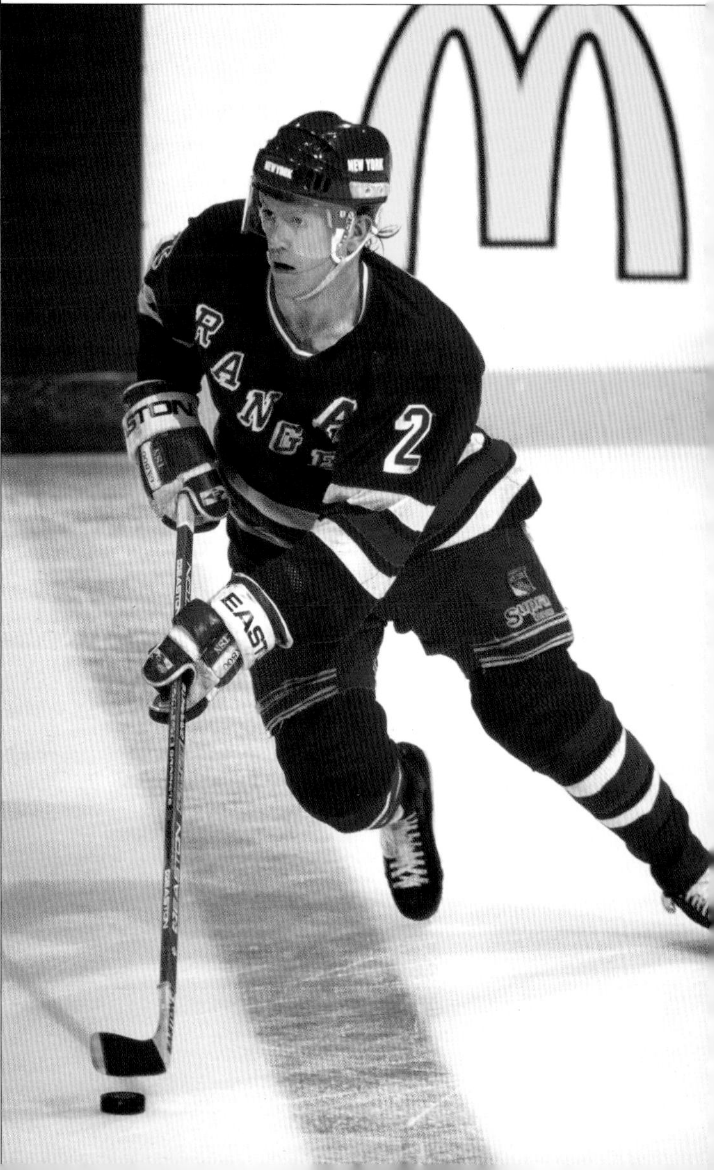

QUICK FACTS

- Holds N.Y. Rangers team record for assists in regular season (80), established in 1991–92
- Holds N.Y. Rangers team records for career goals (240), assists (741) and points (981) by a defenseman
- One of only five defensemen (with Bobby Orr, Paul Coffey, Al MacInnis and Denis Potvin) in NHL history to record more than 100 points in a season
- Last NHL defenseman to register 100 points in regular season (1991–92)
- First American-born and trained player to win the Conn Smythe Trophy (1994)
- Played amateur hockey with Cheshire High Rams (1983–84); Avon Old Farms (1984–86); Boston College (1986–87); U.S.A. National Team (1987–88)

- Hockey East First All-Star Team Defense (1987); NCAA East First All-American Team Defense (1987)
- Led NHL playoffs in assists (23) and points (34) in 1993–94
- Played in NHL All-Star Game (1990, 1991, 1992, 1994, 1996, 1997, 1998, 2000, 2001)
- Finished among NHL top-10 in assists in 1990–91 (72), 1991–92 (80), 1995–96 (70), 1996–97 (58) and 2000–01 (58)
- Signed as a free agent by Boston, August 3, 2005
- Registered 1,000th career NHL point in Boston's 4–3 loss to Montreal Canadiens, October 18, 2005
- Inducted into Avon Old Farms Hall of Fame (2004)

> "I was proud to be a Ranger for my entire career, and I wanted to be here when things got turned around. So I was disappointed and still am."
> — Brian Leetch, on being traded to Toronto in 2004

REGULAR SEASON

Season	Age	Team	Lg	GP	G	A	PTS	+/-	PIM	ESG	PPG	SHG	GWG	SOG	S%
1987-88	19	New York Rangers	NHL	17	2	12	14	5	0	1	1	0	1	40	5.0
1988-89	20	New York Rangers	NHL	68	23	48	71	8	50	12	8	3	1	268	8.6
1989-90	21	New York Rangers	NHL	72	11	45	56	-18	26	6	5	0	2	222	5.0
1990-91	22	New York Rangers	NHL	80	16	72	88	2	42	10	6	0	4	206	7.8
1991-92	23	New York Rangers	NHL	80	22	80	102	25	26	11	10	1	3	245	9.0
1992-93	24	New York Rangers	NHL	36	6	30	36	2	26	3	2	1	1	150	4.0
1993-94	25	New York Rangers	NHL	84	23	56	79	28	67	5	17	1	4	328	7.0
1994-95	26	New York Rangers	NHL	48	9	32	41	0	18	6	3	0	2	182	4.9
1995-96	27	New York Rangers	NHL	82	15	70	85	12	30	8	7	0	3	276	5.4
1996-97	28	New York Rangers	NHL	82	20	58	78	31	49	11	9	0	2	256	7.8
1997-98	29	New York Rangers	NHL	76	17	33	50	-36	32	6	11	0	2	230	7.4
1998-99	30	New York Rangers	NHL	82	13	42	55	-7	42	9	4	0	1	184	7.1
1999-00	31	New York Rangers	NHL	50	7	19	26	-16	20	4	3	0	2	124	5.6
2000-01	32	New York Rangers	NHL	82	21	58	79	-18	34	10	10	1	3	241	8.7
2001-02	33	New York Rangers	NHL	82	10	45	55	14	28	9	1	0	3	202	5.0
2002-03	34	New York Rangers	NHL	51	12	18	30	-3	20	7	5	0	2	150	8.0
2003-04	35	New York Rangers	NHL	57	13	23	36	-5	24	8	4	1	1	165	7.9
2003-04	35	Toronto Maple Leafs	NHL	15	2	13	15	11	10	1	1	0	1	41	4.9
2005-06	37	Boston Bruins	NHL	61	5	27	32	-10	36	1	4	0	0	130	3.8
NHL Career – 18 Seasons				1205	247	781	1028	25	571	128	111	8	38	3640	6.8

PLAYOFFS

Season	Age	Team	Lg	GP	G	A	PTS	+/-	PIM	ESG	PPG	SHG	GWG	SOG	S%
1988-89	20	New York Rangers	NHL	4	3	2	5	-4	2	1	2	0	0	25	12.0
1990-91	22	New York Rangers	NHL	6	1	3	4	-2	0	1	0	0	0	13	7.7
1991-92	23	New York Rangers	NHL	13	4	11	15	-5	4	2	1	1	0	67	6.0
1993-94	25	New York Rangers	NHL	23	11	23	34	19	6	7	4	0	4	88	12.5
1994-95	26	New York Rangers	NHL	10	6	8	14	-1	8	3	3	0	1	46	13.0
1995-96	27	New York Rangers	NHL	11	1	6	7	-11	4	0	1	0	0	34	2.9
1996-97	28	New York Rangers	NHL	15	2	8	10	5	6	1	1	0	1	56	3.6
2003-04	35	Toronto Maple Leafs	NHL	13	0	8	8	1	6	0	0	0	0	23	0.0
NHL Career – 8 Seasons				95	28	69	97	2	36	15	12	1	6	352	8.0

TROPHY CASE

AWARDS

Calder Memorial Trophy (1989)

James Norris Memorial Trophy (1992, 1997)

Conn Smythe Trophy (1994)

Lester Patrick Trophy (2007)

Stanley Cup (1993–94)

ALL-STAR SELECTIONS

All-Rookie Team (1989)

First All-Star Team Defense (1989, 1992, 1997)

Second All-Star Team Defense (1991, 1994, 1996)

INTERNATIONAL AWARDS

World Cup (1996)

1

Hugh Lehman
HOCKEY HALL OF FAME CLASS: 1958

Alternate: 15

Goaltender

Catches: Left

Height: 5'-8"

Weight: 168 lbs.

Born: October 27, 1885: Pembroke, Ontario

Died: April 8, 1961: Toronto, Ontario

Played 22 professional seasons from 1906–28

QUICK FACTS

- Holds PCHA career records for games played by a goaltender (262), wins (142), losses (118) and shutouts (17)
- Only one of two goaltenders (with Percy LeSueur) to challenge for Stanley Cup with two different teams in same season (1909–10)
- Played amateur hockey with Pembroke HC (1902–06)
- Led UOVHL in wins (8), shutouts (1) and goals-against-average (1.67) in 1905–06; led UOVHL playoffs in shutouts (1) in 1905–06
- Member of OPHL champion Berlin Dutchmen (1909–10)

- Led OPHL in wins (17) in 1909–10
- Member of Galt Pro team that challenged Ottawa Senators for Stanley Cup title in January of 1909 — Ottawa won two-game, total-goal series 15–4
- Led PCHA in wins in 1911–12 (9), 1914–15 (13), 1918–19 (12), 1921–22 (12), 1922–23 (16)
- Led PCHA in goals-against-average in 1911–12 (5.07), 1913–14 (4.87), 1914–15 (4.08), 1917–18 (3.05), 1922–23 (2.33) and 1923–24 (2.60)
- Led PCHA in shutouts in 1914–15 (1), 1917–18 (1), 1920–21 (3), 1921–22 (4) and 1922–23 (5)

> "Lehman played hard and worked hard and life had been good to him... Few players can match his nomadic exploits and, quite possibly, there never has been a goalkeeper who can match his ironman career."
> — Canadian Press obituary, April 13, 1961

REGULAR SEASON

Season	Age	Team	Lg	GP	W	L	T	SO	GA	GAA
1906–07	21	Canadian Soo	IHL	24	13	11	0	0	123	5.12
1907–08	22	Pembroke Lumber Kings	OVHL	4	2	2	0	0	22	5.50
1908–09	23	Berlin Professionals	OPHL	15	9	6	0	0	72	4.85
1909–10	24	Berlin Professionals	OPHL	23	17	6	0	3	93	4.12
1910–11	25	Berlin Professionals	OPHL	15	7	8	0	0	87	5.80
1911–12	26	New Westminster Royals	PCHA	15	9	6	0	0	77	5.07
1912–13	27	New Westminster Royals	PCHA	12	4	8	0	0	51	4.14
1913–14	28	New Westminster Royals	PCHA	16	7	9	0	0	81	4.87
1914–15	29	Vancouver Millionaires	PCHA	17	13	4	0	1	71	4.08
1915–16	30	Vancouver Millionaires	PCHA	18	9	9	0	0	69	3.79
1916–17	31	Vancouver Millionaires	PCHA	23	14	9	0	0	124	5.30
1917–18	32	Vancouver Millionaires	PCHA	18	9	9	0	1	60	3.05
1918–19	33	Vancouver Millionaires	PCHA	20	12	8	0	1	55	2.58
1919–20	34	Vancouver Millionaires	PCHA	22	11	11	1	0	65	2.92
1920–21	35	Vancouver Millionaires	PCHA	24	13	11	0	3	78	3.23
1921–22	36	Vancouver Millionaires	PCHA	22	12	10	0	4	62	2.82
1922–23	37	Vancouver Maroons	PCHA	25	16	8	1	5	61	2.33
1923–24	38	Vancouver Maroons	PCHA	30	13	16	1	1	80	2.60
1924–25	39	Vancouver Maroons	WCHL	11	7	4	0	0	29	2.62
1925–26	40	Vancouver Maroons	WHL	30	10	18	2	3	90	2.94
1926–27	41	Chicago Black Hawks	NHL	44	19	22	3	5	116	2.49
1927–28	42	Chicago Black Hawks	NHL	4	1	2	1	1	20	4.80
Career — 22 Seasons				432	227	196	9	28	1586	3.67

PLAYOFFS

Season	Age	Team	Lg	GP	W	L	T	SO	GA	GAA
1909–10	24	Galt Professionals	St-Cup	2	0	2	0	0	15	7.50
1909–10	24	Berlin Professionals	St-Cup	1	0	1	0	0	7	7.00
1914–15	29	Vancouver Millionaires	St-Cup	3	3	0	0	0	8	2.67
1917–18	32	Vancouver Millionaires	PCHA	2	1	0	1	1	2	1.00
1917–18	32	Vancouver Millionaires	St-Cup	5	2	3	0	0	18	3.60
1918–19	33	Vancouver Millionaires	PCHA	2	1	1	0	0	7	3.50
1919–20	34	Vancouver Millionaires	PCHA	2	1	1	0	0	7	3.50
1920–21	35	Vancouver Millionaires	PCHA	2	2	0	0	1	2	1.00
1920–21	35	Vancouver Millionaires	St-Cup	5	2	3	0	0	12	2.40
1921–22	36	Vancouver Millionaires	PCHA	2	2	0	0	2	0	0.00
1921–22	36	Vancouver Millionaires	St-Cup	5	2	3	0	1	16	3.15
1921–22	36	Vancouver Millionaires	West-P	2	1	1	0	0	2	1.00
1922–23	37	Vancouver Maroons	PCHA	2	1	1	0	1	3	1.50
1922–23	37	Vancouver Maroons	St-Cup	4	1	3	0	0	10	2.50
1923–24	38	Vancouver Maroons	PCHA	2	1	1	0	0	3	1.34
1923–24	38	Vancouver Maroons	St-Cup	2	0	2	0	0	5	2.50
1923–24	28	Vancouver Maroons	West-P	3	1	2	0	0	10	3.33
1926–27	41	Chicago Black Hawks	NHL	2	0	1	1	0	10	5.00
Career — 10 Seasons				48	21	25	2	7	137	2.85

TROPHY CASE

AWARDS

Stanley Cup (1914–15)

ALL-STAR SELECTIONS

OPHL First All-Star Team Goaltender (1910)

PCHA First All-Star Team Goaltender (1912, 1914, 1915, 1916, 1918, 1919, 1920, 1921, 1922, 1923, 1924)

Jacques Lemaire

HOCKEY HALL OF FAME CLASS: 1984

Center

Shoots: Left

Height: 5'-10"

Weight: 180 lbs.

Born: September 7, 1945: LaSalle, Quebec

Played 12 NHL seasons from 1967–79

QUICK FACTS

- Played amateur hockey with Lachine Maroons (1962–63); Montreal Jr. Canadiens (1963–66)
- Led QJHL in points (104) in 1962–63
- Played minor pro hockey with Quebec Aces (1964–65); Houston Apollos (1966–67)
- First person in NHL history to play 100 playoff games and coach 100 playoff games
- Scored Stanley Cup-winning overtime goal in Montreal's 2–1 victory over Boston, May 14, 1977; scored Stanley Cup-winning goal in Montreal's 4–1 victory over N.Y. Rangers, May 21, 1979
- One of only five players (with Jack Darragh, Henri Richard, Mike Bossy and Jean Béliveau) to score two Cup-winning goals
- Played in NHL All-Star Game (1970, 1973)

- Runner-up to Boston Bruins Derek Sanderson in voting for rookie of the year in 1967–68
- Scored at least 20 goals in each of his 12 NHL seasons
- Member of Montreal's famed Donut Line with Steve Shutt and Guy Lafleur
- Served as player/coach with HC Sierre (1979–81)
- Served as assistant coach of Plattsburgh State University Cardinals (1981–82)
- Coached Montreal Canadiens (1983–85); coached New Jersey Devils (1993–98, 2009–10); coached Minnesota Wild (2000–09)
- Coached Stanley Cup-winning New Jersey Devils (1995)

> With Montreal, there was a certain way to play the game that other teams didn't know. It came from being with winners. As a youngster, I played on good teams that didn't win, but I went to Montreal and right away, won two Stanley Cups in my first two seasons. It was those other guys who showed me how to win."

REGULAR SEASON

Season	Age	Team	Lg	GP	G	A	PTS	+/-	PIM	ESG	PPG	SHG	GWG	SOG	S%
1967–68	22	Montreal Canadiens	NHL	69	22	20	42	15	16	18	3	1	3	182	12.1
1968–69	23	Montreal Canadiens	NHL	75	29	34	63	31	29	24	5	0	4	330	8.8
1969–70	24	Montreal Canadiens	NHL	69	32	28	60	19	16	19	13	0	5	237	13.5
1970–71	25	Montreal Canadiens	NHL	78	28	28	56	0	18	22	6	0	3	252	11.1
1971–72	26	Montreal Canadiens	NHL	77	32	49	81	37	26	24	8	0	7	266	12.0
1972–73	27	Montreal Canadiens	NHL	77	44	51	95	59	16	35	9	0	5	294	15.0
1973–74	28	Montreal Canadiens	NHL	66	29	38	67	4	10	19	10	0	7	219	13.2
1974–75	29	Montreal Canadiens	NHL	80	36	56	92	25	20	24	12	0	8	260	13.8
1975–76	30	Montreal Canadiens	NHL	61	20	32	52	26	20	14	6	0	3	226	8.8
1976–77	31	Montreal Canadiens	NHL	75	34	41	75	70	22	27	5	2	4	272	12.5
1977–78	32	Montreal Canadiens	NHL	76	36	61	97	54	14	30	6	0	5	310	11.6
1978–79	33	Montreal Canadiens	NHL	50	24	31	55	9	10	17	6	1	4	203	11.8
NHL Career – 12 Seasons				853	366	469	835	349	217	273	89	4	58	3051	12.0

PLAYOFFS

Season	Age	Team	Lg	GP	G	A	PTS	+/-	PIM	ESG	PPG	SHG	GWG	SOG	S%
1967–68	22	Montreal Canadiens	NHL	13	7	6	13		6	5	2	0	2		
1968–69	23	Montreal Canadiens	NHL	14	4	2	6		6	3	1	0	0		
1970–71	25	Montreal Canadiens	NHL	20	9	10	19		17	5	4	0	1		
1971–72	26	Montreal Canadiens	NHL	6	2	1	3		2	2	0	0	0		
1972–73	27	Montreal Canadiens	NHL	17	7	13	20		2	4	3	0	1		
1973–74	28	Montreal Canadiens	NHL	6	0	4	4		2	0	0	0	0		
1974–75	29	Montreal Canadiens	NHL	11	5	7	12		4	4	1	0	0		
1975–76	30	Montreal Canadiens	NHL	13	3	3	6		2	1	1	1	1		
1976–77	31	Montreal Canadiens	NHL	14	7	12	19		6	6	1	0	3		
1977–78	32	Montreal Canadiens	NHL	15	6	8	14		10	6	0	0	1		
1978–79	33	Montreal Canadiens	NHL	16	11	12	23		6	5	6	0	2		
NHL Career – 11 Seasons				145	61	78	139		63	41	19	1	11		

TROPHY CASE

AWARDS

Jack Adams Award (1994, 2003)

Stanley Cup (1967–68, 1968–69, 1970–71, 1972–73, 1975–76, 1976–77, 1977–78, 1978–79)

66

Center	
Shoots: Right	
Height: 6'-4"	
Weight: 230 lbs.	

Born: October 5, 1965: Montreal, Quebec

Drafted by the Pittsburgh Penguins first overall in 1984

Played 17 NHL seasons from 1984–94, 1995–97, 2000–04, 2005–06

Mario Lemieux
HOCKEY HALL OF FAME CLASS: 1997

QUICK FACTS

- Ranks ninth in NHL career goals (690); ranks 10th in NHL career assists (1,033); ranks seventh in NHL career points (1,723)

- Holds NHL record for short-handed goals in regular season (13), established in 1988–89

- Shares NHL record for goals (5) and points (8) in a single playoff game and goals in a single playoff period (4), all established in Pittsburgh's 10–7 victory over Philadelphia Flyers, April 25, 1989

- Played amateur hockey with Montreal Hurricane (1979–80); Montreal-Concordia (1980–81); Laval Voisins (1981–84)

- Led QMJHL in goals (133), assists (149) and points (282) in 1983–84; led QMJHL playoffs in goals (29), assists (23) and points (52) in 1983–84

- QMJHL First All-Star Team Center (1984); QMJHL Second All-Star Team Center (1983); CHL Player of the Year (1984)

- Led NHL in short-handed goals in 1987–88 (10), 1988–89 (13) and 1995–96 (8); led NHL in power-play goals in 1988–89 (31) and 1995–96 (31)

- Only player in NHL history to score five goals in five different ways (even-strength goal, a power-play goal, a shorthanded goal, a penalty-shot goal and an empty-net goal) in a single game, December 31, 1988

- One of only three players (with Gordie Howe and Guy Lafleur) to play in NHL after being inducted into the Hall of Fame

REGULAR SEASON

Season	Age	Team	Lg	GP	G	A	PTS	+/-	PIM	ESG	PPG	SHG	GWG	SOG	S%
1984–85	19	Pittsburgh Penguins	NHL	73	43	57	100	-35	54	32	11	0	2	209	20.6
1985–86	20	Pittsburgh Penguins	NHL	79	48	93	141	-6	43	31	17	0	4	276	17.4
1986–87	21	Pittsburgh Penguins	NHL	63	54	53	107	13	57	35	19	0	4	267	20.2
1987–88	22	Pittsburgh Penguins	NHL	77	70	98	168	23	92	38	22	10	7	382	18.3
1988–89	23	Pittsburgh Penguins	NHL	76	85	114	199	41	100	41	31	13	8	313	27.2
1989–90	24	Pittsburgh Penguins	NHL	59	45	78	123	-18	78	28	14	3	4	226	19.9
1990–91	25	Pittsburgh Penguins	NHL	26	19	26	45	8	30	12	6	1	2	89	21.3
1991–92	26	Pittsburgh Penguins	NHL	64	44	87	131	27	94	28	12	4	5	249	17.7
1992–93	27	Pittsburgh Penguins	NHL	60	69	91	160	55	38	47	16	6	10	286	24.1
1993–94	28	Pittsburgh Penguins	NHL	22	17	20	37	-2	32	10	7	0	4	92	18.5
1995–96	30	Pittsburgh Penguins	NHL	70	69	92	161	10	54	30	31	8	8	338	20.4
1996–97	31	Pittsburgh Penguins	NHL	76	50	72	122	27	65	32	15	3	7	327	15.3
2000–01	35	Pittsburgh Penguins	NHL	43	35	41	76	15	18	18	16	1	5	171	20.5
2001–02	36	Pittsburgh Penguins	NHL	24	6	25	31	0	14	4	2	0	0	75	8.0
2002–03	37	Pittsburgh Penguins	NHL	67	28	63	91	-25	43	14	14	0	4	235	11.9
2003–04	38	Pittsburgh Penguins	NHL	10	1	8	9	-2	6	1	0	0	0	21	4.8
2005–06	40	Pittsburgh Penguins	NHL	26	7	15	22	-16	16	4	3	0	0	77	9.1
NHL Career – 17 Seasons				915	690	1033	1723	115	834	405	236	49	74	3633	19.0

PLAYOFFS

Season	Age	Team	Lg	GP	G	A	PTS	+/-	PIM	ESG	PPG	SHG	GWG	SOG	S%
1988–89	23	Pittsburgh Penguins	NHL	11	12	7	19	-1	16	4	7	1	0	41	29.3
1990–91	25	Pittsburgh Penguins	NHL	23	16	28	44	14	16	8	6	2	0	93	17.2
1991–92	26	Pittsburgh Penguins	NHL	15	16	18	34	6	2	6	8	2	5	69	23.2
1992–93	27	Pittsburgh Penguins	NHL	11	8	10	18	2	10	4	3	1	1	40	20.0
1993–94	28	Pittsburgh Penguins	NHL	6	4	3	7	-4	2	3	1	0	0	23	17.4
1995–96	30	Pittsburgh Penguins	NHL	18	11	16	27	3	33	7	3	1	2	78	14.1
1996–97	31	Pittsburgh Penguins	NHL	5	3	3	6	-4	4	3	0	0	0	19	15.8
2000–01	35	Pittsburgh Penguins	NHL	18	6	11	17	4	4	5	1	0	3	39	15.4
NHL Career – 8 Seasons				107	76	96	172	20	87	40	29	7	11	402	18.9

TROPHY CASE

AWARDS
Calder Memorial Trophy (1985)
Lester B. Pearson Award (1986, 1988, 1993, 1996)
Art Ross Trophy (1988, 1989, 1992, 1993, 1996, 1997)
Hart Memorial Trophy (1988, 1993, 1996)
Conn Smythe Trophy (1991, 1992)
Bill Masterton Memorial Trophy (1993)
Lester Patrick Trophy (2000)
Stanley Cup (1990–91, 1991–92)

ALL-STAR SELECTIONS
First All-Star Team Center (1988, 1989, 1993, 1996, 1997)
Second All-Star Team Center (1986, 1987, 1992, 2001)

INTERNATIONAL AWARDS
Canada Cup (1987)
Silver Medal: World Championships (1985)
Gold Medal: Winter Olympics (2002)

Percy LeSueur

HOCKEY HALL OF FAME CLASS: 1961

Goaltender

Catches: Left

Height: 5'-7"

Weight: 150 lbs.

Born: November 21, 1881: Quebec City, Quebec

Died: January 27, 1962: Hamilton, Ontario

Played 13 elite amateur and professional seasons from 1903–16

"LeSueur was so effective and so capable that it appeared easy. From the top of his head to his toes he was bombarded with drives. He saw most of them when they started and never winked an eye."

— *New York Times*, March 21, 1911 on opening game of $1,000 grudge match between Montreal Wanderers and St. Nicholas Rink

QUICK FACTS

- One of only two goaltenders (with Hugh Lehman) to challenge for Stanley Cup with two different teams (Smiths Falls and Ottawa) in same season (1905–06)

- Career in hockey spanned 50 years as a player, coach, manager, columnist and broadcaster

- Began career as a right winger in his hometown of Quebec City, but became a goalie while playing in Smiths Falls, Ontario

- Attracted attention of Ottawa "Silver Seven" team when they defeated Smith Falls in Stanley Cup challenge series in March of 1906

- Selected as NHA All-Star goaltender in the Hod Stuart Memorial Game, first "Major League" All-Star game in hockey history, January 2, 1908

- Led ECHA in wins (10) in 1908–09

- Member of Stanley Cup-winning Ottawa Senators team that successfully defended title twice in January of 1910

- Served as team captain of Ottawa Senators (1910–11)

- Led NHA in wins (13) in 1910–11

- Nicknamed "Peerless Percy" by *Ottawa Free Press* sportswriter Malcolm Brice

- Playing career ended in 1916 when he volunteered for the Canadian Army in World War I

- Coached Guelph Intermediates to Ontario Hockey Association Intermediate championship (1920–21)

- Coached Hamilton Tigers (1923–24)

LaSueur's stick that he tended goal with for Ottawa and Smith Falls between 1904–09. The stick was dear to LeSueur, who carved the dates of his Stanley Cup wins on the shaft and paddle.

REGULAR SEASON

Season	Age	Team	Lg	GP	W	L	T	SO	GA	GAA
1903–04	22	Smiths Falls Seniors	OHA-Sr.	6	3	3	0	2	13	2.11
1904–05	23	Smiths Falls Seniors	OHA-Sr.							
1905–06	24	Smiths Falls Seniors	FAHL	7	7	0	0	1	16	2.30
1906–07	25	Ottawa Senators	ECAHA	10	7	3	0	0	54	5.38
1907–08	26	Ottawa Senators	ECAHA	10	7	3	0	0	51	4.86
1908–09	27	Ottawa Senators	ECHA	12	10	2	0	0	63	5.19
1909–10	28	Ottawa Senators	CHA	2	2	0	0	0	9	4.50
1909–10	28	Ottawa Senators	NHA	12	9	3	0	0	66	5.42
1910–11	29	Ottawa Senators	NHA	16	13	3	0	1	69	4.18
1911–12	30	Ottawa Senators	NHA	18	9	9	0	0	91	4.85
1912–13	31	Ottawa Senators	NHA	18	7	10	0	0	65	4.18
1913–14	32	Ottawa Senators	NHA	13	6	6	0	1	42	3.26
1914–15	33	Toronto Shamrocks	NHA	19	8	11	0	0	96	5.03
1915–16	34	Toronto Blueshirts	NHA	23	9	13	0	1	92	3.90
Career — 13 Seasons				166	97	66	0	6	729	4.39

PLAYOFFS

Season	Age	Team	Lg	GP	W	L	T	SO	GA	GAA
1905–06	24	Smiths Falls Seniors	St-Cup	2	0	2	0	0	14	7.00
1905–06	24	Ottawa Silver Seven	St-Cup	1	1	0	0	0	3	3.00
1909–10	28	Ottawa Senators	St-Cup	4	4	0	0	0	15	3.75
1910–11	29	Ottawa Senators	St-Cup	2	2	0	0	0	8	4.00
Career — 3 Seasons				9	7	2	0	0	40	4.44

TROPHY CASE

AWARDS

Stanley Cup (1908–09, 1909–10, 1910–11)

Herbie Lewis

HOCKEY HALL OF FAME CLASS: 1989

Alternates: 9, 7

Left Wing

Shoots: Left

Height: 5'-9"

Weight: 163 lbs.

Born: April 17, 1906: Calgary, Alberta

Died: January 20, 1991: Indianapolis, Indiana

Played 11 NHL seasons from 1928–39

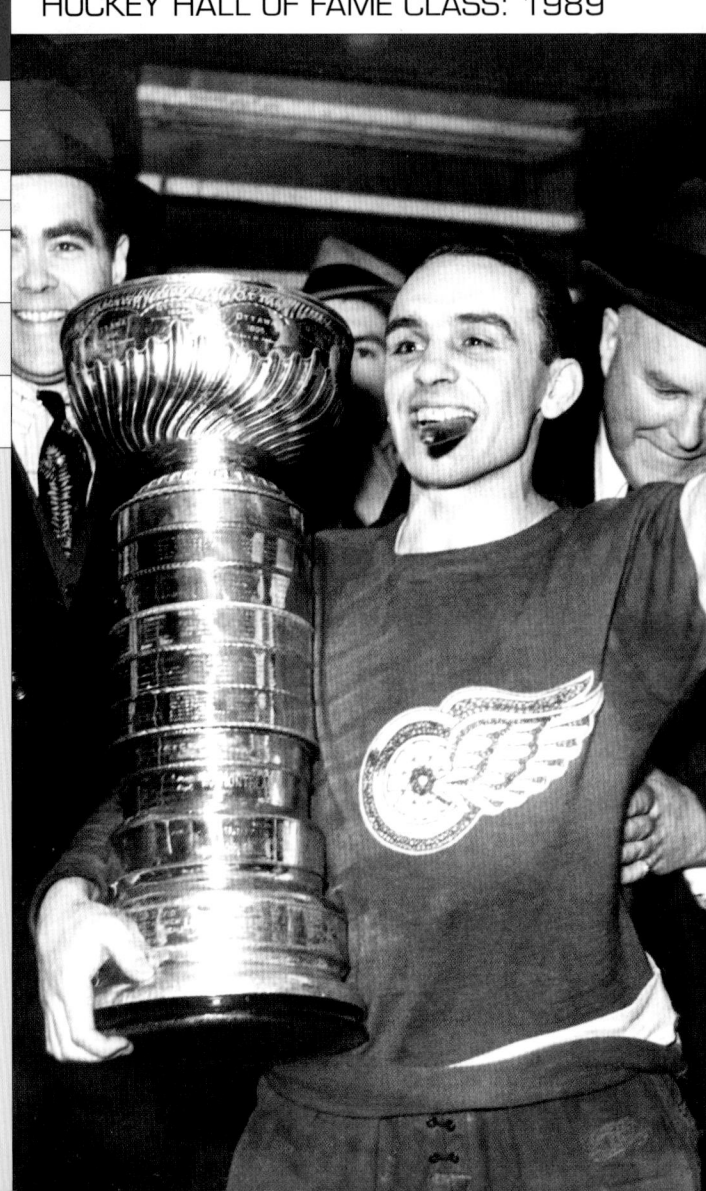

QUICK FACTS

- Nicknamed "The Duke of Duluth"
- Played amateur hockey with Calgary Hustlers (1921–22), Calgary Canadians (1922–24) and Duluth Hornets (1924–28)
- Led Calgary Junior League in goals (17) and points (24) in 1922–23
- Signed as a free agent by Duluth Hornets (CHL), November 4, 1926
- Led CHL in assists (11) and points (28) in 1925–26
- CHL First All-Star Team Left Wing (1926)
- Claimed by Detroit Cougars from Duluth Hornets (AHA) in Inter-League Draft, May 14, 1928
- Played in NHL All-Star Game (1934)
- Led NHL playoffs in goals in 1932–33 (5) and 1936–37 (4)

- Played for all three teams in the history of the Detroit franchise: Cougars (1928–30), Falcons (1930–32) and Red Wings (1932–39)
- Served as captain of Detroit Red Wings (1933–34)
- Held Detroit franchise record for career goals (147); surpassed by Syd Howe during 1943–44 season
- Coached Indianapolis Capitols (1939–43)
- Was the NHL's highest-paid player in 1935 when he received a salary of $8,000
- Times have changed — the Indianapolis Capitols held a "Herbie Lewis Night" on January 10, 1940 and presented Lewis with a picnic basket and two hams

> [He] was a sportsman of the highest type. I defy baseball or football or boxing or any other sport to produce an individual who can eclipse Herbie Lewis as a perfect model of what an athlete should stand for."
> — Jack Adams

REGULAR SEASON

Season	Age	Team	Lg	GP	G	A	PTS	PIM
1928–29	22	Detroit Cougars	NHL	36	9	5	14	33
1929–30	23	Detroit Cougars	NHL	44	20	11	31	36
1930–31	24	Detroit Falcons	NHL	43	15	6	21	38
1931–32	25	Detroit Falcons	NHL	48	5	14	19	21
1932–33	26	Detroit Red Wings	NHL	48	20	14	34	20
1933–34	27	Detroit Red Wings	NHL	43	16	15	31	15
1934–35	28	Detroit Red Wings	NHL	47	16	27	43	26
1935–36	29	Detroit Red Wings	NHL	45	14	23	37	25
1936–37	30	Detroit Red Wings	NHL	45	14	18	32	14
1937–38	31	Detroit Red Wings	NHL	42	13	18	31	12
1938–39	32	Detroit Red Wings	NHL	42	6	10	16	8
NHL Career — 11 Seasons				483	148	161	309	248

PLAYOFFS

Season	Age	Team	Lg	GP	G	A	PTS	PIM
1931–32	25	Detroit Falcons	NHL	2	0	0	0	0
1932–33	26	Detroit Red Wings	NHL	4	1	0	1	0
1933–34	27	Detroit Red Wings	NHL	9	5	2	7	2
1935–36	29	Detroit Red Wings	NHL	7	2	3	5	0
1936–37	30	Detroit Red Wings	NHL	10	4	3	7	4
1938–39	32	Detroit Red Wings	NHL	6	1	2	3	0
NHL Career — 6 Seasons				38	13	10	23	6

TROPHY CASE

AWARDS

Stanley Cup (1935–36, 1936–37)

Alternates: 14, 15	
Left Wing	
Shoots: Left	
Height: 5'-8"	
Weight: 163 lbs.	
Born: July 29, 1925: Renfrew, Ontario	
Played 17 NHL seasons from 1944–60, 1964–65	

Ted Lindsay
HOCKEY HALL OF FAME CLASS: 1966

QUICK FACTS

- Played amateur hockey with Kirkland Lake Lakers (1942–43); St. Michael's Majors (1943–44); Oshawa Generals (1943–44)

- Signed as a free agent by the Detroit Red Wings, October 18, 1944

- Led NHL in goals (33) in 1947–48; led NHL in assists in 1949–50 (55) and 1956–57 (55); led NHL in penalty minutes (184) in 1958–59

- Nicknamed "Terrible Ted" and "Scarface" because of scrappy, chippy play that contributed to more than 400 stitches to his face

- Traded to Chicago by Detroit with Glenn Hall for Johnny Wilson, Forbes Kennedy, Hank Bassen and Bill Preston, July 23, 1957; rights traded to Detroit by Chicago for cash, October 14, 1964

- Attempted to organize the first NHL Players Association in 1957, an activity that led to his trade to the last-place Chicago Black Hawks

- Member of Detroit's famed Production Line with Sid Abel and Gordie Howe

- Played in 11 consecutive NHL All-Star Games (1947–57)

- Ended four-year retirement in 1964–65 to rejoin the Detroit Red Wings and at age 39 ranked second in penalty minutes (173)

- Served as General Manager of Detroit Red Wings (1976–80); coached Detroit Red Wings (1979–80, 1980–81)

- Served as General Manager of Kansas City Red Wings (1977–79)

> " I don't know how I got [my] nickname and tough guy persona because I'm such a nice person. I guess I got rough because I hated to lose. It took me some time to learn the art of losing graciously."

REGULAR SEASON

Season	Age	Team	Lg	GP	G	A	PTS	PIM	ESG	PPG	SHG	GWG
1944–45	19	Detroit Red Wings	NHL	45	17	6	23	43				
1945–46	20	Detroit Red Wings	NHL	47	7	10	17	14				
1946–47	21	Detroit Red Wings	NHL	59	27	15	42	57				
1947–48	22	Detroit Red Wings	NHL	60	33	19	52	95				
1948–49	23	Detroit Red Wings	NHL	50	26	28	54	97				
1949–50	24	Detroit Red Wings	NHL	69	23	55	78	141				
1950–51	25	Detroit Red Wings	NHL	67	24	35	59	110				
1951–52	26	Detroit Red Wings	NHL	70	30	39	69	123				
1952–53	27	Detroit Red Wings	NHL	70	32	39	71	111				
1953–54	28	Detroit Red Wings	NHL	70	26	36	62	110				
1954–55	29	Detroit Red Wings	NHL	49	19	19	38	85				
1955–56	30	Detroit Red Wings	NHL	67	27	23	50	161				
1956–57	32	Detroit Red Wings	NHL	70	30	55	85	103				
1957–58	32	Chicago Blackhawks	NHL	68	15	24	39	110				
1958–59	33	Chicago Blackhawks	NHL	70	22	36	58	184				
1959–60	34	Chicago Blackhawks	NHL	68	7	19	26	91				
1964–65	39	Detroit Red Wings	NHL	69	14	14	28	173	13	1	0	1
NHL Career — 17 Seasons				1068	379	472	851	1808	13	1	0	1

PLAYOFFS

Season	Age	Team	Lg	GP	G	A	PTS	PIM				
1944–45	19	Detroit Red Wings	NHL	14	2	0	2	6				
1945–46	20	Detroit Red Wings	NHL	5	0	1	1	0				
1946–47	21	Detroit Red Wings	NHL	5	2	2	4	10				
1947–48	22	Detroit Red Wings	NHL	10	3	1	4	6				
1948–49	23	Detroit Red Wings	NHL	11	2	6	8	31				
1949–50	24	Detroit Red Wings	NHL	13	4	4	8	16				
1950–51	25	Detroit Red Wings	NHL	6	0	1	1	8				
1951–52	26	Detroit Red Wings	NHL	8	5	2	7	8				
1952–53	27	Detroit Red Wings	NHL	6	4	4	8	6				
1953–54	28	Detroit Red Wings	NHL	12	4	4	8	14				
1954–55	29	Detroit Red Wings	NHL	11	7	12	19	12				
1955–56	30	Detroit Red Wings	NHL	10	6	3	9	22				
1956–57	31	Detroit Red Wings	NHL	5	2	4	6	8				
1958–59	33	Chicago Blackhawks	NHL	6	2	4	6	13				
1959–60	34	Chicago Blackhawks	NHL	4	1	1	2	0				
1964–65	39	Detroit Red Wings	NHL	7	3	0	3	34				
NHL Career — 16 Seasons				133	47	49	96	194				

TROPHY CASE

AWARDS

Art Ross Trophy (1950)

Lester Patrick Trophy (2008)

Stanley Cup (1949–50, 1951–52, 1953–54, 1954–55)

ALL-STAR SELECTIONS

First All-Star Team Left Wing (1948, 1950, 1951, 1952, 1953, 1954, 1956, 1957)

Second All-Star Team Left Wing (1949)

317

Harry Lumley
HOCKEY HALL OF FAME CLASS: 1980

Goaltender

Catches: Left

Height: 6'

Weight: 195 lbs.

Born: November 11, 1926: Owen Sound, Ontario

Died: September 13, 1998: London, Ontario

Played 16 NHL seasons from 1943–56, 1957–60

QUICK FACTS

- Played junior hockey with Barrie Colts (1942–43)

- Loaned to N.Y. Rangers by Detroit to replace injured Ken McAuley, December 23, 1943. Lumley played the third period and didn't allow a goal as the Red Wings defeated the Rangers 5–3

- Recorded league-leading eight wins, three shutouts and 1.86 goals-against-average in backstopping Detroit to the Stanley Cup championship in 1950 playoffs. Despite those impressive statistics, he was traded to Chicago to make room in Detroit for Terry Sawchuk

- Led NHL in shutouts in 1947–48 (7); 1952–53 (10) and 1953–54 (13)

- Led NHL in goals-against-average in 1953–54 (1.86) and 1954–55 (1.94)

- Traded to Chicago by Detroit with Jack Stewart, Al Dewsbury, Pete Babando and Don Morrison for Metro Prystai, Gaye Stewart, Bob Goldham and Jim Henry, July 13, 1950. Trade was largest in NHL history until Calgary and Toronto exchanged ten players — including Doug Gilmour — on January 2, 1992

- Played in NHL All-Star Game (1951, 1954, 1955)

- Traded to Toronto by Chicago for Al Rollins, Gus Mortson, Cal Gardner and Ray Hannigan, September 11, 1952

- Traded to Chicago by Toronto with Eric Nesterenko for $41,000, May 21, 1956

- AHL Second All-Star Team Goaltender (1957)

- Traded to Boston by Chicago for cash, January 16, 1958

> It started when I was a rookie. I was pretty rosy-cheeked and people noticed it. The thing was, if I was playing a good game, the fans would call me Apple Cheeks. But if I was bad on any given night, they'd call me Redneck."
> — Harry Lumley, on his crimson nickname

REGULAR SEASON

Season	Age	Team	Lg	GP	W	L	T	SO	GA	GAA	G	A	PTS	PIM
1943–44	17	Detroit Red Wings	NHL	2	0	2	0	0	13	6.50	0	0	0	0
1943–44	17	New York Rangers	NHL	1	0	0	0	0	0	0.00	0	0	0	0
1944–45	18	Detroit Red Wings	NHL	37	24	10	3	1	119	3.22	0	0	0	0
1945–46	19	Detroit Red Wings	NHL	50	20	20	10	2	159	3.18	0	0	0	6
1946–47	20	Detroit Red Wings	NHL	52	22	20	10	3	159	3.06	0	0	0	4
1947–48	21	Detroit Red Wings	NHL	60	30	18	12	7	147	2.46	0	0	0	8
1948–49	22	Detroit Red Wings	NHL	60	34	19	7	6	145	2.42	0	0	0	12
1949–50	23	Detroit Red Wings	NHL	63	33	16	14	7	148	2.35	0	0	0	10
1950–51	24	Chicago Blackhawks	NHL	64	12	41	10	3	246	3.90	0	0	0	4
1951–52	25	Chicago Blackhawks	NHL	70	17	44	9	2	241	3.46	0	0	0	2
1952–53	26	Toronto Maple Leafs	NHL	70	27	30	13	10	167	2.39	0	0	0	18
1953–54	27	Toronto Maple Leafs	NHL	69	32	24	13	13	128	1.86	0	0	0	6
1954–55	28	Toronto Maple Leafs	NHL	69	23	24	22	8	134	1.94	0	0	0	9
1955–56	29	Toronto Maple Leafs	NHL	59	21	28	10	3	157	2.67	0	0	0	2
1957–58	31	Boston Bruins	NHL	24	11	10	3	1	70	2.92	0	0	0	2
1958–59	32	Boston Bruins	NHL	11	8	2	1	1	27	2.45	0	0	0	0
1959–60	33	Boston Bruins	NHL	42	16	21	5	2	146	3.48	0	0	0	12
NHL Career – 16 Seasons				803	330	329	142	71	2206	2.75	0	0	0	95

PLAYOFFS

Season	Age	Team	Lg	GP	W	L	T	SO	GA	GAA	G	A	PTS	PIM
1944–45	18	Detroit Red Wings	NHL	14	7	7		2	31	2.14	0	0	0	0
1945–46	19	Detroit Red Wings	NHL	5	1	4		1	16	3.10	0	0	0	0
1947–48	21	Detroit Red Wings	NHL	10	4	6		0	30	3.00	0	0	0	10
1948–49	22	Detroit Red Wings	NHL	11	4	7		0	26	2.15	0	0	0	2
1949–50	23	Detroit Red Wings	NHL	14	8	6		3	28	1.85	0	0	0	0
1953–54	27	Toronto Maple Leafs	NHL	5	1	4		0	15	2.80	0	0	0	0
1954–55	28	Toronto Maple Leafs	NHL	4	0	4		0	14	3.50	0	0	0	0
1955–56	29	Toronto Maple Leafs	NHL	5	1	4		1	13	2.57	0	0	0	2
1957–58	31	Boston Bruins	NHL	1	0	1		0	5	5.00	0	0	0	0
1958–59	32	Boston Bruins	NHL	7	3	4		0	20	2.75	0	0	0	4
NHL Career – 10 Seasons				76	29	47		7	198	2.49	0	0	0	18

TROPHY CASE

AWARDS

Vezina Trophy (1954)

Stanley Cup (1949–50)

ALL-STAR SELECTIONS

First All-Star Team Goaltender (1954, 1955)

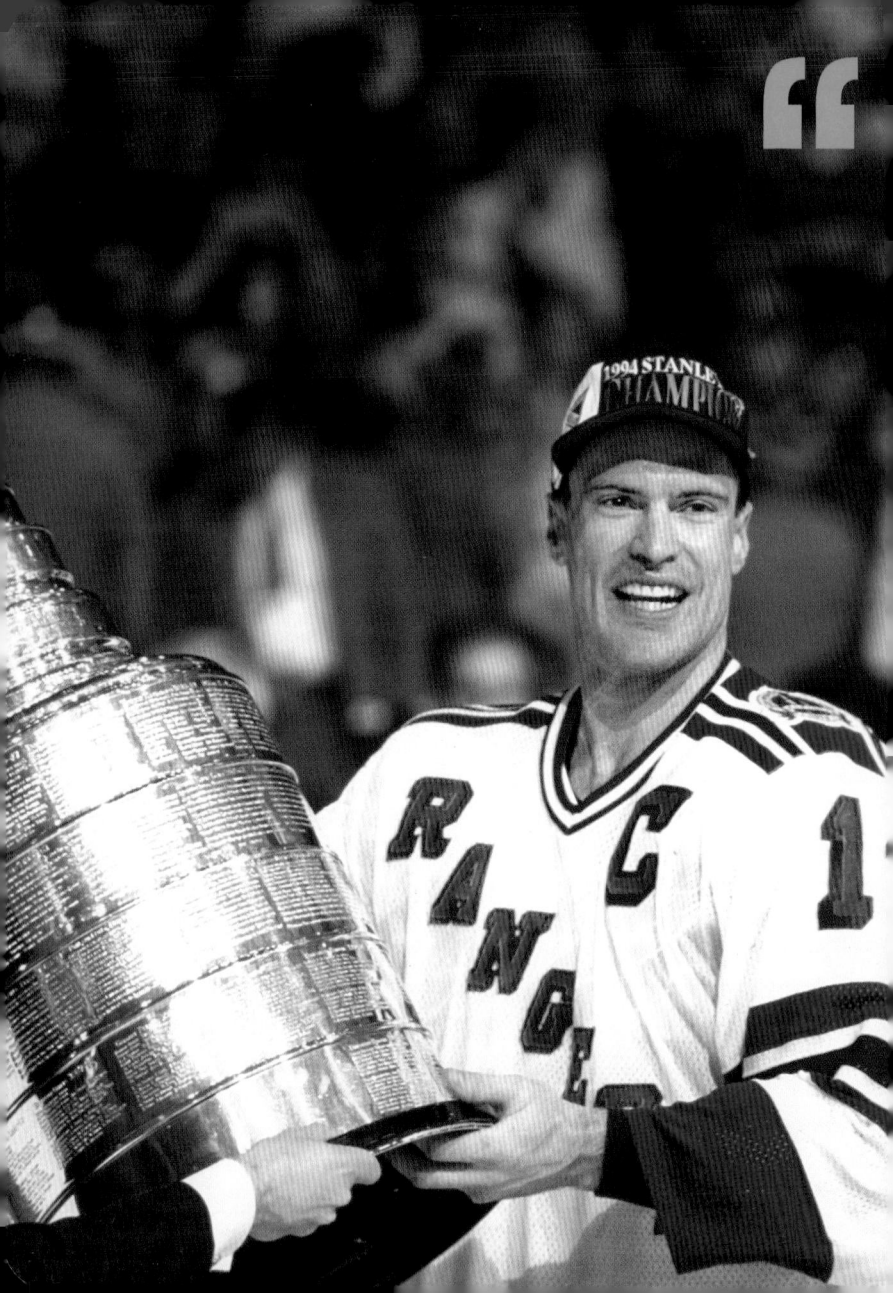

"I had the people and support from the president all the way down to the manager and coaches that shared in my belief, and together, we were part of something that hadn't been done in 54 years. It was an amazing time for us all."

Mark Messier

on winning the Cup with the Rangers

A
B
C
D
E
F
G
H
I
J
K
L
M
N
O
P
Q
R
S
T
U
V
W
X
Y
Z

Al MacInnis

HOCKEY HALL OF FAME CLASS: 2007

Retired by St. Louis

Alternates: 11, 22

Defense

Shoots: Right

Height: 6'-2"

Weight: 204 lbs.

Born: July 11, 1963: Inverness, Nova Scotia

Drafted by the Calgary Flames 15th overall in 1981

Played 23 NHL seasons from 1981–2004

QUICK FACTS

- Holds NHL record for most consecutive playoff games with at least one point by a defenseman (19), established from 1989–90

- Holds Calgary Flames team records for career assists (609), career playoff points (102), career playoff assists (77) and single playoff season points (31)

- Holds St. Louis Blues record for career points by a defenseman (450)

- First defenseman to lead NHL playoffs in points (31) in 1988–89

- Ranks third in NHL career shots-on-goal (5,157); ranks third in NHL career points by a defenseman (1,274)

- One of only five defensemen (with Bobby Orr, Paul Coffey, Brian Leetch and Denis Potvin) in NHL history to record more than 100 points in a season

- Played amateur hockey with Cole Harbour Wings (1978–79); Regina Blues (1979–80); Kitchener Rangers (1980–83)

- OHL First All-Star team Defense (1982, 1983)

- Won Hardest Shot Competition at the NHL All-Star Game (1991, 1992, 1997, 1998, 1999, 2000, 2003)

- Played minor pro hockey with Colorado Flames (1983–84)

> I can remember spending hours just shooting pucks off a sheet of plywood against my Dad's barn. I was just doing it to pass the time, never thinking it would end up the way it did and be known for the slap shot."

REGULAR SEASON

Season	Age	Team	Lg	GP	G	A	PTS	+/-	PIM	ESG	PPG	SHG	GWG	SOG	S%
1981–82	18	Calgary Flames	NHL	2	0	0	0	0	0	0	0	0	0	2	0.0
1982–83	19	Calgary Flames	NHL	14	1	3	4	0	9	1	0	0	0	7	14.3
1983–84	20	Calgary Flames	NHL	51	11	34	45	0	42	4	7	0	2	160	6.9
1984–85	21	Calgary Flames	NHL	67	14	52	66	7	75	6	8	0	0	259	5.4
1985–86	22	Calgary Flames	NHL	77	11	57	68	38	76	7	4	0	0	241	4.6
1986–87	23	Calgary Flames	NHL	79	20	56	76	20	97	13	7	0	2	262	7.6
1987–88	24	Calgary Flames	NHL	80	25	58	83	13	114	16	7	2	2	245	10.2
1988–89	25	Calgary Flames	NHL	79	16	58	74	38	136	8	8	0	3	277	5.8
1989–90	26	Calgary Flames	NHL	79	28	62	90	20	82	13	14	1	3	304	9.2
1990–91	27	Calgary Flames	NHL	78	28	75	103	42	90	11	17	0	1	305	9.2
1991–92	28	Calgary Flames	NHL	72	20	57	77	13	83	9	11	0	0	304	6.6
1992–93	29	Calgary Flames	NHL	50	11	43	54	15	61	4	7	0	4	201	5.5
1993–94	30	Calgary Flames	NHL	75	28	54	82	35	95	15	12	1	5	324	8.6
1994–95	31	St. Louis Blues	NHL	32	8	20	28	19	43	6	2	0	0	110	7.3
1995–96	32	St. Louis Blues	NHL	82	17	44	61	5	88	7	9	1	1	317	5.4
1996–97	33	St. Louis Blues	NHL	72	13	30	43	2	65	6	6	1	1	296	4.4
1997–98	34	St. Louis Blues	NHL	71	19	30	49	6	80	9	9	1	2	227	8.4
1998–99	35	St. Louis Blues	NHL	82	20	42	62	33	70	8	11	1	2	314	6.4
1999–00	36	St. Louis Blues	NHL	61	11	28	39	20	34	5	6	0	7	245	4.5
2000–01	37	St. Louis Blues	NHL	59	12	42	54	23	52	5	6	1	3	218	5.5
2001–02	38	St. Louis Blues	NHL	71	11	35	46	3	52	5	6	0	4	231	4.8
2002–03	39	St. Louis Blues	NHL	80	16	52	68	22	61	6	9	1	2	299	5.4
2003–04	40	St. Louis Blues	NHL	3	0	2	2	-1	6	0	0	0	0	9	0.0
NHL Career – 23 Seasons				1416	340	934	1274	373	1511	164	166	10	44	5157	6.6

PLAYOFFS

Season	Age	Team	Lg	GP	G	A	PTS	+/-	PIM	ESG	PPG	SHG	GWG	SOG	S%
1983–84	20	Calgary Flames	NHL	11	2	12	14	-1	13	0	2	0	1	39	5.1
1984–85	21	Calgary Flames	NHL	4	1	2	3	-1	8	0	1	0	0	13	7.7
1985–86	22	Calgary Flames	NHL	21	4	15	19	11	30	2	2	0	0	79	5.1
1986–87	23	Calgary Flames	NHL	4	1	0	1	-1	0	1	0	0	0	10	10.0
1987–88	24	Calgary Flames	NHL	7	3	6	9	0	18	1	2	0	0	28	10.7
1988–89	25	Calgary Flames	NHL	22	7	24	31	6	46	2	5	0	4	69	10.1
1989–90	26	Calgary Flames	NHL	6	2	3	5	1	8	1	1	0	0	19	10.5
1990–91	27	Calgary Flames	NHL	7	2	3	5	-5	8	0	2	0	0	25	8.0
1992–93	29	Calgary Flames	NHL	6	1	6	7	-4	10	0	1	0	0	25	4.0
1993–94	30	Calgary Flames	NHL	7	2	6	8	5	12	1	1	0	0	32	6.3
1994–95	31	St. Louis Blues	NHL	7	1	5	6	-3	10	1	0	0	0	22	4.5
1995–96	32	St. Louis Blues	NHL	13	3	4	7	2	20	2	1	0	0	48	6.3
1996–97	33	St. Louis Blues	NHL	6	1	2	3	-1	4	0	1	0	0	22	4.5
1997–98	34	St. Louis Blues	NHL	8	2	6	8	1	12	1	1	0	0	27	7.4
1998–99	35	St. Louis Blues	NHL	13	4	8	12	-2	20	2	2	0	0	66	6.1
1999–00	36	St. Louis Blues	NHL	7	1	3	4	-1	14	0	1	0	0	40	2.5
2000–01	37	St. Louis Blues	NHL	15	2	8	10	2	18	0	2	0	0	67	3.0
2001–02	38	St. Louis Blues	NHL	10	0	7	7	3	4	0	0	0	0	30	0.0
2002–03	39	St. Louis Blues	NHL	3	0	1	1	0	0	0	0	0	0	3	0.0
NHL Career – 19 Seasons				177	39	121	160	12	255	13	26	0	5	664	5.9

TROPHY CASE

AWARDS

Conn Smythe Trophy (1989)

James Norris Memorial Trophy (1999)

Stanley Cup (1988–89)

ALL-STAR SELECTIONS

First All-Star Team (1990, 1991, 1999, 2003)

Second All-Star Team (1987, 1989, 1994)

INTERNATIONAL AWARDS

Canada Cup (1991)

Gold Medal: Winter Olympics (2002)

9

Mickey MacKay
HOCKEY HALL OF FAME CLASS: 1952

Alternates:
5, 3, 6, 7, 12

Center

Shoots: Left

Height: 5'-9"

Weight: 162 lbs.

Born: May 25, 1894: Chelsey, Ontario

Died: May 21, 1940: Ymir, British Columbia

Played 16 elite amateur and professional seasons from 1914–30

QUICK FACTS

- Nicknamed "The Wee Scot"
- Played amateur hockey with Chelsey ACC (1910–12); Edmonton Dominions (1912–13); Grand Forks AC (1913–14)
- Led ASHL in playoff goals (8) in 1912–13; led BCBHL in goals (15) and points (15) in 1913–14
- Led PCHA in goals in 1914–15 (33), 1923–24 (21) and 1924–25 (27); led PCHA in assists (12) in 1921–22; led PCHA in goals in 1923–24 (21) and 1924–25 (27)
- Led PCHA playoffs in goals (2) and points (3) in 1916–17; led Stanley Cup tournament in points (10) in 1917–18; led PCHA playoffs in assists (3) in 1920–21
- Signed as a free agent by Vancouver Millionaires (PCHA), November 3, 1914

- Scored four goals and registered six points in the Vancouver Millionaires' Stanley Cup victory over the Ottawa Senators in March 1915
- Traded to Chicago by Vancouver (WHL) for cash, October 4, 1926; traded to Pittsburgh by Chicago for cash, September 1928; traded to Boston by Pittsburgh with $12,000 for Frank Fredrickson, December 21, 1928
- Scored 250 goals in 459 professional games between 1914 and 1930
- Inducted into British Columbia Sports Hall of Fame (1989); inducted into British Columbia Hockey Hall of Fame (2001)
- Suffered heart attack when his car crashed into a telephone pole while driving through the tiny mining community of Ymir, near Nelson, British Columbia

> He was perhaps the greatest center we ever had on the coast. MacKay was a great crowd pleaser. He was clean, splendidly courageous, a happy player with a stylish way of going. He was one of those who helped make pro hockey a great game. He was outstanding in every way."
> — Lester Patrick

REGULAR SEASON

Season	Age	Team	Lg	GP	G	A	PTS	PIM
1914–15	20	Vancouver Millionaires	PCHA	17	33	11	44	9
1915–16	21	Vancouver Millionaires	PCHA	14	12	7	19	32
1916–17	22	Vancouver Millionaires	PCHA	23	22	11	33	37
1917–18	23	Vancouver Millionaires	PCHA	18	10	8	18	31
1918–19	24	Vancouver Millionaires	PCHA	17	9	9	18	9
1919–20	25	Calgary Columbus Club	Big-4	11	4	6	10	14
1920–21	26	Vancouver Millionaires	PCHA	21	10	8	18	15
1921–22	27	Vancouver Millionaires	PCHA	24	14	12	26	20
1922–23	28	Vancouver Maroons	PCHA	30	28	12	40	38
1923–24	29	Vancouver Maroons	PCHA	28	21	4	25	2
1924–25	30	Vancouver Maroons	WCHL	28	27	6	33	17
1925–26	31	Vancouver Maroons	WHL	27	12	4	16	24
1926–27	32	Chicago Black Hawks	NHL	34	14	8	22	23
1927–28	33	Chicago Black Hawks	NHL	36	17	4	21	23
1928–29	34	Pittsburgh Pirates	NHL	10	1	0	1	2
1928–29	34	Boston Bruins	NHL	30	8	2	10	18
1929–30	35	Boston Bruins	NHL	37	4	5	9	13
Career — 16 Seasons				405	246	117	363	327

PLAYOFFS

Season	Age	Team	Lg	GP	G	A	PTS	PIM
1914–15	20	Vancouver Millionaires	St-Cup	3	4	2	6	9
1917–18	23	Vancouver Millionaires	PCHA	2	2	1	3	0
1917–18	23	Vancouver Millionaires	St-Cup	5	5	5	10	12
1920–21	26	Vancouver Millionaires	PCHA	2	0	3	3	0
1920–21	26	Vancouver Millionaires	St-Cup	5	0	1	1	0
1921–22	27	Vancouver Millionaires	PCHA	2	0	0	0	0
1921–22	27	Vancouver Millionaires	West-P	2	0	0	0	0
1921–22	27	Vancouver Millionaires	St-Cup	5	1	0	1	6
1922–23	28	Vancouver Maroons	PCHA	2	2	0	2	12
1922–23	28	Vancouver Maroons	St-Cup	4	1	0	1	4
1923–24	29	Vancouver Maroons	PCHA	2	1	0	1	0
1923–24	29	Vancouver Millionaires	West-P	3	2	0	2	2
1923–24	29	Vancouver Maroons	St-Cup	2	0	0	0	0
1926–27	32	Chicago Black Hawks	NHL	2	0	0	0	0
1928–29	34	Boston Bruins	NHL	3	0	0	0	2
1929–30	35	Boston Bruins	NHL	6	0	0	0	4
Career — 9 Seasons				50	18	12	30	51

TROPHY CASE

AWARDS

Stanley Cup (1914–15, 1928–29)

ALL-STAR SELECTIONS

PCHA First All-Star Team Center (1915, 1917, 1919, 1922, 1923)

PCHA Second All-Star Team Center (1916, 1918, 1921)

WCHL First All-Star Team Center (1925)

WHL First All-Star Team Center (1926)

27

Alternates: 26, 11	
Left Wing	
Shoots: Left	
Height: 6'	
Weight: 205 lbs.	
Born: January 10, 1938: Timmins, Ontario	
Played 22 NHL and WHA seasons from 1956–78	

" Detroit just opened everything up. It was like a piano had been lifted off my back. I finally felt like playing."
— Frank Mahovlich, commenting on his trade to Detroit

Frank Mahovlich

HOCKEY HALL OF FAME CLASS: 1981

QUICK FACTS

- Played amateur hockey with St. Michael's Majors (1953–57)
- Led OHA-Jr. in goals (52) in 1956–57
- Led NHL playoffs in penalty minutes (29) in 1961–62; led NHL playoffs in assists (11) in 1963–64; led NHL playoffs in goals (14) and points (27) in 1970–71
- Finished second in NHL in goals in 1960–61 (48), 1961–62 (33), 1965–66 (32) and 1968–69 (49)
- Played in NHL All-Star Game (1959, 1960, 1961, 1962, 1963, 1964, 1965, 1967, 1968, 1969, 1970, 1971, 1972, 1973, 1974)

- Known as "The Big M" because of his lanky frame and long, flowing skating style
- First former NHL player to be appointed to the Canadian Senate (1998)
- One of only six players in NHL history (with Dick Duff, Red Kelly, Bryan Trottier, Patrick Roy and Larry Murphy) to win two-or-more Stanley Cup championships with two-or-more teams
- Member of the all-WHA Team Canada '74 that played eight game summit series against the Soviet Union

"ALL MY HOCKEY SECRETS"

Mahovlich teaches listeners all the basics about hockey in this 1964 promotional LP distributed by Ford/ Mercury of Canada.

REGULAR SEASON

Season	Age	Team	Lg	GP	G	A	PTS	+/-	PIM	ESG	PPG	SHG	GWG	SOG	S%
1956–57	19	Toronto Maple Leafs	NHL	3	1	0	1		2						
1957–58	20	Toronto Maple Leafs	NHL	67	20	16	36		67						
1958–59	21	Toronto Maple Leafs	NHL	63	22	27	49		94						
1959–60	22	Toronto Maple Leafs	NHL	70	18	21	39		61						
1960–61	23	Toronto Maple Leafs	NHL	70	48	36	84		131						
1961–62	24	Toronto Maple Leafs	NHL	70	33	38	71		87						
1962–63	25	Toronto Maple Leafs	NHL	67	36	37	73		56						
1963–64	26	Toronto Maple Leafs	NHL	70	26	29	55		66	20	6	0	4		
1964–65	27	Toronto Maple Leafs	NHL	59	23	28	51		76	16	7	0	4		
1965–66	28	Toronto Maple Leafs	NHL	68	32	24	56		68	22	10	0	6		
1966–67	29	Toronto Maple Leafs	NHL	63	18	28	46		44	14	4	0	3		
1967–68	30	Toronto Maple Leafs	NHL	50	19	17	36	1	30	17	2	0	4	151	12.6
1967–68	30	Detroit Red Wings	NHL	13	7	9	16	3	2	7	0	0	1	39	17.9
1968–69	31	Detroit Red Wings	NHL	76	49	29	78	46	38	42	7	0	5	293	16.7
1969–70	32	Detroit Red Wings	NHL	74	38	32	70	16	59	22	15	1	5	251	15.1
1970–71	33	Detroit Red Wings	NHL	35	14	18	32	3	30	7	6	1	2	104	13.5
1970–71	33	Montreal Canadiens	NHL	38	17	24	41	4	11	12	4	1	2	100	17.0
1971–72	34	Montreal Canadiens	NHL	76	43	53	96	42	36	25	14	4	4	261	16.5
1972–73	35	Montreal Canadiens	NHL	78	38	55	93	42	51	28	8	2	5	242	15.7
1973–74	36	Montreal Canadiens	NHL	71	31	49	80	16	47	21	8	2	3	221	14.0
1974–75	37	Toronto Toros	WHA	73	38	44	82	8	27	30	8	0		268	14.2
1975–76	38	Toronto Toros	WHA	75	34	55	89	-16	14	27	6	1	1	239	14.2
1976–77	39	Birmingham Bulls	WHA	17	3	20	23	-1	12	1	2	0		45	6.7
1977–78	40	Birmingham Bulls	WHA	72	14	24	38	-5	22	8	6	0		125	11.2
Career — 22 Seasons				1418	622	713	1335	159	1131	319	113	12	49	2339	14.7

PLAYOFFS

Season	Age	Team	Lg	GP	G	A	PTS	+/-	PIM	ESG	PPG	SHG	GWG	SOG	S%
1958–59	21	Toronto Maple Leafs	NHL	12	6	5	11		18						
1959–60	22	Toronto Maple Leafs	NHL	10	3	1	4		27						
1960–61	23	Toronto Maple Leafs	NHL	5	1	1	2		6						
1961–62	24	Toronto Maple Leafs	NHL	12	6	6	12		29						
1962–63	25	Toronto Maple Leafs	NHL	9	0	2	2		8						
1963–64	26	Toronto Maple Leafs	NHL	14	4	11	15		20						
1964–65	27	Toronto Maple Leafs	NHL	6	0	3	3		9						
1965–66	28	Toronto Maple Leafs	NHL	4	1	0	1		10						
1966–67	29	Toronto Maple Leafs	NHL	12	3	7	10		8						
1969–70	32	Detroit Red Wings	NHL	4	0	0	0		2	0	0	0	0		
1970–71	33	Montreal Canadiens	NHL	20	14	13	27		18	11	3	0	0		
1971–72	34	Montreal Canadiens	NHL	6	3	2	5		2	2	1	0	0		
1972–73	35	Montreal Canadiens	NHL	17	9	14	23		6	8	1	0	0		
1973–74	36	Montreal Canadiens	NHL	6	1	2	3		0	1	0	0	0		
1974–75	37	Toronto Toros	WHA	6	3	0	3		2				0		
1977–78	40	Birmingham Bulls	WHA	3	1	1	2	2	0				0		
Career — 16 Seasons				146	55	68	123	2	165	22	5	0	0		

TROPHY CASE

AWARDS

Calder Memorial Trophy (1958)

Stanley Cup (1961–62, 1962–63, 1963–64, 1967–68, 1970–71, 1972–73)

ALL-STAR SELECTIONS

First All-Star Team Left Wing (1961, 1963, 1973)

Second All-Star Team Left Wing (1962, 1964, 1965, 1966, 1969, 1970)

INTERNATIONAL AWARDS

Summit Series (1972)

Joe Malone

HOCKEY HALL OF FAME CLASS: 1950

Alternates: 7, 11, 9

Center/Left Wing

Shoots: Left

Height: 5'-10"

Weight: 150 lbs.

Born: February 28, 1890: Quebec City, Quebec

Died: May 15, 1969: Montreal, Quebec

Played 15 professional seasons from 1909–24

QUICK FACTS

- Holds NHL record for goals in a single game (7), established in Quebec's 10–6 victory over Toronto Arenas, January 31, 1920

- Held NHL record for most goals in regular season (44) from 1917–18 to 1944–45; surpassed by Maurice Richard (50), February 25, 1945

- Held NHL record for most points in regular season (49) from 1919–20 to 1927–28; surpassed by Howie Morenz (59) in 1927–28

- Only player in NHL history to score six-or-more goals in a single game twice (seven goals against Toronto, January 31, 1920; six goals against Ottawa, March 10, 1920)

- Led NHA in goals (43) and points (43) in 1912–13; goals (41) and points (49) in 1916–17

- Led NHL in goals (44) and points (48) in 1917–18; goals (39) and points (49) in 1919–20

- Nicknamed "The Phantom" because of his ability to find openings and "invisibly" weave his way through the opposition defenses

- Played amateur hockey with Quebec Crescents (1907–08); Quebec Bulldogs (1908–10)

- Signed as a free agent by Waterloo (OPHL), January 20, 1910

- Scored nine goals for Quebec Bulldogs in 14–3 Stanley Cup playoff win over Sydney Millionaires on March 8, 1913

- Served as captain of the Quebec Bulldogs (1910–17)

- Served as player/coach of the Hamilton Bulldogs (1920–22)

> In my day, there was no trophy, no bonus, no prize of any kind for leading the league. They didn't even count assists. Now the winner gets a fine cup and $1,000. That's more money than I ever made in a season."
> — Joe Malone, 1961

REGULAR SEASON

Season	Age	Team	Lg	GP	G	A	PTS	PIM
1909–10	19	Quebec Bulldogs	CHA	3	5	0	5	2
1909–10	19	Waterloo Colts	OPHL	12	10	0	10	16
1910–11	20	Quebec Bulldogs	NHA	13	9	0	9	3
1911–12	21	Quebec Bulldogs	NHA	18	21	0	21	0
1912–13	22	Quebec Bulldogs	NHA	20	43	0	43	34
1913–14	23	Quebec Bulldogs	NHA	17	24	4	28	20
1914–15	24	Quebec Bulldogs	NHA	12	16	5	21	21
1915–16	25	Quebec Bulldogs	NHA	24	25	10	35	21
1916–17	26	Quebec Bulldogs	NHA	19	41	8	49	15
1917–18	27	Montreal Canadiens	NHL	20	44	4	48	30
1918–19	28	Montreal Canadiens	NHL	8	7	2	9	3
1919–20	29	Quebec Bulldogs	NHL	24	39	10	49	12
1920–21	30	Hamilton Tigers	NHL	20	28	9	37	6
1921–22	31	Hamilton Tigers	NHL	24	24	7	31	4
1922–23	32	Montreal Canadiens	NHL	20	1	0	1	2
1923–24	33	Montreal Canadiens	NHL	10	0	0	0	0
Career — 15 Seasons				264	337	59	396	189

PLAYOFFS

Season	Age	Team	Lg	GP	G	A	PTS	PIM
1911–12	21	Quebec Bulldogs	St-Cup	2	5	0	5	0
1912–13	22	Quebec Bulldogs	St-Cup	1	9	0	9	0
1917–18	27	Montreal Canadiens	NHL	2	1	0	1	3
1918–19	28	Montreal Canadiens	NHL	5	5	2	7	3
1922–23	32	Montreal Canadiens	NHL	2	0	0	0	0
Career — 5 Seasons				12	20	2	22	6

TROPHY CASE

AWARDS

NHL Scoring Leader (1918, 1920)

Stanley Cup: (1911–12, 1912–13, 1923–24)

Sylvio Mantha

HOCKEY HALL OF FAME CLASS: 1960

Alternate: 8

Defense

Shoots: Right

Height: 5'-10"

Weight: 178 lbs.

Born: April 14, 1902: Montreal, Quebec

Died: August 7, 1974: Montreal, Quebec

Played 14 NHL seasons from 1923–37

QUICK FACTS

- Played amateur hockey with the Notre Dame de Grace (1918–19), Verdun HC (1919–20); Montreal Imperial Tobacco (1920–21); Montreal Northern Electric (1921–22); Montreal Nationales (1922–23)

- Signed as free agent by Montreal Canadiens, December 3, 1923

- Member of the Stanley Cup-winning Montreal Canadiens team that "forgot" the Stanley Cup in a snow bank while changing a flat tire on the team car following a victory reception at the University of Montreal, March 27, 1924

- Scored first goal in history of Boston Garden in Montreal Canadiens' 1–0 victory over Boston Bruins, November 20, 1928

- Missed only 10 games in his first 10 NHL seasons

- Signed as free agent by Boston, February 11, 1937

- Worked as a linesman and referee for the AHL and NHL

- Coached Montreal Canadiens (1935–36)

- Coached Montreal Concordias (1938–39); Laval Nationales (1943–45); Verdun Maple Leafs (1945–47) and St. Jerome Eagles (1947–48)

- After retirement, operated dairy businesses in Ontario and Quebec. Elected member of the Canadian Commodity Exchange in June of 1938

- The Georges and Sylvio Mantha Arenas are part of the Complexe Récréatif Gadbois in Montreal and were dedicated to honor him and his brother, Georges Mantha

> " I think I can relate to players because I've been through the process. I've been sent down to the minors, I've been put on waivers, I've been claimed on waivers, I've been traded, I've played for different coaches and had to learn different styles."
>
> — Sylvio Mantha, commenting on his qualifications as coach

REGULAR SEASON

Season	Age	Team	Lg	GP	G	A	PTS	PIM
1923–24	21	Montreal Canadiens	NHL	24	1	3	4	11
1924–25	22	Montreal Canadiens	NHL	30	2	3	5	18
1925–26	23	Montreal Canadiens	NHL	34	2	1	3	66
1926–27	24	Montreal Canadiens	NHL	43	10	5	15	77
1927–28	25	Montreal Canadiens	NHL	43	4	11	15	61
1928–29	26	Montreal Canadiens	NHL	44	9	4	13	56
1929–30	27	Montreal Canadiens	NHL	44	13	11	24	108
1930–31	28	Montreal Canadiens	NHL	44	4	7	11	75
1931–32	29	Montreal Canadiens	NHL	47	5	5	10	62
1932–33	30	Montreal Canadiens	NHL	48	4	7	11	50
1933–34	31	Montreal Canadiens	NHL	48	4	6	10	24
1934–35	32	Montreal Canadiens	NHL	47	3	11	14	36
1935–36	33	Montreal Canadiens	NHL	42	2	4	6	25
1936–37	34	Boston Bruins	NHL	4	0	0	0	2
Career – 14 Seasons				542	63	78	141	671

PLAYOFFS

Season	Age	Team	Lg	GP	G	A	PTS	PIM
1923–24	21	Montreal Canadiens	NHL	2	0	0	0	0
1923–24	21	Montreal Canadiens	St-Cup	4	0	0	0	0
1924–25	22	Montreal Canadiens	NHL	2	0	1	1	0
1924–25	22	Montreal Canadiens	St-Cup	4	0	0	0	2
1926–27	24	Montreal Canadiens	NHL	4	1	0	1	0
1927–28	25	Montreal Canadiens	NHL	2	0	0	0	6
1928–29	26	Montreal Canadiens	NHL	3	0	0	0	0
1929–30	27	Montreal Canadiens	NHL	6	2	1	3	18
1930–31	28	Montreal Canadiens	NHL	10	2	1	3	26
1931–32	29	Montreal Canadiens	NHL	4	0	1	1	8
1932–33	30	Montreal Canadiens	NHL	2	0	1	1	2
1933–34	31	Montreal Canadiens	NHL	2	0	0	0	2
1934–35	32	Montreal Canadiens	NHL	2	0	0	0	2
Career – 11 Seasons				47	5	5	10	66

TROPHY CASE

AWARDS

Stanley Cup (1923–24, 1929–30, 1930–31)

ALL-STAR SELECTIONS

Second All-Star Team Defense (1931, 1932)

8

Jack Marshall

HOCKEY HALL OF FAME CLASS: 1965

Alternates: 3, 7

Center/Defense

Shoots: Right

Height: 5'-9"

Weight: 160 lbs.

Born: March 14, 1877: Saint-Vallier, Quebec

Died: August 7, 1965: Montreal, Quebec

Played 16 elite amateur and professional seasons from 1900–05, 1906–17

QUICK FACTS

- Only player in hockey history to win the Stanley Cup with four different teams (Winnipeg, Montreal AAA, Montreal Wanderers, Toronto Blueshirts)

- Played amateur hockey with Montreal Pointe Charles (1894–98)

- Renowned as all-around athlete who also starred at football, soccer, baseball, lacrosse and bowling

- Born in Quebec and raised in Montreal, he first came to prominence in hockey in Winnipeg

- Member of Stanley Cup-winning Winnipeg Victorias team that defeated Montreal Shamrocks in January of 1901

- Scored Stanley Cup-winning goal in Montreal AAA's 2–1 victory over Winnipeg Victorias, March 17, 1903

- Led FAHL in goals in 1903–04 (11) and 1904–05 (17)

- Won Stanley Cup as forward with the Montreal Wanderers (1906–07)

- Won Stanley Cup as a defenseman with the Montreal Wanderers (1909–10)

- Served as player/coach of Stanley Cup-winning Toronto Blueshirts (1913–14)

- Retired to serve as NHA referee (1916–17)

- Coached Montreal AAA (1919–23); coached Montreal British Consols (1924–25)

- Played exhibition season with Toronto Pros in 1905–06

> I knew the boys could do it and they played with every ounce that was in them. It was a rough, hard-checking contest from start to finish, but we were always going strong and I was sure that we would make it three straight."
> — Jack Marshall, on Toronto's 1914 Stanley Cup victory

REGULAR SEASON

Season	Age	Team	Lg	GP	G	A	PTS	PIM
1900–01	23	Winnipeg Victorias	WSrHL	2	2	0	2	
1901–02	24	Montreal AAA	CAHL	8	11	0	11	8
1902–03	25	Montreal AAA	CAHL	2	8	0	8	3
1903–04	26	Montreal Wanderers	FAHL	4	11	0	11	6
1904–05	27	Montreal Wanderers	FAHL	8	17	0	17	9
1906–07	29	Ottawa Montagnards	FAHL	3	6	0	6	
1906–07	29	Montreal Wanderers	ECAHA	3	6	0	6	0
1907–08	30	Montreal Shamrocks	ECAHA	9	20	0	20	13
1908–09	31	Montreal Shamrocks	ECHA	12	10	0	10	14
1909–10	32	Montreal Wanderers	NHA	12	2	0	2	8
1910–11	33	Montreal Wanderers	NHA	5	1	0	1	2
1911–12	34	Montreal Wanderers	NHA	3	0	0	0	0
1912–13	35	Toronto Blueshirts	NHA	13	3	0	3	8
1913–14	36	Toronto Blueshirts	NHA	20	3	3	6	16
1914–15	37	Toronto Blueshirts	NHA	4	0	1	1	8
1915–16	38	Montreal Wanderers	NHA	15	1	0	1	2
1916–17	39	Montreal Wanderers	NHA	8	0	0	0	3
Career — 16 Seasons				131	101	4	105	102

PLAYOFFS

Season	Age	Team	Lg	GP	G	A	PTS	PIM
1900–01	23	Winnipeg Victorias	St-Cup	2	0	0	0	
1901–02	24	Montreal AAA	St-Cup	3	2	0	2	8
1902–03	25	Montreal AAA	St-Cup	4	7	0	7	2
1903–04	26	Montreal Wanderers	St-Cup	1	1	0	1	0
1906–07	29	Montreal Wanderers	St-Cup	1	1	0	1	0
1909–10	32	Montreal Wanderers	St-Cup	1	0	0	0	0
1913–14	36	Toronto Blueshirts	NHA	2	0	0	0	0
1913–14	36	Toronto Blueshirts	St-Cup	3	1	0	1	2
Career — 7 Seasons				17	12	0	12	12

TROPHY CASE

AWARDS

Stanley Cup (1900–01, 1901–02, 1902–03, 1906–07, 1909–10, 1913–14)

Fred Maxwell

Rover

Shoots: Unknown

Height: Unknown

Weight: 135 lbs.

Born: May 19, 1890: Winnipeg, Manitoba

Died: September 11, 1975: Winnipeg, Manitoba

Played six elite amateur seasons from 1909–15

QUICK FACTS

- Earned nickname "Steamer" because of his tremendous speed
- Offered $1,500 to turn pro with the Toronto Blueshirts of the National Hockey Association in 1913 and $1,800 to join the PCHA in 1914 but preferred to remain in Winnipeg as an amateur
- Member of Manitoba champion Winnipeg Monarchs (1913–14, 1914–15)
- Member of Allan Cup-winning Winnipeg Monarchs (1914–15) that defeated the Melville Millionaires 7–6 in two-game, total-goal series
- Coached Allan Cup-winning Winnipeg Falcons (1919–20) that represented Canada at Spring Sports Festival during 1920 Antwerp (Summer) Olympics
- Coached Elmwood Millionaires (1929–31); coached Winnipeg Winnipegs (1932–33)
- Coached Winnipeg Monarchs to gold medal victory at 1935 World Championships in Davos, Switzerland
- Continued to coach at both the amateur and professional levels and won several more Manitoba championships in the 1920s and 1930s
- Served as a referee during Memorial Cup and Allan Cup playoffs in the west and in exhibition games for the top professional leagues
- Won eight Winnipeg City League baseball championships between 1908 and 1923 as a player, manager and general manager with the Arena Baseball Club
- MHL-Sr. Second All-Star Team Rover (1911)

> "Although Bert Andrews played a mighty fine game last night, our old friend Steamer Maxwell gave an exhibition of back-checking and all-around skating which was a treat to witness. Steamer ... has made a name for himself that even the mighty Bert will have to travel to equal."
> — *Manitoba Free Press*, February 13, 1914

REGULAR SEASON

Season	Age	Team	Lg	GP	G	A	PTS	PIM
1909–10	19	Winnipeg Winnipegs	MHL-Sr.	1	0	0	0	0
1910–11	20	Winnipeg Monarchs	MHL-Sr.	5	6	0	6	
1911–12	21	Winnipeg Monarchs	MHL-Sr.	8	7	0	7	
1912–13	22	Winnipeg Monarchs	MHL-Sr.	8	2	0	2	
1913–14	23	Winnipeg Monarchs	MHL-Sr.	8	3	2	5	6
1914–15	24	Winnipeg Monarchs	WSrHL	7	3	2	5	22
Career — 6 Seasons				37	21	4	25	28

PLAYOFFS

Season	Age	Team	Lg	GP	G	A	PTS	PIM
1913–14	23	Winnipeg Monarchs	Al-Cup	2	1	0	1	6
1914–15	24	Winnipeg Monarchs	WSrHL	1	1	0	1	6
Career — 2 Seasons				3	2	0	2	12

TROPHY CASE

Lanny McDonald
HOCKEY HALL OF FAME CLASS: 1992

9

Retired by Calgary

Alternate: 7

Right Wing

Shoots: Right

Height: 6'

Weight: 185 lbs.

Born: February 16, 1953: Hanna, Alberta

Drafted by the Toronto Maple Leafs fourth overall in 1973

Played 16 NHL seasons from 1973–89

QUICK FACTS

- Played amateur hockey with Lethbridge Sugar Kings (1969–71); Calgary Centennials (1970–71); Medicine Hat Tigers (1971–73)
- Named AJHL Most Valuable Player (1971); AJHL Second All-Star Team Right Wing (1971)
- Led WCWJHL in playoff goals (18) in 1972–73; WJCHL First All-Star Team Right Wing (1973)
- Holds Calgary Flames' team record for goals in regular season (66), established in 1982–83
- Played in NHL All-Star Game (1977, 1978, 1983, 1984)
- Led NHL in power-play goals (16) in 1976–77; led NHL in even strength goals (49) in 1982–83
- Finished among NHL top-5 in goals in 1976–77 (46), 1977–78 (47) and 1982–83 (66); finished among NHL top-5 in shots-on-goal in 1978–79 (314) and 1979–80 (334); finished among NHL top-5 in short-handed goals in 1975–76 (3) and 1976–77 (4)
- Considered iconic because of his distinctive moustache, his middle name (King) is a tribute Maple Leaf great King Clancy; Inaugural winner of NHL's King Clancy Memorial Trophy (1988)
- Registered 1,000th career NHL point in Calgary's 9–5 victory over Winnipeg Jets, March 19, 1988; recorded 500th career NHL goal in Calgary's 4–1 victory over N.Y. Islanders, March 21, 1989
- Scored series-winning overtime goal in Game 7 of Toronto's 2–1 victory over N.Y. Islanders, April 21, 1978

> My Mom and Dad drove me into Hanna to play hockey. It was so much fun playing the game that not only my father had played, but that my older brother played as well. It was a great way to grow up."

REGULAR SEASON

Season	Age	Team	Lg	GP	G	A	PTS	+/-	PIM	ESG	PPG	SHG	GWG	SOG	S%
1973–74	20	Toronto Maple Leafs	NHL	70	14	16	30	3	43	12	2	0	3	142	9.9
1974–75	21	Toronto Maple Leafs	NHL	64	17	27	44	5	86	14	2	1	1	168	10.1
1975–76	22	Toronto Maple Leafs	NHL	75	37	56	93	24	70	26	6	5	4	270	13.7
1976–77	23	Toronto Maple Leafs	NHL	80	46	44	90	12	77	26	16	4	5	293	15.7
1977–78	24	Toronto Maple Leafs	NHL	74	47	40	87	34	54	36	11	0	5	243	19.3
1978–79	25	Toronto Maple Leafs	NHL	79	43	42	85	12	32	27	16	0	2	314	13.7
1979–80	26	Toronto Maple Leafs	NHL	35	15	15	30	-1	10	9	6	0	2	140	10.7
1979–80	26	Colorado Rockies	NHL	46	25	20	45	-15	43	17	8	0	3	194	12.9
1980–81	27	Colorado Rockies	NHL	80	35	46	81	-27	56	24	11	0	2	298	11.7
1981–82	28	Colorado Rockies	NHL	16	6	9	15	-3	20	6	0	0	1	65	9.2
1981–82	28	Calgary Flames	NHL	55	34	33	67	22	37	23	10	1	3	178	19.1
1982–83	29	Calgary Flames	NHL	80	66	32	98	-2	90	49	17	0	8	272	24.3
1983–84	30	Calgary Flames	NHL	65	33	33	66	-15	64	23	10	0	1	245	13.5
1984–85	31	Calgary Flames	NHL	43	19	18	37	-4	36	10	9	0	2	117	16.2
1985–86	32	Calgary Flames	NHL	80	28	43	71	-2	44	17	11	0	3	227	12.3
1986–87	33	Calgary Flames	NHL	58	14	12	26	-3	54	10	4	0	3	127	11.0
1987–88	34	Calgary Flames	NHL	60	10	13	23	2	57	10	0	0	2	79	12.7
1988–89	35	Calgary Flames	NHL	51	11	7	18	-1	26	11	0	0	3	72	15.3
NHL Career — 16 Seasons				1111	500	506	1006	41	899	350	139	11	53	3444	14.5

PLAYOFFS

Season	Age	Team	Lg	GP	G	A	PTS	+/-	PIM	ESG	PPG	SHG	GWG	SOG	S%
1974–75	21	Toronto Maple Leafs	NHL	7	0	0	0		2	0	0	0	0		
1975–76	22	Toronto Maple Leafs	NHL	10	4	4	8		4	2	2	0	1		
1976–77	23	Toronto Maple Leafs	NHL	9	10	7	17		6	7	3	0	1		
1977–78	24	Toronto Maple Leafs	NHL	13	3	4	7		10	2	1	0	2		
1978–79	25	Toronto Maple Leafs	NHL	6	3	2	5		0	3	0	0	0		
1981–82	28	Calgary Flames	NHL	3	0	1	1		6	0	0	0	0		
1982–83	29	Calgary Flames	NHL	7	3	4	7		19	2	1	0	0		
1983–84	30	Calgary Flames	NHL	11	6	7	13	-2	6	3	3	0	1	31	19.4
1984–85	31	Calgary Flames	NHL	1	0	0	0	0	0	0	0	0	0	1	0.0
1985–86	32	Calgary Flames	NHL	22	11	7	18	5	30	7	4	0	2	70	15.7
1986–87	33	Calgary Flames	NHL	5	0	0	0	-3	2	0	0	0	0	7	0.0
1987–88	34	Calgary Flames	NHL	9	3	1	4	3	6	3	0	0	0	17	17.6
1988–89	35	Calgary Flames	NHL	14	1	3	4	2	29	1	0	0	0	13	7.7
NHL Career — 13 Seasons				117	44	40	84	5	120	30	14	0	7	139	15.1

TROPHY CASE

AWARDS

Bill Masterton Memorial Trophy (1983)

King Clancy Memorial Trophy (1988)

Stanley Cup (1988–89)

ALL-STAR SELECTIONS

Second All-Star Team Right Wing (1977, 1983)

INTERNATIONAL AWARDS

Canada Cup (1976)

Frank McGee

HOCKEY HALL OF FAME CLASS: 1945

Center

Shoots: Right

Height: 5'-6"

Weight: 150 lbs.

Born: November 4, 1880: Ottawa, Ontario

Died: September 16, 1916: Killed in action, Courcelette, France

Played seven elite amateur seasons from 1899–1906

QUICK FACTS

- Played amateur hockey with Ottawa Secords (1899–00); Ottawa Aberdeens (1900–02)

- Holds Stanley Cup playoff record for goals in a single game (14), established in Ottawa's 23–2 victory over Dawson City Nuggets, January 16, 1905

- Nicknamed "One Eyed Frank McGee" after losing sight in left eye when struck by a puck in game against Hawkesbury, March 21, 1900

- Shared FAHL goals scoring lead (17) with future Hall of Fame member Jack Marshall (1904–05)

- Scored Stanley Cup-winning goal in Ottawa's 5–4 victory over Rat Portage Thistles while playing with a broken wrist, March 11, 1905

- Finished third in the ECAHA scoring (28 goals) behind teammate Harry Smith (brother of Hall of Fame members Alf and Tommy Smith) and future Hall of Fame member Dubbie Bowie in 1905–06

- Scored eight goals versus the Montreal Wanderers in an ECAHA league game on March 3, 1906

- Member of prominent Ottawa family — his father (John Joseph McGee) was Clerk of the Privy Council (Canada's highest-ranking civil servant) and his uncle (Thomas D'Arcy McGee) was a "Father of Confederation" who was assassinated in 1868

- Killed in combat while serving in the Canadian Army during World War I

> He was even better than they say he was. He had everything — speed, stick-handling, scoring ability and was a punishing checker. He was strongly built but beautifully proportioned and he had an almost animal rhythm.
> — Hockey Hall of Fame builder Frank Patrick

REGULAR SEASON

Season	Age	Team	Lg	GP	G	A	PTS	PIM
1899–00	19	Ottawa Seconds	CAIHL					
1900–01	20	Ottawa Aberdeens	OCJHL					
1901–02	21	Ottawa Aberdeens	CAIHL					
1902–03	22	Ottawa Silver Seven	CAHL	6	14	0	14	9
1903–04	23	Ottawa Silver Seven	CAHL	4	12	0	12	9
1904–05	24	Ottawa Silver Seven	FAHL	6	17	0	17	14
1905–06	25	Ottawa Silver Seven	ECAHA	7	28	0	28	18
Career – 7 Seasons				23	71	0	71	50

PLAYOFFS

Season	Age	Team	Lg	GP	G	A	PTS	PIM
1902–03	22	Ottawa Silver Seven	CAHL	2	3	0	3	3
1902–03	22	Ottawa Silver Seven	St-Cup	2	4	0	4	
1903–04	23	Ottawa Silver Seven	St-Cup	8	21	0	21	
1904–05	24	Ottawa Silver Seven	St-Cup	4	18	0	18	
1905–06	25	Ottawa Silver Seven	ECAHA	2	2	0	2	9
1905–06	25	Ottawa Silver Seven	St-Cup	4	16	0	16	6
Career – 4 Seasons				22	64	0	64	18

TROPHY CASE

AWARDS

Stanley Cup (1902–03, 1903–04, 1904–05, 1905–06)

Billy McGimsie

HOCKEY HALL OF FAME CLASS: 1962

Center

Shoots: Left

Height: 5'-8"

Weight: 145 lbs.

Born: June 7, 1880:
Woodsville, Ontario

Died: October 28,
1968: Unknown

Played six elite
amateur seasons
from 1901–07

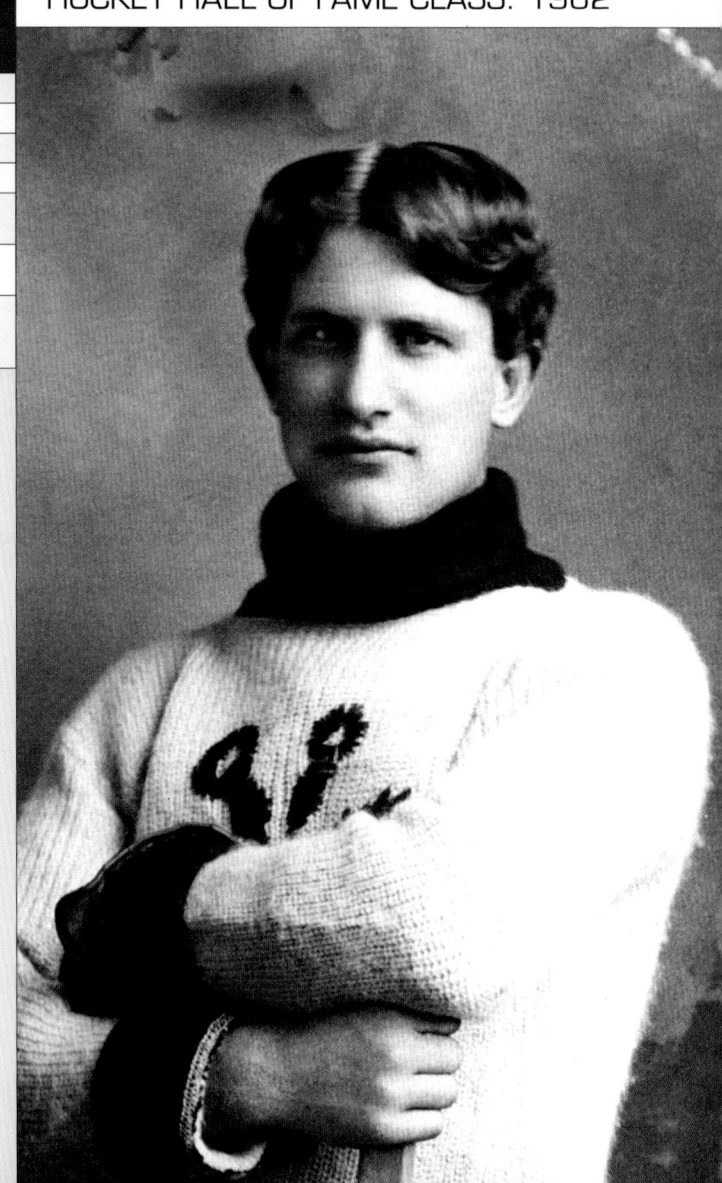

+1962 Punch Broadbent, Harry Cameron, Rusty Crawford, Jack Darragh, Jimmy Gardner, Billy Gilmour, Shorty Green, Riley Hern, Tom Hooper, Bouse Hutton, Harry Hyland, Jack Laviolette, Fred Maxwell, Reg Noble, Didier Pitre, Jack Ruttan, Sweeney Schriner, Joe Simpson, Alf Smith, Barney Stanley, Nels Stewart, Marty Walsh, Harry E. Watson, Harry Westwick, Fred Whitcroft, Phat Wilson

QUICK FACTS

- Family moved to Rat Portage (Kenora) when he was one year old and he grew up to star on local school and junior teams with future Hall of Fame members Tommy Phillips, Si Griffis and Tom Hooper
- Member of Manitoba champion Rat Portage Thistles (1902–03)
- Member of Rat Portage Thistles that lost Stanley Cup challenge to Ottawa "Silver Seven" (1902–03, 1904–05)
- Led the Manitoba and North West Hockey League in goals (28) in 1904–05
- Member of Manitoba champion Kenora Thistles (1905–06)
- Finished third in scoring (21 goals) in the Manitoba Hockey League (1905–06)

- Scored goal in Kenora's 8–6 victory over the Montreal Wanderers that helped clinch Stanley Cup championship, January 21, 1907
- Suffered dislocated shoulder during an exhibition game in Ottawa following Kenora's Stanley Cup victory and never played again
- Coached Fort Williams Forts (1910–11)

> My ambition when I started was to play on a winning Stanley Cup team, and I had three cracks at it."

REGULAR SEASON

Season	Age	Team	Lg	GP	G	A	PTS	PIM
1901–02	21	Rat Portage Thistles	MNWHA-Int	4	8	0	8	0
1902–03	22	Rat Portage Thistles	MNWHA	4	10	0	10	
1903–04	23	Rat Portage Thistles	MNWHA	11	14	2	16	
1904–05	24	Rat Portage Thistles	MHL	8	28	0	28	3
1905–06	25	Kenora Thistles	MHL	9	21	0	21	
1906–07	26	Kenora Thistles	MHL-Pro	2	2	0	2	
Career — 6 Seasons				38	83	2	85	3

PLAYOFFS

Season	Age	Team	Lg	GP	G	A	PTS	PIM
1902–03	22	Rat Portage Thistles	St-Cup	2	3	0	3	
1904–05	24	Rat Portage Thistles	St-Cup	3	0	0	0	
1906–07	26	Kenora Thistles	St-Cup	2	1	0	1	8
Career — 3 Seasons				7	4	0	4	8

TROPHY CASE

AWARDS

Stanley Cup (1906–07)

George McNamara
HOCKEY HALL OF FAME CLASS: 1958

Alternate: 4

Defense

Shoots: Left

Height: 6'-1"

Weight: 220 lbs.

Born: August 26, 1886: Penetanguishene, Ontario

Died: March 10, 1952: Miami, Florida

Played 10 professional seasons from 1906–09, 1910–17

QUICK FACTS

- Played amateur hockey with Sault Ste. Marie Monarchs (1904–06)

- Renowned as a rugged, hard-checking defenseman who was often paired with brother Howard throughout his hockey career

- The McNamara Brothers were known as "The Dynamite Twins" despite being born three years apart

- A third brother — Harold — was often teamed with the "Twins"

- Signed as a free agent by Toronto Tecumsehs, December 12, 1912; traded to Toronto Blueshirts by Toronto Ontarios for cash, January 12, 1914

- Member of Stanley Cup-winning Toronto Blueshirts (1913–14)

- Enlisted in the Canadian army during Word War I and played with the 228th Battalion team that began the 1916–17 season playing in the NHA before being sent overseas

- Credited with naming Sault Ste. Marie team the "Greyhounds" because a "greyhound is much faster than a wolf" in reference to local rivals, the Sudbury Wolves

- Coached Sault Ste. Marie Greyhounds (1920–26)

- Coached Allan Cup-winning Sault Ste. Marie Greyhounds (1924)

- Coached Detroit Greyhounds (1926–27)

- Served on Ontario Athletic Commission (1941–45)

> The McNamara brothers checked well ... In the second period, George McNamara got away for one of his rushes. He bore well in past the Wanderers' defense and scored the winning goal."
> — *Toronto World*, February 10, 1913

REGULAR SEASON

Season	Age	Team	Lg	GP	G	A	PTS	PIM
1906–07	20	Canadian Soo	IHL	3	0	0	0	0
1907–08	21	Montreal Shamrocks	ECAHA	10	3	0	3	34
1908–09	22	Montreal Shamrocks	ECHA	12	4	0	4	60
1910–11	24	Waterloo Colts	OPHL	16	15	0	15	
1911–12	25	Halifax Crescents	MPHL	10	2	0	2	24
1912–13	26	Toronto Tecumsehs	NHA	20	4	0	4	23
1913–14	27	Toronto Ontarios	NHA	9	0	1	1	0
1913–14	27	Toronto Blueshirts	NHA	9	0	1	1	2
1914–15	28	Toronto Shamrocks	NHA	18	4	8	12	67
1915–16	29	Toronto Blueshirts	NHA	23	5	2	7	74
1916–17	30	Toronto 228th Battalion	NHA	11	2	1	3	15
Career — 10 Seasons				141	39	13	52	299

PLAYOFFS

Season	Age	Team	Lg	GP	G	A	PTS	PIM
1910–11	24	Waterloo Colts	OPHL	1	0	0	0	
1913–14	27	Toronto Blueshirts	St-Cup	3	2	0	2	0
Career — 2 Seasons				4	2	0	2	0

TROPHY CASE

AWARDS

Stanley Cup (1913–14)

11

Left Wing/Center

Shoots: Left

Height: 6'-1"

Weight: 210 lbs.

Born: January 18, 1961; Edmonton, Alberta

Drafted by the Edmonton Oilers 48th overall in 1979

Played 26 WHA and NHL seasons from 1978–2004

Mark Messier

HOCKEY HALL OF FAME CLASS: 2007

> I had the people and support from the president all the way down to the manager and coaches that shared in my belief, and together, we were part of something that hadn't been done in 54 years. It was an amazing time for us all."

— Mark Messier, on winning the Cup with the Rangers

QUICK FACTS

- First player to serve as captain on two different Stanley Cup-winning teams (Edmonton, 1990 and N.Y. Rangers, 1994)
- One of only six Hall of Fame members (with Sid Abel, Doug Bentley, Dit Clapper, Neil Colville and Alex Delvecchio) to be selected as an NHL All-Star at two different positions
- Played amateur hockey with Spruce Grove Mets (1976–77); St. Albert Saints (1977–79); Portland Winter Hawks (1977–78)
- Ranks second in NHL career points (1,887); ranks second in NHL career short-handed goals (63)

- Ranks third in NHL career assists (1,193); ranks seventh in NHL career goals (694)
- Registered 1,000th career NHL point in Edmonton's 5–3 victory over Pittsburgh Penguins, January 13, 1991; recorded 500th career NHL goal in N.Y. Rangers' 4–2 victory over Calgary Flames, November 6, 1995
- Played in NHL All-Star Game (1982, 1983, 1984, 1986, 1988, 1989, 1990, 1991, 1992, 1994, 1996, 1997, 1998, 2000, 2004)

Messier collected his 600th career goal wearing these skates in the 1998–99 season with the Vancouver Canucks.

REGULAR SEASON

Season	Age	Team	Lg	GP	G	A	PTS	+/-	PIM	ESG	PPG	SHG	GWG	SOG	S%
1978–79	18	Indianapolis Racers	WHA	5	0	0	0	-4	0	0	0	0		7	0.0
1978#79	18	Cincinnati Stingers	WHA	47	1	10	11	-6	58	1	0	0		55	1.8
1979–80	19	Edmonton Oilers	NHL	75	12	21	33	-10	120	10	1	1	1	113	10.6
1980–81	20	Edmonton Oilers	NHL	72	23	40	63	-12	102	19	4	0	1	179	12.8
1981–82	21	Edmonton Oilers	NHL	78	50	38	88	21	119	40	10	0	3	235	21.3
1982–83	22	Edmonton Oilers	NHL	77	48	58	106	19	72	35	12	1	2	237	20.3
1983–84	23	Edmonton Oilers	NHL	73	37	64	101	40	165	26	7	4	7	219	16.9
1984–85	24	Edmonton Oilers	NHL	55	23	31	54	8	57	14	4	5	1	136	16.9
1985–86	25	Edmonton Oilers	NHL	63	35	49	84	36	68	20	10	5	7	201	17.4
1986–87	26	Edmonton Oilers	NHL	77	37	70	107	21	73	26	7	4	5	208	17.8
1987–88	27	Edmonton Oilers	NHL	77	37	74	111	21	103	22	12	3	7	182	20.3
1988–89	28	Edmonton Oilers	NHL	72	33	61	94	-	130	21	6	6	4	164	20.1
1989–90	29	Edmonton Oilers	NHL	79	45	84	129	19	79	26	13	6	3	211	21.3
1990–91	30	Edmonton Oilers	NHL	53	12	52	64	15	34	8	3	1	2	109	11.0
1991–92	31	New York Rangers	NHL	79	35	72	107	31	76	19	12	4	6	212	16.5
1992–93	32	New York Rangers	NHL	75	25	66	91	-6	72	16	7	2	2	215	11.6
1993–94	33	New York Rangers	NHL	76	26	58	84	25	76	18	6	2	5	216	12.0
1994–95	34	New York Rangers	NHL	46	14	39	53	8	40	8	3	3	2	126	11.1
1995–96	35	New York Rangers	NHL	74	47	52	99	29	122	32	14	1	5	241	19.5
1996–97	36	New York Rangers	NHL	71	36	48	84	12	88	24	7	5	9	227	15.9
1997–98	37	Vancouver Canucks	NHL	82	22	38	60	-10	58	12	8	2	2	139	15.8
1998–99	38	Vancouver Canucks	NHL	59	13	35	48	-12	33	7	4	2	2	97	13.4
1999–00	39	Vancouver Canucks	NHL	66	17	37	54	-15	30	11	6	0	4	131	13.0
2000–01	40	New York Rangers	NHL	82	24	43	67	-25	89	9	12	3	2	131	18.3
2001–02	41	New York Rangers	NHL	41	7	16	23	-1	32	5	2	0	2	69	10.1
2002–03	42	New York Rangers	NHL	78	18	22	40	-2	30	9	8	1	5	117	15.4
2003–04	43	New York Rangers	NHL	76	18	25	43	3	42	15	1	2	3	104	17.3
Career – 26 Seasons				1808	695	1203	1898	200	1968	453	179	63	92	4281	16.2

PLAYOFFS

Season	Age	Team	Lg	GP	G	A	PTS	+/-	PIM	ESG	PPG	SHG	GWG	SOG	S%
1979–80	19	Edmonton Oilers	NHL	3	1	2	3		2	0	0	1	0		
1980–81	20	Edmonton Oilers	NHL	9	2	5	7		13	2	0	0	0		
1981–82	21	Edmonton Oilers	NHL	5	1	2	3		8	1	0	0	0		
1982–83	22	Edmonton Oilers	NHL	15	15	6	21		14	9	4	2	0		
1983–84	23	Edmonton Oilers	NHL	19	8	18	26	9	19	6	1	1	2	63	12.7
1984–85	24	Edmonton Oilers	NHL	18	12	13	25	13	12	10	1	1	1	56	21.4
1985–86	25	Edmonton Oilers	NHL	10	4	6	10	1	18	2	0	2	0	23	17.4
1986–87	26	Edmonton Oilers	NHL	21	12	16	28	13	16	9	1	2	1	62	19.4
1987–88	27	Edmonton Oilers	NHL	19	11	23	34	9	29	3	7	1	0	42	26.2
1988–89	28	Edmonton Oilers	NHL	7	1	11	12	-1	8	1	0	0	0	23	4.3
1989–90	29	Edmonton Oilers	NHL	22	9	22	31	5	20	7	1	1	1	47	19.1
1990–91	30	Edmonton Oilers	NHL	18	4	11	15	2	16	3	1	0	0	41	9.8
1991–92	31	New York Rangers	NHL	11	7	7	14	-4	6	3	2	2	0	27	25.9
1993–94	33	New York Rangers	NHL	23	12	18	30	14	33	9	2	1	4	75	16.0
1994–95	34	New York Rangers	NHL	10	3	10	13	-11	8	1	2	0	1	26	11.5
1995–96	35	New York Rangers	NHL	11	4	7	11	-10	16	2	2	0	1	41	9.8
1996–97	36	New York Rangers	NHL	15	3	9	12	2	6	3	0	0	1	43	7.0
Career – 17 Seasons				236	109	186	295	42	244	71	24	14	12	569	15.8

21

Center/Right Wing

Shoots: Right

Height: 5'-9"

Weight: 169 lbs.

Born: May 20, 1940: Sokolce, Czechoslovakia

Played 22 NHL seasons from 1959–80

Stan Mikita

HOCKEY HALL OF FAME CLASS: 1983

QUICK FACTS

- Played amateur hockey with St. Catharines Tee Pees (1956–59)
- Led OHA-Jr. in assists (59) and points (97)
- First player in NHL history to win three individual awards in the same season (1967, 1968)
- Holds Chicago Blackhawks' team records for seasons (22), games (1,394), assists (926), and career points (1,467)
- Ranks fourteenth in career NHL points (1,467)
- Renowned for making dramatic change in style of play from aggressive agitator to pacifist point producer

- One of only four players (with Alex Delvecchio, Steve Yzerman and Mike Modano) to play at least 20 seasons with only one organization
- Led NHL in points in 1963–64 (89), 1964–65 (87), 1966–67 (97) and 1967–68 (87)
- Led NHL playoffs in goals (6) in 1960–61; led NHL playoffs in assists (15) and points (1961–62); led NHL playoffs in penalty minutes (53) in 1964–65
- Led NHL in power-play goals (14) in 1963–64; led NHL in game-winning goals in 1967–68 (8) and 1969–70 (8)
- Led NHL in assists in 1964–65 (59), 1965–66 (48) and 1966–67 (62)

> One year, I must have had five or more [misconducts]. That's 50 minutes right there! So, I said, 'Keep your mouth shut. Don't change your style of play but don't take those lazy penalties and let's see what happens.' The next season, in the first 20 games, I only had one penalty. It was unbelievable!"
>
> — Stan Mikita, reflecting on becoming a gentleman player

REGULAR SEASON

Season	Age	Team	Lg	GP	G	A	PTS	+/-	PIM	ESG	PPG	SHG	GWG	SOG	S%
1959–60	19	Chicago Black Hawks	NHL	67	8	18	26		229						
1960–61	20	Chicago Black Hawks	NHL	66	19	34	53		100						
1961–62	21	Chicago Black Hawks	NHL	70	25	52	77		97						
1962–63	22	Chicago Black Hawks	NHL	65	31	45	76		69						
1963–64	23	Chicago Black Hawks	NHL	70	39	50	89		146	24	14	1	7		
1964–65	24	Chicago Black Hawks	NHL	70	28	59	87		154	20	8	0	6		
1965–66	25	Chicago Black Hawks	NHL	68	30	48	78		58	18	11	1	1		
1966–67	26	Chicago Black Hawks	NHL	70	35	62	97		12	26	8	1	5		
1967–68	27	Chicago Black Hawks	NHL	72	40	47	87	-3	14	25	13	2	8	303	13.2
1968–69	28	Chicago Black Hawks	NHL	74	30	67	97	17	52	20	7	3	2	299	10.0
1969–70	29	Chicago Black Hawks	NHL	76	39	47	86	29	50	32	7	0	8	352	11.1
1970–71	30	Chicago Black Hawks	NHL	74	24	48	72	21	85	17	7	0	4	220	10.9
1971–72	31	Chicago Black Hawks	NHL	74	26	39	65	16	46	21	5	0	6	185	14.1
1972–73	32	Chicago Black Hawks	NHL	57	27	56	83	31	32	19	7	1	5	177	15.3
1973–74	33	Chicago Black Hawks	NHL	76	30	50	80	24	46	22	6	2	1	171	17.5
1974–75	34	Chicago Black Hawks	NHL	79	36	50	86	14	48	24	12	0	6	253	14.2
1975–76	35	Chicago Black Hawks	NHL	48	16	41	57	-4	37	10	6	0	1	159	10.1
1976–77	36	Chicago Black Hawks	NHL	57	19	30	49	-9	20	12	6	1	4	128	14.8
1977–78	37	Chicago Black Hawks	NHL	76	18	41	59	18	35	12	6	0	2	202	8.9
1978–79	38	Chicago Black Hawks	NHL	65	19	36	55	3	34	15	4	0	1	147	12.9
1979–80	39	Chicago Black Hawks	NHL	17	2	5	7	2	12	2	0	0	0	28	7.1
NHL Career — 22 Seasons				1394	541	926	1467	159	1270	319	127	12	67	2624	12.4

PLAYOFFS

Season	Age	Team	Lg	GP	G	A	PTS	+/-	PIM	ESG	PPG	SHG	GWG	SOG	S%
1959–60	19	Chicago Black Hawks	NHL	3	0	1	1		2						
1960–61	20	Chicago Black Hawks	NHL	12	6	5	11		21						
1961–62	21	Chicago Black Hawks	NHL	12	6	15	21		19						
1962–63	22	Chicago Black Hawks	NHL	6	3	2	5		2						
1963–64	23	Chicago Black Hawks	NHL	7	3	6	9		8						
1964–65	24	Chicago Black Hawks	NHL	14	3	7	10		53						
1965–66	25	Chicago Black Hawks	NHL	6	1	2	3		2						
1966–67	26	Chicago Black Hawks	NHL	6	2	2	4		2						
1967–68	27	Chicago Black Hawks	NHL	11	5	7	12		6	2	3	0	0		
1969–70	29	Chicago Black Hawks	NHL	8	4	6	10		2	1	3	0	1		
1970–71	30	Chicago Black Hawks	NHL	18	5	13	18		16	4	1	0	1		
1971–72	31	Chicago Black Hawks	NHL	8	3	1	4		4	3	0	0	0		
1972–73	32	Chicago Black Hawks	NHL	15	7	13	20		8	6	1	0	2		
1973–74	33	Chicago Black Hawks	NHL	11	5	6	11		8	4	1	0	1		
1974–75	34	Chicago Black Hawks	NHL	8	3	4	7		12	2	1	0	1		
1975–76	35	Chicago Black Hawks	NHL	4	0	0	0		0	0	0	0	0		
1976–77	36	Chicago Black Hawks	NHL	2	0	1	1		0	0	0	0	0		
1977–78	37	Chicago Black Hawks	NHL	4	3	0	3		0	1	2	0	0		
NHL Career — 18 Seasons				155	59	91	150		169	23	12	0	6		

TROPHY CASE

AWARDS

Art Ross Trophy (1964, 1965, 1967, 1968)

Hart Memorial Trophy (1967, 1968)

Lady Byng Memorial Trophy (1967, 1968)

Stanley Cup (1960–61)

Lester Patrick Trophy (1976)

ALL-STAR SELECTIONS

First All-Star Team Center (1962, 1963, 1964, 1966, 1967, 1968)

Second All-Star Team Center (1965, 1970)

INTERNATIONAL AWARDS

Summit Series (1972)

12

Dickie Moore

HOCKEY HALL OF FAME CLASS: 1974

Alternate: 16

Left Wing

Shoots: Left

Height: 5'-10"

Weight: 168 lbs.

Born: January 6, 1931: Montreal, Quebec

Played 14 NHL seasons from 1951–63, 1964–65, 1967–68

"When Toe [Blake] became coach, I was elated. He kept me on the team. I was lucky to have a guy who believed in me. You're only as good as how somebody can lift you up to the heights where he thinks you can play."

QUICK FACTS

- Shares NHL record for most points (4) in one playoff period, established in Montreal's 8–1 victory over Boston, March 25, 1954

- Played amateur hockey with Montreal Jr. Royals (1947–50); Montreal Jr. Canadiens (1949–51); Montreal Royals (1951–52, 1953–54)

- QJHL First All-Star Team Left Wing (1951); QJHL Second All-Star Team Left Wing (1950)

- Member of Memorial Cup-winning Montreal Jr. Royals (1949) and Montreal Jr. Canadiens (1950)

- Led QJHL playoffs in assists (13) and penalty minutes (51); led Memorial Cup playoffs in penalty minutes (41)

- Scored Stanley Cup-winning goal in Montreal's 5–1 victory over Boston Bruins, April 16, 1957

- Established NHL record for points in regular season (96) in 1958–59 while playing with a broken wrist. He wore a specially designed cast to protect his injured hand

- Played only 13 games in 1953–54 season recovering from a collarbone injury suffered in game vs. Boston, October 10, 1953

- Led NHL in goals (36) and points (84) in 1957–58; led NHL in assists (55) and points (96) in 1958–59

- Played in NHL All-Star Game (1953, 1956, 1957, 1958, 1959, 1960)

- Signed as a free agent by St. Louis Blues, December 3, 1967

38 Dickie Moore

Moore's 1960–61 Parkhurst hockey card.

REGULAR SEASON

Season	Age	Team	Lg	GP	G	A	PTS	+/-	PIM	ESG	PPG	SHG	GWG	SOG	S%
1951–52	21	Montreal Canadiens	NHL	33	18	15	33		44						
1952–53	22	Montreal Canadiens	NHL	18	2	6	8		19						
1953–54	23	Montreal Canadiens	NHL	13	1	4	5		12						
1954–55	24	Montreal Canadiens	NHL	67	16	20	36		32						
1955–56	25	Montreal Canadiens	NHL	70	11	39	50		55						
1956–57	26	Montreal Canadiens	NHL	70	29	29	58		56						
1957–58	27	Montreal Canadiens	NHL	70	36	48	84		65						
1958–59	28	Montreal Canadiens	NHL	70	41	55	96		61						
1959–60	29	Montreal Canadiens	NHL	62	22	42	64		54						
1960–61	30	Montreal Canadiens	NHL	57	35	34	69		62						
1961–62	31	Montreal Canadiens	NHL	57	19	22	41		54						
1962–63	32	Montreal Canadiens	NHL	67	24	26	50		61						
1964–65	34	Toronto Maple Leafs	NHL	38	2	4	6		68	2	0	0	0		
1967–68	37	St. Louis Blues	NHL	27	5	3	8	-8	9	4	1	0	1	37	13.5
NHL Career – 14 Seasons				719	261	347	608	-8	652	6	1	0	1	37	13.5

PLAYOFFS

Season	Age	Team	Lg	GP	G	A	PTS	+/-	PIM	ESG	PPG	SHG	GWG	SOG	S%
1951–52	21	Montreal Canadiens	NHL	11	1	1	2		12						
1952–53	22	Montreal Canadiens	NHL	12	3	2	5		13						
1953–54	23	Montreal Canadiens	NHL	11	5	8	13		8						
1954–55	24	Montreal Canadiens	NHL	12	1	5	6		22						
1955–56	25	Montreal Canadiens	NHL	10	3	6	9		12						
1956–57	26	Montreal Canadiens	NHL	10	3	7	10		4						
1957–58	27	Montreal Canadiens	NHL	10	4	7	11		4						
1958–59	28	Montreal Canadiens	NHL	11	5	12	17		8						
1959–60	29	Montreal Canadiens	NHL	8	6	4	10		4						
1960–61	30	Montreal Canadiens	NHL	6	3	1	4		4						
1961–62	31	Montreal Canadiens	NHL	6	4	2	6		8						
1962–63	32	Montreal Canadiens	NHL	5	0	1	1		2						
1964–65	34	Toronto Maple Leafs	NHL	5	1	1	2		6						
1967–68	37	St. Louis Blues	NHL	18	7	7	14		15	5	2	0	1		
NHL Career – 14 Seasons				135	46	64	110		122	5	2	0	1		

TROPHY CASE

AWARDS

Art Ross Trophy (1958, 1959)

Stanley Cup (1952–53, 1955–56, 1956–57, 1957–58, 1958–59, 1959–60)

ALL-STAR SELECTIONS

First All-Star Team Left Wing (1958, 1959)

Second All-Star Team Left Wing (1961)

Paddy Moran

HOCKEY HALL OF FAME CLASS: 1958

Goaltender

Catches: Left

Height: 5'-11"

Weight: 180 lbs.

Born: March 11, 1877: Quebec City, Quebec

Died: January 24, 1966: Quebec City, Quebec

Played 16 elite amateur and professional seasons from 1901–17

QUICK FACTS

- Played amateur hockey with Quebec Dominions (1898–99); Quebec Crescents (1899–01); Quebec Athletics (1901–05)

- Led CAHL in wins in 1903–04 (5) and 1904–05 (7)

- Member of Canadian Intermediate champion Quebec Crescents (1900–01)

- Played majority of career with Quebec Bulldogs in era when goaltenders were required to remain standing at all times, retiring a year before the formation of the NHL

- ECAHA First All-Star Team Goaltender (1908)

- Signed as a free agent by Haileybury HC, January 16, 1910 when Quebec was denied entry into the National Hockey Association

- Rejoined Quebec club when team was admitted to the NHA (1910–11)

- Member of Stanley Cup-winning Quebec Bulldogs (1911–12, 1912–13); led Stanley Cup playoffs in wins (2) in 1911–12

- Led NHA in wins in 1911–12 (10) and 1912–13 (16); led NHA in shutouts in 1912–13 (1) and 1913–14 (1)

- Selected to play on NHA All-Star Team in a postseason series against PCHA All-Stars in March of 1913

- Renowned as a clutch goaltender who was difficult to beat in important games

> "Paddy stopped them from all angles, and his brilliant work put heart into the players in front of him and sent them after Wanderers in a style that threatened to take the champions off their feet."
> — *Montreal Gazette*, January 18, 1909

REGULAR SEASON

Season	Age	Team	League	GP	W	L	T	SO	GA	GAA
1901–02	24	Quebec Athletics	CAHL	8	4	4	0	0	34	4.25
1902–03	25	Quebec Athletics	CAHL	7	3	4	0	0	46	6.57
1903–04	26	Quebec Athletics	CAHL	6	5	1	0	0	37	6.17
1904–05	27	Quebec Athletics	CAHL	9	7	2	0	0	45	5.00
1905–06	28	Quebec Bulldogs	ECAHA	10	3	7	0	0	70	6.79
1906–07	29	Quebec Bulldogs	ECAHA	6	0	6	0	0	58	9.61
1907–08	30	Quebec Bulldogs	ECAHA	10	5	5	0	0	74	7.38
1908–09	31	Quebec Bulldogs	ECHA	12	3	9	0	0	106	8.83
1909–10	32	All-Montreal	CHA	4	2	2	0	0	24	6.00
1909–10	32	Haileybury Comets	NHA	11	3	8	0	0	80	7.22
1910–11	33	Quebec Bulldogs	NHA	16	4	12	0	0	97	5.92
1911–12	34	Quebec Bulldogs	NHA	18	10	8	0	0	78	4.26
1912–13	35	Quebec Bulldogs	NHA	20	16	4	0	1	75	3.70
1913–14	36	Quebec Bulldogs	NHA	20	12	8	0	1	73	3.58
1914–15	37	Quebec Bulldogs	NHA	20	11	9	0	0	85	3.91
1915–16	38	Quebec Bulldogs	NHA	22	10	10	0	0	82	3.54
1916–17	39	Quebec Bulldogs	NHA	7	1	5	0	0	35	6.84
Career – 16 Seasons				206	99	104	0	2	1099	5.33

PLAYOFFS

Season	Age	Team	League	GP	W	L	T	SO	GA	GAA
1911–12	34	Quebec Bulldogs	St-Cup	2	2	0	0	1	3	1.50
1912–13	35	Quebec Bulldogs	St-Cup	2	2	0	0	0	5	2.50
Career – 2 Seasons				4	4	0	0	1	8	2.00

TROPHY CASE

AWARDS

Stanley Cup (1911–12, 1912–13)

Howie Morenz
HOCKEY HALL OF FAME CLASS: 1945

7

Alternates: 3, 6, 12

Center

Shoots: Left

Height: 5'-9"

Weight: 165 lbs.

Born: September 21, 1902: Mitchell, Ontario

Died: March 8, 1937: Montreal, Quebec

Played 14 NHL seasons from 1923–37

> "The old spirit is back. There was something missing inside when I was away the last two seasons. I got it back when I came back with the Canadiens. I'm giving the fans everything I've got. The end may be in sight but the heart is still sound."
> — Howie Morenz, on his return to Montreal

+1945 Dan Bain, Hobey Baker, Dubbie Bowie, Chuck Gardiner, Eddie Gerard, Frank McGee, Tommy Phillips, Harvey Pulford, Art Ross, Hod Stuart, Georges Vezina

QUICK FACTS

- Nicknamed the "Stratford Streak," "Canadiens Comet" and "Mitchell Meteor" because of his tremendous speed and agility with the puck

- Named the top hockey player of the first half of the 20th century by Canadian Press

- First player to have his number retired by the Montreal Canadiens (1937)

- Played amateur hockey with Stratford Midgets (1919–22); Stratford Indians (1921–23)

- Led OHA-Jr. in assists (12) and points (31) in 1920–21; led OHA-Jr. in playoff goals (38), assists (18) and points (56) in 1919–20

- Led OHA-Jr. in playoff goals (17), assists (4) and points (21) in 1921–22; led OHA-Sr. in playoff goals (15), assists (8) and points (23) in 1921–22

- Led NHL in points in 1927–28 (51) and 1930–31 (51); led NHL in assists (18) in 1927–28; led NHL in goals (33) in 1927–28

- Scored Stanley Cup-winning goal in Montreal Canadiens' 3–0 victory over Calgary Tigers, March 25, 1924

- Played in NHL All-Star Game (1934)

- Traded to Chicago by Montreal Canadiens with Lorne Chabot and Marty Burke for Leroy Goldsworthy, Lionel Conacher and Roger Jenkins, October 3, 1934

- Traded to N.Y. Rangers by Chicago for Glenn Brydson, January 26, 1936; traded to Montreal Canadiens by N.Y. Rangers for cash, September 1, 1936

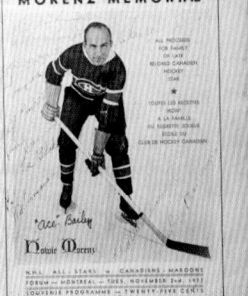

MORENZ MEMORIAL

Morenz Memorial program autographed by NHL All-Stars. Memorial proceeds went to the Morenz family to help cope with the star's sudden death.

REGULAR SEASON

Season	Age	Team	Lg	GP	G	A	PTS	PIM
1923–24	21	Montreal Canadiens	NHL	24	13	3	16	20
1924–25	22	Montreal Canadiens	NHL	30	28	11	39	46
1925–26	23	Montreal Canadiens	NHL	31	23	3	26	39
1926–27	24	Montreal Canadiens	NHL	44	25	7	32	49
1927–28	25	Montreal Canadiens	NHL	43	33	18	51	66
1928–29	26	Montreal Canadiens	NHL	42	17	10	27	47
1929–30	27	Montreal Canadiens	NHL	44	40	10	50	72
1930–31	28	Montreal Canadiens	NHL	39	28	23	51	49
1931–32	29	Montreal Canadiens	NHL	48	24	25	49	46
1932–33	30	Montreal Canadiens	NHL	46	14	21	35	32
1933–34	31	Montreal Canadiens	NHL	39	8	13	21	21
1934–35	32	Chicago Black Hawks	NHL	48	8	26	34	21
1935–36	33	Chicago Black Hawks	NHL	23	4	11	15	20
1935–36	33	New York Rangers	NHL	19	2	4	6	6
1936–37	34	Montreal Canadiens	NHL	30	4	16	20	12
Career — 14 Seasons				550	271	201	472	546

PLAYOFFS

Season	Age	Team	Lg	GP	G	A	PTS	PIM
1923–24	21	Montreal Canadiens	NHL	2	3	1	4	6
1923–24	21	Montreal Canadiens	St-Cup	4	4	2	6	4
1924–25	22	Montreal Canadiens	NHL	2	3	0	3	4
1924–25	22	Montreal Canadiens	St-Cup	4	4	1	5	4
1926–27	24	Montreal Canadiens	NHL	4	1	0	1	4
1927–28	25	Montreal Canadiens	NHL	2	0	0	0	12
1928–29	26	Montreal Canadiens	NHL	3	0	0	0	6
1929–30	27	Montreal Canadiens	NHL	6	3	0	3	10
1930–31	28	Montreal Canadiens	NHL	10	1	4	5	10
1931–32	29	Montreal Canadiens	NHL	4	1	0	1	4
1932–33	30	Montreal Canadiens	NHL	2	0	3	3	2
1933–34	31	Montreal Canadiens	NHL	2	1	1	2	0
1934–35	32	Chicago Black Hawks	NHL	2	0	0	0	0
Career — 11 Seasons				47	21	12	33	66

TROPHY CASE

AWARDS

NHL Scoring Leader (1928, 1931)

Hart Memorial Trophy (1928, 1931, 1932)

Stanley Cup (1923–24, 1929–30, 1930–31)

ALL-STAR SELECTIONS

First All-Star Team Center (1931, 1932)

Second All-Star Team Center (1933)

8

Bill Mosienko

HOCKEY HALL OF FAME CLASS: 1965

Alternates: 10, 19

Right Wing

Shoots: Right

Height: 5'-8"

Weight: 160 lbs.

Born: November 2, 1921: Winnipeg, Manitoba

Died: July 9, 1994: Winnipeg, Manitoba

Played 14 NHL seasons from 1941–55

"It was quite an accomplishment, I hope [the record] stays. After I scored the third goal, Jim Peters skated up to me and told me to keep the puck because I had set a new record. I was very happy and proud. It was like being on cloud nine."

– Bill Mosienko, reflecting on his 3 goals in 21 seconds record

QUICK FACTS

- Scored his first two NHL goals in 21 seconds in Chicago's 4–3 loss to N.Y. Rangers on February 8, 1942

- Holds NHL record for scoring fastest three goals (21 seconds) in a single game, established in Chicago's 7–6 victory over N.Y. Rangers, March 23, 1952

- Played amateur hockey with Winnipeg Sherburn-Juvenile (1938–39) and Winnipeg Monarchs (1939–40)

- Signed as a free agent by Chicago, October 27, 1940

- Made professional debut with Kansas City Americans (1940–41)

- Right winger on the Pony Line with Max and Doug Bentley

- Played in NHL All-Star Game (1947, 1949, 1950, 1952, 1953)

- Finished among NHL top-5 in goals in 1944–45 (28) and 1951–52 (31)

- Finished among NHL top-5 in points in 1944–45 (54) and 1945 (48)

- WHL Prairie First All-Star Team (1957–59)

- Member of WHL champion Winnipeg Warriors (1956); member of Edinburgh Trophy (top minor professional team in Canada) champion Winnipeg Warriors (1956)

- Led WHL in playoff assists (12) in 1956; led Edinburgh Trophy series in goals (6) in 1956

- Coached WHL's Winnipeg Warriors (1959–61)

- Named Manitoba's Athlete of the Year (1957)

Painting commemorating Mosienko's 3 goals in 21 seconds by unknown artist "Thompson."

REGULAR SEASON

Season	Age	Team	Lg	GP	G	A	PTS	PIM
1941–42	20	Chicago Black Hawks	NHL	12	6	8	14	4
1942–43	21	Chicago Black Hawks	NHL	2	2	0	2	0
1943–44	22	Chicago Black Hawks	NHL	50	32	38	70	10
1944–45	23	Chicago Black Hawks	NHL	50	28	26	54	0
1945–46	24	Chicago Black Hawks	NHL	40	18	30	48	12
1946–47	25	Chicago Black Hawks	NHL	59	25	27	52	2
1947–48	26	Chicago Black Hawks	NHL	40	16	9	25	0
1948–49	27	Chicago Black Hawks	NHL	60	17	25	42	6
1949–50	28	Chicago Black Hawks	NHL	69	18	28	46	10
1950–51	29	Chicago Black Hawks	NHL	65	21	15	36	18
1951–52	30	Chicago Black Hawks	NHL	70	31	22	53	10
1952–53	31	Chicago Black Hawks	NHL	65	17	20	37	8
1953–54	32	Chicago Black Hawks	NHL	65	15	19	34	17
1954–55	33	Chicago Black Hawks	NHL	64	12	15	27	24
NHL Career — 14 Seasons				711	258	282	540	121

PLAYOFFS

Season	Age	Team	Lg	GP	G	A	PTS	PIM
1941–42	20	Chicago Black Hawks	NHL	3	2	0	2	0
1942–44	22	Chicago Black Hawks	NHL	8	2	2	4	6
1945–46	24	Chicago Black Hawks	NHL	4	2	0	2	2
1952–53	31	Chicago Black Hawks	NHL	7	4	2	6	7
NHL Career — 4 Seasons				22	10	4	14	15

TROPHY CASE

AWARDS

Lady Byng Memorial Trophy (1945)

ALL-STAR SELECTIONS

Second All-Star Team Right Wing (1945, 1946)

Joseph Mullen

HOCKEY HALL OF FAME CLASS: 2000

Alternate: 11

Right Wing

Shoots: Right

Height: 5'-9"

Weight: 180 lbs.

Born: February 26, 1957: New York, New York

Played 17 NHL seasons from 1979–80, 1981–97

" I could look out my window and see Madison Square Garden, which was half a block up the street from me. We had a schoolyard right across the street from us where we played roller hockey. So, the combination of all that gave me my love for the game."

QUICK FACTS

- First American-born and trained player to record 500 goals and 1,000 points
- Played amateur hockey with New York 14 Precinct (1971–72); New York Westsiders (1971–75); Boston College Eagles (1975–79)
- Led NYJHL in goals (110) and points (182) in 1974–75; led NYJHL playoffs in goals (27) and points (37) in 1974–75
- ECAC First All-Star Team Right Wing (1978, 1979); NCAA East First All-American Team (1978, 1979)
- Named CHL Rookie of the Year (1980); named CHL Most Valuable Player (1981)
- CHL Second All-Star Team Right Wing (1980); CHL First All-Star Team Right Wing (1981)
- Led CHL in playoff goals (9) in 1979–80; led CHL in points (117) in 1980–81
- Signed as a free agent by St. Louis, August 16, 1979
- Played in NHL All-Star Game (1989, 1990, 1994)
- Led NHL playoffs in goals in 1985–86 (12) and 1988–89 (16)
- Registered 1,000th career NHL point in Pittsburgh's 7–3 victory over Florida Panthers, February 7, 1995; recorded 500th career NHL goal in Pittsburgh's 6–3 loss to Colorado Avalanche, March 14, 1997
- Nicknamed "Slippery Rock Joe" by Pittsburgh Penguins' broadcaster Mike Lange for his agility and toughness on the ice

Mullen wore these gloves on March 14, 1997, when he became the first American-born player to score 500 goals.

REGULAR SEASON

Season	Age	Team	Lg	GP	G	A	PTS	+/-	PIM	ESG	PPG	SHG	GWG	SOG	S%
1981–82	24	St. Louis Blues	NHL	45	25	34	59	11	4	15	10	0	3	141	17.7
1982–83	25	St. Louis Blues	NHL	49	17	30	47	-5	6	12	5	0	0	128	13.3
1983–84	26	St. Louis Blues	NHL	80	41	44	85	-8	19	28	13	0	6	228	18.0
1984–85	27	St. Louis Blues	NHL	79	40	52	92	5	6	27	13	0	4	252	15.9
1985–86	28	St. Louis Blues	NHL	48	28	24	52	-7	10	19	9	0	4	142	19.7
1985–86	28	Calgary Flames	NHL	29	16	22	38	2	11	11	5	0	4	61	26.2
1986–87	29	Calgary Flames	NHL	79	47	40	87	18	14	32	15	0	12	206	22.8
1987–88	30	Calgary Flames	NHL	80	40	44	84	28	30	28	12	0	5	205	19.5
1988–89	31	Calgary Flames	NHL	79	51	59	110	51	16	37	13	1	7	270	18.9
1989–90	32	Calgary Flames	NHL	78	36	33	69	6	24	25	8	3	5	236	15.3
1990–91	33	Pittsburgh Penguins	NHL	47	17	22	39	6	6	8	8	0	2	85	20.0
1991–92	34	Pittsburgh Penguins	NHL	77	42	45	87	12	30	28	14	0	4	226	18.6
1992–93	35	Pittsburgh Penguins	NHL	72	33	37	70	19	14	21	9	3	3	175	18.9
1993–94	36	Pittsburgh Penguins	NHL	84	38	32	70	9	41	30	6	2	9	231	16.5
1994–95	37	Pittsburgh Penguins	NHL	45	16	21	37	15	6	9	5	2	3	78	20.5
1995–96	38	Boston Bruins	NHL	37	8	7	15	-2	0	4	4	0	1	60	13.3
1996–97	39	Pittsburgh Penguins	NHL	54	7	15	22	0	4	6	1	0	1	63	11.1
NHL Career — 16 Seasons				1062	502	561	1063	163	241	341	150	11	73	2787	18.0

PLAYOFFS

Season	Age	Team	Lg	GP	G	A	PTS	+/-	PIM	ESG	PPG	SHG	GWG	SOG	S%
1979–80	22	St. Louis Blues	NHL	1	0	0	0		0	0	0	0	0		
1981–82	24	St. Louis Blues	NHL	10	7	11	18		4	6	1	0	0		
1983–84	26	St. Louis Blues	NHL	6	2	0	2	0	0	2	0	0	0	21	9.5
1984–85	27	St. Louis Blues	NHL	3	0	0	0	1	0	0	0	0	0	10	0.0
1985–86	28	Calgary Flames	NHL	21	12	7	19	-3	4	8	4	0	2	53	22.6
1986–87	29	Calgary Flames	NHL	6	2	1	3	-4	0	1	1	0	1	12	16.7
1987–88	30	Calgary Flames	NHL	7	2	4	6	0	10	2	0	0	0	21	9.5
1988–89	31	Calgary Flames	NHL	21	16	8	24	8	4	10	6	0	1	91	17.6
1989–90	32	Calgary Flames	NHL	6	3	0	3	-4	0	2	0	1	0	12	25.0
1990–91	33	Pittsburgh Penguins	NHL	22	8	9	17	17	4	7	1	0	1	44	18.2
1991–92	34	Pittsburgh Penguins	NHL	9	3	1	4	-4	4	2	1	0	0	21	14.3
1992–93	35	Pittsburgh Penguins	NHL	12	4	2	6	4	6	3	0	1	1	32	12.5
1993–94	36	Pittsburgh Penguins	NHL	6	1	0	1	-1	2	1	0	0	0	6	16.7
1994–95	37	Pittsburgh Penguins	NHL	12	0	3	3	-5	4	0	0	0	0	12	0.0
1996–97	39	Pittsburgh Penguins	NHL	1	0	0	0	0	0	0	0	0	0	0	
NHL Career — 15 Seasons				143	60	46	106	9	42	44	14	2	6	335	15.8

TROPHY CASE

AWARDS

Lady Byng Memorial Trophy (1987, 1989)

Lester Patrick Trophy (1995)

Stanley Cup (1988–89, 1990–91, 1991–92)

ALL-STAR SELECTIONS

First NHL All-Star Team Right Wing (1989)

55

Larry Murphy
HOCKEY HALL OF FAME CLASS: 2004

Alternates: 8, 5

Defense

Shoots: Right

Height: 6'-2"

Weight: 210 lbs.

Born: March 8, 1961: Scarborough, Ontario

Drafted by the Los Angeles Kings fourth overall in 1980

Played 21 NHL seasons from 1980–2001

QUICK FACTS

- Holds NHL record for points by a rookie defenseman (76), established in 1980–81
- Holds NHL record for assists by a defenseman in Stanley Cup Finals (9), established in 1990–91
- Holds Washington Capitals' record for assists (60) and points (81) by a defenseman in regular season, established in 1986–87
- Played on four Stanley Cup-winning teams in the 1990s, the most of any NHL player in that decade
- One of only six players in NHL history (with Red Kelly, Frank Mahovlich, Bryan Trottier, Patrick Roy and Dick Duff) to win two-or-more Stanley Cup championships with two-or-more teams
- Ranks seventh in NHL career games played (1,615)
- Ranks fourth in NHL career assists by a defenseman (929)
- Ranks fifth in NHL career points by a defenseman (1,216)

> "Once you get your hands on the Stanley Cup, it gets so much tougher to lose, and you ache to get at it again."

REGULAR SEASON

Season	Age	Team	Lg	GP	G	A	PTS	+/-	PIM	ESG	PPG	SHG	GWG	SOG	S%
1980–81	19	Los Angeles Kings	NHL	80	16	60	76	17	79	10	5	1	1	153	10.5
1981–82	20	Los Angeles Kings	NHL	79	22	44	66	-13	95	13	8	1	2	191	11.5
1982–83	21	Los Angeles Kings	NHL	77	14	48	62	2	81	5	9	0	2	172	8.1
1983–84	22	Los Angeles Kings	NHL	6	0	3	3	-4	0	0	0	0	0	11	0.0
1983–84	22	Washington Capitals	NHL	72	13	33	46	12	50	11	2	0	2	138	9.4
1984–85	23	Washington Capitals	NHL	79	13	42	55	21	51	10	3	0	0	153	8.5
1985–86	24	Washington Capitals	NHL	78	21	44	65	2	50	12	8	1	2	180	11.7
1986–87	25	Washington Capitals	NHL	80	23	58	81	25	39	15	8	0	4	226	10.2
1987–88	26	Washington Capitals	NHL	79	8	53	61	2	72	1	7	0	1	201	4.0
1988–89	27	Washington Capitals	NHL	65	7	29	36	-5	70	4	3	0	0	129	5.4
1988–89	27	Minnesota North Stars	NHL	13	4	6	10	5	12	1	3	0	1	31	12.9
1989–90	28	Minnesota North Stars	NHL	77	10	58	68	-13	44	6	4	0	1	173	5.8
1990–91	29	Minnesota North Stars	NHL	31	4	11	15	-8	38	3	1	0	2	103	3.9
1990–91	29	Pittsburgh Penguins	NHL	44	5	23	28	2	30	3	2	0	0	85	5.9
1991–92	30	Pittsburgh Penguins	NHL	77	21	56	77	33	48	12	7	2	3	206	10.2
1992–93	31	Pittsburgh Penguins	NHL	83	22	63	85	45	73	14	6	2	2	230	9.6
1993–94	32	Pittsburgh Penguins	NHL	84	17	56	73	10	44	10	7	0	4	236	7.2
1994–95	33	Pittsburgh Penguins	NHL	48	13	25	38	12	18	9	4	0	3	124	10.5
1995–96	34	Toronto Maple Leafs	NHL	82	12	49	61	-2	34	4	8	0	1	182	6.6
1996–97	35	Toronto Maple Leafs	NHL	69	7	32	39	1	20	3	4	0	0	137	5.1
1996–97	35	Detroit Red Wings	NHL	12	2	4	6	2	0	1	1	0	1	21	9.5
1997–98	36	Detroit Red Wings	NHL	82	11	41	52	35	37	8	2	1	2	129	8.5
1998–99	37	Detroit Red Wings	NHL	80	10	42	52	21	42	4	5	1	2	168	6.0
1999–00	38	Detroit Red Wings	NHL	81	10	30	40	4	45	3	7	0	0	148	6.8
2000–01	39	Detroit Red Wings	NHL	57	2	19	21	-6	12	2	0	0	1	81	2.5
NHL Career — 21 Seasons				1615	287	929	1216	200	1084	164	114	9	37	3606	8.0

PLAYOFFS

Season	Age	Team	Lg	GP	G	A	PTS	+/-	PIM	ESG	PPG	SHG	GWG	SOG	S%
1980–81	19	Los Angeles Kings	NHL	4	3	0	3	2	2	1	0	0	0		
1981–82	20	Los Angeles Kings	NHL	10	2	8	10	12	1	1	0	0	0		
1983–84	22	Washington Capitals	NHL	8	0	3	3	6	0	0	0	0	0	20	0.0
1984–85	23	Washington Capitals	NHL	5	2	3	5	0	0	2	0	0	0	17	11.8
1985–86	24	Washington Capitals	NHL	9	1	5	6	6	0	1	0	0	0	21	4.8
1986–87	25	Washington Capitals	NHL	7	2	2	4	6	2	0	0	0	1	25	8.0
1987–88	26	Washington Capitals	NHL	13	4	4	8	33	2	2	0	0	1	21	19.0
1988–89	27	Minnesota North Stars	NHL	5	0	2	2	8	0	0	0	0	0	9	0.0
1989–90	28	Minnesota North Stars	NHL	7	1	2	3	1	1	0	0	0	0	16	6.3
1990–91	29	Pittsburgh Penguins	NHL	23	5	18	23	44	1	4	0	0	1	86	1.6
1991–92	30	Pittsburgh Penguins	NHL	21	6	10	16	19	3	3	0	0	1	59	10.2
1992–93	31	Pittsburgh Penguins	NHL	12	2	11	13	10	0	2	0	0	1	26	7.7
1993–94	32	Pittsburgh Penguins	NHL	6	0	5	5	0	0	0	0	0	0	13	0.0
1994–95	33	Pittsburgh Penguins	NHL	12	2	13	15	0	1	0	0	0	1	35	5.7
1995–96	34	Toronto Maple Leafs	NHL	6	0	2	2	4	0	0	0	0	0	16	0.0
1996–97	35	Detroit Red Wings	NHL	20	2	9	11	8	1	0	0	0	1	51	3.9
1997–98	36	Detroit Red Wings	NHL	22	3	12	15	2	0	1	2	2	1	36	8.3
1998–99	37	Detroit Red Wings	NHL	10	0	2	2	8	0	0	0	0	0	14	0.0
1999–00	38	Detroit Red Wings	NHL	9	2	3	5	2	0	1	1	1	0	16	12.5
2000–01	39	Detroit Red Wings	NHL	6	0	1	1	0	0	0	0	0	0	7	0.0
NHL Career — 20 Seasons				215	37	115	152	201	14	20	3	3	7	468	6.8

TROPHY CASE

AWARDS

Stanley Cup (1990–91, 1991–92, 1996–97, 1997–98)

ALL-STAR SELECTIONS

Second All-Star Team Defenseman (1987, 1993, 1995)

INTERNATIONAL AWARDS

Canada Cup (1987, 1991)

Silver Medal: World Championships (1985)

You don't have to be crazy to be a goalie,
but it helps."
Bernie Parent

8

Cam Neely

HOCKEY HALL OF FAME CLASS: 2005

Alternate: 21

Right Wing

Shoots: Right

Height: 6'-1"

Weight: 218 lbs.

Born: June 6, 1965: Comox, British Columbia

Drafted by the Vancouver Canucks ninth overall in 1983

Played 13 NHL seasons from 1983–96

QUICK FACTS

- Holds Boston Bruins team record for career playoff goals (55) and career playoff power-play goals (24)

- Holds Boston Bruins team record for goals in regular season by a right wing (55), established in 1988–89

- Played amateur hockey with Ridge Meadows Lightning (1981–82); Portland Winter Hawks (1982–84)

- Member of Memorial Cup-winning Portland Winter Hawks (1983); led Memorial Cup tournament in goals (5) in 1983

- Traded to Boston by Vancouver with Vancouver's first round choice (Glen Wesley) in 1987 Entry Draft for Barry Pederson, June 6, 1986

- Led NHL in powerplay goals (16) in 1994–95

- Led NHL in game-winning goals in 1989–90 (12) and 1993–94 (13)

- Led NHL in shooting percentage (27%) in 1993–94

- Played in NHL All-Star Game (1988, 1989, 1990, 1991, 1996)

- Only second player (with Phil Esposito) in Boston team history to record back-to-back 50-goal seasons

- Developed a condition called myositis ossificans, which causes abnormal bone formation within deep muscle tissue, forcing his premature retirement

- Made cameo appearances in the movies *Dumb and Dumber*, *Me, Myself and Irene*, and *Stuck on You* and the television series *Rescue Me*

> It meant as much to me to give a big hit as it did to score a big goal. And to leave a mark for being that kind of player is special to me."

REGULAR SEASON

Season	Age	Team	Lg	GP	G	A	PTS	+/-	PIM	ESG	PPG	SHG	GWG	SOG	S%
1983–84	18	Vancouver Canucks	NHL	56	16	15	31	0	57	13	3	0	1	87	18.4
1984–85	19	Vancouver Canucks	NHL	72	21	18	39	-26	137	17	4	0	1	138	15.2
1985–86	20	Vancouver Canucks	NHL	73	14	20	34	-30	126	8	6	0	3	113	12.4
1986–87	21	Boston Bruins	NHL	75	36	36	72	-23	143	29	7	0	3	206	17.5
1987–88	22	Boston Bruins	NHL	69	42	27	69	30	175	31	11	0	3	207	20.3
1988–89	23	Boston Bruins	NHL	74	37	38	75	14	190	19	18	0	6	235	15.7
1989–90	24	Boston Bruins	NHL	76	55	37	92	10	117	30	25	0	12	271	20.3
1990–91	25	Boston Bruins	NHL	69	51	40	91	26	98	32	18	1	8	262	19.5
1991–92	26	Boston Bruins	NHL	9	9	3	12	9	16	8	1	0	2	30	30.0
1992–93	27	Boston Bruins	NHL	13	11	7	18	4	25	5	6	0	1	45	24.4
1993–94	28	Boston Bruins	NHL	49	50	24	74	12	54	30	20	0	13	185	27.0
1994–95	29	Boston Bruins	NHL	42	27	14	41	7	72	11	16	0	5	178	15.2
1995–96	30	Boston Bruins	NHL	49	26	20	46	3	31	19	7	0	3	191	13.6
NHL Career – 13 Seasons				726	395	299	694	82	1241	252	142	1	61	2148	18.4

PLAYOFFS

Season	Age	Team	Lg	GP	G	A	PTS	+/-	PIM	ESG	PPG	SHG	GWG	SOG	S%
1983–84	18	Vancouver Canucks	NHL	4	2	0	2	-4	2	1	1	0	0	7	28.6
1985–86	20	Vancouver Canucks	NHL	3	0	0	0	-3	6	0	0	0	0	4	0.0
1986–87	21	Boston Bruins	NHL	4	5	1	6	-1	8	2	3	0	0	19	26.3
1987–88	22	Boston Bruins	NHL	23	9	8	17	1	51	7	2	0	2	71	12.7
1988–89	23	Boston Bruins	NHL	10	7	2	9	-2	8	3	4	0	2	24	29.2
1989–90	24	Boston Bruins	NHL	21	12	16	28	7	51	7	4	1	2	65	18.5
1990–91	25	Boston Bruins	NHL	19	16	4	20	-3	36	7	9	0	4	72	22.2
1992–93	27	Boston Bruins	NHL	4	4	1	5	0	4	3	1	0	0	16	25.0
1994–95	29	Boston Bruins	NHL	5	2	0	2	-4	2	1	1	0	1	13	15.4
NHL Career – 9 Seasons				93	57	32	89	-9	168	31	25	1	11	291	19.6

TROPHY CASE

AWARDS

Bill Masterton Memorial Trophy (1994)

ALL-STAR SELECTIONS

Second All-Star Team Right Wing (1988, 1990, 1991, 1994)

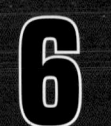

6

Frank Nighbor

HOCKEY HALL OF FAME CLASS: 1947

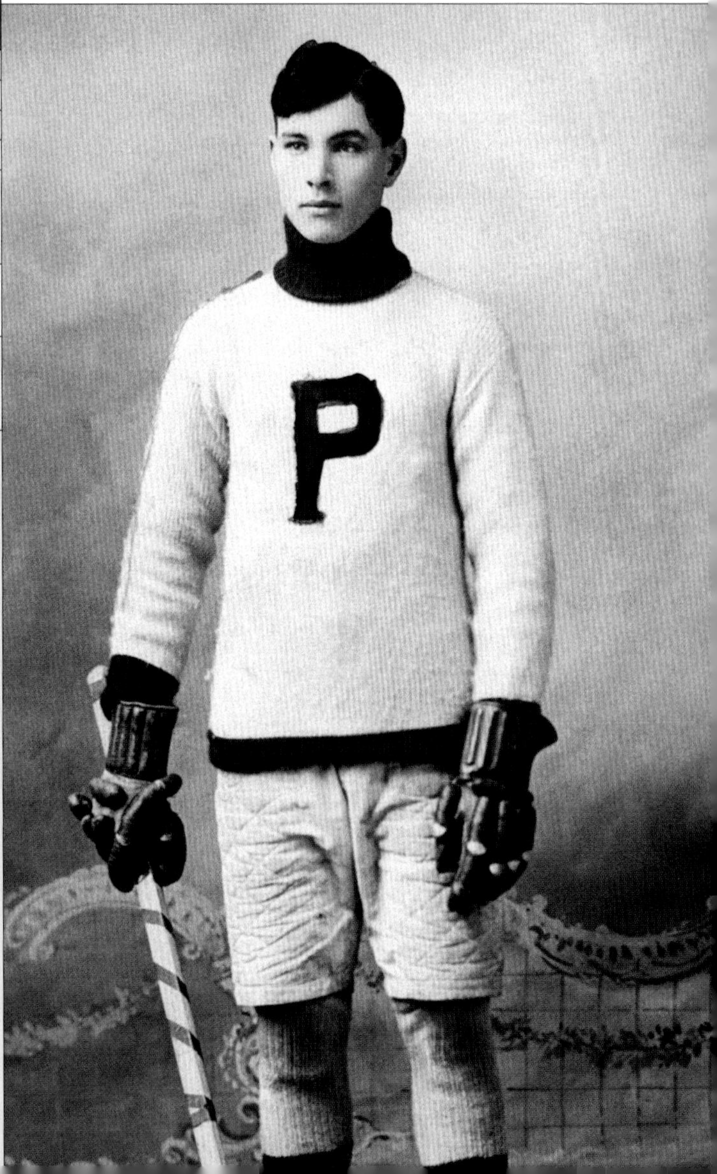

Alternate: 7

Center

Shoots: Right

Height: 5'-9"

Weight: 160 lbs.
Born: January 26, 1893: Pembroke, Ontario

Died: April 13, 1966: Pembroke, Ontario

Played 18 professional seasons from 1912–30

QUICK FACTS

- First player to win the Hart Trophy and the Lady Byng Trophy

- Nicknamed "The Pembroke Peach" because of his sweet and smooth style of play

- Played amateur hockey with Pembroke Debators (1910–11)

- Made professional debut with the Port Arthur Bearcats of the Northern Ontario Hockey League in 1911

- Scored six goals in Toronto Blueshirts' 10–3 victory over Montreal Wanderers, February 15, 1913

- Signed as a free agent by Vancouver (PCHA), October 22, 1915; jumped contract to sign with Ottawa (NHA), November 12, 1915

- Member of Stanley Cup-winning Vancouver Millionaires in 1914–15

- Led NHA in goals (41) and points (51) in 1916–17

- Led NHL in assists (15) in 1919–20; led NHL in assists (13) in 1925–26

- Finished among NHL top-5 in goals in 1918–19 (19), 1919–20 (26) and 1920–21 (19)

- Finished among NHL top-5 in assists in 1918–19 (9), 1919–20 (15), 1920–21 (10), 1923–24 (6) and 1925–26 (13)

- Finished among NHL top-5 in points in 1918–19 (28), 1919–20 (41) and 1920–21 (29)

- Noted for being a master of the sweep check, a common defensive maneuver now but an innovative and pioneering move during Nighbor's playing days

> They hand out a $1,000 check with the Byng award today, but I wouldn't trade this for $10,000."
>
> — Frank Nighbor, commenting on the trophy he was given by Lady Byng in 1925

REGULAR SEASON

Season	Age	Team	Lg	GP	G	A	PTS	PIM
1912–13	20	Toronto Blueshirts	NHA	19	25	0	25	9
1913–14	21	Vancouver Millionaires	PCHA	11	10	5	15	6
1914–15	22	Vancouver Millionaires	PCHA	17	23	7	30	12
1915–16	23	Ottawa Senators	NHA	23	19	5	24	26
1916–17	24	Ottawa Senators	NHA	19	41	10	51	24
1917–18	25	Ottawa Senators	NHL	10	11	8	19	6
1918–19	26	Ottawa Senators	NHL	18	19	9	28	27
1919–20	27	Ottawa Senators	NHL	23	26	15	41	18
1920–21	28	Ottawa Senators	NHL	24	19	10	29	10
1921–22	29	Ottawa Senators	NHL	20	8	10	18	4
1922–23	30	Ottawa Senators	NHL	22	11	7	18	14
1923–24	31	Ottawa Senators	NHL	20	11	6	17	16
1924–25	32	Ottawa Senators	NHL	26	5	5	10	18
1925–26	33	Ottawa Senators	NHL	35	12	13	25	40
1926–27	34	Ottawa Senators	NHL	38	6	6	12	26
1927–28	35	Ottawa Senators	NHL	42	8	5	13	46
1928–29	36	Ottawa Senators	NHL	30	1	4	5	22
1929–30	37	Ottawa Senators	NHL	19	0	0	0	0
1929–30	37	Toronto Maple Leafs	NHL	22	2	0	2	2
Career — 18 Seasons				438	257	125	382	326

PLAYOFFS

Season	Age	Team	Lg	GP	G	A	PTS	PIM
1914–15	22	Vancouver Millionaires	St-Cup	3	4	6	10	6
1916–17	24	Ottawa Senators	NHA	2	1	1	2	6
1918–19	26	Ottawa Senators	NHL	2	0	2	2	3
1919–20	27	Ottawa Senators	St-Cup	5	6	1	7	2
1920–21	28	Ottawa Senators	NHL	2	1	3	4	2
1920–21	28	Ottawa Senators	St-Cup	5	0	1	1	0
1921–22	29	Ottawa Senators	NHL	2	2	1	3	4
1922–23	30	Ottawa Senators	NHL	2	0	1	1	0
1922–23	30	Ottawa Senators	St-Cup	6	1	1	2	10
1923–24	31	Ottawa Senators	NHL	2	0	1	1	0
1925–26	33	Ottawa Senators	NHL	2	0	0	0	2
1926–27	34	Ottawa Senators	NHL	6	1	1	2	0
1927–28	35	Ottawa Senators	NHL	2	0	0	0	2
Career — 11 Seasons				41	16	19	35	37

TROPHY CASE

AWARDS

Hart Memorial Trophy (1924)

Lady Byng Memorial Trophy (1925, 1926)

Stanley Cup (1914–15, 1919–20, 1920–21, 1922–23, 1926–27)

ALL-STAR SELECTIONS

PCHA First All-Star Team Center (1915)

Reg Noble

HOCKEY HALL OF FAME CLASS: 1962

Alternates:
3, 12, 15, 7, 11, 6

Center/Defense

Shoots: Left

Height: 5'-8"

Weight: 180 lbs.

Born: June 23,
1896: Collingwood,
Ontario

Died: January 19,
1962: Alliston,
Ontario

Played 17
professional
seasons from
1916–33

QUICK FACTS

- Played amateur hockey with Collingwood ACC (1912–15); St. Michael's College (1915–16); Toronto Riversides (1915–16)
- OHA-Jr. First All-Star Team Center (1915)
- Led NHL in assists (10) in 1917–18; led NHL in penalty minutes (79) in 1923–24
- Finished among NHL top-5 in goals in 1917–18 (30), 1919–20 (24) and 1920–21 (19)
- Finished among NHL top-5 in assists in 1917–18 (10), 1922–23 (11) and 1925–26 (9)
- Traded to Montreal Maroons by Toronto St. Pats for $8,000, December 9, 1924
- Served as captain of Detroit Cougars (1927–30)
- Traded to Detroit Cougars by Montreal Maroons for $7,500, October 4, 1927

- Suffered a fractured skull when clipped by the stick of Ottawa's Hooley Smith in a 1925–26 game, but was back in the Maroons lineup after missing just four games
- Played for all three teams in the history of the Detroit franchise — Cougars (1927–30), Falcons (1930–32) and Red Wings (1932–33)
- Traded to Montreal Maroons by Detroit Falcons for John Gallagher, December 9, 1932
- Last player from inaugural NHL season of 1917–18 to be an active player in the league
- Worked as an NHL referee (1937–39)
- His niece, Gayle Noble, is a member of the McGill University Sports Hall of Fame for her contributions to the school in the sport of soccer

> He had an iron constitution and my players told me that every time they came in bodily contact with him, they were jarred from head to heels. He gave back with interest anything anybody was able to hand out."
> — Frank Selke

REGULAR SEASON

Season	Age	Team	Lg	GP	G	A	PTS	PIM
1916–17	19	Toronto Blueshirts	NHA	14	7	5	12	41
1916–17	20	Montreal Canadiens	NHA	6	4	0	4	15
1917–18	21	Toronto Arenas	NHL	20	30	10	40	35
1918–19	22	Toronto Arenas	NHL	17	10	5	15	35
1919–20	23	Toronto St. Patricks	NHL	24	24	9	33	52
1920–21	24	Toronto St. Patricks	NHL	24	19	8	27	54
1921–22	25	Toronto St. Patricks	NHL	24	17	11	28	19
1922–23	26	Toronto St. Patricks	NHL	24	12	11	23	47
1923–24	27	Toronto St. Patricks	NHL	24	12	5	17	79
1924–25	28	Toronto St. Patricks	NHL	3	1	0	1	8
1924–25	28	Montreal Maroons	NHL	27	8	11	19	56
1925–26	29	Montreal Maroons	NHL	33	9	9	18	96
1926–27	30	Montreal Maroons	NHL	43	3	3	6	112
1927–28	31	Detroit Cougars	NHL	44	6	8	14	63
1928–29	32	Detroit Cougars	NHL	43	6	4	10	52
1929–30	33	Detroit Cougars	NHL	43	6	4	10	72
1930–31	34	Detroit Falcons	NHL	44	2	5	7	42
1931–32	35	Detroit Falcons	NHL	48	3	3	6	72
1932–33	36	Detroit Red Wings	NHL	5	0	0	0	8
1932–33	36	Montreal Maroons	NHL	20	0	0	0	16
Career — 17 Seasons				530	179	111	290	972

PLAYOFFS

Season	Age	Team	Lg	GP	G	A	PTS	PIM
1916–17	20	Montreal Canadiens	NHA	2	0	1	1	3
1917–18	21	Toronto Arenas	NHL	2	1	1	2	9
1917–18	21	Toronto Arenas	St-Cup	5	2	1	3	12
1920–21	24	Toronto St. Patricks	NHL	2	0	0	0	0
1921–22	25	Toronto St. Patricks	NHL	2	0	0	0	12
1921–22	25	Toronto St. Patricks	St-Cup	5	0	1	1	9
1925–26	29	Montreal Maroons	NHL	4	1	1	2	6
1925–26	29	Montreal Maroons	St-Cup	4	0	0	0	4
1926–27	30	Montreal Maroons	NHL	2	0	0	0	2
1928–29	32	Detroit Cougars	NHL	2	0	0	0	2
1931–32	35	Detroit Falcons	NHL	2	0	0	0	0
1932–33	36	Montreal Maroons	NHL	2	0	0	0	2
Career — 9 Seasons				34	4	5	9	61

TROPHY CASE

AWARDS

Stanley Cup (1917–18, 1921–22, 1925–26)

10

Buddy O'Connor

HOCKEY HALL OF FAME CLASS: 1988

Alternates: 5, 21	
Center	
Shoots: Right	
Height: 5'-8"	
Weight: 142 lbs.	
Born: June 21, 1916: Montreal, Quebec	
Died: August 24, 1977: Montreal, Quebec	
Played 10 NHL seasons from 1941–51	

"I never met a finer person than Buddy. We played hockey together as kids and over the many years of association, he was always a gentleman and devoted family man."

— Pete Morin, member of the famed Razzle Dazzle Line with O'Connor and Gerry Heffernan

QUICK FACTS

- First player to win Hart Trophy and Lady Byng Trophy in the same year (1948)
- Named Canadian Athlete of the Year (1948)
- Played amateur hockey with Montreal Crane Juniors (1933–34); Montreal Jr. Royals (1934–35); Montreal Sr. Royals (1934–42)
- Led Montreal Junior League in goals (15) and points (22) in 1934–35
- Led Quebec Senior League in assists (23) and points (36) in 1938–39
- Led Quebec Senior League in assists in 1936–37 (17) and 1940–41 (38)
- Member of Allan Cup-winning Montreal Royals in 1939; registered 10 goals and 10 assists in Allan Cup playoffs
- Traded to Montreal Canadiens by Montreal Maroons for cash, September 24, 1938

- Member of Razzle Dazzle Line with Pete Morin and Gerry Heffernan. During the 1941–42 season, the entire line was promoted from the Quebec Senior League and brought up to play with the Canadiens
- Finished among NHL top-5 in assists in 1942–43 (43), 1943–44 (42) and 1947–48 (36)
- Rights traded to Montreal Maroons by Montreal Canadiens for Sammy McManus, September 10, 1936
- QSHL First All-Star Team Center (1937, 1941)
- Collected 210 points (78 goals and 132 assists) in 168 regular season games with the Royals and 98 points (42 goals and 56 assists) in 71 playoff games

O'Conner won his Cups in Montreal, but his best statistical season came in New York in 1947–48.

REGULAR SEASON

Season	Age	Team	Lg	GP	G	A	PTS	PIM
1941–42	25	Montreal Canadiens	NHL	36	9	16	25	4
1942–43	26	Montreal Canadiens	NHL	50	15	43	58	2
1943–44	27	Montreal Canadiens	NHL	44	12	42	54	6
1944–45	28	Montreal Canadiens	NHL	50	21	23	44	2
1945–46	29	Montreal Canadiens	NHL	45	11	11	22	2
1946–47	30	Montreal Canadiens	NHL	46	10	20	30	6
1947–48	31	New York Rangers	NHL	60	24	36	60	8
1948–49	32	New York Rangers	NHL	46	11	24	35	0
1949–50	33	New York Rangers	NHL	66	11	22	33	4
1950–51	34	New York Rangers	NHL	66	16	20	36	0
NHL Career – 10 Seasons				509	140	257	397	34

PLAYOFFS

Season	Age	Team	Lg	GP	G	A	PTS	PIM
1941–42	25	Montreal Canadiens	NHL	3	0	1	1	0
1942–43	26	Montreal Canadiens	NHL	5	4	5	9	0
1943–44	27	Montreal Canadiens	NHL	8	1	2	3	2
1944–45	28	Montreal Canadiens	NHL	2	0	0	0	0
1945–46	29	Montreal Canadiens	NHL	9	2	3	5	0
1946–47	30	Montreal Canadiens	NHL	8	3	4	7	0
1947–48	31	New York Rangers	NHL	6	1	4	5	0
1949–50	33	New York Rangers	NHL	12	4	2	6	4
NHL Career – 8 Seasons				53	15	21	36	6

TROPHY CASE

AWARDS

Lady Byng Memorial Trophy (1948)

Hart Memorial Trophy (1948)

Stanley Cup (1943–44, 1945–46)

ALL-STAR SELECTIONS

Second All-Star Team Center (1948)

9

Harry Oliver

HOCKEY HALL OF FAME CLASS: 1967

Alternates:
8, 10, 7, 6

Right Wing

Shoots: Right

Height: 5'-8"

Weight: 155 lbs.

Born: October 26, 1898: Selkirk, Manitoba

Died June 16, 1985: Winnipeg, Manitoba

Played 16 professional seasons from 1921–37

QUICK FACTS

- Played amateur hockey with Selkirk Jr. Fishermen (1915–18); Selkirk Sr. Fishermen (1918–20); Calgary Canadians (1920–21)

- Led WCHL in assists (13) and points (33) in 1924–25

- Inducted in Manitoba Hockey Hall of Fame (1985)

- Nicknamed "Pee-Wee" because of his diminutive size

- Signed as a free agent by Calgary Tigers (WCHL), December 22, 1921

- Traded to Boston by Calgary Tigers (WHL) for cash, September 4, 1926; traded to N.Y. Americans by Boston for cash, November 2, 1934

- Played on a line with scoring ace Frank Fredrickson and Perk Galbraith in Boston

- Scored the opening goal and set up the Stanley Cup-winning goal in Boston's 2–1 victory over the N.Y. Rangers, March 26, 1929

- Played on a line with Art Chapman and Lorne Carr as a member of the N.Y. Americans

- Renowned for his gentlemanly conduct on the ice and impeccable decorum outside of the rink

> "When I was a kid, there was no organized hockey. We just went out and played, sometimes on an outdoor rink, but mostly on the river."

REGULAR SEASON

Season	Age	Team	Lg	GP	G	A	PTS	PIM
1921–22	23	Calgary Tigers	WCHL	20	10	4	14	7
1922–23	24	Calgary Tigers	WCHL	29	25	7	32	10
1923–24	25	Calgary Tigers	WCHL	27	22	12	34	14
1924–25	26	Calgary Tigers	WCHL	24	20	13	33	23
1925–26	27	Calgary Tigers	WHL	30	13	12	25	14
1926–27	28	Boston Bruins	NHL	42	18	6	24	17
1927–28	29	Boston Bruins	NHL	43	13	5	18	20
1928–29	30	Boston Bruins	NHL	43	17	6	23	24
1929–30	31	Boston Bruins	NHL	40	16	5	21	12
1930–31	32	Boston Bruins	NHL	44	16	14	30	18
1931–32	33	Boston Bruins	NHL	44	13	7	20	22
1932–33	34	Boston Bruins	NHL	47	11	7	18	10
1933–34	35	Boston Bruins	NHL	48	5	9	14	6
1934–35	36	New York Americans	NHL	47	7	9	16	4
1935–36	37	New York Americans	NHL	45	9	16	25	12
1936–37	38	New York Americans	NHL	20	2	1	3	2
Career — 16 Seasons				593	217	133	350	215

PLAYOFFS

Season	Age	Team	Lg	GP	G	A	PTS	PIM
1921–22	23	Calgary Tigers	WCHL	2	1	0	1	0
1923–24	25	Calgary Tigers	St-Cup	2	0	0	0	0
1923–24	25	Calgary Tigers	WCHL	2	0	1	1	2
1923–24	25	Calgary Tigers	West-P	3	2	1	3	2
1924–25	26	Calgary Tigers	WCHL	2	0	0	0	2
1926–27	28	Boston Bruins	NHL	8	4	2	6	4
1927–28	29	Boston Bruins	NHL	2	2	0	2	4
1928–29	30	Boston Bruins	NHL	5	1	1	2	8
1929–30	31	Boston Bruins	NHL	6	2	1	3	6
1930–31	32	Boston Bruins	NHL	4	0	0	0	2
1932–33	34	Boston Bruins	NHL	5	0	0	0	0
1935–36	37	New York Americans	NHL	5	1	2	3	0
Career — 10 Seasons				46	13	8	21	30

TROPHY CASE

AWARDS

Stanley Cup (1928–29)

ALL-STAR SELECTIONS

WCHL Second Team
All-Star Right Wing
(1923, 1924, 1925)

15

Bert Olmstead
HOCKEY HALL OF FAME CLASS: 1985

Alternates:
16, 14, 19

Left Wing

Shoots: Left

Height: 6'-1"

Weight: 180 lbs.

Born: September
4, 1926: Sceptre,
Saskatchewan

Played 14 NHL
seasons from
1948–62

QUICK FACTS

I'm a hockey man through and through. I have a lot of love for the game and for what it means."

- Held NHL record for assists in regular season (56); surpassed by Jean Béliveau (58) in 1960–61

- Shared NHL record (with Maurice Richard) for most points in a regular season game (8); surpassed by Darryl Sittler (10), February 7, 1976

- Played amateur hockey with Moose Jaw Canucks (1944–46)

- Played minor pro hockey with Kansas City Pla-Mors (1946–49); Milwaukee Seagulls (1950–51)

- Played in NHL All-Star Game (1953, 1956, 1957, 1959)

- Led NHL in assists in 1954–55 (48) and 1955–56 (56); led NHL in playoff assists (10) in 1955–56

- Finished among NHL top-5 in points in 1953–54 (52) and 1955–56 (70)

- Traded to Detroit by Chicago with Vic Stasiuk for Lee Fogolin and Steve Black, December 2, 1950; traded to Montreal by Detroit for Leo Gravelle, December 19, 1950

- Claimed by Toronto from Montreal in Intra-League Draft, June 3, 1958

- Renowned for skills as a ferocious, antagonistic checker — an early version of today's power forward

- Served as player/assistant coach with Toronto (1958–59)

- Coached (WHL) Vancouver Canucks (1965–67)

- Served as coach and General Manager of Oakland Seals (1967–68)

REGULAR SEASON

Season	Age	Team	Lg	GP	G	A	PTS	PIM
1948–49	22	Chicago Black Hawks	NHL	9	0	2	2	4
1949–50	23	Chicago Black Hawks	NHL	70	20	29	49	40
1950–51	24	Chicago Black Hawks	NHL	15	2	1	3	0
1950–51	24	Montreal Canadiens	NHL	39	16	22	38	50
1951–52	25	Montreal Canadiens	NHL	69	7	28	35	49
1952–53	26	Montreal Canadiens	NHL	69	17	28	45	83
1953–54	27	Montreal Canadiens	NHL	70	15	37	52	85
1954–55	28	Montreal Canadiens	NHL	70	10	48	58	103
1955–56	29	Montreal Canadiens	NHL	70	14	56	70	94
1956–57	30	Montreal Canadiens	NHL	64	15	33	48	74
1957–58	31	Montreal Canadiens	NHL	57	9	28	37	71
1958–59	32	Toronto Maple Leafs	NHL	70	10	31	41	74
1959–60	33	Toronto Maple Leafs	NHL	53	15	21	36	63
1960–61	34	Toronto Maple Leafs	NHL	67	18	34	52	84
1961–62	35	Toronto Maple Leafs	NHL	56	13	23	36	10
NHL Career – 14 Seasons				848	181	421	602	884

PLAYOFFS

Season	Age	Team	Lg	GP	G	A	PTS	PIM
1950–51	24	Montreal Canadiens	NHL	11	2	4	6	9
1951–52	25	Montreal Canadiens	NHL	11	0	1	1	4
1952–53	26	Montreal Canadiens	NHL	12	2	2	4	4
1953–54	27	Montreal Canadiens	NHL	11	0	1	1	19
1954–55	28	Montreal Canadiens	NHL	12	0	4	4	21
1955–56	29	Montreal Canadiens	NHL	10	4	10	14	8
1956–57	30	Montreal Canadiens	NHL	10	0	9	9	13
1957–58	31	Montreal Canadiens	NHL	9	0	3	3	0
1958–59	32	Toronto Maple Leafs	NHL	12	4	2	6	13
1959–60	33	Toronto Maple Leafs	NHL	10	3	4	7	0
1960–61	34	Toronto Maple Leafs	NHL	3	1	2	3	10
1961–62	35	Toronto Maple Leafs	NHL	4	0	1	1	0
NHL Career – 12 Seasons				115	16	43	59	101

TROPHY CASE

AWARDS

Stanley Cup (1952–53, 1955–56, 1956–57, 1957–58, 1961–62)

ALL-STAR SELECTIONS

Second All-Star Team Left Wing (1953, 1956)

Retired by Boston

Defense	
Shoots: Left	
Height: 6'	
Weight: 197 lbs.	

Born: March 20, 1948: Parry Sound, Ontario

Played 12 NHL seasons from 1966–77, 1978–79

" I never thought there could be such a day. This is what every kid dreams of, scoring the winning goal in a Stanley Cup overtime final. Wow! I can't find words to express what I feel."

— Bobby Orr, on his famous 1970 overtime goal

Bobby Orr
HOCKEY HALL OF FAME CLASS: 1979

QUICK FACTS

- First and only defenseman in NHL history to win league scoring title (1970, 1975)
- First defenseman in NHL history to record 100 points in regular season (1969–70)
- First player in NHL history to win Conn Smythe Trophy twice (1970, 1972)
- Holds NHL record for regular season assists (102) and points (139) by a defenseman, established in 1970–71
- Holds NHL record for plus/minus rating in regular season (+124), established in 1970–71
- Shares NHL record for assists in a regular season game by a defenseman (6), January 1, 1973
- Played in NHL All-Star Game (1968, 1969, 1970, 1971, 1972, 1973, 1975)
- Played amateur hockey with Oshawa Generals (1962–66)
- Scored Stanley Cup-winning overtime goal in Boston's 4–3 victory over St. Louis Blues, May 10, 1970
- Led NHL in assists in 1969–70 (87), 1970–71 (102), 1971–72 (80), 1973–74 (90) and 1974–75 (89); led NHL playoffs in assists (19) and points (24) in 1971–72; led NHL in shots-on-goal in 1969–70 (413) and 1974–75 (384)
- Led Canada Cup Tournament in points (9) in 1976; named Canada Cup MVP (1976)
- Burdened by knee injuries through the majority of career; missed 1972 Summit Series and entire 1977–78 season recovering from off-season surgery

Bobby Orr stars in Bally's "Power Play" pinball game.

REGULAR SEASON

Season	Age	Team	Lg	GP	G	A	PTS	+/-	PIM	ESG	PPG	SHG	GWG	SOG	S%
1966–67	18	Boston Bruins	NHL	61	13	28	41		102	9	3	1	0		
1967–68	19	Boston Bruins	NHL	46	11	20	31	30	63	8	3	0	1	172	6.4
1968–69	20	Boston Bruins	NHL	67	21	43	64	65	133	17	4	0	2	285	7.4
1969–70	21	Boston Bruins	NHL	76	33	87	120	54	125	18	11	4	3	413	8.0
1970–71	22	Boston Bruins	NHL	78	37	102	139	124	91	29	5	3	5	392	9.4
1971–72	23	Boston Bruins	NHL	76	37	80	117	86	106	22	11	4	4	353	10.5
1972–73	24	Boston Bruins	NHL	63	29	72	101	56	99	21	7	1	3	282	10.3
1973–74	25	Boston Bruins	NHL	74	32	90	122	84	82	21	11	0	4	384	8.3
1974–75	26	Boston Bruins	NHL	80	46	89	135	80	101	28	16	2	4	384	12.0
1975–76	27	Boston Bruins	NHL	10	5	13	18	10	22	1	3	1	0	57	8.8
1976–77	28	Chicago Black Hawks	NHL	20	4	19	23	6	25	2	2	0	0	55	7.3
1978–79	30	Chicago Black Hawks	NHL	6	2	2	4	2	4	2	0	0	0	18	11.1
NHL Career – 12 Seasons				657	270	645	915	597	953	178	76	16	26	2795	9.2

PLAYOFFS

Season	Age	Team	Lg	GP	G	A	PTS	+/-	PIM	ESG	PPG	SHG	GWG	SOG	S%
1967–68	19	Boston Bruins	NHL	4	0	2	2		2	0	0	0	0		
1968–69	20	Boston Bruins	NHL	10	1	7	8		10	1	0	0	1		
1969–70	21	Boston Bruins	NHL	14	9	11	20		14	5	3	1	2		
1970–71	22	Boston Bruins	NHL	7	5	7	12		25	3	1	1	1		
1971–72	23	Boston Bruins	NHL	15	5	19	24		19	2	3	0	1		
1972–73	24	Boston Bruins	NHL	5	1	1	2		7	1	0	0	0		
1973–74	25	Boston Bruins	NHL	16	4	14	18		28	3	1	0	2		
1974–75	26	Boston Bruins	NHL	3	1	5	6		2	0	0	1	0		
NHL Career – 8 Seasons				74	26	66	92		107	15	8	3	7		

TROPHY CASE

AWARDS

Calder Memorial Trophy (1967)

James Norris Memorial Trophy (1968, 1969, 1970, 1971, 1972, 1973, 1974, 1975)

Art Ross Trophy (1970, 1975)

Conn Smythe Trophy (1970, 1972)

Hart Memorial Trophy (1970, 1971, 1972)

Lester B. Pearson Award (1975)

Lester Patrick Trophy (1979)

Stanley Cup (1969–70, 1971–72)

ALL-STAR SELECTIONS

First All-Star Team Defense (1968, 1969, 1970, 1971, 1972, 1973, 1974, 1975)

Second All-Star Team Defense (1967)

INTERNATIONAL AWARDS

Canada Cup (1976)

1

Retired by Philadelphia

Alternate: 30
Goaltender
Catches: Left
Height: 5'-10"
Weight: 180 lbs.
Born: April 3, 1945: Montreal, Quebec
Played 14 NHL and WHA seasons from 1965–79

" You don't have to be crazy to be a goalie, but it helps."

Bernie Parent

HOCKEY HALL OF FAME CLASS: 1984

QUICK FACTS

- Held NHL record for wins in regular season (47); surpassed by Martin Brodeur (48) in 2006–07
- First player in NHL history to win Conn Smythe Trophy in back-to-back seasons
- Holds Philadelphia Flyers team records for career shutouts (50) and single season shutouts (12)
- Played amateur hockey with Rosemount Raiders (1962–63); Niagara Falls Flyers (1963–65)
- Led OHA-Jr. in goals-against-average in 1963–64 (2.86) and 1964–65 (2.58); led OHA-Jr. playoffs in wins (6) and goals-against-average (1.86) in 1964–65
- Member of Memorial Cup-winning Niagara Falls Flyers (1964–65); led Memorial Cup playoffs in wins (10) and goals-against-average (1.63)

- OHA-Jr. First All-Star Team Goaltender (1965); OHA-Jr. Second All-Star Team Goaltender (1964)
- Played minor pro hockey with Oklahoma City Blazers (1965–67)
- Led CPHL in shutouts (4) in 1966–67
- Played in NHL All-Star Game (1969, 1970, 1974, 1975, 1977)
- Led NHL in goals-against-average in 1973–74 (1.89) and 1974–75 (2.03)
- Led NHL in shutouts in 1973–74 (12), 1974–75 (12) and 1977–78 (7); led NHL in wins in 1973–74 (47) and 1974–75 (44)
- Led WHA in wins (33) in 1972–73; WHA Second All-Star Team Goaltender (1973)
- Suffered career-ending eye injury in game vs. N.Y. Rangers, February 17, 1979

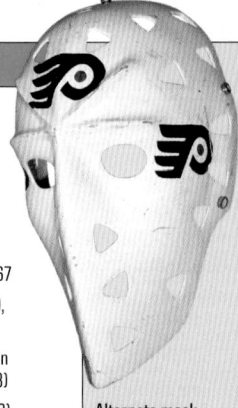

Alternate mask Parent wore toward the end of his NHL career.

REGULAR SEASON

Season	Age	Team	Lg	GP	W	L	T	SO	GA	GAA	G	A	PTS	PIM
1965–66	20	Boston Bruins	NHL	39	11	20	3	1	128	3.69	0	0	0	4
1966–67	21	Boston Bruins	NHL	18	4	12	2	0	62	3.64	0	0	0	2
1967–68	22	Philadelphia Flyers	NHL	38	16	17	5	4	93	2.48	0	1	1	23
1968–69	23	Philadelphia Flyers	NHL	58	17	23	16	1	151	2.69	0	0	0	4
1969–70	24	Philadelphia Flyers	NHL	62	13	29	20	3	171	2.79	0	3	3	14
1970–71	25	Philadelphia Flyers	NHL	30	9	12	6	2	73	2.76	0	2	2	5
1970–71	25	Toronto Maple Leafs	NHL	18	7	7	4	0	46	2.65	0	0	0	0
1971–72	26	Toronto Maple Leafs	NHL	47	17	18	9	3	116	2.56	0	1	1	6
1972–73	27	Philadelphia Blazers	WHA	63	33	28	0	2	220	3.61	0	1	1	36
1973–74	28	Philadelphia Flyers	NHL	73	47	13	12	12	136	1.89	0	3	3	24
1974–75	29	Philadelphia Flyers	NHL	68	44	14	10	12	137	2.03	0	0	0	16
1975–76	30	Philadelphia Flyers	NHL	11	6	2	3	0	24	2.34	0	0	0	2
1976–77	31	Philadelphia Flyers	NHL	61	35	13	12	5	159	2.71	0	0	0	0
1977–78	32	Philadelphia Flyers	NHL	49	29	6	13	7	108	2.22	0	0	0	0
1978–79	33	Philadelphia Flyers	NHL	36	16	12	7	4	89	2.70	0	2	2	8
Career – 14 Seasons				671	304	226	121	56	1713	2.55	0	13	13	148

PLAYOFFS

Season	Age	Team	Lg	GP	W	L	T	SO	GA	GAA	G	A	PTS	PIM
1967–68	22	Philadelphia Flyers	NHL	5	2	3		0	8	1.35	0	0	0	0
1968–69	23	Philadelphia Flyers	NHL	3	0	3		0	12	4.00	0	0	0	0
1970–71	25	Toronto Maple Leafs	NHL	4	2	2		0	9	2.30	0	0	0	0
1971–72	26	Toronto Maple Leafs	NHL	4	1	3		0	13	3.21	0	0	0	0
1972–73	27	Philadelphia Blazers	WHA	1	0	1		0	3	2.57	0	0	0	0
1973–74	27	Philadelphia Flyers	NHL	17	12	5		2	35	2.02	0	0	0	4
1974–75	29	Philadelphia Flyers	NHL	15	10	5		4	29	1.89	0	0	0	0
1975–76	30	Philadelphia Flyers	NHL	8	4	4		0	27	3.38	0	0	0	0
1976–77	31	Philadelphia Flyers	NHL	3	0	3		0	8	3.90	0	0	0	0
1977–78	32	Philadelphia Flyers	NHL	12	7	5		0	33	2.74	0	0	0	0
Career – 10 Seasons				72	38	34		6	177	2.46	0	0	0	4

TROPHY CASE

AWARDS

Conn Smythe Trophy winner (1974, 1975)

Vezina Trophy (1974, 1975)

Stanley Cup (1973–74, 1974–75)

ALL-STAR SELECTIONS

First All-Star Team Goaltender (1974, 1975)

2

Brad Park

HOCKEY HALL OF FAME CLASS: 1988

Alternate: 22

Defense

Shoots: Left

Height: 6'

Weight: 200 lbs.

Born: July 6, 1948;
Toronto, Ontario

Drafted by
the New York
Rangers second
overall in 1966

Played 17 NHL
seasons from
1968–85

" I never
thought
I'd get to a
thousand games
and quite a few
other people
didn't think I
would either.
There was just no
indication how
much hockey was
left in my knees.
Even though
there was a lot
of damage done
to my knees, they
held together
remarkably well
through the
years."

QUICK FACTS

- Held NHL record for career points by a defenseman (896); surpassed by Denis Potvin in 1986–87
- Held NHL record for consecutive years appearing in the playoffs (17); surpassed by Larry Robinson in 1999–2000
- Played amateur hockey with Scarborough Lions (1959–63); Eglington Aces (1963–65); Toronto Westclairs (1965–66); Toronto Marlboros (1965–68)
- OHA-Jr. Second All-Star Team Defense (1968)
- Member of Memorial Cup-winning Toronto Marlboros (1967)
- First defenseman in N.Y. Rangers history to record a hat-trick in N.Y. Rangers' 6–1 victory over Pittsburgh Penguins, December 12, 1971

- One of only seven players to play every game in 1972 Canada–Soviet Union Summit Series
- Named Player of the Game (with Paul Henderson) in Game 8 of 1972 Summit Series
- Played in nine consecutive NHL All-Star Games from 1970–78
- Finished among NHL top-10 in assists in 1973–74 (57), 1976–77 (55) and 1977–78 (57)
- Finished as runner-up to Bobby Orr in Norris Trophy voting six times
- Named N.Y. Rangers MVP after leading team in scoring with 82 points in 1973–74
- Coached Detroit Red Wings (1985–86)

Park's Daoust 301 skates, a popular choice for NHL stars in the early 1980s.

REGULAR SEASON

Season	Age	Team	Lg	GP	G	A	PTS	+/-	PIM	ESG	PPG	SHG	GWG	SOG	S%
1968–69	20	New York Rangers	NHL	54	3	23	26	12	70	1	2	0	0	103	2.9
1969–70	21	New York Rangers	NHL	60	11	26	37	23	98	4	6	1	2	161	6.8
1970–71	22	New York Rangers	NHL	68	7	37	44	25	114	4	3	0	0	199	3.5
1971–72	23	New York Rangers	NHL	75	24	49	73	62	130	14	8	2	4	263	9.1
1972–73	24	New York Rangers	NHL	52	10	43	53	31	51	6	4	0	1	142	7.0
1973–74	25	New York Rangers	NHL	78	25	57	82	18	148	21	4	0	4	227	11.0
1974–75	26	New York Rangers	NHL	65	13	44	57	6	104	5	8	0	2	189	6.9
1975–76	27	New York Rangers	NHL	13	2	4	6	-4	23	2	0	0	1	28	7.1
1975–76	27	Boston Bruins	NHL	43	16	37	53	23	95	8	7	1	2	163	9.8
1976–77	28	Boston Bruins	NHL	77	12	55	67	47	67	7	4	1	4	238	5.0
1977–78	29	Boston Bruins	NHL	80	22	57	79	68	79	13	9	0	3	225	9.8
1978–79	30	Boston Bruins	NHL	40	7	32	39	28	10	4	3	0	0	96	7.3
1979–80	31	Boston Bruins	NHL	32	5	16	21	11	27	3	2	0	2	67	7.5
1980–81	32	Boston Bruins	NHL	78	14	52	66	21	111	4	10	0	2	201	7.0
1981–82	33	Boston Bruins	NHL	75	14	42	56	11	82	6	8	0	1	159	8.8
1982–83	34	Boston Bruins	NHL	76	10	26	36	20	82	5	5	0	0	127	7.9
1983–84	35	Detroit Red Wings	NHL	80	5	53	58	-29	85	1	4	0	0	140	3.6
1984–85	36	Detroit Red Wings	NHL	67	13	30	43	-15	53	7	6	0	0	92	14.1
NHL Career — 17 Seasons				1113	213	683	896	358	1429	115	93	5	28	2820	7.6

PLAYOFFS

Season	Age	Team	Lg	GP	G	A	PTS	+/-	PIM	ESG	PPG	SHG	GWG	SOG	S%
1968–69	20	New York Rangers	NHL	4	0	2	2		7	0	0	0	0		
1969–70	21	New York Rangers	NHL	5	1	2	3		11	0	1	0	0		
1970–71	22	New York Rangers	NHL	13	0	4	4		42	0	0	0	0		
1971–72	23	New York Rangers	NHL	16	4	7	11		21	2	2	0	1		
1972–73	24	New York Rangers	NHL	10	2	5	7		8	1	1	0	1		
1973–74	25	New York Rangers	NHL	13	4	8	12		38	2	2	0	1		
1974–75	26	New York Rangers	NHL	3	1	4	5		2	1	0	0	0		
1975–76	27	Boston Bruins	NHL	11	3	8	11		14	1	1	1	0		
1976–77	28	Boston Bruins	NHL	14	2	10	12		4	2	0	0	0		
1977–78	29	Boston Bruins	NHL	15	9	11	20		14	5	4	0	0		
1978–79	30	Boston Bruins	NHL	11	1	4	5		8	1	0	0	1		
1979–80	31	Boston Bruins	NHL	10	3	6	9		4	3	0	0	0		
1980–81	32	Boston Bruins	NHL	3	1	3	4		11	0	1	0	0		
1981–82	33	Boston Bruins	NHL	11	1	4	5		4	1	0	0	1		
1982–83	34	Boston Bruins	NHL	16	3	9	12		18	2	1	0	1		
1983–84	35	Detroit Red Wings	NHL	3	0	3	3	0	0	0	0	0	0	5	0.0
1984–85	36	Detroit Red Wings	NHL	3	0	0	0	-8	11	0	0	0	0	5	0.0
NHL Career — 17 Seasons				161	35	90	125	-8	217	21	13	1	6	10	0.0

Lester Patrick
HOCKEY HALL OF FAME CLASS: 1947

Alternates: 3, 16

Defense/
Goaltender/Rover

Shoots: Left

Height: 6'-1"

Weight: 180 lbs.

Born: December 31, 1883: Drummondville, Quebec

Died: June 1, 1960: Victoria, British Columbia

Played 22 elite amateur and professional seasons from 1903–22, 1925–27, 1927–28

> "Without doubt, Lester Patrick had something on every one of the remaining players. The big fellow is in a class without opposition as a defenseman ... Patrick at point would make any second-rate team look formidable."
> — Malcolm Brice, *Ottawa Free Press*, December 1908

QUICK FACTS

- Brother of Hall of Fame member Frank Patrick (inducted as a builder), who played 19 elite amateur and professional seasons from 1901–24

- Father of Hall of Fame member Lynn Patrick, who played in NHL with N.Y. Rangers from 1934–46; father of Muzz Patrick, who played in NHL with N.Y. Rangers from 1937–46

- Learned to play hockey in Montreal but came to prominence with Brandon, Manitoba, team that lost Stanley Cup challenge to the Ottawa "Silver Seven" in March of 1904

- Played with future Hall of Fame members Frank Patrick, Cyclone Taylor, Newsy Lalonde and Fred Whitcroft on the Renfrew Millionaires of the National Hockey Association in 1909–10

- Scored final two goals in 12–10 two-game, total-goal series that clinched Montreal Wanderers' Stanley Cup victory over Ottawa in March of 1906

- Helped form and launch Pacific Coast Hockey Association in 1911–12 with brother Frank Patrick

- Served as player, coach, General Manager and owner of Victoria Aristocrats and Victoria Cougars (1911–16, 1918–26)

- Coached Stanley Cup-winning Victoria Cougars — last non-NHL team to win the Stanley Cup in 1924–25

- Coached N.Y. Rangers (1926–39); served as General Manager of N.Y. Rangers (1926–45)

- Replaced an injured Lorne Chabot in goal during N.Y. Rangers' 2–1 victory over Montreal Maroons, April 7, 1928

Patrick as a member of the Renfrew Millionaires.

REGULAR SEASON

Season	Age	Team	Lg	GP	G	A	PTS	PIM
1903–04	20	Brandon Hockey Club	MNWHA	12	4	2	6	
1904–05	21	Westmount Hockey Club	CAHL	8	4	0	4	
1905–06	22	Montreal Wanderers	ECAHA	9	17	0	17	26
1906–07	23	Montreal Wanderers	ECAHA	9	11	0	11	11
1907–08	24	Nelson HC	BCBHL	3	3	0	3	
1908–09	25	Nelson HC	BCBHL	22	6	0	6	
1909–10	26	Renfrew Hockey Club	NHA	12	24	0	24	25
1910–11	27	Nelson HC	BCBHL	11	5	0	5	
1911–12	28	Victoria Aristocrats	PCHA	16	10	0	10	9
1912–13	29	Victoria Aristocrats	PCHA	15	14	5	19	12
1913–14	30	Victoria Aristocrats	PCHA	9	5	5	10	0
1914–15	31	Victoria Aristocrats	PCHA	17	12	5	17	15
1915–16	32	Victoria Aristocrats	PCHA	18	13	11	24	27
1916–17	33	Spokane Canaries	PCHA	23	10	11	21	15
1917–18	34	Seattle Metropolitans	PCHA	17	2	8	10	15
1918–19	35	Victoria Aristocrats	PCHA	9	2	5	7	0
1919–20	36	Victoria Aristocrats	PCHA	11	2	2	4	3
1920–21	37	Victoria Aristocrats	PCHA	5	2	3	5	13
1921–22	38	Victoria Aristocrats	PCHA	2	0	0	0	0
1925–26	42	Victoria Cougars	WHL	23	5	8	13	20
1926–27	43	New York Rangers	NHL	1	0	0	0	2
Career — 18 Seasons				252	151	65	403	213

PLAYOFFS

Season	Age	Team	Lg	GP	G	A	PTS	PIM
1903–04	20	Brandon Hockey Club	St-Cup	2	0	0	0	0
1905–06	22	Montreal Wanderers	ECAHA	2	3	0	3	3
1906–07	23	Montreal Wanderers	St-Cup	6	10	0	10	32
1907–08	24	Nelson Seniors	BCHL	2	1	0	1	
1908–09	25	Edmonton Professionals	St-Cup	2	1	1	2	3
1913–14	30	Victoria Aristocrats	St-Cup	3	2	0	2	0
1917–18	34	Seattle Metropolitans	PCHA	2	0	1	1	0
1925–26	42	Victoria Cougars	WHL	2	0	0	0	2
1927–28	44	New York Rangers	NHL	1	0	0	0	0
Career — 9 Seasons				22	17	2	19	40

TROPHY CASE

AWARDS

Stanley Cup (1905–06, 1906–07, 1927–28)

ALL-STAR SELECTIONS

PCHA First All-Star Team Defense (1913, 1915, 1916, 1917)

PCHA Second All-Star Team Defense (1918, 1920)

First All-Star Team Coach (1931, 1932, 1933, 1934, 1935, 1936, 1938)

Lynn Patrick

HOCKEY HALL OF FAME CLASS: 1980

Alternate: 18

Center/Left Wing

Shoots: Left

Height: 6'-1"

Weight: 192 lbs.

Born: February 3, 1912: Victoria, British Columbia

Died: January 26, 1980: St. Louis, Missouri

Played 10 NHL seasons from 1934–43, 1945–46

QUICK FACTS

- Played amateur hockey with Montreal Royals (1933–34)
- Played basketball with Vancouver Blue Ribbons, Dominion of Canada champions (1933)
- Played basketball with Montreal Nationales (1934)
- Played football with the Montreal Football Club (1934)
- Signed as a free agent by N.Y. Rangers, November 4, 1934
- Led NHL in goals (32) in 1941–42
- Finished second in NHL points in 1940–41 (44) and 1941–42 (54)
- Member of N.Y. Rangers' Powerhouse Line with Phil Watson and Bryan Hextall

- Coached New Haven Ramblers (1946–48); coached Los Angeles Blades (1965–66)
- Coached N.Y. Rangers (1948–50); coached Boston Bruins (1950–55)
- Coached St. Louis Blues (1967–68, 1974–75, 1975–76)
- Served as General Manager of Boston Bruins (1954–64); served as General Manager of St. Louis Blues (1967–68, 1971–72)
- Subject of a *Time Magazine* story, "The Boss's Son," in the January 3, 1949 issue
- Brother of Muzz Patrick, who played in the NHL with N.Y. Rangers from 1937–46
- Father of Craig Patrick, who played in the NHL with California, St. Louis, Kansas City and Washington from 1971–79

> I was never judged on my merit as a hockey player. The fans felt the only reason I made the Rangers was because my dad Lester was the big man."
> — Lynn Patrick, on accusations of nepotism

REGULAR SEASON

Season	Age	Team	Lg	GP	G	A	PTS	PIM
1934–35	22	New York Rangers	NHL	48	9	13	22	17
1935–36	23	New York Rangers	NHL	48	11	14	25	29
1936–37	24	New York Rangers	NHL	45	8	16	24	23
1937–38	25	New York Rangers	NHL	48	15	19	34	24
1938–39	26	New York Rangers	NHL	35	8	21	29	25
1939–40	27	New York Rangers	NHL	48	12	16	28	34
1940–41	28	New York Rangers	NHL	48	20	24	44	12
1941–42	29	New York Rangers	NHL	47	32	22	54	18
1942–43	30	New York Rangers	NHL	50	22	39	61	28
1945–46	33	New York Rangers	NHL	38	8	6	14	30
NHL Career — 10 Seasons				455	145	190	335	240

PLAYOFFS

Season	Age	Team	Lg	GP	G	A	PTS	PIM
1934–35	22	New York Rangers	NHL	4	2	2	4	0
1936–37	24	New York Rangers	NHL	9	3	0	3	2
1937–38	25	New York Rangers	NHL	3	0	1	1	2
1938–39	26	New York Rangers	NHL	7	1	1	2	0
1939–40	27	New York Rangers	NHL	12	2	2	4	4
1940–41	28	New York Rangers	NHL	3	1	0	1	14
1941–42	29	New York Rangers	NHL	6	1	0	1	0
NHL Career — 7 Seasons				44	10	6	16	22

TROPHY CASE

AWARDS

Lester Patrick Trophy (1989)

Stanley Cup (1939–40)

ALL-STAR SELECTIONS

First All-Star Team Left Wing (1942)

Second All-Star Team Left Wing (1943)

11

Retired by Buffalo

Center

Shoots: Right

Height: 6'-1"

Weight: 180 lbs.

Born: November 13, 1950; Victoriaville, Quebec

Drafted by the Buffalo Sabres first overall in 1970

Played 17 NHL seasons from 1970–87

Gilbert Perreault
HOCKEY HALL OF FAME CLASS: 1990

QUICK FACTS

- Holds Buffalo team records for career games (1,191), goals (512), assists (814) and points (1,326)

- Holds Buffalo team record for points in a single game (7), established in Buffalo's 9–5 victory over Oakland, February 1, 1976

- Played amateur hockey with Thetford Mines Canadiens (1966–67); Montreal Jr. Canadiens (1967–70)

- Member of Memorial Cup-winning Montreal Jr. Canadiens (1969, 1970)

- Led Memorial Cup playoffs in goals (17), assists (21) and points (38) in 1970

- OHA-Jr. First All-Star Team Center (1969, 1970); named OHA-Jr. MVP (1969–70)

- Member of Buffalo's famed French Connection Line with Rick Martin and Rene Robert

- Led NHL in game-winning goals (9) in 1976–77

- Finished among NHL top-5 in points in 1975–76 (113), 1976–77 (95) and 1979–80 (106); finished among NHL top-5 in assists in 1972–73 (60), 1975–76 (69) and 1979–80 (66)

- Registered 1,000th career NHL point in Buffalo's 5–4 victory over Montreal Canadiens, April 3, 1982; recorded 500th career NHL goal in Buffalo's 4–3 victory over New Jersey, March 9, 1986

- Member of Team NHL that played Soviet Union in 1979 Challenge Cup Series

- Member of Team Canada in 1981 Canada Cup Tournament — Canada finished second to the Soviet Union

> In my first seasons, [General Manager/ coach Punch] Imlach told me to go for goals and not worry about checking. That really helped me get my confidence. The first few years I was there, I was loose. I was rushing the puck a lot. We had style."

REGULAR SEASON

Season	Age	Team	Lg	GP	G	A	PTS	+/-	PIM	ESG	PPG	SHG	GWG	SOG	S%
1970–71	20	Buffalo Sabres	NHL	78	38	34	72	-39	19	24	14	0	5	210	18.1
1971–72	21	Buffalo Sabres	NHL	76	26	48	74	-40	24	15	11	0	1	218	11.9
1972–73	22	Buffalo Sabres	NHL	78	28	60	88	11	10	20	8	0	7	234	12.0
1973–74	23	Buffalo Sabres	NHL	55	18	33	51	-8	10	12	6	0	7	163	11.0
1974–75	24	Buffalo Sabres	NHL	68	39	57	96	1	36	27	12	0	8	245	15.9
1975–76	25	Buffalo Sabres	NHL	80	44	69	113	17	36	30	14	0	4	237	18.6
1976–77	26	Buffalo Sabres	NHL	80	39	56	95	10	30	30	7	2	9	195	20.0
1977–78	27	Buffalo Sabres	NHL	79	41	48	89	18	20	34	7	0	7	192	21.4
1978–79	28	Buffalo Sabres	NHL	79	27	58	85	12	20	21	6	0	4	172	15.7
1979–80	29	Buffalo Sabres	NHL	80	40	66	106	32	57	30	10	0	5	180	22.2
1980–81	30	Buffalo Sabres	NHL	56	20	39	59	3	56	15	5	0	3	150	13.3
1981–82	31	Buffalo Sabres	NHL	62	31	42	73	19	40	29	2	0	4	155	20.0
1982–83	32	Buffalo Sabres	NHL	77	30	46	76	-10	34	20	8	2	5	192	15.6
1983–84	33	Buffalo Sabres	NHL	73	31	59	90	19	32	21	8	2	7	165	18.8
1984–85	34	Buffalo Sabres	NHL	78	30	53	83	9	42	19	10	1	1	172	17.4
1985–86	35	Buffalo Sabres	NHL	72	21	39	60	-10	28	15	5	1	3	164	12.8
1986–87	36	Buffalo Sabres	NHL	20	9	7	16	-2	6	8	1	0	1	35	25.7
NHL Career — 17 Seasons				1191	512	814	1326	42	500	370	134	8	81	3079	16.6

PLAYOFFS

Season	Age	Team	Lg	GP	G	A	PTS	+/-	PIM	ESG	PPG	SHG	GWG	SOG	S%
1972–73	22	Buffalo Sabres	NHL	6	3	7	10		2	2	1	0	1		
1974–75	24	Buffalo Sabres	NHL	17	6	9	15		10	2	4	0	1		
1975–76	25	Buffalo Sabres	NHL	9	4	4	8		4	4	0	0	0		
1976–77	26	Buffalo Sabres	NHL	6	1	8	9		4	1	0	0	0		
1977–78	27	Buffalo Sabres	NHL	8	3	2	5		0	3	0	0	1		
1978–79	28	Buffalo Sabres	NHL	3	1	0	1		2	1	0	0	0		
1979–80	29	Buffalo Sabres	NHL	14	10	11	21		8	7	3	0	2		
1980–81	30	Buffalo Sabres	NHL	8	2	10	12		2	2	0	0	0		
1981–82	31	Buffalo Sabres	NHL	4	0	7	7		0	0	0	0	0		
1982–83	32	Buffalo Sabres	NHL	10	0	7	7		8	0	0	0	0		
1984–85	34	Buffalo Sabres	NHL	5	3	5	8	2	4	2	1	0	0	10	30.0
NHL Career — 11 Seasons				90	33	70	103	2	44	23	10	0	5	10	30.0

TROPHY CASE

AWARDS

Calder Memorial Trophy (1971)

Lady Byng Memorial Trophy (1973)

ALL-STAR SELECTIONS

Second All-Star Team Center (1975, 1976)

INTERNATIONAL AWARDS

Summit Series (1972)

Canada Cup (1976)

Tommy Phillips

HOCKEY HALL OF FAME CLASS: 1945

Left Wing

Shoots: Right

Height: 5'-9"

Weight: 168 lbs.

Born: May 22, 1883: Rat Portage, Ontario

Died: November 30, 1923: Toronto, Ontario

Played 8 elite amateur and professional seasons from 1901–09, 1911–12

QUICK FACTS

- Considered by many to be the greatest player of his era

- Starred on local school and junior teams in Rat Portage (Kenora) with future Hall of Fame members Si Griffis, Tommy Hooper and Billy McGimisie

- Attended McGill University while he was a member of the Stanley Cup-winning Montreal Amateur Athletic Association (1902–03)

- Attended business school in Toronto while he was a member of Ontario Senior champion Toronto Marlboros (1903–04)

- Member of Manitoba champion Rat Portage Thistles (1904–05); member of Stanley Cup-winning Kenora Thistles (1905–06)

- Served as captain/playing coach of Stanley Cup-winning Kenora Thistles (1905–07)

- Led Manitoba Pro League in goals (18) in 1906–07; led Stanley Cup playoffs in goals (9) and penalty minutes (16) in 1906–07

- MHL-Pro First All-Star Team Left Wing (1907)

- Scored all four goals in Kenora's 4–2 victory over Montreal Wanderers in Game One of 1907 Stanley Cup playoffs, January 17, 1907

- Scored three goals in Kenora's 8–6 victory over Montreal Wanderers in Game Two of 1907 Stanley Cup playoffs, January 21, 1907

- ECAHA First All-Star Team Left Wing (1908)

- Retired and worked in lumber business in Vancouver (1909–11)

- Returned to play final season with Vancouver Millionaires in inaugural season of Pacific Coast Hockey Association and finished among top-10 in goals (17) in 1911–12

> He is the best in the game; that's what I think of him. Let me tell you that Tom Phillips is very, very far from all in."
>
> — Lester Patrick to the *Ottawa Citizen*, December 22, 1909

REGULAR SEASON

Season	Age	Team	Lg	GP	G	A	PTS	PIM
1901–02	18	Rat Portage Thistles	MNWHA-Int	9	7	0	7	7
1902–03	19	Montreal AAA	CAHL	4	6	0	6	
1903–04	20	Toronto Marlboros	OHA-Sr.	4	5	0	5	21
1904–05	21	Rat Portage Thistles	MHL	8	26	0	26	
1905–06	22	Kenora Thistles	MHL	9	24	0	24	
1906–07	23	Kenora Thistles	MHL-Pro	6	18	0	18	
1907–08	24	Ottawa Senators	ECAHA	10	26	0	26	40
1908–09	25	Edmonton Professional Exhibition	ECAHA	1	0	2	2	3
1911–12	28	Vancouver Millionaires	PCHA	17	17	0	17	38
Career – 8 Seasons				68	129	2	131	109

PLAYOFFS

Season	Age	Team	Lg	GP	G	A	PTS	PIM
1902–03	19	Montreal AAA	St-Cup	4	3	0	3	
1903–04	20	Toronto Marlboros	OHA-Sr.	2	6	6	12	9
1903–04	20	Toronto Marlboros	St-Cup	2	1	2	3	6
1904–05	21	Rat Portage Thistles	St-Cup	3	8	0	8	
1906–07	23	Kenora Thistles	MHL-Pro	2	4	0	4	9
1906–07	23	Kenora Thistles	St-Cup	4	9	0	9	16
1908–09	25	Edmonton Professionals	St-Cup	1	1	0	1	0
Career – 5 Seasons				18	32	8	40	40

TROPHY CASE

AWARDS

Stanley Cup (1902–03, 1906–07)

3

Alternates: 21, 2

Defense

Shoots: Left

Height: 5'-10"

Weight: 178 lbs.

Born: December 11, 1931: Kenogami, Quebec

Played 14 NHL seasons from 1955–69

Pierre Pilote
HOCKEY HALL OF FAME CLASS: 1975

QUICK FACTS

- Held NHL record for regular season points by a defenseman (59); surpassed by Bobby Orr (68) in 1968–69
- Played amateur hockey with St. Catharines Tee Pees (1950–52)
- Led OHA-Jr. in penalty minutes (230) in 1950–51; led OHA-Jr. playoffs in penalty minutes (50) in 1951–52
- Played minor pro hockey with Buffalo Bisons (1951–56)
- Played 376 consecutive NHL games from 1956–61
- Led NHL in penalty minutes (165) in 1960–61; led NHL playoffs in assists (12) and points (15) in 1960–61
- Served as captain of Chicago Black Hawks (1961–68)
- Played in NHL All-Star Game (1960, 1961, 1962, 1963, 1964, 1965, 1966, 1967, 1968)
- Finished among NHL top-5 in assists in 1963–64 (46), 1964–65 (45) and 1966–67 (46)
- Traded to Toronto by Chicago for Jim Pappin, May 23, 1968
- Number 3 jersey retired by Chicago Blackhawks, November 12, 2008
- Legacy honored by Canada Post, who issued a stamp featuring his image in 2005
- Renowned as a tough, physical hitter and pinpoint passer

> "I always believed that if I had the puck, the other team didn't have it. My first instinct was always playing forward. I'm what you call 'Mr. Xerox'—I copy. If it's good for you, it's mine. My hero was Doug Harvey. I picked up tricks from him and from other guys and that's how I learned."

REGULAR SEASON

Season	Age	Team	Lg	GP	G	A	PTS	+/-	PIM	ESG	PPG	SHG	GWG	SOG	S%
1955-56	24	Chicago Black Hawks	NHL	20	3	5	8		34						
1956-57	25	Chicago Black Hawks	NHL	70	3	14	17		117						
1957-58	26	Chicago Black Hawks	NHL	70	6	24	30		91						
1958-59	27	Chicago Black Hawks	NHL	70	7	30	37		79						
1959-60	28	Chicago Black Hawks	NHL	70	7	38	45		100						
1960-61	29	Chicago Black Hawks	NHL	70	6	29	35		165						
1961-62	30	Chicago Black Hawks	NHL	59	7	35	42		97						
1962-63	31	Chicago Black Hawks	NHL	59	8	18	26		57						
1963-64	32	Chicago Black Hawks	NHL	70	7	46	53		84	7	0	0	2		
1964-65	33	Chicago Black Hawks	NHL	68	14	45	59		162	6	7	1	2		
1965-66	34	Chicago Black Hawks	NHL	51	2	34	36		60	1	1	0	0		
1966-67	35	Chicago Black Hawks	NHL	70	6	46	52		90	2	4	0	2		
1967-68	36	Chicago Black Hawks	NHL	74	1	36	37	-8	69	1	0	0	0	69	1.4
1968-69	37	Toronto Maple Leafs	NHL	69	3	18	21	5	46	2	1	0	0	48	6.3
NHL Career — 14 Seasons				890	80	418	498	-3	1251	19	13	1	6	117	3.4

PLAYOFFS

Season	Age	Team	Lg	GP	G	A	PTS	+/-	PIM	ESG	PPG	SHG	GWG	SOG	S%
1958-59	27	Chicago Black Hawks	NHL	6	0	2	2		10						
1959-60	28	Chicago Black Hawks	NHL	4	0	1	1		8						
1960-61	29	Chicago Black Hawks	NHL	12	3	12	15		8						
1961-62	30	Chicago Black Hawks	NHL	12	0	7	7		8						
1962-63	31	Chicago Black Hawks	NHL	6	0	8	8		8						
1963-64	32	Chicago Black Hawks	NHL	7	2	6	8		6						
1964-65	33	Chicago Black Hawks	NHL	12	0	7	7		22						
1965-66	34	Chicago Black Hawks	NHL	6	0	2	2		10						
1966-67	35	Chicago Black Hawks	NHL	6	2	4	6		6						
1967-68	36	Chicago Black Hawks	NHL	11	1	3	4		12	0	1	0	0		
1968-69	37	Toronto Maple Leafs	NHL	4	0	1	1		4	0	0	0	0		
NHL Career — 11 Seasons				86	8	53	61		102	0	1	0	0		

TROPHY CASE

AWARDS

James Norris Trophy (1963, 1964, 1965)

Stanley Cup (1960–61)

ALL-STAR SELECTIONS

First All-Star Team Defense (1963, 1964, 1965, 1966, 1967)

Second All-Star Team Defense (1960, 1961, 1962)

Didier Pitre

HOCKEY HALL OF FAME CLASS: 1962

Alternate: 10

Right Wing/
Defense/Rover

Shoots: Right

Height: 5'-11"

Weight: 185 lbs.

Born: September 1,
1883: Valleyfield,
Quebec

Died: July 29,
1934: Sault Ste.
Marie, Michigan

Played 19
professional
seasons from
1904–23

QUICK FACTS

- Nicknamed "Cannonball" because of his rambunctious and explosive style of play and the sound his shot made when it crashed into the end boards. Also known as "Bullet Shot," "Old Folks" and "Pit"

- Played amateur hockey with Montreal Nationals (1903–05)

- First player signed by Jack Laviolette for the new Montreal Canadiens franchise in 1909

- Signed as a free agent by American Soo (IHL), January 5, 1905

- Led IHL in goals (41) and points (41) in 1905–06

- Led NHA in assists (15) and points (39) in 1915–16

- One of the fastest skaters of his time, it was said that he could skate as fast backward as he could forward

- Led NHA in playoff scoring with four goals in five games, including a hat trick against the Pacific Coast League's Portland Rosebuds in helping the Montreal Canadiens win the first Stanley Cup in franchise history. The winner's share for winning the Cup in 1916 was $238

- He was embroiled in numerous contract controversies between professional leagues from coast to coast because of his tendency to jump from league to league. In his career, he jumped from Edmonton to Renfrew, from Montreal Nationals to Montreal Canadiens and from New Westminster to Quebec

- Played 12 seasons of professional lacrosse with the Montreal Nationals

> "Pitre earns every cent he gets. He would play until he dropped out of sheer exhaustion. I consider him one of the greatest athletes in the country."
> — George Kennedy, Montreal Canadiens manager, 1917

REGULAR SEASON

Season	Age	Team	Lg	GP	G	A	PTS	PIM
1903–04	20	Montreal Nationals	FAHL	2	1	0	1	0
1904–05	21	Montreal Nationals	CAHL	2	0	0	0	0
1904–05	21	American Soo Indians	IHL	13	11	0	11	6
1905–06	22	American Soo Indians	IHL	22	41	0	41	29
1906–07	23	American Soo Indians	IHL	23	25	11	36	28
1907–08	24	Montreal Shamrocks	ECAHA	10	3	0	3	15
1908–09	25	Renfrew Creamery Kings	FAHL	5	5	0	5	16
1909–10	26	Les Canadiens (Montreal)	NHA	13	11	0	11	11
1910–11	27	Montreal Canadiens	NHA	16	19	0	19	22
1911–12	28	Montreal Canadiens	NHA	18	27	0	27	40
1912–13	29	Montreal Canadiens	NHA	17	24	0	24	80
1913–14	30	Vancouver Millionaires	PCHA	16	14	2	16	12
1914–15	31	Montreal Canadiens	NHA	20	30	4	34	15
1915–16	32	Montreal Canadiens	NHA	24	24	15	39	42
1916–17	33	Montreal Canadiens	NHA	20	21	6	27	50
1917–18	34	Montreal Canadiens	NHL	20	17	6	23	29
1918–19	35	Montreal Canadiens	NHL	17	14	4	18	15
1919–20	36	Montreal Canadiens	NHL	22	14	12	26	6
1920–21	37	Montreal Canadiens	NHL	23	16	5	21	25
1921–22	38	Montreal Canadiens	NHL	23	2	4	6	12
1922–23	39	Montreal Canadiens	NHL	22	1	2	3	0
Career — 19 Seasons				348	320	71	391	453

PLAYOFFS

Season	Age	Team	Lg	GP	G	A	PTS	PIM
1908–09	25	Edmonton Professionals	St-Cup	2	0	0	0	11
1915–16	32	Montreal Canadiens	St-Cup	5	4	0	4	18
1916–17	33	Montreal Canadiens	NHA	2	2	2	4	32
1916–17	33	Montreal Canadiens	St-Cup	4	5	0	5	6
1917–18	34	Montreal Canadiens	NHL	2	0	1	1	13
1918–19	35	Montreal Canadiens	NHL	5	2	3	5	6
1918–19	35	Montreal Canadiens	St-Cup	5	0	3	3	0
1922–23	39	Montreal Canadiens	NHL	2	0	0	0	0
Career — 6 Seasons				27	13	9	22	86

TROPHY CASE

AWARDS

Stanley Cup (1915–16)

ALL-STAR SELECTIONS

IHL First All-Star Team Right Wing (1906, 1907)

NHA First All-Star Team Right Wing (1917)

Jacques Plante

HOCKEY HALL OF FAME CLASS: 1978

1

Retired by Montreal

Alternates: 31, 30

Goaltender

Catches: Left

Height: 6'

Weight: 175 lbs.

Born: January 17, 1929: Shawinigan Falls, Quebec

Died: February 27, 1986: Geneva, Switzerland

Played 19 NHL and WHA seasons from 1952–65, 1968–73, 1974–75

"Hockey is an art. It requires speed, precision, and strength like other sports, but it also demands an extraordinary intelligence to develop a logical sequence of movements, a technique which is smooth, graceful and in rhythm with the rest of the game."

QUICK FACTS

- First goaltender to regularly wear a facemask after he was struck by a shot in game against N.Y. Rangers, November 1, 1959

- Designed and produced numerous masks during his career, constantly improving their strength, visibility and lightness

- Won record seven Vezina Trophies, including five in a row during the seasons when the Montreal Canadiens won five consecutive Stanley Cups

- Ranks sixth in NHL career wins (437)

- Ranks fifth in NHL career shutouts (82)

- Played amateur hockey with Shawinigan Cataracts (1946–47); Quebec Citadelle (1947–48); Montreal Jr. Canadiens (1947–48); Montreal Sr. Royals (1949–50)

- Led QJHL in wins (35) in 1948–49

- QJHL First All-Star Team Goaltender (1948, 1949)

- Played in NHL All-Star Game (1956, 1957, 1958, 1959, 1960, 1962, 1969, 1970)

- Led NHL in wins in 1955–56 (42), 1957–58 (34), 1958–59 (38), 1959–60 (40), 1961–62 (42)

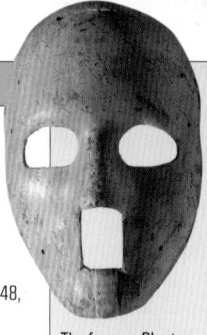

The famous Plante mask that changed the face of the goaltending position.

REGULAR SEASON

Season	Age	Team	Lg	GP	W	L	T	SO	GA	GAA	G	A	PTS	PIM
1952-53	24	Montreal Canadiens	NHL	3	2	0	1	0	4	1.33	0	0	0	0
1953-54	25	Montreal Canadiens	NHL	17	7	5	5	5	27	1.59	0	0	0	0
1954-55	26	Montreal Canadiens	NHL	52	33	12	7	5	110	2.14	0	0	0	2
1955-56	27	Montreal Canadiens	NHL	64	42	12	10	7	119	1.86	0	0	0	10
1956-57	28	Montreal Canadiens	NHL	61	31	18	12	9	122	2.00	0	0	0	16
1957-58	29	Montreal Canadiens	NHL	57	34	14	8	9	119	2.11	0	0	0	13
1958-59	30	Montreal Canadiens	NHL	67	38	16	13	9	144	2.16	0	1	1	11
1959-60	31	Montreal Canadiens	NHL	69	40	17	12	3	175	2.54	0	0	0	2
1960-61	32	Montreal Canadiens	NHL	40	23	11	6	2	112	2.80	0	0	0	2
1961-62	33	Montreal Canadiens	NHL	70	42	14	14	4	166	2.37	0	0	0	14
1962-63	34	Montreal Canadiens	NHL	56	22	14	19	5	138	2.49	0	1	1	2
1963-64	35	New York Rangers	NHL	65	22	36	7	3	220	3.38	0	1	1	6
1964-65	36	New York Rangers	NHL	33	10	17	5	2	109	3.37	0	1	1	6
1968-69	40	St. Louis Blues	NHL	37	18	12	6	5	70	1.96	0	0	0	2
1969-70	41	St. Louis Blues	NHL	32	18	9	5	5	67	2.19	0	2	2	0
1970-71	42	Toronto Maple Leafs	NHL	40	24	11	4	4	73	1.88	0	0	0	2
1971-72	43	Toronto Maple Leafs	NHL	34	16	13	2	2	86	2.63	0	0	0	2
1972-73	44	Toronto Maple Leafs	NHL	32	8	14	6	1	87	3.04	0	0	0	0
1972-73	44	Boston Bruins	NHL	8	7	1	0	2	16	2.00	0	2	2	2
1974-75	46	Edmonton Oilers	WHA	31	15	14	1	1	88	3.32	0	1	1	2
Career – 19 Seasons				868	452	260	146	83	2052	2.36	0	9	9	94

PLAYOFFS

Season	Age	Team	Lg	GP	W	L	T	SO	GA	GAA	G	A	PTS	PIM
1952-53	24	Montreal Canadiens	NHL	4	3	1		1	7	1.75	0	0	0	0
1953-54	25	Montreal Canadiens	NHL	8	5	3		2	15	1.88	0	0	0	0
1954-55	26	Montreal Canadiens	NHL	12	6	3		0	30	2.82	0	0	0	0
1955-56	27	Montreal Canadiens	NHL	10	8	2		2	18	1.80	0	0	0	2
1956-57	28	Montreal Canadiens	NHL	10	8	2		1	17	1.66	0	0	0	4
1957-58	29	Montreal Canadiens	NHL	10	8	2		1	20	1.94	0	0	0	2
1958-59	30	Montreal Canadiens	NHL	11	8	3		0	26	2.33	0	0	0	0
1959-60	31	Montreal Canadiens	NHL	8	8	0		3	11	1.35	0	0	0	0
1960-61	32	Montreal Canadiens	NHL	6	2	4		0	16	2.33	0	0	0	2
1961-62	33	Montreal Canadiens	NHL	6	2	4		0	19	3.17	0	0	0	2
1962-63	34	Montreal Canadiens	NHL	5	1	4		0	14	2.80	0	0	0	0
1968-69	40	St. Louis Blues	NHL	10	8	2		3	14	1.43	0	1	1	0
1969-70	41	St. Louis Blues	NHL	6	4	1		1	8	1.48	0	0	0	2
1970-71	42	Toronto Maple Leafs	NHL	3	0	2		0	7	3.13	0	0	0	0
1971-72	43	Toronto Maple Leafs	NHL	1	0	1		0	5	5.00	0	0	0	0
1972-73	44	Boston Bruins	NHL	2	0	2		0	10	5.00	0	0	0	0
Career – 16 Seasons				112	71	36		14	237	2.14	0	1	1	12

TROPHY CASE

AWARDS

Vezina Trophy (1956, 1957, 1958, 1959, 1960, 1962, 1969)

Hart Memorial Trophy (1962)

Stanley Cup (1952–53, 1955–56, 1956–57, 1957–58, 1958–59, 1959–60)

ALL-STAR SELECTIONS

First All-Star Team Goaltender (1956, 1959, 1962)

Second All-Star Team Goaltender (1957, 1958, 1960, 1971)

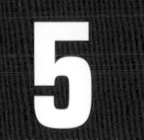

5

Retired by the N.Y. Islanders

Denis Potvin

HOCKEY HALL OF FAME CLASS: 1991

Defense

Shoots: Left

Height: 6'

Weight: 205 lbs.

Born: October 29, 1953: Ottawa, Ontario

Drafted by the New York Islanders first overall in 1973

Played 15 NHL seasons from 1973–88

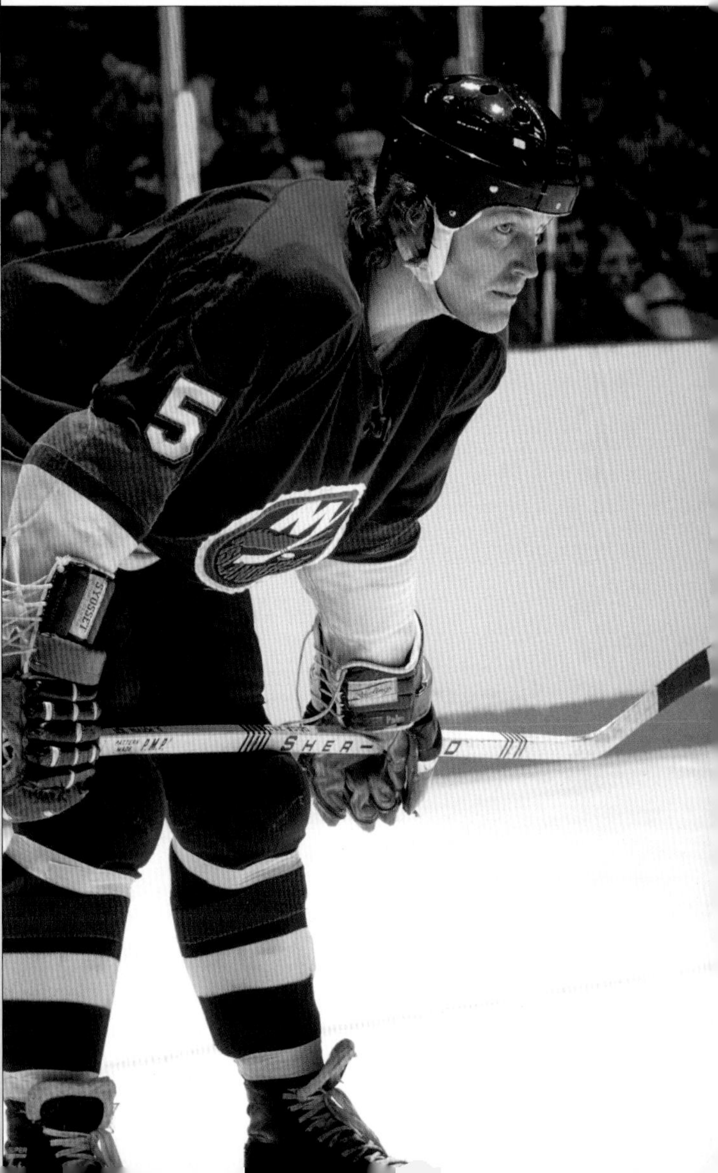

QUICK FACTS

- Holds NHL record most power-play goals by a defenseman (3) in single playoff game, established in N.Y. Islanders' 6–3 victory over Edmonton, April 17, 1981
- Holds nine N.Y. Islander team records for scoring by a defenseman
- Ranks fifth in career NHL goals by an defenseman (310); ranks sixth in career NHL points by a defenseman (1,052)
- Played amateur hockey with Ottawa 67's (1968–73)
- OMJHL First All-Star Team Defense (1971, 1972, 1973)
- First NHL defenseman to register 1,000 career points
- Registered 1,000th career NHL point in N.Y. Islanders' 6–6 tie with Buffalo Sabres, April 4, 1987

- Second defenseman (after Bobby Orr) in NHL history to record 30 goals in a season (1977–78) and register 100 points in a season (1978–79)
- Played in NHL All-Star Game (1974, 1975, 1976, 1977, 1978, 1981,1983,1984,1988)
- Served as captain of N.Y. Islanders (1979–87)
- Brother of Jean Potvin, who played in NHL with L.A. Kings, Philadelphia, N.Y. Islanders, Cleveland Barons and Minnesota North Stars from 1970–81
- Served as color commentator for Florida Panthers television broadcasts (1993–2009)
- Inducted into Canada's Sports Hall of Fame (2001)

> "Often I'm asked which Cup I fancy the most and I often reply by saying, 'It's like having four children. Which one do you love the most?' All are totally different but the first one is always very special because it is the first one."

REGULAR SEASON

Season	Age	Team	Lg	GP	G	A	PTS	+/-	PIM	ESG	PPG	SHG	GWG	SOG	S%
1973–74	20	New York Islanders	NHL	77	17	37	54	-16	175	11	6	0	3	209	8.1
1974–75	21	New York Islanders	NHL	79	21	55	76	28	105	14	5	2	4	211	10.0
1975–76	22	New York Islanders	NHL	78	31	67	98	12	100	13	18	0	4	256	12.1
1976–77	23	New York Islanders	NHL	80	25	55	80	42	103	17	7	1	4	241	10.4
1977–78	24	New York Islanders	NHL	80	30	64	94	57	81	21	9	0	6	288	10.4
1978–79	25	New York Islanders	NHL	73	31	70	101	71	58	16	12	3	2	237	13.1
1979–80	26	New York Islanders	NHL	31	8	33	41	13	44	4	4	0	0	98	8.2
1980–81	27	New York Islanders	NHL	74	20	56	76	38	104	11	9	0	4	206	9.7
1981–82	28	New York Islanders	NHL	60	24	37	61	38	83	12	11	1	4	169	14.2
1982–83	29	New York Islanders	NHL	69	12	54	66	32	60	7	4	1	1	191	6.3
1983–84	30	New York Islanders	NHL	78	22	63	85	55	87	10	11	1	3	246	8.9
1984–85	31	New York Islanders	NHL	77	17	51	68	36	96	11	6	0	1	198	8.6
1985–86	32	New York Islanders	NHL	74	21	38	59	34	78	12	8	1	4	168	12.5
1986–87	33	New York Islanders	NHL	58	12	30	42	-6	70	4	8	0	1	147	8.2
1987–88	34	New York Islanders	NHL	72	19	32	51	26	112	10	9	0	3	188	10.1
NHL Career – 15 Seasons				1060	310	742	1052	460	1356	173	127	10	44	3053	10.2

PLAYOFFS

Season	Age	Team	Lg	GP	G	A	PTS	+/-	PIM	ESG	PPG	SHG	GWG	SOG	S%
1974–75	21	New York Islanders	NHL	17	5	9	14		30	1	3	1	0		
1975–76	22	New York Islanders	NHL	13	5	14	19		32	3	2	0	1		
1976–77	23	New York Islanders	NHL	12	6	4	10		20	4	2	0	0		
1977–78	24	New York Islanders	NHL	7	2	2	4		6	2	0	0	0		
1978–79	25	New York Islanders	NHL	10	4	7	11		8	4	0	0	1		
1979–80	26	New York Islanders	NHL	21	6	13	19		24	2	4	0	1		
1980–81	27	New York Islanders	NHL	18	8	17	25		16	1	6	1	2		
1981–82	28	New York Islanders	NHL	19	5	16	21		30	2	3	0	0		
1982–83	29	New York Islanders	NHL	20	8	12	20		22	4	4	0	1		
1983–84	30	New York Islanders	NHL	20	1	5	6	-5	28	0	1	0	0	56	1.8
1984–85	31	New York Islanders	NHL	10	3	2	5	0	10	2	1	0	1	22	13.6
1985–86	32	New York Islanders	NHL	3	0	1	1	-2	0	0	0	0	0	4	0.0
1986–87	33	New York Islanders	NHL	10	2	2	4	-7	21	1	1	0	0	22	9.1
1987–88	34	New York Islanders	NHL	5	1	4	5	-3	6	0	1	0	0	15	6.7
NHL Career – 14 Seasons				185	56	108	164	-17	253	26	28	2	7	119	5.9

TROPHY CASE

AWARDS

Calder Memorial Trophy (1974)

James Norris Memorial Trophy (1976, 1978, 1979)

Stanley Cup (1979–80, 1980–81, 1981–82, 1982–83)

ALL-STAR SELECTIONS

First All-Star Team Defense (1975, 1976, 1978, 1979, 1981)

Second All-Star Team Defense (1977, 1984)

INTERNATIONAL AWARDS

Canada Cup (1976)

Bronze Medal: World Championships (1986)

2

Babe Pratt

HOCKEY HALL OF FAME CLASS: 1966

Alternates: 11, 21, 12

Defense

Shoots: Left

Height: 6'-3"

Weight: 212 lbs.

Born: January 7, 1916: Stony Mountain, Manitoba

Died: December 16, 1988: Vancouver, British Columbia

Played 12 NHL seasons from 1935–47

QUICK FACTS

- Held NHL record for regular season assists (40) and points (57) by a defenseman; assists record surpassed by Bill Gadsby (46) in 1958–59; points record surpassed by Pierre Pilote (59) in 1964–65
- Played amateur hockey with Elmwood Millionaires (1932–33); Kenora Thistles (1933–35); Brandon Wheat Kings (1933–35)
- Led MJHL in assists (23) and points (42) in 1934–35
- Nicknamed "Babe" at age of 10 because of his love for baseball and the obvious connection to Babe Ruth
- Member of Can-Am champion Philadelphia Ramblers (1936)
- Traded to Toronto by N.Y. Rangers for Hank Goldup and Red Garrett, November 27, 1942

- Scored Stanley Cup-winning goal in Toronto's 2–1 victory over Detroit Red Wings, April 22, 1945
- Suspended by NHL President Red Dutton for gambling violations, January 29, 1946; suspension lifted, February 15, 1946
- Traded to Boston by Toronto for the rights to Eric Pogue and cash, June 19, 1946
- Played minor pro hockey with New Westminster Royals (1948–51); Tacoma Rockets (1951–52)
- Served as player/coach of New Westminster Royals (1949–51, 1951–52)
- Coached New Westminster Royals (1952–53)
- PCHL North First All-Star Team Defense (1949, 1950); PCHL First All-Star Team Defense (1951)

> It was a different kind of game then. Today, they stress board-checking and checking from behind, both unheard of when we played. We'd hit a man standing right up and now the players don't seem to want to take that kind of check. The only check they want is on the first and fifteenth of the month.

REGULAR SEASON

Season	Age	Team	Lg	GP	G	A	PTS	PIM
1935-36	20	New York Rangers	NHL	17	1	1	2	16
1936-37	21	New York Rangers	NHL	47	8	7	15	23
1937-38	22	New York Rangers	NHL	47	5	14	19	56
1938-39	23	New York Rangers	NHL	48	2	19	21	20
1939-40	24	New York Rangers	NHL	48	4	13	17	61
1940-41	25	New York Rangers	NHL	47	3	17	20	52
1941-42	26	New York Rangers	NHL	47	4	24	28	55
1942-43	27	New York Rangers	NHL	4	0	2	2	6
1942-43	27	Toronto Maple Leafs	NHL	40	12	25	37	44
1943-44	28	Toronto Maple Leafs	NHL	50	17	40	57	30
1944-45	29	Toronto Maple Leafs	NHL	50	18	23	41	39
1945-46	30	Toronto Maple Leafs	NHL	41	5	20	25	36
1946-47	31	Boston Bruins	NHL	31	4	4	8	25
NHL Career — 12 Seasons				517	83	209	292	463

PLAYOFFS

Season	Age	Team	Lg	GP	G	A	PTS	PIM
1936-37	21	New York Rangers	NHL	9	3	1	4	11
1937-38	22	New York Rangers	NHL	2	0	0	0	2
1938-39	23	New York Rangers	NHL	7	1	2	3	9
1939-40	24	New York Rangers	NHL	12	3	1	4	18
1940-41	25	New York Rangers	NHL	3	1	1	2	6
1941-42	26	New York Rangers	NHL	6	1	3	4	24
1942-43	27	Toronto Maple Leafs	NHL	6	1	2	3	8
1943-44	28	Toronto Maple Leafs	NHL	5	0	3	3	4
1944-45	29	Toronto Maple Leafs	NHL	13	2	4	6	8
NHL Career — 9 Seasons				63	12	17	29	90

TROPHY CASE

AWARDS

Hart Memorial Trophy (1944)

Stanley Cup (1939–40, 1944–45)

ALL-STAR SELECTIONS

First All-Star Team Defense (1944)

Second All-Star Team Defense (1945)

10

Joe Primeau
HOCKEY HALL OF FAME CLASS: 1963

Alternates: 12, 15

Center

Shoots: Left

Height: 5'-11"

Weight: 153 lbs.

Born: January 29, 1906: Lindsay, Ontario

Died: May 14, 1989: Toronto, Ontario

Played nine NHL seasons from 1927–36

QUICK FACTS

- Nicknamed "Gentleman Joe" because of his classy and calm demeanor on the ice
- Played amateur hockey with St. Michael's Majors (1923–24); Toronto St. Mary's (1924–26); Toronto Marlboros (1925–26)
- Signed as a free agent by Toronto Maple Leafs, July 17, 1928
- Member of Toronto Maple Leafs' famed Kid Line with Charlie Conacher and Busher Jackson
- Led OHA-Jr. goals (15) and points (17) in 1925–26
- Made professional debut with the Toronto Ravinas of the Canadian-Professional Hockey League (1927–28)
- Led NHL in assists in 1930–31 (32), 1931–32 (37) and 1933–34 (32)
- Finished among NHL top-5 in points in 1931–32 (50) and 1933–34 (46)
- Played in NHL All-Star Game (1934)
- Retired at age 30 to operate Joe Primeau Block (later known as Primeau-Argo Block) — a concrete business that eventually expanded to include five plants across the country
- Coached West Toronto Juniors (1932–33); coached Upper Canada College Blues (1938–43); St. Michael's Majors (1943–48); Toronto Marlboros (1948–50); Toronto Maple Leafs (1950–52)
- Coached Toronto St. Michael's Majors to Memorial Cup championship (1944–45). St. Michael's defeated the Porcupine Combines, Montreal Royals and Moose Jaw Warriors to win the title

> "Times have certainly changed in hockey since the antics of our Leaf team on the late 1920s and early 1930s. A 70-game schedule would have provided just that much more time to cook up gags."

REGULAR SEASON

Season	Age	Team	Lg	GP	G	A	PTS	PIM
1927–28	22	Toronto Maple Leafs	NHL	2	0	0	0	0
1928–29	23	Toronto Maple Leafs	NHL	6	0	1	1	2
1929–30	24	Toronto Maple Leafs	NHL	43	5	21	26	22
1930–31	25	Toronto Maple Leafs	NHL	38	9	32	41	18
1931–32	26	Toronto Maple Leafs	NHL	46	13	37	50	25
1932–33	27	Toronto Maple Leafs	NHL	48	11	21	32	4
1933–34	28	Toronto Maple Leafs	NHL	45	14	32	46	8
1934–35	29	Toronto Maple Leafs	NHL	37	10	20	30	16
1935–36	30	Toronto Maple Leafs	NHL	45	4	13	17	10
NHL Career – 9 Seasons				310	66	177	243	105

PLAYOFFS

Season	Age	Team	Lg	GP	G	A	PTS	PIM
1930–31	25	Toronto Maple Leafs	NHL	2	0	0	0	0
1931–32	26	Toronto Maple Leafs	NHL	7	0	6	6	2
1932–33	27	Toronto Maple Leafs	NHL	8	0	1	1	4
1933–34	28	Toronto Maple Leafs	NHL	5	2	4	6	6
1934–35	29	Toronto Maple Leafs	NHL	7	0	3	3	0
1935–36	30	Toronto Maple Leafs	NHL	9	3	4	7	0
NHL Career – 6 Seasons				38	5	18	23	12

TROPHY CASE

AWARDS

Lady Byng Memorial Trophy (1932)

Stanley Cup (1931–32)

ALL-STAR SELECTIONS

Second All-Star Team Center (1934)

3

Marcel Pronovost

HOCKEY HALL OF FAME CLASS: 1978

Alternates:
18, 23, 22

Defense

Shoots: Left

Height: 6'

Weight: 190 lbs.

Born: June 15,
1930: Lac-de-
Tortue, Quebec

Played 20 NHL
seasons from
1950–70

QUICK FACTS

- Played amateur hockey with Windsor Spitfires (1947–49); Detroit Auto Club (1947–48)
- Played left wing and center for Windsor Spitfires (1947–48)
- Named USHL Rookie of the Year (1950)
- USHL First All-Star Team Defense (1950); AHL Second All-Star Team Defense (1951)
- Played in NHL All-Star Game (1950, 1954, 1955, 1957, 1958, 1959, 1960, 1961, 1963, 1965, 1968)
- Traded to Toronto by Detroit with Aut Erickson, Larry Jeffrey, Eddie Joyal and Lowell MacDonald for Billy Harris, Gary Jarrett and Andy Bathgate, May 20, 1965
- Coached Tulsa Oilers (1969–72)
- Coached Chicago Cougars (1972–73)
- Coached Hull Festivals (1975–77, 1979–80)
- Coached Buffalo Sabres (1977–79)
- Coached Windsor Spitfires (1981–83)
- Brother of Jean Pronovost, who played in NHL with Pittsburgh, Washington and Atlanta from 1968–82
- Brother of goaltender Claude Pronovost, who played in NHL with Boston (1955–56) and Montreal (1958–59)
- Served as scout with New Jersey Devils (1989–2009)
- Number 4 jersey honored by Windsor Spitfires (2005)

> Making a dangerous play on the ice didn't make me any more nervous than crossing the street might make someone else. He doesn't worry about getting hit by a car and I don't worry about getting hurt on the ice. If I did, I'd probably go crazy."

TROPHY CASE

AWARDS

Stanley Cup (1949–50, 1951–52, 1953–54, 1954–55, 1966–67)

ALL-STAR SELECTIONS

First All-Star Team Defense (1960, 1961)

Second All-Star Team Defense (1958, 1959)

REGULAR SEASON

Season	Age	Team	Lg	GP	G	A	PTS	+/-	PIM	ESG	PPG	SHG	GWG	SOG	S%
1950–51	20	Detroit Red Wings	NHL	37	1	6	7		20						
1951–52	21	Detroit Red Wings	NHL	69	7	11	18		50						
1952–53	22	Detroit Red Wings	NHL	68	8	19	27		72						
1953–54	23	Detroit Red Wings	NHL	57	6	12	18		50						
1954–55	24	Detroit Red Wings	NHL	70	9	25	34		90						
1955–56	25	Detroit Red Wings	NHL	68	4	13	17		46						
1956–57	26	Detroit Red Wings	NHL	70	7	9	16		38						
1957–58	27	Detroit Red Wings	NHL	62	2	18	20		52						
1958–59	28	Detroit Red Wings	NHL	69	11	21	32		44						
1959–60	29	Detroit Red Wings	NHL	69	7	17	24		38						
1960–61	30	Detroit Red Wings	NHL	70	6	11	17		44						
1961–62	31	Detroit Red Wings	NHL	70	4	14	18		38						
1962–63	32	Detroit Red Wings	NHL	69	4	9	13		48						
1963–64	33	Detroit Red Wings	NHL	67	3	17	20		42	3	0	0	0		
1964–65	34	Detroit Red Wings	NHL	68	1	15	16		45	1	0	0	1		
1965–66	35	Toronto Maple Leafs	NHL	54	2	8	10		34	2	0	0	0		
1966–67	36	Toronto Maple Leafs	NHL	58	2	12	14		28	2	0	0	0		
1967–68	37	Toronto Maple Leafs	NHL	70	3	17	20	0	48	3	0	0	1	70	4.3
1968–69	38	Toronto Maple Leafs	NHL	34	1	2	3	-2	20	1	0	0	0	18	5.6
1969–70	39	Toronto Maple Leafs	NHL	7	0	1	1	5	4	0	0	0	0	2	0.0
NHL Career – 20 Seasons				1206	88	257	345	3	851	12	0	0	2	90	4.4

PLAYOFFS

Season	Age	Team	Lg	GP	G	A	PTS	+/-	PIM	ESG	PPG	SHG	GWG	SOG	S%
1949–50	19	Detroit Red Wings	NHL	9	0	1	1		10						
1950–51	20	Detroit Red Wings	NHL	6	0	0	0		0						
1951–52	21	Detroit Red Wings	NHL	8	0	1	1		10						
1952–53	22	Detroit Red Wings	NHL	6	0	0	0		6						
1953–54	23	Detroit Red Wings	NHL	12	2	3	5		12						
1954–55	24	Detroit Red Wings	NHL	11	1	2	3		6						
1955–56	25	Detroit Red Wings	NHL	10	0	2	2		8						
1956–57	26	Detroit Red Wings	NHL	5	0	0	0		6						
1957–58	27	Detroit Red Wings	NHL	4	0	1	1		4						
1959–60	29	Detroit Red Wings	NHL	6	1	1	2		2						
1960–61	30	Detroit Red Wings	NHL	9	2	3	5		0						
1962–63	32	Detroit Red Wings	NHL	11	1	4	5		8						
1963–64	33	Detroit Red Wings	NHL	14	0	2	2		14						
1964–65	34	Detroit Red Wings	NHL	7	0	3	3		4						
1965–66	35	Toronto Maple Leafs	NHL	4	0	0	0		6						
1966–67	36	Toronto Maple Leafs	NHL	12	1	0	1		8						
NHL Career – 16 Seasons				134	8	23	31		104						

20

Bob Pulford
HOCKEY HALL OF FAME CLASS: 1991

Left Wing

Shoots: Left

Height: 5'-11"

Weight: 188 lbs.

Born: March 31, 1936: Newton Robinson, Ontario

Played 16 NHL seasons from 1956–72

QUICK FACTS

- Played amateur hockey with Weston Dukes (1953–54); Toronto Marlboros (1953–56)
- Member of Memorial Cup-winning Toronto Marlboros (1955, 1956)
- Led Memorial Cup playoffs in goals (16) and points (24) in 1955–56
- Led NHL in playoff assists (10) in 1966–67
- Led NHL in short-handed goals (4) in 1963–64
- Awarded assist on Bobby Baun's game-winning overtime goal in Toronto's 4–3 victory over Detroit Red Wings in Game 6 of the 1964 Stanley Cup finals even though he wasn't on the ice at the time, April 23, 1964
- Played in NHL All-Star Game (1960, 1962, 1963, 1964, 1968)

- Served as President of the NHL Players' Association (1967–72)
- Traded to L.A. Kings by Toronto for Garry Monahan and Brian Murphy, September 3, 1970
- Served as captain of Los Angeles Kings (1971–73)
- Coached Los Angeles Kings (1972–77)
- Coached Chicago Blackhawks (1977–79, 1981–82, 1984–85, 1985–87, 1999–2000)
- Served as General Manager of Chicago Blackhawks (1977–89, 1992–93, 1993–97, 1999–2000, 2003–04, 2004–05)

> My story is this: A Canadian kid who can play the game well is the luckiest kid in the world. There is no limit."

REGULAR SEASON

Season	Age	Team	Lg	GP	G	A	PTS	+/-	PIM	ESG	PPG	SHG	GWG	SOG	S%
1956–57	20	Toronto Maple Leafs	NHL	65	11	11	22		32						
1957–58	21	Toronto Maple Leafs	NHL	70	14	17	31		48						
1958–59	22	Toronto Maple Leafs	NHL	70	23	14	37		53						
1959–60	23	Toronto Maple Leafs	NHL	70	24	28	52		81						
1960–61	24	Toronto Maple Leafs	NHL	40	11	18	29		41						
1961–62	25	Toronto Maple Leafs	NHL	70	18	21	39		98						
1962–63	26	Toronto Maple Leafs	NHL	70	19	25	44		49						
1963–64	27	Toronto Maple Leafs	NHL	70	18	30	48		73	13	1	4	1		
1964–65	28	Toronto Maple Leafs	NHL	65	19	20	39		46	13	2	4	4		
1965–66	29	Toronto Maple Leafs	NHL	70	28	28	56		51	15	11	2	2		
1966–67	30	Toronto Maple Leafs	NHL	67	17	28	45		28	15	1	1	1		
1967–68	31	Toronto Maple Leafs	NHL	74	20	30	50	-7	40	13	4	3	3	229	8.7
1968–69	32	Toronto Maple Leafs	NHL	72	11	23	34	-9	20	7	3	1	1	179	6.1
1969–70	33	Toronto Maple Leafs	NHL	74	18	19	37	-24	31	15	3	0	1	227	7.9
1970–71	34	Los Angeles Kings	NHL	59	17	26	43	-15	53	10	6	1	2	170	10.0
1971–72	35	Los Angeles Kings	NHL	73	13	24	37	-25	48	10	2	1	0	170	7.6
NHL Career — 16 Seasons				1079	281	362	643	-80	792	111	33	17	15	975	8.1

PLAYOFFS

Season	Age	Team	Lg	GP	G	A	PTS	+/-	PIM	ESG	PPG	SHG	GWG	SOG	S%
1958–59	22	Toronto Maple Leafs	NHL	12	4	4	8		8						
1959–60	23	Toronto Maple Leafs	NHL	10	4	1	5		10						
1960–61	24	Toronto Maple Leafs	NHL	5	0	0	0		8						
1961–62	25	Toronto Maple Leafs	NHL	12	7	1	8		24						
1962–63	26	Toronto Maple Leafs	NHL	10	2	5	7		14						
1963–64	27	Toronto Maple Leafs	NHL	14	5	3	8		20						
1964–65	28	Toronto Maple Leafs	NHL	6	1	1	2		16						
2965–66	29	Toronto Maple Leafs	NHL	4	1	1	2		12						
1966–67	30	Toronto Maple Leafs	NHL	12	1	10	11		12						
1968–69	32	Toronto Maple Leafs	NHL	4	0	0	0		2	0	0	0	0		
NHL Career — 10 Seasons				89	25	26	51		126	0	0	0	0		

TROPHY CASE

AWARDS

Jack Adams Award (1975)

Stanley Cup (1961–62, 1962–63, 1963–64, 1966–67)

Harvey Pulford

HOCKEY HALL OF FAME CLASS: 1945

Defense

Shoots: Unknown

Height: 6'

Weight: 180 lbs.

Born: April 22, 1875: Toronto, Ontario

Died: October 31, 1940: Ottawa, Ontario

Played 15 elite amateur seasons from 1893–1908

QUICK FACTS

- Renowned as a versatile athlete who was named All-Around Sports Champion while attending Ottawa's Model School

- Starred in football, lacrosse, boxing, paddling and rowing

- Served as captain of Ottawa "Silver Seven" (1900–05)

- Member of Stanley Cup-winning Ottawa "Silver Seven" (1902–03, 1903–04, 1904–05, 1905–06)

- ECAHA Second All-Star Team Defense (1907, 1908)

- Led Stanley Cup playoffs in penalty minutes (24) in 1905–06

- Renowned as a solid checker and effective rusher who could consistently carry the puck out of danger in his own end

- Helped Ottawa successfully defend the Stanley Cup in eight consecutive challenge matches — more than any other championship team during his era

- Member of Canadian football champion Ottawa Rough Riders (1898, 1899, 1900)

- Member of Ottawa Capitals lacrosse club (1897–1900)

- Won numerous national and international championships with the Ottawa Rowing Club from 1905–12 and competed in the English Henley Regatta

- Served as NHA (1912–17) and NHL (1917–18) on-ice official

"Without Pulford, the team would be sorely handicapped. His all-around knowledge of the game, capability as a stick-handler, great defense work and aggressiveness on the attack have proved him the backbone of the team."

— *The Pittsburgh Press*, December 31, 1906

REGULAR SEASON

Season	Age	Team	Lg	GP	G	A	PTS	PIM
1893–94	18	Ottawa Hockey Club	AHAC	6	0	0	0	
1894–95	19	Ottawa Hocky Club	AHAC	7	0	0	0	
1895–96	20	Ottawa Hockey Club	AHAC	8	0	0	0	
1896–97	21	Ottawa Hockey Club	AHAC	8	0	0	0	
1897–98	22	Ottawa Hockey Club	AHAC	7	0	0	0	
1898–99	23	Ottawa Hockey Club	AHAC	5	0	0	0	
1899–00	24	Ottawa Hockey Club	CAHL	6	1	0	1	
1899–00	24	Ottawa Aberdeens	CAIHL	5	1	0	1	
1900–01	25	Ottawa Hockey Club	CAHL	5	0	0	0	
1901–02	26	Ottawa Hockey Club	CAHL	5	0	0	0	
1902–03	27	Ottawa Silver Seven	CAHL	7	0	0	0	15
1903–04	28	Ottawa Silver Seven	CAHL	2	0	0	0	3
1904–05	29	Ottawa Silver Seven	FAHL	6	1	0	1	6
1905–06	30	Ottawa Silver Seven	ECAHA	10	3	0	3	27
1906–07	31	Ottawa Senators	ECAHA	10	0	0	0	31
1907–08	32	Ottawa Senators	ECAHA	9	1	0	1	32
Career – 15 Seasons				106	7	0	7	114

PLAYOFFS

Season	Age	Team	Lg	GP	G	A	PTS	PIM
1893–94	18	Ottawa Hockey Club	AHAC	1	0	0	0	0
1902–03	27	Ottawa Silver Seven	CAHL	2	0	0	0	6
1902–03	27	Ottawa Silver Seven	St-Cup	2	0	0	0	3
1903–04	28	Ottawa Silver Seven	St-Cup	7	1	0	1	12
1904–05	29	Ottawa Silver Seven	St-Cup	4	0	0	0	6
1905–06	30	Ottawa Silver Seven	ECAHA	2	0	0	0	12
1905–06	30	Ottawa Silver Seven	St-Cup	4	1	0	1	24
Career – 5 Seasons				22	2	0	2	63

TROPHY CASE

AWARDS

Stanley Cup (1902–03, 1903–04, 1904–05, 1905–06)

I can't hear what Jeremy says,
because I've got my two Stanley
Cup rings plugging my ears."

Patrick Roy

responding to negative comments made by Chicago's
Jeremy Roenick during 1996 playoffs

A
B
C
D
E
F
G
H
I
J
K
L
M
N
O
P
Q
R
S
T
U
V
W
X
Y
Z

11

Bill Quackenbush
HOCKEY HALL OF FAME CLASS: 1976

Alternates:
3, 16, 15

Defense

Shoots: Left

Height: 5'-11"

Weight: 190 lbs.

Born: March 2, 1922: Toronto, Ontario

Died: September 12, 1999: Newtown, Pennsylvania

Played 14 NHL seasons from 1942–56

"I wasn't a body-checker. I was a poke checker, I had to play a certain style. I found that if I did a lot of body checking, I got tired very easily. I was on the ice an awful lot because I didn't get penalties."

QUICK FACTS

- First defenseman to win the Lady Byng Trophy

- Played amateur hockey with Toronto Western High (1939–40); Toronto Native Sons (1940–41); Toronto Campbell's (1940–41); Brantford Lions (1941–42); Toronto Tip Top Tailors (1941–42)

- Signed as a free agent by Detroit, October 19, 1942

- Played the entire 1948–49 season (and a total of 131 consecutive games over three seasons) without recording a single penalty; record finally broken when he was penalized for tripping Chicago's Jim Conacher in a 5–1 loss to the Black Hawks on January 24, 1950

- Finished among top-10 in scoring by NHL defensemen 11 times in 14 NHL seasons

- Recorded only 95 minutes in penalties in 774 NHL games

- Played in eight consecutive NHL All-Star Games from 1947 to 1954

- Traded to Boston by Detroit with Pete Horeck for Pete Babando, Lloyd Durham, Clare Martin and Jimmy Peters, August 16, 1949

- Coached Princeton University Tigers (1967–73). Led team to their best season since 1936 in 1967–68 when the team compiled a 13–10–1 record, won the ECAC Christmas tournament championship and earned a berth in the ECAC playoffs

- Coached Princeton University Women's Hockey Team (1978–85); coached Princeton University Golf Team (1969–85)

Quackenbush's 1952 Parkhurst card.

REGULAR SEASON

Season	Age	Team	Lg	GP	G	A	PTS	PIM
1942–43	20	Detroit Red Wings	NHL	10	1	1	2	4
1943–44	21	Detroit Red Wings	NHL	43	4	14	18	6
1944–45	22	Detroit Red Wings	NHL	50	7	14	21	10
1945–46	23	Detroit Red Wings	NHL	48	11	10	21	6
1946–47	24	Detroit Red Wings	NHL	44	5	17	22	6
1947–48	25	Detroit Red Wings	NHL	58	6	16	22	17
1948–49	26	Detroit Red Wings	NHL	60	6	17	23	0
1949–50	27	Boston Bruins	NHL	70	8	17	25	4
1950–51	28	Boston Bruins	NHL	70	5	24	29	12
1951–52	29	Boston Bruins	NHL	69	2	17	19	6
1952–53	30	Boston Bruins	NHL	69	2	16	18	6
1953–54	31	Boston Bruins	NHL	45	0	17	17	6
1954–55	32	Boston Bruins	NHL	68	2	20	22	8
1955–56	33	Boston Bruins	NHL	70	3	22	25	4
NHL Career – 14 Seasons				774	62	222	284	95

PLAYOFFS

Season	Age	Team	Lg	GP	G	A	PTS	PIM
1943–44	21	Detroit Red Wings	NHL	2	1	0	1	0
1944–45	22	Detroit Red Wings	NHL	14	0	2	2	2
1945–46	23	Detroit Red Wings	NHL	5	0	1	1	0
1946–47	24	Detroit Red Wings	NHL	5	0	0	0	2
1947–48	25	Detroit Red Wings	NHL	10	0	2	2	0
1948–49	26	Detroit Red Wings	NHL	11	1	1	2	0
1950–51	28	Boston Bruins	NHL	6	0	1	1	0
1951–52	29	Boston Bruins	NHL	7	0	3	3	0
1952–53	30	Boston Bruins	NHL	11	0	4	4	4
1953–54	31	Boston Bruins	NHL	4	0	0	0	0
1954–55	32	Boston Bruins	NHL	5	0	5	5	0
NHL Career – 11 Seasons				80	2	19	21	8

TROPHY CASE

AWARDS

Lady Byng Memorial Trophy (1949)

ALL-STAR SELECTIONS

First All-Star Team Defense (1948, 1949, 1951)

Second All-Star Team Defense (1947, 1953)

Frank Rankin

HOCKEY HALL OF FAME CLASS: 1961

Rover

Shoots: Right

Height: 5'-5"

Weight: 145 lbs.

Born: April 1, 1891:
Stratford, Ontario

Died: July 23,
1932: Stratford,
Ontario

Played 10 elite
amateur seasons
from 1904–14

QUICK FACTS

- Member of prominent sports family from Stratford, Ontario
- Member of Ontario Junior champion Stratford Hockey Club (1907, 1908, 1909)
- Member of Ontario Senior champion Toronto Eatons (1910–11, 1911–12)
- Led St. Michael's to the OHA senior finals in 1912–13 and 1913–14
- OHA-Sr. First All-Star Team Rover (1910, 1911, 1913)
- OHA-Sr. Second All-Star Team Rover (1912, 1914, 1915)
- Led OHA-Sr. in goals (15) in 1910–11; led OHA-Sr. playoffs in goals (4) in 1910–11
- Led OHA-Sr. in goals (22) in 1912–13
- Served in the Canadian Armed Forces during World War I
- Coached Toronto Granites to gold medal finish at first Winter Olympic Games in Chamonix, France (1924)

> "The professionals have offered him twenty-five hundred dollars, but he refuses to make the jump. His work in mid-ice this year has been positively sensational."
> — *Lethbridge Daily Herald*, reporting on the Toronto hockey scene, January 11, 1913

TROPHY CASE

REGULAR SEASON

Season	Age	Team	Lg	GP	G	A	PTS	PIM
1904–05	13	Stratford Hockey Club	OHA-Sr					
1905–06	14	Stratford Hockey Club	OHA-Sr					
1906–07	15	Stratford Hockey Club	OHA-Sr					
1907–08	16	Stratford Hockey Club	OHA-Sr					
1908–09	17	Stratford Hockey Club	OHA-Sr					
1909–10	18	Stratford Hockey Club	Exhib.	2	4	0	4	
1910–11	19	Toronto Eaton's	OHA-Sr.	4	15	0	15	
1911–12	20	Toronto Eaton's	OHA-Sr.	6	6	0	6	
1912–13	21	Toronto St. Michael's	OHA-Sr.	5	22	0	22	
1913–14	22	Toronto St. Michael's	OHA-Sr.	2	10	0	10	
Career – 10 Seasons				19	57	0	57	

PLAYOFFS

Season	Age	Team	Lg	GP	G	A	PTS	PIM
1910–11	19	Toronto Eaton's	OHA-Sr.	2	4	0	4	
1911–12	20	Toronto Eaton's	OHA-Sr.	4	3	0	3	12
1912–13	21	Toronto St. Michael's	OHA-Sr.	4	4	0	4	
1913–14	22	Toronto St. Michael's	OHA-Sr.	2	3	0	3	
Career – 4 Seasons				12	14	0	14	12

19

Jean Ratelle
HOCKEY HALL OF FAME CLASS: 1985

Alternates: 10, 14

Center

Shoots: Left

Height: 6'-1"

Weight: 180 lbs.

Born: October 3, 1940: Lac St-Jean, Quebec

Played 21 NHL seasons from 1960–81

"Management in New York put a lot of pressure on me. They wanted me to play a more aggressive brand of hockey, but that just wasn't the way I played the game."

QUICK FACTS

- Played amateur hockey with Guelph Biltmores (1958–61)
- Led OHA-Jr. in assists (61) in 1960–61
- OHA-Jr. Second All-Star Team Center (1961)
- Played minor pro hockey with Trois-Rivieres Lions (1959–60)
- Member of N.Y. Rangers' famed GAG (Goal-a-Game) Line with Rod Gilbert and Vic Hadfield
- Played in NHL All-Star Game (1970, 1971, 1972, 1973, 1980)

- Led NHL in shooting percentage (25.1%) in 1971–72; led NHL in even strength goals (40) in 1971–72
- Finished among NHL top-5 in points in 1967–69 (78) and 1971–72 (109); finished among NHL top-5 in assists in 1967–68 (46), 1971–72 (63) and 1975–76 (69)
- Renowned for sportsmanship and smooth style that was often compared to Montreal's Jean Béliveau

Gloves worn by Ratelle when playing for Team Canada in the 1972 Summit Series.

REGULAR SEASON

Season	Age	Team	Lg	GP	G	A	PTS	+/-	PIM	ESG	PPG	SHG	GWG	SOG	S%
1960–61	20	New York Rangers	NHL	3	2	1	3		0						
1961–62	21	New York Rangers	NHL	31	4	8	12		4						
1962–63	22	New York Rangers	NHL	48	11	9	20		8						
1963–64	23	New York Rangers	NHL	15	0	7	7		6	0	0	0	0		
1964–65	24	New York Rangers	NHL	54	14	21	35		14	12	2	0	1		
1965–66	25	New York Rangers	NHL	67	21	30	51		10	17	4	0	2		
1966–67	26	New York Rangers	NHL	41	6	5	11		4	4	2	0	1		
1967–68	27	New York Rangers	NHL	74	32	46	78	23	18	22	10	0	5	180	17.8
1968–69	28	New York Rangers	NHL	75	32	46	78	16	26	24	8	0	4	204	15.7
1969–70	29	New York Rangers	NHL	75	32	42	74	8	28	22	10	0	6	198	16.2
1970–71	30	New York Rangers	NHL	78	26	46	72	28	14	19	6	1	3	203	12.8
1971–72	31	New York Rangers	NHL	63	46	63	109	61	4	40	5	1	6	183	25.1
1972–73	32	New York Rangers	NHL	78	41	53	94	24	12	30	11	0	4	241	17.0
1973–74	33	New York Rangers	NHL	68	28	39	67	5	16	22	6	0	3	165	17.0
1974–75	34	New York Rangers	NHL	79	36	55	91	1	26	21	15	0	6	205	17.6
1975–76	35	New York Rangers	NHL	13	5	10	15	2	2	3	2	0	1	28	17.9
1975–76	35	Boston Bruins	NHL	67	31	59	90	17	16	15	15	1	3	186	16.7
1976–77	36	Boston Bruins	NHL	78	33	61	94	19	22	24	8	1	6	186	17.7
1977–78	37	Boston Bruins	NHL	80	25	59	84	49	10	22	3	0	5	158	15.8
1978–79	38	Boston Bruins	NHL	80	27	45	72	17	12	16	11	0	5	137	19.7
1979–80	39	Boston Bruins	NHL	67	28	45	73	11	8	14	14	0	1	145	19.3
1980–81	40	Boston Bruins	NHL	47	11	26	37	18	16	7	4	0	2	62	17.7
NHL Career – 21 Seasons				1281	491	776	1267	299	276	334	136	4	64	2481	17.5

PLAYOFFS

Season	Age	Team	Lg	GP	G	A	PTS	+/-	PIM	ESG	PPG	SHG	GWG	SOG	S%
1966–67	26	New York Rangers	NHL	4	0	0	0		2						
1967–68	27	New York Rangers	NHL	6	0	4	4		2	0	0	0	0		
1968–69	28	New York Rangers	NHL	4	1	0	1		0	0	1	0	0		
1969–70	29	New York Rangers	NHL	6	1	3	4		0	1	0	0	0		
1970–71	30	New York Rangers	NHL	13	2	9	11	8	2	0	0	0	0		
1971–72	31	New York Rangers	NHL	6	0	1	1	0	0	0	0	0	0		
1972–73	32	New York Rangers	NHL	10	2	7	9	0	0	1	1	0	0		
1973–74	33	New York Rangers	NHL	13	2	4	6	0	2	0	0	0	1		
1974–75	34	New York Rangers	NHL	3	1	5	6	2	0	1	0	0	0		
1975–76	35	Boston Bruins	NHL	12	8	8	16	4	3	5	0	0	1		
1976–77	36	Boston Bruins	NHL	14	5	12	17	4	4	1	0	0	1		
1977–78	37	Boston Bruins	NHL	15	3	7	10	0	3	0	0	0	0		
1978–79	38	Boston Bruins	NHL	11	7	6	13	2	5	2	0	0	2		
1979–80	39	Boston Bruins	NHL	3	0	0	0	0	0	0	0	0	0		
1980–81	40	Boston Bruins	NHL	3	0	0	0	0	0	0	0	0	0		
NHL Career – 15 Seasons				123	32	66	98		24	21	11	0	5		

TROPHY CASE

AWARDS

Bill Masterton Memorial Trophy (1971)

Lady Byng Memorial Trophy (1972, 1976)

Lester B. Pearson Award (1972)

ALL-STAR SELECTIONS

Second All-Star Team Center (1972)

INTERNATIONAL AWARDS

Summit Series (1972)

1

Chuck Rayner
HOCKEY HALL OF FAME CLASS: 1973

Goaltender

Catches: Left

Height: 5'-11"

Weight: 190 lbs.

Born: August 11, 1920: Sutherland, Saskatchewan

Died: October 6, 2002: Langley, British Columbia

Played 10 NHL seasons from 1940–42, 1945–53

QUICK FACTS

- Played amateur hockey with Saskatoon Wesleys (1936–37); Kenora Thistles (1937–40); Nelson Maple Leafs (1954–56)

- Was part of a unique "platoon" goaltending tandem during the 1945–46 season. N.Y. Rangers coach Frank Boucher played Rayner and Sugar Jim Henry in alternate games and sometimes would switch them from shift to shift like regular forwards or defensemen

- First goaltender since Roy Worters (1929) to be awarded the Hart Trophy as NHL MVP

- Led Manitoba Junior League in wins (15) and shutouts (1) in 1939–40

- Led AHL in shutouts (6) and goals-against-average (2.29) in 1940–41

- AHL Second All-Star Team Goaltender (1941)

- Played with Victoria Navy and Halifax RCAF during World War II

- While playing for a touring Royal Canadian Armed Forces All-Star team in Halifax during World War II, Rayner became the first goaltender to skate the length of the ice and score a goal

- Led NHL in shutouts (5) in 1946–47

- Played in All-Star Game (1949, 1950, 1951)

- Used as an extra forward in the closing stages of a February 1, 1947 game against Montreal. With the Rangers down a goal, Rayner played the minute and a half as a forward

- Coached Edmonton Flyers (1962–63)

- Played minor pro hockey with Springfield Indians (1940–42); New Haven Ramblers (1947–48); Saskatoon Quakers (1953–54)

> I stopped a shot and the puck bounced straight out. I skated out to get clear, found myself alone and went the rest of the way. When I got about 15 feet from the other goal, I shot and scored."
>
> — Chuck Rayner, describing his infamous goal

REGULAR SEASON

Season	Age	Team	Lg	GP	W	L	T	SO	GA	GAA	G	A	PTS	PIM
1940–41	20	New York Americans	NHL	12	2	7	3	0	44	3.42	0	0	0	0
1941–42	21	Brooklyn Americans	NHL	36	13	21	2	1	129	3.47	0	0	0	0
1945–46	25	New York Rangers	NHL	40	12	21	7	1	149	3.76	0	0	0	6
1946–47	26	New York Rangers	NHL	58	22	30	6	5	177	3.05	0	0	0	0
1947–48	27	New York Rangers	NHL	12	4	7	0	0	42	3.65	0	0	0	0
1948–49	28	New York Rangers	NHL	58	16	31	11	7	168	2.90	0	0	0	2
1949–50	29	New York Rangers	NHL	69	28	30	11	6	181	2.62	0	0	0	6
1950–51	30	New York Rangers	NHL	66	19	28	19	2	187	2.85	0	0	0	6
1951–52	31	New York Rangers	NHL	53	18	25	10	2	159	3.00	0	0	0	4
1952–53	32	New York Rangers	NHL	20	4	8	8	1	58	2.90	0	0	0	2
NHL Career – 10 Seasons				424	138	208	77	25	1294	3.05	0	0	0	26

PLAYOFFS

Season	Age	Team	Lg	GP	W	L	T	SO	GA	GAA	G	A	PTS	PIM
1947–48	27	New York Rangers	NHL	6	2	4		0	17	2.83	0	0	0	0
1949–50	29	New York Rangers	NHL	12	7	5		1	29	2.25	0	0	0	0
NHL Career – 2 Seasons				18	9	9		1	46	2.43	0	0	0	0

TROPHY CASE

AWARDS

Hart Memorial Trophy (1950)

ALL-STAR SELECTIONS

Second All-Star Team Goaltender (1949, 1950, 1951)

Kenny Reardon

HOCKEY HALL OF FAME CLASS: 1966

Alternate: 4

Defense

Shoots: Left

Height: 5'-10"

Weight: 180 lbs.

Born: April 1, 1921: Winnipeg, Manitoba

Died: March 15, 2008: Saint-Sauveur, Quebec

Played seven NHL seasons from 1940–42, 1945–50

QUICK FACTS

> When I was playing it was hard to stay in the league if you were the least bit shy. Some could, but if they weren't fighters, they had to be able to take [the punishment]."

- Played amateur hockey with Blue River Rebels (1937–38); Edmonton Athletic Club (1938–40)

- Nicknamed "Beans" because he was "full of it" on the ice

- Signed as a free agent by Montreal Canadiens, October 26, 1940

- Made NHL debut in 1–1 tie against Boston Bruins, November 3, 1940. It was the first time Reardon had ever skated in the Montreal Forum

- Played in NHL All-Star Game (1947, 1948, 1949)

- Played with Ottawa Commandos and Ottawa Army during World War II

- Awarded Field Marshall Montgomery Certificate of Merit for bravery in battle during World War II

- Member of Allan Cup-winning Ottawa Commandos (1943); Ottawa defeated the Ottawa RCAF Flyers and Victoria Army to win the title

- Managed Cincinnati Mohawks to five consecutive IHL championships (1952–57). During that time, the club lost only five games in the five championship finals they played

- Coached Kitchener-Waterloo Jr. Greenshirts (1954–55)

- In his capacity as Eastern Canada scout, he helped sign and develop future Montreal Canadiens stars such as Ralph Backstrom, Terry Harper, Dave Balon, Bill Hicke, and Red Berenson

REGULAR SEASON

Season	Age	Team	Lg	GP	G	A	PTS	PIM
1940–41	19	Montreal Canadiens	NHL	34	2	8	10	41
1941–42	20	Montreal Canadiens	NHL	41	3	12	15	93
1945–46	24	Montreal Canadiens	NHL	43	5	4	9	45
1946–47	25	Montreal Canadiens	NHL	52	5	17	22	84
1947–48	26	Montreal Canadiens	NHL	58	7	15	22	129
1948–49	27	Montreal Canadiens	NHL	46	3	13	16	103
1949–50	28	Montreal Canadiens	NHL	67	1	27	28	109
NHL Career – 7 Seasons				341	26	96	122	604

PLAYOFFS

Season	Age	Team	Lg	GP	G	A	PTS	PIM
1940–41	19	Montreal Canadiens	NHL	3	0	0	0	4
1941–42	20	Montreal Canadiens	NHL	3	0	0	0	4
1945–46	24	Montreal Canadiens	NHL	9	1	1	2	4
1946–47	25	Montreal Canadiens	NHL	7	1	2	3	20
1948–49	27	Montreal Canadiens	NHL	7	0	0	0	18
1949–50	28	Montreal Canadiens	NHL	2	0	2	2	12
NHL Career – 6 Seasons				31	2	5	7	62

TROPHY CASE

AWARDS

Stanley Cup (1945–46)

ALL-STAR SELECTIONS

First All-Star Team Defense (1947, 1950)

Second All-Star Team Defense (1946, 1948, 1949)

16

Retired by Montreal

Center

Shoots: Right

Height: 5'-7"

Weight: 160 lbs.

Born: February 29, 1936: Montreal, Quebec

Played 20 NHL seasons from 1955–75

Henri Richard

HOCKEY HALL OF FAME CLASS: 1979

QUICK FACTS

- Holds NHL record for most Stanley Cup championships won by a player (11)
- Shares record (with Boston Celtics' Bill Russell) for most championships won by a professional athlete (11)
- Nicknamed "The Pocket Rocket"
- Played amateur hockey with Montreal Nationale (1951–52); Joliette Cyclones (1951–52); St. Laurent Castors (1951–52); Montreal Jr. Canadiens (1952–54); Montreal Royals (1952–53)
- Led QJHL in goals (53), assists (56) and points (109) in 1953–54; led QJHL in goals (33) and points (66) in 1954–55
- Led NHL in assists in 1957–58 (52) and 1962–63 (50)

- Played in NHL All-Star Game (1956, 1957, 1958, 1959, 1960, 1961, 1963, 1965, 1967, 1974)
- Served as captain of Montreal Canadiens (1971–75)
- Scored Stanley Cup-winning overtime goal in Montreal's 3–2 victory over Detroit, May 5, 1966; scored Stanley Cup-winning goal in Montreal's 3–2 victory over Chicago, May 18, 1971
- Registered 1,000th career NHL point in Montreal's 2–2 tie with Buffalo Sabres, December 20, 1973
- Brother of Hall of Fame member Maurice "Rocket" Richard who played in the NHL with Montreal from 1942–60

> "There were a lot of people who told me that playing with Maurice was going to add a lot of pressure but I never felt any pressure. I never thought about my brother Maurice being a big star. It was normal for me."

REGULAR SEASON

Season	Age	Team	Lg	GP	G	A	PTS	+/-	PIM	ESG	PPG	SHG	GWG	SOG	S%
1955–56	19	Montreal Canadiens	NHL	64	19	21	40		46						
1956–57	20	Montreal Canadiens	NHL	63	18	36	54		71						
1957–58	21	Montreal Canadiens	NHL	67	28	52	80		56						
1958–59	22	Montreal Canadiens	NHL	63	21	30	51		33						
1959–60	23	Montreal Canadiens	NHL	70	30	43	73		66						
1960–61	24	Montreal Canadiens	NHL	70	24	44	68		91						
1961–62	25	Montreal Canadiens	NHL	54	21	29	50		48						
1962–63	26	Montreal Canadiens	NHL	67	23	50	73		57						
1963–64	27	Montreal Canadiens	NHL	66	14	39	53		73	13	1	0	1		
1964–65	28	Montreal Canadiens	NHL	53	23	29	52		43	18	5	0	5		
1965–66	29	Montreal Canadiens	NHL	62	22	39	61		47	19	3	0	7		
1966–67	30	Montreal Canadiens	NHL	65	21	34	55		28	19	2	0	1		
1967–68	31	Montreal Canadiens	NHL	54	9	19	28	4	16	7	2	0	3	123	7.3
1968–69	32	Montreal Canadiens	NHL	64	15	37	52	25	45	13	2	0	0	210	7.1
1969–70	33	Montreal Canadiens	NHL	62	16	36	52	24	61	14	2	0	4	204	7.8
1970–71	34	Montreal Canadiens	NHL	75	12	37	49	13	46	11	1	0	1	226	5.3
1971–72	35	Montreal Canadiens	NHL	75	12	32	44	10	48	12	0	0	1	175	6.9
1972–73	36	Montreal Canadiens	NHL	71	8	35	43	34	21	8	0	0	2	133	6.0
1973–74	37	Montreal Canadiens	NHL	75	19	36	55	7	28	18	1	0	3	175	10.9
1974–75	38	Montreal Canadiens	NHL	16	3	10	13	9	4	3	0	0	0	33	9.1
NHL Career — 20 Seasons				1256	358	688	1046	126	928	155	19	0	28	1279	7.3

PLAYOFFS

Season	Age	Team	Lg	GP	G	A	PTS	+/-	PIM	ESG	PPG	SHG	GWG	SOG	S%
1955–56	19	Montreal Canadiens	NHL	10	4	4	8		21						
1956–57	20	Montreal Canadiens	NHL	10	2	6	8		10						
1957–58	21	Montreal Canadiens	NHL	10	1	7	8		11						
1958–59	22	Montreal Canadiens	NHL	11	3	8	11		13						
1959–60	23	Montreal Canadiens	NHL	8	3	9	12		9						
1960–61	24	Montreal Canadiens	NHL	6	2	4	6		22						
1962–63	26	Montreal Canadiens	NHL	5	1	1	2		2						
1963–64	27	Montreal Canadiens	NHL	7	1	1	2		9						
1964–65	28	Montreal Canadiens	NHL	13	7	4	11		24						
1965–66	29	Montreal Canadiens	NHL	8	1	4	5		2						
1966–67	30	Montreal Canadiens	NHL	10	4	6	10		2						
1967–68	31	Montreal Canadiens	NHL	13	4	4	8		4	3	1	0	0		
1968–69	32	Montreal Canadiens	NHL	14	2	4	6		8	2	0	0	0		
1970–71	34	Montreal Canadiens	NHL	20	5	7	12		20	5	0	0	1		
1971–72	35	Montreal Canadiens	NHL	6	0	3	3		4	0	0	0	0		
1972–73	36	Montreal Canadiens	NHL	17	6	4	10		14	6	0	0	2		
1973–74	37	Montreal Canadiens	NHL	6	2	2	4		2	2	0	0	0		
1974–75	38	Montreal Canadiens	NHL	6	1	2	3		4	1	0	0	0		
NHL Career — 18 Seasons				180	49	80	129		181	19	1	0	3		

TROPHY CASE

AWARDS

Bill Masterton Memorial Trophy (1974)

Stanley Cup (1955–56, 1956–57, 1957–58, 1958–59, 1959–60, 1964–65, 1965–66, 1967–68, 1968–69, 1970–71, 1972–73)

ALL-STAR SELECTIONS

First All-Star Team Center (1958)

Second All-Star Team Center (1959, 1961, 1963)

419

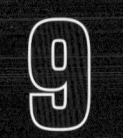

9

Retired by Montreal

Alternate: 15

Right Wing

Shoots: Left

Height: 5'-10"

Weight: 170 lbs.

Born: August 4, 1921: Montreal, Quebec

Died: May 27, 2000: Montreal, Quebec

Played 18 NHL seasons from 1942–1960

Maurice Richard

HOCKEY HALL OF FAME CLASS: 1961

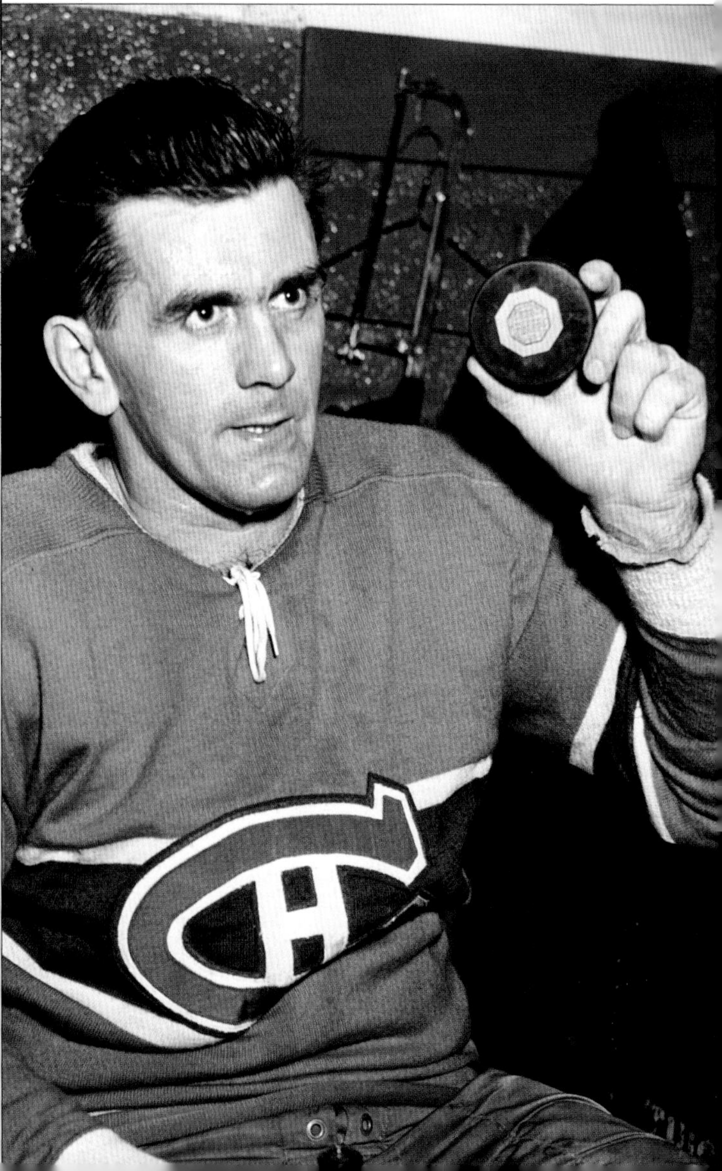

Syl Apps, Charlie Conacher, Hap Day, George Hainsworth, Joe Hall, Percy LeSueur, Frank Rankin, Milt Schmidt, Oliver Seibert, Bruce Stuart

QUICK FACTS

> *His dark eyes glowed like embers as he bore down on the opposing goaltender."*
> — Jack Adams

- Nicknamed "The Rocket" by teammate Ray Getliffe

- Became first player in NHL history to record 500 career NHL goals in Montreal's 3–1 victory over Chicago Black Hawks, October 19, 1957

- First NHL player to score 50 goals in regular season (1944–45)

- Held NHL record for goals in regular season (50); surpassed by Bobby Hull, March 12, 1965

- Held NHL record for most career regular season goals (544); surpassed by Gordie Howe, November 10, 1963

- Held NHL record for most career regular season points (965); surpassed by Gordie Howe, January 16, 1960

- Held NHL record for career playoff overtime goals (6); surpassed by Joe Sakic, April 24, 2006

- Shares NHL record for most goals in a single playoff game (5), established in Montreal's 5–1 victory over Toronto Maple Leafs, March 23, 1944

- Shares NHL record (with Mud Bruneteau) for most overtime goals in a single playoff season (3), established in 1951

- Played amateur hockey with Verdun Maple Leafs (1938–40); Montreal Paquette Midgets (1938–39); Montreal Sr. Canadiens (1940–42)

- Served as captain of Montreal Canadiens (1956–60)

- Played in 13 consecutive NHL All-Star Games (1947–59)

REGULAR SEASON

Season	Age	Team	Lg	GP	G	A	PTS	PIM
1942–43	21	Montreal Canadiens	NHL	16	5	6	11	4
1943–44	22	Montreal Canadiens	NHL	46	32	22	54	45
1944–45	23	Montreal Canadiens	NHL	50	50	23	73	46
1945–46	24	Montreal Canadiens	NHL	50	27	21	48	50
1946–47	25	Montreal Canadiens	NHL	60	45	26	71	69
1947–48	26	Montreal Canadiens	NHL	53	28	25	53	89
1948–49	27	Montreal Canadiens	NHL	59	20	18	38	110
1949–50	28	Montreal Canadiens	NHL	70	43	22	65	114
1950–51	29	Montreal Canadiens	NHL	65	42	24	66	97
1951–52	30	Montreal Canadiens	NHL	48	27	17	44	44
1952–53	31	Montreal Canadiens	NHL	70	28	33	61	112
1953–54	32	Montreal Canadiens	NHL	70	37	30	67	112
1954–55	33	Montreal Canadiens	NHL	67	38	36	74	125
1955–56	34	Montreal Canadiens	NHL	70	38	33	71	89
1956–57	35	Montreal Canadiens	NHL	63	33	29	62	74
1957–58	36	Montreal Canadiens	NHL	28	15	19	34	28
1958–59	37	Montreal Canadiens	NHL	42	17	21	38	27
1959–60	38	Montreal Canadiens	NHL	51	19	16	35	50
NHL Career – 18 Seasons				978	544	421	965	1285

PLAYOFFS

Season	Age	Team	Lg	GP	G	A	PTS	PIM
1943–44	22	Montreal Canadiens	NHL	9	12	5	17	10
1944–45	23	Montreal Canadiens	NHL	6	6	2	8	10
1945–46	24	Montreal Canadiens	NHL	9	7	4	11	15
1946–47	25	Montreal Canadiens	NHL	10	6	5	11	44
1948–49	27	Montreal Canadiens	NHL	7	2	1	3	14
1949–50	28	Montreal Canadiens	NHL	5	1	1	2	6
1950–51	29	Montreal Canadiens	NHL	11	9	4	13	13
1951–52	30	Montreal Canadiens	NHL	11	4	2	6	6
1952–53	31	Montreal Canadiens	NHL	12	7	1	8	2
1953–54	32	Montreal Canadiens	NHL	11	3	0	3	22
1955–56	34	Montreal Canadiens	NHL	10	5	9	14	24
1956–57	35	Montreal Canadiens	NHL	10	8	3	11	8
1957–58	36	Montreal Canadiens	NHL	10	11	4	15	10
1958–59	37	Montreal Canadiens	NHL	4	0	0	0	2
1959–60	38	Montreal Canadiens	NHL	8	1	3	4	2
NHL Career – 15 Seasons				133	82	44	126	188

TROPHY CASE

AWARDS

Hart Memorial Trophy (1947)

Stanley Cup (1943–44, 1945–46, 1952–53, 1955–56, 1956–57, 1957–58, 1958–59, 1959–60)

ALL-STAR SELECTIONS

First All-Star Team Right Wing (1945, 1946, 1947, 1948, 1949, 1950, 1955, 1956)

Second All-Star Team Right Wing (1944, 1951, 1952, 1953, 1954, 1957)

George Richardson

HOCKEY HALL OF FAME CLASS: 1950

Left Wing

Shoots: Right

Height: Unknown

Weight: Unknown

Born: September 14, 1886: Kingston, Ontario

Died: February 9, 1916: Killed in action, Bailleul, France

Played nine elite amateur seasons from 1902–10, 1911–12

QUICK FACTS

- Was a member of a prominent and wealthy family in Kingston, Ontario
- Renowned as a clean and gentlemanly player who was a fine stickhandler and prolific scorer
- Member of Queen's University club that defeated Princeton and Yale to win the 1903 intercollegiate title of America
- Member of Canadian University champion Queen's Golden Gaels (1903–04, 1905–06)
- Member of Ontario Hockey Association senior champion Kingston's 14th Regiment (1907–08)
- Scored seven goals in Kingston's 9–7 victory over Stratford that clinched 1908 OHA senior title
- Led OHA-Sr. playoffs in goals in 1907–08 (18) and 1908–09 (13)
- Led OHA-Sr. in goals (8) in 1908–09
- Served on the executive of the Kingston Frontenacs team that captured OHA junior championship in 1910–11
- Served as captain in the Canadian Army with the 14th P.W.O. Riles when he was killed in action in World War I
- Legacy honored by Richardson Stadium, erected on the campus of Queen's University in his name (1920)
- Awarded La legion d'honneur Croix de Guerre by France, March 10, 1916

> "A hero in sport and war. Those who recall his play will remember how he seemed to start instantaneously at full speed in one stroke."
> — *Toronto Telegram* tribute, 1921

REGULAR SEASON

Season	Age	Team	Lg	GP	G	A	PTS	PIM
1902–03	16	Queen's University	CIHU					
1903–04	17	Queen's University	CIHU	4	6	0	6	3
1904–05	18	Queen's University	CIHU	4	6	0	6	0
1905–06	19	Queen's University	CIHU	4	11	0	11	2
1906–07	20	Kingston 14th Regiment	OHA-Sr.	7	23	0	23	0
1907–08	21	Kingston 14th Regiment	OHA-Sr.	3	9	3	12	12
1908–09	22	Kingston 14th Regiment	OHA-Sr.	4	8	0	8	9
Career – 7 Seasons				25	63	3	66	26

PLAYOFFS

Season	Age	Team	Lg	GP	G	A	PTS	PIM
1905–06	19	Queen's University	St-Cup	2	3	0	3	0
1906–07	20	Kingston 14th Regiment	OHA-Sr.	2	2	0	2	0
1907–08	21	Kingston 14th Regiment	OHA-Sr.	4	18	0	18	9
1908–09	22	Kingston 14th Regiment	OHA-Sr.	2	13	0	13	0
1909–10	23	Kingston Frontenacs	Exhib.	2	8	0	8	0
1911–12	25	Kingston Frontenacs	OHA-Sr.	1	1	0	1	0
Career – 6 Seasons				13	45	0	45	9

TROPHY CASE

Gordon Roberts

HOCKEY HALL OF FAME CLASS: 1971

Alternates: 8, 7

Left Wing

Shoots: Left

Height: 5'-11"

Weight: 180 lbs.

Born: September 5, 1891: Ottawa, Ontario

Died: September 2, 1966: Oakland, California

Played 11 elite amateur and professional seasons from 1908–18, 1919–20

GORDON ROBERTS

QUICK FACTS

- Played amateur hockey with Stratford HC (1906–07); Ottawa Emmetts (1908–09); Ottawa Seconds (1909–10)
- Led Ottawa City Senior League in goals (19) in 1908–09
- Played with Montreal Wanderers while studying medicine at McGill University
- Obtained medical degree from McGill University (1916)
- Finished among league leaders in NHA scoring every season from 1911–12 to 1915–16
- Finished second in NHA goals in 1913–14 (31) and 1914–15 (29)

- Signed as a free agent by Seattle Metropolitans, December 25, 1917
- Led PCHA in goals (43) in 1916–17
- Retired to operate medical practice (1918)
- Signed as a free agent by Vancouver Millionaires, December 12, 1919
- Attracted interest from the NHL's Senators while in Ottawa in 1922 doing post-graduate work in medicine but decided against making another comeback

> "Gordon Roberts ... was the real sensation of the night ... Roberts checked Millar to a standstill, and in addition notched no less than four of the Ottawa goals — a phenomenal performance for a youngster."
>
> — *Ottawa Citizen*, January 19, 1910, recapping the Senators' 8–4 win over Edmonton in a Stanley Cup game

REGULAR SEASON

Season	Age	Team	Lg	GP	G	A	PTS	PIM
1908–09	17	Ottawa Emmetts	OCHL	6	19	0	19	8
1909–10	18	Ottawa Senators	CHA	1	3	0	3	6
1909–10	18	Ottawa Senators	NHA	9	13	0	13	34
1909–10	18	Ottawa Seconds	OCHL	1	3	0	3	5
1910–11	19	Montreal Wanderers	NHA	4	1	0	1	3
1911–12	20	Montreal Wanderers	NHA	18	16	0	16	28
1912–13	21	Montreal Wanderers	NHA	16	16	0	16	22
1913–14	22	Montreal Wanderers	NHA	20	31	13	44	15
1914–15	23	Montreal Wanderers	NHA	19	29	5	34	74
1915–16	24	Montreal Wanderers	NHA	21	18	7	25	64
1916–17	25	Vancouver Millionaires	PCHA	23	43	10	53	42
1917–18	26	Seattle Metropolitans	PCHA	18	20	3	23	24
1919–20	28	Vancouver Millionaires	PCHA	22	16	3	19	13
Career — 11 Seasons				178	228	41	269	338

PLAYOFFS

Season	Age	Team	Lg	GP	G	A	PTS	PIM
1908–09	17	Ottawa Emmetts	OCHL	2	2	0	2	0
1909–10	18	Ottawa Senators	St-Cup	2	7	0	7	0
1914–15	23	Montreal Wanderers	NHA	2	0	0	0	15
1917–18	26	Seattle Metropolitans	PCHA	2	0	0	0	3
1919–20	28	Vancouver Millionaires	PCHA	2	1	0	1	0
Career — 5 Seasons				10	10	0	10	18

TROPHY CASE

AWARDS

Stanley Cup (1909–10)

ALL-STAR SELECTIONS

NHA First All-Star Team Left Wing (1914)

PCHA First All-Star Team Left Wing (1917)

19

Retired by Montreal

Defense

Shoots: Left

Height: 6'-4"

Weight: 225 lbs.

Born: June 2, 1951: Winchester, Ontario

Drafted by the Montreal Canadiens 20th overall in 1971

Played 20 NHL seasons from 1972–92

Larry Robinson

HOCKEY HALL OF FAME CLASS: 1995

QUICK FACTS

- Holds NHL record for most consecutive years appearing in the playoffs (20)

- Holds Montreal Canadiens' team record for career games played (1,202), goals (197), assists (686) and points (883) by a defenseman

- Holds Montreal Canadiens' team record for assists (66) and points (85) by a defenseman in regular season

- Played amateur hockey with Hull Castors (1968–69); Brockville Braves (1969–70); Kitchener Rangers (1970–71)

- Scored 22 goals as a left winger and center with OJHL's Brockville Braves

- Played minor pro hockey with Nova Scotia Voyageurs (1971–73)

- Led NHL in plus/minus (+120) in 1976–77, second highest regular season plus/minus rating in NHL history

- Played in NHL All-Star Game (1974, 1976, 1977, 1978, 1980, 1982, 1986, 1988, 1989, 1992)

- Nicknamed "Big Bird" because his height and gangly posture resembled the character on *Sesame Street* TV show

- Member of Montreal's famed defensive trio with Serge Savard and Guy Lapointe collectively known as "Les Trois Gros" (The Big Three)

> Speed only means you might be able to catch somebody, but if you don't have any mobility you're going to stick out like a sore thumb."

REGULAR SEASON

Season	Age	Team	Lg	GP	G	A	PTS	+/-	PIM	ESG	PPG	SHG	GWG	SOG	S%
1972–73	21	Montreal Canadiens	NHL	36	2	4	6	3	20	2	0	0	1	36	5.6
1973–74	22	Montreal Canadiens	NHL	78	6	20	26	32	66	6	0	0	1	98	6.1
1974–75	23	Montreal Canadiens	NHL	80	14	47	61	61	76	13	1	0	2	102	13.7
1975–76	24	Montreal Canadiens	NHL	80	10	30	40	50	59	8	2	0	0	130	7.7
1976–77	25	Montreal Canadiens	NHL	77	19	66	85	120	45	16	3	0	3	199	9.5
1977–78	26	Montreal Canadiens	NHL	80	13	52	65	71	39	8	3	2	5	154	8.4
1978–79	27	Montreal Canadiens	NHL	67	16	45	61	50	33	12	4	0	1	147	10.9
1979–80	28	Montreal Canadiens	NHL	72	14	61	75	38	39	8	6	0	3	133	10.5
1980–81	29	Montreal Canadiens	NHL	65	12	38	50	46	37	5	7	0	2	130	9.2
1981–82	30	Montreal Canadiens	NHL	71	12	47	59	57	41	6	5	1	0	141	8.5
1982–83	31	Montreal Canadiens	NHL	71	14	49	63	33	33	8	6	0	1	147	9.5
1983–84	32	Montreal Canadiens	NHL	74	9	34	43	4	39	5	4	0	1	141	6.4
1984–85	33	Montreal Canadiens	NHL	76	14	33	47	33	44	8	6	0	3	120	11.7
1985–86	34	Montreal Canadiens	NHL	78	19	63	82	29	39	9	10	0	1	167	11.4
1986–87	35	Montreal Canadiens	NHL	70	13	37	50	24	44	7	6	0	3	122	10.7
1987–88	36	Montreal Canadiens	NHL	53	6	34	40	26	30	4	2	0	1	96	6.3
1988–89	37	Montreal Canadiens	NHL	74	4	26	30	23	22	4	0	0	0	79	5.1
1989–90	38	Los Angeles Kings	NHL	64	7	32	39	7	34	6	1	0	1	80	8.8
1990–91	39	Los Angeles Kings	NHL	62	1	22	23	22	16	1	0	0	0	70	1.4
1991–92	40	Los Angeles Kings	NHL	56	3	10	13	1	37	3	0	0	0	46	6.5
NHL Career — 20 Seasons				1384	208	750	958	730	793	139	66	3	29	2338	8.9

PLAYOFFS

Season	Age	Team	Lg	GP	G	A	PTS	+/-	PIM	ESG	PPG	SHG	GWG	SOG	S%
1972–73	21	Montreal Canadiens	NHL	11	1	4	5		9	1	0	0	1		
1973–74	22	Montreal Canadiens	NHL	6	0	1	1		26	0	0	0	0		
1974–75	23	Montreal Canadiens	NHL	11	0	4	4		27	0	0	0	0		
1975–76	24	Montreal Canadiens	NHL	13	3	3	6		10	3	0	0	1		
1976–77	25	Montreal Canadiens	NHL	14	2	10	12		12	1	1	0	0		
1977–78	26	Montreal Canadiens	NHL	15	4	17	21		6	2	2	0	0		
1978–79	27	Montreal Canadiens	NHL	16	6	9	15		8	5	1	0	1		
1979–80	28	Montreal Canadiens	NHL	10	0	4	4		2	0	0	0	0		
1980–81	29	Montreal Canadiens	NHL	3	0	1	1		2	0	0	0	0		
1981–82	30	Montreal Canadiens	NHL	5	0	1	1		8	0	0	0	0		
1982–83	31	Montreal Canadiens	NHL	3	0	0	0		2	0	0	0	0		
1983–84	32	Montreal Canadiens	NHL	15	0	5	5	6	22	0	0	0	0	27	0.0
1984–85	33	Montreal Canadiens	NHL	12	3	8	11	0	8	2	1	0	0	20	15.0
1985–86	34	Montreal Canadiens	NHL	20	0	13	13	4	22	0	0	0	0	42	0.0
1986–87	35	Montreal Canadiens	NHL	17	3	17	20	4	6	1	2	0	0	40	7.5
1987–88	36	Montreal Canadiens	NHL	11	1	4	5	-3	4	1	0	0	0	10	10.0
1988–89	37	Montreal Canadiens	NHL	21	2	8	10	9	12	2	0	0	0	15	13.3
1989–90	38	Los Angeles Kings	NHL	10	2	3	5	2	10	2	0	0	0	12	16.7
1990–91	39	Los Angeles Kings	NHL	12	1	4	5	7	15	1	0	0	0	15	6.7
1991–92	40	Los Angeles Kings	NHL	2	0	0	0	-2	0	0	0	0	0	1	0.0
NHL Career — 20 Seasons				227	28	116	144	27	211	21	7	0	3	182	6.6

TROPHY CASE

AWARDS

James Norris Memorial Trophy (1977, 1980)

Conn Smythe Trophy (1978)

Stanley Cup (1972–73, 1975–76, 1976–77, 1977–78, 1978–79, 1985–86)

ALL-STAR SELECTIONS

First Team All-Star Team Defense (1977, 1979, 1980)

Second All-Star Team Defense (1978, 1981, 1986)

INTERNATIONAL AWARDS

Canada Cup (1976, 1984)

427

20

Left Wing

Shoots: Left

Height: 6'-1"

Weight: 215 lbs.

Born: February 17, 1966: Montreal, Quebec

Drafted by the Los Angeles Kings 171st overall in 1984

Played 19 NHL seasons from 1986–2004, 2005–06

Luc Robitaille

HOCKEY HALL OF FAME CLASS: 2009

QUICK FACTS

- Holds NHL record for career goals (668) and points (1,394) by a left wing
- Holds NHL record for goals (63) and points (125) by a left wing in regular season, established in 1992–93
- Holds L.A. Kings' team record for points by a rookie (84), established in 1986–87
- Ranks fourth in NHL career power-play goals (247)
- Played amateur hockey with Bourassa Angevins (1982–83); Hull Olympiques (1983–86)
- Led QMJHL in assists (123) and points (191) in 1985–86; led QMJHL playoffs in points (44) in 1985–86
- Named CHL Player of the Year (1986); led Memorial Cup Tournament in goals (8) in 1985–86
- QMJHL First All-Star Team Left Wing (1986); QMJHL Second All-Star Team Left Wing (1985)
- Played in NHL All-Star Game (1988, 1989, 1990, 1991, 1992, 1993, 1999, 2001)
- Led NHL in shooting percentage (24.8%) in 1989–90
- Finished among NHL top-5 in points in 1987–88 (111) and 1991–92 (107)
- Finished among NHL top-5 in goals in 1987–88 (53) and 1992–93 (63)
- Registered 1,000th career NHL point in L.A. Kings' 5–3 victory over Calgary Flames, January 29, 1998; recorded 500th career NHL goal in L.A. Kings' 4–2 victory over Buffalo Sabres, January 7, 1999

> "As a hockey player, you play for the team and for your teammates. You never play for yourself or think about yourself. This is not tennis, where you're alone on the court. Hockey is a team game."

REGULAR SEASON

Season	Age	Team	Lg	GP	G	A	PTS	+/-	PIM	ESG	PPG	SHG	GWG	SOG	S%
1986–87	20	Los Angeles Kings	NHL	79	45	39	84	-18	28	27	18	0	3	199	22.6
1987–88	21	Los Angeles Kings	NHL	80	53	58	111	-9	82	36	17	0	6	220	24.1
1988–89	22	Los Angeles Kings	NHL	78	46	52	98	5	65	36	10	0	4	237	19.4
1989–90	23	Los Angeles Kings	NHL	80	52	49	101	8	38	32	20	0	7	210	24.8
1990–91	24	Los Angeles Kings	NHL	76	45	46	91	28	68	34	11	0	5	229	19.7
1991–92	25	Los Angeles Kings	NHL	80	44	63	107	-4	95	18	26	0	6	240	18.3
1992–93	26	Los Angeles Kings	NHL	84	63	62	125	18	100	37	24	2	8	265	23.8
1993–94	27	Los Angeles Kings	NHL	83	44	42	86	-20	86	20	24	0	3	267	16.5
1994–95	28	Pittsburgh Penguins	NHL	46	23	19	42	10	37	18	5	0	3	109	21.1
1995–96	29	New York Rangers	NHL	77	23	46	69	13	80	12	11	0	4	223	10.3
1996–97	30	New York Rangers	NHL	69	24	24	48	16	48	19	5	0	4	200	12.0
1997–98	31	Los Angeles Kings	NHL	57	16	24	40	5	66	11	5	0	7	130	12.3
1998–99	32	Los Angeles Kings	NHL	82	39	35	74	-1	54	28	11	0	7	292	13.4
1999–00	33	Los Angeles Kings	NHL	71	36	38	74	11	68	23	13	0	7	221	16.3
2000–01	34	Los Angeles Kings	NHL	82	37	51	88	10	66	20	16	1	4	235	15.7
2001–02	35	Detroit Red Wings	NHL	81	30	20	50	-2	38	17	13	0	5	190	15.8
2002–03	36	Detroit Red Wings	NHL	81	11	20	31	4	50	8	3	0	0	148	7.4
2003–04	37	Los Angeles Kings	NHL	80	22	29	51	4	56	10	12	0	4	221	10.0
2005–06	39	Los Angeles Kings	NHL	65	15	9	24	-6	52	12	3	0	2	125	12.0
NHL Career — 19 Seasons				1431	668	726	1394	72	1177	418	247	3	89	3961	16.9

PLAYOFFS

Season	Age	Team	Lg	GP	G	A	PTS	+/-	PIM	ESG	PPG	SHG	GWG	SOG	S%
1986–87	20	Los Angeles Kings	NHL	5	1	4	5	-7	2	1	0	0	0	5	20.0
1987–88	21	Los Angeles Kings	NHL	5	2	5	7	-8	18	0	2	0	1	6	33.3
1988–89	22	Los Angeles Kings	NHL	11	2	6	8	0	10	2	0	0	1	24	8.3
1989–90	23	Los Angeles Kings	NHL	10	5	5	10	-5	12	4	1	0	1	28	17.9
1990–91	24	Los Angeles Kings	NHL	12	12	4	16	-2	22	7	5	0	2	44	27.3
1991–92	25	Los Angeles Kings	NHL	6	3	4	7	-1	12	2	1	0	1	28	10.7
1992–93	26	Los Angeles Kings	NHL	24	9	13	22	-13	28	5	4	0	2	71	12.7
1994–95	28	Pittsburgh Penguins	NHL	12	7	4	11	5	26	7	0	0	2	33	21.2
1995–96	29	New York Rangers	NHL	11	1	5	6	1	8	1	0	0	0	36	2.8
1996–97	30	New York Rangers	NHL	15	4	7	11	7	4	4	0	0	0	43	9.3
1997–98	31	Los Angeles Kings	NHL	4	1	2	3	1	6	1	0	0	0	13	7.7
1999–00	33	Los Angeles Kings	NHL	4	2	2	4	-1	6	2	0	0	0	8	25.0
2000–01	34	Los Angeles Kings	NHL	13	4	3	7	1	10	3	1	0	1	24	16.7
2001–02	35	Detroit Red Wings	NHL	23	4	5	9	4	10	3	1	0	1	43	9.3
2002–03	36	Detroit Red Wings	NHL	4	1	0	1	1	0	1	0	0	0	12	8.3
NHL Career — 15 Seasons				159	58	69	127	-17	174	43	15	0	12	418	13.9

TROPHY CASE

AWARDS

Calder Memorial Trophy (1987)

Stanley Cup (2001–02)

ALL-STAR SELECTIONS

All-Rookie Team (1987)

First All-Star Team Left Wing (1988, 1989, 1990, 1991, 1993)

Second All-Star Team Left Wing (1987, 1992, 2001)

INTERNATIONAL AWARDS

Canada Cup (1991)

Gold Medal: World Championships (1994)

Art Ross

HOCKEY HALL OF FAME CLASS: 1945

Alternate: 2

Defense

Shoots: Left

Height: 5'-11"

Weight: 190 lbs.

Born: January 13, 1886: Naughton, Ontario

Died: August 5, 1964: Boston, Massachusetts

Played 14 elite amateur and professional seasons from 1904–18

QUICK FACTS

- Renowned as a top defensemen, went on to become a pivotal coach, manager, inventor and strategist throughout a lifetime of service to hockey
- First came to prominence as an athlete playing hockey and football in Montreal suburb of Westmount
- Loaned to the Kenora Thistles and became a member of Stanley Cup-winning team (January 1907)
- MHL-Pro First All-Star Team Defense (1907)
- Member of Stanley Cup-winning Montreal Wanderers (1907–08)
- ECAHA First All-Star Team Defense (1908)
- Served as player/coach with Montreal Wanderers (1913–14)
- Playing career ended when the Montreal Wanderers withdrew from league during inaugural NHL season of 1917–18
- Coached Hamilton Tigers (1922–23); coached Boston Bruins (1924–28, 1929–34, 1936–39, 1941–45)
- Served as General Manager of Boston Bruins (1924–54)
- Responsible for improving the design of the puck and goal nets used in the NHL
- Donated Art Ross Trophy to league, which has gone to the NHL's leading scorer since 1947–48

> "Hockey isn't a gentle pastime — not as it is played by the big teams. If it were, people wouldn't go to see it ... With the possible exception of football ... hockey is the most strenuous game I know."
> — Art Ross (who also played football), 1910

REGULAR SEASON

Season	Age	Team	Lg	GP	G	A	PTS	PIM
1904–05	19	Westmount Hockey Club	CAHL	8	10	0	10	
1905–06	20	Brandon Elks	MHL	7	6	0	6	
1906–07	21	Brandon Elks	MHL-Pro	10	6	3	9	11
1907–08	22	Montreal Wanderers	ECAHA	10	8	0	8	27
1907–08	22	Pembroke Lumber Kings	UOHVL	1	5	0	5	
1908–09	23	Montreal Wanderers	ECHA	9	2	0	2	30
1909–10	24	All-Montreal	CHA	4	4	0	4	3
1909–10	24	Haileybury Comets	NHA	12	6	0	6	25
1910–11	25	Montreal Wanderers	NHA	11	4	0	4	24
1911–12	26	Montreal Wanderers	NHA	18	16	0	16	35
1912–13	27	Montreal Wanderers	NHA	19	11	0	11	58
1913–14	28	Montreal Wanderers	NHA	18	4	5	9	74
1914–15	29	Ottawa Senators	NHA	16	3	1	4	55
1915–16	30	Ottawa Senators	NHA	21	8	8	16	69
1916–17	31	Montreal Wanderers	NHA	16	6	2	8	66
1917–18	32	Montreal Wanderers	NHL	3	1	0	1	12
Career – 14 Seasons				183	100	19	119	492

PLAYOFFS

Season	Age	Team	Lg	GP	G	A	PTS	PIM
1906–07	21	Brandon Elks	MHL-Pro	2	1	0	1	3
1906–07	21	Kenora Thistles	St-Cup	2	0	0	0	10
1907–08	22	Montreal Wanderers	St-Cup	5	3	0	3	23
1908–09	23	Montreal Wanderers	St-Cup	2	0	0	0	13
1908–09	23	Cobalt Silver Kings	TPHL	2	1	0	1	0
1914–15	29	Ottawa Senators	NHA	5	2	0	2	0
Career – 4 Seasons				18	7	0	7	49

TROPHY CASE

AWARDS

Lester Patrick Trophy (1984)

Stanley Cup (1906–07, 1907–08)

ALL-STAR SELECTIONS

First All-Star Team Coach (1939)

Second All-Star Team Coach (1938, 1943)

Patrick Roy

HOCKEY HALL OF FAME CLASS: 2006

33

Retired by Montreal & Colorado

Goaltender

Catches: Left

Height: 6'-2"

Weight: 185 lbs.

Born: October 5, 1965: Quebec City, Quebec

Drafted by the Montreal Canadiens 51st overall in 1984

Played 19 NHL seasons from 1984–2003

QUICK FACTS

- Only player to win Conn Smythe Trophy on three different occasions (1986, 1993, 2001)
- Only player to win Conn Smythe Trophy with two different teams (Montreal, Colorado)
- Only second player (with Ken Dryden) to win Conn Smythe Trophy and Stanley Cup as a rookie (1986)
- Holds NHL records for most playoff games played by a goaltender (247), most playoff wins (151) and most combined (regular season and playoff) wins (702)
- Shares NHL record (with Martin Brodeur) for career playoff shutouts (23)
- Led NHL in wins in 1989-90 (31) and 1996-97 (38)
- Ranks second in NHL career wins (551); ranks second in NHL career games played by a goaltender (1,029)
- Holds Colorado Avalanche team records for career games by a goalie (478); career shutouts (37); career wins (262) and wins in a single season (40)
- Played amateur hockey with Ste. Foy Gouvernors (1981-82); Granby Bisons (1982-85)
- Played in NHL All-Star Game (1988, 1990, 1991, 1992, 1993, 1994, 1997, 1998, 2001, 2002, 2003)
- Led NHL in shutouts in 1991-92 (5), 1993-94 (7) and 2001-02 (9)

> "I can't hear what Jeremy says, because I've got my two Stanley Cup rings plugging my ears."
> — Patrick Roy, responding to negative comments made by Chicago's Jeremy Roenick during 1996 playoffs

REGULAR SEASON

Season	Age	Team	Lg	GP	W	L	T	SO	GA	GAA	G	A	PTS	PIM
1984-85	19	Montreal Canadiens	NHL	1	1	0	0	0	0	0.00	0	0	0	0
1985-86	20	Montreal Canadiens	NHL	47	23	18	3	1	148	3.35	0	3	3	4
1986-87	21	Montreal Canadiens	NHL	46	22	16	6	1	131	2.93	0	1	1	8
1987-88	22	Montreal Canadiens	NHL	45	23	12	9	3	125	2.90	0	2	2	14
1988-89	23	Montreal Canadiens	NHL	48	33	5	6	4	113	2.47	0	6	6	2
1989-90	24	Montreal Canadiens	NHL	54	31	16	5	3	134	2.53	0	5	5	0
1990-91	25	Montreal Canadiens	NHL	48	25	15	6	1	128	2.71	0	2	2	6
1991-92	26	Montreal Canadiens	NHL	67	36	22	8	5	155	2.36	0	5	5	4
1992-93	27	Montreal Canadiens	NHL	62	31	25	5	2	192	3.20	0	2	2	16
1993-94	28	Montreal Canadiens	NHL	68	35	17	11	7	161	2.50	0	1	1	30
1994-95	29	Montreal Canadiens	NHL	43	17	20	6	1	127	2.97	0	1	1	20
1995-96	30	Montreal Canadiens	NHL	22	12	9	1	1	62	2.95	0	0	0	6
1995-96	30	Colorado Avalanche	NHL	39	22	15	1	1	103	2.68	0	0	0	4
1996-97	31	Colorado Avalanche	NHL	62	38	15	7	7	143	2.32	0	1	1	15
1997-98	32	Colorado Avalanche	NHL	65	31	19	13	4	153	2.39	0	3	3	39
1998-99	33	Colorado Avalanche	NHL	61	32	19	8	5	139	2.29	0	2	2	28
1999-00	34	Colorado Avalanche	NHL	63	32	21	8	2	141	2.28	0	3	3	10
2000-01	35	Colorado Avalanche	NHL	62	40	13	7	4	132	2.21	0	5	5	10
2001-02	36	Colorado Avalanche	NHL	63	32	23	8	9	122	1.94	0	3	3	26
2002-03	37	Colorado Avalanche	NHL	63	35	15	13	5	137	2.18	0	0	0	20
NHL Career — 19 Seasons				1029	551	315	131	66	2546	2.54	0	45	45	262

PLAYOFFS

Season	Age	Team	Lg	GP	W	L	T	SO	GA	GAA	G	A	PTS	PIM
1985-86	20	Montreal Canadiens	NHL	20	15	5		1	39	1.92	0	0	0	10
1986-87	21	Montreal Canadiens	NHL	6	4	2		0	22	4.00	0	0	0	0
1987-88	22	Montreal Canadiens	NHL	8	3	4		0	24	3.35	0	0	0	0
1988-89	23	Montreal Canadiens	NHL	19	13	6		2	42	2.09	0	2	2	16
1989-90	24	Montreal Canadiens	NHL	11	5	6		1	26	2.43	0	1	1	0
1990-91	25	Montreal Canadiens	NHL	13	7	5		0	40	3.06	0	0	0	2
1991-92	26	Montreal Canadiens	NHL	11	4	7		1	30	2.62	0	0	0	2
1992-93	27	Montreal Canadiens	NHL	20	16	4		0	46	2.13	0	1	1	4
1993-94	28	Montreal Canadiens	NHL	6	3	3		0	16	2.56	0	0	0	0
1995-96	30	Colorado Avalanche	NHL	22	16	6		3	51	2.10	0	0	0	0
1996-97	31	Colorado Avalanche	NHL	17	10	7		3	38	2.21	0	0	0	12
1997-98	32	Colorado Avalanche	NHL	7	3	4		0	18	2.51	0	1	1	0
1998-99	33	Colorado Avalanche	NHL	19	11	8		1	52	2.66	0	2	2	4
1999-00	34	Colorado Avalanche	NHL	17	11	6		3	31	1.79	0	1	1	4
2000-01	35	Colorado Avalanche	NHL	23	16	7		4	41	1.70	0	1	1	0
2001-02	36	Colorado Avalanche	NHL	21	11	10		3	52	2.51	0	2	2	0
2002-03	37	Colorado Avalanche	NHL	7	3	4		1	16	2.27	0	0	0	0
NHL Career — 17 Seasons				247	151	94		23	584	2.30	0	11	11	54

TROPHY CASE

AWARDS

Vezina Trophy (1989, 1990, 1992)

Conn Smythe Trophy (1986, 1993, 2001)

William M. Jennings Trophy (1987, 1988, 1989, 1992, 2002)

Stanley Cup (1985-86, 1992-93, 1995-96, 2000-01)

ALL-STAR SELECTIONS

All-Rookie Team (1986)

First All-Star Team Goaltender (1989, 1990, 1992, 2002)

Second All-Star Team Goaltender (1988, 1991)

Blair Russel

HOCKEY HALL OF FAME CLASS: 1965

Left Wing

Shoots: Left

Height: Unknown

Weight: Unknown

Born: September 17, 1880: Montreal, Quebec

Died: December 7, 1961: Unknown

Played 11 elite amateur and professional seasons from 1899–1910

QUICK FACTS

- Played as an amateur throughout his career, like Montreal Victorias teammate and future Hall of Fame member Russell (Dubbie) Bowie

- Renowned for his two-way play, he was an aggressive defender and productive forward

- Scored seven goals in a game on January 2, 1904 and also had a six-goal game and a five-goal game during his career

- Refused all offers to become professional with the Montreal Wanderers when the Eastern Canada Amateur Hockey Association became fully professional after the 1907–08 season

- Scored four goals in Montreal Victorias' 13–5 loss to Ottawa, February 16, 1907; scored four goals in Montreal Victorias' 13–8 victory over Montreal AAA, February 27, 1907

- ECAHA First All-Star Team Left Wing (1907)

- Served as president of both the Montreal Victorias and the Inter-Provincial Amateur Hockey Union (1908–09)

- Played amateur hockey with Montreal Jr. Victorias (1894–99); Montreal Royal-Queen (1897–99)

> He was probably the most useful member of the club [Montreal Victorias] for he was a tireless skater, a great back checker and a fine scorer in his own right."
> — *Montreal Gazette*, April 14, 1934

REGULAR SEASON

Season	Age	Team	Lg	GP	G	A	PTS	PIM
1899–00	19	Montreal Victorias	CAHL	7	9	0	9	
1900–01	20	Montreal Victorias	CAHL	8	8	0	8	
1901–02	21	Montreal Victorias	CAHL	8	9	0	9	3
1902–03	22	Montreal Victorias	CAHL	8	7	0	7	6
1903–04	23	Montreal Victorias	CAHL	8	17	0	17	15
1904–05	24	Montreal Victorias	CAHL	8	19	0	19	6
1905–06	25	Montreal Victorias	ECAHA	4	7	0	7	0
1906–07	26	Montreal Victorias	ECAHA	10	25	0	25	6
1907–08	27	Montreal Victorias	ECAHA	6	8	0	8	26
1908–09	28	Montreal Victorias	IPAHU	1	2	0	2	1
1909–10	29	Montreal Victorias	IPAHU	1	2	0	2	2
Career — 11 Seasons				69	113	0	113	65

PLAYOFFS

Season	Age	Team	Lg	GP	G	A	PTS	PIM
1902–03	22	Montreal Victorias	St-Cup	2	0	0	0	6
Career — 1 Season				2	0	0	0	6

TROPHY CASE

Ernie Russell

HOCKEY HALL OF FAME CLASS: 1965

Center/Rover

Shoots: Right

Height: 5'-6"

Weight: 160 lbs.

Born: October 21, 1883: Montreal, Quebec

Died: February 23, 1963: Montreal, Quebec

Played nine elite amateur and professional seasons from 1904–08, 1909–14

QUICK FACTS

- Starred in both football and hockey while growing up in Montreal
- Served as captain of Sterling Athletics, Canadian Junior hockey champions (1903)
- Served as captain of Montreal Amateur Athletic Association, Canadian Junior football champions (1904)
- Member of Stanley Cup-winning Montreal Wanderers (1907)
- Member of Canadian Senior Football champion Montreal AAA (1907)
- Played his first year of senior hockey with the Montreal AAA in 1904–05 before joining the Wanderers
- Led the Eastern Canada Amateur Hockey Association in goals (43) in 1906–07

- ECAHA First All-Star Team Rover (1907); ECHA Second All-Star Team Center (1908)
- Scored eight goals in Montreal Wanderers' 18–5 victory over Montreal Shamrocks, February 19, 1907
- Scored eight goals in Montreal Wanderers' 16–5 victory over Montreal Shamrocks, March 6, 1907
- Scored at least three goals in five straight games in 1906–07
- Did not play 1908–09 season because of dispute over his amateur status
- Scored a goal in 10 straight games during the 1911–12 season

"[Jimmy] Gardner, an all-time great himself, picked Ernie Russell, Russell Bowie, Frank McGee and Art Farrell as among the best he ever saw. He rated Georges Vezina the greatest goaltender and Cyclone Taylor the fastest skater of them all."

— Montreal Gazette, November 7, 1940

REGULAR SEASON

Season	Age	Team	Lg	GP	G	A	PTS	PIM
1904-05	21	Montreal AAA	CAHL	8	11	0	11	
1905-06	22	Montreal Wanderers	ECAHA	6	21	0	21	13
1906-07	23	Montreal Wanderers	ECAHA	9	43	0	43	26
1907-08	24	Montreal Wanderers	ECHA	9	20	0	20	37
1909-10	26	Montreal Wanderers	NHA	13	35	0	35	57
1910-11	27	Montreal Wanderers	NHA	11	18	0	18	56
1911-12	28	Montreal Wanderers	NHA	18	27	0	27	110
1912-13	29	Montreal Wanderers	NHA	15	7	0	7	48
1913-14	30	Montreal Wanderers	NHA	12	2	4	6	21
Careers — 9 Seasons				101	184	4	188	368

PLAYOFFS

Season	Age	Team	Lg	GP	G	A	PTS	PIM
1905-06	22	Montreal Wanderers	St-Cup	2	4	0	4	6
1906-07	23	Montreal Wanderers	St-Cup	5	12	0	12	35
1907-08	24	Montreal Wanderers	St-Cup	3	11	0	11	7
1909-10	26	Montreal Wanderers	St-Cup	1	4	0	4	3
Career — 4 Seasons				11	31	0	31	51

TROPHY CASE

AWARDS

Stanley Cup (1905–06, 1906–07, 1907–08, 1909–10)

Jack Ruttan

HOCKEY HALL OF FAME CLASS: 1962

Defense

Shoots: Unknown

Height: Unknown

Weight: Unknown

Born: April 5, 1889: Winnipeg, Manitoba

Died: January 7, 1973: Winnipeg, Manitoba

Played nine elite amateur seasons from 1905–13, 1917–18

QUICK FACTS

- Played amateur hockey with Armstrong Point (1905–06); Winnipeg Rustlers (1906–07); Winnipeg St. John's (1905–08)

- Legendary figure in Winnipeg hockey during a time when the city was one of the most important hockey centers in Canada

- Member of Winnipeg Juvenile champion Armstrong Point (1905–06) and Winnipeg Rustlers (1906–07)

- Member of Manitoba University hockey champion St. John's College (1907–08)

- Member of Winnipeg Senior champion University of Manitoba (1909–10)

- Member of Allan Cup-winning Winnipeg Winnipegs (1912–13)

- Served as a captain in Canadian Army during World War I and ran the Military Hockey League in Winnipeg

- Coached University of Manitoba (1923–24)

- Active in hockey as a referee and coach in Winnipeg for many years after the War

- Inducted into Manitoba Hockey Hall of Fame (1985)

> "Jack Ruttan enjoyed a long and illustrious career in hockey, both as a player and coach, all of it in amateur ranks. His stature in Winnipeg … was such that he became an example for younger players."
> — Thumbnail sketch from early Hockey Hall of Fame yearbook

REGULAR SEASON

Season	Age	Team	Lg	GP	G	A	PTS	PIM
1905–06	16	St. John's College	MAHA					
1906–07	17	St. John's College	MAHA					
1907–08	18	St. John's College	MAHA					
1908–09	19	University of Manitoba	WSrHL	7	10	0	10	
1909–10	20	University of Manitoba	WSrHL	1	0	0	0	0
1910–11	21	U. of Manitoba Varsity	MHL-Sr.	4	2	0	2	
1911–12	22	University of Manitoba	WSrHL	8	4	0	4	
1912–13	23	Winnipeg Winnipegs	MHL-Sr.	6	4	0	4	
1917–18	28	Winnipeg Somme	WNDHL	1	0	0	0	2
Career — 9 Seasons				27	20	0	20	2

PLAYOFFS

Season	Age	Team	Lg	GP	G	A	PTS	PIM
1912–13	23	Winnipeg Winnipegs	Al-Cup	4	2	0	2	
1913–14	24	Winnipeg Winnipegs	MHL-Sr.	1	0	0	0	4
Career — 2 Seasons				5	2	0	2	4

TROPHY CASE

In the 80s, when Wayne Gretzky and Mario Lemieux were breaking all kinds of records, I thought one of those guys would break it. But now the game has changed so much. You hardly see five or six-goal games between two teams, let alone one player."

Darryl Sittler

on the longevity of his 10-point record

A
B
C
D
E
F
G
H
I
J
K
L
M
N
O
P
Q
R
S
T
U
V
W
X
Y
Z

21

Borje Salming

HOCKEY HALL OF FAME CLASS: 1996

Defense

Shoots: Left

Height: 6'-1"

Weight: 193 lbs.

Born: April 17, 1951: Kiruna, Sweden

Played 17 NHL seasons from 1973–90

QUICK FACTS

- First Swedish-born and trained player to earn an NHL All-Star berth
- First Swedish-born and trained player to be inducted into Hockey Hall of Fame
- Holds Toronto Maple Leafs team record for career assists (620)
- Holds Toronto Maple Leafs team records for career goals (148), assists (620) and points (768) by a defenseman
- Holds Toronto Maple Leafs team record for assists in regular season by a defenseman (66), established in 1976–77
- Played amateur hockey with Brynas IF Gavle (1970–73)
- Discovered by Maple Leaf scout Gerry McNamara (along with winger Inge Hammarstrom) during a holiday tournament in Sweden

- Signed as a free agent by Toronto, May 12, 1973
- Played in NHL All-Star Game (1976, 1977, 1978)
- Renowned as one of the first European-born players to make an impact on the North American game and helping open the NHL door to players born and trained in Europe
- Signed as a free agent by Detroit, June 12, 1989
- Played in Sweden with AIK Solna (1990–93) after retiring from the NHL

> "Borje was a once-in-a-lifetime find. Here is a player you can mention in the same sentence with Bobby Orr, Brad Park and Larry Robinson when you're talking about the great defensemen of the modern era."
> — Gerry McNamara

REGULAR SEASON

Season	Age	Team	Lg	GP	G	A	PTS	+/-	PIM	ESG	PPG	SHG	GWG	SOG	S%
1973–74	22	Toronto Maple Leafs	NHL	76	5	34	39	38	48	2	3	0	0	130	3.8
1974–75	23	Toronto Maple Leafs	NHL	60	12	25	37	4	34	7	4	1	1	136	8.8
1975–76	24	Toronto Maple Leafs	NHL	78	16	41	57	33	70	8	8	0	1	194	8.2
1976–77	25	Toronto Maple Leafs	NHL	76	12	66	78	45	46	11	1	0	0	186	6.5
1977–78	26	Toronto Maple Leafs	NHL	80	16	60	76	30	70	10	6	0	5	258	6.2
1978–79	27	Toronto Maple Leafs	NHL	78	17	56	73	36	76	13	4	0	2	230	7.4
1979–80	28	Toronto Maple Leafs	NHL	74	19	52	71	4	94	15	4	0	1	222	8.6
1980–81	29	Toronto Maple Leafs	NHL	72	5	61	66	0	154	3	1	1	1	210	2.4
1981–82	30	Toronto Maple Leafs	NHL	69	12	44	56	4	170	11	1	0	0	175	6.9
1982–83	31	Toronto Maple Leafs	NHL	69	7	38	45	-3	104	4	2	1	0	110	6.4
1983–84	32	Toronto Maple Leafs	NHL	68	5	38	43	-34	92	2	2	1	0	160	3.1
1984–85	33	Toronto Maple Leafs	NHL	73	6	33	39	-26	76	3	3	0	0	181	3.3
1985–86	34	Toronto Maple Leafs	NHL	41	7	15	22	-7	48	3	3	1	1	71	9.9
1986–87	35	Toronto Maple Leafs	NHL	56	4	16	20	17	42	3	0	1	1	71	5.6
1987–88	36	Toronto Maple Leafs	NHL	66	2	24	26	7	82	1	1	0	0	92	2.2
1988–89	37	Toronto Maple Leafs	NHL	63	3	17	20	7	86	2	1	0	0	58	5.2
1989–90	38	Detroit Red Wings	NHL	49	2	17	19	20	52	0	2	0	0	52	3.8
NHL Career — 17 Seasons				1148	150	637	787	175	1344	98	46	6	13	2536	5.9

PLAYOFFS

Season	Age	Team	Lg	GP	G	A	PTS	+/-	PIM	ESG	PPG	SHG	GWG	SOG	S%
1973–74	22	Toronto Maple Leafs	NHL	4	0	1	1		4	0	0	0	0		
1974–75	23	Toronto Maple Leafs	NHL	7	0	4	4		6	0	0	0	0		
1975–76	24	Toronto Maple Leafs	NHL	10	3	4	7		9	2	1	0	0		
1976–77	25	Toronto Maple Leafs	NHL	9	3	6	9		6	1	2	0	0		
1977–78	26	Toronto Maple Leafs	NHL	6	2	2	4		6	2	0	0	1		
1978–79	27	Toronto Maple Leafs	NHL	6	0	1	1		8	0	0	0	0		
1979–80	28	Toronto Maple Leafs	NHL	3	1	1	2		2	0	1	0	0		
1980–81	29	Toronto Maple Leafs	NHL	3	0	2	2		4	0	0	0	0		
1982–83	31	Toronto Maple Leafs	NHL	4	1	4	5		10	0	1	0	0		
1985–86	34	Toronto Maple Leafs	NHL	10	1	6	7	13	14	1	0	0	0	23	4.3
1986–87	35	Toronto Maple Leafs	NHL	13	0	3	3	-1	14	0	0	0	0	20	0.0
1987–88	36	Toronto Maple Leafs	NHL	6	1	3	4	1	8	1	0	0	0	16	6.3
NHL Career — 12 Seasons				81	12	37	49	13	91	7	5	0	1	59	3.4

TROPHY CASE

ALL-STAR SELECTIONS

First All-Star Team Defense (1977)

Second All-Star Team Defense (1975, 1976, 1978, 1979, 1980)

INTERNATIONAL AWARDS

Bronze Medal: World Championships (1972)

Silver Medal: World Championships (1973)

18

Retired by Chicago

Alternates: 9

Center

Shoots: Right

Height: 5'-10"

Weight: 175 lbs.

Born: February 4, 1961: Pointe Gatineau, Quebec

Drafted by the Chicago Black Hawks third overall in 1980

Played 17 NHL seasons from 1980–97

Denis Savard

HOCKEY HALL OF FAME CLASS: 2000

QUICK FACTS

- Shares NHL record (with Claude Provost) for fastest goal from the start of a period (4 seconds), established in third period of Chicago's 4–2 victory over Hartford Whalers, January 12, 1986

- Holds Chicago Blackhawks' team record for assists (87) and points (131) in regular season

- Holds Chicago Blackhawks' team record for assists (20) and points (29) in one playoff season, established in 1984–85

- Played amateur hockey with Montreal Juniors (1977–80)

- QMJHL Rookie of the Year (with Normand Rochefort) in 1977–78

- QMJHL First All-Star Team Center (1980); QMJHL Third All-Star Team Center (1977)

- Named QMJHL MVP (1979–80)

- Led QMJHL in assists (112) in 1978–79

- Member of the Les Trois Denis Line with Denis Cyr and Denis Tremblay on the Montreal Juniors. All three players shared the same birthday and all were born in the same hospital

- Played in NHL All-Star Game (1982, 1983, 1984, 1986, 1988, 1991, 1996)

- Served as co-captain (with Dirk Graham) of Chicago Blackhawks (1988–89)

- Registered 1,000th career NHL point in Chicago's 6–4 loss to St. Louis Blues, March 11, 1990

- Traded to Montreal by Chicago for Chris Chelios and Montreal's 2nd round choice (Michael Pomichter) in 1991 Entry Draft, June 29, 1990

> I've learned that it doesn't matter how many goals you get or how many points. One-on-one doesn't win the Cup, and that's what you play for."

REGULAR SEASON

Season	Age	Team	Lg	GP	G	A	PTS	+/-	PIM	ESG	PPG	SHG	GWG	SOG	S%
1980–81	19	Chicago Black Hawks	NHL	76	28	47	75	27	47	24	4	0	3	159	17.6
1981–82	20	Chicago Black Hawks	NHL	80	32	87	119	0	82	24	8	0	4	231	13.9
1982–83	21	Chicago Black Hawks	NHL	78	35	86	121	26	99	22	13	0	4	213	16.4
1983–84	22	Chicago Black Hawks	NHL	75	37	57	94	-13	71	25	12	0	5	210	17.6
1984–85	23	Chicago Black Hawks	NHL	79	38	67	105	16	56	31	7	0	1	266	14.3
1985–86	24	Chicago Black Hawks	NHL	80	47	69	116	7	111	32	14	1	8	279	16.8
1986–87	25	Chicago Blackhawks	NHL	70	40	50	90	15	108	33	7	0	7	237	16.9
1987–88	26	Chicago Blackhawks	NHL	80	44	87	131	4	95	23	14	7	6	270	16.3
1988–89	27	Chicago Blackhawks	NHL	58	23	59	82	-5	110	11	7	5	1	182	12.6
1989–90	28	Chicago Blackhawks	NHL	60	27	53	80	8	56	15	10	2	4	181	14.9
1990–91	29	Montreal Canadiens	NHL	70	28	31	59	-1	52	19	7	2	0	187	15.0
1991–92	30	Montreal Canadiens	NHL	77	28	42	70	6	73	15	12	1	5	174	16.1
1992–93	31	Montreal Canadiens	NHL	63	16	34	50	1	90	11	4	1	2	99	16.2
1993–94	32	Tampa Bay Lightning	NHL	74	18	28	46	-1	106	15	2	1	2	181	9.9
1994–95	33	Tampa Bay Lightning	NHL	31	11	17	17	-6	10	5	1	0	1	56	10.7
1994–95	33	Chicago Blackhawks	NHL	12	4	4	8	3	8	3	1	0	0	26	15.4
1995–96	34	Chicago Blackhawks	NHL	69	13	35	48	20	102	11	2	0	1	110	11.8
1996–97	35	Chicago Blackhawks	NHL	64	9	18	27	-10	60	7	2	0	2	82	11.0
NHL Career — 17 Seasons				1196	473	865	1338	97	1336	326	127	20	56	3143	15.0

PLAYOFFS

Season	Age	Team	Lg	GP	G	A	PTS	+/-	PIM	ESG	PPG	SHG	GWG	SOG	S%
1980–81	19	Chicago Black Hawks	NHL	3	0	0	0		0	0	0	0	0		
1981–82	20	Chicago Black Hawks	NHL	15	11	7	18		52	6	5	0	2		
1982–83	21	Chicago Black Hawks	NHL	13	8	9	17		22	5	3	0	1		
1983–84	22	Chicago Black Hawks	NHL	5	1	3	4	3	9	1	0	0	0	8	12.5
1984–85	23	Chicago Black Hawks	NHL	15	9	20	29	4	20	6	3	0	0	49	18.4
1985–86	24	Chicago Black Hawks	NHL	3	4	1	5	-1	6	2	2	0	0	16	25.0
1986–87	25	Chicago Blackhawks	NHL	4	1	0	1	-3	12	1	0	0	0	8	12.5
1987–88	26	Chicago Blackhawks	NHL	5	4	3	7	3	17	3	0	1	1	13	30.8
1988–89	27	Chicago Blackhawks	NHL	16	8	11	19	8	10	5	2	1	1	68	11.8
1989–90	28	Chicago Blackhawks	NHL	20	7	15	22	0	41	3	4	0	1	69	10.1
1990–91	29	Montreal Canadiens	NHL	13	2	11	13	-1	35	1	1	0	0	33	6.1
1991–92	30	Montreal Canadiens	NHL	11	3	9	12	1	8	2	1	0	0	33	9.1
1992–93	31	Montreal Canadiens	NHL	14	0	5	5	-3	4	0	0	0	0	15	0.0
1994–95	33	Chicago Blackhawks	NHL	16	7	11	18	12	10	4	3	0	0	39	17.9
1995–96	34	Chicago Blackhawks	NHL	10	1	2	3	0	8	1	0	0	0	12	8.3
1996–97	35	Chicago Blackhawks	NHL	6	0	2	2	-3	2	0	0	0	0	14	0.0
NHL Career — 16 Seasons				169	66	109	175	20	256	40	24	2	6	377	12.5

TROPHY CASE

AWARDS

Stanley Cup (1992–93)

ALL-STAR SELECTIONS

Second All-Star Team Center (1983)

Retired by Montreal

Alternate: 24

Defense

Shoots: Left

Height: 6'-3"

Weight: 210 lbs.

Born: January 22, 1946: Montreal, Quebec

Played 17 NHL seasons from 1966–83

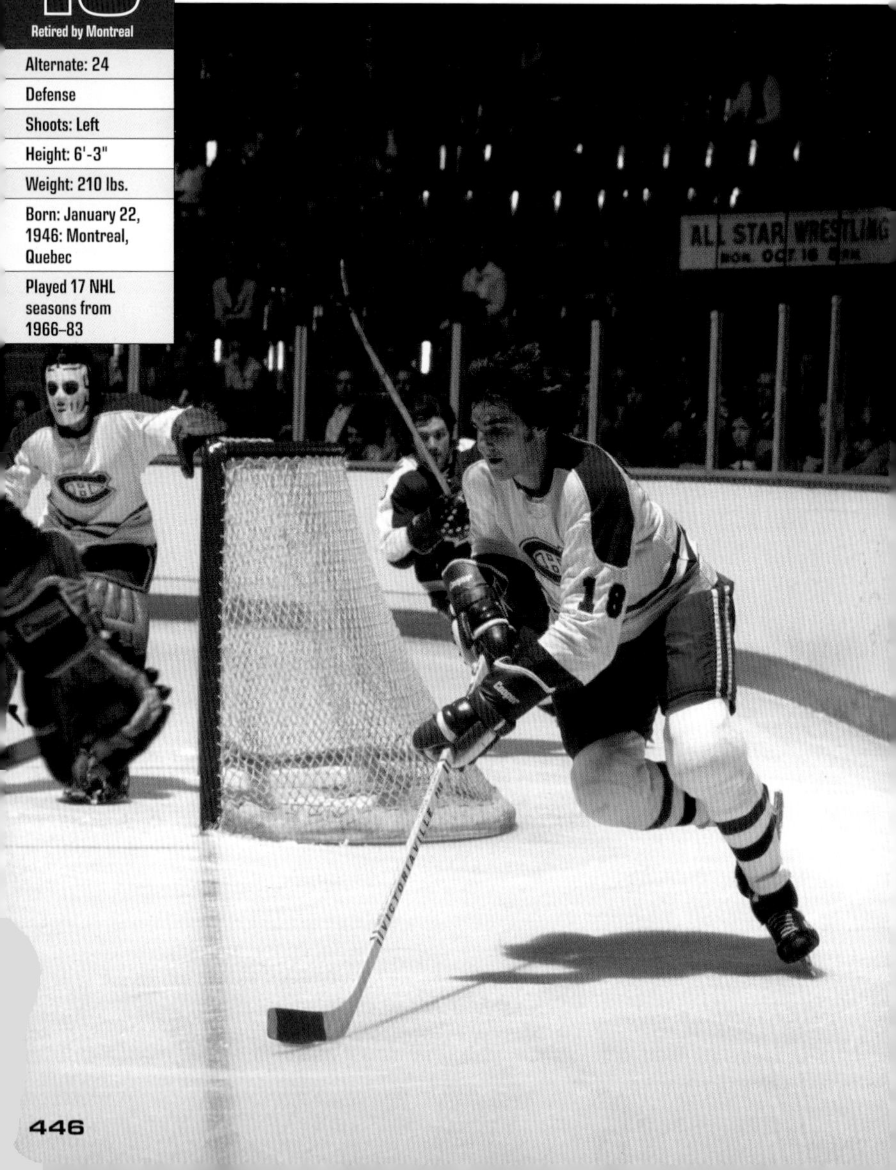

Serge Savard

HOCKEY HALL OF FAME CLASS: 1986

QUICK FACTS

- Played amateur hockey with Montreal Jr. Canadiens (1963–66)
- OHA-Jr. Second All-Star Team Defense (1966)
- Played minor pro hockey with Omaha Knights (1964–65)
- CPHL Second All-Star Team Defense (1967)
- Nicknamed "The Senator" and "Minister of Defense"
- Renowned for the "Savardian Spinnerama" — a 360-degree maneuver used to avoid opposing checkers
- Key component in Team Canada's Summit Series victory; the team won every game that Savard played in

- Served as captain of Montreal Canadiens (1979–81)
- Served as General Manager of Montreal Canadiens (1983–96)
- Played in NHL All-Star Game (1970, 1973, 1977, 1978)
- Missed remainder of 1970–71 season and majority of 1971–72 season recovering from leg injury suffered in game vs. Toronto, January 30, 1971.
- Claimed by Winnipeg Jets from Montreal in Waiver Draft, October 5, 1981
- Member of Montreal's "Big Three" on defense with Guy Lapointe and Larry Robinson

> "Your goal when you're a kid is to make the National Hockey League. Your second goal after is to win the Stanley Cup. Having your number retired? That's something that's never even in your dreams as an athlete."

REGULAR SEASON

Season	Age	Team	Lg	GP	G	A	PTS	+/-	PIM	ESG	PPG	SHG	GWG	SOG	S%
1966–67	21	Montreal Canadiens	NHL	2	0	0	0		0	0	0	0	0		
1967–68	22	Montreal Canadiens	NHL	67	2	13	15	13	34	1	1	0	0	59	3.4
1968–69	23	Montreal Canadiens	NHL	74	8	23	31	33	73	8	0	0	2	98	8.2
1969–70	24	Montreal Canadiens	NHL	64	12	19	31	4	38	4	5	3	2	151	7.9
1970–71	25	Montreal Canadiens	NHL	37	5	10	15	11	30	4	0	1	0	55	9.1
1971–72	26	Montreal Canadiens	NHL	23	1	8	9	21	16	1	0	0	0	45	2.2
1972–73	27	Montreal Canadiens	NHL	74	7	32	39	70	58	4	2	1	0	106	6.6
1973–74	28	Montreal Canadiens	NHL	67	4	14	18	20	49	3	1	0	1	98	4.1
1974–75	29	Montreal Canadiens	NHL	80	20	40	60	71	64	12	7	1	2	165	12.1
1975–76	30	Montreal Canadiens	NHL	71	8	39	47	52	38	6	1	1	1	112	7.1
1976–77	31	Montreal Canadiens	NHL	78	9	33	42	79	35	9	0	0	1	110	8.2
1977–78	32	Montreal Canadiens	NHL	77	8	34	42	62	24	4	4	0	1	103	7.8
1978–79	33	Montreal Canadiens	NHL	80	7	26	33	46	30	4	1	2	0	82	8.5
1979–80	34	Montreal Canadiens	NHL	46	5	8	13	-2	18	5	0	0	1	45	11.1
1980–81	35	Montreal Canadiens	NHL	77	4	13	17	12	30	4	0	0	1	63	6.3
1981–82	36	Winnipeg Jets	NHL	47	2	5	7	-8	26	2	0	0	1	41	4.9
1982–83	37	Winnipeg Jets	NHL	76	4	16	20	-24	29	4	0	0	0	51	7.8
NHL Career — 17 Seasons				1040	106	333	439	460	592	75	22	9	13	1384	7.7

PLAYOFFS

Season	Age	Team	Lg	GP	G	A	PTS	+/-	PIM	ESG	PPG	SHG	GWG	SOG	S%
1967–68	22	Montreal Canadiens	NHL	6	2	0	2		0	0	0	2	1		
1968–69	23	Montreal Canadiens	NHL	14	4	6	10		24	3	1	0	1		
1971–72	26	Montreal Canadiens	NHL	6	0	0	0		10	0	0	0	0		
1972–73	27	Montreal Canadiens	NHL	17	3	8	11		22	3	0	0	0		
1973–74	28	Montreal Canadiens	NHL	6	1	1	2		4	1	0	0	0		
1974–75	29	Montreal Canadiens	NHL	11	1	7	8		2	1	0	0	0		
1975–76	30	Montreal Canadiens	NHL	13	3	6	9		6	1	1	1	2		
1976–77	31	Montreal Canadiens	NHL	14	2	7	9		2	1	1	0	1		
1977–78	31	Montreal Canadiens	NHL	15	1	7	8		8	1	0	0	0		
1978–79	33	Montreal Canadiens	NHL	16	2	7	9		6	1	1	0	1		
1979–80	34	Montreal Canadiens	NHL	2	0	0	0		0	0	0	0	0		
1980–81	35	Montreal Canadiens	NHL	3	0	0	0		0	0	0	0	0		
1981–82	36	Winnipeg Jets	NHL	4	0	0	0		2	0	0	0	0		
1982–83	37	Winnipeg Jets	NHL	3	0	0	0		2	0	0	0	0		
NHL Career — 14 Seasons				130	19	49	68		88	12	4	3	6		

TROPHY CASE

AWARDS

Conn Smythe Trophy (1969)

Bill Masterton Memorial Trophy (1979)

Stanley Cup (1967–68, 1968–69, 1972–73, 1975–76, 1976–77, 1977–78, 1978–79)

ALL-STAR SELECTIONS

Second All-Star Team Defense (1979)

INTERNATIONAL AWARDS

Summit Series (1972)

Canada Cup (1976)

Terry Sawchuk

HOCKEY HALL OF FAME CLASS: 1971

1

Retired by Detroit

Alternates:
30, 24, 29

Goaltender

Catches: Left

Height: 5'-11"

Weight: 195 lbs.

Born: December
28, 1929:
Winnipeg,
Manitoba

Died: May 31,
1970: New York
City, New York

Played 21 NHL
seasons from
1949–70

" I don't think
people
understood
the suffering he
went through.
He shouldn't have
been an athlete.
He was a freak
of nature and was
driven by two
things — fear and
adrenaline."
— Jerry Sawchuk,
Terry's son

QUICK FACTS

- Ranks second in NHL career shutouts (103)
- Ranks third in NHL career games played by a goaltender (971)
- Ranks fifth in NHL career wins by a goaltender (477)
- Played amateur hockey with Winnipeg Rangers (1945–46); Galt Red Wings (1946–47); Windsor Spitfires (1947–48); Windsor Hettche (1947–48)
- Named USHL Rookie of the Year (1948); named AHL Rookie of the Year (1949)
- Played in NHL All-Star Game (1950, 1951, 1952, 1953, 1954, 1955, 1956, 1959, 1963, 1964, 1968)
- Led NHL in shutouts in 1950–51 (11), 1951–52 (12) and 1954–55 (40)

- Led NHL in wins in 1950–51 (44), 1951–52 (44), 1952–53 (32), 1953–54 (35) and 1954–55 (40)
- Won all eight playoff games he played in 1951–52, recording four shutouts and goals-against average of 0.62
- Claimed by Toronto from Detroit in the 1964 Intra-League Draft and won the Vezina Trophy with Johnny Bower in 1964–65
- Died on May 31, 1970 of heart failure following two operations that were the result of a wrestling match with teammate Ron Stewart on April 29
- Elected into the Hall of Fame in 1971 without having to wait the minimum three-year period

Sawchuk's late-career gloves: a Cooper GM12 blocker and a custom catcher.

REGULAR SEASON

Season	Age	Team	Lg	GP	W	L	T	SO	GA	GAA	G	A	PTS	PIM
1949–50	20	Detroit Red Wings	NHL	7	4	3	0	1	16	2.29	0	0	0	0
1950–51	21	Detroit Red Wings	NHL	70	44	13	13	11	139	1.99	0	0	0	2
1951–52	22	Detroit Red Wings	NHL	70	44	14	12	12	133	1.90	0	0	0	2
1952–53	23	Detroit Red Wings	NHL	63	32	15	16	9	120	1.90	0	0	0	5
1953–54	24	Detroit Red Wings	NHL	67	35	19	13	12	129	1.93	0	1	1	31
1954–55	25	Detroit Red Wings	NHL	68	40	17	11	12	132	1.96	0	1	1	10
1955–56	26	Boston Bruins	NHL	68	22	33	13	9	177	2.60	0	0	0	20
1956–57	27	Boston Bruins	NHL	34	18	10	6	2	81	2.38	0	0	0	12
1957–58	28	Detroit Red Wings	NHL	70	29	29	12	3	206	2.94	0	0	0	39
1958–59	29	Detroit Red Wings	NHL	67	23	36	8	5	207	3.09	0	0	0	12
1959–60	30	Detroit Red Wings	NHL	58	24	20	14	5	155	2.67	0	0	0	22
1960–61	31	Detroit Red Wings	NHL	37	12	16	8	2	112	3.13	0	1	1	8
1961–62	32	Detroit Red Wings	NHL	43	14	21	8	5	141	3.28	0	0	0	12
1962–63	33	Detroit Red Wings	NHL	48	22	16	7	3	118	2.55	0	0	0	14
1963–64	34	Detroit Red Wings	NHL	53	25	20	7	5	138	2.64	0	0	0	0
1964–65	35	Toronto Maple Leafs	NHL	36	17	13	6	1	92	2.56	0	2	2	24
1965–66	36	Toronto Maple Leafs	NHL	27	10	11	3	1	80	3.16	0	1	1	12
1966–67	37	Toronto Maple Leafs	NHL	28	15	5	4	2	66	2.81	0	0	0	2
1967–68	38	Los Angeles Kings	NHL	36	11	14	6	2	99	3.07	0	0	0	0
1968–69	39	Detroit Red Wings	NHL	13	3	4	3	0	28	2.62	0	0	0	0
1969–70	40	New York Rangers	NHL	8	3	1	2	1	20	2.91	0	1	1	0
NHL Career — 21 Seasons				971	447	330	172	103	2389	2.51	0	7	7	229

PLAYOFFS

Season	Age	Team	Lg	GP	W	L	T	SO	GA	GAA	G	A	PTS	PIM
1950–51	21	Detroit Red Wings	NHL	6	2	4		1	13	1.68	0	0	0	0
1951–52	22	Detroit Red Wings	NHL	8	8	0		4	5	0.62	0	0	0	0
1952–53	23	Detroit Red Wings	NHL	6	2	4		1	21	3.39	0	0	0	10
1953–54	24	Detroit Red Wings	NHL	12	8	4		2	20	1.60	0	0	0	2
1954–55	25	Detroit Red Wings	NHL	11	8	3		1	26	2.36	0	0	0	12
1957–58	28	Detroit Red Wings	NHL	4	0	4		0	19	4.52	0	0	0	0
1959–60	30	Detroit Red Wings	NHL	6	2	4		0	20	2.96	0	0	0	0
1960–61	31	Detroit Red Wings	NHL	8	5	3		1	18	2.32	0	0	0	0
1962–63	33	Detroit Red Wings	NHL	11	5	6		0	35	3.18	0	0	0	0
1963–64	34	Detroit Red Wings	NHL	13	6	5		1	31	2.75	0	0	0	2
1964–65	35	Toronto Maple Leafs	NHL	1	0	1		0	3	3.00	0	0	0	0
1965–66	36	Toronto Maple Leafs	NHL	2	0	2		0	6	3.00	0	0	0	0
1966–67	37	Toronto Maple Leafs	NHL	10	6	4		0	25	2.65	0	0	0	0
1967–68	38	Los Angeles Kings	NHL	5	2	3		1	18	3.86	0	0	0	0
1969–70	40	New York Rangers	NHL	3	0	1		0	6	4.50	0	0	0	0
NHL Career — 15 Seasons				106	54	48		12	266	2.54	0	0	0	26

TROPHY CASE

AWARDS

Calder Memorial Trophy (1951)

Vezina Trophy (1952, 1953, 1955, 1965)

Lester Patrick Trophy (1971)

Stanley Cup (1951–52, 1953–54, 1954–55, 1966–67)

ALL-STAR SELECTIONS

First All-Star Team Goaltender (1951, 1952, 1953)

Second All-Star Team Goaltender (1954, 1955, 1959, 1963)

Fred Scanlan

HOCKEY HALL OF FAME CLASS: 1965

Left Wing

Shoots: Unknown

Height: Unknown

Weight: Unknown

Born: May 5, 1877:
Montreal, Quebec

Died: November 11,
1950: Unknown

Played six elite
amateur seasons
from 1897–1903

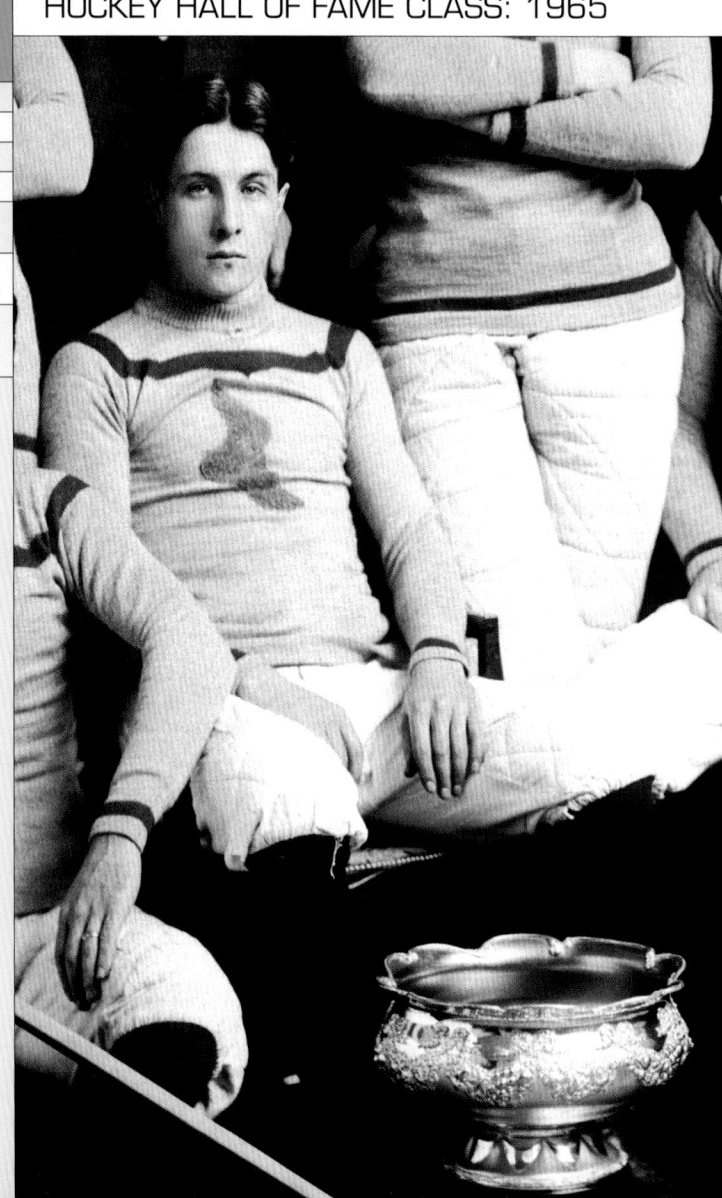

Marty Barry, Clint Benedict, Arthur Farrell, Red Horner, Syd Howe,
Jack Marshall, Bill Mosienko, Blair Russel, Ernie Russell

QUICK FACTS

- Renowned for his skating speed and skill as a stickhandler who was considered one of the top forwards in Canada

- Member of Montreal Shamrocks' outstanding forward line with future Hall of Fame members Harry Trihey and Arthur Farrell

- Member of Stanley Cup-winning Montreal Shamrocks team that defeated Queen's University (March, 1899), Winnipeg (February, 1900) and Halifax (March, 1900) to win and retain championship

- Employment opportunity with the Canadian Northern Railway brought him to Winnipeg where he joined the Victorias hockey team

- Member of Stanley Cup-winning Winnipeg Victorias team that defeated Toronto Wellingtons 5–3 and 5–3 to capture championship, January 29–31, 1901

- Moved to San Francisco in the fall of 1903 and survived the 1906 earthquake

> 'Frindy' has always had the reputation of being one of the best forwards in the Dominion. He is a fast skater and a splendid stickhandler."
> — *Montreal Gazette*, December 19, 1901

REGULAR SEASON .

Season	Age	Team	Lg	GP	G	A	PTS
1897–98	20	Montreal Shamrocks	AHAC	8	2	0	2
1889–99	21	Montreal Shamrocks	CAHL	8	4	0	4
1899–00	22	Montreal Shamrocks	CAHL	7	6	0	6
1900–01	23	Montreal Shamrocks	CAHL	8	5	0	5
1901–02	24	Winnipeg Victorias	MNWHA	3	5	0	5
1902–03	25	Winnipeg Victorias	WSrHL	6	6	2	8
Career – 6 Seasons				40	28	2	30

PLAYOFFS

Season	Age	Team	Lg	GP	G	A	PTS
1898–99	21	Montreal Shamrocks	St-Cup	1	1	0	1
1899–00	22	Montreal Shamrocks	St-Cup	5	2	0	2
1900–01	23	Montreal Shamrocks	St-Cup	2	0	0	0
1901–02	24	Winnipeg Victorias	St-Cup	5	2	0	2
1902–03	25	Winnipeg Victorias	St-Cup	4	1	0	1
Career – 5 Seasons				17	6	0	6

TROPHY CASE

AWARDS

Stanley Cup (1898–99, 1899–1900, 1901–02)

Milt Schmidt

HOCKEY HALL OF FAME CLASS: 1961

Center/Defense

Shoots: Left

Height: 6'

Weight: 185 lbs.

Born: March 5, 1918: Kitchener, Ontario

Played 16 NHL seasons from 1936–42, 1945–55

QUICK FACTS

- Played amateur hockey with Kitchener Empires (1933–34); Kitchener Greenshirts (1934–36); Ottawa RCAF Flyers (1941–42)
- Led OHA-Jr. playoffs in goals (4) and points (5) in 1935–36
- Signed as a free agent by Boston, October 9, 1936
- Member of Allan Cup-winning Ottawa RCAF Flyers (1941–42); recorded 6 goals and 16 assists in 13 games in Allan Cup playoffs
- Member of Boston's famed Kraut Line with Bobby Bauer and Woody Dumart
- Entire line finished 1–2–3 in scoring (Schmidt, Dumart, Bauer) in 1939–40, first time in NHL history three teammates accomplished that feat
- Led NHL in assists (30) and points (52) in 1939–40

- Led NHL playoffs in points (11) in 1940–41
- Finished among NHL top-5 in points in 1939–40 (52), 1946–47 (62) and 1950–51 (61)
- Played in NHL All-Star Game (1947, 1948, 1951, 1952)
- Served as captain of Boston Bruins (1951–54)
- Officially announced retirement, December 25, 1954 and named coach of Boston Bruins
- Coached Boston Bruins (1954–55, 1955–61, 1962–63, 1963–66)
- Served as General Manager of Boston Bruins (1967–72)
- Coached Washington Capitals (1974–76)
- Served as General Manager of Washington Capitals (1974–76)

> "I was 18 years of age when I signed my contract and started playing with the Boston Bruins in 1936–37. Two years later, in 1938–39, we won the Stanley Cup. It was the greatest charge I ever got out of playing hockey."

REGULAR SEASON

Season	Age	Team	Lg	GP	G	A	PTS	PIM
1936–37	18	Boston Bruins	NHL	26	2	8	10	15
1937–38	19	Boston Bruins	NHL	44	13	14	27	15
1938–39	20	Boston Bruins	NHL	41	15	17	32	13
1939–40	21	Boston Bruins	NHL	48	22	30	52	37
1940–41	22	Boston Bruins	NHL	45	13	25	38	23
1941–42	23	Boston Bruins	NHL	36	14	21	35	34
1945–46	27	Boston Bruins	NHL	48	13	18	31	21
1946–47	28	Boston Bruins	NHL	59	27	35	62	40
1947–48	29	Boston Bruins	NHL	33	9	17	26	28
1948–49	30	Boston Bruins	NHL	44	10	22	32	25
1949–50	31	Boston Bruins	NHL	68	19	22	41	41
1950–51	32	Boston Bruins	NHL	62	22	39	61	33
1951–52	33	Boston Bruins	NHL	69	21	29	50	57
1952–53	34	Boston Bruins	NHL	68	11	23	34	30
1953–54	35	Boston Bruins	NHL	62	14	18	32	28
1954–55	36	Boston Bruins	NHL	23	4	8	12	26
NHL Career — 16 Seasons				776	229	346	575	466

PLAYOFFS

Season	Age	Team	Lg	GP	G	A	PTS	PIM
1936–37	18	Boston Bruins	NHL	3	0	0	0	0
1937–38	19	Boston Bruins	NHL	3	0	0	0	0
1938–39	20	Boston Bruins	NHL	12	3	3	6	2
1939–40	21	Boston Bruins	NHL	6	0	0	0	0
1940–41	22	Boston Bruins	NHL	11	5	6	11	9
1945–46	27	Boston Bruins	NHL	10	3	5	8	2
1946–47	28	Boston Bruins	NHL	5	3	1	4	4
1947–48	29	Boston Bruins	NHL	5	2	5	7	2
1948–49	30	Boston Bruins	NHL	4	0	2	2	8
1950–51	32	Boston Bruins	NHL	6	0	1	1	7
1951–52	33	Boston Bruins	NHL	7	2	1	3	0
1952–53	34	Boston Bruins	NHL	10	5	1	6	6
1953–54	35	Boston Bruins	NHL	4	1	0	1	20
NHL Career — 13 Seasons				86	24	25	49	60

TROPHY CASE

AWARDS

NHL Scoring Leader (1940)

Hart Memorial Trophy (1951)

Lester Patrick Trophy (1996)

Stanley Cup (1938–39, 1940–41)

ALL-STAR SELECTIONS

First All-Star Team Center (1940, 1947, 1951)

Second All-Star Team Center (1952)

11

Sweeney Schriner

HOCKEY HALL OF FAME CLASS: 1962

Alternate: 14

Left Wing

Shoots: Left

Height: 6'

Weight: 185 lbs.

Born: November 30, 1911: Saratov, Russian Federation

Died: July 4, 1990: Calgary, Alberta

Played 11 NHL seasons from 1934–43, 1944–46

Punch Broadbent, Harry Cameron, Rusty Crawford, Jack Darragh, Jimmy Gardner, Billy Gilmour, Shorty Green, Riley Hern, Tom Hooper, Bouse Hutton, Harry Hyland, Jack Laviolette, Didier Pitre, Fred Maxwell, Billy McGimsie, Reg Noble, Jack Ruttan, Joe Simpson, Alf Smith, Barney Stanley, Nels Stewart, Marty Walsh, Harry E. Watson, Harry Westwick, Fred Whitcroft, Phat Wilson

QUICK FACTS

> He was the best left winger I ever saw. That includes everybody: Frank Mahovlich, Busher Jackson, Bobby Hull, everybody."
> — Conn Smythe

- Nicknamed "Sweeney" because of his devotion to a semi-pro baseball player named Bill Sweeney

- Played amateur hockey with Calgary North Hill (1925–28), Calgary Canadians (1928–31) and Calgary Bronks (1931–33)

- Led ASHL in goals (19) and points (22) in 1931–32; goals (22) and points (26) in 1932–33

- Played in NHL All-Star Game (1937)

- Traded to Toronto by N.Y. Americans for Busher Jackson, Buzz Boll, Doc Romnes, Jimmy Fowler and Murray Armstrong, May 18, 1939

- Finished among NHL top-5 in goals in 1935–36 (19), 1936–37 (21), 1937–38 (21) and 1940–41 (24)

- Finished among NHL top-5 in assists in 1935–36 (26), 1936–37 (25) and 1938–39 (31)

- Finished among NHL top-5 in points in 1935–36 (45), 1936–37 (46) and 1938–39 (44)

- Played with Calgary Combines and Vancouver St. Regis Hotel (1943–44) during World War II

- ANDHL Second All-Star Team Left Wing (1943–44)

- Coached Lethbridge Maple Leafs (1946–48); Crow's Nest Pass Coalers (1951–52)

- Played with Regina Capitals (1948–49) and helped team advance to the Allan Cup Finals

- WCSHL Second All-Star Team Left Wing (1949)

REGULAR SEASON

Season	Age	Team	Lg	GP	G	A	PTS	PIM
1934–35	23	New York Americans	NHL	48	18	22	40	6
1935–36	24	New York Americans	NHL	48	19	26	45	8
1936–37	25	New York Americans	NHL	48	21	25	46	17
1937–38	26	New York Americans	NHL	48	21	17	38	22
1938–39	27	New York Americans	NHL	48	13	31	44	20
1939–40	28	Toronto Maple Leafs	NHL	39	11	15	26	10
1940–41	29	Toronto Maple Leafs	NHL	48	24	14	38	6
1941–42	30	Toronto Maple Leafs	NHL	47	20	16	36	21
1942–43	31	Toronto Maple Leafs	NHL	37	19	17	36	13
1944–45	33	Toronto Maple Leafs	NHL	26	22	15	37	10
1945–46	34	Toronto Maple Leafs	NHL	47	13	6	19	15
NHL Career – 11 Seasons				484	201	204	405	148

PLAYOFFS

Season	Age	Team	Lg	GP	G	A	PTS	PIM
1935–36	24	New York Americans	NHL	5	3	1	4	2
1937–38	26	New York Americans	NHL	6	1	0	1	0
1938–39	27	New York Americans	NHL	2	0	0	0	30
1939–40	28	Toronto Maple Leafs	NHL	9	1	3	4	4
1940–41	29	Toronto Maple Leafs	NHL	7	2	1	3	4
1941–42	30	Toronto Maple Leafs	NHL	13	6	3	9	10
1942–43	31	Toronto Maple Leafs	NHL	4	2	2	4	0
1944–45	33	Toronto Maple Leafs	NHL	13	3	1	4	4
NHL Career – 8 Seasons				59	18	11	29	54

TROPHY CASE

AWARDS

Calder Memorial Trophy (1935)

NHL Scoring Leader (1936, 1937)

Stanley Cup (1941–42, 1944–45)

ALL-STAR SELECTIONS

First All-Star Team Left Wing (1936, 1941)

Second All-Star Team Left Wing (1937)

17

Earl Seibert

HOCKEY HALL OF FAME CLASS: 1963

Alternates: 2, 21

Defense

Shoots: Right

Height: 6'-2"

Weight: 198 lbs.

Born: December 7, 1911: Berlin, Ontario

Died: May 20, 1990: Agawam, Massachusetts

Played 15 NHL seasons from 1931–46

QUICK FACTS

- Played amateur hockey with Kitchener Greenshirts (1927–29)

- Along with father Oliver Seibert, became first father-son duo to be honored as members of the Hockey Hall of Fame. The elder Seibert played for the Western Ontario Senior champion Berlin HC

- Can-Am First All-Star Team Defense (1931)

- Traded to N.Y. Rangers by Springfield Indians (Can-Am) for cash, May 9, 1931

- Traded to Chicago by N.Y. Rangers for Art Coulter, January 15, 1936

- Scored five goals and added two assists in 10 playoff games to help the Black Hawks upset the Toronto Maple Leafs and win the Stanley Cup in 1938. He scored only eight goals in 48 regular season games during the 1937–38 season

- A pugnacious, hard-hitting defender, it was Seibert who upended Howie Morenz in a game on January 28, 1937, causing the Montreal Canadiens star to slide feet first into the end boards. Seibert fell on top of Morenz' leg, breaking it in four places. Morenz would never play again, and six weeks later he died of complications from the injury

- Played in NHL All-Star Game (1939)

- Served as captain of Chicago Black Hawks (1940–42)

- Traded to Detroit by Chicago with future considerations (Fido Purpur, January 4, 1945) for Cully Simon, Don Grosso and Butch McDonald, January 2, 1945

- Coached Indianapolis Capitols (1945–46); coached Springfield Indians (1946–51)

> Let's put it this way, no one wanted any part of 'Si' in a fight. Even Eddie Shore and Red Horner steered clear of him, and Shore and Horner were considered the toughest guys in the league at the time.
> — Ching Johnson

REGULAR SEASON

Season	Age	Team	Lg	GP	G	A	PTS	PIM
1931-32	20	New York Rangers	NHL	46	4	6	10	88
1932-33	21	New York Rangers	NHL	45	2	3	5	92
1933-34	22	New York Rangers	NHL	48	13	10	23	66
1934-35	23	New York Rangers	NHL	48	6	19	25	86
1935-36	24	New York Rangers	NHL	17	2	3	5	6
1935-36	24	Chicago Black Hawks	NHL	15	3	6	9	19
1936-37	25	Chicago Black Hawks	NHL	43	9	6	15	46
1937-38	26	Chicago Black Hawks	NHL	48	8	13	21	38
1938-39	27	Chicago Black Hawks	NHL	48	4	11	15	57
1939-40	28	Chicago Black Hawks	NHL	36	3	7	10	35
1940-41	29	Chicago Black Hawks	NHL	46	3	17	20	52
1941-42	30	Chicago Black Hawks	NHL	46	7	14	21	52
1942-43	31	Chicago Black Hawks	NHL	44	5	27	32	48
1943-44	32	Chicago Black Hawks	NHL	50	8	25	33	20
1944-45	33	Chicago Black Hawks	NHL	22	7	8	15	13
1944-45	33	Detroit Red Wings	NHL	25	5	9	14	10
1945-46	34	Detroit Red Wings	NHL	18	0	3	3	18
NHL Career — 15 Seasons				645	89	196	276	746

PLAYOFFS

Season	Age	Team	Lg	GP	G	A	PTS	PIM
1931-32	20	New York Rangers	NHL	7	1	2	3	14
1932-33	21	New York Rangers	NHL	8	1	0	1	14
1933-34	22	New York Rangers	NHL	2	0	0	0	4
1934-35	23	New York Rangers	NHL	4	0	0	0	6
1935-36	24	Chicago Black Hawks	NHL	2	2	0	2	0
1937-38	26	Chicago Black Hawks	NHL	10	5	2	7	12
1939-40	28	Chicago Black Hawks	NHL	2	0	1	1	8
1940-41	29	Chicago Black Hawks	NHL	5	0	0	0	12
1941-42	30	Chicago Black Hawks	NHL	3	0	0	0	0
1943-44	32	Chicago Black Hawks	NHL	9	0	2	2	2
1944-45	33	Detroit Red Wings	NHL	14	2	1	3	4
NHL Career — 11 Seasons				66	11	8	19	76

TROPHY CASE

AWARDS

Stanley Cup (1932–33, 1937–38)

ALL-STAR SELECTIONS

First All-Star Team Defense (1935, 1942, 1943, 1944)

Second All-Star Team Defense (1936, 1937, 1938, 1939, 1940, 1941)

Oliver Seibert

HOCKEY HALL OF FAME CLASS: 1961

Center

Shoots: Unknown

Height: Unknown

Weight: 180 lbs.

Born: March 18, 1881: Berlin, Ontario

Died: May 15, 1944: Kitchener, Ontario

Played six elite amateur and professional seasons from 1899–1905

QUICK FACTS

- Renowned as being among the first Canadian players to skate on artificial ice as a member of the Berlin Rangers in an exhibition game in St. Louis
- Father of Hall of Fame member Earl Seibert, who played in NHL with N.Y. Rangers, Detroit and Chicago from 1931–46
- First father-and-son team to be inducted into the Hall of Fame in the player category
- Member of prominent sports family in Berlin (now Kitchener), Ontario, where he once played on the All-Seibert Team with brothers Edward, Nelson, Clarence, Bert and Shannon
- Father "Butch" Seibert was reputed to have beaten a horse in a one-mile race on the frozen Grand River
- Began his career as a goaltender before moving to forward

- Played five games as a goaltender for the Berlin Pros posting a 2-2-1 record with a 6.72 goals-against average in 1906–07
- Member of Western Ontario Hockey champion Berlin Rangers (1899–00, 1900–01, 1901–02, 1903–04)
- Led WOHA in goals (17) in 1901–02
- Signed as a free agent by Canadian Soo, January 31, 1905
- Suffered broken leg in the first game of the season with the Canadian Soo team in the professional International Hockey League in 1904–05

> "Oliver Seibert of the old 'Flying Dutchmen' brought hockey fame many years ago to Kitchener."
>
> — *Ottawa Citizen*, March 30, 1932, in a story about his son—future Hall of Famer Earl Seibert

REGULAR SEASON

Season	Age	Team	Lg	GP	G	A	PTS
1899–00	18	Berlin Hockey Club	WOHA	8	10	0	10
1900–01	19	Berlin Hockey Club	WOHA	6	13	0	13
1901–02	20	Berlin Hockey Club	WOHA	8	17	0	17
1902–03	21	Guelph OAC	OHA-Sr				
1903–04	22	Berlin Hockey Club	WOHA				
1904–05	23	Canadian Soo	IHL	1	0	0	0
Career — 6 Seasons				23	40	0	40

TROPHY CASE

Eddie Shore

HOCKEY HALL OF FAME CLASS: 1947

Defense

Shoots: Right

Height: 5'-11"

Weight: 190 lbs.

Born: November 25, 1902: Fort Qu'Appelle, Saskatchewan

Died: March 16, 1985: Springfield, Massachusetts

Played 16 professional seasons from 1924–40

" I'm not sorry about anything I've done."
— Eddie Shore, 1985

QUICK FACTS

- His #2 jersey was retired by the Boston Bruins, April 1, 1947

- First player to win the Hart Trophy as NHL MVP four times; only defenseman to win the Hart Trophy as NHL MVP four times

- Nicknamed "The Edmonton Express"

- Played amateur hockey with Melville Millionaires (1923–24)

- Signed as a free agent by Regina Caps (WCHL), December 2, 1924; transferred to Portland (WHL) after Regina (WHL) franchise relocated, September 1, 1925; traded to Edmonton (WHL) by Portland (WHL) with Art Gagne for Joe McCormick and Bob Trapp, October 7, 1925

- Traded to Boston Bruins by Edmonton (WHL) for cash, August 20, 1926

- Led NHL in penalty minutes (165) in 1927–28

- Finished among NHL top-10 in assists in 1930–31 (16), 1932–33 (27) and 1934–35 (26); finished among NHL top-10 in points in 1928–29 (19) and 1932–33 (35)

- Traded to N.Y. Americans by Boston for Ed Wiseman and $5,000, January 25, 1940

- Renowned as the toughest and dirtiest player of his era

- When Shore owned and managed the AHL's Springfield Indians, his players went on strike in December of 1966 to protest his "constant harassment" and the suspensions of four Springfield players. The strike was settled with the help of lawyer Allan Eagleson, who later helped form the NHLPA

- Played in NHL All-Star Game (1934, 1937, 1939)

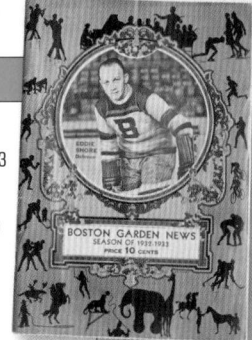

Shore featured on the cover of the *Boston Garden News* in 1932–33.

REGULAR SEASON								
Season	Age	Team	Lg	GP	G	A	PTS	PIM
1924–25	22	Regina Capitals	WCHL	24	6	0	6	75
1925–26	23	Edmonton Eskimos	WHL	30	12	2	14	86
1926–27	24	Boston Bruins	NHL	40	12	6	18	130
1927–28	25	Boston Bruins	NHL	43	11	6	17	165
1928–29	26	Boston Bruins	NHL	39	12	7	19	96
1929–30	27	Boston Bruins	NHL	42	12	19	31	105
1930–31	28	Boston Bruins	NHL	44	15	16	31	105
1931–32	29	Boston Bruins	NHL	45	9	13	22	80
1932–33	30	Boston Bruins	NHL	48	8	27	35	102
1933–34	31	Boston Bruins	NHL	30	2	10	12	57
1934–35	32	Boston Bruins	NHL	48	7	26	33	32
1935–36	33	Boston Bruins	NHL	45	3	16	19	61
1936–37	34	Boston Bruins	NHL	20	3	1	4	12
1937–38	35	Boston Bruins	NHL	48	3	14	17	42
1938–39	36	Boston Bruins	NHL	44	4	14	18	47
1939–40	37	Boston Bruins	NHL	4	2	1	3	4
Career — 16 Seasons				604	123	181	304	1208

PLAYOFFS								
Season	Age	Team	Lg	GP	G	A	PTS	PIM
1925–26	23	Edmonton Eskimos	WHL	2	0	0	0	8
1926–27	24	Boston Bruins	NHL	8	1	1	2	40
1927–28	25	Boston Bruins	NHL	2	0	0	0	8
1928–29	26	Boston Bruins	NHL	5	1	1	2	28
1929–30	27	Boston Bruins	NHL	6	1	0	1	26
1930–31	28	Boston Bruins	NHL	5	2	1	3	24
1932–33	30	Boston Bruins	NHL	5	1	0	1	14
1934–35	32	Boston Bruins	NHL	4	0	1	1	2
1935–36	33	Boston Bruins	NHL	2	1	1	2	12
1937–38	35	Boston Bruins	NHL	3	0	1	1	6
1938–39	36	Boston Bruins	NHL	12	0	4	4	19
1939–40	37	New York Americans	NHL	3	0	2	2	2
Career — 12 Seasons				57	7	12	22	195

TROPHY CASE

AWARDS

Hart Memorial Trophy (1933, 1935, 1936, 1938)

Stanley Cup (1928–29, 1938–39)

Lester Patrick Trophy (1970)

ALL-STAR SELECTIONS

WHL First All-Star Team Defense (1925)

First All-Star Team Defense (1931, 1932, 1933, 1935, 1936, 1938, 1939)

Second All-Star Team Defense (1934)

Steve Shutt

HOCKEY HALL OF FAME CLASS: 1993

Alternate: 11

Left Wing

Shoots: Left

Height: 5'-11"

Weight: 185 lbs.

Born: July 1, 1952:
Toronto, Quebec

Drafted by
the Montreal
Canadiens fourth
overall in 1972

Played 13 NHL
seasons from
1972–85

QUICK FACTS

- Played amateur hockey with North York Rangers (1968–69); Toronto Marlboros (1968–72)
- Led OHA-Jr. in goals (63) in 1971–72
- OHA-Jr. First Team All-Star Left Wing (1972); OHA-Jr. Second Team All-Star Left Wing (1971)
- Holds Montreal Canadiens team record for career goals (408) and points (776) by a left wing
- Shares Montreal Canadiens team record (with Guy Lafleur) for goals in regular season (60), established in 1976–77
- Held NHL record for most goals by a left wing in regular season (60); surpassed by Luc Robitaille in 1992–93

- Led NHL in goals (60) in 1976–77; led NHL in even-strength goals (52) in 1976–77
- Led NHL in game-winning goals (9) in 1976–77
- Played in NHL All-Star Game (1976, 1978, 1981)
- Traded to L.A. Kings by Montreal for future considerations, November 19, 1984
- Claimed on waivers by Montreal from L.A. Kings, June 18, 1985
- Nicknamed "Bullet" because of his powerful shot

> When you're playing, you don't worry about being in the Hall of Fame. When they come up and say, 'Hey, you've been inducted,' it was a thrill for everybody. You're being acknowledged by your peers and the people within the industry, and that's impressive because they're the hardest ones to convince. That, more than anything, gave me the greatest satisfaction."

REGULAR SEASON

Season	Age	Team	Lg	GP	G	A	PTS	+/-	PIM	ESG	PPG	SHG	GWG	SOG	S%
1972-73	20	Montreal Canadiens	NHL	50	8	8	16	5	24	7	1	0	2	55	14.5
1973-74	21	Montreal Canadiens	NHL	70	15	20	35	19	17	12	3	0	1	131	11.5
1974-75	22	Montreal Canadiens	NHL	77	30	35	65	40	40	27	3	0	5	165	18.2
1975-76	23	Montreal Canadiens	NHL	80	45	34	79	73	47	38	7	0	7	223	20.2
1976-77	24	Montreal Canadiens	NHL	80	60	45	105	88	28	52	8	0	9	294	20.4
1977-78	25	Montreal Canadiens	NHL	80	49	37	86	56	24	33	16	0	7	243	20.2
1978-79	26	Montreal Canadiens	NHL	72	37	40	77	37	31	27	10	0	6	192	19.3
1979-80	27	Montreal Canadiens	NHL	77	47	42	89	45	34	30	17	0	4	224	21.0
1980-81	28	Montreal Canadiens	NHL	77	35	38	73	30	51	28	7	0	3	232	15.1
1981-82	29	Montreal Canadiens	NHL	57	31	24	55	24	40	26	5	0	3	154	20.1
1982-83	30	Montreal Canadiens	NHL	78	35	22	57	8	26	27	8	0	0	202	17.3
1983-84	31	Montreal Canadiens	NHL	63	14	23	37	-18	29	10	4	0	2	146	9.6
1984-85	32	Montreal Canadiens	NHL	10	2	0	2	2	9	1	1	0	0	17	11.8
1984-85	32	Los Angeles Kings	NHL	59	16	25	41	-16	10	11	5	0	1	127	12.6
NHL Career – 13 Seasons				930	424	393	817	393	410	329	95	0	50	2405	17.6

PLAYOFFS

Season	Age	Team	Lg	GP	G	A	PTS	+/-	PIM	ESG	PPG	SHG	GWG	SOG	S%
1972-73	20	Montreal Canadiens	NHL	1	0	0	0		0	0	0	0	0		
1973-74	21	Montreal Canadiens	NHL	6	5	3	8		9	4	1	0	0		
1974-75	22	Montreal Canadiens	NHL	9	1	6	7		4	1	0	0	0		
1975-76	23	Montreal Canadiens	NHL	13	7	8	15		2	4	3	0	0		
1976-77	24	Montreal Canadiens	NHL	14	8	10	18		2	6	2	0	3		
1977-78	25	Montreal Canadiens	NHL	15	9	8	17		20	6	3	0	0		
1978-79	26	Montreal Canadiens	NHL	11	4	7	11		6	3	1	0	0		
1979-80	27	Montreal Canadiens	NHL	10	6	3	9		6	4	2	0	2		
1980-81	28	Montreal Canadiens	NHL	3	2	1	3		4	2	0	0	0		
1982-83	30	Montreal Canadiens	NHL	3	1	0	1		0	1	0	0	0		
1983-84	31	Montreal Canadiens	NHL	11	7	2	9	5	8	5	2	0	0	26	26.9
1984-85	32	Los Angeles Kings	NHL	3	0	0	0	-4	4	0	0	0	0	6	0.0
NHL Career – 12 Seasons				99	50	48	98	1	65	36	14	0	5	32	21.9

TROPHY CASE

AWARDS

Stanley Cup (1972–73, 1975–76, 1976–77, 1977–78, 1978–79)

ALL-STAR SELECTIONS

First All-Star Team Left Wing (1977)

Second All-Star Team Left Wing (1978, 1980)

INTERNATIONAL AWARDS

Canada Cup (1976)

Babe Siebert

HOCKEY HALL OF FAME CLASS: 1964

Alternates: 12, 4, 1

Left Wing/Defense

Shoots: Left

Height: 5'-10"

Weight: 182 lbs.
Born: January 14,
1904: Plattsville,
Ontario

Died: August 25,
1939: Zurich,
Ontario

Played 14 NHL
seasons from
1925–39

QUICK FACTS

- Played amateur hockey with Zurich Intermediates (1920–21); Exeter Hawks (1921–22); Kitchener Greenshirts (1922–23); Kitchener Twin Cities (1923–24); Niagara Falls Cataracts (1925–26)

- Signed as a free agent by Montreal Maroons, March 16, 1925

- Member of Montreal Maroons famed "S Line" with Hooley Smith and Nels Stewart

- Began career as a rover — a player used as both a forward and defender in the era of seven-man hockey — before becoming an offensively talented left winger with the Montreal Maroons

- Moved back to defense when he joined the Boston Bruins and earned three All-Star team berths as a defenseman

- Played in NHL All-Star Game (1937)

- Traded to N.Y. Rangers by Montreal Maroons for cash, July 2, 1932; traded to Boston by N.Y. Rangers for Vic Ripley and Roy Burmeister, December 18, 1933; traded to Montreal by Boston with Roger Jenkins for Leroy Goldsworthy, Sammy McManus and $10,000, September 10, 1936.

- Served as captain of Montreal Canadiens (1936–39)

- Named head coach of the Montreal Canadiens (June 9, 1939)

- Drowned while swimming with family on Lake Huron, near Zurich, Ontario (August 25, 1939)

- Third NHL Memorial All-Star Game was played in his honor. The Babe Siebert Memorial Game was held at the Montreal Forum on Sunday, October 29, 1939

> When I was put on defense and began having 40 and 45 minutes of play each game, I was alright again. That was all there was to it. I hadn't lost what ability I had — I just wasn't getting the opportunity to use it."
> — Babe Siebert, reflecting on his "amazing" comeback

REGULAR SEASON

Season	Age	Team	Lg	GP	G	A	PTS	PIM
1925–26	21	Montreal Maroons	NHL	35	16	8	24	108
1926–27	22	Montreal Maroons	NHL	42	5	3	8	116
1927–28	23	Montreal Maroons	NHL	39	8	9	17	109
1928–29	24	Montreal Maroons	NHL	40	3	5	8	52
1929–30	25	Montreal Maroons	NHL	39	14	19	33	94
1930–31	26	Montreal Maroons	NHL	43	16	12	28	76
1931–32	27	Montreal Maroons	NHL	48	21	18	39	64
1932–33	28	New York Rangers	NHL	43	9	10	19	38
1933–34	29	New York Rangers	NHL	13	0	1	1	18
1933–34	29	Boston Bruins	NHL	32	5	6	11	31
1934–35	30	Boston Bruins	NHL	48	6	18	24	80
1935–36	31	Boston Bruins	NHL	45	12	9	21	66
1936–37	32	Montreal Canadiens	NHL	44	8	20	28	38
1937–38	33	Montreal Canadiens	NHL	37	8	11	19	56
1938–39	34	Montreal Canadiens	NHL	44	9	7	16	36
Career — 14 Seasons				592	140	156	296	982

PLAYOFFS

Season	Age	Team	Lg	GP	G	A	PTS	PIM
1925–26	21	Montreal Maroons	NHL	4	1	0	1	4
1925–26	21	Montreal Maroons	St-Cup	4	1	2	3	2
1926–27	22	Montreal Maroons	NHL	2	1	0	1	2
1927–28	23	Montreal Maroons	NHL	9	2	0	2	26
1929–30	25	Montreal Maroons	NHL	3	0	0	0	0
1930–31	26	Montreal Maroons	NHL	2	0	0	0	6
1931–32	27	Montreal Maroons	NHL	4	0	1	1	4
1932–33	28	New York Rangers	NHL	8	1	0	1	12
1934–35	30	Boston Bruins	NHL	4	0	0	0	6
1935–36	31	Boston Bruins	NHL	2	0	1	1	0
1936–37	32	Montreal Canadiens	NHL	5	1	2	3	2
1937–38	33	Montreal Canadiens	NHL	3	1	1	2	0
1938–39	34	Montreal Canadiens	NHL	3	0	0	0	0
Career — 12 Seasons				53	8	7	15	64

TROPHY CASE

AWARDS

Hart Memorial Trophy (1937)

Stanley Cup (1925–26, 1932–33)

ALL-STAR SELECTIONS

First All-Star Team Defense (1936, 1937, 1938)

Joe Simpson

HOCKEY HALL OF FAME CLASS: 1962

Alternate: 4

Defense

Shoots: Right

Height: 5'-10"

Weight: 175 lbs.

Born: August 13, 1893: Selkirk, Manitoba

Died: December 25, 1973: Coral Gables, Florida

Played 10 professional seasons from 1921–31

QUICK FACTS

- Played amateur hockey with the Winnipeg Strathconas (1912-13); Selkirk Fishermen (1913–14); Winnipeg Victorias (1914–15); Winnipeg 61st Battalion (1915–16)

- Nicknamed "Bullet Joe" because of his blinding speed and in reference to the wounds he suffered during World War I

- Member of Allan Cup-winning Winnipeg 61st Battalion team that defeated the Regina Capitals 13–3 in the two game total goal series in 1916. Simpson scored four goals and registered two assists in five playoff games

- During World War I, he served with the 43rd Cameron Highlanders in a battalion commanded by Major Winston Churchill

- Twice wounded in the war — at the Battle of the Somme and Amiens — he was awarded the Military Medal for Valor

- Signed as a free agent by Edmonton Eskimos (WCHL), November 4, 1921

- Big-4 First All-Star team Defense (1921)

- Established WCHL record for goals (21) and points (33) by a defenseman (1921–22)

- Established WCHL record for assists (14) by a defenseman (1922–23)

- Traded to N.Y. Americans by Edmonton (WHL) with John Morrison and Roy Rickey for $10,000, September 18, 1925

- Coached N.Y. Americans (1931–34); New Haven Eagles (1934–36); Minneapolis Millers (1936–38); Miami Clippers (1938–39)

- The Marine Museum of Manitoba in Selkirk restored a 1963 flat-bottomed freighter; renamed the vessel *Harold Bullet Joe Simpson*

> "Simpson was a great skater, a defenseman whose end-to-end rushes wowed fans wherever he went. The nickname 'Bullet Joe' was well deserved and his fame well understood by everyone who watched him play the game at another level than most."
> — Canadian Sports Hall of Fame

REGULAR SEASON

Season	Age	Team	Lg	GP	G	A	PTS	PIM
1921–22	28	Edmonton Eskimos	WCHL	25	21	12	33	15
1922–23	29	Edmonton Eskimos	WCHL	30	15	14	29	6
1923–24	30	Edmonton Eskimos	WCHL	30	10	4	14	6
1924–25	31	Edmonto Eskimos	WCHL	28	11	12	23	16
1925–26	32	New York Americans	NHL	32	2	2	4	2
1926–27	33	New York Americans	NHL	43	4	2	6	39
1927–28	34	New York Americans	NHL	24	2	0	2	32
1928–29	35	New York Americans	NHL	43	3	2	5	29
1929–30	36	New York Americans	NHL	44	8	13	21	41
1930–31	37	New York Americans	NHL	42	2	0	2	13
Career – 10 Seasons				341	78	61	139	199

PLAYOFFS

Season	Age	Team	Lg	GP	G	A	PTS	PIM
1921–22	28	Edmonton Eskimos	WCHL	2	1	0	1	2
1922–23	29	Edmonton Eskimos	St-Cup	2	0	1	1	0
1922–23	29	Edmonton Eskimos	WCHL	2	0	0	0	0
1928–29	35	New York Americans	NHL	2	0	0	0	0
Career – 3 Seasons				8	1	1	2	2

TROPHY CASE

ALL-STAR SELECTIONS

WCHL First All-Star Team Defense (1922, 1923, 1925)

WCHL Second All-Star Team Defense (1924)

27

Honored by Toronto

Darryl Sittler
HOCKEY HALL OF FAME CLASS: 1989

Alternate: 9

Center

Shoots: Left

Height: 6'

Weight: 190 lbs.

Born: September 18, 1950: Kitchener, Ontario

Drafted by the Toronto Maple Leafs eighth overall in 1970

Played 15 NHL seasons from 1970–85

QUICK FACTS

- Holds NHL record for points in a single game (10), established in Toronto's 11–4 victory over Boston, February 7, 1976

- Shares NHL record for goals in a single playoff game (5), established in Toronto's 8–5 victory over Philadelphia, April 22, 1976

- Played amateur hockey with Elmira Sugar Kings (1966–67); London Nationals/Knights (1967–68); London Knights (1968–70)

- OHA-Jr. Second Team All-Star Center (1969)

- Scored Canada Cup-winning overtime goal in Canada's 5–4 victory over Czechoslovakia, September 15, 1976

- Led NHL in shots-on-goal (311) in 1977–78

- Served as Toronto Maple Leafs captain (1975–81)

- Son Ryan was drafted 7th overall by Philadelphia Flyers in 1992 Entry Draft

- Canada Cup All-Star Team (1976)

- Played in NHL All-Star Game (1975, 1978, 1980, 1983)

- Registered 1,000th career NHL point in Philadelphia's 5–2 victory over Calgary Flames, January 20, 1983

- Traded to Philadelphia by Toronto for the rights to Rich Costello, Hartford's 2nd round choice (previously acquired, Toronto selected Peter Ihnacak) in 1982 Entry Draft and future considerations (Ken Strong, May, 1982), January 20, 1982

- Traded to Detroit by Philadelphia for Murray Craven and Joe Paterson, October 10, 1984

> In the 80s, when Wayne Gretzky and Mario Lemieux were breaking all kinds of records, I thought one of those guys would break it. But now the game has changed so much. You hardly see five or six-goal games between two teams, let alone one player."
>
> — Darryl Sittler, on the longevity of his 10-point record

REGULAR SEASON

Season	Age	Team	Lg	GP	G	A	PTS	+/-	PIM	ESG	PPG	SHG	GWG	SOG	S%
1970–71	21	Toronto Maple Leafs	NHL	49	10	8	18	3	37	7	3	0	3	131	7.6
1971–72	21	Toronto Maple Leafs	NHL	74	15	17	32	-4	44	14	1	0	4	174	8.6
1972–73	22	Toronto Maple Leafs	NHL	78	29	48	77	-11	69	21	8	0	1	331	8.8
1973–74	23	Toronto Maple Leafs	NHL	78	38	46	84	12	55	27	11	0	6	270	14.1
1974–75	24	Toronto Maple Leafs	NHL	72	36	44	80	-10	47	23	12	1	2	273	13.2
1975–76	25	Toronto Maple Leafs	NHL	79	41	59	100	12	90	29	11	1	2	346	11.8
1976–77	26	Toronto Maple Leafs	NHL	73	38	52	90	8	89	25	12	1	5	307	12.4
1977–78	27	Toronto Maple Leafs	NHL	80	45	72	117	34	100	31	14	0	8	311	14.5
1978–79	28	Toronto Maple Leafs	NHL	70	36	51	87	9	69	24	12	0	4	290	12.4
1979–80	29	Toronto Maple Leafs	NHL	73	40	57	97	3	62	22	17	1	5	315	12.7
1980–81	30	Toronto Maple Leafs	NHL	80	43	53	96	-8	77	27	14	2	2	267	16.1
1981–82	31	Toronto Maple Leafs	NHL	38	18	20	38	-14	24	11	5	2	0	127	14.2
1981–82	31	Philadelphia Flyers	NHL	35	14	18	32	-1	50	8	5	1	2	114	12.3
1982–83	32	Philadelphia Flyers	NHL	80	43	40	83	17	60	33	10	0	8	231	18.6
1983–84	33	Philadelphia Flyers	NHL	76	27	36	63	13	38	15	11	1	3	212	12.7
1984–85	34	Detroit Red Wings	NHL	61	11	16	27	-10	37	7	4	0	2	113	9.7
NHL Career — 15 Seasons				1096	484	637	1121	53	948	324	150	10	57	3812	12.7

PLAYOFFS

Season	Age	Team	Lg	GP	G	A	PTS	+/-	PIM	ESG	PPG	SHG	GWG	SOG	S%
1970–71	20	Toronto Maple Leafs	NHL	6	2	1	3		31	1	1	0	0		
1971–72	21	Toronto Maple Leafs	NHL	3	0	0	0		2	0	0	0	0		
1973–74	23	Toronto Maple Leafs	NHL	4	2	1	3		6	1	1	0	0		
1974–75	24	Toronto Maple Leafs	NHL	7	2	1	3		15	1	1	0	0		
1975–76	25	Toronto Maple Leafs	NHL	10	5	7	12		19	3	2	0	1		
1976–77	26	Toronto Maple Leafs	NHL	9	5	16	21		4	2	3	0	0		
1977–78	27	Toronto Maple Leafs	NHL	13	3	8	11		12	1	2	0	0		
1978–79	28	Toronto Maple Leafs	NHL	6	5	4	9		17	3	2	0	0		
1979–80	29	Toronto Maple Leafs	NHL	3	1	2	3		10	0	1	0	0		
1980–81	30	Toronto Maple Leafs	NHL	3	0	0	0		4	0	0	0	0		
1981–82	31	Philadelphia Flyers	NHL	4	3	1	4		6	2	1	0	0		
1982–83	32	Philadelphia Flyers	NHL	3	1	0	1		4	1	0	0	0		
1983–84	33	Philadelphia Flyers	NHL	3	0	2	2	-1	7	0	0	0	0	6	0.0
1984–85	34	Detroit Red Wings	NHL	2	0	2	2	0	0	0	0	0	0	2	0.0
NHL Career — 14 Seasons				76	29	45	74	-1	137	15	14	0	1	8	0.0

TROPHY CASE

ALL-STAR SELECTIONS

Second All-Star Team Center (1978)

INTERNATIONAL AWARDS

Canada Cup (1976)

Bronze Medal: World Championships (1982, 1983)

Alf Smith

HOCKEY HALL OF FAME CLASS: 1962

Right Wing

Shoots: Right

Height: 5'-7"

Weight: 165 lbs.

Born: June 3, 1873: Ottawa, Ontario

Died: August 21, 1953: Ottawa, Ontario

Played 12 elite amateur and professional seasons from 1894–97, 1899–1900, 1901–09

+1962 Punch Broadbent, Harry Cameron, Rusty Crawford, Jack Darragh, Jimmy Gardner, Billy Gilmour, Shorty Green, Riley Hern, Tom Hooper, Bouse Hutton, Harry Hyland, Jack Laviolette, Fred Maxwell, Billy McGimsie, Reg Noble, Didier Pitre, Jack Ruttan, Sweeney Schriner, Joe Simpson, Barney Stanley, Nels Stewart, Marty Walsh, Harry E. Watson, Harry Westwick, Fred Whitcroft, Phat Wilson

QUICK FACTS

- Played amateur hockey with Ottawa HC (1894–99); Ottawa Capitals (1899–1901)
- Renowned for his all-round athletic ability, he played quarterback with Ottawa Rough Rider football club and lacrosse with Ottawa Capitals
- Led AHAC in goals (12) in 1896–97
- Led WPHL in assists (9) and points (20) in 1901–02
- WPHL First All-Star Team Right Wing (1902)
- FAHL Second All-Star Team Right Wing (1905)
- ECAHA Second All-Star Team Right Wing (1907)
- Signed as a free agent by Kenora Thistles, March, 1907

- Served as player/coach of Stanley Cup-winning Ottawa "Silver Seven" team that won and retained championship on eight separate occasions between 1903 and 1906
- Member of Stanley Cup-winning Kenora Thistles team that defeated Brandon Wheat Kings in March, 1907
- Coached Renfrew Creamery Kings (1908); coached Pittsburgh Duquesne (1908–09); coached Ottawa Cliffsides (1910–11)
- Coached Montreal Canadiens (1912–13); coached Ottawa Senators (1918–19); coached N.Y. Americans (1925–26)
- Brother of Hall of Fame member Tommy Smith, who played 15 seasons of elite amateur and professional hockey

"That was the way Alf Smith played, all-out and to win. He made allowances for inability, but he had no time or patience for the athlete who did not give his best."
— *Ottawa Citizen*, August 24, 1953

TROPHY CASE

AWARDS

Stanley Cup (1903–04, 1904–05, 1905–06, 1906–07)

REGULAR SEASON

Season	Age	Team	Lg	GP	G	A	PTS	PIM
1894–95	21	Ottawa Hockey Club	AHAC	8	5	0	5	
1895–96	22	Ottawa Hockey Club	AHAC	8	7	0	7	
1896–97	23	Ottawa Hockey Club	AHAC	8	12	0	12	
1899–00	26	Ottawa Capitals	AHA-Sr.					
1901–02	28	Pittsburgh PAC	WPHL	14	11	9	20	17
1902–03	29	Ottawa Silver Seven	CAHL					
1903–04	30	Ottawa Silver Seven	CAHL	4	8	0	8	6
1904–05	31	Ottawa Silver Seven	FAHL	8	13	0	13	30
1905–06	32	Ottawa Silver Seven	ECAHA	10	13	0	13	36
1906–07	33	Ottawa Senators	ECAHA	9	17	0	17	19
1906–07	33	Kenora Thistles	MHL-Pro	1	2	0	2	
1907–08	34	Ottawa Senators	ECAHA	9	12	0	12	20
1908–09	35	Pittsburgh Duquesne	WPHL	2	3	0	3	
1908–09	35	Pittsburgh Bankers	WPHL	3	2	0	2	
1908–09	35	Ottawa Senators	FAHL	1	1	0	1	0
Career – 12 Seasons				85	106	9	115	128

PLAYOFFS

Season	Age	Team	Lg	GP	G	A	PTS	PIM
1903–04	30	Ottawa Silver Seven	St-Cup	7	13	0	13	20
1904–05	31	Ottawa Silver Seven	St-Cup	5	11	0	11	9
1905–06	32	Ottawa Silver Seven	St-Cup	6	6	0	8	6
1906–07	33	Kenora Thistles	MHL-Pro	2	1	0	1	3
1906–07	33	Kenora Thistles	St-Cup	2	2	0	2	3
Career – 4 Seasons				22	35	0	35	41

31

Billy Smith

HOCKEY HALL OF FAME CLASS: 1993

Alternate: 29

Goaltender

Catches: Left

Height: 5'-10"

Weight: 185 lbs.

Born: December 12, 1950: Perth, Ontario

Drafted by the Los Angeles Kings 59th overall in 1970

Played 18 NHL seasons from 1971–89

"I knew as soon as it went in, I was the last guy to touch the puck. It's pretty exciting but unfortunately the way we've been playing took all the excitement out of it."

— Billy Smith, on his "infamous" goal

QUICK FACTS

- First NHL goaltender to be credited with scoring a goal in Colorado Rockies' 7–4 victory over N.Y. Islanders, November 28, 1979

- Held NHL record for career playoff wins (88); surpassed by Patrick Roy (96) in 1996–97

- Played amateur hockey with Smiths Falls Bears (1968–69); Hull Castors (1968–69); Cornwall Royals (1969–70)

- Played minor pro hockey with Springfield Kings (1970–72)

- Led AHL in shutouts (4) in 1971–72; led AHL in playoff wins (11), shutouts (1) and goals-against-average (2.56) in 1970–71

- Played in NHL All-Star Game (1978)

- Led NHL in wins (32) in 1981–82

- Led NHL playoffs in shutouts (1) and goals-against-average (1.90) in 1978–79; shutouts (1) and goals-against-average (2.52) in 1981–82; shutouts (2) and goals-against-average (2.68) in 1982–83

- Nicknamed "Battlin' Billy" and "Hatchet Man" because of his active stick work and refusal to back down from physical play

- Served as assistant coach of N.Y. Islanders (1989–93); served as assistant coach of Florida Panthers (1999–2001)

- Brother of Gord Smith, who played in NHL with Washington and Winnipeg from 1974–80

A late 1970s model mask that Smith wore before switching to the helmet-and-cage style head gear.

REGULAR SEASON

Season	Age	Team	Lg	GP	W	L	T	SO	GA	GAA	G	A	PTS	PIM
1971–72	21	Los Angeles Kings	NHL	5	1	3	1	0	23	4.60	0	0	0	5
1972–73	22	New York Islanders	NHL	37	7	24	3	0	147	4.16	0	0	0	42
1973–74	23	New York Islanders	NHL	46	9	23	12	0	134	3.07	0	0	0	11
1974–75	24	New York Islanders	NHL	58	21	18	17	3	156	2.78	0	0	0	14
1975–76	25	New York Islanders	NHL	39	19	10	9	3	98	2.61	0	1	1	10
1976–77	26	New York Islanders	NHL	36	21	8	6	2	87	2.50	0	1	1	12
1977–78	27	New York Islanders	NHL	38	20	8	8	2	95	2.65	0	0	0	35
1978–79	28	New York Islanders	NHL	40	25	8	4	1	108	2.87	0	2	2	54
1979–80	29	New York Islanders	NHL	38	15	14	7	2	104	2.95	1	0	1	39
1980–81	30	New York Islanders	NHL	41	22	10	8	2	129	3.28	0	0	0	33
1981–82	31	New York Islanders	NHL	46	32	9	4	0	133	2.97	0	1	1	24
1982–83	32	New York Islanders	NHL	41	18	14	7	1	112	2.87	0	0	0	41
1983–84	33	New York Islanders	NHL	42	23	13	2	2	130	3.42	0	2	2	23
1984–85	34	New York Islanders	NHL	37	18	14	3	0	133	3.82	0	0	0	25
1985–86	35	New York Islanders	NHL	41	20	14	4	1	143	3.72	0	3	3	49
1986–87	36	New York Islanders	NHL	40	14	18	5	1	132	3.52	0	2	2	37
1987–88	37	New York Islanders	NHL	38	17	14	5	2	113	3.22	0	0	0	20
1988–89	38	New York Islanders	NHL	17	3	11	0	0	54	4.44	0	0	0	8
NHL Career – 18 Seasons				680	305	233	105	22	2031	3.17	1	12	13	489

PLAYOFFS

Season	Age	Team	Lg	GP	W	L	T	SO	GA	GAA	G	A	PTS	PIM
1974–75	24	New York Islanders	NHL	6	1	4		0	23	4.14	0	0	0	6
1975–76	25	New York Islanders	NHL	8	4	3		0	21	2.88	0	0	0	11
1976–77	26	New York Islanders	NHL	10	7	3		0	27	2.79	0	0	0	8
1977–78	27	New York Islanders	NHL	1	0	0		0	1	1.28	0	0	0	9
1978–79	28	New York Islanders	NHL	5	4	1		1	10	1.90	0	0	0	4
1979–80	29	New York Islanders	NHL	20	15	4		1	56	2.80	0	0	0	11
1980–81	30	New York Islanders	NHL	17	14	3		0	42	2.54	0	1	1	2
1981–82	31	New York Islanders	NHL	18	15	3		1	47	2.52	0	0	0	6
1982–83	32	New York Islanders	NHL	17	13	3		2	43	2.68	0	1	1	9
1983–84	33	New York Islanders	NHL	21	12	8		0	54	2.72	0	0	0	17
1984–85	34	New York Islanders	NHL	6	3	3		0	19	3.33	0	0	0	6
1985–86	35	New York Islanders	NHL	1	0	1		0	4	4.00	0	0	0	0
1986–87	36	New York Islanders	NHL	2	0	0		0	1	0.90	0	0	0	0
NHL Career – 13 Seasons				132	88	36		5	348	2.73	0	2	2	89

TROPHY CASE

AWARDS

Vezina Trophy (1982)

Conn Smythe Trophy (1983)

William M. Jennings Trophy (1983)

Stanley Cup (1979–80, 1980–81, 1981–82, 1982–83)

ALL-STAR SELECTIONS

First All-Star Team Goaltender (1982)

Clint Smith

HOCKEY HALL OF FAME CLASS: 1991

Alternates:
3, 14, 20

Center

Shoots: Left

Height: 5'-8"

Weight: 165 lbs.

Born: December 12, 1913: Assiniboia, Saskatchewan

Died: May 19, 2009: Vancouver, British Columbia

Played 11 NHL seasons from 1936–47

> I can't explain the feeling of winning the Stanley Cup. It's the ultimate. It's something you always strive for — just to get into the Stanley Cup Final. And then when you win — it's something you always remember."

QUICK FACTS

- Shares NHL record for most goals in a period (4), established in third period of Chicago Black Hawks' 6–4 win over Montreal Canadiens, March 4, 1945

- Held NHL record for assists (49) in regular season in 1943–44; surpassed by Elmer Lach (54) in 1944–45

- Credited with scoring first empty-net goal in NHL history in Chicago Black Hawks' 6–4 win over Boston on November 11, 1943

- Nicknamed "Snuffy" after the character Snuffy Smith in the 1930s comic strip "Barney Google"

- Played amateur hockey with Saskatoon Wesleys (1930–32); Saskatoon Crescents (1932–34); Saskatoon Indians (1932–33); Vancouver Lions (1933–36)

- Led NHL in assists (49) in 1943–44

- Led Northern Saskatchewan Junior League in goals (5) and points (6) in 1931–32; led Northern Saskatchewan Senior League in goals (19) in 1931–32

- Led North West Hockey League in goals (25) in 1933–34; led NWHL in assists (22) and points (44) in 1934–35; led NWHL in assists (32) and points (53) in 1935–36

- Signed as a free agent by N.Y. Rangers, October 13, 1932 and assigned to Vancouver Lions

- Finished among NHL top-5 in goals in 1938–39 (21) and 1945–46 (26)

- Finished among NHL top-5 in points in 1938–39 (41), 1943–44 (72), 1944–45 (54) and 1945–46 (50)

Smith's tube skates feature extra ankle and toe protection.

REGULAR SEASON

Season	Age	Team	Lg	GP	G	A	PTS	PIM
1936–37	23	New York Rangers	NHL	2	1	0	1	0
1937–38	24	New York Rangers	NHL	48	14	23	37	0
1938–39	25	New York Rangers	NHL	48	21	20	41	2
1939–40	26	New York Rangers	NHL	41	8	16	24	2
1940–41	27	New York Rangers	NHL	48	14	11	25	0
1941–42	28	New York Rangers	NHL	47	10	24	34	4
1942–43	29	New York Rangers	NHL	47	12	21	33	4
1943–44	30	Chicago Black Hawks	NHL	50	23	49	72	4
1944–45	31	Chicago Black Hawks	NHL	50	23	31	54	0
1945–46	32	Chicago Black Hawks	NHL	50	26	24	50	2
1946–47	33	Chicago Black Hawks	NHL	52	9	17	26	6
NHL Career – 11 Seasons				483	161	236	397	24

PLAYOFFS

Season	Age	Team	Lg	GP	G	A	PTS	PIM
1937–38	24	New York Rangers	NHL	3	2	0	2	0
1938–39	25	New York Rangers	NHL	7	1	2	3	0
1939–40	26	New York Rangers	NHL	11	1	3	4	2
1940–41	27	New York Rangers	NHL	3	0	0	0	0
1941–42	28	New York Rangers	NHL	5	0	0	0	0
1943–44	30	Chicago Black Hawks	NHL	9	4	8	12	0
1945–46	32	Chicago Black Hawks	NHL	4	2	1	3	0
NHL Career – 7 Seasons				42	10	14	24	2

TROPHY CASE

AWARDS

Lady Byng Memorial Trophy (1939, 1944)

Stanley Cup (1939–40)

Hooley Smith

HOCKEY HALL OF FAME CLASS: 1972

Alternates: 17, 5, 6

Center/Right Wing/Defense

Shoots: Right

Height: 5'-10"

Weight: 155 lbs.

Born: January 7, 1903: Toronto, Ontario

Died: August 24, 1963: Montreal, Quebec

Played 17 NHL seasons from 1924–41

QUICK FACTS

- Played amateur hockey with Parkdale Canoe Club (1920–21); Toronto Granites (1921–24)

- Member of Allan Cup-champion Toronto Granites (1922, 1923)

- As a member of the Toronto Granites, he represented Canada at the 1924 Olympic Games, registering a tournament-high 16 assists as Canada captured the gold medal

- Signed as a free agent by Ottawa Senators, October 31, 1924; traded to Montreal Maroons by Ottawa for Punch Broadbent and $22,500, October 7, 1927

- Made NHL debut in Ottawa Senators' 5–3 loss to Hamilton Tigers, November 30, 1924

- Member of Montreal Maroons' famed S Line with Babe Siebert and Nels Stewart

- A physically dominant player who played with a "bitter edge", Smith was renowned for his defensive skills and was an expert at utilizing the "hook" check to sweep the puck off opposing players sticks

- Renowned for his skills as an oarsman, amateur boxer and rugby player, he also played football with the Toronto Argonauts and Balmy Beach

- Played in NHL All-Star Game (1934)

- Traded to Boston by Montreal Maroons for cash and future considerations (Gerry Shannon, December 4, 1936), October 26, 1936; traded to N.Y. Americans by Boston for cash, November 5, 1937

- Finished among NHL top-5 in assists in 1924–25 (13), 1925–26 (9) and 1931–32 (33)

> There was a popular cartoon in the papers when I was a kid called Happy Hooligan. One day, my dad called me Hooligan, then he shortened it to Hooley and the name stuck. I mean, what kid would want to go through life with a tag like Reginald?"

REGULAR SEASON

Season	Age	Team	Lg	GP	G	A	PTS	PIM
1924–25	22	Ottawa Senators	NHL	30	10	13	23	81
1925–26	23	Ottawa Senators	NHL	28	16	9	25	53
1926–27	24	Ottawa Senators	NHL	43	9	6	15	125
1927–28	25	Montreal Maroons	NHL	34	14	5	19	72
1928–29	26	Montreal Maroons	NHL	41	10	9	19	120
1929–30	27	Montreal Maroons	NHL	42	21	9	30	83
1930–31	28	Montreal Maroons	NHL	39	12	14	26	68
1931–32	29	Montreal Maroons	NHL	43	11	33	44	49
1932–33	30	Montreal Maroons	NHL	48	20	21	41	66
1933–34	31	Montreal Maroons	NHL	47	18	19	37	58
1934–35	32	Montreal Maroons	NHL	46	5	22	27	41
1935–36	33	Montreal Maroons	NHL	47	19	19	38	75
1936–37	34	Boston Bruins	NHL	44	8	10	18	36
1937–38	35	New York Americans	NHL	47	10	10	20	23
1938–39	36	New York Americans	NHL	48	8	11	19	18
1939–40	37	New York Americans	NHL	47	7	8	15	41
1940–41	38	New York Americans	NHL	41	2	7	9	4
NHL Career — 17 Seasons				715	200	225	425	1013

PLAYOFFS

Season	Age	Team	Lg	GP	G	A	PTS	PIM
1925–26	23	Ottawa Senators	NHL	2	0	0	0	14
1926–27	24	Ottawa Senators	NHL	6	1	0	1	16
1927–28	25	Montreal Maroons	NHL	9	2	1	3	23
1929–30	27	Montreal Maroons	NHL	4	1	1	2	14
1931–32	29	Montreal Maroons	NHL	4	2	1	3	2
1932–33	30	Montreal Maroons	NHL	2	2	0	2	2
1933–34	31	Montreal Maroons	NHL	4	0	1	1	6
1934–35	32	Montreal Maroons	NHL	6	0	0	0	14
1935–36	33	Montreal Maroons	NHL	3	0	0	0	2
1936–37	34	Boston Bruins	NHL	3	0	0	0	0
1937–38	35	New York Americans	NHL	6	0	3	3	0
1938–39	36	New York Americans	NHL	2	0	0	0	14
1939–40	37	New York Americans	NHL	3	3	1	4	2
NHL Career — 13 Seasons				54	11	8	19	109

TROPHY CASE

AWARDS

Stanley Cup (1926–27, 1934–35)

ALL-STAR SELECTIONS

First All-Star Team Center (1936)

Second All-Star Team Center (1932)

INTERNATIONAL AWARDS

Gold Medal: Winter Olympics (1924)

477

Tommy Smith

HOCKEY HALL OF FAME CLASS: 1973

Alternates: 11, 5, 2

Center/Right Wing

Shoots: Left

Height: 5'-6"

Weight: 150 lbs.

Born: September 27, 1885: Ottawa, Ontario

Died: August 1, 1966: Unknown

Played 13 elite amateur and professional seasons from 1905–17, 1919–20

QUICK FACTS

- Led FAHL in goals (12) in 1905–06
- FAHL First Team All-Star Center (1906)
- Scored eight goals in a single game against Brockville, February 23, 1906
- Led OPHL in goals (40) in 1908–09
- OPHL First Team All-Star Center (1909)
- Played in unsuccessful Stanley Cup challenges with Galt Pros in 1911 and Moncton Victorias in 1912
- Signed as a free agent by Quebec Bulldogs, December 1, 1912
- Led NHA in goals (39) and points (45) in 1913–14; goals (40) and points (44) in 1914–15
- Scored at least one goal in 10 consecutive games (1912–13)

- Tied NHA single game record with nine goals in Quebec's 12–6 victory over Montreal Wanderers, January 21, 1914
- One of seven hockey-playing brothers (George, Alf, Dan, Jack, Harry and Willie) from Ottawa who formed their own "All-Smith" team
- Member of Stanley Cup-winning Quebec Bulldogs (1912–13)
- Member of NHA champion Montreal Canadiens team that lost Stanley Cup Final to Seattle Metropolitans (1916–17)
- Returned briefly as a player in 1919–20 when Quebec Bulldogs entered the NHL but retired permanently after the season

Tommy Smith, the brilliant little rover of the Pittsburgh hockey team, is known by nearly all those who attend the games as "Snake," and the name fits him like a new glove for when he secures the puck one might as well try to catch and hold a reptile as he."

— *Pittsburgh Press*, March 6, 1907

REGULAR SEASON

Season	Age	Team	Lg	GP	G	A	PTS	PIM
1905–06	19	Ottawa Vics	FAHL	8	12	0	12	
1905–06	19	Ottawa Silver Seven	ECAHA	3	6	0	6	12
1906–07	20	Pittsburgh Professionals	IHL	23	31	13	44	47
1907–08	21	Pittsburgh Lyceum	WPHL	16	33	0	33	
1908–09	22	Brantford Professionals	OPHL	13	40	0	40	30
1908–09	22	Pittsburgh Lyceum	WPHL	6	15	0	15	
1908–09	22	Haileybury Hockey Club	TPHL	1	3	0	3	2
1909–10	23	Branford Redmen	OPHL	2	1	0	1	3
1910–11	24	Galt Professionals	OPHL	18	22	0	22	
1911–12	25	Moncton Victorias	MPHL	18	53	0	53	48
1912–13	26	Quebec Bulldogs	NHA	18	39	0	39	30
1913–14	27	Quebec Bulldogs	NHA	20	39	6	45	35
1914–15	28	Toronto Shamrocks	NHA	10	17	2	19	14
1914–15	28	Quebec Bulldogs	NHA	9	23	2	25	29
1915–16	29	Quebec Bulldogs	NHA	22	16	3	19	30
1916–17	30	Montreal Canadiens	NHA	14	7	4	11	32
1919–20	33	Quebec Bulldogs	NHL	10	0	1	1	14
Career — 13 Seasons				200	357	31	388	323

PLAYOFFS

Season	Age	Team	Lg	GP	G	A	PTS	PIM
1905–06	19	Ottawa Silver Seven	St-Cup	1	0	0	0	9
1907–08	21	Pittsburgh Lyceum	WPHL	1	2	0	2	
1908–09	22	Haileybury Hockey Club	TPHL	2	3	0	3	0
1908–09	22	Pittsburgh Bankers	WPHL	3	3	0	3	3
1910–11	24	Galt Professionals	OPHL	3	10	0	10	0
1910–11	24	Galt Professionals	St-Cup	1	1	0	1	0
1911–12	25	Moncton Victorias	St-Cup	2	2	0	2	3
1912–13	26	Quebec Bulldogs	St-Cup	2	4	0	4	0
1916–17	30	Montreal Canadiens	NHA	2	2	0	2	11
1916–17	30	Montreal Canadiens	St-Cup	4	2	0	2	3
Career — 7 Seasons				21	29	0	29	29

TROPHY CASE

AWARDS

Stanley Cup (1905–06, 1912–13)

Allan Stanley

HOCKEY HALL OF FAME CLASS: 1981

Alternates:
8, 4, 10, 6

Defense

Shoots: Left
Height: 6'-1"

Weight: 170 lbs.
Born: March 1,
1926: Timmins,
Ontario

Played 21 NHL
seasons from
1948–69

" I was just a kid, but I remember asking my Uncle Barney what hockey players drink between periods to make them play hockey better. He said, 'We usually drink tea with honey,' so I drank tea and honey for years after that. It seems to have helped."

QUICK FACTS

- Played amateur hockey with Holman Pluggers (1939–43); Boston Olympics (1943–44, 1945–46, 1947–48); Porcupine Combines (1944–45); Port Arthur Navy (1944–45)
- Member of the Ontario Juvenile champion Holman Pluggers (1942–43, 1943–44)
- Played minor pro hockey with Providence Reds (1947–49); Vancouver Canucks (1953–54)
- Played in NHL All-Star Game (1955, 1957, 1960, 1962, 1963, 1967, 1968)
- Awarded the J.P. Bickell Trophy by the Toronto Maple Leafs' board of directors for outstanding achievement on and off the ice (1965, 1966)
- Led all NHL defensemen in goals (10) in 1959–60

- Nicknamed "Snowshoes" because of plodding skating style
- Booed out of New York and considered too old to play in Boston, his career was rejuvenated in Toronto
- Traded to N.Y. Rangers by Providence (AHL) for Eddie Kullman, Moe Morris, cash and future considerations (Buck Davies, June 1949), December 9, 1948
- Traded to Boston by Chicago for cash, October 8, 1956; traded to Toronto by Boston for Jim Morrison, October 8, 1958
- Claimed by Philadelphia (Quebec-AHL) from Toronto in Reverse Draft, June 13, 1968

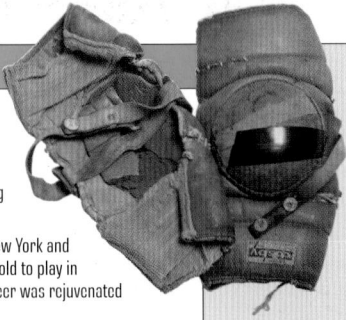

Stanley's battered elbow pads.

REGULAR SEASON

Season	Age	Team	Lg	GP	G	A	PTS	+/-	PIM	ESG	PPG	SHG	GWG	SOG	S%
1948–49	22	New York Rangers	NHL	40	2	8	10		22						
1949–50	23	New York Rangers	NHL	55	4	4	8		58						
1950–51	24	New York Rangers	NHL	70	7	14	21		75						
1951–52	25	New York Rangers	NHL	50	5	14	19		75						
1952–53	26	New York Rangers	NHL	70	5	12	17		52						
1953–54	27	New York Rangers	NHL	10	0	2	2		11						
1954–55	28	New York Rangers	NHL	12	0	1	1		2						
1954–55	28	Chicago Black Hawks	NHL	52	10	15	25		22						
1955–56	29	Chicago Black Hawks	NHL	59	4	14	18		70						
1956–57	30	Boston Bruins	NHL	60	6	25	31		45						
1957–58	31	Boston Bruins	NHL	69	6	25	31		37						
1958–59	32	Toronto Maple Leafs	NHL	70	1	22	23		47						
1959–60	33	Toronto Maple Leafs	NHL	64	10	23	33		22						
1960–61	34	Toronto Maple Leafs	NHL	68	9	25	34		42						
1961–62	35	Toronto Maple Leafs	NHL	60	9	26	35		24						
1962–63	36	Toronto Maple Leafs	NHL	61	4	15	19		22						
1963–64	37	Toronto Maple Leafs	NHL	70	6	21	27		60	5	1	0	1		
1964–65	38	Toronto Maple Leafs	NHL	64	2	15	17		30	2	0	0	0		
1965–66	39	Toronto Maple Leafs	NHL	59	4	14	18		35	3	1	0	0		
1966–67	40	Toronto Maple Leafs	NHL	53	1	12	13		20	1	0	0	0		
1967–68	41	Toronto Maple Leafs	NHL	64	1	13	14	6	16	1	0	0	0	61	1.6
1968–69	42	Philadelphia Flyers	NHL	64	4	13	17	-4	28	2	2	0	0	75	5.3
NHL Career — 21 Seasons				1244	100	333	433	2	792	14	4	0	1	136	3.7

PLAYOFFS

Season	Age	Team	Lg	GP	G	A	PTS	+/-	PIM	ESG	PPG	SHG	GWG	SOG	S%
1949–50	23	New York Rangers	NHL	12	2	5	7		10						
1957–58	31	Boston Bruins	NHL	12	1	3	4		6						
1958–59	32	Toronto Maple Leafs	NHL	12	0	3	3		2						
1959–60	33	Toronto Maple Leafs	NHL	10	2	3	5		2						
1960–61	34	Toronto Maple Leafs	NHL	5	0	3	3		0						
1961–62	35	Toronto Maple Leafs	NHL	12	0	3	3		6						
1962–63	36	Toronto Maple Leafs	NHL	10	1	6	7		8						
1963–64	37	Toronto Maple Leafs	NHL	14	1	6	7		20						
1964–65	38	Toronto Maple Leafs	NHL	6	0	1	1		12						
1965–66	39	Toronto Maple Leafs	NHL	1	0	0	0		0						
1966–67	40	Toronto Maple Leafs	NHL	12	0	2	2		10						
1968–69	42	Philadelphia Flyers	NHL	3	0	1	1		4	0	0	0	0		
NHL Career — 12 Seasons				109	7	36	43		80	0	0	0	0		

TROPHY CASE

AWARDS

Stanley Cup (1961–62, 1962–63, 1963–64, 1966–67)

ALL-STAR SELECTIONS

Second All-Star Team Defense (1960, 1961, 1966)

Barney Stanley

HOCKEY HALL OF FAME CLASS: 1962

Alternates:
3, 4, 6, 7, 8

Right Wing

Shoots: Left

Height: 6'

Weight: 175 lbs.

Born: January 1, 1893: Paisley, Ontario

Died: May 16, 1971: Edmonton, Alberta

Played 14 elite amateur and professional seasons from 1914–28

Punch Broadbent, Harry Cameron, Rusty Crawford, Jack Darragh, Jimmy Gardner, Billy Gilmour, Shorty Green, Riley Hern, Tom Hooper, Bouse Hutton, Harry Hyland, Jack Laviolette, Didier Pitre, Fred Maxwell, Billy McGimsie, Reg Noble, Jack Ruttan, Sweeney Schriner, Joe Simpson, Alf Smith, Nels Stewart, Marty Walsh, Harry E. Watson, Harry Westwick, Fred Whitcroft, Phat Wilson

QUICK FACTS

- Played amateur hockey with Edmonton Maritmers (1911–12); Edmonton Dominions (1912–14); Edmonton Albertans (1914–15)

- Signed as free agent by Vancouver Millionaires (PCHA), February, 1915

- Scored five goals and recorded six points in the 1915 Stanley Cup championship series against Ottawa Senators

- Led PCHA in assists (18) in 1916–17

- Signed as a free agent by Calgary Tigers (WCHL), November 30, 1921; traded to Regina Capitals (WCHL) by Calgary Tigers (WCHL) for cash, November 13, 1922

- Signed as a free agent by Edmonton Eskimos (WCHL), November 7, 1924; named playing coach of Winnipeg Maroons (AHA) after resigning position with Edmonton Eskimos (AHA), October 28, 1926

- Signed as free agent by Chicago Black Hawks and appointed coach, April 4, 1927; coached Chicago Black Hawks (1927–28)

- Coached Edmonton Eskimos (1925–26); coached Winnipeg Maroons (1926–27); coached Edmonton Poolers (1929–31)

- Father of Don Stanley, who won a gold medal at the IIHF World Championships as a member of the Edmonton Mercurys in 1950; uncle of Hall of Fame member Allan Stanley, who won four Stanley Cup championships with the Toronto Maple Leafs in the 1960s

- Designed a hockey helmet and presented it at a NHL Board of Governors meeting after Chicago Black Hawk captain Dick Irvin suffered a fractured skull in a game during the 1927–28 season. There was no interest in his creation

> It is a great source of pleasure to me to have you write as you did about my hockey career and as you say I did have some terrific teammates. I enjoy reading [Charles Coleman's] 'The Trail of the Stanley Cup' and relive many moments tabulated therein."
>
> — Barney Stanley, in a letter to a devoted fan

REGULAR SEASON

Season	Age	Team	Lg	GP	G	A	PTS	PIM
1914–15	22	Vancouver Millionaires	PCHA	5	7	1	8	0
1915–16	23	Vancouver Millionaires	PCHA	14	6	6	12	9
1916–17	24	Vancouver Millionaires	PCHA	23	28	18	46	9
1917–18	25	Vancouver Millionaires	PCHA	18	11	6	17	9
1918–19	26	Vancouver Millionaires	PCHA	20	10	6	16	19
1919–20	27	Edmonton Eskimos	Big-4	12	10	12	22	20
1920–21	28	Calgary Tigers	Big-4	15	11	10	21	5
1921–22	29	Calgary Tigers	WCHL	24	26	5	31	17
1922–23	30	Regina Capitals	WCHL	29	14	7	21	10
1923–24	31	Regina Capitals	WCHL	30	15	11	26	27
1924–25	32	Edmonton Eskimos	WCHL	25	12	5	17	36
1925–26	33	Edmonton Eskimos	WHL	29	14	8	22	47
1926–27	34	Winnipeg Maroons	AHA	35	8	8	16	78
1927–28	35	Chicago Black Hawks	NHL	1	0	0	0	0
Career – 14 Seasons				280	172	103	275	286

PLAYOFFS

Season	Age	Team	Lg	GP	G	A	PTS	PIM
1914–15	22	Vancouver Millionaires	St-Cup	3	5	1	6	0
1917–18	25	Vancouver Millionaires	PCHA	2	1	0	1	3
1917–18	25	Vancouver Millionaires	St-Cup	5	2	0	2	6
1918–19	26	Vancouver Millionaires	PCHA	2	0	0	0	0
1919–20	27	Edmonton Eskimos	Big-4	2	0	1	1	5
1921–22	29	Calgary Tigers	WCHL	2	0	0	0	0
1922–23	30	Regina Capitals	WCHL	2	1	0	1	2
1923–24	31	Regina Capitals	WCHL	2	1	0	1	2
1925–26	33	Edmonton Eskimos	WHL	2	1	0	1	0
Career – 8 Seasons				29	12	2	14	22

TROPHY CASE

AWARDS

Stanley Cup (1914–15)

ALL-STAR SELECTIONS

PCHA Second All-Star Team Right Wing (1918)

WCHL First All-Star Team Right Wing (1922, 1923)

26

Alternate: 29

Center

Shoots: Left

Height: 6'-1"

Weight: 200 lbs.

Born: September 18, 1956; Bratislava, Czechoslovkia

Played 15 NHL seasons from 1980–95

Peter Stastny
HOCKEY HALL OF FAME CLASS: 1998

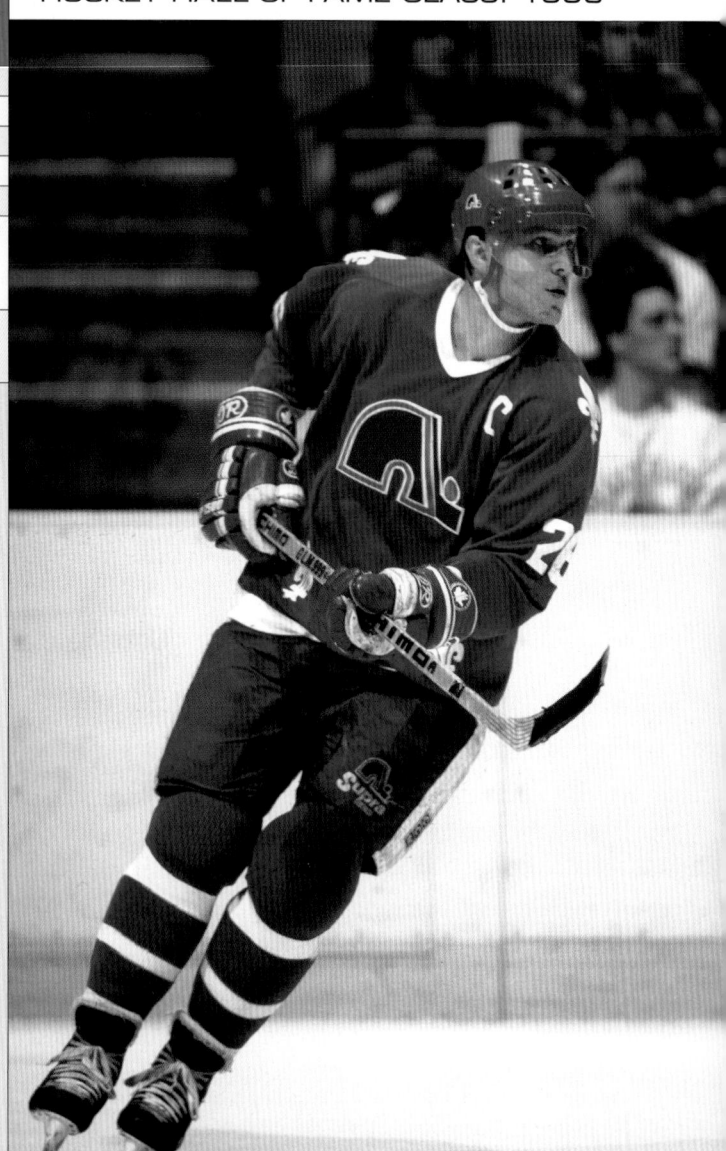

QUICK FACTS

- Shares NHL record (with Anton Stastny) for points in a regular season road game (8), established in Quebec's 11–7 victory over Washington Capitals, February 22, 1981

- Shares NHL record (with Joe Juneau) for assists in regular season by a rookie (70), established in 1980–81

- First player in NHL history to record 100 points in rookie season (109), established in 1980–81

- First European-born and trained player in NHL history to register 1,000 career points

- Registered 1,000th career NHL point in Quebec's 5–3 victory over Chicago Blackhawks, October 19, 1989

- Ranked second (behind Wayne Gretzky) for most points from 1979–80 to 1988–89 (986)

- Played amateur hockey with Slovan Bratislava (1974–80)

- Named Czechoslovakian Player of the Year (1980)

- Signed as a free agent by Quebec, August 26, 1980

- Finished among NHL top-5 in points in 1981–82 (139), 1982–83 (124), 1983–84 (119) and 1987–88 (111)

- Named Best Forward at World-B Championships (1995); World-B Championships All-Star Team Center (1995)

- Brother of Anton Stastny, who played in NHL with Quebec from 1980–89; brother of Marian Stastny, who played in NHL with Quebec and Toronto from 1981–86

> "We'd watched the '72 series and we saw the Czechs and Canada tie 3–3 right after. We [Czechoslovakia] were the only country that could compete with the Russians at the World Championships, but we also learned how strong [Canadian] desire can beat pure skill."

REGULAR SEASON

Season	Age	Team	Lg	GP	G	A	PTS	+/-	PIM	ESG	PPG	SHG	GWG	SOG	S%
1980–81	24	Quebec Nordiques	NHL	77	39	70	109	11	37	26	11	2	4	232	16.8
1981–82	25	Quebec Nordiques	NHL	80	46	93	139	-10	91	27	16	3	3	227	20.3
1982–83	26	Quebec Nordiques	NHL	75	47	77	124	28	78	42	5	0	4	201	23.4
1983–84	27	Quebec Nordiques	NHL	80	46	73	119	22	73	35	11	0	4	189	24.3
1984–85	28	Quebec Nordiques	NHL	75	32	68	100	23	95	24	7	1	9	207	15.5
1985–86	29	Quebec Nordiques	NHL	76	41	81	122	2	60	26	15	0	8	207	19.8
1986–87	30	Quebec Nordiques	NHL	64	24	53	77	-21	43	12	12	0	4	157	15.3
1987–88	31	Quebec Nordiques	NHL	76	46	65	111	2	69	26	20	0	2	199	23.1
1988–89	32	Quebec Nordiques	NHL	72	35	50	85	-23	117	22	13	0	5	195	17.9
1989–90	33	Quebec Nordiques	NHL	62	24	38	62	-45	24	14	10	0	0	131	18.3
1989–90	33	New Jersey Devils	NHL	12	5	6	11	-1	16	3	2	0	1	25	20.0
1990–91	34	New Jersey Devils	NHL	77	18	42	60	0	53	14	4	0	3	117	15.4
1991–92	35	New Jersey Devils	NHL	66	24	38	62	6	42	13	10	1	3	142	16.9
1992–93	36	New Jersey Devils	NHL	62	17	23	40	-5	22	10	7	0	3	106	16.0
1993–94	37	St. Louis Blues	NHL	17	5	11	16	-2	4	3	2	0	1	30	16.7
1994–95	38	St. Louis Blues	NHL	6	1	1	2	1	0	1	0	0	0	9	11.1
NHL Career – 15 Seasons				977	450	789	1239	-12	824	298	145	7	54	2374	19.0

PLAYOFFS

Season	Age	Team	Lg	GP	G	A	PTS	+/-	PIM	ESG	PPG	SHG	GWG	SOG	S%
1980–81	24	Quebec Nordiques	NHL	5	2	8	10		7	1	1	0	0		
1981–82	25	Quebec Nordiques	NHL	12	7	11	18		10	3	4	0	1		
1982–83	26	Quebec Nordiques	NHL	4	3	2	5		10	2	1	0	0		
1983–84	27	Quebec Nordiques	NHL	9	2	7	9	3	31	0	2	0	0	18	11.1
1984–85	28	Quebec Nordiques	NHL	18	4	19	23	1	24	3	1	0	2	27	14.8
1985–86	29	Quebec Nordiques	NHL	3	0	1	1	-5	2	0	0	0	0	10	0.0
1986–87	30	Quebec Nordiques	NHL	13	6	9	15	3	12	3	2	1	1	24	25.0
1989–90	33	New Jersey Devils	NHL	6	3	2	5	-1	2	2	1	0	1	9	33.3
1990–91	34	New Jersey Devils	NHL	7	3	4	7	-2	2	2	1	0	2	7	42.9
1991–92	35	New Jersey Devils	NHL	7	3	7	10	1	19	3	0	0	0	12	25.0
1992–93	36	New Jersey Devils	NHL	5	0	2	2	0	2	0	0	0	0	3	0.0
1993–94	37	St. Louis Blues	NHL	4	0	0	0	-4	2	0	0	0	0	3	0.0
NHL Career – 12 Seasons				93	33	72	105	-4	123	19	13	1	7	113	18.6

TROPHY CASE

AWARDS

Calder Memorial Trophy (1981)

INTERNATIONAL AWARDS

Gold Medal: World Championships (1976, 1977)

Silver Medal: World Championships (1978, 1979)

4

Alternates: 3, 2

Defense

Shoots: Left

Height: 6'-2"

Weight: 215 lbs.

Born: April 1, 1964: Kitchener, Ontario

Drafted by the Washington Capitals fifth overall in 1982

Played 22 NHL seasons from 1982–2004

Scott Stevens

HOCKEY HALL OF FAME CLASS: 2007

QUICK FACTS

- Played amateur hockey with Kitchener Ranger B's (1980–81); Kitchener Rangers (1980–82)
- Member of Memorial Cup-winning Kitchener Rangers (1982)
- Ranks second in career NHL games played by a defenseman (1,635)
- Played in NHL All-Star Game (1985, 1989, 1991. 1992, 1993, 1994, 1996, 1997, 1998, 1999, 2000, 2001, 2003)
- Led NHL in plus/minus (+53) in 1993–94
- Served as captain of New Jersey Devils (1992–2003)
- Finished among NHL top-5 in power-play goals (16) in 1984–85
- Renowned for his devastating open-ice body-checks
- Scored first NHL goal in first NHL game on first NHL shot in Washington's 5–4 victory over N.Y. Rangers, October 6, 1982
- Signed as a free agent by St. Louis, July 16, 1990
- Transferred to New Jersey from St. Louis as compensation for St. Louis' signing of free agent Brendan Shanahan, September 3, 1991

> "I'm a firm believer that a big hit could change momentum in a game, just like a big goal could. I'm proud of [my reputation]."

REGULAR SEASON

Season	Age	Team	Lg	GP	G	A	PTS	+/-	PIM	ESG	PPG	SHG	GWG	SOG	S%
1982–83	18	Washington Capitals	NHL	77	9	16	25	14	195	9	0	0	0	121	7.4
1983–84	19	Washington Capitals	NHL	78	13	32	45	26	201	6	7	0	2	155	8.4
1984–85	20	Washington Capitals	NHL	80	21	44	65	19	221	5	16	0	5	170	12.4
1985–86	21	Washington Capitals	NHL	73	15	38	53	0	165	12	3	0	2	121	12.4
1986–87	22	Washington Capitals	NHL	77	10	51	61	13	283	8	2	0	0	165	6.1
1987–88	23	Washington Capitals	NHL	80	12	60	72	14	184	6	5	1	2	231	5.2
1988–89	24	Washington Capitals	NHL	80	7	61	68	0	225	1	6	0	3	195	3.6
1989–90	25	Washington Capitals	NHL	56	11	29	40	1	154	4	7	0	0	143	7.7
1990–91	26	St. Louis Blues	NHL	78	5	44	49	23	150	4	1	0	1	160	3.1
1991–92	27	New Jersey Devils	NHL	68	17	42	59	24	124	9	7	1	2	156	10.9
1992–93	28	New Jersey Devils	NHL	81	12	45	57	14	120	4	8	0	1	146	8.2
1993–94	29	New Jersey Devils	NHL	83	18	60	78	53	112	12	5	1	4	215	8.4
1994–95	30	New Jersey Devils	NHL	48	2	20	22	4	56	1	1	0	1	111	1.8
1995–96	31	New Jersey Devils	NHL	82	5	23	28	7	100	2	2	1	1	174	2.9
1996–97	32	New Jersey Devils	NHL	79	5	19	24	26	70	5	0	0	1	166	3.0
1997–98	33	New Jersey Devils	NHL	80	4	22	26	19	80	3	1	0	1	94	4.3
1998–99	34	New Jersey Devils	NHL	75	5	22	27	29	64	5	0	0	1	111	4.5
1999–00	35	New Jersey Devils	NHL	78	8	21	29	30	103	7	0	1	1	133	6.0
2000–01	36	New Jersey Devils	NHL	81	9	22	31	40	71	6	3	0	2	171	5.3
2001–02	37	New Jersey Devils	NHL	82	1	16	17	15	44	1	0	0	1	121	0.8
2002–03	38	New Jersey Devils	NHL	81	4	16	20	18	41	4	0	0	2	113	3.5
2003–04	39	New Jersey Devils	NHL	38	3	9	12	3	22	2	1	0	1	68	4.4
NHL Career — 22 Seasons				1635	196	712	908	393	2785	116	75	5	34	3240	6.0

PLAYOFFS

Season	Age	Team	Lg	GP	G	A	PTS	+/-	PIM	ESG	PPG	SHG	GWG	SOG	S%
1982–83	18	Washington Capitals	NHL	4	1	0	1		26	1	0	0	0		
1983–84	19	Washington Capitals	NHL	8	1	8	9	2	21	0	1	0	0	21	4.8
1984–85	20	Washington Capitals	NHL	5	0	1	1	-4	20	0	0	0	0	11	0.0
1985–86	21	Washington Capitals	NHL	9	3	8	11	9	12	1	2	0	2	17	17.6
1986–87	22	Washington Capitals	NHL	7	0	5	5	4	19	0	0	0	0	19	0.0
1987–88	23	Washington Capitals	NHL	13	1	11	12	-1	46	1	0	0	0	42	2.4
1988–89	24	Washington Capitals	NHL	6	1	4	5	-2	11	1	0	0	0	16	6.3
1989–90	25	Washington Capitals	NHL	15	2	7	9	-1	25	1	1	0	0	35	4.7
1990–91	26	St. Louis Blues	NHL	13	0	3	3	8	36	0	0	0	0	17	0.0
1991–92	27	New Jersey Devils	NHL	7	2	1	3	-5	29	2	0	0	1	9	22.2
1992–93	28	New Jersey Devils	NHL	5	2	2	4	-2	10	1	1	0	0	21	9.5
1993–94	29	New Jersey Devils	NHL	20	2	9	11	-1	42	0	2	0	1	56	3.6
1994–95	30	New Jersey Devils	NHL	20	1	7	8	10	24	1	0	0	1	54	1.9
1996–97	32	New Jersey Devils	NHL	10	0	4	4	-2	2	0	0	0	0	27	0.0
1997–98	33	New Jersey Devils	NHL	6	1	0	1	4	8	1	0	0	0	11	9.1
1998–99	34	New Jersey Devils	NHL	7	2	1	3	-2	10	0	2	0	0	14	14.3
1999–00	35	New Jersey Devils	NHL	23	3	8	11	9	6	3	0	0	2	29	10.3
2000–01	36	New Jersey Devils	NHL	25	1	7	8	3	37	1	0	0	0	34	2.9
2001–02	37	New Jersey Devils	NHL	6	0	0	0	5	4	0	0	0	0	7	0.0
2002–03	38	New Jersey Devils	NHL	24	3	6	9	14	14	2	1	0	1	33	9.1
NHL Career — 20 Seasons				233	26	92	118	48	402	14	12	0	8	473	5.3

TROPHY CASE

AWARDS

Conn Smythe Trophy (1990)

Stanley Cup (1994–95, 1999–2000, 2002–03)

ALL-STAR SELECTIONS

All-Rookie Team (1983)

First Team All-Star Team Defense (1988, 1994)

Second All-Star Team Defense (1992, 1997, 2001)

INTERNATIONAL AWARDS

Bronze Medal: World Championships (1983)

Silver Medal: World Championships (1985, 1989)

2

Jack Stewart

HOCKEY HALL OF FAME CLASS: 1964

Alternate: 19

Defense

Shoots: Left

Height: 5'-10"

Weight: 190 lbs.

Born: May 6, 1917: Pilot Mound, Manitoba

Died: May 26, 1983: Detroit, Michigan

Played 12 NHL seasons from 1938–43, 1945–52

QUICK FACTS

- Nicknamed "Black Jack" because of his bruising body checks, he was known as the hardest-hitting defenseman in the NHL during his career

- Known for using the heaviest stick in the league. When asked how he could shoot with a stick so heavy, he replied, "I don't use it for shooting, I use it for breaking arms."

- Played amateur hockey with Portage Terriers (1935–37)

- Signed as a free agent by Detroit, October 27, 1937

- Played with Montreal RCAF and Winnipeg RCAF during World War II

- Led NHL in penalty minutes (73) in 1945–46

- Played in NHL All-Star Game (1947, 1948, 1949, 1950)

- Traded to Chicago by Detroit with Harry Lumley, Al Dewsbury, Pete Babando and Don Morrison for Metro Prystai, Bob Goldham, Gaye Stewart and Jim Henry, July 13, 1950. Nine-player trade was the largest in NHL history until Calgary-Toronto 10-player trade in January of 1992

- Served as captain of the Chicago Black Hawks (1950–52)

- Served as player/coach with Chatham Maroons (1953–54)

- Coached Kitchener-Waterloo Dutchmen (1955–56); Windsor Bulldogs (1957–59); Sault Ste-Marie Greyhounds (1959–60); Pittsburgh Hornets (1962–63)

- Inducted into Manitoba Sports Hall of Fame (1997)

> I bodychecked some fellow one night and when he woke up the next day in the hospital he asked who'd hit him with a blackjack."
>
> — Black Jack Stewart, on how he got his moniker

REGULAR SEASON

Season	Age	Team	Lg	GP	G	A	PTS	PIM
1938–39	21	Detroit Red Wings	NHL	32	0	1	1	18
1939–40	22	Detroit Red Wings	NHL	48	1	0	1	40
1940–41	23	Detroit Red Wings	NHL	47	2	6	8	56
1941–42	24	Detroit Red Wings	NHL	44	4	7	11	93
1942–43	25	Detroit Red Wings	NHL	44	2	9	11	68
1945–46	28	Detroit Red Wings	NHL	47	4	11	15	73
1946–47	29	Detroit Red Wings	NHL	55	5	9	14	83
1947–48	30	Detroit Red Wings	NHL	60	5	14	19	91
1948–49	31	Detroit Red Wings	NHL	60	4	11	15	96
1949–50	32	Detroit Red Wings	NHL	65	3	11	14	86
1950–51	33	Chicago Black Hawks	NHL	26	0	2	2	49
1951–52	34	Chicago Black Hawks	NHL	37	1	3	4	12
NHL Career – 12 Seasons				565	31	84	115	785

PLAYOFFS

Season	Age	Team	Lg	GP	G	A	PTS	PIM
1939–40	22	Detroit Red Wings	NHL	5	0	0	0	4
1940–41	23	Detroit Red Wings	NHL	9	1	2	3	8
1941–42	24	Detroit Red Wings	NHL	12	0	1	1	12
1942–43	25	Detroit Red Wings	NHL	10	1	2	3	35
1945–46	28	Detroit Red Wings	NHL	5	0	0	0	14
1946–47	29	Detroit Red Wings	NHL	5	0	1	1	12
1947–48	30	Detroit Red Wings	NHL	9	1	3	4	6
1948–49	31	Detroit Red Wings	NHL	11	1	1	2	32
1949–50	32	Detroit Red Wings	NHL	14	1	4	5	20
NHL Career – 9 Seasons				80	5	14	19	143

TROPHY CASE

AWARDS

Stanley Cup (1942–43, 1949–50)

ALL-STAR SELECTIONS

First All-Star Team Defense (1943, 1948, 1949)

Second All-Star Team Defense (1946, 1947)

5

Nels Stewart

HOCKEY HALL OF FAME CLASS: 1962

Alternates: 7, 6, 19

Center

Shoots: Left

Height: 6'-1"

Weight: 195 lbs.

Born: December 29, 1902: Montreal, Quebec

Died: August 21, 1957: Wasaga Beach, Ontario

Played 15 NHL seasons from 1925–40

"He was terrific in front of the net, a big strong fellow who had moves like a cat. Stewart never seemed to be paying any attention to where the puck was and, if you were checking him, he'd even hold a little conversation with you. But the minute he'd see the puck coming his way he'd bump you, take the puck and go off and score."
— Hall of Fame referee Cooper Smeaton

QUICK FACTS

- Held NHL record for career goals (324) from 1936–37 until 1952; surpassed by Maurice Richard, November 8, 1952

- Held NHL record for career points (515) from 1936–37 until 1945; surpassed by Syd Howe. March 8, 1945

- Shares NHL record (with Deron Quint of the Winnipeg Jets) for fastest two goals (four seconds) in a game, January 3, 1931

- Played amateur hockey with Parkdale Canoe Club (1919–20); Cleveland Indians (1920–24); Cleveland Blues (1924–25)

- Earned the nickname "Old Poison" because of his deadly accurate shot; also known as "Big Sam" during his NHL career

- Led USAHA in goals in 1920–21 (23), 1922–23 (22) and 1924–25 (21); led USAHA in goals (21) and points (28) in 1923–24

- Signed as a free agent by Montreal Maroons, June 25, 1925

- Led NHL in goals (34) and points (42) in 1925–26; led NHL in penalty minutes (133) in 1926–27; led NHL in goals (23) in 1936–37

- Member of the Montreal Maroons' famous S Line with Babe Siebert and Hooley Smith

- Finished among NHL top-5 in goals in eight different seasons (1925–26, 1928–29 to 1930–31, 1933–34 to 1936–37)

- Finished among NHL top-5 in points in 1925–26 (42), 1927–28 (34), 1928–29 (29) and 1933–34 (39)

All-Star jersey worn by Stewart during the 1934 Ace Bailey Benefit Game; Stewart notched a goal and an assist.

REGULAR SEASON

Season	Age	Team	Lg	GP	G	A	PTS	PIM
1925–26	23	Montreal Maroons	NHL	36	34	8	42	119
1926–27	24	Montreal Maroons	NHL	43	17	4	21	133
1927–28	25	Montreal Maroons	NHL	41	27	7	34	104
1928–29	26	Montreal Maroons	NHL	44	21	8	29	74
1929–30	27	Montreal Maroons	NHL	44	39	16	55	81
1930–31	28	Montreal Maroons	NHL	42	25	14	39	75
1931–32	29	Montreal Maroons	NHL	38	22	11	33	61
1932–33	30	Boston Bruins	NHL	47	18	18	36	62
1933–34	31	Boston Bruins	NHL	48	22	17	39	68
1934–35	32	Boston Bruins	NHL	47	21	18	39	45
1935–36	33	New York Americans	NHL	48	14	15	29	16
1936–37	34	Boston Bruins	NHL	11	3	2	5	6
1936–37	34	New York Americans	NHL	32	20	10	30	31
1937–38	35	New York Americans	NHL	48	19	17	36	29
1938–39	36	New York Americans	NHL	46	16	19	35	43
1939–40	37	New York Americans	NHL	35	6	7	13	6
NHL Career — 15 Seasons				650	324	191	515	953

PLAYOFFS

Season	Age	Team	Lg	GP	G	A	PTS	PIM
1925–26	23	Montreal Maroons	NHL	4	0	2	2	10
1925–26	23	Montreal Maroons	NHL	4	6	1	7	16
1926–27	24	Montreal Maroons	NHL	2	0	0	0	4
1927–28	25	Montreal Maroons	NHL	9	2	2	4	13
1929–30	27	Montreal Maroons	NHL	4	1	1	2	2
1930–31	28	Montreal Maroons	NHL	2	1	0	1	6
1931–32	29	Montreal Maroons	NHL	4	0	1	1	2
1932–33	30	Boston Bruins	NHL	5	2	0	2	4
1934–35	32	Boston Bruins	NHL	4	0	1	1	0
1935–36	33	New York Americans	NHL	5	1	2	3	4
1937–38	35	New York Americans	NHL	6	2	3	5	2
1938–39	36	New York Americans	NHL	2	0	0	0	0
1939–40	37	New York Americans	NHL	3	0	0	0	0
NHL Career — 12 Seasons				54	15	13	28	63

TROPHY CASE

AWARDS

NHL Scoring Leader (1926)

Hart Memorial Trophy (1926, 1930)

Stanley Cup (1925–26)

Bruce Stuart

HOCKEY HALL OF FAME CLASS: 1961

Center/Rover

Shoots: Right

Height: 6'-2"

Weight: 180 lbs.

Born: November 30, 1881: Ottawa, Ontario

Died: October 28, 1961: Ottawa, Ontario

Played 13 elite amateur and professional seasons from 1898–1911

QUICK FACTS

- Brother of Hall of Fame member Hod Stuart, who played nine elite amateur and professional seasons between 1895 and 1907

- Among the first Canadians to play professionally when he signed with Pittsburgh Victorias (1902)

- Led WPHL in goals (16) and points (22) in 1902–03

- WPHL First All-Star Team Center (1903)

- Capable of playing any forward position, he was renowned for his skills as a rover during the seven-man era

- Member of IHL champion Portage Lakes (1903–04, 1905–06, 1906–07)

- Signed as a free agent by Montreal Wanderers, December 10, 1907

- Member of Stanley Cup-winning Montreal Wanderers team that defeated Ottawa (January, 1908); Winnipeg (March, 1908); Toronto (March, 1908); Edmonton (December, 1908)

- ECHA First All-Star Team Rover (1909)

- Served as captain of Stanley Cup-winning Ottawa Senators (1909–10)

- Coached Ottawa Stewartons (1912–13)

> "Give us a couple of good, square officials and we will beat the champions with two or three goals to spare."
>
> — Bruce Stuart, before a key game against the Wanderers in Montreal on February 6, 1909. (The Senators won the game 9–8, then later wrapped up the Stanley Cup with an 8–3 win back home in Ottawa.)

REGULAR SEASON

Season	Age	Team	Lg	GP	G	A	PTS	PIM
1898–99	17	Ottawa Hockey Club	CAHL	1	1	0	1	
1899–00	18	Ottawa Hockey Club	CAHL	5	11	0	11	
1900–01	19	Quebec Bulldogs	CAHL	6	5	0	5	
1901–02	20	Ottawa Hockey Club	CAHL	8	9	0	9	
1902–03	21	Pittsburgh Victorias	WPHL	10	16	6	22	20
1903–04	22	Portage Lakes	Exhib.	14	44	0	44	6
1904–05	23	Portage Lakes	IHL	22	33	0	33	59
1905–06	24	Portage Lakes	IHL	20	15	0	15	22
1906–07	25	Portage Lakes	IHL	23	20	9	29	81
1907–08	26	Montreal Wanderers	ECAHA	3	3	0	3	18
1908–09	27	Ottawa Senators	ECHA	11	22	0	22	30
1909–10	28	Ottawa Senators	CHA	2	4	0	4	0
1909–10	28	Ottawa Senators	NHA	7	14	0	14	17
1910–11	29	Ottawa Senators	NHA	3	0	0	0	0
Career — 13 Seasons				135	197	15	212	253

PLAYOFFS

Season	Age	Team	Lg	GP	G	A	PTS	PIM
1903–04	22	Portage Lakes	Exhib.	9	28	0	28	13
1907–08	26	Montreal Wanderers	St-Cup	3	8	0	8	18
1909–10	28	Ottawa Senators	St-Cup	4	10	0	10	6
Career — 3 Seasons				16	46	0	46	37

TROPHY CASE

AWARDS

Stanley Cup (1907–08, 1908–09, 1909–10, 1910–11)

ALL-STAR SELECTIONS

IHL First All-Star Team Center (1906)

IHL Second All-Star Team Center (1905)

Hod Stuart

HOCKEY HALL OF FAME CLASS: 1945

Defense

Shoots: Unknown

Height: 6'

Weight: 190 lbs.

Born: February 20, 1879: Ottawa, Ontario

Died: June 23, 1907: Belleville, Ontario

Played nine elite amateur and professional seasons from 1898–1907

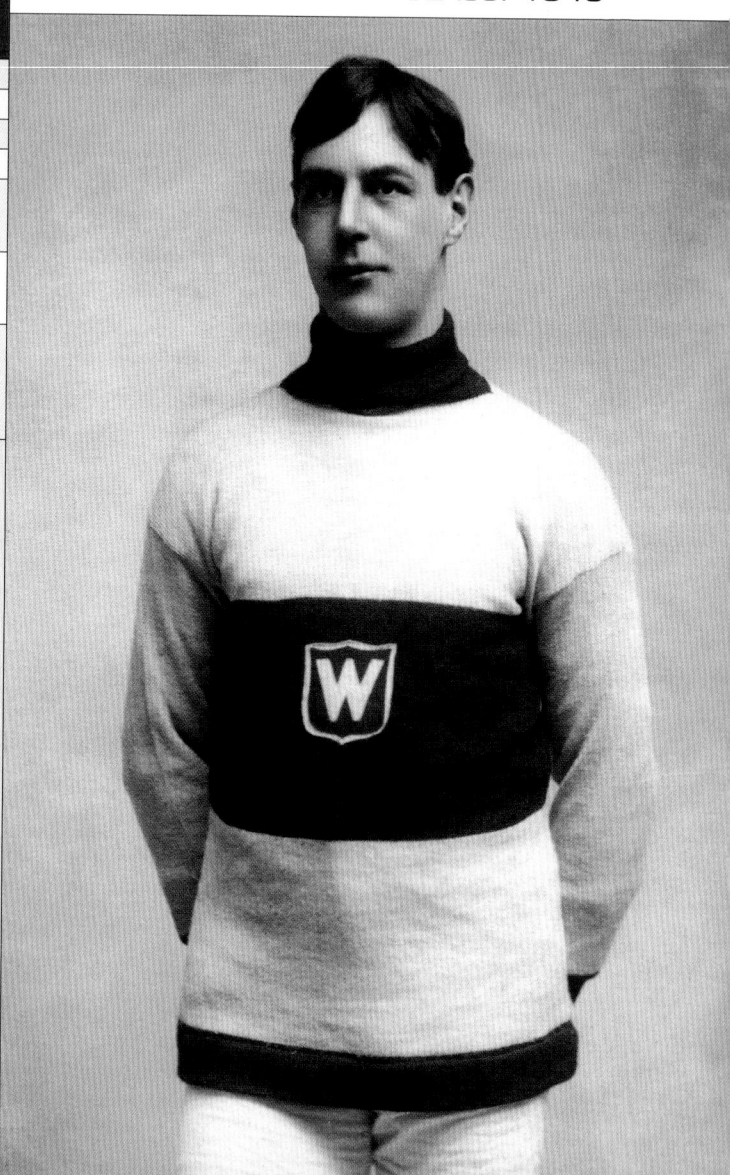

QUICK FACTS

- Played senior hockey with Rat Portage Thistles (1895–96)
- Brother of Hall of Fame member Bruce Stuart, who played 13 elite amateur and professional seasons from 1898–1911
- Member of WPHL champion Calumet Miners (1903); member of United States Pro champion Portage Lakes (1904)
- Served as player/coach of IHL champion Calumet Miners (1905)
- Renowned as one of the best defensemen in hockey during his career
- Signed as a free agent by Pittsburgh Pros, December 3, 1906
- Jumped contract with Pittsburgh to sign as a free agent with Montreal Wanderers, January 3, 1907

- Member of Stanley Cup-winning Montreal Wanderers team that defeated Kenora Thistles, March 23–25, 1907
- ECAHA First All-Star Team Defense (1907)
- Died three months after Stanley Cup victory when he broke his neck in a diving accident while swimming near Belleville, Ontario
- Hod Stuart Memorial All-Star Game between Montreal Wanderers and NHA All-Stars was played to raise funds for his wife and two children, January 2, 1908. Wanderers won game 10–7
- Seven future Hall of Fame members (Riley Hern, Art Ross, Ernie Russell, Moose Johnson, Percy LeSueur, Jack Marshall and Frank Patrick) played in the game

> "We won the Cup in the most gentlemanly manner we could and I am glad to see that Montrealers appreciate it. We will do our best to keep the Cup in our possession."
> — Hod Stuart to the crowd outside Montreal's Savoy hotel before a dinner to honor the Wanderers' 1907 Stanley Cup victory in Kenora.

REGULAR SEASON

Season	Age	Team	Lg	GP	G	A	PTS	PIM
1898–99	19	Ottawa Hockey Club	CAHL	3	1	0	1	
1899–00	20	Ottawa Hockey Club	CAHL	7	5	0	5	
1900–01	21	Quebec Bulldogs	CAHL	7	2	0	2	
1901–02	22	Quebec Bulldogs	CAHL	8	5	0	5	
1902–03	23	Pittsburgh Bankers	WPHL	13	7	8	15	29
1903–04	24	Portage Lakes	Exhib.	14	13	0	13	23
1904–05	25	Calumet Miners	IHL	22	18	0	18	19
1905–06	26	Pittsburgh Professionals	IHL	20	11	0	11	50
1905–06	26	Calumet Miners	IHL	1	0	0	0	0
1906–07	27	Pittsburgh Professionals	IHL	4	1	3	4	19
1906–07	27	Montreal Wanderers	ECAHA	8	3	0	3	21
Career – 9 Seasons				107	66	11	77	161

PLAYOFFS

Season	Age	Team	Lg	GP	G	A	PTS	PIM
1902–03		Pittsburgh Bankers	WPHL	4	1	2	3	2
1903–04		Portage Lakes	Exhib.	9	4	0	4	12
1906–07		Montreal Wanderers	St-Cup	4	0	0	0	8
Career – 3 Seasons				17	5	2	7	22

TROPHY CASE

AWARDS

Stanley Cup (1906–07)

When I was holding the Cup. I could
feel all the names. My senses peaked.
I could hear everyone. The crowd was
incredible, one continuous roar."

Bryan Trottier

A
B
C
D
E
F
G
H
I
J
K
L
M
N
O
P
Q
R
S
T
U
V
W
X
Y
Z

Cyclone Taylor

HOCKEY HALL OF FAME CLASS: 1947

Defense/Rover

Shoots: Left

Height: 5'-8"

Weight: 165 lbs.

Born: June 23, 1884: Tara, Ontario

Died: June 9, 1979: Vancouver, British Columbia

Played 17 professional seasons from 1905–21, 1922–23

QUICK FACTS

- Holds PCHA record for career assists (104)
- Given name was Frederick; earned nickname "Cyclone" for his matchless speed as a skater and the furious rushes he led during his time with the Ottawa Senators
- Member of IHL champion Portage Lakes (1905–06, 1906–07)
- Played mainly as a forward until moving back to defense with the Ottawa Senators in 1907–08 and helped them win the Stanley Cup the following season
- ECAHA First All-Star team Defense (1908)
- Contract with Renfrew Millionaires for the inaugural season of the National Hockey Association was said to be worth $5,250 for a 12-game season at a time when Ty Cobb earned $6,500 to play 154 games with baseball's Detroit Tigers
- Signed as a free agent by Vancouver Millionaires, February 1, 1916
- Member of Stanley Cup-winning Vancouver Millionaires (1914–15); led Stanley Cup playoffs in goals (8) in 1914–15
- Set a PCHA record with six goals in game against Victoria, February 1, 1916
- Led PCHA in goals in 1913–14 (24), 1917–18 (32) and 1918–19 (23)
- Recorded 16 hat-tricks and seven four-goal games during PCHA career
- Served as President of PCHL (1936–39)
- Legacy honored by Cyclone Taylor Cup — the championship trophy awarded to British Columbia's top Junior "B" hockey club

> I don't think I'd like to play the game now. I was used to going on at the start of the game and playing to the finish. I think any man between the ages of 18 and 35 who can't play 60 minutes of hockey — well, he just doesn't want to play, that's all."

REGULAR SEASON

Season	Age	Team	Lg	GP	G	A	PTS	PIM
1905–06	21	Portage-la-Prairie	MHL	4	3	1	4	
1905–06	21	Portage Lakes	IHL	6	11	0	11	4
1906–07	22	Portage Lakes	IHL	23	18	7	25	31
1907–08	23	Ottawa Senators	ECAHA	10	9	0	9	40
1908–09	24	Pittsburgh Professionals	WPHL	3	0	0	0	
1908–09	24	Ottawa Senators	ECHA	11	9	0	9	28
1909–10	25	Renfrew Hockey Club	NHA	13	10	0	10	19
1910–11	26	Renfrew Hockey Club	NHA	16	12	0	12	21
1911–12	27	Ottawa Senators	NHA	1	0	0	0	0
1912–13	28	Vancouver Millionaires	PCHA	14	10	8	18	5
1913–14	29	Vancouver Millionaires	PCHA	16	24	15	39	18
1914–15	30	Vancouver Millionaires	PCHA	16	23	22	45	9
1915–16	31	Vancouver Millionaires	PCHA	18	22	13	35	9
1916–17	32	Vancouver Millionaires	PCHA	11	14	15	29	12
1917–18	33	Vancouver Millionaires	PCHA	18	32	11	43	0
1918–19	34	Vancouver Millionaires	PCHA	20	23	13	36	12
1919–20	35	Vancouver Millionaires	PCHA	10	6	6	12	0
1920–21	36	Vancouver Millionaires	PCHA	6	5	1	6	0
1922–23	38	Vancouver Maroons	PCHA	1	0	0	0	0
Career — 17 Seasons				217	231	112	343	208

PLAYOFFS

Season	Age	Team	Lg	GP	G	A	PTS	PIM
1914–15	30	Vancouver Millionaires	St-Cup	3	8	2	10	3
1917–18	33	Vancouver Millionaires	PCHA	2	0	1	1	0
1917–18	33	Vancouver Millionaires	St-Cup	5	9	0	9	15
1918–19	34	Vancouver Millionaires	PCHA	2	1	0	1	0
1919–20	35	Vancouver Millionaires	PCHA	2	0	0	0	0
1920–21	36	Vancouver Millionaires	PCHA	2	0	0	0	0
1920–21	36	Vancouver Millionaires	St-Cup	3	0	1	1	5
Career — 5 Seasons				19	18	4	22	23

TROPHY CASE

AWARDS

Stanley Cup (1908–09, 1914–15)

ALL-STAR SELECTIONS

IHL First All-Star Team Rover (1907)

PCHA First All-Star Team Rover (1913, 1914, 1915, 1918)

Tiny Thompson

HOCKEY HALL OF FAME CLASS: 1959

1

Goaltender

Catches: Left

Height: 5'-10"

Weight: 160 lbs.

Born: May 31, 1905: Sandon, British Columbia

Died: February 9, 1981: Calgary, Alberta

Played 12 NHL seasons from 1928–40

"Never make a move until the man with the puck makes his. There's no room for guesswork in goaltending."

QUICK FACTS

- Ranks sixth in all-time NHL career shutouts (81)
- First goaltender to win Vezina Trophy four times
- Earned nickname because of the size of his goals-against-average, not his physical dimensions
- Played amateur hockey with Calgary Monarchs (1919–20); Calgary Alberta Grain (1920–21); Belleville Colts (1921–22); Belleville Bulldogs (1922–24); Duluth Hornets (1924–25)
- Signed as a free agent by Minneapolis Millers (AHA), June 8, 1926; traded to Boston by Minneapolis (AHA) for cash, May 12, 1928
- Led NHL in shutouts in 1931–32 (9); 1932–33 (11); 1935–36 (10); 1936–37 (6)
- Recorded 1–0 shutout victory over the Pittsburgh Pirates in his NHL debut, November 15, 1928
- Led NHL in wins in 1928–29 (26); 1929–30 (38); 1930–31 (28); 1932–33 (25); 1937–38 (30)
- Led NHL in goals-against-average in 1929–30 (2.19); 1932–33 (1.76); 1935–36 (1.68); 1937–38 (1.80)
- Played in NHL All-Star Game (1937)
- First goaltender to be awarded an assist for actually passing the puck to a teammate. In a game during the 1935–36 season, he passed the puck to Babe Siebert who skated down the ice and scored
- Wore the same goal pads from the beginning of his professional career in Duluth until he retired in 1940

Thompson's hockey card from the 1933 Ice Kings collection produced by the Montreal World Wide Gum Company.

REGULAR SEASON

Season	Age	Team	Lg	GP	W	L	T	SO	GA	GAA	G	A	PTS	PIM
1928–29	25	Boston Bruins	NHL	44	26	13	5	12	52	1.15	0	0	0	0
1929–30	26	Boston Bruins	NHL	44	38	5	1	3	98	2.19	0	0	0	0
1930–31	27	Boston Bruins	NHL	44	28	10	6	3	90	1.98	0	0	0	0
1931–32	28	Boston Bruins	NHL	43	13	19	11	9	103	2.29	0	0	0	0
1932–33	29	Boston Bruins	NHL	48	25	15	8	11	88	1.76	0	0	0	0
1933–34	30	Boston Bruins	NHL	48	18	25	5	5	130	2.62	0	0	0	0
1934–35	31	Boston Bruins	NHL	48	26	16	6	8	112	2.26	0	0	0	0
1935–36	32	Boston Bruins	NHL	48	22	20	6	10	82	1.68	0	1	1	0
1936–37	33	Boston Bruins	NHL	48	23	18	7	6	110	2.22	0	0	0	0
1937–38	34	Boston Bruins	NHL	48	30	11	7	7	89	1.80	0	0	0	0
1938–39	35	Boston Bruins	NHL	5	3	1	1	0	8	1.55	0	0	0	0
1938–39	35	Detroit Red Wings	NHL	39	16	17	6	4	101	2.53	0	0	0	0
1939–40	36	Detroit Red Wings	NHL	46	16	24	6	3	120	2.54	0	0	0	0
NHL Career – 12 Seasons				553	284	194	75	81	1183	2.08	0	1	1	0

PLAYOFFS

Season	Age	Team	Lg	GP	W	L	T	SO	GA	GAA	G	A	PTS	PIM
1928–29	25	Boston Bruins	NHL	5	5	0	0	3	3	0.60	0	0	0	0
1929–30	26	Boston Bruins	NHL	6	3	3	0	0	12	1.67	0	0	0	0
1930–31	27	Boston Bruins	NHL	5	2	3	0	0	13	2.27	0	0	0	0
1932–33	29	Boston Bruins	NHL	5	2	3	0	0	9	1.23	0	0	0	0
1934–35	31	Boston Bruins	NHL	4	1	3	0	1	7	1.53	0	0	0	0
1935–36	32	Boston Bruins	NHL	2	1	1	0	1	8	4.00	0	0	0	0
1936–37	33	Boston Bruins	NHL	3	1	2		1	8	2.67	0	0	0	0
1937–38	34	Boston Bruins	NHL	3	0	3		0	6	1.70	0	0	0	0
1938–39	35	Detroit Red Wings	NHL	6	3	3		1	15	2.41	0	0	0	0
1939–40	36	Detroit Red Wings	NHL	5	2	3		0	12	2.40	0	0	0	0
NHL Career – 10 Seasons				44	20	24	0	7	93	1.88	0	0	0	0

TROPHY CASE

AWARDS

Vezina Trophy (1930, 1933, 1936, 1938)

Stanley Cup (1928–29)

ALL-STAR SELECTIONS

First All-Star Team Goaltender (1936, 1938)

Second All-Star Team Goaltender (1931, 1935)

20

Vladislav Tretiak

HOCKEY HALL OF FAME CLASS: 1989

Goaltender

Catches: Left

Height: 6'-1"

Weight: 202 lbs.

Born: April 25, 1952; Dmitrov, Union of Soviet Socialist Republics

Drafted by the Montreal Canadiens 143rd overall in 1983

Played 16 seasons of Russian elite amateur hockey with CSKA Moscow from 1968–84

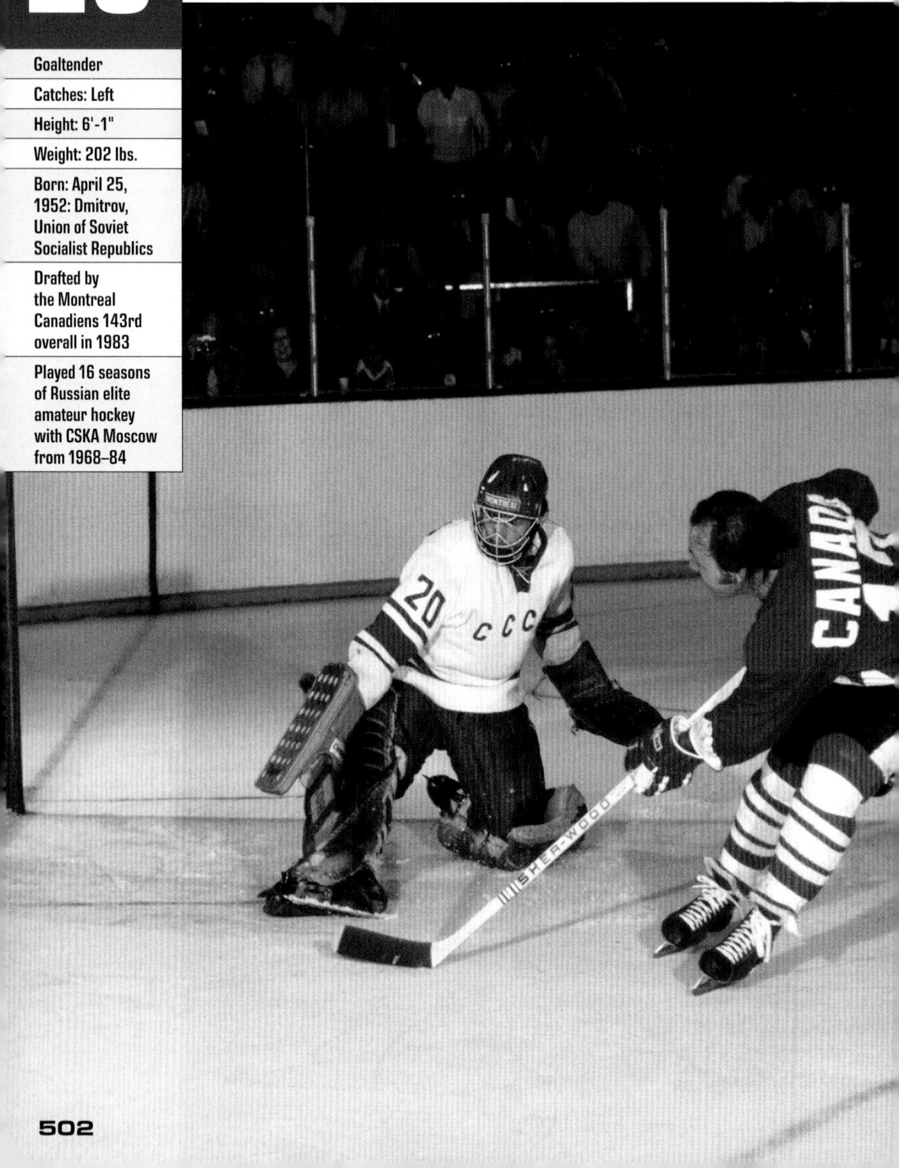

QUICK FACTS

- Only athlete in Olympic hockey history to win three gold medals (1972, 1976, 1984) and one silver medal (1980)

- First European-born player without NHL experience and first Russian-born and trained player to be inducted into Hockey Hall of Fame

- USSR First All-Star Team Goaltender (1971, 1972, 1973, 1974, 1975, 1976, 1977, 1978, 1979, 1980, 1981, 1982, 1983)

- Named USSR Elite League MVP (1974, 1975, 1976, 1981, 1983)

- Named World Championships Best Goaltender (1974, 1979, 1981, 1983)

- Canada Cup First All-Star Team Goaltender (1981)

- World Championships First All-Star Team Goaltender (1975, 1979, 1983)

- Named Best Russian Hockey Player of 20th century by the IIHF and Russian Hockey Federation (2000)

- Named Goalkeeper of the Century on the IIHF Centennial All-Star Team (2008)

- Won Golden Stick Award (European Player of Year) in 1981, 1982 and 1984

- Served as Chicago Blackhawks goaltending consultant (1990–92, 2000–04)

- Served as Chicago Blackhawks goaltending coach (1992–2000)

- Montreal Canadiens' General Manager Serge Savard traveled to Soviet Union in 1984 but failed to secure permission from Soviet authorities for Tretiak to leave Russia and play in the NHL

> I would have loved to play in the [Montreal] Forum. I was hoping to one day play in the NHL. I would have liked to do it even for just one season. Unfortunately, it didn't work out that way. I regret not having the chance."

REGULAR SEASON

Season	Age	Team	Lg	GP	W	L	T	SO	GA	GAA
1968–69	16	CSKA Moscow	USSR	3					2	0.67
1969–70	17	CSKA Moscow	USSR	34					76	2.24
1970–71	18	CSKA Moscow	USSR	40					81	2.03
1971–72	19	CSKA Moscow	USSR	30					78	2.60
1972–73	20	CSKA Moscow	USSR	30					80	2.67
1973–74	21	CSKA Moscow	USSR	27					94	3.48
1974–75	22	CSKA Moscow	USSR	35					104	2.97
1975–76	23	CSKA Moscow	USSR	33					100	3.03
1976–77	24	CSKA Moscow	USSR	35					98	2.80
1977–78	25	CSKA Moscow	USSR	29					72	2.48
1978–79	26	CSKA Moscow	USSR	40					111	2.78
1979–80	27	CSKA Moscow	USSR	36					85	2.36
1980–81	28	CSKA Moscow	USSR	18					32	1.78
1981–82	29	CSKA Moscow	USSR	41	34	4	3	6	65	1.59
1982–83	30	CSKA Moscow	USSR	29	25	3	1	6	40	1.38
1983–84	31	CSKA Moscow	USSR	22	22	0	0	4	40	1.82
Career – 16 Seasons				482	81	7	4	16	1158	2.40

TROPHY CASE

INTERNATIONAL AWARDS

Summit Series (1974)

Challenge Cup (1979)

Canada Cup (1981)

Gold Medal: World Championships (1970, 1971, 1973, 1974, 1975, 1978, 1979, 1981, 1982, 1983)

Silver Medal: World Championships (1972, 1977)

Gold Medal: Winter Olympics (1972, 1976, 1984)

Silver Medal: Winter Olympics (1980)

Harry Trihey

HOCKEY HALL OF FAME CLASS: 1950

Center

Shoots: Unknown

Height: Unknown

Weight: Unknown

Born: December 25, 1877: Montreal, Quebec

Died: December 9, 1942: Montreal, Quebec

Played six elite amateur seasons from 1895–1901

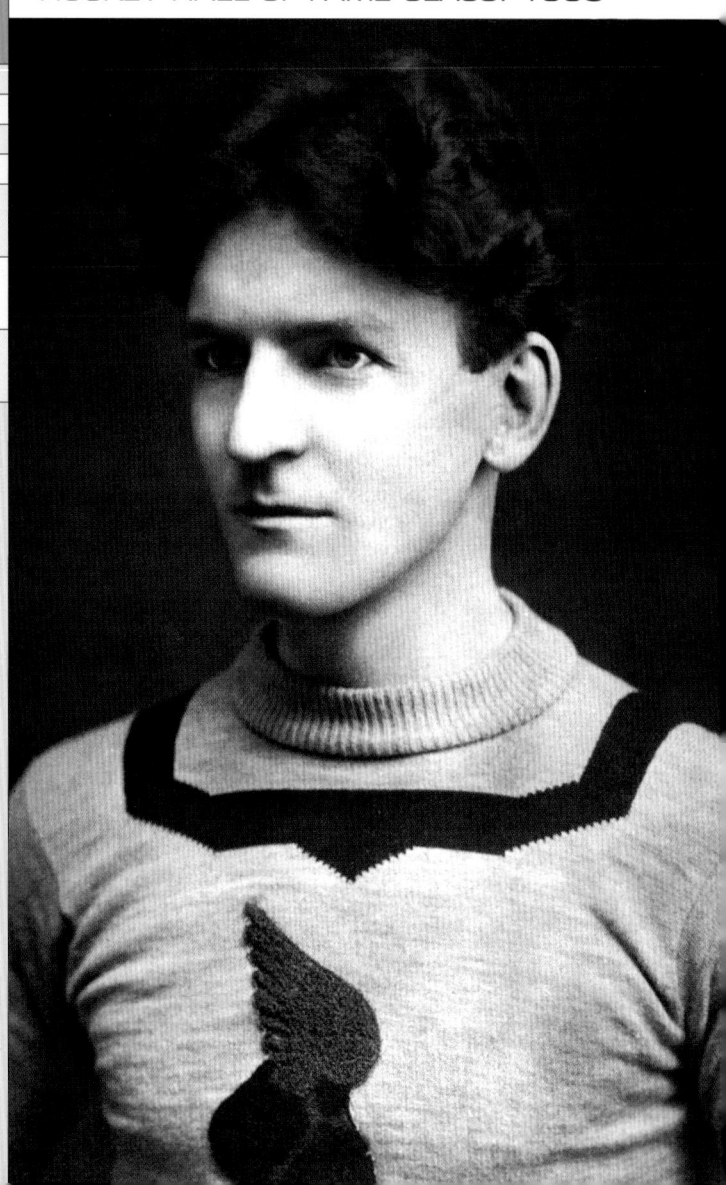

QUICK FACTS

- Member of forward line with the Montreal Shamrocks that included future Hall of Fame members Art Farrell and Fred Scanlan
- Renowned for helping introduce teamwork and strategy to the game of hockey
- Served as captain of Montreal Shamrocks (1898–1901)
- Member of Stanley Cup-winning Montreal Shamrocks (1898–99, 1899–00)
- Led CAHL in goals in 1898–99 (19) and 1899–00 (17)
- Scored CAHL-record 10 goals in Montreal Shamrocks' 13–4 victory over Quebec, February 4, 1899
- Scored three goals in Montreal Shamrocks' 6–2 victory over Queen's University in team's first successful Stanley Cup defense, March 14, 1899

- Scored 12 goals in five Stanley Cup games during the 1899–00 season
- Injuries limited his effectiveness in 1900–01 when the Shamrocks lost Stanley Cup challenge to the Winnipeg Victorias
- Retired due to injuries in 1901 but remained active in hockey as a referee, executive with the CAHL and advisor to the Montreal Wanderers
- Operated a successful law practice in Montreal
- Served as Lieutenant-Colonel with the 199th Battalion Irish Canadian Rangers during World War I

> In Canada, Farrell and Trihey are considered two of the best forwards that have ever played hockey."
> — *New York Times*, March 17, 1899

REGULAR SEASON

Season	Age	Team	Lg	GP	G	A	PTS	PIM
1895–96	18	Montreal Orioles	QAHA					
1896–97	19	Montreal Shamrocks	QAHA					
1896–97	19	Montreal Shamrocks	MCSHL	1	0	0	0	
1897–98	20	Montreal Shamrocks	CAHL	8	3	0	3	
1898–99	21	Montreal Shamrocks	CAHL	7	19	0	19	
1899–00	22	Montreal Shamrocks	CAHL	7	17	0	17	
1900–01	23	Montreal Shamrocks	CAHL	7	7	0	7	
Career – 6 Seasons				30	46	0	46	

PLAYOFFS

Season	Age	Team	Lg	GP	G	A	PTS	PIM
1898–99	21	Montreal Shamrocks	St-Cup	1	3	0	3	
1899–00	22	Montreal Shamrocks	St-Cup	5	12	0	12	
1900–01	23	Montreal Shamrocks	St-Cup	2	1	0	1	
Career – 3 Seasons				8	16	0	16	

TROPHY CASE

AWARDS

Stanley Cup (1898–99, 1899–1900)

Bryan Trottier
HOCKEY HALL OF FAME CLASS: 1997

Center

Shoots: Left

Height: 5'-11"

Weight: 195 lbs.

Born: July 17, 1956: Val Marie, Saskatchewan

Drafted by the New York Islanders 22nd overall in 1974

Played 18 NHL seasons from 1975–92, 1993–94

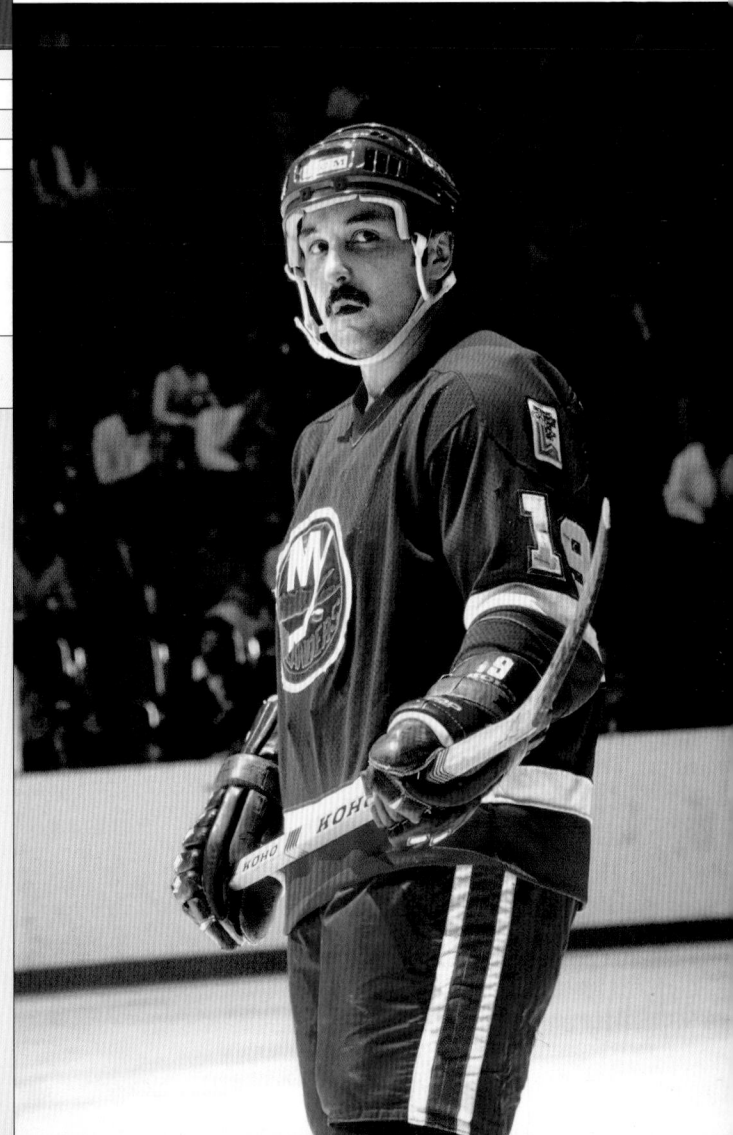

QUICK FACTS

- Holds NHL record for most points in a regular season period (6), established in N.Y. Islanders' 9–4 victory over N.Y. Rangers, December 23, 1978

- Holds NHL record for longest consecutive point-scoring streak in playoffs (27 games), established from 1980 through 1982; holds NHL record for longest consecutive point-scoring streak in one playoff season (18 games), established in 1981

- Holds N.Y. Islanders' team records for career games (1,123), assists (853), points (1,353), regular season assists (87), points in a regular season game (6) and points by a rookie (95)

- Played amateur hockey with Humboldt Broncos (1971–72); Swift Current Broncos (1972–74); Lethbridge Broncos (1974–75)

- Led WCJHL in assists (98) in 1974–75; WCJHL First All-Star Team Center (1975)

- One of only six players in NHL history (with Dick Duff, Red Kelly, Frank Mahovlich, Patrick Roy and Larry Murphy) to win two-or-more Stanley Cup championships with two-or-more teams

- Played for Team USA at 1984 Canada Cup tournament

- Led NHL in points (134) in 1978–79; led NHL in assists in 1977–78 (77) and 1978–79 (87); led NHL in plus/minus (+76) in 1978–79

- Registered 1,000th career NHL point in N.Y. Islanders' 4–4 tie with Minnesota North Stars, January 29, 1985; recorded 500th career NHL goal in N.Y. Islanders' 4–2 loss to Calgary Flames, February 13, 1990

> "When I was holding the Cup, I could feel all the names. My senses peaked. I could hear everyone. The crowd was incredible, one continuous roar."

REGULAR SEASON

Season	Age	Team	Lg	GP	G	A	PTS	+/-	PIM	ESG	PPG	SHG	GWG	SOG	S%
1975–76	19	New York Islanders	NHL	80	32	63	95	28	21	20	11	1	5	178	18.0
1976–77	20	New York Islanders	NHL	76	30	42	72	28	34	18	11	1	6	175	17.1
1977–78	21	New York Islanders	NHL	77	46	77	123	52	46	31	13	2	6	193	23.8
1978–79	22	New York Islanders	NHL	76	47	87	134	76	50	32	15	0	8	187	25.1
1979–80	23	New York Islanders	NHL	78	42	62	104	31	68	27	15	0	6	186	22.6
1980–81	24	New York Islanders	NHL	73	31	72	103	49	74	20	9	2	5	156	19.9
1981–82	25	New York Islanders	NHL	80	50	79	129	70	88	30	18	2	10	217	23.0
1982–83	26	New York Islanders	NHL	80	34	55	89	37	68	21	13	0	5	179	19.0
1983–84	27	New York Islanders	NHL	68	40	71	111	70	59	30	7	3	4	194	20.6
1984–85	28	New York Islanders	NHL	68	28	31	59	5	47	19	4	5	3	159	17.6
1985–86	29	New York Islanders	NHL	78	37	59	96	29	72	31	5	1	3	185	20.0
1986–87	30	New York Islanders	NHL	80	23	64	87	3	50	10	13	0	1	194	11.9
1987–88	31	New York Islanders	NHL	77	30	52	82	10	48	15	15	0	3	176	17.0
1988–89	32	New York Islanders	NHL	73	17	28	45	-7	44	12	5	0	3	163	10.4
1989–90	33	New York Islanders	NHL	59	13	11	24	-11	29	9	4	0	0	84	15.5
1990–91	34	Pittsburgh Penguins	NHL	52	9	19	28	5	24	8	0	1	0	68	13.2
1991–92	35	Pittsburgh Penguins	NHL	63	11	18	29	-11	54	7	3	1	0	102	10.8
1993–94	37	Pittsburgh Penguins	NHL	41	4	11	15	-12	36	4	0	0	0	45	8.9
NHL Career – 18 Seasons				1279	524	901	1425	452	912	344	161	19	68	2841	18.4

PLAYOFFS

Season	Age	Team	Lg	GP	G	A	PTS	+/-	PIM	ESG	PPG	SHG	GWG	SOG	S%
1975–76	19	New York Islanders	NHL	13	1	7	8		8	1	0	0	0		
1976–77	20	New York Islanders	NHL	12	2	8	10		2	2	0	0	0		
1977–78	21	New York Islanders	NHL	7	0	3	3		4	0	0	0	0		
1978–79	22	New York Islanders	NHL	10	2	4	6		13	2	0	0	1		
1979–80	23	New York Islanders	NHL	21	12	17	29		16	6	4	2	2		
1980–81	24	New York Islanders	NHL	18	11	18	29		34	5	4	2	1		
1981–82	25	New York Islanders	NHL	19	6	23	29		40	4	2	0	2		
1982–83	26	New York Islanders	NHL	17	8	12	20		18	5	3	0	1		
1983–84	27	New York Islanders	NHL	21	8	6	14	2	49	7	1	0	0	39	20.5
1984–85	28	New York Islanders	NHL	10	4	2	6	0	8	3	1	0	1	25	16.0
1985–86	29	New York Islanders	NHL	3	1	1	2	-1	2	1	0	0	0	10	10.0
1986–87	30	New York Islanders	NHL	14	8	5	13	-6	12	5	3	0	2	46	17.4
1987–88	31	New York Islanders	NHL	6	0	0	0	-9	10	0	0	0	0	11	0.0
1989–90	33	New York Islanders	NHL	4	1	0	1	-4	4	1	0	0	0	7	14.3
1990–91	34	Pittsburgh Penguins	NHL	23	3	4	7	-1	49	3	0	0	0	16	18.8
1991–92	35	Pittsburgh Penguins	NHL	21	4	3	7	0	8	4	0	0	0	30	13.3
1993–94	37	Pittsburgh Penguins	NHL	2	0	0	0	0	0	0	0	0	0	1	0.0
NHL Career – 17 Seasons				221	71	113	184	-19	277	49	18	4	12	185	15.7

TROPHY CASE

AWARDS

Calder Memorial Trophy (1976)

Art Ross Trophy (1979)

Hart Memorial Trophy (1979)

Conn Smythe Trophy (1980)

King Clancy Memorial Trophy (1989)

Stanley Cup (1979–80, 1980–81, 1981–82, 1982–83, 1990–91, 1991–92)

ALL-STAR SELECTIONS

First NHL All-Star Team Center (1978, 1979)

Second NHL All-Star Team Center (1982, 1984)

7

Norm Ullman

HOCKEY HALL OF FAME CLASS: 1982

Alternates: 9, 16

Center

Shoots: Left

Height: 5'-10"

Weight: 175 lbs.

Born: December 26, 1935; Provost, Alberta

Played 22 NHL and WHA seasons from 1955–77

QUICK FACTS

- Played amateur hockey with Edmonton Oil Kings (1951–54)
- Led WCJHL in assists (47) and points (76) in 1952–53; led WCJHL in goals (56) and points (101) in 1953–54; led WCJHL playoffs in assists (26) and points (37) in 1953–54
- Led Memorial Cup playoffs in assists (18) and points (30) in 1953–54
- Played minor pro hockey with Edmonton Flyers (1953–55)
- Led NHL in goals (42) in 1964–65
- Led NHL playoffs in assists (12) and points (16) in 1962–63; led NHL playoffs in goals (6) and points (15) in 1965–66
- Led NHL in game-winning goals (10) in 1964–65; led NHL in even-strength goals (32) in 1964–65
- Played in NHL All-Star Game (1955, 1960, 1961, 1962, 1963, 1964,1965, 1967, 1968, 1969, 1974)
- Registered 1,000th career NHL point in Toronto's 5–3 loss to N.Y. Rangers, October 16, 1971
- Involved in one of the biggest transactions in NHL history when he was traded to Toronto by Detroit with Floyd Smith, Paul Henderson and Doug Barrie for Frank Mahovlich, Pete Stemkowski, Garry Unger and the rights to Carl Brewer, March 3, 1968

> "It's the biggest accolade you can get to be honored as one of the best in the game. All of a sudden you sit back and say, 'My God, I'm in the Hockey Hall of Fame!' It is a great honor and really caps off a career for a player."

REGULAR SEASON

Season	Age	Team	Lg	GP	G	A	PTS	+/-	PIM	ESG	PPG	SHG	GWG	SOG	S%
1955–56	20	Detroit Red Wings	NHL	66	9	9	18		26						
1956–57	21	Detroit Red Wings	NHL	64	16	36	52		47						
1957–58	22	Detroit Red Wings	NHL	69	23	28	51		38						
1958–59	23	Detroit Red Wings	NHL	69	22	36	58		42						
1959–60	24	Detroit Red Wings	NHL	70	24	34	58		46						
1960–61	25	Detroit Red Wings	NHL	70	28	42	70		34						
1961–62	26	Detroit Red Wings	NHL	70	26	38	64		54						
1962–63	27	Detroit Red Wings	NHL	70	26	30	56		53						
1963–64	28	Detroit Red Wings	NHL	61	21	30	51		55	17	3	1	5		
1964–65	29	Detroit Red Wings	NHL	70	42	41	83		70	32	9	1	10		
1965–66	30	Detroit Red Wings	NHL	70	31	41	72		35	24	7	0	2		
1966–67	31	Detroit Red Wings	NHL	68	26	44	70		26	20	5	1	3		
1967–68	32	Detroit Red Wings	NHL	58	30	25	55	-13	26	23	7	0	4	189	15.9
1967–68	32	Toronto Maple Leafs	NHL	13	5	12	17	12	2	4	1	0	0	39	12.8
1968–69	33	Toronto Maple Leafs	NHL	75	35	42	77	19	41	22	13	0	2	247	14.2
1969–70	34	Toronto Maple Leafs	NHL	74	18	42	60	20	37	13	4	1	0	207	8.7
1970–71	35	Toronto Maple Leafs	NHL	73	34	51	85	14	24	22	11	1	4	226	15.0
1971–72	36	Toronto Maple Leafs	NHL	77	23	50	73	8	26	14	9	0	1	204	11.3
1972–73	37	Toronto Maple Leafs	NHL	65	20	35	55	-18	10	17	3	0	1	174	11.5
1973–74	38	Toronto Maple Leafs	NHL	78	22	47	69	10	12	18	4	0	2	178	12.4
1974–75	39	Toronto Maple Leafs	NHL	80	9	26	35	-12	8	8	1	0	0	117	7.7
1975–76	40	Edmonton Oilers	WHA	77	31	56	87	-21	12	17	13	1	1	158	19.6
1976–77	41	Edmonton Oilers	WHA	67	16	27	43	-23	28	12	4	0		107	15.0
Career — 22 Seasons				1554	537	822	1359	-4	752	263	94	6	35	1846	13.2

PLAYOFFS

Season	Age	Team	Lg	GP	G	A	PTS	+/-	PIM	ESG	PPG	SHG	GWG	SOG	S%
1955–56	20	Detroit Red Wings	NHL	10	1	3	4		13						
1956–57	21	Detroit Red Wings	NHL	5	1	1	2		6						
1957–58	22	Detroit Red Wings	NHL	4	0	2	2		4						
1959–60	24	Detroit Red Wings	NHL	6	2	2	4		0						
1960–61	25	Detroit Red Wings	NHL	11	0	4	4		4						
1962–63	27	Detroit Red Wings	NHL	11	4	12	16		14						
1963–64	28	Detroit Red Wings	NHL	14	7	10	17		6						
1964–65	29	Detroit Red Wings	NHL	7	6	4	10		2						
1965–66	30	Detroit Red Wings	NHL	12	6	9	15		12						
1968–69	33	Toronto Maple Leafs	NHL	4	1	0	1		0	1	0	0	0		
1970–71	35	Toronto Maple Leafs	NHL	6	0	2	2		2	0	0	0	0		
1971–72	36	Toronto Maple Leafs	NHL	5	1	3	4		2	1	0	0	0		
1973–74	38	Toronto Maple Leafs	NHL	4	1	1	2		0	1	0	0	0		
1974–75	39	Toronto Maple Leafs	NHL	7	0	0	0		2	0	0	0	0		
1975–76	40	Edmonton Oilers	WHA	4	1	3	4	3	2						
1976–77	41	Edmonton Oilers	WHA	5	0	3	3	-2	0	0	0	0	0		
Career — 16 Seasons				115	31	59	90	1	69	3	0	0	0		

TROPHY CASE

ALL-STAR SELECTIONS

First All-Star Team
Center (1965)

Second All-Star Team
Center (1967)

Georges Vezina

HOCKEY HALL OF FAME CLASS: 1945

Goaltender

Catches: Left

Height: 5'-6"

Weight: 185 lbs.

Born: January 21, 1887: Chicoutimi, Quebec

Died: March 27, 1926: Chicoutimi, Quebec

Played 16 professional seasons from 1910–26

"He stood upright in the net and scarcely ever left his feet; he simply played all his shots in a standing position. Vezina was a pale, narrow-featured fellow, almost frail looking, yet remarkably good with his stick. He'd pick off more shots with it than he did with his glove."

— Frank Boucher, Hall of Fame player

QUICK FACTS

- Nicknamed "The Chicoutimi Cucumber" because of his poise and cool demeanor in the nets
- Played amateur hockey with Chicoutimi Sagueneens (1909–10)
- Signed by Montreal Canadiens after he shutout the Canadiens in an exhibition game while playing with a Chicoutimi intermediate team on February 17, 1910
- Never missed a single regular season or playoff game from the time he joined the Montreal Canadiens in 1910–11 until he became ill during a game on November 25, 1925
- Led NHA in wins (13), goals-against-average (3.14) and shutouts (1) in 1913–14; led NHA in wins (16) in 1915–16

- Led NHL in wins (12), shutouts (1) and goals-against-average (3.93) in 1917–18; led NHL in shutouts (3) and goals-against-average (1.97) in 1923–24; led NHL in goals-against-average (1.81) in 1924–25
- Recorded first shutout in NHL history with 9–0 victory over the Toronto Arenas on February 18, 1918
- First goaltender to be awarded an assist when Canadiens teammate Newsy Lalonde took a rebound that Vezina stopped, skated up ice and scored in Montreal's 6–3 victory over Toronto Arenas, December 28, 1918
- The ownership of the Canadiens donated the Vezina Trophy — awarded to the league's top goaltender — to the NHL in his honor

The final pair of skates Vezina wore before leaving his 325th consecutive game after only 20 minutes, and retiring immediately thereafter due to tuberculosis.

REGULAR SEASON

Season	Age	Team	Lg	GP	W	L	T	SO	GA	GAA	G	A	PTS	PIM
1910–11	24	Montreal Canadiens	NHA	16	8	8	0	0	62	3.80				
1911–12	25	Montreal Canadiens	NHA	18	8	10	0	0	66	3.57				
1912–13	26	Montreal Canadiens	NHA	20	11	9	0	1	81	3.99				
1913–14	27	Montreal Canadiens	NHA	20	13	7	0	1	64	3.14				
1914–15	28	Montreal Canadiens	NHA	20	6	14	0	0	81	3.87				
1915–16	29	Montreal Canadiens	NHA	24	16	7	1	0	76	3.08				
1916–17	30	Montreal Canadiens	NHA	20	10	10	0	0	80	3.94				
1917–18	31	Montreal Canadiens	NHL	21	12	9	0	1	84	3.93	0	0	0	0
1918–19	32	Montreal Canadiens	NHL	18	10	8	0	1	78	4.19	0	1	1	0
1919–20	33	Montreal Canadiens	NHL	24	13	11	0	0	113	4.66	0	0	0	0
1920–21	34	Montreal Canadiens	NHL	24	13	11	0	1	99	4.12	0	0	0	0
1921–22	35	Montreal Canadiens	NHL	24	12	11	1	0	94	3.84	0	0	0	2
1922–23	36	Montreal Canadiens	NHL	24	13	9	2	2	61	2.46	0	0	0	0
1923–24	37	Montreal Canadiens	NHL	24	13	11	0	3	48	1.97	0	0	0	0
1924–25	38	Montreal Canadiens	NHL	30	17	11	2	5	56	1.81	0	0	0	0
1925–26	39	Montreal Canadiens	NHL	1	0	0	0	0	0	0.00	0	0	0	0
Career – 16 Seasons				328	175	146	6	15	1143	3.48	0	1	1	2

PLAYOFFS

Season	Age	Team	Lg	GP	W	L	T	SO	GA	GAA	G	A	PTS	PIM
1913–14	27	Montreal Canadiens	NHA	2	1	1	0	1	6	3.00				
1915–16	29	Montreal Canadiens	St-Cup	5	3	2	0	0	13	2.60				
1916–17	30	Montreal Canadiens	NHA	2	1	1	0	0	6	3.00				
1916–17	30	Montreal Canadiens	St-Cup	4	1	3	0	0	23	5.75				
1917–18	31	Montreal Canadiens	NHL	2	1	1	0	0	10	5.00	0	0	0	0
1918–19	32	Montreal Canadiens	St-Cup	5	2	2	1	1	19	3.39				
1918–19	32	Montreal Canadiens	NHL	5	4	1	0	0	18	3.60	0	0	0	0
1922–23	36	Montreal Canadiens	NHL	2	1	1	0	0	3	1.50	0	0	0	0
1923–24	37	Montreal Canadiens	St-Cup	4	4	0	0	1	4	1.00				
1923–24	37	Montreal Canadiens	NHL	2	2	0	0	1	2	1.00	0	0	0	0
1924–25	38	Montreal Canadiens	St-Cup	4	1	3	0	0	16	4.00				
1924–25	38	Montreal Canadiens	NHL	2	2	0	0	1	2	1.00	0	0	0	0
Career – 8 Seasons				39	23	15	1	5	122	3.13	0	0	0	0

TROPHY CASE

AWARDS

Stanley Cup (1915–16, 1923–24)

ALL-STAR SELECTIONS

NHA First All-Star Team Goaltender (1914)

7

Jack Walker

HOCKEY HALL OF FAME CLASS: 1960

Alternate: 6

Center

Shoots: Left

Height: 5'-8"

Weight: 153 lbs.

Born: November 29, 1888: Silver Mountain, Ontario

Died: February 16, 1950: Unknown

Played 18 elite amateur and professional seasons from 1910–28

QUICK FACTS

- Played amateur hockey with Port Arthur East Greys (1905–07); Port Arthur Lake City (1907–12)
- Credited with inventing the hook and sweep check that enabled him to become one of the best defensive forwards of his era
- Associated with hockey for more than 30 years, but spent all but two years of his playing career in leagues that either predated or rivaled the NHL
- Won Stanley Cup championship three times with three different teams from three different leagues (Toronto Blueshirts, NHA; Seattle Metropolitans, PCHA; Victoria Cougars, WCHL)
- Jumped contract with Toronto (NHA) to sign with Seattle (PCHA), November 12, 1915
- Led NHA in assists (16) in 1913–14
- Member of Stanley Cup-winning Seattle Metropolitans (1916–17)
- Signed as a free agent by Victoria (WCHL), November 10, 1924
- Traded to Detroit by Victoria (WHL) for cash, May 15, 1926
- Member of Stanley Cup-winning Victoria Cougars (1924–25) – last non-NHL club to win the Stanley Cup
- Led WCHL playoffs in goals (4) in 1924–25; led Stanley Cup playoffs in goals (4) and points (6) in 1924–25
- Played minor pro hockey with Seattle Eskimos (1928–31); Hollywood Stars (1931–32); Oakland Sheiks (1932–33)

> **Walker, like Frank Nighbor of the champion Senators, is the type of player who plays the puck and not the man. Like Nighbor, he is a poke-check expert and is a clean-living athlete and a credit to the game. Hockey owes much to players like Jack Walker."**
>
> — *Ottawa Citizen,*
> May 3, 1927

REGULAR SEASON

Season	Age	Team	Lg	GP	G	A	PTS	PIM
1910–11	22	Port Arthur Lake City	NOHL	14	30	0	30	
1911–12	23	Port Arthur Lake City	NOHL	13	17	0	17	0
1912–13	24	Toronto Blueshirts	NHA	1	0	0	0	0
1912–13	24	Moncton Victorias	MPHL	15	21	0	21	9
1913–14	25	Toronto Blueshirts	NHA	20	20	16	36	17
1914–15	26	Toronto Blueshirts	NHA	19	12	7	19	11
1915–16	27	Seattle Metropolitans	PCHA	18	13	6	19	6
1916–17	28	Seattle Metropolitans	PCHA	24	11	15	26	3
1917–18	29	Seattle Metropolitans	PCHA	1	0	0	0	0
1918–19	30	Seattle Metropolitans	PCHA	20	9	6	15	9
1919–20	31	Seattle Metropolitans	PCHA	22	4	8	12	3
1920–21	32	Seattle Metropolitans	PCHA	23	6	4	10	6
1921–22	33	Seattle Metropolitans	PCHA	20	8	4	12	0
1922–23	34	Seattle Metropolitans	PCHA	29	13	10	23	4
1923–24	35	Seattle Metropolitans	PCHA	29	18	5	23	0
1924–25	36	Victoria Cougars	WCHL	28	7	7	14	6
1925–26	27	Victoria Cougars	WHL	30	9	8	17	16
1926–27	38	Detroit Cougars	NHL	37	3	4	7	6
1927–28	39	Detroit Cougars	NHL	43	2	4	6	12
Career — 18 Seasons				406	203	104	307	108

PLAYOFFS

Season	Age	Team	Lg	GP	G	A	PTS	PIM
1910–11	22	Port Arthur Lake City	NOHL	2	2	0	2	0
1910–11	22	Port Arthur Lake City	St-Cup	1	1	0	1	0
1911–12	23	Port Arthur Lake City	NOHL	2	3	0	3	0
1913–14	25	Toronto Blueshirts	NHA	2	3	0	3	2
1913–14	25	Toronto Blueshirts	St-Cup	3	1	0	1	3
1916–17	28	Seattle Metropolitans	St-Cup	4	1	2	3	0
1918–19	30	Seattle Metropolitans	PCHA	2	0	2	2	0
1918–19	30	Seattle Metropolitans	St-Cup	5	3	0	3	9
1919–20	31	Seattle Metropolitans	PCHA	2	1	1	2	0
1919–20	31	Seattle Metropolitans	St-Cup	5	1	3	4	0
1920–21	32	Seattle Metropolitans	PCHA	2	0	0	0	0
1921–22	33	Seattle Metropolitans	PCHA	2	0	0	0	0
1923–24	35	Seattle Metropolitans	PCHA	2	0	1	1	0
1924–25	36	Victoria Cougars	St-Cup	4	4	2	6	0
1924–25	36	Victoria Cougars	WCHL	4	4	0	4	0
1925–26	37	Victoria Cougars	WHL	4	0	0	0	2
Career — 11 Seasons				46	24	11	35	16

TROPHY CASE

AWARDS

Stanley Cup (1913–14, 1916–17, 1924–25)

ALL-STAR SELECTIONS

PCHA First All-Star Team Center (1921, 1922, 1923)

PCHA Second All-Star Team Center (1917, 1919, 1920)

Marty Walsh

HOCKEY HALL OF FAME CLASS: 1962

Center

Shoots: Left

Height: 5'-7"

Weight: 155 lbs.

Born: October 16, 1884: Ottawa, Ontario

Died: March 27, 1915: Muskoka, Ontario

Played 10 elite amateur and professional seasons from 1902–12

QUICK FACTS

- Member of Canadian University champion Queen's University (1903–04, 1905–06)

- Led Canadian University League in goals (9) and penalty minutes (30) in 1903–04

- Led Canadian University League in goals (15) in 1905–06

- Signed as a free agent by Canadian Soo Algonquins, December 4, 1906

- Signed as a free agent by Ottawa Senators, December 3, 1907

- ECAHA First All-Star Team Center (1908); ECHA First All-Star Team Center (1909)

- Member of Stanley Cup-winning Ottawa Senators (1908–09, 1909–10, 1910–11)

- Led ECHA in goals (42) in 1908–09; finished second in ECAHA in goals (27) in 1907–08

- Scored six goals in Ottawa's 12–3 Stanley Cup series victory over Galt, January 5, 1910

- Scored 10 goals in Ottawa's 14–4 Stanley Cup series victory over Port Arthur, March 16, 1911 — the second-highest total in Stanley Cup history behind Frank McGee's 14 goals against Dawson City in 1905

- Coached Edmonton Sr. Eskimos (1913–14)

- Led CIHU in goals in 1905–06 (15); led NHA in goals in 1910–11 (35); led Stanley Cup playoffs in goals in 1910–11 (13)

> "One of the best hockey players Kingston ever produced and a player who was a distinct credit to the game. He … was admired for his straightforward, upright qualities as well as for his great skill as a player."
> — *The Toronto Daily Star*, March 29, 1915.

REGULAR SEASON

Season	Age	Team	Lg	GP	G	A	PTS	PIM
1902–03	18	Queen's University	CIHU					
1903–04	19	Queen's University	CIHU	4	9	0	9	30
1903–04	19	Kingston A.C.	OHA-Int.					
1904–05	20	Queen's University	CIHU	4	9	0	9	15
1905–06	21	Queen's University	CIHU	4	15	0	15	12
1906–07	22	Canadian Soo	IHL	7	4	5	9	0
1907–08	23	Ottawa Senators	ECAHA	9	27	0	27	30
1908–09	24	Ottawa Senators	ECHA	12	42	0	42	41
1909–10	25	Ottawa Senators	CHA	2	9	0	9	18
1909–10	25	Ottawa Senators	NHA	11	19	0	19	44
1910–11	26	Ottawa Senators	NHA	16	35	0	35	51
1911–12	27	Ottawa Senators	NHA	12	9	0	9	0
Career — 10 Seasons				81	178	5	183	249

PLAYOFFS

Season	Age	Team	Lg	GP	G	A	PTS	PIM
1905–06	21	Queen's University	St-Cup	2	4	0	4	3
1909–10	25	Ottawa Senators	St-Cup	4	8	0	8	12
1910–11	26	Ottawa Senators	St-Cup	2	13	0	13	0
Career — 3 Seasons				8	25	0	25	15

TROPHY CASE

AWARDS

Stanley Cup (1908–09, 1909–10, 1910–11)

Harry E. Watson

HOCKEY HALL OF FAME CLASS: 1962

Left Wing

Shoots: Left

Height: Unknown

Weight: 165 lbs.

Born: July 14, 1898: St. John's, Newfoundland

Died: September 11, 1957: Toronto, Ontario

Played 13 elite amateur seasons from 1916–17, 1918–28, 1929–30, 1931–32

QUICK FACTS

- Played amateur hockey with Whitby Athletics (1913–14); Toronto St. Andrews (1914–15); Toronto Aura Lee (1915–17)
- OHA-Jr. First All-Star Team Left Wing (1915)
- Led OHA-Sr. in goals in 1916–17 (18) and 1922–23 (21)
- Named OHA-Sr. Most Valuable Player (1922, 1923)
- OHA-Sr. First All-Star Team Left Wing (1922, 1923); OHA-Sr. Second All-Star Team Left Wing (1920)
- Led OHA-Sr. playoffs in goals in 1921–22 (5), 1922–23 (3)
- Member of Allan Cup-winning Toronto Granites (1922, 1923); led Allan Cup playoffs in goals (11) and points (15) in 1922–23
- Led Winter Olympics in goals (36) and points (50) in 1924
- Served as a fighter pilot with the Royal Flying Corps during World War I
- Member of OHA-Sr. champion Toronto Granites (1919–20, 1921–22, 1922–23)
- Turned down offer of $30,000 to turn professional and play with the NHL's Montreal Maroons in 1925
- Coached Toronto National "Sea Fleas" (1930–32); coached Toronto City Hall (1931–32)
- Guided the Toronto National "Sea Fleas" to the Allan Cup championship in 1932 but retired before the team earned a silver medal at the 1933 World Championships

> Savoie, the Swiss goalkeeper, was peppered with bullet-like shots throughout the three periods today. On coming off the ice he said with a grim smile he would about as soon face a machine gun as a hot one off Watson, Munro or McCaffrey.
> — *Toronto Daily Star*, January 30, 1924, on Canada's 33–0 Olympic victory over Switzerland in which Watson scored 12 goals

REGULAR SEASON

Season	Age	Team	Lg	GP	G	A	PTS	PIM
1916–17	18	Toronto Aura Lee	OHA-Sr.	8	18	0	18	
1918–19	20	Toronto Dentals	OHA-Sr.					
1919–20	21	Toronto Granites	OHA-Sr.	8	17	4	21	
1920–21	22	Toronto Granites	OHA-Sr.	9	10	4	14	
1921–22	23	Toronto Granites	OHA-St.	10	18	4	22	
1922–23	24	Toronto Granites	OHA-Sr.	12	21	4	25	
1923–24	25	Canada	Exhib.	14	24	6	30	
1923–24	25	Canada	Olympics	5	36	14	50	2
1924–25	26	Parkdale Canoe Club	OHA-Sr.	6	6	2	8	
1925–26	27	Parkdale Canoe Club	OHA-Sr.	1	1	1	2	
1926–27	28	Parkdale Canoe Club	OHA-Sr.	1	2	0	2	
1927–28	29	Toronto Marlboros	OHA-Sr.	2	1	1	2	2
1929–30	31	Toronto Nationals	OHA-Sr.	1	0	0	0	0
1931–32	33	Toronto Nationals	OHA-Sr.	2	0	0	0	0
Career – 13 Seasons				79	154	40	194	4

PLAYOFFS

Season	Age	Team	Lg	GP	G	A	PTS	PIM
1918–19	20	Toronto Dentals	OHA-Sr.	1	1	0	1	
1919–20	21	Toronto Granites	Al-Cup	2	1	0	1	
1919–20	21	Toronto Granites	OHA-Sr.	5	4	1	5	
1920–21	22	Toronto Granites	OHA-Sr.	2	2	0	2	
1921–22	23	Toronto Granites	Al-Cup	5	13	2	15	
1921–22	23	Toronto Granites	OHA-Sr.	2	5	0	5	
1922–23	24	Toronto Granites	Al-Cup	6	11	4	15	2
1922–23	24	Toronto Granites	OHA-Sr.	2	3	0	3	0
1925–26	27	Parkdale Canoe Club	OHA-Sr.	2	0	0	0	
Career – 6 Seasons				27	40	7	47	2

TROPHY CASE

INTERNATIONAL AWARDS

Gold Medal: Winter Olympics (1924)

4

Harry Percival Watson

HOCKEY HALL OF FAME CLASS: 1994

Alternates:
5, 17, 18, 19

Left Wing

Shoots: Left

Height: 6'-1"

Weight: 207 lbs.
Born: May 6, 1923
in Saskatoon,
Saskatchewan

Died: November
19, 2002:
Toronto, Ontario

Played 14 NHL
seasons from
1941–43, 1945–57

QUICK FACTS

"He was a larger man than many players of our era, very strong, and a solid bodychecker. He was a clean player who did not have to resort to fouls because of his skill level."

— Bill Ezinicki, Watson's teammate with the Maple Leafs from 1946–50

- Played amateur hockey with Saskatoon Wesleys (1934–38); Saskatoon Chiefs (1938–40); Saskatoon Dodgers (1939–40); Saskatoon Quakers (1940–41)

- Signed as a free agent by Brooklyn Americans, October 10, 1941

- Made NHL debut in 1–0 loss to Chicago Black Hawks, November 6, 1941

- Played with Montreal RCAF, Saskatoon Navy and Winnipeg RCAF during World War II

- Rights transferred to Detroit from Brooklyn in Special Dispersal Draft October 9, 1942; traded to Toronto by Detroit for Billy Taylor, September 21, 1946

- Assisted on Bill Barilko's Stanley Cup-winning goal in Game Five of the 1951 Stanley Cup Finals against Montreal goaltender Gerry McNeil, April 2, 1951

- Finished second in NHL goals in 1948–49 (26)

- Scored Stanley Cup-winning goal in Toronto's 7–2 victory over Detroit Red Wings, April 14, 1948

- Played the entire 1948–49 season without registering a single minute in penalties and received only 150 minutes in penalties in 809 NHL games

- Traded to Chicago by Toronto for cash, December 10, 1954

- Nicknamed "Whipper" because of his resemblance to famous wrestler "Whipper" Billy Watson

- Played in NHL All-Star Game (1947, 1948, 1949, 1951, 1952, 1953, 1955)

TROPHY CASE

AWARDS

Stanley Cup (1942–43, 1946–47, 1947–48, 1948–49, 1950–51)

REGULAR SEASON

Season	Age	Team	Lg	GP	G	A	PTS	PIM
1941–42	18	Brooklyn Americans	NHL	47	10	8	18	6
1942–43	19	Detroit Red Wings	NHL	50	13	18	31	10
1945–46	22	Detroit Red Wings	NHL	44	14	10	24	4
1946–47	23	Detroit Red Wings	NHL	44	19	15	34	10
1947–48	24	Toronto Maple Leafs	NHL	57	21	20	41	16
1948–49	25	Toronto Maple Leafs	NHL	60	26	19	45	0
1949–50	26	Toronto Maple Leafs	NHL	60	19	16	35	11
1950–51	27	Toronto Maple Leafs	NHL	68	18	19	37	18
1951–52	28	Toronto Maple Leafs	NHL	70	22	17	39	18
1952–53	29	Toronto Maple Leafs	NHL	63	16	8	24	8
1953–54	30	Toronto Maple Leafs	NHL	70	21	7	28	30
1954–55	31	Toronto Maple Leafs	NHL	8	1	1	2	0
1954–55	31	Chicago Black Hawks	NHL	43	14	16	30	4
1955–56	32	Chicago Black Hawks	NHL	55	11	14	25	6
1956–57	33	Chicago Black Hawks	NHL	70	11	19	30	9
NHL Career — 14 Seasons				809	236	217	443	150

PLAYOFFS

Season	Age	Team	Lg	GP	G	A	PTS	PIM
1942–43	19	Detroit Red Wings	NHL	7	0	0	0	0
1945–46	22	Detroit Red Wings	NHL	5	2	0	2	0
1946–47	23	Toronto Maple Leafs	NHL	11	3	2	5	6
1947–48	24	Toronto Maple Leafs	NHL	9	5	2	7	9
1948–49	25	Toronto Maple Leafs	NHL	9	4	2	6	2
1949–50	26	Toronto Maple Leafs	NHL	7	0	0	0	2
1950–51	27	Toronto Maple Leafs	NHL	5	1	2	3	4
1951–52	28	Toronto Maple Leafs	NHL	4	1	0	1	2
1953–54	30	Toronto Maple Leafs	NHL	5	0	1	1	2
NHL Career — 9 Seasons				62	16	9	25	27

Cooney Weiland

HOCKEY HALL OF FAME CLASS: 1971

Alternate: 14

Center

Shoots: Left

Height: 5'-7"

Weight: 150 lbs.

Born: November 5, 1904; Edmondville, Ontario

Died: July 3, 1985; Boston, Massachusetts

Played 11 NHL seasons from 1928–39

QUICK FACTS

- Held NHL record for points (73) in regular season (1929–30). Record tied by Doug Bentley in 1942–43 and surpassed by Herb Cain (82) in 1943–44

- Played amateur hockey with Seaforth Highlanders (1918–22); Owen Sound Greys (1922–24); Minneapolis Rockets (1924–25)

- Led OHA-Jr. in goals (33) and points (38) in 1923–24

- Member of the Memorial Cup-winning Owen Sound Greys (1924); led Memorial Cup playoffs in goals (37) and points (46) in 1923–24

- Led AHA in goals (21) in 1927–28; led AHA playoffs in goals (4) and points (5) in 1926–27; led AHA playoffs in assists (2) and points (4) in 1927–28

- Signed as a free agent by Minneapolis Millers (AHA), November 1, 1926

- Traded to Boston by Minneapolis (AHA) for cash, December 23, 1927; traded to Ottawa by Boston for Joe Lamb and $7,000, July 25, 1932; traded to Detroit by Ottawa for Carl Voss and cash, November 26, 1933; traded to Boston by Detroit with Walt Buswell for Marty Barry and Art Giroux, June 30, 1938

- Led NHL in goals (43) and points (73) in 1929–30

- Finished among NHL top-5 in goals in 1929–30 (43) and 1930–31 (25)

- Coached Boston Bruins (1939–41), Hershey Bears (1941–45) and New Haven Nighthawks (1945–46)

- AHL First All-Star Team Coach (1943)

> I definitely believe there is a place for bodychecking in the game of hockey, but I'd just like to see it out in the open. So long as a player is checked in the open, he has room to elude his opponent."

REGULAR SEASON

Season	Age	Team	Lg	GP	G	A	PTS	PIM
1928–29	24	Boston Bruins	NHL	42	11	7	18	16
1929–30	25	Boston Bruins	NHL	44	43	30	73	27
1930–31	26	Boston Bruins	NHL	44	25	13	38	14
1931–32	27	Boston Bruins	NHL	46	14	12	26	20
1932–33	28	Ottawa Senators	NHL	48	16	11	27	4
1933–34	29	Ottawa Senators	NHL	9	2	0	2	4
1933–34	29	Detroit Red Wings	NHL	39	11	19	30	6
1934–35	30	Detroit Red Wings	NHL	48	13	25	38	10
1935–36	31	Boston Bruins	NHL	48	14	13	27	15
1936–37	32	Boston Bruins	NHL	48	6	9	15	6
1937–38	33	Boston Bruins	NHL	48	11	12	23	16
1938–39	34	Boston Bruins	NHL	45	7	9	16	9
NHL Career — 11 Seasons				509	173	160	333	147

PLAYOFFS

Season	Age	Team	Lg	GP	G	A	PTS	PIM
1928–29	24	Boston Bruins	NHL	5	2	0	2	2
1929–30	25	Boston Bruins	NHL	6	1	5	6	2
1930–31	26	Boston Bruins	NHL	5	6	3	9	2
1933–34	29	Detroit Red Wings	NHL	9	2	2	4	4
1935–36	31	Boston Bruins	NHL	2	1	0	1	2
1936–37	32	Boston Bruins	NHL	3	0	0	0	0
1937–38	33	Boston Bruins	NHL	3	0	0	0	0
1938–39	34	Boston Bruins	NHL	12	0	0	0	0
NHL Career — 8 Seasons				45	12	10	22	12

TROPHY CASE

AWARDS

NHL Scoring Leader (1930)

Stanley Cup (1928–29, 1938–39)

Lester Patrick Trophy (1972)

ALL-STAR SELECTIONS

Second All-Star Team Center (1935)

First All-Star Team Coach (1941)

Harry Westwick

Rover

Shoots: Unknown

Height: Unknown

Weight: Unknown

Born: April 22, 1876: Ottawa, Ontario

Died: April 3, 1957: Ottawa, Ontario

Played 14 elite amateur and professional seasons from 1894–98, 1899–1909

QUICK FACTS

- Earned nickname "Rat" because of his small stature, aggressive nature and elusive style
- Member of World Lacrosse Champion Ottawa Capitals (1900)
- Began career as a goaltender before switching to rover and averaged a goal a game over the course of his career
- FAHL Second Team All-Star Rover (1905)
- Recorded career-best 24 goals in 13 regular-season and Stanley Cup challenge games during 1904–05 season
- Member of Stanley Cup-winning Ottawa "Silver Seven" (1902–03, 1903–04, 1904–05, 1905–06)

- Helped Ottawa capture Stanley Cup title for three straight seasons from 1902–03 to 1904–05 and defend it successfully in two challenges during the 1905–06 season
- Signed as a free agent by Kenora Thistles, March 1, 1907
- Member of Stanley Cup-winning Kenora Thistles team that defeated Brandon 8–6 and 6–1 in best-of-three challenge series, March 17–18, 1907
- Inducted into Ottawa Sports Hall of Fame (1968)

> "No one was killed, but there was hardly one of the 14 players at the end of the match who couldn't show some bruise or cut."
> — Harry Westwick, recalling a particularly rough game between Ottawa's "Silver Seven" and the Montreal Wanderers

REGULAR SEASON

Season	Age	Team	Lg	GP	G	A	PTS	PIM
1894–95	18	Ottawa Hockey Club	AHAC	5	1	0	1	
1895–96	19	Ottawa Hockey Club	AHAC	8	8	0	8	
1896–97	20	Ottawa Hockey Club	AHAC	8	6	0	6	
1897–98	21	Ottawa Hockey Club	AHAC	5	1	0	1	
1899–00	23	Ottawa Capitals	OHA-Sr.					
1900–01	24	Ottawa Hockey Club	CAHL	7	6	0	6	
1901–02	25	Ottawa Hockey Club	CAHL	8	11	0	11	6
1902–03	26	Ottawa Silver Seven	CAHL	6	6	0	6	9
1903–04	27	Ottawa Silver Seven	CAHL	2	5	0	5	0
1904–05	28	Ottawa Silver Seven	FAHL	8	15	0	15	9
1905–06	29	Ottawa Silver Seven	ECAHA	8	6	0	6	15
1906–07	30	Ottawa Senators	ECAHA	9	14	0	14	12
1906–07	30	Kenora Thistles	MHL-Pro	1	0	0	0	0
1907–08	31	Ottawa Senators	ECAHA	10	10	0	10	20
1908–09	32	Ottawa Senators	ECHA	6	3	0	3	8
Career — 14 Seasons				91	92	0	92	79

PLAYOFFS

Season	Age	Team	Lg	GP	G	A	PTS	PIM
1902–03	26	Ottawa Silver Seven	CAHL	1	0	0	0	0
1903–04	27	Ottawa Silver Seven	St-Cup	8	6	0	6	6
1904–05	28	Ottawa Silver Seven	St-Cup	5	9	0	9	3
1905–06	29	Ottawa Silver Seven	ECAHA	2	1	0	1	0
1905–06	29	Ottawa Silver Seven	St-Cup	4	7	0	7	9
1906–07	30	Kenora Thistles	MHL-Pro	2	2	0	2	6
1906–07	30	Kenora Thistles	St-Cup	2	0	0	0	6
Career — 5 Seasons				24	25	0	25	30

TROPHY CASE

AWARDS

Stanley Cup (1902–03, 1903–04, 1904–05, 1905–06, 1906–07)

Fred Whitcroft

HOCKEY HALL OF FAME CLASS: 1962

Rover

Shoots: Right

Height: 5'-10"

Weight: 165 lbs.

Born: December 20, 1882: Port Perry, Ontario

Died: August 9, 1931: Edmonton, Alberta

Played eight elite amateur and professional seasons from 1902–10

QUICK FACTS

- Played amateur hockey with Peterborough Jr. Colts (1899–1902); Midland HC (1904–05); Peterborough Colts (1902–04, 1905–07)

- Member of Ontario Hockey Association Junior champion Peterborough Jr. Colts (1901)

- Served as captain of OHA Intermediate champion Peterborough Colts (1906)

- Signed as a free agent by Kenora Thistles, February 1, 1907

- Led MHL-Pro League playoffs in goals (5) in 1906–07

- Member of Stanley Cup-winning Kenora Thistles team that defeated Brandon 8–6 and 6–1 to retain Stanley Cup title, March 17–18, 1907

- Signed as a free agent by Edmonton, December 22, 1907

- Led Alberta Pro League in goals (35), assists (7) and points (42) in 1907–08

- APHL First All-Star Team Rover (1908)

- Led Edmonton to unsuccessful Stanley Cup challenges in December of 1908 versus the Montreal Wanderers and January of 1910 versus Ottawa Senators

- Played with future Hall of Fame members Frank and Lester Patrick, Cyclone Taylor and Newsy Lalonde in Renfrew

- Returned to Edmonton in 1910 to coach, operate local arena and scout for Lester and Frank Patrick in the Pacific Coast Hockey Association

> Whitcroft, on top of having to manage the team, played up to the top of his form.... His reputation had suffered some [but] he made a new name for himself.... His handling of the team on the ice and his own individual work as a member of the team, places him in the front rank of hockey players anywhere."
> — *Edmonton Bulletin*, January 12, 1909

REGULAR SEASON

Season	Age	Team	Lg	GP	G	A	PTS	PIM
1902–03	20	Peterborough Colts	OHA-Int.					
1903–04	21	Peterborough Colts	OHA-Int.					
1904–05	22	Midland Hockey Club	OHA-Int.					
1905–06	23	Peterborough Colts	OHA-Int.					
1906–07	24	Peterborough Colts	OHA-Int.	5	13	0	13	33
1906–07	24	Kenora Thistles	MHL-Pro	4	3	0	3	
1907–08	25	Edmonton Professionals	APHL	10	35	7	42	12
1908–09	26	Edmonton Professionals	Exhib.	10	27	0	27	12
1909–10	27	Renfrew Hockey Club	NHA	5	3	0	3	13
Career — 8 Seasons				34	81	7	88	70

PLAYOFFS

Season	Age	Team	Lg	GP	G	A	PTS	PIM
1906–07	24	Kenora Thistles	MHL-Pro	2	5	0	5	0
1906–07	24	Kenora Thistles	St-Cup	2	2	0	2	3
1907–08	25	Edmonton Professionals	APHL	8	24	7	31	12
1908–09	26	Edmonton Professionals	Exhib.	7	19	0	19	14
1908–09	27	Edmonton Professionals	St-Cup	2	2	0	2	18
1909–10	28	Edmonton Professionals	St-Cup	2	5	0	5	2
Career — 4 Seasons				23	57	7	64	49

TROPHY CASE

AWARDS

Stanley Cup (1906–07)

Phat Wilson

HOCKEY HALL OF FAME CLASS: 1962

Defense

Shoots: Left

Height: Unknown

Weight: Unknown

Born: December 29, 1895: Port Arthur, Ontario

Died: July 26, 1970: Thunder Bay, Ontario

Played 16 elite amateur seasons from 1915–17, 1918–32

QUICK FACTS

- Renowned for his skills as a baseball player in his youth and became a top baseball organizer in the Port Arthur (Thunder Bay) area

- Didn't learn to skate until he joined a local church league team in 1914

- Played amateur hockey throughout his career despite several offers to turn professional

- Considered one of the greatest amateur players of all time and one of the finest defensemen of his era

- Inducted into Northwestern Ontario Sports Hall of Fame (1982)

- Led MTBHL in assists (9) in 1928–29; led TSBHL in assists in 1929–30 (8); led TSBHL in assists (8) and points (17) in 1930–31

- Member of Allan Cup-winning Port Arthur Hockey Club (1925, 1926, 1929)

- Coached Port Arthur Ports (1932–42)

- Served as coach and General Manager of numerous Port Arthur senior teams in the 1930s and 40s and was a co-founder of a local girls hockey league

"A brilliant defenseman remembered for his rink-long rushes, he won several scoring titles throughout his career ... Given the fact that he was 30 years of age when he captained the Seniors to their first Allan Cup title in 1926, his accomplishments on the ice were that much more impressive."
— Northwestern Ontario Sports Hall of Fame

REGULAR SEASON

Season	Age	Team	Lg	GP	G	A	PTS	PIM
1915–16	20	Port Arthur Shuniahs	TBSHL	8	2	0	2	23
1916–17	21	Port Arthur 141st Battalion	TBSHL	1	0	0	0	0
1918–19	23	Port Arthur Columbus Club	TBSHL	13	8	2	10	42
1919–20	24	Port Arthur War Vets	TBSHL	11	9	0	9	10
1920–21	25	Port Arthur Hockey Club	TBSHL	15	11	5	16	
1921–22	26	Iroquois Falls Flyers	NOHA					
1922–23	27	Port Arthur Hockey Club	MHL-Sr.	16	5	6	11	32
1923–24	28	Port Arthur Hockey Club	MHL-Sr.	15	6	5	11	19
1924–25	29	Port Arthur Hockey Club	MHL-Sr.	19	7	1	8	
1925–26	30	Port Arthur Hockey Club	TBSHL	19	8	5	13	22
1926–27	31	Port Arthur Ports	TBSHL	20	11	5	16	24
1927–28	32	Port Arthur Ports	MTBHL	17	7	6	13	19
1928–29	33	Port Arthur Hockey Club	MTBHL	20	12	9	21	25
1929–30	34	Port Arthur Hockey Club	TBSHL	19	9	8	17	22
1930–31	35	Port Arthur Hockey Club	TBSHL	21	9	8	17	32
1931–32	36	Port Arthur Ports	TBSHL	15	5	2	7	26
Career — 16 Seasons				229	109	62	171	296

PLAYOFFS

Season	Age	Team	Lg	GP	G	A	PTS	PIM
1918–19	23	Port Arthur Columbus Club	Al-Cup	1	0	0	0	0
1920–21	25	Port Arthur Hockey Club	TBSHL	2	1	0	1	5
1920–21	25	Port Arthur Hockey Club	Al-Cup	4	4	1	5	0
1922–23	27	Port Arthur Hockey Club	MHL-Sr.	2	0	0	0	2
1923–24	28	Port Arthur Hockey Club	MHL-Sr.	2	1	1	2	4
1924–25	29	Port Arthur Hockey Club	MHL-Sr.	10	9	3	12	24
1924–25	29	Port Arthur Hockey Club	Al-Cup	6	0	2	2	18
1925–26	30	Port Arthur Hockey Club	TBSHL	3	0	0	0	10
1925–26	30	Port Arthur Hockey Club	Al-Cup	8	0	2	2	18
1926–27	31	Port Arthur Ports	TBSHL	2	0	0	0	4
1928–29	33	Port Arthur Hockey Club	MTBHL	2	0	0	0	6
1928–29	33	Port Arthur Hockey Club	Al-Cup	7	3	1	4	20
1929–30	34	Port Arthur Hockey Club	TBSHL	4	4	1	5	11
1929–30	34	Port Arthur Hockey Club	Al-Cup	6	1	1	2	7
1930–31	35	Port Arthur Hockey Club	TBSHL	2	0	0	0	2
1931–32	36	Port Arthur Ports	TBSHL	2	1	1	2	10
Career — 11 Seasons				61	24	13	37	141

TROPHY CASE

Gump Worsley

HOCKEY HALL OF FAME CLASS: 1980

Alternate: 30

Goaltender

Catches: Left

Height: 5'-7"

Weight: 180 lbs.

Born: May 14, 1929: Montreal, Quebec

Died: January 26, 2007: St-Hyacinthe, Quebec

Played 21 NHL seasons from 1952–53, 1954–74

QUICK FACTS

> The only job worse [than goaltending] is javelin catcher at a track-and-field meet."

- Nicknamed "Gump" as a youngster because his hair "style" was similar to comic book character Andy Gump

- Played amateur hockey with Verdun Cyclones (1946–49); N.Y. Rovers (1948–50)

- QJHL Second All-Star Team Goaltender (1949)

- Led EAHL in shutouts (7) in 1949–50; led EAHL in playoff wins (8), shutouts (1) and goals-against-average (2.25)

- EAHL First All-Star Team Goaltender (1950); USHL First All-Star Team Goaltender (1951); WHL First All-Star Team Goaltender (1954)

- PCHL Second All-Star Team Goaltender (1952); AHL Second All-Star Team Goaltender (1964)

- Played minor pro with New Haven Ramblers (1949–50); St. Paul Saints (1950–51); Saskatoon Quakers (1951–1953); Edmonton Flyers (1952–53); Vancouver Canucks (1953–54); Quebec Aces (1963–65)

- Led USHL in shutouts (3) and goals-against-average (2.82) in 1950–51; led WHL in wins (39) and goals-against-average (2.40) in 1953–54

- Named USHL Rookie of the Year (1951)

- Named USHL Top Goaltender (1951); named WHL Top Goaltender (1954); named WHL MVP (1954)

- Led NHL in goals-against-average (1.98) in 1967–68; finished second in NHL shutouts (6) in 1967–68

- Last Hall of Fame goaltender to play in the NHL without wearing a mask

REGULAR SEASON

Season	Age	Team	Lg	GP	W	L	T	SO	GA	GAA	G	A	PTS	PIM
1952–53	23	New York Rangers	NHL	50	13	29	8	2	153	3.06	0	0	0	2
1954–55	25	New York Rangers	NHL	65	15	33	17	4	197	3.03	0	0	0	2
1955–56	26	New York Rangers	NHL	70	32	28	10	4	198	2.83	0	0	0	2
1956–57	27	New York Rangers	NHL	68	26	28	14	3	216	3.18	0	0	0	19
1957–58	28	New York Rangers	NHL	37	21	10	6	4	86	2.32	0	0	0	10
1958–59	29	New York Rangers	NHL	67	26	30	11	2	198	2.97	0	0	0	10
1959–60	30	New York Rangers	NHL	39	7	23	8	0	135	3.52	0	0	0	12
1960–61	31	New York Rangers	NHL	59	20	29	8	1	190	3.28	0	0	0	12
1961–62	32	New York Rangers	NHL	60	22	27	9	2	172	2.92	0	0	0	12
1962–63	33	New York Rangers	NHL	67	22	34	10	2	217	3.27	0	0	0	14
1963–64	34	Montreal Canadiens	NHL	8	3	2	2	1	22	2.97	0	0	0	0
1964–65	35	Montreal Canadiens	NHL	19	10	7	1	1	50	2.94	0	0	0	0
1965–66	36	Montreal Canadiens	NHL	51	29	14	6	2	114	2.36	0	1	1	4
1966–67	37	Montreal Canadiens	NHL	18	9	6	2	1	47	3.18	0	0	0	4
1967–68	38	Montreal Canadiens	NHL	40	19	9	8	6	73	1.98	0	0	0	10
1968–69	39	Montreal Canadiens	NHL	30	19	5	4	5	64	2.25	0	0	0	0
1969–70	40	Montreal Canadiens	NHL	6	3	1	2	0	14	2.33	0	0	0	0
1969–70	40	Minnesota North Stars	NHL	8	5	1	1	1	20	2.65	0	0	0	0
1970–71	41	Minnesota North Stars	NHL	24	4	10	8	0	57	2.50	0	0	0	10
1971–72	42	Minnesota North Stars	NHL	34	16	10	7	2	68	2.12	0	1	1	2
1972–73	43	Minnesota North Stars	NHL	12	6	2	3	0	30	2.88	0	1	1	22
1973–74	44	Minnesota North Stars	NHL	29	8	14	5	0	86	3.22	0	0	0	0
NHL Career — 21 Seasons				861	335	352	150	43	2407	2.88	0	3	3	145

Season	Age	Team	Lg	GP	W	L	T	SO	GA	GAA	G	A	PTS	PIM
1955–56	26	New York Rangers	NHL	3	0	3		0	14	4.67	0	0	0	2
1956–57	27	New York Rangers	NHL	5	1	4		0	21	3.99	0	0	0	0
1957–58	28	New York Rangers	NHL	6	2	4		0	28	4.60	0	0	0	0
1961–62	32	New York Rangers	NHL	6	2	4		0	21	3.28	0	0	0	0
1964–65	35	Montreal Canadiens	NHL	8	5	3		2	14	1.68	0	0	0	0
1965–66	36	Montreal Canadiens	NHL	10	8	2		1	20	1.99	0	0	0	0
1966–67	37	Montreal Canadiens	NHL	2	0	1		0	2	1.50	0	0	0	0
1967–68	38	Montreal Canadiens	NHL	12	11	0		1	21	1.88	0	0	0	10
1968–69	39	Montreal Canadiens	NHL	7	5	1		0	14	2.27	0	0	0	5
1969–70	40	Minnesota North Stars	NHL	3	1	2		0	14	4.67	0	0	0	0
1970–71	41	Minnesota North Stars	NHL	4	3	1		0	13	3.25	0	0	0	0
1971–72	42	Minnesota North Stars	NHL	4	2	1		1	7	2.16	0	0	0	0
NHL Career — 12 Seasons				70	40	26		5	189	2.78	0	0	0	17

TROPHY CASE

AWARDS

Calder Memorial Trophy (1953)

Vezina Trophy (1966, 1968)

Stanley Cup (1964–65, 1965–66, 1967–68, 1968–69)

ALL-STAR SELECTIONS

First All-Star Team Goaltender (1968)

Second All-Star Team Goaltender (1966)

Roy Worters

HOCKEY HALL OF FAME CLASS: 1969

1

Goaltender

Catches: Left

Height: 5'-3"

Weight: 135 lbs.

Born: October 19, 1900: Toronto, Ontario

Died: November 7, 1957: Toronto, Ontario

Played 12 NHL seasons from 1925–37

QUICK FACTS

- Nicknamed "Shrimp" because of his diminutive (5'-3") height. He was the shortest goaltender to ever play in the NHL

- Played amateur hockey with Parkdale Canoe Club Paddlers (1918–20); Porcupine Miners (1920–22); Toronto Argonauts (1922–23); Pittsburgh Yellow Jackets (1923–25)

- Member of Memorial Cup-winning Parkdale Canoe Club Paddlers that defeated the Selkirk Fishermen 13–3 in a two-game, total-goal series (1920)

- Led USAHA in wins (15), shutouts (7) and goals-against-average (1.23) in 1923–24; led USAHA in playoff wins (9), shutouts (5) and goals-against-average (0.86) in 1924

- Led USAHA in wins (25), shutouts (17) and goals-against-average (0.81) in 1924–25; led USAHA playoffs in wins (6) and goals-against-average (1.20) in 1925

- Member of the two-time USAHA champion Pittsburgh Yellow Jackets team that defeated Boston AA in 1924 and the Fort Pitt Pirates in 1925

- Signed as a free agent by Pittsburgh Pirates, September 26, 1925

- Traded to N.Y. Americans by Pittsburgh for Joe Miller and $20,000, November 1, 1928

- Led NHL in goals-against-average in 1930–31 (1.61)

- First goaltender to win the Hart Trophy (1929) as the league's most valuable player

- Stopped 70 shots in 3–1 loss to the New York Americans on December 26, 1926. The Pirates and Americans combined for 141 shots in the game, which is still a NHL record

> He was called the Mighty Mite and I think he was the first goalie to adopt the style of steering the puck into the corners [with his blocker]."
> — Toe Blake

REGULAR SEASON

Season	Age	Team	Lg	GP	W	L	T	SO	GA	GAA	G	A	PTS	PIM
1925–26	25	Pittsburgh Pirates	NHL	35	18	16	1	7	68	1.90	0	0	0	0
1926–27	26	Pittsburgh Pirates	NHL	44	15	26	3	4	108	2.39	0	0	0	0
1927–28	27	Pittsburgh Pirates	NHL	44	19	17	8	11	76	1.66	0	0	0	0
1928–29	28	New York Americans	NHL	38	16	12	10	13	46	1.15	0	0	0	0
1929–30	29	New York Americans	NHL	36	11	21	4	2	135	3.57	0	0	0	0
1929–30	29	Montreal Canadiens	NHL	1	1	0	0	0	2	2.00	0	0	0	0
1930–31	30	New York Americans	NHL	44	18	16	10	8	74	1.61	0	0	0	0
1931–32	31	New York Americans	NHL	40	12	20	8	5	110	2.68	0	0	0	0
1932–33	32	New York Americans	NHL	47	15	22	10	5	116	2.34	0	0	0	0
1933–34	33	New York Americans	NHL	36	12	13	10	4	75	2.01	0	0	0	0
1934–35	34	New York Americans	NHL	48	12	27	9	3	142	2.84	0	0	0	0
1935–36	35	New York Americans	NHL	48	16	25	7	3	122	2.44	0	0	0	0
1936–37	36	New York Americans	NHL	23	6	14	3	2	69	2.90	0	0	0	0
NHL Career – 12 Seasons				484	171	229	83	67	1143	2.36	0	0	0	0

PLAYOFFS

Season	Age	Team	Lg	GP	W	L	T	SO	GA	GAA	G	A	PTS	PIM
1925–26	25	Pittsburgh Pirates	NHL	2	0	1	1	1	6	3.00	0	0	0	0
1927–28	27	Pittsburgh Pirates	NHL	2	1	1	0	0	6	3.00	0	0	0	0
1928–29	28	New York Americans	NHL	2	0	1	1	1	1	0.40	0	0	0	0
1925–36	35	New York Americans	NHL	5	2	3	0	2	11	2.20	0	0	0	0
NHL Career – 4 Seasons				11	3	6	2	3	24	2.09	0	0	0	0

TROPHY CASE

AWARDS

Hart Memorial Trophy (1929)

Vezina Trophy (1931)

ALL-STAR SELECTIONS

Second All-Star Team Goaltender (1932, 1934)

19

Center

Shoots: Right

Height: 5'-11"

Weight: 185 lbs.

Born: May 9, 1965: Cranbrook, British Columbia

Drafted by the Detroit Red Wings fourth overall in 1983

Played 22 NHL seasons from 1983–2004, 2005–06

" When you're on the ice, you have very little time, you see very little, and everything happens really quick."

Steve Yzerman
HOCKEY HALL OF FAME CLASS: 2009

QUICK FACTS

- Played amateur hockey with Nepean Raiders (1980–81); Peterborough Petes (1981–83)
- Led CJHL in assists (54) in 1980–81
- One of only four players (with Alex Delvecchio, Stan Mikita and Mike Modano) to play at least 20 seasons with only one organization
- Holds Detroit Red Wings team records for goals (65), assists (90) and points (155) in regular season, established in 1988–89; holds Detroit Red Wings team record for points by a rookie in the regular season (87), established in 1983–84
- Ranks third in NHL career short-handed goals (50); ranks sixth in NHL career points (1,755)
- Ranks seventh in NHL career assists (1,063); ranks eighth in NHL career goals (692)
- Led NHL in short-handed goals in 1989–90 (7), 1991–92 (8) and 1992–93 (7)
- Led NHL in shots-on-goal (388) in 1988–89; led NHL in even-strength goals (45) in 1988–89
- Served as captain of Detroit Red Wings (1986–2006)

Yzerman's battle-worn helmet.

REGULAR SEASON

Season	Age	Team	Lg	GP	G	A	PTS	+/-	PIM	ESG	PPG	SHG	GWG	SOG	S%
1983–84	18	Detroit Red Wings	NHL	80	39	48	87	-17	33	26	13	0	2	177	22.0
1984–85	19	Detroit Red Wings	NHL	80	30	59	89	-17	58	21	9	0	3	231	13.0
1985–86	20	Detroit Red Wings	NHL	51	14	28	42	-24	16	11	3	0	3	132	10.6
1986–87	21	Detroit Red Wings	NHL	80	31	59	90	-1	43	21	9	1	2	217	14.3
1987–88	22	Detroit Red Wings	NHL	64	50	52	102	30	44	34	10	6	6	242	20.7
1988–89	23	Detroit Red Wings	NHL	80	65	90	155	17	61	45	17	3	7	388	16.8
1989–90	24	Detroit Red Wings	NHL	79	62	65	127	-6	79	39	16	7	8	332	18.7
1990–91	25	Detroit Red Wings	NHL	80	51	57	108	-2	34	33	12	6	4	326	15.6
1991–92	26	Detroit Red Wings	NHL	79	45	58	103	26	64	28	9	8	9	295	15.3
1992–93	27	Detroit Red Wings	NHL	84	58	79	137	33	44	38	13	7	6	307	18.9
1993–94	28	Detroit Red Wings	NHL	58	24	58	82	11	36	14	7	3	3	217	11.1
1994–95	29	Detroit Red Wings	NHL	47	12	26	38	6	40	8	4	0	1	134	9.0
1995–96	30	Detroit Red Wings	NHL	80	36	59	95	29	64	18	16	2	8	220	16.4
1996–97	31	Detroit Red Wings	NHL	81	22	63	85	22	78	14	8	0	3	232	9.5
1997–98	32	Detroit Red Wings	NHL	75	24	45	69	3	46	16	6	2	0	188	12.8
1998–99	33	Detroit Red Wings	NHL	80	29	45	74	8	42	14	13	2	4	231	12.6
1999–00	34	Detroit Red Wings	NHL	78	35	44	79	28	34	18	15	2	6	234	15.0
2000–01	35	Detroit Red Wings	NHL	54	18	34	52	4	18	13	5	0	7	155	11.6
2001–02	36	Detroit Red Wings	NHL	52	13	35	48	11	10	7	5	1	6	104	12.5
2002–03	37	Detroit Red Wings	NHL	16	2	6	8	6	8	1	1	0	1	13	15.4
2003–04	38	Detroit Red Wings	NHL	75	18	33	51	10	46	11	7	0	3	141	12.8
2005–06	40	Detroit Red Wings	NHL	61	14	20	34	8	18	10	4	0	3	86	16.3
NHL Career – 22 Seasons				1514	692	1063	1755	185	924	440	202	50	94	4602	15.0

PLAYOFFS

Season	Age	Team	Lg	GP	G	A	PTS	+/-	PIM	ESG	PPG	SHG	GWG	SOG	S%
1983–84	18	Detroit Red Wings	NHL	4	3	3	6	1	0	2	1	0	1	9	33.3
1984–85	19	Detroit Red Wings	NHL	3	2	1	3	-5	2	2	0	0	0	11	18.2
1986–87	21	Detroit Red Wings	NHL	16	5	13	18	-2	8	4	1	0	0	41	12.2
1987–88	22	Detroit Red Wings	NHL	3	1	3	4	-3	6	1	0	0	0	12	8.3
1988–89	23	Detroit Red Wings	NHL	6	5	5	10	-7	2	3	2	0	0	35	14.3
1990–91	25	Detroit Red Wings	NHL	7	3	3	6	-1	4	2	1	0	0	27	11.1
1991–92	26	Detroit Red Wings	NHL	11	3	5	8	-3	12	2	0	1	1	48	6.3
1992–93	27	Detroit Red Wings	NHL	7	4	3	7	-4	4	2	1	1	1	24	16.7
1993–94	28	Detroit Red Wings	NHL	3	1	3	4	4	0	1	0	0	0	8	12.5
1994–95	29	Detroit Red Wings	NHL	15	4	8	12	-2	0	2	2	0	1	37	10.8
1995–96	30	Detroit Red Wings	NHL	18	8	12	20	-1	4	4	4	0	1	52	15.4
1996–97	31	Detroit Red Wings	NHL	20	7	6	13	3	4	4	3	0	2	65	10.8
1997–98	32	Detroit Red Wings	NHL	22	6	18	24	10	22	2	3	1	0	65	9.2
1998–99	33	Detroit Red Wings	NHL	10	9	4	13	2	0	5	4	0	2	41	22.0
1999–00	34	Detroit Red Wings	NHL	8	0	4	4	-4	0	0	0	0	0	20	0.0
2000–01	35	Detroit Red Wings	NHL	1	0	0	0	0	0	0	0	0	0	0	0.0
2001–02	36	Detroit Red Wings	NHL	23	6	17	23	4	10	2	4	0	2	52	11.5
2002–03	37	Detroit Red Wings	NHL	4	0	1	1	0	2	0	0	0	0	10	0.0
2003–04	38	Detroit Red Wings	NHL	11	3	2	5	-1	0	3	0	0	1	18	16.7
2005–06	40	Detroit Red Wings	NHL	4	0	4	4	-2	4	0	0	0	0	10	0.0
NHL Career – 20 Seasons				196	70	115	185	-11	84	41	26	3	12	585	12.0

TROPHY CASE

AWARDS

Lester B. Pearson Award (1989)

Conn Smythe Trophy (1998)

Frank J. Selke Trophy (2000)

Bill Masterton Memorial Trophy (2003)

Lester Patrick Trophy (2006)

Stanley Cup (1996–97, 1997–98, 2001–02)

ALL-STAR SELECTIONS

All-Rookie Team (1984)

First All-Star Team Center (2000)

INTERNATIONAL AWARDS

Canada Cup (1984)

Gold Medal: Winter Olympics (2002)

Silver Medal: World Championships (1985)

Silver Medal: World Championships (1989)

NHL Trophies

Team Awards

PRESIDENTS' TROPHY

Presented to the NHL by the Board of Governors for the 1985–86 season, the Presidents' Trophy is awarded annually to the team with the best regular-season record. In the case of a tie, the trophy goes to the team with the most wins.

First Winner: Edmonton Oilers

Most Wins: Detroit Red Wings (6)

CLARENCE S. CAMPBELL BOWL

Introduced by the NHL in 1968 in recognition of the services of Clarence S. Campbell, president of the NHL from 1946 to 1977, the Bowl was originally presented to the regular season champions of the West Division. Beginning in 1975 it was awarded to the regular-season champion of the Campbell Conference, and from 1982–93 the bowl was awarded to the Campbell Conference playoff champion. Since 1993–94 the trophy has been presented to the playoff champion of the Western Conference.

First Winner: Philadelphia Flyers

Most Wins: Edmonton Oilers, Philadelphia Flyers (6)

PRINCE OF WALES TROPHY

The Prince of Wales donated this trophy to the NHL in 1924. From 1927–28 through 1937–38 the award was presented to the winner of the American Division. From 1938–39 to 1966–67 the team with the best regular-season record claimed the trophy. With expansion in 1967–68 the trophy was awarded to the regular season East Division champion. Beginning in 1974–75 the regular season winner of the Prince of Wales Conference claimed the trophy, and from 1981–82 to 1992–93 the playoff champion of the Wales Conference was presented the hardware. Since 1993–94, the trophy has been presented to the playoff champion of the Eastern Conference.

First Winner: Montreal Canadiens

Most Wins: Montreal Canadiens (25)

STANLEY CUP

The most coveted prize in sports, the Stanley Cup is the oldest trophy awarded to professional athletes in North America. The Cup was donated by Lord Stanley of Preston in 1892 to be awarded to "the championship hockey club of the Dominion of Canada." The National Hockey Association took possession of the Stanley Cup in 1910 and it has been awarded to NHL teams exclusively since 1927.

First Winner: Montreal Amateur Athletic Association

Most Wins: Montreal Canadiens (24)

Individual Awards

HART MEMORIAL TROPHY

The Hart Trophy is one of the NHL's longest standing prizes, donated in 1923 by Dr. David Hart, father of Montreal Canadiens coach Cecil Hart. The trophy is presented to the most valuable player of the regular season. Voting is conducted by the Professional Hockey Writers' Association.

First Winner: Frank Nighbor

Most Wins: Wayne Gretzky (9)

TED LINDSAY AWARD

The National Hockey League Players' Association has named a "most outstanding player" since 1970–71. In 1971–72, this distinction was marked with the presentation of the Lester B. Pearson Award, in honor of the Canadian Prime Minister from 1963–67. Carrying on the tradition established by the Pearson Award, the Ted Lindsay Award was created as a replacement in 2010. The award is named in honor of Hall of Famer Ted Lindsay and his role in establishing the original Players' Association. All previous winners are recognized together on the Ted Lindsay Award.

First Winner: Phil Esposito

Most Wins: Wayne Gretzky (5)

CONN SMYTHE TROPHY

In 1964 Maple Leaf Gardens donated a trophy in honor of Conn Smythe, former coach, general manager and owner of the Toronto Maple Leafs. It is awarded to the most valuable player of the playoffs. The award is most often given to a player on the team winning the Stanley Cup, but five times it has been given to a player on a losing squad. Voting is conducted by the Professional Hockey Writers' Association.

First Winner: Jean Béliveau

Most Wins: Patrick Roy (3)

ART ROSS TROPHY

In 1947, Art Ross, the legendary Boston Bruins executive, donated a trophy to the NHL. It is awarded to the player who scores the most points during the regular season. Wayne Gretzky posted the highest-ever points total in 1985–86, registering 215 points.

First Winner: Elmer Lach

Most Wins: Wayne Gretzky (10)

MAURICE "ROCKET" RICHARD TROPHY

The newest NHL trophy was donated by the Montreal Canadiens in 1999, to honor Maurice Richard. Richard was the first player to have a 50-goal season and was the league's top goal-scorer five times. Accordingly, this trophy is presented to the league's leading goal-scorer.

First Winner: Teemu Selanne

Most Wins: Pavel Bure, Jarome Iginla, Alex Ovechkin (2)

JAMES NORRIS MEMORIAL TROPHY

The James Norris Memorial Trophy, first awarded in 1954, was named after long-time Detroit Red Wings owner James Norris, whose family controlled the Wings from 1932–82. Every year it is presented to the defenseman who demonstrates the greatest all-around ability in his position. The winner is selected in a poll of the Professional Hockey Writers' Association.

First Winner: Red Kelly

Most Wins: Bobby Orr (8)

VEZINA TROPHY

In 1926–27, Leo Dandurand, Louis Letourneau and Joe Cattarinich, former owners of the Montreal Canadiens, donated a trophy in memory of Habs goaltender Georges Vezina to be awarded to the goalkeeper(s) of the team allowing the fewest number of goals during the regular season. The trophy's definition changed in 1981–82, with the prize being awarded to the NHL's best overall goalkeeper as voted by the league's GMs.

First Winner (1926–27): George Hainsworth

Most Wins (1926–27 to 1980–81): Jacques Plante (7)

First Winner (1981–82): Billy Smith

Most Wins (1981–82 to present): Dominik Hasek (6)

FRANK J. SELKE TROPHY

The Selke Trophy was introduced in 1977 to recognize the top defensive forward in the league. The trophy was named for Frank J. Selke, a former executive with both the Toronto Maple Leafs and the Montreal Canadiens, who was instrumental in building Maple Leaf Gardens. The winner is selected in a poll by the Professional Hockey Writers' Association.

First Winner: Bob Gainey

Most Wins: Bob Gainey (4)

LADY BYNG MEMORIAL TROPHY

Lady Byng, wife of Canada's then-Governor-General, The Viscount Byng, donated her trophy in 1925 to be awarded to the player exhibiting the most gentlemanly conduct and sportsmanship, combined with excellent skill. Frank Boucher of the New York Rangers won the award seven times in eight seasons, and was given the original trophy. Lady Byng donated a second trophy in 1936, and after her death in 1949, the NHL presented a third trophy: the Lady Byng Memorial Trophy. Voting is conducted by the Professional Hockey Writers' Association.

First Winner: Frank Nighbor

Most Wins: Frank Boucher (7)

CALDER MEMORIAL TROPHY

The NHL announced the "Rookie of the Year" beginning in 1933, but it wasn't until the 1936–37 season that a trophy was awarded. The trophy was named the Calder Trophy, after then-president Frank Calder. After Calder's sudden death in 1943, the award became known as the Calder Memorial Trophy. The winner is selected in a poll by the Professional Hockey Writers' Association.

First Winner: Syl Apps

BILL MASTERTON MEMORIAL TROPHY

Bill Masterton, an All-American, and MVP of the NCAA tournament of 1961, retired from professional hockey in 1964, having played in the minors his entire career. In 1967, while a member of the U.S. National Team, Masterton's rights were bought by the expansion Minnesota North Stars. 38 games into the season Masterton was bodychecked, hitting his head on the ice, knocking him unconscious. He never woke from his coma and died two days later on January 15, 1968. The NHL introduced this trophy in his honor at the end of the 1967–68 season. It is awarded to the player who best exhibits the dedication and sportsmanship Masterton embodied. Voting is conducted by the Professional Hockey Writers' Association.

First Winner: Claude Provost

Most Wins: No multiple winners

KING CLANCY MEMORIAL TROPHY

The King Clancy Memorial Trophy was introduced in 1988, in honor of the late King Clancy, who had been a player, official, coach and executive. The trophy is awarded to the player who best exemplifies leadership, on and off the ice, and who has made notable humanitarian contributions. The winner is selected in a poll by the Professional Hockey Writers' Association.

First Winner: Lanny MacDonald

Most Wins: No multiple winners

JACK ADAMS AWARD

Though inducted into the Hockey Hall of Fame as a player, Jack Adams is best remembered as the Detroit Red Wings' coach during the 1940s and 1950s. In 1974 the NHL Broadcaster's Association created this award in his honor to be given to the NHL coach judged to have contributed most to his team's success during the season. The winner is voted by the NHL Broadcasters' Association.

First Winner: Fred Shero

Most Wins: Pat Burns (3)

WILLIAM M. JENNINGS TROPHY

This trophy was introduced during the 1981–82 season in honor of William M. Jennings, longtime governor and owner of the New York Rangers. It replaced the Vezina Trophy as the prize for the goaltender(s) of the team allowing the fewest number of goals during the regular season.

First Winner(s): Denis Hero and Rick Wamsley

Most Wins: Patrick Roy (5)

Early Challenge Cup Era: 1892–93 to 1908–09

The Stanley Cup was donated by Lord Stanley of Preston and was to be given to the "the championship hockey club of the Dominion of Canada." The Montreal Amateur Athletic Association captured the first Stanley Cup by finishing first in the Amateur Hockey Association — the first official holders of the Cup. Under Lord Stanley's rules, any Canadian hockey team could challenge for the Cup, but none dared.

1892–93
AHA Champion/Cup Winner
Montreal Amateur Athletic Association

1893–94
Challenge 1: Single Elimination Game
Cup Holder: Montreal AAA 3
Challenger: Montreal Victorias 2
Challenge 2: Single Elimination Game
Cup Holder: Montreal AAA 3
Challenger: Ottawa Capitals 1

1894–95
Challenge: Single Elimination Game
Cup Holder: Montreal AAA 5
Challenger: Queen's University 1
Cup claimed by Montreal Victorias*
* The 1894–95 AHA champion Montreal Victorias challenged Montreal AAA for the Cup, only to find that a challenge by Queen's University had already been accepted. In a bizarre twist it was decided that if the Montreal AAA defeated Queen's, the Victorias would claim the Cup.

1895–96
Challenge 1: Single Elimination Game
Cup Holder: Montreal Victorias 0
Challenger: Winnipeg Victorias 2
Challenge 2: Single Elimination Game
Cup Holder: Winnipeg Victorias 5
Challenger: Montreal Victorias 6

1896–97
Challenge: Single Elimination Game
Cup Holder: Montreal Victorias 15
Challenger: Ottawa Capitals 2

1897–98
Cup Holder: Montreal Victorias*
* Montreal Victorias retain Cup after finishing first in AHA. No challenges issued.

1898–99
Challenge 1: Two Game Series
Cup Holder: Montreal Victorias 2
Challenger: Winnipeg Victorias 0
Challenge 2: Single Elimination Game
Cup Holder: Montreal Shamrocks* 6
Challenger: Queen's University 2
* The AHA disbanded after the Montreal-Winnipeg challenge and the Canadian Amateur Hockey League took its place. The Shamrocks finished first in the CAHL, ahead of the Cup-holding Montreal Victorias, and became holders of the Cup.

1899–1900
Challenge 1: Best-of-Three
Cup Holder: Montreal Shamrocks 2
Challenger: Winnipeg Victorias 1
Challenge 2: Two Game Series
Cup Holder: Montreal Shamrocks 2
Challenger: Halifax Crescents 0

1900–01
Challenge: Best-of-Three
Cup Holder: Montreal Shamrocks 0
Challenger: Winnipeg Victorias 2

1901–02
Challenge 1: Two Game Series
Cup Holder: Winnipeg Victorias 2
Challenger: Toronto Wellingtons 0
Challenge 2: Best-of-Three
Cup Holder: Winnipeg Victorias 1
Challenger: Montreal AAA 2

1902–03
Challenge 1: Best-of-Three
Cup Holder: Montreal AAA 2
Challenger: Winnipeg Victorias 1
Challenge 2: Two Game – Total Goals*
Challenger 1: Montreal Victorias 1
Challenger 2: Ottawa Silver Seven 9
* Montreal AAA failed to finish first in the CAHL after Cup challenge with Winnipeg; the two top CAHL teams competed.
Challenge 3: Two Game – Total Goals
Cup Holder: Ottawa Silver Seven 10
Challenger: Rat Portage Thistles 4

1903–04
Challenge 1: Best-of-Three
Cup Holder: Ottawa Silver Seven 2
Challenger: Winnipeg Rowing Club 1
Challenge 2: Two Game Series
Cup Holder: Ottawa Silver Seven* 2
Challenger: Toronto Marlboros 0
* Ottawa defects from CAHL and takes Cup with them.

Challenge 3: Two Game – Total Goals
Cup Holder: Ottawa Silver Seven 5
Challenger: Montreal Wanderers* 5
* Montreal Wanderers forfeit series, refusing to play games in Ottawa.
Challenge 4: Two Game – Total Goals
Cup Holder: Ottawa Silver Seven 15
Challenger: Brandon Hockey Club 6

1904–05
Challenge 1: Two Game Series
Cup Holder: Ottawa Silver Seven* 2
Challenger: Dawson City Nuggets 0
* Ottawa joins Federal Amateur Hockey League; brings Cup with them.

Challenge 2: Best-of-Three
Cup Holder: Ottawa Silver Seven 2
Challenger: Rat Portage Thistles 1

1905–06
Challenge 1: Two Game Series
Cup Holder: Ottawa Silver Seven* 2
Challenger: Queen's University 0
* Ottawa joins Eastern Canada Amateur Hockey Association; Cup now awarded within the ECAHA.

Challenge 2: Two Game Series
Cup Holder: Ottawa Silver Seven 2
Challenger: Smith Falls Seniors 1
Challenge 3: Two Game – Total Goals
Cup Holder: Ottawa Silver Seven 10
Challenger: Montreal Wanderers 12
Challenge 4: Two Game – Total Goals
Cup Holder: Montreal Wanderers 17
Challenger: New Glasgow Hockey Club 5

1906–07
Challenge 1: Two Game – Total Goals
Cup Holder: Montreal Wanderers 8
Challenger: Kenora Thistles* 12
* Formerly Rat Portage

Challenge 2: Two Game Series
Cup Holder: Kenora Thistles 2
Challenger: Brandon Hockey Club 0
Challenge 3: Two Game – Total Goals
Cup Holder: Kenora Thistles 8
Challenger: Montreal Wanderers 12

1907–08
Challenge 1: Two Game – Total Goals
Cup Holder: Montreal Wanderers 22
Challenger: Ottawa Victorias 4
Challenge 2: Two Game – Total Goals
Cup Holder: Montreal Wanderers 20
Challenger: Winnipeg Maple Leafs 8
Challenge 3: Single Elimination Game
Cup Holder: Montreal Wanderers 6
Challenger: Toronto Maple Leafs (OPHL) 4

Challenge 4: Two Game – Total Goals

Cup Holder: Montreal Wanderers	13
Challenger: Edmonton Eskimos	10

1908–09*

* Ottawa Senators captured the East Coast Hockey Association (formerly ECAHA) league title and claimed the Cup. A challenge was accepted from Winnipeg but mild weather prevented playable ice from being available.

1909–10

Challenge 1: Two Game – Total Goals

Cup Holder: Ottawa Senators*	15
Challenger: Galt Professionals	4

* Formerly Ottawa Silver Seven.

Challenge 2: Two Game – Total Goals

Cup Holder: Ottawa Senators	21
Challenger: Edmonton Eskimos	11

* Challenges took place in January 1910, before the semblance of the NHA and the new challenge format.

NHA Challenge Cup Era: 1909–10 to 1916–17

The ECAHA folded and the new National Hockey Association took control of the Cup, which was to go to the champion of the NHA season. Afterward, challenges for the Cup could take place.

1909–10

NHA Champion: Montreal Wanderers
Challenge: Single Elimination Game

Cup Holder: Montreal Wanderers	7
Challenger: Berlin Professionals	3

1910–11

NHA Champion: Ottawa Senators
Challenge 1: Single Elimination Game

Cup Holder: Ottawa Senators	7
Challenger: Galt Professionals	4

Challenge 2: Single Elimination Game

Cup Holder: Ottawa Senators	14
Challenger: Port Arthur Bearcats	4

1911–12

NHA Champion: Quebec Bulldogs
Challenge: Best-of-Three

Cup Holder: Quebec Bulldogs	2
Challenger: Moncton Victorias	0

1912–13

NHA Champion: Quebec Bulldogs
Challenge: Best-of-Three

Cup Holder: Quebec Bulldogs	2
Challenger: Sydney Miners	0

1913–14

No NHA Champion: Top two clubs play for Cup and Championship.
NHA Championship:
Two Game – Total Goals

Challenger 1: Montreal Canadiens	2
Challenger 2: Toronto Blueshirts*	6

* Predecessor of Maple Leafs

Challenge 1: Best-of-Five*

Cup Holder: Toronto Blue Shirts	3
Challenger: Victoria Cougars	0

* Deemed illegitimate series by Cup Trustees because Victoria officials did no submit proper paperwork.

1914–15

NHA Champion: Ottawa Senators
Challenge: Best-of-Five

Cup Holder: Ottawa Senators	0
Challenger: Vancouver Millionaires*	3

* PCHA champion

1915–16

NHA Champion: Montreal Canadiens
Challenge: Best-of-Five

Cup Holder: Montreal Canadiens	3
Challenger: Portland Rosebuds*	2

* PCHA champion

1916–17

NHA Champion: Montreal Canadiens
Challenge: Best-of-Five

Cup Holder: Montreal Canadiens	1
Challenger: Seattle Metropolitans*	3

* PCHA champion

The NHL, PCHA and WCHL Challenge Cup Era: 1917–18 to 1925–26

The NHA dissolved and the National Hockey League was formed. From 1917–18 to 1920–21, the NHL champion played the Pacific Coast Hockey Association champion for the Cup. In 1921–22 the Western Canadian Hockey League was formed and the WCHL champion and the PCHA champion battled for the right to play the NHL champion for the Cup. From 1922–23 to 1923–24, the best teams from the PCHA and the WCHL took part in games against the NHL champion for the Cup. Prior to the start of the 1924–25 season the PCHA merged with the WCHL, with the league winner vying for the Cup with the top NHL club. The WCHL became the WHL for its last season of operation, 1925–26.

1917–18

Best-of-Five

Toronto Arenas (NHL)*	3
Vancouver Millionaires (PCHA)	2

* Predecessor of Maple Leafs

1918–19*

Best-of-Five

Montreal Canadiens (NHL)
Seattle Metropolitans (PCHA)

* No winner. The series, tied in Game 5, was cancelled due to Spanish Influenza.

1919–20

Best-of-Five

Ottawa Senators (NHL)	3
Seattle Metropolitans (PCHA)	2

1920–21

Best-of-Five

Ottawa Senators (NHL)	3
Vancouver Millionaires (PCHA)	2

1921–22

Best-of-Five

Toronto St. Pats (NHL)*	3
Vancouver Millionaires (PCHA)	2

* Predecessor of Maple Leafs

1922–23

Semifinals/Finals Format
Semifinals: Best-of-Five

Ottawa Senators (NHL)	3
Vancouver Maroons* (PCHA)	1

* Formerly Millionaires

Finals: Best-of-Three

Ottawa Senators (NHL)	2
Edmonton Eskimos (WCHL)	0

1923–24

Semifinals/Finals Format
Semifinals: Best-of-Three

Montreal Canadiens (NHL)	2
Vancouver Maroons (WCHL)	0

Finals: Best-of-Three

Montreal Canadiens (NHL)	2
Calgary Tigers (PCHA)	0

1924—25
Best-of-Five

Montreal Canadiens (NHL)	1
Victoria Cougars (WCHL)	3

1925—26
Best-of-Five

Montreal Maroons (NHL)	3
Victoria Cougars (WHL)	1

Early NHL Stanley Cup Finals

After the PCHA and WCHL folded, the NHL remained the only viable professional league to claim the Cup. From this point on, only NHL clubs would compete for the Stanley Cup.

1926—27
Best-of-Five*

Ottawa Senators	2
Boston Bruins	0

* Two games ended in ties.

1927—28
Best-of-Five

New York Rangers	3
Montreal Maroons	2

1928—29
Best-of-Three

Boston Bruins	2
New York Rangers	1

1929—30
Best-of-Three

Montreal Canadiens	2
Boston Bruins	0

1930—31
Best-of-Five

Montreal Canadiens	3
Chicago Black Hawks	2

1931—32
Best-of-Five

Toronto Maple Leafs	3
New York Rangers	0

1932—33
Best-of-Five

New York Rangers	3
Toronto Maple Leafs	1

1933—34
Best-of-Five

Chicago Black Hawks	3
Detroit Red Wings	1

1934—35
Best-of-Five

Montreal Maroons	3
Toronto Maple Leafs	0

1935—36
Best-of-Five

Detroit Red Wings	3
Toronto Maple Leafs	1

1936—37
Best-of-Five

Detroit Red Wings	3
New York Rangers	2

1937—38
Best-of-Five

Chicago Black Hawks	3
Toronto Maple Leafs	1

NHL Modern Format Best-of-Seven Stanley Cup Finals

1938—39

Boston Bruins	4
Toronto Maple Leafs	1

1939—40

New York Rangers	4
Toronto Maple Leafs	2

1940—41

Boston Bruins	4
Detroit Red Wings	0

1941—42

Toronto Maple Leafs	4
Detroit Red Wings	3

1942—43

Detroit Red Wings	4
Boston Bruins	0

1943—44

Montreal Canadiens	4
Chicago Black Hawks	0

1944—45

Toronto Maple Leafs	4
Detroit Red Wings	3

1945—46

Montreal Canadiens	4
Boston Bruins	1

1946—47

Toronto Maple Leafs	4
Montreal Canadiens	2

1947—48

Toronto Maple Leafs	4
Detroit Red Wings	0

1948—49

Toronto Maple Leafs	4
Detroit Red Wings	0

1949—50

Detroit Red Wings	4
New York Rangers	3

1950—51

Toronto Maple Leafs	4
Montreal Canadiens	1

1951—52

Detroit Red Wings	4
Montreal Canadiens	0

1952—53

Montreal Canadiens	4
Boston Bruins	1

1953—54

Detroit Red Wings	4
Montreal Canadiens	3

1954—55

Detroit Red Wings	4
Montreal Canadiens	3

1955—56

Montreal Canadiens	4
Detroit Red Wings	1

1956—57

Montreal Canadiens	4
Boston Bruins	1

1957—58

Montreal Canadiens	4
Boston Bruins	2

1958—59

Montreal Canadiens	4
Toronto Maple Leafs	1

1959—60

Montreal Canadiens	4
Toronto Maple Leafs	0

1960—61

Chicago Blackhawks	4
Detroit Red Wings	2

1961—62

Toronto Maple Leafs	4
Chicago Black Hawks	2

1962–63	
Toronto Maple Leafs	4
Detroit Red Wings	1

1963–64	
Toronto Maple Leafs	4
Detroit Red Wings	3

1964–65	
Montreal Canadiens	4
Chicago Black Hawks	3

1965–66	
Montreal Canadiens	4
Detroit Red Wings	2

1966–67	
Toronto Maple Leafs	4
Montreal Canadiens	2

1967–68	
Montreal Canadiens	4
St. Louis Blues	0

1968–69	
Montreal Canadiens	4
St. Louis Blues	0

1969–70	
Boston Bruins	4
St. Louis Blues	0

1970–71	
Montreal Canadiens	4
Chicago Black Hawks	3

1971–72	
Boston Bruins	4
New York Rangers	2

1972–73	
Montreal Canadiens	4
Chicago Black Hawks	2

1973–74	
Philadelphia Flyers	4
Boston Bruins	2

1974–75	
Philadelphia Flyers	4
Buffalo Sabres	2

1975–76	
Montreal Canadiens	4
Philadelphia Flyers	0

1976–77	
Montreal Canadiens	4
Boston Bruins	0

1977–78	
Montreal Canadiens	4
Boston Bruins	2

1978–79	
Montreal Canadiens	4
New York Rangers	1

1979–80	
New York Islanders	4
Philadelphia Flyers	2

1980–81	
New York Islanders	4
Minnesota North Stars	1

1981–82	
New York Islanders	4
Vancouver Canucks	0

1982–83	
New York Islanders	4
Edmonton Oilers	0

1983–84	
Edmonton Oilers	4
New York Islanders	1

1984–85	
Edmonton Oilers	4
Philadelphia Flyers	1

1985–86	
Montreal Canadiens	4
Calgary Flames	1

1986–87	
Edmonton Oilers	4
Philadelphia Flyers	3

1987–88	
Edmonton Oilers	4
Boston Bruins	0

1988–89	
Calgary Flames	4
Montreal Canadiens	2

1989–90	
Edmonton Oilers	4
Boston Bruins	1

1990–91	
Pittsburgh Penguins	4
Minnesota North Stars	2

1991–92	
Pittsburgh Penguins	4
Chicago Blackhawks	0

1992–93	
Montreal Canadiens	4
Los Angeles Kings	1

1993–94	
New York Rangers	4
Vancouver Canucks	3

1994–95	
New Jersey Devils	4
Detroit Red Wings	0

1995–96	
Colorado Avalanche	4
Florida Panthers	0

1996–97	
Detroit Red Wings	4
Philadelphia Flyers	0

1997–98	
Detroit Red Wings	4
Washington Capitals	0

1998–99	
Dallas Stars	4
Buffalo Sabres	2

1999–00	
New Jersey Devils	4
Dallas Stars	2

2000–01	
Colorado Avalanche	4
New Jersey Devils	3

2001–02	
Detroit Red Wings	4
Carolina Hurricanes	1

2002–03	
New Jersey Devils	4
Mighty Ducks of Anaheim	3

2003–04	
Tampa Bay Lightning	4
Calgary Flames	3

2005–06	
Carolina Hurricanes	4
Edmonton Oilers	3

2006–07	
Anaheim Ducks	4
Ottawa Senators	1

2007–08	
Detroit Red Wings	4
Pittsburgh Penguins	2

2008–09	
Pittsburgh Penguins	4
Detroit Red Wings	3

2009–10	
Chicago Blackhawks	4
Philadelphia Flyers	2

Hockey Leagues

AAHL Alberta Amateur Hockey League

AHA Amateur Hockey Association

AHAC Amateur Hockey Association of Canada

AHL American Hockey League

Al-Cup Allan Cup

APHL Alberta Professional Hockey League

BCHL British Columbia Hockey League

Big-4 Big-4 Hockey League

CAHL Canadian Amateur Hockey League

Can-Am Canadian-American Hockey League

Can-Pro Canadian Professional Hockey League

CCSHL Central Canada Senior Hockey League

CHA Canadian Hockey Association

CHL Central Hockey League

CIHU Canadian Intercollegiate Hockey Union

COWHL Central Ontario Women's Hockey League

ECAC Eastern College Athletic Conference

ECAHA Eastern Canada Amateur Hockey Association

ECHA Eastern Canada Hockey Association

Exhib Exhibition Games

FAHL Federal Amateur Hockey League

High-NH High School – New Hampshire

IAHL International-American Hockey League

IHL International Pro Hockey League (1903-1907)

IPAHU Inter-Provincial Amateur Hockey Union

Ivy Ivy League Collegiate Hockey Division

M-Cup Memorial Cup

MCHL Montreal City Hockey League

MCJHL Montreal City Junior Hockey League

MHL Manitoba Hockey League

MHL-Pro Manitoba Professional Hockey League

MHL-Sr. Manitoba Senior Hockey League

MIHA Maritime Intermediate Hockey Association

MJHL Manitoba Junior Hockey League

MNWHA Manitoba Northwest Hockey Association

MNWHA-Int. Manitoba Northwest Intermediate Hockey Association

MPHL Maritime Professional Hockey League

MTBHL Manitoba-Thunder Bay Hockey League

Nat-Team National Team

NHA National Hockey Association

NHL National Hockey League

NOHA Northern Ontario Hockey Association

NOHL New Ontario Hockey League

NWHL National Women's Hockey League

OCAA Ontario Colleges Athletic Association

OCJHL Ottawa City Junior Hockey League

OHA Ontario Hockey Association

OHA-Int. Ontario Intermediate Hockey Association

OHA-Jr. Ontario Junior Hockey Association

OHA-Sr. Ontario Senior Hockey Association

OPHL Ontario Professional Hockey League

Pacific Rim Pacific Rim Championships

PCHA Pacific Coast Hockey Association

PCHL Pacific Coast Hockey League

QSSF Quebec Student Sports Federation

Sask-Pro Saskatchewan Professional Hockey League

SSHL Saskatchewan Senior Hockey League

St-Cup Stanley Cup Challenge Series

TPHL Temiskaming Professional Hockey League

TBSHL Thunder Bay Senior Hockey League

UOVHL Upper Ottawa Valley Hockey League

USAHA United States Amateur Hockey Association

USHL United States Hockey League

USSR Union of Soviet Socialist Republics (1946–1992)

WCAHA Western Canada Amateur Hockey Association

WCHL Western Canada Hockey League

WHA World Hockey Association

WHL Western Hockey League

West-P Western Playoffs

WOHA Western Ontario Hockey Association

WPHL Western Pennsylvania Hockey League

W-S World Series of Hockey

WSrHL Winnipeg Senior Hockey League

WWC Women's World Championships

Player Profile Index

Photo Credits